MINUTES

OF THE

Seventh Biennial Convention

OF

The United Lutheran Church in America

MILWAUKEE, WISCONSIN
October 7-14, 1930

THE UNITED LUTHERAN PUBLICATION HOUSE
PHILADELPHIA, PA.

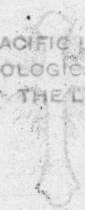

THE UNITED LUTHERAN CHURCH IN AMERICA

CALENDAR, 1930-1932

OFFICERS

President—Rev. F. H. Knubel, D.D., LL.D., S.T.D.
39 East 35th Street, New York City.

Secretary—Rev. M. G. G. Scherer, D.D.,
39 East 35th Street, New York City.

Treasurer—Mr. E. Clarence Miller, LL.D.,
1508 Walnut Street, Philadelphia, Pa.

EXECUTIVE BOARD

Term Expires 1934

Rev. Marion Justus Kline, D.D., 1407 Twelfth Avenue, Altoona, Pa.
Rev. Jacob L. Morgan, D.D., 612 S. Main Street, Salisbury, N. C.
Rev. Rees Edgar Tulloss, Ph.D., D.D., 1817 Woodedge Rd., Springfield, O.
Mr. John Greiner, Jr., 1317 Myrtle Street, Scranton, Pa.
B. B. Miller, Esq., Salisbury, N. C.
Mr. Wm. H. Stackel, 68 Crosman Terrace, Rochester, N. Y.

Term Expires 1932

Rev. A. Charles R. Keiter, 940 Cumberland Street, Lebanon, Pa.
Rev. Charles D. Trexler, D.D., 28 East 73rd Street, New York City.
Rev. Abdel Ross Wentz, Ph.D., D.D., Gettysburg, Pa.
Hon. Wm. E. Hirt, Erie, Pa.
Hon. John F. Kramer, 3-5 Blymyer Building, Mansfield, Ohio.
George E. Neff, Esq., 29 S. Duke Street, York, Pa.

Members Ex-Officio

Rev. F. H. Knubel, President.
Rev. M. G. G. Scherer, Secretary.
Mr. E. Clarence Miller, Treasurer.

Place of next Convention—Philadelphia, Pennsylvania

Minutes of the Seventh Biennial Convention of the United Lutheran Church In America

THE SERVICE—INTRODUCTORY

CHURCH OF THE EPIPHANY
Milwaukee, Wisconsin.
Tuesday, October 7, 1930, 8 P. M.

Preparatory to the Opening of the Seventh Biennial Convention of The United Lutheran Church in America, delegates-elect from the Constituent Synods, a large number of visitors and many members of the churches of the Convention City assembled to participate in The Service, at the Church of the Epiphany, Milwaukee, Wisconsin, on Tuesday evening, October 7, 1930, at eight o'clock. The Secretary conducted The Service, including the Order for Public Confession, and the Reverends Samuel Trexler, President of the United Synod of New York, and W. A. Wade, President of the Synod of Maryland, had charge of the Administration of the Sacrament of the Altar.

The text of the Sermon, which was preached by the President, was "I am come": the theme, "What the United Lutheran Church Stands For."

FIRST MEETING

Morning Session

HOTEL SCHROEDER
Milwaukee, Wisconsin.
Wednesday, October 8, 1930, 8:45 o'clock.

Matins were conducted by the Rev. A. H. Smith.

The President called the convention to order, and, after the use of the Order for the Opening of Synods, declared the Seventh Biennial Convention of The United Lutheran Church in America open for business.

Moved and carried, that beginning this afternoon the three central blocks of seats be set aside for delegates, and that no one will be recognized who asks for the floor unless he is seated within these three central blocks.

By general consent the report of the completed roll of delegates was deferred.

The roll, as finally established, follows:

ROLL OF DELEGATES BY SYNODS

1. Ministerium of Pennsylvania

Organized August 15, 1748

Clerical	Lay
Rev. E. P. Pfatteicher, Ph.D., D.D.	E. Clarence Miller, LL.D.
Rev. F. K. Fretz, Ph.D., D.D.	Hon. Claude T. Reno
Rev. N. R. Melhorn, D.D., Litt.D.	Mr. O. W. Osterlund
Rev. C. M. Jacobs, D.D., LL.D., L.H.D.	Mr. Peter P. Hagan
	Mr. H. Torrey Walker
Rev. G. S. Kressley, Litt.D.	Mr. A. Raymond Bard
Rev. George Gebert, D.D.	Mr. Daniel F. Yost
Rev. W. L. Stough, D.D.	Mr. Frank D. Bittner
Rev. J. A. W. Haas, D.D., LL.D.	Mr. William H. Hager
Rev. J. C. Mattes, D.D.	Mr. William M. Mearig
Rev. A. Charles R. Keiter	Mr. James M. Snyder
Rev. F. M. Urich, DD..	Mr. Charles H. Esser
Rev. F. T. Esterly	John L. Potteiger, Esq.
Rev. J. J. Schindel, D.D.	James F. Henninger, Esq.
Rev. W. C. Schaeffer, Jr., D.D.	Mr. Samuel W. Deininger
Rev. A. B. MacIntosh, D.D.	Mr. Wm. P. M. Braun
Rev. G. A. Kercher	Mr. John Greiner, Jr.
Rev. A. L. Benner, D.D.	Grant Hultberg, D.C.L.
Rev. I. B. Kurtz, D.D.	Mr. Leon M. Brobst
Rev. E. F. Bachmann, D.D.	Ralph Schatz, Esq.
Rev. L. D. Ulrich, D.D.	Geo. F. Seiberling, M.D.
Rev. G. H. Kinard	Mr. C. S. Eisenbrown
Rev. C. Wilker	Mr. Allen R. Shimer
Rev. E. E. Fischer, D.D.	Mr. J. Milton Deck
Rev. L. E. Wein	Mr. P. S. Trumbauer
Rev. James F. Lambert, D.D.	Mr. Oscar W. Schmidt
Rev. J. H. Waidelich, D.D.	Mr. Harry Hodges
Rev. C. E. Kistler, D.D.	Mr. A. F. Ritter
Rev. P. A. Laury, D.D.	Mr. J. H. Wisler
Rev. E. W. Weber	Mr. D. M. Reitz
Rev. J. C. Fisher, D.D.	Dr. E. D. Funk
Rev. W. H. Kline	Mr. W. C. Boyer
Rev. J. F. Stolte, Ph.D.	Mr. H. W. Cressman
Rev. I. F. Frankenfield	Mr. R. D. Raeder

Rev. G. H. Bechtold
Rev. C. M. Snyder
Rev. W. C. Beck, D.D.
Rev. R. E. Kern
Rev. G. F. Gehr, D.D.

Mr. C. A. Scheuringer
Mr. H. F. Heuer
Mr. R. L. Neugard
Mr. W. H. Williams

2. United Synod of New York

*October 23, 1786

Clerical	Lay
Rev. Samuel Trexler, D.D.	Mr. Fred H. Wefer
Rev. F. H. Knubel, D.D., LL.D., S.T.D.	Heiby W. Ungerer, Esq.
	Geo. A. W. Achenbach, Esq.
Rev. Paul Andrew Kirsch	Mr. William Eck
Rev. Wm. M. Horn, D.D.	Herbert C. Yeckel, M.D.
Rev. Charles D. Trexler, D.D.	Mr. William H. Stackel
Rev. Paul E. Scherer, D.D.	Mr. George Bohrer
Rev. Herman Brezing, D.D.	Mr. Clarence C. Dittmer
Rev. F. A. Kahler, D.D., LL.D.	Dr. Richard Moldenke
Rev. Chas. W. Leitzell, D.D.	Mr. Philip Machemer
Rev. Geo. Linn Kieffer, D.D., Litt.D.	Mr. Frederick Henrich
Rev. Augustus Steimle, D.D.	Mr. William Richters a.
Rev. Franklin F. Fry, D.D.	Mr. William J. Roser
Rev. Theo. O. Posselt, D.D.	Hon. E. F. Eilert, C.S.D. a.
Rev. Andrew L. Dillenbeck, D.D.	Mr. Fred W. Rettenmeyer
Rev. Walter Krumwiede, S.T.M.	Mr. Joseph M. Lotsch
Rev. Ernest Heyd, D.D.	Ellwood M. Rabenold, Esq.
Rev. Harold S. Miller	Mr. James Gear a.
Rev. H. T. Weiskotten, Ph.D.	Mr. H. A. Weymann
Rev. Fred B. Clausen	Mr. Charles F. Obenhack
Rev. Arthur S. Hardy, D.D.	Mr. Louis T. Henrich a.
Rev. Frederick Noeldeke	Mr. I. Searles Runyon a.
Rev. Frederick R. Knubel	Mr. Martin Wulff
Rev. John A. Weyl, D.D.	Mr. Frank Kalmbach
Rev. Chas. F. Dapp, D.D., Ph.D.	Chas. G. Schamu, M.D.
Rev. Chalmers E. Frontz, D.D.	Mr. Charles W. Ackerman
Rev. Clarence E. Krumbholz	Mr. Henry Beisler
Rev. F. E. Oberlander, D.D.	Mr. Charles A. Emerich
Rev. Wm. H. Stutts, D.D.	Mr. Albert E. J. Krauss a.
Rev. A. Walter Baker	Mr. Henry G. Pfeil
Rev. Raymond C. Deitz, D.D.	Mr. Henry Streibert
Rev. Geo. E. Hipsley, D.D.	Mr. A. N. Steiner
Rev. Stephen M. Paulson, D.D.	Mr. Jacob H. Smith
Rev. Henry J. Pflum, M.A., D.D.	Mr. Fred Kreisel
Rev. Henry H. Wahl	Mr. Chas J. Hurst
Rev. Frank Wolford, D.D.	Mr. Ludolph H. Eppers
Rev Wm. G. Boomhower, D.D.	Mr. E. B. Fernschild
Rev. F. H. Bosch, D.D.	Mr. Elliot Springstead

* Date of organization of the Ministerium of New York and Adjacent States and Countries, which on June 5, 1929, merged with the Evangelical Lutheran Synod of New York (organized 1830, see Minutes U. L. C. 1926, p. 8) and the Evangelical Lutheran Synod of New York and New England (organized in 1902), to form The United Lutheran Synod of New York.

Rev. Henry C. Wasmund, D.D.
Rev. Carl B. Schuchard
Rev. Arthur H. Schmoyer

Mr. Louis A. Wilke
Mr. Benj. H. Ertell

3. United Synod of North Carolina
May 2, 1803

Clerical	Lay
Rev. J. L. Morgan, D.D.	Mr. Chas. S. Heilig
Rev. M. L. Stirewalt, D.D.	Mayor J. L. Fisher
Rev. J. M. Senter, D.D.	Judge A. L. Starr a.
Rev. G. H. Rhodes	Mr. Avery R. Rhyne a.
Rev. F. L. Conrad	Prof. H. A. Fisher
Rev. A. G. Voigt, D.D., LL.D.	Mr. J. H. Rehder
Rev. E. J. Sox, D.D.	Mr. H. E. Isenhour
Rev. C. N. Yount	Prof. W. T. Whitsett, Ph.D.
Rev. C. R. Patterson	Mr. J. W. Futchs

* Date of organization of the Evangelical Lutheran Synod and Ministerium of North Carolina, which cn March 2, 1921, with the Evangelical Lutheran Tennessee Synod (organized July 17, 1820) merged into the United Evangelical Lutheran Synod of North Carolina under an amended charter of the former of the two synods which merged.

4. Maryland Synod
Organized October 11, 1820

Clerical	Lay
Rev. William A. Wade, D.D.	L. Russell Alden, Esq.
Rev. J. W. Ott, D.D.	Harry T. Domer, Litt.D.
Rev. Charles H. Corbett	Mr. Virgil W. Doub
Rev. A. R. Wentz, Ph.D., D.D.	Mr. F. W. Kakel
Rev. Charles P. Wiles, D.D.	Mr. J. Henry Frick
Rev. John Weidley, D.D.	H. C. Poffenberger, Esq.
Rev. John C. Bowers, D.D.	Mr. M. P. Moller, Jr.
Rev. Richard Schmidt, D.D.	Mr. L. S. Birely
Rev. James Oosterling	Edwin Herrmann, Esq.
Rev. Frederick R. Wagner, D.D.	Mr. H. T. Wentz

5. Synod of South Carolina
Organized January 14, 1824

Clerical	Lay
Rev. Chas J. Shealy	Prof. Jas. C. Kinard, LL.D.
Rev. M. G. G. Scherer, D.D.	Hon. C. M. Efird, LL.D.
Rev. W. H. Greever, D.D., LL.D.	Mr. B. B. Hare, M.C. a.
Rev. P. D. Brown, D.D.	Mr. S. P. Frick
Rev. W. C. Davis, D.D.	Mr. E. H. Schirmer
Rev. C. A. Freed, D.D.	Mr. R. C. Counts

6. Synod of West Pennsylvania
Organized September 5, 1825

Clerical	Lay
Rev. John S. Tome	Mr. Alvin R. Nissly
Rev. M. E. Smith	Hon. D. Edward Long
Rev. C. H. Hershey	Mr. R. M. Saubel
Rev. Oliver D. Coble	George E. Neff, Esq.
Rev. M. R. Hamsher	Hon. Franklin Menges
Rev. W. H. Traub, D.D.	Mr. William H. Menges
Rev. H. C. Alleman, D.D.	Mr. George B. Hoover
Rev. C. E. Walter, D.D.	Mr. Morgan F. Leader
Rev. H. B. Burkholder	Hon. E. P. Miller

7. Synod of Virginia
*August 10, 1829

Clerical	Lay
Rev. J. J. Scherer, Jr., D.D.	Mr. E. L. Keiser
Rev. C. W. Cassell	Mr. Harry E. Pugh
Rev. R. H. Anderson	W. T. Stauffer, Esq.
Rev. C. M. Teufel, D.D.	Mr. H. L. Snyder
Rev. J. L. Sieber, D.D.	Mr. A. D. Smith
Rev. Paul L. Royer	Mr. B. E. Copenhaver
Rev. P. E. Shealy	Mr. H. L. Bonham
Rev. L. W. Strickler	Mr. R. E. Mapes

* Date of organization of the Evangelical Lutheran Synod and Ministerium of Virginia, which, on March 17, 1922, with the Evangelical Lutheran Synod and Ministerium of Southwestern Virginia (composed of the former Evangelical Lutheran Synod and Ministerium of Southwestern Virginia, organized September 20, 1842, and the Evangelical Lutheran Holston Synod, organized September 29, 1860), merged into the Lutheran Synod of Virginia.

8. Synod of Ohio
*November 7, 1836

Clerical	Lay
Rev. Joseph Sittler, D.D.	Mr. J. W. Kahler
Rev. A. E. Bell, D.D.	Hon. J. L. Zimmerman, LL.D.
Rev. H. C. Getter	Mr. A. W. Ulrici
Rev. A. H. Smith, D.D.	Judge C. F. Ribble
Rev. W. M. Hackenberg, D.D.	Mr. A. H. Homrighaus
Rev. H. C. Roehner, D.D.	Mr. H. L. Hess
Rev. R. E. Tulloss, D.D., Ph.D., LL.D.	Mr. M. W. Lutz
	Mr. W. W. Miller
Rev. E. E. Snyder, D.D.	Mr. W. C. Shott
Rev. C. F. Sheriff	Mr. Geo. W. Sieber a.
Rev. O. C. Kramer, D.D.	Mr. H. C. Kistler a.
Rev. R. L. Lubold	Judge W. C. Wiseman
Rev. H. C. Brillhart, D.D.	Mr. Niel Byers
Rev. C. S. Foust	Mr. John Toedtman
Rev. E. C. Herman, D.D.	Mr. E. J. Welling
Rev. L. P. Speaker	Mr. Ralph Hatfield
Rev. W. K. Himes	Mr. S. O. Burton

* Date of organization of East Ohio Synod which, on November 3, 1920, with the Synod of Miami (organized October 16, 1844), Wittenberg Synod (organized June 8, 1847) and the District Synod of Ohio (organized August 26, 1857) merged into the Synod of Ohio of the United Lutheran Church.

Rev. F. F. Secrist
Rev. J. L. Smith
Rev. J. E. Zimmerman
Rev. S. D. Myers

Mr. S. A. Pfau
Mr. Ralph Bowman
Mr. E. H. Misch

9. East Pennsylvania Synod
Organized May 2, 1842

Clerical

Rev. C. G. Leatherman, D.D.
Rev. W. C. Dunlap, D.D., Ph.D.
Rev. George A. Greiss, D.D.
Rev. Stanley Billheimer, D.D.
Rev. E. A. Chamberlin
Rev. C. P. Swank, S.T.D.
Rev. J. D. Krout
Rev. S. W. Herman, D.D.
Rev. A. Pohlman, D.D., M.D.
Rev. F. C. Sternat
Rev. R. C. Miller
Rev. E. M. Grove
Rev. A. C. Harris
Rev. W. C. Ney

Lay

Mr. B. B. Slifer
Mr. Luther Minter
Mr. E. G. Hoover
W. H. Emhardt, Esq.
Mr. R. O. Frankenfield
Croll Keller, M.D.
Mr. Roy Dougherty
Mr. J. G. Kurzenknabe
Mr. Harold Landis
Mr. P. C. Fuhrmann
Mr. A. K. Jacks
D. P. Deatrick, D.D.S.
Mr. Karl Karmany
Mr. A. H. Durborow

10. Alleghany Synod
Organized September 9, 1842

Clerical

Rev. H. M. Petrea
Rev. M. J. Ross
Rev. L. G. Shannon
Rev. C. E. Berkey
Rev. Fred R. Greninger
Rev. J. Luther Frantz
Rev. George N. Lauffer, D.D.

Lay

Mr. C. W. Woods
Hon. John T. Matt
Mr. H. W. Ramer
Mr. J. P. Martin
Mr. W. B. Miller
Mr. F. P. Reiter
Prof. H. S. Fleck

11. Pittsburgh Synod
Organized January 15, 1845

Clerical

Rev. Henry H. Bagger
Rev. Martin L. Clare, D.D.
Rev. Ellis B. Burgess, D.D., LL.D.
Rev. G. E. Swoyer
Rev. A. J. Turkle, D.D.
Rev. Theodore Buch
Rev. J. Kent Rizer, D.D.
Rev. C. E. Schweickert
Rev. E. F. Dickey
Rev. F. P. Fisher
Rev. William E. Frey, D.D.
Rev. E. A. Tappert, D.D.
Rev. William E. Bauer
Rev. I. Noble Dundore
Rev. Elmer F. Rice
Rev. M. M. Allbeck, D.D.

Lay

Mr. Jesse Martsolf
Paul H. Baldwin, Esq.
Mr. J. A. Hill
Mr. W. J. Shaughnessy
Mr. Arthur N. Steinmark
Mr. George Schneider
Mr. Chas. F. Gongaware
Robbin B. Wolf, Esq.
Mr. A. M. Hartzel
Mr. Michael Alexi
Mr. W. B. Keller
Mr. W. J. Daugherty
Mr. J. A. A. Geidel
Mr. Andrew Schilling, Jr.
Mr. A. J. Gosser
Mr. F. I. Bossart

Rev. B. F. Hankey, D.D.
Rev. A. W. Steinfurth
Rev. B. F. Bieber, D.D.
Rev. A. J. Holl, D.D.
Rev. R. W. Doty, D.D.
Rev. G. Arthur Fry, D.D.
Rev. Luther A. Krouse

Mr. J. L. Frederick
Mr. John Van Dyke
Mr. John S. Lowry
Mr. John V. Laver
Mr. M. E. Studer
Mr. L. T. Shaner
Mr. Harry E. Cope

12. Indiana Synod

October 28, 1848

Clerical

Rev. R. H. Benting, D.D.
Rev. F. M. Hanes
Rev. Ira R. Ladd, D.D.
Rev. G. C. Leonard
Rev. H. E. Turney, S.T.M.
Rev. F. A. Dressel, D.D.

Lay

Mr. M. L. Zerkel
Mr. A. F. Sittloh
Mr. Chas. E. Seng
Mr. Paul Stohler
Mr. C. J. Rollman
Mr. A. G. Renau

* Date of organization of the Olive Branch Synod which, on June 24, 1920, with portions of the Chicago Synod (organized 1896), united to form the Indiana Synod of The United Lutheran Church in America.

13. Illinois Synod

September 8, 1851

Clerical

Rev. J. M. Bramkamp, D.D.
Rev. P. E. Bishop
Rev. J. B. Moose, Ph.D.
Rev. J. A. Leas, D.D.
Rev. J. R. E. Hunt, D.D
Rev. O. G. Beckstrand
Rev. Ed. A. A. Kreppert
Rev. L. J. Powell, D.D.
Rev. T. B. Uber, D.D.
Rev. C. R. Dunlap, Ph.D.
Rev. C. H. Hightower

Lay

Mr. C. J. Driever
Mr. C. W. Howe
Mr. C. G. Swanson
Mr. C. J. Swensen
Mr. J. C. Skoog
Mr. L. W. Nelson
Mr. Henry Luedinghaus
Mr. C. A. Kober
Mr. F. W. Strube
Mr. W. A. Hillman
Mr. A. T. Schmidt

* Date of organization of the Northern Illinois Synod which on June 10, 1920, with the Southern Illinois (organized 1856), the Central Illinois (organized 1862), and portions of the Chicago (organized 1896) Synods, formed the Illinois Synod of The United Lutheran Church in America.

14. Texas Synod

Organized November 10, 1851

Clerical

Rev. J. C. A. Pfenninger
Rev. Oscar Krauch

Lay

Mr. P. R. Boubel
Mr. W. A. Miller

15. Susquehanna Synod of Central Pennsylvania
February 21, 1855

Clerical	Lay
Rev. John Wagner, D.D.	Mr. E. E. Breininger
Rev. Carl R. Simon	Hon. B. F. Apple
Rev. Walter E. Brown	Mr. E. M. Huyett
Rev. Albert F. Klepfer	Prof. George C. Lyter
Rev. C. H. Stein, D.D.	Mr. John Oberdorf
Rev. G. H. Middlesworth	Mr. W. A. Nicely
Rev. C. E. Arnold	George B. Reimensnyder, Esq.
Rev. Harry W. Miller	Mr. Chas. A. Foulke

* Date of organization of the Synod of Central Pennsylvania which, on September 5, 1923, with the Susquehanna Synod (organized November 5, 1867) merged under the name of the Susquehanna Synod of Central Pennsylvania of the Evangelical Lutheran Church. The newly organized synod held its first session May 22, 1924.

16. Mississippi Synod
Organized July 25, 1855

Clerical	Lay
Rev. E. K. Counts	Mr. F. R. Epting

17. Synod of Iowa
Organized September 3, 1855

Clerical	Lay
Rev. J. O. Simon, D.D.	Mr. Lester F. Martin
Rev. W. H. Blancke, D.D.	Mr. A. T. Peterson
Rev. J. Hamilton Dawson, Ph.D.	Mr. William F. Boldt

18. Michigan Synod
October 27, 1855

Clerical	Lay
Rev. A. H. Keck, D.D.	Mr. Fred E. Buergin
Rev. C. F. Stickles	Hon. E. K. Strong
Rev. E. Huenergard	Mr. George J. Lehman
Rev. H. J. Fennig	Mr. J. P. Lantz
Rev. Paul M. Brosy	Mr. Chas A. Croop
Rev. Paul H. Krauss	Mr. G. A. Dehn a.

* Date of organization of the Northern Indiana Synod which on June 10, 1920, with portions of the Chicago Synod (organized 1896), formed the Michigan Synod of The United Lutheran Church in America.

19. Georgia-Alabama Synod
Organized July 20, 1860

Clerical	Lay
Rev. W. A. Reiser	Mr. D. E. Wilson
Rev. S. N. Carpenter, D.D.	R. L. Gnann, D.D.S.

20. Synod of Canada
*July 21, 1861

Clerical	Lay
Rev. J. H. Reble	Mr. J. C. Casselman
Rev. Theo. A. Iseler, B.A.	Mr. Emil Christiansen a.
Rev. C. H. Little, D.D., S.T.D	Mr. A. Ramsperger
Rev. J. Maurer, D.D.	Mr. Fred Dobrindt
Rev. J. Schmieder, B.A.	Mr. John H. Siegler

* Date of organization of the Evangelical Lutheran Synod of Canada with which, on June 12, 1925, the Synod of Central Canada (organized November 11, 1908) united.

21. Synod of Kansas
Organized November 5, 1868

Clerical	Lay
Rev. C. N. Swihart, D.D.	Mr. C. H. Wortz
Rev. Charles Puls	Mr. L. T. Bang
Rev. I. B. Heisey	Mr. A. G. Sabol
Rev. H. J. McGuire, D.D.	Mr. E. E. Sterling

22. Synod of Nebraska
Organized September 1, 1871

Clerical	Lay
Rev. R. E. Rangeler	Mr. Albert Hedelund
Rev. A. O. Frank	Mr. A. T. Yost
Rev. W. A. Klink	Mr. B. M. Boals
Rev. J. L. Sawyer	Mr. I. M. Augustine
Rev. W. I. Guss, D.D.	Mr. Ernest Enke

23. Wartburg Synod
Organized 1875

Clerical	Lay
Rev. R. Neumann, D.D., Litt.D.	Mr. Christ Hummel
Rev. Geo. Schulz, D.D.	Mr. Martin Kottman a.
Rev. R. B. Garten, D.D.	Mr. W. F. Dehn a.
Rev. F. Werhahn	Mr. John Black a.
Rev. Gottfried Kempf	Mr. Rudolph Lang

24. German Synod of Nebraska
Organized July 24, 1890

Clerical	Lay
Rev. F. C. Schuldt	Mr. Geo. H. Hilbers
Rev. J. Huebner, S.T.M.	Mr. Albert Siemers
Rev. E. Klotsche, Ph.D., D.D.	Mr. John Wagner
Rev. Wm. Harder	Mr. L. J. Siekman
Rev. H. A. Teckhaus, S.T.M.	Mr. W. H. Weiss
Rev. J. A. Bahnsen	Mr. R. G. Jenny
Rev. E. C. Hansen	Mr. H. S. Monke
Rev. M. Schroeder	Mr. Fred Bartels

25. Synod of California
Organized April 2, 1891

Clerical	Lay
Rev. Jesse W. Ball, Ph.D.	Mr. William B. Scheehl
Rev. David R. Huber, D.D.	Mr. John Esterly
Rev. John E. Hoick	Mr. J. Joergensen
Rev. Chas F. Oehler, D.D.	Mr. Clarence B. Runkle ?

26. Rocky Mountain Synod
Organized May 6, 1891

Clerical	Lay
Rev. Charles S. Bream	Mr. Peter Frandsen
Rev. Wilson P. Ard	Mr. J. N. Hiller

27. Synod of the Northwest
Organized September 22, 1891

Clerical	Lay
Rev. R. H. Gerberding	Mr. Clayton Berdal
Rev. P. H. Roth, D.D.	Mr. George Hemsing
Rev. C. E. Fritz	Mr. J. A. Krenske
Rev. Wm. F. Bacher, D.D.	Mr. J. W. Jouno
Rev. Wm. H. Gable	Mr. J. K. Jensen
Rev. Edwin F. Marker	Mr. Wm. Siegman
Rev. S. H. Roth	Mr. Martin Veaux
Rev. Webster H. Clement	Mr. Chas J. Christenson

28. Manitoba Synod
Organized July 16, 1897

Clerical	Lay
Rev. Thos. Hartig	
Rev. H. W. Harms	
Rev. Geo. C. Weidenhammer	

29. Pacific Synod
Organized September 26, 1901

Clerical	Lay
Rev. D. D. Kistler	Mr. W. H. Hoover
Rev. F. W. Bussard	Mr. John Hartman
Rev. T. A. Jansen	Mr. H. H. Petershagen

30. Nova Scotia Synod
Organized July 10, 1903

Clerical	Lay
Rev. Geo. P. Endy	Mr. J. E. Hirtle

31. Synod of West Virginia
Organized April 17, 1912

Clerical	*Lay*
Rev. C. G. Aurand	Mr. Glen R. Edgar
Rev. C. A. Shilke	Mr. R. E. Roberts

32. Slovak Lutheran "Zion" Synod
Organized June 10, 1919

Clerical	*Lay*
Rev. John Body, D.D.	Mr. Martin Pavella
Rev. Andrew Balaska	
Rev. Gustav J. Chernansky	

33. Synod of Florida
Organized September 24, 1928

Clerical	*Lay*
Rev. B. D. Wessinger	E. J. Etheredge, D.D.S.

(Associate Bodies)
The Evangelical Lutheran Church in the Andhra Country, India

Clerical	*Lay*
Rev. C. H. Swavely	Mr. V. Ch. John

Japan Mission and Church
Rev. D. G. M. Bach

a. Absent.

On motion the reports as printed in the Bulletin were received.

In accordance with a rule of the previous convention (see Minutes 1928, page 15) it was, by common consent, decided that reports shall not be adopted as a whole, action being taken only upon resolutions.

On motion the order of business was adopted as follows:

PROGRAM OF THE CONVENTION

All meetings and services will be held in the convention hall at the Hotel Schroeder with the exception of the opening service which will be held at the Church of the Epiphany, Second and Clarke Streets.

The offerings at all evening services will be applied to the deficit in the treasury of the Board of Foreign Missions.

TUESDAY, OCTOBER 7—Night, 8 o'clock.
The Service. President's Sermon. Sacrament of the Altar.

WEDNESDAY, OCTOBER 8—Morning, 8.45 to 12 o'clock.
1. Devotions. (Matins will be used. The Committee on Devotions will appoint those who are to conduct all devotions.)
2. Formal opening of the Convention.
3. Organization of the convention—Roll. Receipt of reports as printed in the Bulletin. Order of Business. Appointment of special Committees. General rules of procedure.
4. Action upon items in Executive Board's report concerning the roll of Constitutent Synods.
5. Approval of minutes of last convention.
6. Reports of the President and of the Secretary.
7. Election of the President and of the Secretary.
8. Treasurer's Report, with audit.
9. Election of the Treasurer.
10. Report of the Executive Board.

Actions at this and succeeding sessions to be taken on the following items. Any delegate may call up for consideration or question other items of the report, not included in the following. These are given in the order in which they are found in the report.

Restudy of the Use of Asterisks. Convention Calendar. Proposed Merger of Board of American Missions and Inner Mission Board and Work for Deaf Mutes. United Lutheran Synod of New York: enrollment of. Hartwick Seminary. Pacific Synod. Board of American Missions: Home Missions Council. Siebenburger Saxons. International Jewish Missions. Policy of Bi-lingual Education. International Inner Mission Federation. Leadership Training School Corporation of Parish and Church School Board. Budget. Report of Committee of Fifteen. Permission to use musical setting of the Common Service. Recommendations of delegates to Lutheran World Convention. (Address by Dr. J. A. Morehead) Recommendations of Commissioners to the World Conference on Faith and Order. Invitations for next convention—Special Committee.

WEDNESDAY, OCTOBER 8—Afternoon, 2 to 5 o'clock.
1. Devotions.
2. Continuation of action on the Executive Board's report.

WEDNESDAY, OCTOBER 8—Night, 8 o'clock.
> Celebration of the Quadricentennial of the Augsburg Confession.
>> Addresses by Dr. John A. W. Haas; subject, The Augsburg Confession in the Light of Modern Tendencies.
>> The Rev. Ralph H. Long; subject, Why I Love the Augsburg Confession.

THURSDAY, OCTOBER 9—Morning, 8.45 to 11.45 o'clock.
> (Before the opening of the morning session the chairmen of synodical delegations must secure ballots in the voting room for those elections which are to be held this day at noon. Each chairman will distribute the ballots to his delegation.)

1. Devotions.
2. Minutes.
3. Reports of Nominating Committees as to members of the Executive Board, of the Commission of Adjudication, of the Church Paper Committee, and of the Executive Committee of the Laymen's Movement.
4. Report of the Committee on Moral and Social Welfare.
5. Unfinished Business.

> (Immediately after the close of the session at 11.45 the election will be held for membership on the Executive Board, the Commission of Adjudication, the Church Paper Committee, and the Executive Committee of the Laymen's Movement. Each delegate must deposit his own ballots, giving his name to the tellers. Polls will close at two o'clock.)

THURSDAY, OCTOBER 9—Afternoon, 2 to 5 o'clock.
1. Devotions.
2. Representatives and General Resolutions (as arranged by the Committee of Reference and Counsel for this place and for stated places on following days.)
3. Report of the Commission of Adjudication.
4. Report of the Laymen's Movement.
5. Report of the Church Papers Committee.
6. Report of the Commission on Lutheran Church Unity.
7. Report of the Committee on Memorials from Constituent Synods.
8. Unfinished Business.

THURSDAY, OCTOBER 9—Evening.
> Banquet arranged by the Laymen's Movement.

FRIDAY, OCTOBER 10—Morning, 8.45 to 12 o'clock.
1. Devotions.

2. Minutes.
3. Report of tellers upon Thursday's election.
4. Report of the Board of Foreign Missions.
5. Unfinished Business.

FRIDAY, OCTOBER 10—Afternoon, 2 to 5 o'clock.
1. Devotions.
2. Representatives and General Resolutions.
3. Report of the Board of American Missions.
4. Report of the Committee on Evangelism.
5. Unfinished Business.

FRIDAY, OCTOBER 10—Night, 8 o'clock.
Program prepared by the Board of Education.

SATURDAY, OCTOBER 11—Morning, 8.45 to 11.45 o'clock.
(Before the opening of the morning session the chairmen of delegations must secure ballots for today's elections.)
1. Devotions.
2. Minutes.
3. Report of Nominating Committee for today's elections.
4. Report of the Committee on Lutheran Brotherhood.
Hearing of the representative of the Brotherhood.
5. Report of the Committee on Women's Work. Hearing of the
representative of the Women's Missionary Society.
6. Report of the Committee on Associations of Young People.
Hearing of the representative of the Luther League of America.
7. Report of Commission on Investment of Endowments.
8. Recognition of the Centennial of the Virginia and New York
Synods.
9. Unfinished Business.
(Immediately after adjournment at 11.45 the election will be held for
membership on all boards and elective committees not included
in the Thursday election. Polls will close at 2 o'clock.)

SATURDAY, OCTOBER 11—Afternoon, 2 to 5 o'clock.
1. Devotions.
2. Representatives and General Resolutions.
3. Report of the Board of Education.
4. Report of the Commission on Theological Education.
5. Report of the Parish and Church School Board.
6. Unfinished Business.

SUNDAY, OCTOBER 12.
The Milwaukee committee has arranged and will announce the preachers at all church services.

MONDAY, OCTOBER 13—Morning, 8.45 to 12 o'clock.
1. Devotions.
2. Minutes.
3. Report of tellers upon Saturday's elections.
4. Report of the Board of Publication.
5. Report of the Committee on Common Service Book.
6. Report of the Committee on Church Music.
7. Report of the Committee on Church Architecture.
8. Report of the Committee on Statistics and Church Year Book, including the reports of the Statistical Secretary and of the editor of the Year Book.
9. Unfinished Business.

MONDAY, OCTOBER 13—Afternoon, 2 to 5 o'clock.
1. Devotions.
2. Representatives and General Resolutions.
3. Report of the Inner Mission Board, with Inner Mission institutions.
4. Report of the National Lutheran Home for the Aged.
5. Report of the Board of Deaconess Work.
6. Report of the Board of Ministerial Pensions and Relief.
7. At 4.30—Report of the Necrologist.

MONDAY, OCTOBER 13—Night, 8 o'clock.
Program prepared by the Inner Mission Board.

TUESDAY, OCTOBER 14—Morning, 8.45 to 12 o'clock; afternoon, 2 to 5 o'clock; night, 8 o'clock. (As may be necessary to complete all business.)
1. Devotions.
2. Minutes.
3. Representatives and General Resolutions.
4. Report of Commissioners to the National Lutheran Council, including report on special publicity.
5. Report of the Executive Committee of the Lutheran World Convention.
6. Report of the Committee on German Interests.
7. Report of the Committee on President's Report.
8. Report of the Committee on Army and Navy Work.
9. Report of the representative to the American Bible Society.
10. Report of the Committee on Conference with Y. M. C. A.
11. Report of the Committee on Church and State.
12. Report of the Committee on Transportation.
13. Report of the Archivist.
14. Report of the Committee on Leave of Absence.

15. Report of the Lutheran Historical Society.
16. Report of the Lutheran Church Book and Literature Society.
17. Unfinished Business.
18. Printing of Minutes.
19. Final Minutes.
20. Formal close of the Convention.

There being no objection, the President ruled that Special Committees stand as appointed, without reading them.

SPECIAL COMMITTEES

COMMITTEE OF REFERENCE AND COUNSEL

This committee is appointed to consider all general resolutions before they are submitted to the Convention; to arrange with the President for the hearing of representatives sent to the Convention; generally to assist the President in the daily program.

Rev. J. A. Leas
Rev. E. W. Weber
Rev. F. E. Oberlander
Rev. A. G. Voigt
Rev. R. Schmidt
Rev. R. H. Anderson
Rev. William E. Frey
Rev. F. A. Dressel
Rev. Oscar Krauch
Rev. C. F. Stickles
Rev. J. Maurer

Mr. J. K. Jensen
Prof. J. C. Kinard
Hon. Franklin Menges
Hon. J. L. Zimmerman
Mr. J. G. Kurzenknabe
Mr. W. B. Miller
George B. Reimensnyder, Esq.
Mr. C. H Wortz
Mr. I. M. Augustine
Mr. Glenn R. Edgar

COMMITTEE ON PRESIDENT'S REPORT

Rev. C. P. Swank
Rev. Andrew Balaska
Rev. Geo. P. Endy
Rev. Webster H. Clement
Rev. John E. Hoick
Rev. Gottfried Kempf
Rev. A. O. Frank
Rev. Charles Puls
Rev. S. N. Carpenter
Rev. Carl R. Simon
Rev. Andrew L. Dillenbeck
Rev. C. H. Stein

Mr. Peter Frandsen
Mr. W. H. Weiss
Mr. F. P. Reiter
Judge W. C. Wiseman
Hon. D. Edward Long
Mr. L. S. Birely
George A. W. Achenbach, Esq.
Ellwood M. Rabenold, Esq.
James F. Henninger, Esq.
John L. Potteiger, Esq.

COMMITTEE ON LEAVE OF ABSENCE

Rev. W. C. Davis
Rev. F. T. Esterly
Rev. W. H. Stutts
Rev. W. Krumwiede
Rev. J. S. Tome

Mr. J. H. Rehder
Edwin Herrmann, Esq.
Mr. Alvin R. Nissly
Mr. Roy Dougherty
Mr. George Schneider

Rev. L. P. Speaker
Rev. Fred R. Greninger
Rev. Elmer F. Rice
Rev. I. B. Heisey

Mr. C. A. Kober
Mr. W. H. Hoover
Mr. Oscar W. Schmidt

COMMITTEE ON MEMORIALS FROM CONSTITUENT SYNODS

Rev. M. L. Stirewalt
Rev. W. C. Schaeffer, Jr.
Rev. H. C. Alleman
Rev. W. M. Hackenberg
Rev. E. M. Grove
Rev. J. Luther Frantz
Rev. Martin L. Clare
Rev. E. K. Counts
Rev. W. H. Blancke
Rev. E. Klotsche
Rev. W. F. Bacher

Mr. F. W. Kakel
Mr. Harry E. Pugh
Mr. A. F. Sittloh
Mr. Albert Hedelund
Mr. William B. Scheehl
E. J. Etheredge, D.D.S.

COMMITTEE TO NOMINATE EXECUTIVE COMMITTEE OF LAYMEN'S MOVEMENT

Rev. D. R. Huber
Rev. R. E. Rangeler
Rev. B. D. Wessinger

Mr. D. E. Wilson
Mr. A. G. Sabol
Mr. J. E. Hirtle

COMMITTEE TO NOMINATE MEMBERS OF EXECUTIVE BOARD, COMMISSION OF ADJUDICATION, AND CHURCH PAPER COMMITTEE

Rev. Chalmers E. Frontz
Rev. J. J. Schindel
Rev. John C. Bowers
Rev. Chas. J. Shealy
Rev. W. C. Ney
Rev. Theodore Buch
Rev. H. A. Teckhaus
Rev. Charles S. Brean.
Rev. C. A. Shilke

Judge C. F. Ribble
Hon. B. F. Apple
Mr. F. R. Epting
Mr. Fred E. Buergin
Mr. George Hemsing
Mr. W. P. M. Braun
Mr. R. C. Counts

COMMITTEE TO NOMINATE MEMBERS OF ALL OTHER BOARDS

Rev. Theo. O. Posselt
Rev. G. H. Rhodes
Rev. W. H. Traub
Rev. L. W. Strickler
Rev. E. E. Snyder
Rev. Ira R. Ladd
Rev. T. B. Uber
Rev. F. Werhahn
Rev. F. W. Bussard

Mr. James M. Snyder
Mr. R. O. Frankenfield
Mr. H. W. Ramer
Paul H. Baldwin, Esq.
Mr. Lester F. Martin
Mr. Martin Pavella
Mr. C. C. Dittmer
Mr. Frank D. Bittner

COMMITTEE ON DEVOTIONAL SERVICES

Its duties are to name and secure men to conduct opening and closing devotions at the sessions of the Convention.

Rev. A. J. Turkle
Rev. G. S. Kressley
Rev. J. W. Ott
Rev. H. C. Brillhart
Rev. J. R. E. Hunt
Rev. E. Huenergard
Rev. C. H. Little

Mr. H. L. Snyder
R. L. Gnann, D.D.S.
Mr. H. S. Monke
Mr. J. N. Hiller
Mr. Charles W. Ackerman

COMMITTEE OF TELLERS No. 1

To conduct the election of the President and of the Secretary, and also the Thursday elections.

Mr. W. H. Hager
Mr. Joseph M. Lotsch
Mr. Virgil W. Doub
Mr. A. K. Jacks
Mr. Jesse Martsolf
Mr. H. L. Zerkel

Mr. C. J. Swensen
Prof. George C. Lyter
Mr. Christ Hummel
Mr. John Esterly
Mr. H. L. Hess

COMMITTEE OF TELLERS No. 2

To conduct the election of the Treasurer, and also the Saturday elections.

Mr. William H. Menges
Mr. Chas. S. Heilig
Mr. George B. Hoover
Mr. C. W. Woods
Mr. W. J. Daugherty
Mr. Edward B. Fernschild
Mr. A. T. Peterson

Mr. A. Ramsperger
Mr. A. T. Yost
Mr. J. L. Siekman
Mr. Wm. Siegman
Mr. R. E. Roberts
Mr. John Toedtman
Mr. Wm. A. Miller

The following rules of procedure were adopted:

(1) That any delegate may from the floor move a resolution which fits perfectly to any report coming before the convention, but that resolutions of a general character must be handed to the Committee of Reference and Counsel, with whom the mover may confer;

(2) That in discussion the time of speakers be limited to five minutes; and

(3) That the privilege of the floor be granted to members of the Executive Board, to all members of the Commission of Adjudication and to officers of other boards when their reports are before the convention.

The President called for the next order and the Secretary prsented the

REPORT OF THE EXECUTIVE BOARD

I. CONCERNING THE EXECUTIVE BOARD

Members

Ex-Officio: Rev. F. H. Knubel, Rev. M. G. G. Scherer, Mr. E. Clarence Miller.

Term Expires 1932: Rev. A. Charles R. Keiter, Rev. Charles D. Trexler, Rev. Abdel Ross Wentz, Hon. Wm. E. Hirt, Hon. John F. Kramer, George E. Neff, Esq.

Term Expires 1930: Rev. Ellis B. Burgess, Rev. W. H. Greever, Rev. Arthur H. Smith, Mr. John Greiner, Jr., B. B. Miller, Esq., Mr. Wm. H. Stackel.

1. Committees of the Executive Board:

At the beginning of the biennium the following committees of the Executive Board were appointed by the President:

Committee on Constituent Synods

Rev. A. R. Wentz   Rev. W. H. Greever
                        Rev. A. C. R. Keiter

Committee on Boards and Committees

Rev. E. B. Burgess   Rev. M. G. G. Scherer
Rev. A. H. Smith   Rev. C. D. Trexler
                        Mr. W. H. Stackel

Finance Committee

Mr. E. Clarence Miller   Mr. George E. Neff
                        Mr. John Greiner, Jr.

Legal Committee

Hon. J. F. Kramer   Hon. B. B. Miller
                        Hon. Wm. E. Hirt

2. Nominations to Fill Vacancies:

At this convention the terms of the following six members of the Executive Board expire, namely: Rev. Ellis B. Burgess, Rev. W. H. Greever, Rev.

Arthur H. Smith, Hon. B. B. Miller, Mr. John Greiner, Jr., Mr. Wm. H. Stackel. Of these the Messrs. B. B. Miller, John Greiner, Jr., and Wm. H. Stackel are eligible for re-election.

To fill vacancies occurring at this convention, the Board places the following in nomination: Rev. Marion J. Kline; Rev. J. L. Morgan; Rev. Joseph Sittler; Mr. John Greiner, Jr.; Mr. B. B. Miller and Mr. Wm. H. Stackel.

II. MATTERS REFERRED

1. **Minutes; Approval, Printing and Distribution:**

The Executive Board approved the Minutes for the last two sessions of the Erie Convention at its meeting held December 13, 1928, and ordered that 4,200 copies of the Minutes of the Sixth Biennial Convention be printed and distributed. This work was done by our Publication House. The Minutes were mailed, according to a list prepared by the Secretary, early in January, 1929.

2. **Establishment of a Bureau of Architecture:** See IV, C, 5, of this report.

3. **Request of the Pacific Synod to appoint representatives on School of Religion in connection with the University of Oregon:** See III, B, 4, of this report.

4. **Suomi Synod and Work in Canada:** See VIII, 2, of this report.

5. **Celebrations of 1929 and 1930:**

(a) Luther's Small Catechism:

At its February meeting in 1929 the Executive Board took up for consideration the celebration of the quadricentennial of Luther's Small Catechism. Following the suggestion of a daily calendar issued by the pastors in Charleston, S. C., focusing thought upon the parts of the Catechism, the Board arranged with the Publication House for the publication of a similar calendar for use in congregations during the Fall and particularly in connection with the celebration of the Reformation Festival. This calendar was prepared by the Rev. Paul J. Hoh and was issued in due time for its intended use.

(b) The Augsburg Confession:

Inasmuch as the National Lutheran Council had undertaken to make provision for the celebration of the Augsburg Confession in the year 1930, the Executive Board deemed it unnecessary to provide further plans for the celebration throughout the year. Arrangements have been made for a suitable celebration at this convention.

6. **Restudy of the Use of Asterisks, etc.:**

The following shows the procedure and the action taken with regard to this matter:

At the Erie Convention a resolution was proposed that at elections in future conventions, no stars or other distinguishing marks, except such abbreviations as denote synodical affiliations, be placed beside names upon the ballots, and that the resolution of the Chicago Convention providing such distinguishing marks be herewith rescinded. (See Minutes 1928, page 403). The resolution was referred to the Executive Board for consideration and by it to the Secretary who reported as follows: "This matter has been under consideration in almost every biennium since the first and for reasons which seemed cogent, the Executive Board recommended to the Chicago Convention a series of standing resolutions among which was the following: 'In the preparation of ballots for an election, the nominations made by the Board concerned are to stand first, arranged in alphabetical order. Also an asterisk shall be used to indicate nominations made by the Board; in case of a renomination, a double asterisk. Then will follow the nominations, arranged alphabetically, made by the Nominating Committee. In the case of each nominee the Synod of which he is a member shall be indicated.' This recommendation was adopted as a standing resolution. As the reasons which suggested it are as strong as they were at that time, it is the judgment of your Secretary that the Executive Board should recommend to the United Lutheran Church that the rule adopted at Chicago remain in force."

The recommendation of the Secretary was approved and the action of the Executive Board is herewith submitted to the convention.

7. Convention Calendar:

The course pursued and the action taken upon this matter is exhibited in the following:

A resolution found on page 206 of the Minutes of the Erie Convention together with an amendment thereto found on page 284 relative to the preparation, printing and distribution of a Convention Calendar was referred to the Executive Board for consideration and by the Board to the Secretary who reported as follows: "The object of this resolution evidently was to provide delegates to the convention with convenient material for use in arriving at an understanding of the questions or issues involved in the resolutions, recommendations and findings of boards and other agencies of the Church. It is the judgment of your Secretary that this end may be more effectively accomplished by certain provisions inserted in the Bulletin than by the issuance of a separate pamphlet or of leaflets containing the resolutions or recommendations of the several agencies, as suggested in the resolution under consideration. It is very important that the delegates read all reports from beginning to end both for the sake of the general information which they usually contain and for the purpose of acquainting themselves with the specific facts and considerations upon which resolutions or recommendations are based. It is greatly to be feared that a pamphlet or leaflets, as suggested in the resolution, would tend to defeat the purpose sought. It would be inconvenient for delegates to handle two or more documents in order to secure the information needed. Besides, the preparation, printing and distribution of a separate pamphlet would involve considerable expense.

Your Secretary offers the following recommendations:

(a) That the table of contents printed at the beginning of the Bulletin shall give two columns of references; the first indicating the page on which a report begins, and the other the page on which resolutions or recommendations may be found.

(b) That, if possible, the same references be printed in the Program of the Convention.

(c)   That boards, commissions, committees and other agencies be re-quested to insert in parentheses, at the proper places in their reports, refer-ences in bold-faced type to resolutions or recommendations; thus **(See reso-lution 1)**.

(d)   That items in the Report of the Executive Board requiring the action of the Convention be indicated by an asterisk prefixed in distinguish-ing type.

These recommendations were adopted and the action of the Executive Board is submitted to the convention.

8.   Proposed Merger of Board of American Missions and Inner Mis-sion Board and Work for Deaf Mutes:

The following report of the Committee on Boards and Committees in regard to these matters was adopted by items:

"At the Erie Convention of The United Lutheran Church in America, two memorials were received, each of which raised the question of existing rela-tionships between the Board of American Missions and the Inner Mission Board.   The first, which came from the Synod of New York, raised the question of the desirability of a merger of these two Boards of the Church: the second, which originated in the Synod of Kansas, requested that the Board of American Missions open a department of work among deaf-mutes, and give consideration to Rev. E. C. Sibberson to head this work.   The final action of the United Lutheran Church on both memorials was to refer them to the Executive Board, with power to act, in conference with the Board of American Missions and the Inner Mission Board.   In harmony with this action of the Church, accredited representatives of the two Boards met with the Committee on Boards and Committees in New York, December 12, 1928, and gave careful consideration to the questions of American Church polity involved.

Your Committee recommends the following action:

(a)   In regard to the memorial of the Synod of New York, the Executive Board is of opinion that the work of the Board of American Missions and of the Inner Mission Board should remain separate and distinct.   Something of distinctive value in both Boards would be lost in a federation.   The Board of American Missions is primarily engaged in the establishment of Christian congregations; the Inner Mission Board is primarily engaged in the stimu-lation of the Church in its work of mercy.   Where the labor of the Church in home lands may reasonably be expected to produce self-sustaining congre-gations of believers, whose chief concern will be the preaching of the gospel and the administration of the sacraments, it should be placed under the care of the Board of American Missions; where organization of congrega-tions is a secondary consideration, and the work is designed chiefly to furnish opportunity to many Christians in different parishes for the expression of their faith in deeds of serving love, the supervision properly belongs to the Inner Mission Board.

(b)   In answer to the memorial from the Synod of Kansas, the Executive Board is of opinion that the work of the Church among the deaf, together with the selection of suitable leaders, should be assigned to the Inner Mission Board.   There is good reason to believe that this important work would prosper in the hands of either Board; and the Inner Mission Board is selected as the proper agency only because it is considered desirab'e to place the emphasis upon the duty of every Christian to engage in such deeds of serving love, regardless of any hope of return to the Church in the form of self-sustaining congregations.

This action is recommended to the Convention for approval.

9. **Alternative Plan for Annuities for all Boards:** See VI, 3, of this report.
10. **Plans of Committee on Evangelism to send Representatives to Synodical Meetings:**
The request of the Committee on Evangelism for the privilege of sending representatives to meetings of Synods was answered by the suggestion that the Committee select men in each Synod specially equipped to make such a presentation and instruct them in the matter to be presented.
11. **Request of Committee on Associations of Young People for an Increased Appropriation for the Luther League:** See IV, C, 9, of this report.
12. **Commission on Lutheran Church Unity:** See IV, C, 7, of this report.
13. **Commission on Investment of Trust and Endowment Funds:** See IV, C, 8, of this report.
14. **Commission on Theological Education:** See IV, C, 6, of this report.
15. **Restudy of Distribution of Apportionment:** See IV, B, 2, (c), of this report.

III.   SYNODS
A.   In General

1. **Conference of Presidents:**
The Conference of Presidents of Constituent Synods was held at Harrisburg, Pa., January 7 and 8, 1930. Twenty-six synodical presidents and the President and Secretary of the United Lutheran Church were in attendance. It was generally agreed that the Conference was very helpful in several important respects.
2. **Apportionment to Synods, 1930 and 1931:**
The budget of $2,400,000 adopted at Erie for the years 1930 and 1931 was apportioned among the Constituent Synods as follows:

For the year 1930:

	Communing Membership	Appor- tionment
Ministerium of Pennsylvania	141,229	$511,329
Ministerium of New York	44,940	162,708
North Carolina	18,504	66,996
Maryland	31,873	115,399
South Carolina	13,358	48,364
West Pennsylvania	34,338	124,322

	Communing Membership	Appor-tionment
Virginia	11,801	42,727
New York	23,233	84,117
Ohio	47,793	173,037
East Pennsylvania	34,183	123,763
Alleghany	21,315	77,172
Pittsburgh	51,300	185,736
Indiana	8,768	31,744
Illinois	24,364	88,212
Texas	2,753	9,967
Susquehanna Synod of Central Pennsylvania	26,646	96,472
Mississippi	270	976
Iowa	6,358	23,020
Michigan	9,315	33,724
Georgia	2,606	9,434
Canada	11,684	42,302
Kansas	5,236	18,957
Nebraska	8,252	29,877
Wartburg	4,485	16,238
German Synod of Nebraska	6,335	22,936
California	4,170	15,098
Rocky Mountain	1,623	5,875
Northwest	21,407	77,505
Manitoba	4,447	16,101
Pacific	2,179	7,888
New York and New England	25,491	92,292
Nova Scotia	1,361	4,927
West Virginia	3,294	11,925
Slovak "Zion"	6,943	25,137
Florida	1,024	3,708
Total	662,878	$2,400,000

For the year 1931:

Ministerium of Pennsylvania	141,335	$510,256
United Synod of New York	94,630	341,640
North Carolina	17,764	64,132
Maryland	30,761	111,055
South Carolina	13,251	47,839
West Pennsylvania	34,128	123,211
Virginia	12,092	43,656
Ohio	48,133	173,772
East Pennsylvania	34,183	123,410
Alleghany	20,988	75,772
Pittsburgh	51,740	186,794
Indiana	8,660	31,264
Illinois	25,336	91,468
Texas	2,753	9,938
Susquehanna Synod of Central Pennsylvania	26,699	96,391
Mississippi	286	1,032
Iowa	6,356	22,946
Michigan	9,461	34,156
Georgia	2,702	9,756

Canada	12,589	45,448
Kansas	5,081	18,343
Nebraska	8,436	30,456
Wartburg	5,102	18,420
German Synod of Nebraska	6,335	22,872
California	4,193	15,136
Rocky Mountain	1,638	5,913
Northwest	22,194	80,126
Manitoba	5,037	18,184
Pacific	2,177	7,860
Nova Scotia	1,628	5,877
West Virginia	3,229	11,656
Slovak "Zion"	4,849	17,505
Florida	1,024	3,696
Total	**664,770**	**$2,400,000**

3. Model Constitution for Congregations, German:

A Model Constitution for Congregations using the German language, prepared in co-operation with the Committee on German Interests, was approved and submitted to the Board of Publication.

B. In Particular
1. United Lutheran Synod of New York:

(a) On the fifth day of June, 1929, in St. John's Church, at Albany, N. Y., the Ministerium of New York and Adjacent States and Countries (organized in 1786), the Evangelical Lutheran Synod of New York (organized in 1830, see Minutes U. L. C. 1926, p. 8), and the Evangelical Lutheran Synod of New York and New England (organized in 1902), formally merged into a new synod under the name and title of The United Lutheran Synod of New York. The secretary of the merged body submitted a printed copy of its Constitution and reported that the Synod took action recording its choice of the date of the organization of the New York Ministerium (1786) as the date of organization of The United Lutheran Synod of New York.

The Committee on Constituent Synods reported that it had examined the Constitution of The United Lutheran Synod of New York and Minutes of its organization meeting on June 5, 1929, and that nothing had been found in conflict with The United Lutheran Church in America. It is recommended that The United Lutheran Synod of New York be enrolled as a constituent synod of The United Lutheran Church in America with 1786 as the date of organization and that the delegates, properly certified by the officers of the Synod, be accorded all rights and privileges of representatives of a constituent synod.

(b) Knowledge having come to the Executive Board of the contemplated removal of Hartwick Seminary to Brooklyn, N. Y., the following resolution was offered:

Whereas, The United Lutheran Synod of New York has taken action,

June 19, 1930, looking to the relocation of Hartwick Seminary in the metropolitan district of New York; and

Whereas, The United Lutheran Church, on recommendation of the Commission on Theological Education, has taken action, "That it be the sense of the convention that no synod or group of synods should hereafter organize or locate a theological seminary without first securing the consent of the United Lutheran Church" and

Whereas, It is evident that the problem of theological education in the United Lutheran Synod of New York is but a part of the larger problem of the number and location of theological seminaries in The United Lutheran Church in America; therefore be it

Resolved, That the Executive Board recommends to the United Lutheran Church in America that the United Lutheran Synod of New York be requested to take no further steps at this time that might interfere with future plans of the Church for theological education.

Pending the consideration of the above resolution, it was voted to refer the same to the Commission of Adjudication, with the request that a decision be rendered on the following points:

(1) Whether The United Lutheran Church in America has any authority at all in the matter of organization or location or relocation of theological seminaries.

(2) Whether the United Lutheran Church has definitely stated that no Synod shall have authority to locate or change a location without the approval of The United Lutheran Church in America. (For rewording of the questions, see afternoon session, Thursday, October 9th.—Secy.)

2. Ministerium of Pennsylvania and East Pennsylvania Synod:

The Ministerium of Pennsylvania and the East Pennsylvania Synod memorialized the Executive Board of the United Lutheran Church to consider the advisability of establishing a corporation to insure the church properties of Lutheran churches against fire and storm. These memorials were referred to the Finance Committee for report and recommendation. The Committee reported that it did not think it wise that the Church should enter into commercial activities and the report was adopted by the Executive Board.

3. Iowa Synod:

The Synod of Iowa requested permission to enter into a general Lutheran commission for consultation and co-operation in that state, especially as to home mission work. This request was approved, the attention of the Synod being called, however, to the policy concerning co-operation with Lutheran Bodies approved by the United Lutheran Church in 1924, Minutes, page 73.

4. Pacific Synod and the School of Religion at Oregon University:

The Committee on Boards and Committees reported upon the request of the Pacific Synod to appoint representatives on the School of Religion in connection with the University of Oregon as follows:

"During the last biennium a request was received from the Pacific Synod, that it be permitted to elect two directors of a school of religion, to be established in connection with the University of Oregon. In our report to the United Lutheran Church in America, the Executive Board expressed the opinion that important civic and religious principles were involved in this request, and recommended that it be referred to the Board of Education, in conference with the Executive Board, for examination and answer. In harmony with this recommendation, adopted by the Erie Convention, the Board of Education referred the matter to its University Committee, with instructions to submit a statement of policy to the Executive Board. This statement, submitted under date of December 6, 1928, with a few minor changes, reads as follows:

The University Committee has had before it for several years the question of participating in these schools of religion at various universities, and we have made individually and collectively a careful study of the situation, and also of the success or failure of these schools where they have been in operation.

As a result of this study we submit the following conclusions:

(a) A study of the work at three universities, carefully prepared but confidentially given, indicates that in all of them there has been a great deal of discord. The teaching of religion has been emasculated; comparatively few students have been enrolled; and the work has not been satisfactory either to the university or the Church.

(b) We believe that it is the duty of the university to teach religion as a part of phenomena, and also in the spirit of investigation; but we do not believe that the university can ever satisfactorily take up the educational work of the Church.

(c) Co operation in the conduct of such schools of religion is contrary to our Lutheran traditions, involves us in situations over which we have no control, and jeopardizes Lutheran unity. We are of the opinion, therefore, that such co-operation will prove both inadvisable and unsatisfactory to any of our Constituent Synods.

(d) The efficient way to teach religion on the part of the Church is not through participation in the management of such schools, but rather in the calling of specially qualified men to serve as university pastors in well located and adequately equipped churches.

Your Committee on Boards and Committees recommends that the Executive Board concur in the general principles of religious education, embodied in the above statement, and recommends that the Board of Education answer the request of the Pacific Synod in accordance therewith.

The report and recommendation of the Committee on Boards and Committees was adopted and this action is recommended for adoption by the Convention.

5. Pittsburgh Synod:

The Pittsburgh Synod requested the Executive Board of the United Lutheran Church to permit the sending of a representative of the Synod to the National Inner Mission Conference held annually in some metropolitan center of the country. It was the judgment of the Executive Board that a practice such as that requested by the Pittsburgh Synod would tend to destroy the character of the National Lutheran Inner Mission Conference as a free conference (see Constitution of National Lutheran Inner Mission Conference, Article II) and to effect an official intersynodical organization that would be inadvisable.

6. Georgia-Alabama Synod:

Official information was received that the Synod of Georgia and Adjacent States had by formal action changed its name to the Georgia-Alabama Synod and that the Synod had been duly incorporated under its new name. The Synod has been so listed in the roll of delegates to this convention.

IV. BOARDS AND COMMITTEES

A. In General

Restudy of the Use of Asterisks, etc.: See II, 6.

B. In Particular

1. Commission of Adjudication:

Vacancy filled: Judge Henry W. Harter, having been elected by the Erie Convention as a member of the Board of Ministerial Pensions and Relief, resigned from the Commission of Adjudication in order to accept the new position. Upon nomination of the Commission, Robbin B. Wolf, Esq., was elected by the Executive Board, December 13, 1928, to fill the vacancy.

2. Board of Foreign Missions:

(a) **Request for an appeal to the churches for full apportionment:** A request from the Foreign Mission Board, asking the Executive Board to consider the advisability of making during the fall months of 1929 an earnest, vigorous appeal to the church at large to meet in full the apportionment, was referred to the Committee of Fifteen appointed at Erie to devise plans for the raising of the full amount of the budget adopted.

(b) **Incomes from Hottenstein and Pflaum Trusts:** Upon recommendation of the Finance Committee the undesignated income from the Hottenstein Trust and the Pflaum Trust was given for the biennium to the Board of Foreign Missions.

(c) **Restudy of Distribution of Apportionment:** The Executive Board was instructed to restudy the subject of the distribution of the apportionment among the various causes with a view to increasing the percentage allotted to the Board of Foreign Missions. (Minutes 1928, page 168.) This matter was taken under consideration in the preparation of the budget summitted in this report. (See VI, 6.)

(d) **Offerings:** The Executive Board took action assigning the offerings to be taken at this convention to the use of the Board of Foreign Missions.

(e) **International Lutheran Relationships:** At a meeting of the Lutheran Foreign Missions Conference of America, March 5, 1930, the following action was taken:

Resolved, That the Lutheran Foreign Missions Conference of America respectfully requests the Executive Committee of the Lutheran World Convention to constitute a standing sub-committee on Foreign Missions, one of whose duties shall be to arrange through said Executive Committee, either in connection with the regular meetings of the Lutheran World Convention, or at other stated times, a World Lutheran Foreign Missions Conference.

While this action was under consideration by the Board of Foreign Missions, the Executive Board gave the following advice: Inasmuch as the question of external relationships is involved and also inasmuch as the question has been raised whether it is a wise policy for the United Lutheran Church to concentrate all her international relationships in one organization, the Board of Foreign Missions be advised that it is the judgment of the Executive Board that international Foreign Mission contacts be formed direct with the Foreign Mission agencies of other lands.

(f) **Proposed Constitution of the Evangelical Lutheran Church in Japan:** Representatives of the Committee on Boards and Committees conferred with the Committee on Fields of the Board of Foreign Missions in regard to this proposed Constitution. The Committee on Boards and Committees reported that while this document is not regarded as an ideal body of law, it is a necessary step in that direction; and that its approval at this time by the United Lutheran Church in America is considered highly important by the entire group of our missionaries in Japan, as well as by the Board of Foreign Missions. In accordance with the report of the Committee, the Executive Board recommends to the United Lutheran Church in America the approval of the certified copy of the Constitution of the Evangelical Lutheran Church in Japan. (See Report of the Board of Foreign Missions.—Secretary.)

(g) **Vacancy filled:** The Rev. J. T. Huddle, having resigned as a member of the Board of Foreign Missions, the Board nominated the Rev. Samuel T. Nicholas, to fill his place and Dr. Nicholas was duly elected by the Executive Board at its meeting February 28, 1929.

3. Board of American Missions:

(a) **Establishment of a Council of Lutheran Home Mission Boards:** The following action taken by the Board of American Missions at a meeting held July 18-19, 1929, was submitted to the Executive Board:

Whereas, it seems the time has come when we should approach other Lutheran bodies regarding the administration of mission activities, and *whereas* we believe establishing such a contact will result in the doing away with misunderstandings, the prevention of duplication of work, and the saving of men and means for all, the Board of American Missions therefore respectfully petitions the Executive Board of The United Lutheran Church in America to grant it the right to approach the mission boards of other Lutheran bodies in this country, with a view of establishing a council to confer concerning comity and co-operation in the occupation and development of the vast field which lies before the American Lutheran Church.

Acting in harmony with the statement of policy concerning co-operation with other Lutheran bodies adopted by The United Lutheran Church in America (Minutes 1924, page 73) the Executive Board granted this petition.

(b) **Siebenburger Saxons:** In regard to the work of the Pittsburgh Synod among the Siebenburger Saxons, the Board of American Missions requested the Executive Board to consider the wisdom of allocating the work to synods on whose territory it is being conducted. Inasmuch as the allocation of this work concerns intersynodical rather than interboard relationships, the request of the Board of American Missions was referred to the Committee on Constituent Synods. This Committee having given thorough consideration to the entire matter recommended that the Executive Board reply to the Board of American Missions that it cannot see the wisdom at present of making any change in the synodical allocation of the work among the Siebenburger Saxons. The Board of American Missions thereupon asked the Executive Board to reconsider this action of February 28, 1929, concerning work among the Siebenburger Saxons, and that a conference be had upon the subject between representatives of the Executive Board and the Board of American Missions. At its meeting May 9, 1929, the Executive Board took action asking the Board of American Missions to supply any additional information and instructing the officers to arrange for a conference. Such conference was held with the representatives of the Board of American Missions and the officers reported as follows:

It became evident that some misunderstanding existed concerning our synodical principles and concerning linguistic policies. The conference unanimously recognized that our present linguistic methods of operation are not to be regarded as ideal and lasting ones from the standpoint of synodical organization, but are of distinct value for present circumstances. Furthermore the conference recognized clearly the bearing of the action of the Richmond Convention concerning the Siebenburger work (Minutes 1926, page 87), as follows: "When congregations are to be established on the territory of another synod permission shall be obtained from such synod." In view of the above, the officers believe that no action is needed by the Executive Board further than the approval of these findings.

The findings of the officers in regard to this matter were approved by the Executive Board.

(c) **International Jewish Missions:** In the interest of its Jewish Missions, the Board of American Missions desired the establishment of relations with the International Missionary Council. Although this is a Foreign Missionary Council, our Jewish Mission work has been definitely committed to the Board of American Missions. The Executive Board therefore recommends that this relationship to the International Missionary Council be approved.

(d) **Vacancies filled:** Upon nomination of the Board of American Missions, the Rev. Paul H. Krauss was elected by the Executive Board to succeed the Rev. George Gebert, resigned; later, the Rev. L. W. Steckel, to succeed the Rev. Paul H. Krauss, resigned; Mr. Charles H. Lehman to succeed Mr. Wm. E. Black, resigned, and John A. Hoober, Esq., to succeed Mr. W. L. Glatfelter, deceased.

4. Board of Northwestern Missions:

The Minutes of this Board were received and filed with the archives of the Church.

5. West Indies Mission Board:

Vacancies filled: Upon nomination of the West Indies Mission Board Mr. Charles H. Lehmann was elected to fill a vacancy occasioned by the resignation of Mr. I. Searles Runyon; the Rev. Jacob Maurer to fill a vacancy caused by the death of the Rev. J. H. Meyer; and Mr. H. F. Heuer to fill a vacancy caused by the death of Mr. W. L. Glatfelter.

6. Board of Education:

(a) **Day of Prayer:** The following resolution was submitted to the Executive Board by the Board of Education:

"That we recommend to the Executive Board of The United Lutheran Church in America the holding of 'College Sunday' (or 'Day of Prayer for Colleges, Universities, etc.,' as commonly called and to which phraseology there is objection) in connection with the Sunday of American Education Week, and ask said Board for permission to make the change from Reformation Sunday."

The Executive Board adopted the report of the Committee on Boards and Committees as follows: Your Committee on Boards and Committees has given careful consideration to this request of the Board of Education; to the special rubric governing the use of the day in the Calendar of Special Days and Seasons, adopted by the Erie Convention, (See Minutes of 1928, page 54); and to the necessity of keeping the month of November as free as possible for the every member canvass in all the churches; and recommends to the Executive Board that no changes be made in the Calendar of Special Days and Seasons at the present time.

(b) **Policy of Bi-lingual Education,** which was submitted by representatives of certain boards and committees, was approved by the Executive Board and is recommended to the Convention for adoption.

At a meeting of the Board of American Missions, January 17, 1930, action was taken, looking toward the establishment of a more definite policy of bi-lingual education of men for the ministry. In harmony with this action, representatives of the Board of American Missions, the Board of Education, the Committee on German Interests, and the Committee on Boards and Committees of the Executive Board, met in Philadelphia, February 12, 1930, at which time a sub-committee on policy was appointed. This sub-committee reported at a meeting in New York, May 6, 1930, when the following was adopted:

Policy for the Training of Men in Bi-lingual Work

I. Some Principles.

(1) The high educational standards for entrance into the ministry, heretofore recognized in our Church, of four years college and three years seminary training, or its equivalent, should be maintained in the preparation of men for the ministry.

(2) This standard should be observed no less in the preparation of men who are to minister in two languages than for those ministering in one language.

(3) The bi-lingual pastor should have an effective knowledge of the English language and literature, as well as the language, literature and traditions of the people to whom he ministers.

(4) It is a NORMAL condition of the Church that, for its own welfare, its ministry should be recruited from its own parishes, and trained in its own schools.

II. Some Applications of the Above Principles.

In order to provide for the training of such a ministry it is recommended:

(1) That the Board of Education be instructed to enter into negotiations with colleges to arrange for an adequate linguistic preparation of students for the ministry.

(2) That the Board of Education in consultation with the Commission on Theological Education enter into negotiations with theological seminaries, to arrange if possible for the establishment of courses for the bi-lingual training of students for the ministry.

(3) That the Board of Education be authorized in special cases to send students of theology, who are pursuing a course of training in a foreign language, to institutions abroad.

(4) That students of theology, coming from European institutions, shall continue their studies in an institution of the United Lutheran Church, under the direction of the Board of Education.

(c) **Vacancies filled:** Upon nomination of the Board of Education, the Rev. M. L. Stirewalt was elected by the Executive Board to succeed the

Rev. W. M. Horn, resigned, and the Rev. H. H. Bagger to succeed the Rev. A. J. Holl, resigned.

7. Inner Mission Board:

(a) **Proposed Merger of Board of American Missions and Inner Mission Board and Work for Deaf Mutes:** See II, 8.

(b) **Vacancy filled:** Upon nomination of the Inner Mission Board, Mr. Thos. P. Hickman was elected to fill a vacancy occurring through the ineligibility of one who had been elected at the Erie Convention.

(c) **Relationship with the International Inner Mission Federation:** In accordance with a request from the International Inner Mission Federation and the desire of our Inner Mission Board, the Rev. H. Brueckner was appointed as a visitor to a meeting of the Federation in Germany. An appropriation of $200 was made toward the payment of the visitor's expenses.

Upon the basis of the report made by Dr. Brueckner, the Inner Mission Board took the following action which was referred to the Committee on Boards and Committees for study and recommendation:

"This is an international federation of evangelical organizations engaged in the general work of the Inner Mission. Its last meeting, convened in Bonn, Germany, August 29, 1929, was attended by 150 delegates from twenty different countries. Dr. Herman Brueckner was present as the accredited representative of the Inner Mission Board of the United Lutheran Church.

"The objects of the federation are: to further mutual understanding in the work of the Inner Mission in different parts of the world; to facilitate the spread of information concerning this work by the exchange of reports; to represent the Inner Mission and the Diaconate at international meetings, where the negotiations touch upon their problems; and to initiate common action in case of extraordinary emergencies.

"The following associations are eligible to membership in the federation:

"a. Independent central organizations for Inner Mission and the Diaconate, being evangelical and legally organized.

"b. Committees and Boards, organized by Evangelical Churches for Inner Mission and the Diaconate.

"c. Associations and societies devoted in a general way to the work of the Inner Mission may be admitted to advisory or regular membership at the discretion of the General Committee, so long as their countries are not represented under a or b.

"The administrative agencies of the Federation are the General Committee and the Executive Committee. The General Committee consists of representatives of organizations as defined above; the Executive Committee is selected by and from the members of the General Committee. The proportion of voters from each country is determined by the General Committee, according to a standard based on Protestant population. In the carefully prepared report of Doctor Brueckner, addressed to both the Inner Mission Board and the Executive Board, are five specific recommendations, which were adopted by the Inner Mission Board, December 5, 1929, as follows:

"(1) That The United Lutheran Church in America, in consideration of the common battlefront forced upon the Inner Mission Work of the Churches by secular attempts to exclude it, join the International Federation for Inner Mission and the Diaconate.

"(2) That the Inner Mission Board of The United Lutheran Church in America be authorized to acquire membership and cast the votes for the United Lutheran Church.

"(3) That, since under the conditions prevailing in the United States of America we cannot claim votes in proportion to the protestant population of our country, the Federation for Inner Mission and the Diaconate be asked to allot to the United Lutheran Church in America a number of votes according to its baptized membership.

"(4) That the desideria submitted by the Federation be received and presented to the Church.

"(5) That the outline of general statistics prepared by the Federation be handed over through this Board to the statistician of the United Lutheran Church with the request to co-operate through this Board with the International Federation toward the procuring of world-wide statistics of the service of love of the protestant churches."

This was referred to the Committee on Boards and Committees for study and recommendation. The following report of the Committee was approved by the Executive Board and is submitted to the Convention:

Your Committee on Boards and Committees recommends the following action by the Executive Board:

(A) That the Inner Mission Board be granted permission, in its own name, to enter this desired relationship with the International Federation for Inner Mission and the Diaconate, with the understanding that the costs will be financed through its treasury.

(B) That the desideria, submitted by the International Federation, be presented to The United Lutheran Church in America only after formal approval by the Inner Mission Board.

(C) That the Inner Mission Board be advised that its work in the International Federation must not interfere with the work of the United Lutheran Church through the National Lutheran Council.

(D) That the Statistical Secretary of the United Lutheran Church be requested to co-operate, through the Inner Mission Board, with the International Federation in the collection and dissemination of statistics on the Inner Mission and the Diaconate.

8. Parish and Church School Board:

The Parish and Church School Board, having formed a holding corporation under the name of "The Leadership Training School Corporation of the Parish and Church School Board of The United Lutheran Church in America," this action of the Parish and Church School Board was referred by the Executive Board to its Legal Committee for study and report. The following report of the Legal Committee was approved by the Executive Board:

"The purpose of the Parish and Church School Board, as set forth in its charter, is as follows:

" 'Second. Said corporation is formed for the purpose of developing and executing a system or systems of literature for use in the home, and the Church School, to organize schools for weekday Christian training; to plan methods of school administration; to recommend books for the library; to outline programs for Summer Assemblies, Sunday School Conventions, and Normals, and all festival occasions of the Church; to prepare hymnals; to have oversight over and control of whatever pertains to the best interests of the Parish and the Church School. It shall carry on its work in the name of The United Lutheran Church in America, and in accordance with the Doctrinal Basis, Constitution, Acts and Rulings of said United Lutheran Church in America, and to this end the Board shall have power to prosecute the work entrusted to it.'

"Prior to 1928 it acquired land in Adams County, Pennsylvania, and a holding corporation was formed under the name of 'The Leadership Training School Corporation of the Parish and Church School Board of The United Lutheran Church in America.' The charter, as granted, states the purpose of the holding corporation as follows:

" 'The acquisition, improvement and maintenance of real estate necessary for the conduct of an outdoor school or camp for education and instruction in Christian leadership in accordance with the purpose, policies and regulations of the Parish and Church School Board of the United Lutheran Church in America and for such purpose to lease, buy, sell, mortgage, hold and otherwise acquire, manage, improve and dispose of real estate, all of which real estate shall be located in Adams County, Pennsylvania.'

"The Parish and Church School Board made report of the extension of its work and the formation of the holding company to the convention of the United Lutheran Church but did not ask for approval of its acts.

"It has been questioned, (1) was the action of the Parish and Church School Board, in creating the holding corporation, legal; and (2) if legal, was it wise that a member should proceed in the manner in which this Board proceeded?

"As to legality there can be little question; but inasmuch as the stated purposes of the two corporations are not repugnant but, on the contrary, are of similar intent, the necessity or expediency of forming the holding company is not apparent; the charter of the Parish and Church School Board might have been amended to permit this extension of its work.

"Although the character of extension of activities in this case cannot be criticized, yet this procedure violates Sections 1 and 3 of Article XIII and Section 5, Subdivision C, Item 1, of the Constitution and By-Laws of The United Lutheran Church in America in that a major expansion has been undertaken without consent of this Executive Board and the Board of the new Corporation is not amenable to The United Lutheran Church in America except through its control by the Parish and Church School Board.

"We, therefore, recommend that in this instance the action of the Parish and Church School Board, in the extension of its work and the formation of the holding company, be approved but that for the future the Executive Board declare as its policy that such approval must be obtained prior to commitments for expansion of activities by the Boards of the Church.

"We further recommend that the Parish and Church School Board consider the advisability of amending its charter, if necessary, and of taking over the work of the Leadership Training School, and its assets and dissolving the latter corporation and that the Parish and Church School Board report its action to the Executive Board."

9. Committee on Church Papers:

Vacancies filled: Upon nomination of the Committee on Church Papers, the Rev. P. D. Brown was elected to fill a vacancy occasioned by the resignation of the Rev. W. H. Greever, and the Rev. M. R. Hamsher to fill a vacancy caused by the resignation of the Rev. Henry Anstadt.

C. Standing Committees—Commissions

1. Statistical and Church Year Book Committee:

(a) **Statistical Secretary:** The Rev. George L. Kieffer was elected as Statistical Secretary for the biennium at a salary of $800 per annum.

(b) **Agreement as to compensation of Editor of Year Book:** Through the agency of the Committee on Boards and Committees an agreement was reached with representatives of the Board of Publication as to the compensation of the Editor of the Year Book of the United Lutheran Church by the Board of Publication.

2. Committee on German Interests:

Upon request of this committee the Executive Board authorized the holding of a general German Conference in October, 1929.

3. Committee on Women's Work:

The Rev. A. H. Smith resigned as chairman and member of the United Lutheran Church's Committee on Women's Work and the Rev. Frank M. Urich was appointed to fill the vacancy.

4. Committee on Evangelism:

Request to send representatives to synodical meetings: See II, 10.

5. Committee on Church Architecture:

A report was received from the Committee on Church Architecture outlining a plan of organization and operation of a Bureau of Architecture. This report was examined by the Finance Committee and upon recommendation of the Committee it was resolved that an appropriation of $5,000.00 be made provided that $3,000.00 be secured from some other source.

6. Commission on Theological Education:

It was resolved by the Erie Convention that the Commission on Theological Education should be enlarged to a membership of fifteen and that the Commission should be appointed by the Executive Board. The Board decided that at least two members of this Commission should be named from the membership of the Board of Education, and that nominations be submitted by the President. The election by the Executive Board resulted as follows:

Rev. John Aberly
Rev. R. D. Clare
Rev. F. O. Evers
Rev. L. F. Gruber
Rev. J. A. W. Haas
Rev. A. S. Hardy
Hon. H. W. Harter

Rev. C. M. Jacobs
Rev. L. H. Larimer
Rev. J. Sittler
Rev. G. Morris Smith
Rev. A. Steimle (Convener)
Rev. A. G. Voigt
Robbin B. Wolf, Esq.

Rev. A. A. Zinck

Mr. Robbin B. Wolf, having asked to be excused from service on this Commission, Judge J. W. King was chosen to fill the vacancy.

7. Commission on Lutheran Church Unity:
As instructed by the Erie Convention (see Minutes 1928, page 518) the Executive Board appointed the Commission on Lutheran Church Unity as follows:

Rev. Paul E. Scherer (Convener)
Rev. C. M. Jacobs
Rev. R. E. Tulloss

Dr. W. A. Granville
Hon. E. F. Eilert
Mr. J. K. Jensen

8. Commission on Investment of Trust and Endowment Funds:
As instructed by the Erie Convention (see Minutes 1928, page 322) the Executive Board appointed the Commission on Investment of Trust and Endowment Funds as follows:

Mr. Wm. H. Stackel (Convener)
Mr. Peter P. Hagan
Mr. E. Clarence Miller

Mr. P. A. Myers
Robbin B. Wolf, Esq.
Carl M. Distler, Esq.

Mr. Geo. A. W. Achenbach

9. Luther League:
(a) **Request of Committee on Associations of Young People for Increased Appropriation:** A request of the Committee on Associations of Young People for an appropriation of $10,000 for the Luther League (Minutes 1928, page 317) was referred by the Erie Convention to the Executive Board. By the Executive Board it was referred to the Finance Committee for consideration and report. Upon report and recommendation of the Finance Committee the appropriation for the Luther League was continued at $6,000.

(b) **Permission to exchange delegates with Lutheran Young People's Organizations:** Permission was granted to the Luther League to exchange fraternal delegates with other American Lutheran Young People's Organizations.

(c) **Training School in Porto Rico:** The Board also approved the request of the Luther League to adopt as its missionary project for the biennium the erection of a native training school in Porto Rico at a cost of $25,000.

10. Lutheran Brotherhood:

Upon request of the Brotherhood permission was granted for it to enter into co-operative arrangements with the Federation of Lutheran Brotherhoods whereby the official organ *Lutheran Men* of the former may be also the official organ of the latter.

V. LUTHERAN CHURCH HOUSE

Report of Treasurer F. H. Knubel

CASH ACCOUNT
For the year ended June 30, 1929

Balance, July 1, 1928 ....$ 584.63
Receipts:
From the Executive Board:
For maintenance expenses ....$ 3,030.00
For telephone service ....   143.51 $ 3,173.51

Other receipts, as annexed:
Board of American Missions ....$ 2,184.71
Board of Education 545.21
Board of Inner Missions 794.23
National Lutheran Council 3,983.71
New York and New England Synod .. 1,112.50
Ministerial Pensions Campaign 43.86
Lutheran Hospital Campaign 18.78
Miscellaneous 477.50   9,160.50   12,334.01

$12,918.64

Disbursements, as annexed:
For furniture and equipment 815.56
Operating disbursements 9,634.79
Cost of repairs due to fire 460.00   10,910.35

Balance, June 30, 1929...............................*$ 2,008.29
* On deposit, Corn Exchange Bank of New York.. 1,758.29
Petty cash fund held by the
Superintendent of the building..............   250.00

$2,008.29

OTHER RECEIPTS
For the year ended June 30, 1929

	For Maintenance	For Telephone Service	Totals
Board of American Missions	$2,007.50	$177.21	$2,184.71
Board of Education	510.00	35.21	545.21
Board of Inner Missions	725.00	69.23	794.23
National Lutheran Council	3,617.50	366.21	3,983.71
New York and New England Synod	990.00	122.50	1,112.50
Ministerial Pensions Campaign	—	43.86	43.86
Lutheran Hospital Campaign	—	18.78	18.78
Proceeds of fire insurance	—	460.00	460.00
Miscellaneous telephone receipts	—	17.50	17.50
	$7,850.00	$1,310.50	$9,160.50

DETAILS OF CASH DISBURSEMENTS
For the year ended June 30, 1929

For furniture and equipment:
Furniture, etc., for bedrooms on fifth floor	$227.56	
Storm vestibule	588.00	
		$815.56

Operating expenses:
Wages for care and upkeep of building	$3,434.50	
Interest on mortgage	2,500.00	
Insurance	286.71	
Telephone	970.72	
Supplies and miscellaneous expenses	1,014.17	
Water rent and permits	36.00	
Gas	35.19	
Electric Current	474.50	
Fuel Oil	635.00	
Elevator maintenance service	100.00	
Painting	148.00	9,634.79

Cost of repairs due to fire (recovered from insurance companies)	460.00
	$10,910.35

LUTHERAN CHURCH HOUSE
Balance Sheet at June 30, 1930

ASSETS

Cash: On deposit, Corn Exchange Bank of New York	$2,823.46	
Petty cash fund	250.00	
		$3,073.46
Fixtures and equipment, at cost		3,722.19
Real estate, 39 E. 35th St., New York	196 079.25	
Less mortgage payable	50,000.00	
		146,079.25
		$152,874.90

FUND

General Fund $152,874.90

Subject to depreciation of buildings, fixtures and equipment.

CASH ACCOUNT
For the year ended June 30, 1930

Balance, July 1, 1929 .... $2,008.29

RECEIPTS

From the Executive Board:

For Maintenance	$3,030.00	
For telephone service	146.47	
		$3,176.47

From others, as annexed:

Board of American Missions	2,440.05	
Board of Education	97.30	
Board of Inner Missions	974.79	
National Lutheran Council	4,666.91	
New York Synod	1,588.40	
Silver Spruce Camp Campaign	22.85	
Lutheran Hospital Campaign	52.96	
Lutheran World Convention	76.09	
Miscellaneous	30.00	
	9,949.35	
		13,125.82
		15,134.11

DISBURSEMENTS

Furniture and equipment, as annexed	273.00	
Operating disbursements, as annexed	11,787.65	
		12,060.65

Balance, June 30, 1930 .... $3,073.46

On deposit, Corn Exchange Bank of New York....	2,823.46	
Petty cash fund	250.00	
		$3,073.46

DETAILS OF RECEIPTS FROM OTHERS
For the year ended June 30, 1930

	For Maintenance	For Telephone Service	Totals
Board of American Missions	$2,260.00	$180.05	$2,440.05
Board of Education	85.00	12.30	97.30
Board of Inner Missions	870.00	104.79	974.79
National Lutheran Council	4,290.00	376.91	4,666.91
New York Synod	1,400.83	187.57	1,588.40
Silver Spruce Camp Campaign		22.85	22.85
Lutheran Hospital Campaign		52.96	52.96
Lutheran World Convention	72.00	4.09	76.09
Miscellaneous		30.00	30.00
	$8,977.83	$971.52	$9,949.35

DETAILS OF CASH DISBURSEMENTS

For the year ended June 30, 1930

Furniture and equipment:

Radiator enclosures	136.50	
Chapel gowns	45.00	
Bronze tablet	91.50	
		$273.00

Operating expenses:

Wages for care and upkeep of building	3,598.00	
Interest on mortgage	2,500.00	
Insurance	122.40	
Telephone	1,081.58	
Supplies and miscellaneous expenses	1,440.63	
Water rents and permits	36.00	
Gas	47.61	
Electric current	582.68	
Fuel oil	699.65	
Elevator maintenance service	100.00	
Painting	925.00	
Repairs to building, etc.	654.10	
		$11,787.65

VI. FINANCE

1. Auditors:

The firm of Lybrand, Ross Bros. & Montgomery was retained as auditors of boards for the biennium.

2. Incomes from Hottenstein and Pflaum Trusts: See IV, B, 2 (b).

3. Alternative Plans for Annuities for all Boards:

The Executive Board was "requested to prepare and submit to the several Boards of the Church issuing annuity bonds, a two-fold annuity plan, the one of which shall obligate the Board to a fixed amount of interest at a rate approximating the interest earned, and the other to the rates now prevailing and which graduate according to the age of the annuitant." (See Minutes 1928, p. 518).

This matter was referred to the Finance Committee which reported as follows:

In regard to the preparation of an alternative schedule of annuity rates, we would call attention to the present provision "that Boards be given authority to make lower rates when requested to do so by annuitants" believing it provides the opportunities desired by the proposer of the motion.

The report was approved.

4. Apportionment to Synods, 1930 and 1931: See III, A, 2.

5. Bequest of Naomi Smoots:

The Finance Committee reported to the Executive Board that the litigation of Alta M. Smoots, et al, of Licking County, Ohio, (see Minutes 1928, page 68) over the last Will and Testament of Naomi Smoots, had been closed and that $917.71 was realized and turned over by the attorney to the treasurer of the United Lutheran Church.

6. Budget:

The budget for the years 1932 and 1933, approved by the Executive Board and recommended to the Convention, is as follows:

Board of	Amount	Percentage
Foreign Missions	$720,000	30.00
American Missions	912,000	38.00
Education	216,000	9.00
Parish and Church School	22,800	.95
Inner Missions	37,680	1.57
Ministerial Pensions and Relief	282,000	11.75
Deaconess Work	48,000	2.00
National Home for the Aged	14,400	.60
Tabitha Home	9,600	.40
Lowman Home	2,160	.09
National Lutheran Council	27,600	1.15
American Bible Society	6,000	.25
United Lutheran Church Treasury	101,760	4.24
	$2,400,000	100.00

7. Committee of Fifteen Concerning Budget:

The following report is here incorporated by action of the Executive Board:

Pursuant to a motion approved by the Erie Convention, (Minutes p. 105), a Committee of Fifteen laymen — to act in connection with the Finance Committee of the Executive Board—was named by the Rev. Frederick H. Knubel, D.D., President of The United Lutheran Church in America, to devise plans to raise the apportionment 100 per cent.

The initial meeting of the Committee was held in Philadelpha, January 9, 1929, wth the following members present:

Dr. F. H. Knubel   Peter P. Hagan
Dr. E. P. Pfatteicher   Dr. E. Clarence Miller
Dr. Ellis B. Burgess   Harvey C. Miller
Hon. E. F. Eilert   Hon. Charles Steele
Hon. John L. Zimmerman   Horace W. Bikle
John Greiner, Jr.   George E. Neff
Grant Hultberg   Arthur P. Black
                    W. L. Glatfelter

Members absent: Rev. Herman Brezing, J. L. Clark, E. J. Young, William H. Hager.

The Committee organized by electing Peter P. Hagan chairman, and Arthur P. Black secretary.

PLAN TO PROMOTE BENEVOLENCES APPROVED

Dr. Knubel offered prayer, and Chairman Hagan explained the origin and objective of the Committee, subsequently calling upon each member to state his personal views on the apportionment problem, and to offer any sug‑gestion he had in mind. After all the members had been heard, Mr. Neff remarked: "The talking all points to one thing—the Laymen's Movement is the organization to handle our situation. Mr. Chairman, I present the following resolutions:

1. "*Resolved,* that it is the sense of this Committee our present plan (the Every Member Canvass plan) is the most feasible for promoting the benevolent work of the Church.

2. "*Resolved,* that we urge the Laymen's Movement to give every prefer‑ence to raising the apportionment of our United Lutheran Church in America through the medium of the Every Member Canvass and its aides— the Duplex Envelope, the Budget, the Pledge Card, and the Quarterly Statement.

3. "*Resolved,* that a Committee of Four be appointed to summarize all the definite suggestions made at this meeting, for presentation to the Laymen's Movement, the Board of Publication, and the Presidents of Synods, said Committee of Four to consist of Dr. Knubel, Mr. Hultberg, and the two officers of this Committee, Chairman Hagan, and Secretary Black."

These three resolutions were unanimously approved, and the Committee adjourned subject to the call of the Chairman.

PLAN OF ACTION SUBMITTED AND APPROVED

A second meeting of the Committee was held in Philadelphia, May 15, 1929, with eleven members present, and five members of the Laymen's Movement Executive Committee participating upon invitation of Chairman Hagan. In the meantime the summary referred to in the third resolution had been prepared by Dr. Knubel, and distributed, as directed, by the Secretary. Also, officers of the Laymen's Movement had worked out a Proposed Plan in accordance with the first and second resolutions, which had been approved by its Executive Committee.

This Proposed Plan was unanimously approved by the Committee, upon motion of Dr. E. P. Pfatteicher, President of the Ministerium of Pennsylvania, after Dr. Knubel had stressed the imperative need of making education the major consideration, and had offered two recommendations incorporating his views and the views of Dr. E. Clarence Miller, Church Treasurer, both of which were accepted without debate, and made the first three paragraphs. As thus amended and approved the Proposed Plan is here printed in full:

I. EDUCATION OF FUNDAMENTAL IMPORTANCE

"It is of fundamental importance that our people be educated in the general work of the Church to which they are asked to contribute, and be inspired to respond regularly and liberally. No financial plan, however effective, can be successful unless full information is given, and a sympathetic attitude of mind and heart is first developed. This being an incontrovertible fact, it is recommended that the following educational efforts be made:

(a) "That appeal be made to the Board of Publication to assist in the education of the Church by plans for the wider distribution of the official Church papers, said Board seeking also in its plans the co-operation of other Boards of the Church.

(b) "That the Board of Publication be urged to consider with other Boards of the Church the desirability of establishing a Bureau of Promotion under the direction of the Board of Publication and with the assistance of the other Boards.

II. PLAN FOR INTENSIVE ACTION BY THE LAYMEN'S MOVEMENT

1. *Four Letters Recommended*

(a) "That Dr. Knubel, as President of the United Lutheran Church in America, write a letter to the pastor of every deficit congregation setting forth the facts as to the state of our Church, with special reference to its benevolent program.

(b) "That each President of Synod write a letter to the pastor of every deficit congregation in his Synod, calling attention to President Knubel's letter, and emphasizing the imperative need of every congregation meeting its apportionment in full if the Synod is to meet its goal—a 100 per cent Synod.

(c) "That each President of Conference write a letter to the pastor of every deficit congregation in his Conference, calling attention to the letters already received from President Knubel and the President of Synod, emphasizing the imperative need for loyalty to those officials in their efforts to carry out our Church Program if his Conference is to reach its goal—a 100 per cent Conference.

(d) . "That the Secretary of the Laymen's Movement follow up with a letter supporting the preceding three letters, and explaining the plan approved by our Church—the Every Member Canvass—and its aides, the Duplex Envelope, the Budget, the Pledge Card, and the Quarterly Statement, citing concrete illustrations showing how the plan works.

2. *Division of Territory*
"That the geographical territory covered by the United Lutheran Church in America be divided into zones, each zone to include one or more synods.

3. *Set-Up Meeting in Each Zone*
"That the (a) Presidents of Synods (b) Presidents of Conferences (c) Synodical Stewardship Secretaries (d) Synodical Brotherhood Representatives (e) Representatives of Ministerial Pension Campaign Committees and (f) all members of the Laymen's Movement, in each zone, be called together at a central point for a meeting with Mr. Clark, Mr. Young, and Mr. Hagan.

4. *Set-Up Meeting for Congregation*
"That in each of these zone meetings there shall be worked out a plan whereby teams made up of one or more representatives of all groups named in the preceding paragraph personally visit every deficit congregation on its territory, for the purpose of conferring with the pastor, councilmen, and outstanding laymen, to explain our Church Program, and to pledge them to make the Every Member Canvass, and to use the Duplex Envelope, the Budget, the Pledge Card, and the Quarterly Statement—this contact to be followed up by the secretary of the Laymen's Movement, who is to grant all possible aid.

5. *The Two Objectives*
"That this program be not considered or worked as a 'drive' but be made continuous, throughout the years, with the view not only of (a) raising the apportionment 100 per cent, but (b) effecting a permanent, co-operative, church-wide organization available at all times for use in promoting our Church Program—whatever it may be."

EDUCATIONAL PLANS BEING WORKED OUT
It was left with the President of the United Lutheran Church to bring the three educational paragraphs (I above) to the attention of the General Conference on Parish Education, which the Parish and Church School Board fostered in accordance with instructions from the Erie Convention. In this way the attention of the Board of Publication was called to these three paragraphs, also. Plans for the building of their thought and purpose into the program of the United Lutheran Church are in the making.

VII. NATIONAL LUTHERAN COUNCIL
Approval of Appeal:
The appeals of the National Lutheran Council for Lutheran World Service have been made each year in the month of May in accordance with

the provisions in the Calendar of Special Days and Seasons. Contributions of the United Lutheran Church for the year 1929 amounted to $26,654.44; for 1930, to June 30, $8,329.60.

VIII. RELATIONS WITH OTHER LUTHERAN CHURCH BODIES IN AMERICA

1.   Official Visitors to Augustana Synod:

The Secretary of the United Lutheran Church, the Rev. Dr. M. G. G. Scherer, was appointed official visitor to the Augustana Synod for the year 1929. He attended the meeting of the Augustana Synod at Rockford, Ill., on June 8, 1929, and conveyed to that body the greetings of the United Lutheran Church. He assured them of our appreciation of the spirit of cordial, Christian co-operation shown by the Synod in such tasks as are of common concern to all Lutherans and particularly of their co-operation with us in foreign mission work in India, in the work of our Board of American Missions in the West Indies and that of the Board of Education in the care of Lutheran students in state universities, and said to them that when we think of the larger work of the Kingdom and the ways of promoting it our interest in them and in the things which concern their greater efficiency is as our interest in our own. He was most cordially received and assurances given him of most fraternal relations existing toward us on the part of that great body.

By appointment of the President of the United Lutheran Church, the Rev. Paul E. Scherer, D.D., was present at Rock Island, Illinois, June 10, 1930, as fraternal delegate to the 71st convention of the Augustana Synod. In the course of the afternoon session he was accorded the privilege of the floor, and in a brief address referred to the position of leadership possible to the Lutheran Church and the increasing desirability of oneness of aim and solidarity of movement, voicing the earnest hope that the existing fellowship between Augustana Synod and the United Lutheran Church might be marked by still closer co-operation. President Brandelle in his response gave assurance of the deepest friendliness and a greater willingness than ever to move hand in hand toward the achievement of united Lutheranism.

It was a disappointment to learn in the morning session that the recommendations of the joint sub-committee of the Commissions on Unity of Augustana and the United Lutheran Church had on the Saturday previous already been acted on to the effect that Augustana's Commission be requested to confine itself to the matter of co-operation as over against any plan for definite merger. In addition to this, action was taken looking toward the affiliation of Augustana Synod with the American Lutheran Conference.

2.   Suomi Synod and Work in Canada:

In accordance with instructions of the United Lutheran Church (Minutes 1928, page 249, recommendation 3) a conference was held December 7, 1928, between representatives of the Suomi Synod, representatives of the Board of American Missions, and the officers of the Church. The topic discussed was the request of the Suomi Synod that the United Lutheran Church in America take over the Finnish work in Canada. While no final conclusions were reached, it was decided that the Board of American Missions be requested to make a larger appropriation temporarily for Finnish work, with the idea of covering the full cost of such work in Canada for the present. The President of the Suomi Synod invited the presence of an official representative of the United Lutheran Church to the meeting of the Synod in June, 1929, at which time the matter under consideration might be more definitely canvassed. In pursuance of this understanding, the Rev. Dr. M. G. G. Scherer was appointed as our official representative to the meeting of the Suomi Synod. Dr. Scherer was present at the convention of the Suomi Synod at Ishpeming, June 11 and 12, 1929 and together with Dr. F. F. Fry, Executive Secretary of the Board of American Missions, who was also present, conveyed the greetings of the United Lutheran Church to that body. The matter of relations with the Suomi Synod was fully discussed. The representatives of the United Lutheran Church were most cordially received and were notified that some definite action would be taken at the meeting of the Synod in 1930.

The Suomi Synod celebrated its Fortieth Anniversary in Calumet, Michigan, June 4-8, 1930. In honor of the event, the Archbishop of Finland sent Dr. Kares as his personal representative from that land. Dr. F. H. Knubel had expected to attend the convention, but was unavoidably prevented. He appointed the Rev. F. F. Fry, D.D., to represent the United Lutheran Church in America. In bringing the felicitations of this body, a plea was made for closer relationship with the request that a Commission be appointed for this purpose. This met with the approval of the Suomi Synod and President A. Haapanen, Dr. J. Wargelin and Missionary Superintendent John F. Saarinen were named as the Commission on Closer Co-operation. These Commissioners plan to be present at the Milwaukee Convention. President Haapanen will bring the official greetings of the Suomi Synod.

3. Official Visitor to the Icelandic Synod:

President Knubel appointed the Rev. N. J. Gould Wickey, Ph.D., as our representative to the Icelandic Synod. Dr. Wickey attended the meeting of that body at Minneota, Minn., in June, 1930. He reported at length including a report of his visit to the institution of the Icelandic Synod at Winnipeg, Manitoba.

4. Intersynodical Hymnal Committee:

The Intersynodical Hymnal Committee, which had prepared the American Lutheran Hymnal, requested permission to use the musical setting of the Common Service for the Service or Communion, for Matins and for Vespers. After conference with officers of the Common Service Book Committee and of the Board of Publication, the President gave consent to this on condition that the music be used in its entirety and that somewhere in the new hymnal unobtrusive acknowledgment be made. The Executive Board gave its approval to this action of the President.

IX. FEDERAL COUNCIL OF CHURCHES OF CHRIST IN AMERICA

The committee of friendly visitors to the Quadrennial Meeting of the Federal Council of the Churches of Christ in America, appointed during the previous biennium (Minutes 1928, page 73) reported as follows:

We, the representatives of the United Lutheran Church in America to the Sixth Quadrennial Meeting of the Federal Council of the Churches of Christ in America held at Rochester, New York, December 5 to 11, 1928, would report:

First, That the program for the convention was of unusual significance, commemorating the twentieth anniversary of the organization of the Council; that it was a source of personal profit to us to attend these meetings; that we received much information and inspiration concerning the work of the Protestant Churches in America and that we desire to express our sincere appreciation for the privilege which was given to us to attend this convention.

Second, That all ot your representatives attended some of the sessions of the convention and some of them were in attendance upon all of the sessions, so that the entire proceedings came under our observation. We would also gladly report that we were received cordially, shown every consideration and treated with sincere Christian courtesy.

Third, That after our attendance upon this convention and after some study of the aims, scope and plans of the Federal Council and with due consideration of the relationship of the United Lutheran Church to this body, we would offer to the Executive Board of the United Lutheran Church, as a matter of information and to be dealt with as they see fit, the following impressions and convictions concerning the work of the Council of the Churches of Christ in America.

First: That the members here assembled were leaders and pastors of marked ability in their respective denominations; that they were men of sincerity of purpose, and deeply consecrated to the work of the Kingdom; that they manifested but one great desire and aim, namely, to help the church to make more effective the principles of Christianity in all departments of life by means of a closer spirit of co-operation among the forces of Protestantism.

Second: That these representatives of the churches gave evidence of an earnest desire to devise plans and methods which would secure this co-operation without interference with the autonomy and integrity of the various units which compose the Council. It was most evident that they were not unmindful of or indifferent to the many and serious difficulties in the way of securing so desirable a thing.

Third: That the purpose of the Council, at least for the present, is not to bring about organic union of all Protestant denominations, but rather the securing of that real spirit of unity in the work of the Church for which Christ prayed—which unity alone will enable the Church to fulfil her God-given mission in this day and age.

Fourth: That while the objects and plans of the Council are many and varied, covering a wide scope, so much so that some of the work must be superficial, yet we are persuaded that many of the departments and much of the work is invaluable. The Department of Research alone, it would seem, justifies the existence of the Council. Its staff of students does collective work such as no denomination could do by itself. The reports at the recent meeting on the country and urban church are not only informative but suggestive and inspirational.

Fifth: That while it must be apparent to all that there is much need for some plan in making more effective the voice and influence of the Church in civic, national and international problems, and that while the Council may be sincere in its purpose to do so, yet its attempts at influencing legislation many times seem ill-advised, inefficient and ineffective.

Sixth: That the enactments of the Council in many cases, inasmuch as they are an endeavor to placate large divergent groups, lack conclusive value. The representatives which the different denominations send are truly representative, although it might be better if there were fewer denominational leaders and more pastors and laymen. The whole meeting, however, is permeated with a fine spirit of sincerity and of a purpose to bring in the Kingdom of God.

Seventh: That the United Lutheran Church in America has done well in associating herself with the Federal Council of Churches in a consultative way; that such relationship should be continued and strengthened in order that our Church may make her contribution in the solution of the many great problems before the Council and that we may assist in bringing about a better understanding and a closer spirit of co-operation among all our churches. We would, therefore, recommend a continued and careful study of the work of the Council and our relationship thereto.

Respectfully submitted,
CHARLES W. LEITZELL
HERMAN BREZING
SAMUEL TREXLER

X. LUTHERAN WORLD CONVENTION

1. Budget:

For each of the years, 1928 and 1929, the Executive Board authorized a payment of $1,702.84 toward the budget of the Lutheran World Convention.

2. Delegates:

Of the delegates elected at the Erie Convention to the Second Lutheran World Convention, Drs. E. B. Burgess, R. E. Tulloss and Charles M. Jacobs resigned. Their respective alternates, the Rev. Drs. F. P. Manhart, P. W. Koller and J. A. W. Haas attended the Convention.

3. Appropriation to Delegates:

An appropriation of $600 per delegate was authorized by the Executive Board.

4. Report of Delegates:

Report of the U. L. C. A. Delegation to the
Second Lutheran World Convention
—1929

At the Second Lutheran World Convention, which met in Copenhagen, Denmark, June 26 to July 4, 1929, the United Lutheran Church in America was officially represented by the following delegation: President F. H. Knubel, Chairman; J. A. W. Haas, P. W. Koller, E. C. J. Kraeling, F. P. Manhart, E. C. Miller, J. A. Morehead, J. J. Scherer, Jr., N. Willison and A. R. Wentz, Secretary. This delegation was chosen by the Executive Board as authorized by the United Lutheran Church (see Minutes,1926, p. 567, and Minutes 1928, p. 72). The delegation held a preliminary meeting in Philadelphia, December 28, 1928, and another in connection with the delegations of the other American Lutheran bodies in Copenhagen during the Convention itself.

The Convention was constituted of about 140 delegates representing forty Church bodies in twenty-one countries. Other American Lutheran bodies officially represented were the Norwegian Lutheran Church, the Swedish Augustana Synod, the Lutheran Free Church, the United Danish Church, the Danish Lutheran Church, the Icelandic Synod, the Joint Synod of Ohio, and the Iowa Synod. We note also that our United Lutheran Church Mission in India was represented by Mr. Samuel John, M.D., and the Rev. Dr. Isaac Cannaday, and our Mission in Japan by Pastor H. Inadomi and Pastor C. W. Hepner.

The Convention organized by electing Dr. Morehead President. Among the Vice-Presidents was Dr. Knubel and among the Secretaries Dr. Wentz.

The program of the Convention gave special recognition to the four hundredth anniversary of Luther's Catechism and of the Marburg Colloquy. It also provided for the formal discussion of certain practical problems, such as the furthering of inner unity among Lutherans, our attitude towards social problems, cultivating the devotional life, prosecuting our missionary work, and helping the needy. There was abundant opportunity, too, for personal fellowship among the delegates and for meetings of special groups representing the several branches of the Church's work. A volume containing the proceedings of the Convention has been issued in English and in German. The English volume is from the press of the United Lutheran Publication House in Philadelphia. It embraces a full account of all the formal addresses, reports and actions of the Convention, together with a complete program, the roll of delegates, and a sketch of the informal discussions and devotional services.

A. WORK OF THE EXECUTIVE COMMITTEE

The Executive Committee for Continuation Work (consisting of Dr. Morehead, President, and Dr. L. W. Boe, for America; Bishop Ihmels and Baron v. Pechmann, for Germany; and Dr. A. Th. Joergensen and Dr. Per

Pehrsson, for the Scandinavian lands) presented a full report of its work during the six years that have elapsed since the First Lutheran World Convention. From this report we learn

(a) That the Committee held annual meetings in various European countries and in connection with these annual meetings carried on deputation work among the weaker Lutheran Churches.

(b) That the Committee carried on an international Lutheran press service in the form of a News Exchange Bulletin.

(c) That the Committee provided for the production of a handbook of World Lutheranism under the title, "The Lutheran Churches of the World." This was published in English, German and Danish.

(d) That the Committee has continued the support of the weak, distressed and endangered Evangelical Lutheran Churches as far as the opportunity and means were available. This work was carried on in various ways but chiefly through financial aid. The chief object of this help was the Lutheran Church in Russia. The total amount expended on the program of relief was $133,237.27. This was contributed by the Lutherans of sixteen nations.

(e) That the Committee made far-reaching and thorough-going preparations for the Second Lutheran World Convention. The thoroughness of these preparations was evident not only from the varied character of the Convention program and the high standard of the addresses delivered, but also from the full representation in the official list of delegates.

(f) That the Committee expended 74,440.07 Danish Crowns in financing its operations during the six years (exclusive of the amount expended for Lutheran World Service and relief work as indicated above). Of this amount the American Lutheran Churches contributed 59,584.85 Danish Crowns. The United Lutheran Church in America contributed 32,215.83 Danish Crowns.

The Committee conducted all of its activities in harmony with the doctrinal statement adopted by the First Lutheran World Convention at Eisenach in 1923 and earnestly sought to discover and further true unity in the faith among Lutherans everywhere. This work was not easy. There were the general adversaries of the faith, such as materialism, unbelief, indifferentism, and false ecclesiasticism. And there were special difficulties, such as the lack of a central agency to carry out the policies of the Committee, the diversity in the languages of Lutheran peoples, and an exaggerated form of nationalism. But in spite of these difficulties an enormous volume of work was accomplished and genuine progress was made in every one of the objects of the World Convention movement.

B. GENERAL PRINCIPLES

In the course of the activities of the Executive Committee during the six years certain definite general principles emerged. These were adopted by the Copenhagen Convention for the regulation of the policies and programs of the continuation work. They are important as helping to define the nature and mission of the World Convention movement. They are as follows:

"1. The continuation work of the Lutheran World Convention shall be spiritual and churchly in character, being governed and determined by the truth as it is in Jesus Christ, revealed in the Holy Scriptures and witnessed to positively by Luther's Small Catechism and the Augsburg Confession. The discovery and furtherance of inner unity in the truth in loyalty to the confessional principle therefore is a primary object.

"2. The Lutheran World Convention shall be of the nature of a free conference or a free association of Lutheran Churches and organizations.

"3. The complete autonomy of all existing organized Evangelical Churches shall be fully recognized and shall under no circumstances be interfered with.

"4. The Lutheran World Convention shall exclude politics, national or international from its programs of discussion and work, confining its activities to the spiritual interests of the Church and the Kingdom of God.

"5. In all of its work of serving love, the Lutheran World Convention and its Committees shall, so far as the means are available, assist the needy and deserving Churches of the faith without respect to race, language or political alignment.

"6. Looking unto God for wisdom and strength, it shall be the declared purpose of the Lutheran World Convention and its authorized committee or committees to become the servant of all in the Gospel and in the faith that worketh by love.

"7. Since the power is of God and His Word, the utmost simplicity in organization is right in principle and wise in the present situation."

In the opening session of the Convention three special committees were appointed, a Committee on Resolutions, a Committee on Organization, and a Committee on Nominations. These Committees reported during the closing sessions.

C. The Committee on Resolutions
The report of the Committee on Resolutions was adopted as follows:

"1. Confessional Declaration
"The Second Lutheran World Convention's confessional declaration can only contain a statement which clearly and emphatically expresses the convention's unconditional and unchanged adherence to the Holy Scriptures and the confession given by our Lutheran fathers before God and before the entire world.

"This expression of firm and unchanging adherence to the faith of our fathers must not be diluted with modifications and admonitions which are motivated by present conditions, but which would divert attention from the confessional content itself.

"The Convention's statement must be expressed so clearly that it cannot be misunderstood, but also so briefly that it will indelibly imprint itself on mind and conscience.

"The Eisenach Convention expressed this adherence to Scripture and confession in such a way. Therefore, we recommend the re-enactment of that Confessional Declaration as follows:

"The Lutheran World Convention acknowledges the Holy Scriptures of the Old and New Testaments as the only source and infallible norm of all church doctrine and practice, and sees in the Confessions of the Lutheran Church, especially in the Unaltered Augsburg Confession and Luther's Small Catechism, a pure exposition of the Word of God.

"II. 'Luther's Small Catechism

"'The Lutheran World Convention joins with all of Lutheran Christendom in grateful recognition of the 400th anniversary of Luther's Small Catechism.

"It joyfully confesses its adherence to the presentation of divine revelation as given in the Catechism, because it is genuinely Biblical both in form and content. The Convention regards such a presentation not only as necessary for the instruction of youth, but also for the guidance and edification of the adults in the Church.

"It should be the aim of the Lutheran bodies to further the cordial acceptance of this blessed book in home, school and church. We earnestly hope and pray that this may succeed! Especially should it be our aim that in the religious instruction in the school the Catechism should secure and maintain the place it deserves both as to its content and as to its importance.

"III. Works of Brotherly Love

"The Lutheran World Convention, which is concerned with the promoting of fellowship among the Lutheran Churches in faith and confession, declares it an urgent necessity, that the self sacrificing love which was manifested in such a splendid manner during and immediately after the war should be kept alive and active in the years to come. We pray earnestly that all Lutheran Christians may continue and not grow weary in such love for their brethren in the faith.

"In view of the difficult position of many Lutheran Churches the World Convention considers organized assistance as necessary. It is recommended that the Executive Committee, which has directed this work with such definite results in the past, continue this leadership of the activity of the Lutheran Churches through such measures as it considers proper, while at the same time it keeps in touch with the existing organizations for help.

"IV. Promoting the Unity of the Lutheran Church

"Since the Second Lutheran World Convention regards the present unity in faith and confession as the only right ground for the fellowship of the different Lutheran Churches and since it regards the living testimony concerning this common faith as the most important and in fact the only practical means of furthering the consciousness of this unity, it is recommended that the Executive Committee adopt measures through which the different church bodies may more intimately learn of the faith, life and conditions of other Lutheran bodies, so that personal testimony may be employed for common instruction and admonition. As such measures special mention has been made at this Convention of the following: exchange of visits of leaders in the respective churches, organized activity for information through the Lutheran Press Bureau and through literature, and support for Lutheran theological students of minority churches for further theological study in other Lutheran centers.

"V. As to the Social Problem

"The World Convention recommends to the Executive Committee that the committee work out an answer to the question as to the attitude of the Lutheran Church towards social problems and that it do this in thorough-going fashion and with a comprehensive declaration, so that the inner character of the Kingdom of God may be emphasized. In the meantime, however, the Convention itself calls upon all Lutheran Church bodies to exercise intensive activity in the solution of the social problems of the present day in order that thereby practical Christianity in the evangelical sense may be manifested in every sphere of practical living.

"VI. Commemorating the Augsburg Confession

"As to the matter of celebrating the four hundredth anniversary of the Augsburg Confession, the Committee on Resolutions resolved, on motion of Bishop Behm, to lay before the president the suggestion that the World Convention adopt the following resolution:

"The Second Lutheran World Convention is mindful of the fact that the year 1930 marks the four hundredth anniversary of the delivery of the Augsburg Confession. The Convention expresses its gratitude to Almighty God that He gave the Lutheran Church this Confession. The Convention takes it for granted that the Lutheran Churches throughout the world will unite in expressing their gratitude for their confessional basis and in this way will strengthen the bond of unity among them.

"VII. Special Questions Before the Convention

"From the special conferences held during the convention the following subjects have been submitted to the Committee on Resolutions:

"(a)   On Foreign Missions:

"(1)   The work of foreign missions is based upon the ordinance of the Lord, and the Lutheran Churches of the world have not yet given it the place that it deserves among the various branches of Church work. The Lutheran World Convention, therefore, calls on all Lutherans everywhere to do their utmost to further the great cause of spreading the Gospel.

"(2)   The various Lutheran missions could accomplish their purpose more effectively if there were more unity and co-operation among them. Moreover, these qualities would strengthen the influence of Lutheranism in international missionary circles.

"(3)   It would constitute a permanent bond of unity among the several Lutheran missionary societies if they were to issue a common year book of missions. The representatives of foreign missions gathered in Copenhagen are ready to support such a year book by contributing material and by helping to circulate it.

"(4)   Dr. Knubel has suggested that the message of Lutheranism to the world should be wrought out with greater clarity. This suggestion is a call to the theologians at home to give more support to the missionaries on the field by setting forth the relation of the Gospel to the several Christian communions.

"(5)   Steps should be taken to have Lutheran missions more strongly represented henceforth in the International Missionary Council.

"(b)   On Inner Missions:

" 'The Committee on Resolutions is asked to secure the appointment of a committee on inner missions to be constituted of members from the various Lutheran Churches that belong to the World Convention. It is to be the duty of the proposed committee to co-operate with the Executive Committee in securing in connection with the meetings of the World Convention an exchange of experiences by various representatives of inner mission work, and in the interims between meetings of the Convention to further a sense of fellowship among the inner mission workers of the various Lutheran countries and bodies.'

"(c)   On Missions Among Sailors and Emigrants:
" 'Recognizing that it is the duty of every Lutheran to be energetically active in social affairs as an expression of his gratitude to God for the grace which he has received, the Second Lutheran World Convention in Copenhagen calls the special attention of all Lutheran Churches and organizations to the great evils that can be met successfully only by international co-operation, particularly the dire distress that befalls emigrants and sailors. The Convention earnestly entreats all officers of Church and State to use every proper lawful means to combat the exploitation of emigrants and sailors in the harbors, to further and support in every possible way the work that for many decades our Churches have been doing among sailors and emigrants, and to make possible for the sailors the observance of the Lord's Day.'

"(d)   On the Work of the Lutheran Press:
" 'The committe for publicity is convinced that the Lutheran press of the whole world should co-operate more closely in order that the cause of the Lutheran Church may everywhere be strengthened. To that end the committee suggests the following resolutions:
" '(1)   In every Lutheran Church there should be a press bureau if at all possible. This bureau should labor in the interest of the Lutheran World Convention and in the interest of the Churches that hold to the Lutheran Confession.
" '(2)   On the basis of the work done by these bureaus in the several countries, three central bureaus might be established, one for Germany, one for the northern countries, and one for America. These central bureaus might then exchange materials with one another.
" '(3)   The chief object would be to secure an ecumenical Lutheran publicity exchange, whose materials might be published in the three main languages, German, English, and Scandinavian. Moreover, it would be desirable to have an exchange of pictures. Perhaps this could be accomplished by expanding the Dresden Bilderkammer.
" '(4)   There shall be prepared as soon as possible a register of all the Lutheran papers that now exist anywhere in the world. This shall include the addresses of the editors and a description of the special character of each paper. It shall be known as "The Handbook of the Lutheran Press." This would make possible the exchange of Lutheran papers and would promote common sympathy and understanding.'

"The Committee on Resolutions recommends that all these matters be referred to the Executive Committee without definite recommendation, but with the request that the Executive Committee give each of them the careful consideration that it deserves.

"VIII.   Resolution of Thanks
"The Second Lutheran World Convention first of all expresses its profound gratitude to the Executive Committee of the Lutheran World Convention consisting of Dr. Morehead, Bishop Ihmels, Professor Joergensen,

Baron von Pechmann, Dr. Pehrsson, and Dr. Boe. The Convention recognizes how very difficult and varied the activities of this committee have been during the past six years and how blessed have been the results of those activities. The Convention therefore expresses its most hearty thanks to this committee and asks that this expression of gratitude be included in the protocol.

"Likewise, the Second Lutheran World Convention expresses its profound gratitude to the Danish Committee of Copenhagen and its chairmen, Bishop Ostenfeld and Professor Joergensen, for their splendid preparations for the Convention, for their arduous labors during the days of the meeting itself, for the interesting program of addresses, and for the cordial hospitality which they have shown. The Convention asks that this expression of gratitude also be made a matter of record.

"Finally, the Convention expresses its special thanks to the city government of Copenhagen, to the city mission for the use of Bethesda, and to all the hosts and friends who have helped to entertain the Convention with their hospitality.'

"In order that the resolutions here adopted may be realized the Executive Committee is requested to call the attention of the different Lutheran bodies to these recommendations and to urge that the delegates here present bring this to the knowledge of their respective church bodies, and that they use their personal influence to impress the importance of these actions upon their constituencies."

D. The Committee on Organization

The Committee on Organization was asked to consider the twelve Recommendations for the Organization of the Continuation Work which were presented by the Executive Committee in its report. Upon the recommendation of the Committee on Organization, the Convention adopted the following principles of organization:

"1. The foundations laid at Eisenach are to be preserved. This applies, above all, to the three Fundamental Resolutions (German ed., page 244, American ed., page 15) ; but it includes also the organization.

"2. Accordingly the World Convention is and shall continue to be a free assembly, without binding power. Its organization shall not and dare not go beyond what is absolutely required for its purpose. It shall and may be changed only in so far as the changed conditions and experience—especially the experiences of the standing Executive Committee—may show to be urgently necessary.

"3. Three organizations were created at Eisenach, to wit: (a) The World Convention itself, as a recurring assembly of delegates from all Lutheran Church-groups and Churches; (b) the Large Committee; (c) a smaller, standing Execu'ive Committee. The mandate of both these committees expired at the beginning of the Second Lutheran World Convention.

"4. The World Convention as such remains unchanged. As heretofore, it shall convene at longer intervals; regular meetings shall be held at in'ervals of about six years; special meetings may be called when deemed necessary by the standing Executive Committee. The number of the delegates and their distribution among the three main groups of the World Convention (Germany, Scandinavia, America) and the remaining larger, smaller and smallest groups, remains the same as in the past. The Standing Committee, however, is authorized to increase or shift the distribution of delegates in case of altered conditions in the various countries and groups, when such altered conditions urgently demand a change, as for instance, when new Churches on the mission field become self-supporting.

"5. The Executive Committee, likewise, remains unchanged. It is to be newly elected at each meeting of the World Convention. The members of the Executive Committee shall hold office until their successors have been elected and have qualified. From among its members the committee shall elect a president, two vice-presidents, a treasurer, an assistant treasurer and a secretary. The office of president should, as a rule, alternate among the three groups. In case a member is temporarily or permanently unable to perform his duties or in case of his death the Executive Committee is hereby authorized to elect a substitute from the same group.

"6. The work of the standing Executive Committee shall be done in part by continued correspondence and in part by convening at regular intervals. The latter are to be held, if possible, at least once every year. The place of meeting is to vary. It is to be chosen as far as possible with a view to visitations of Lutheran Churches and congregations in the vicinity or even within a larger range of adjacent territory. The cultivation of these visits is to be emphasized. They are of value for the Executive Committee and for the Churches and congregations that are visited, and of all means they are the most effective in strengthening and implanting more deeply, as time goes on, the consciousness of Lutheran solidarity.

"In addition to the foregoing, the standing Executive Committee shall do everything possible to promote unity among Lutherans everywhere. This object may be furthered by joint conferences of neighboring Churches, to be promoted by the committee or its members, by the exchange of pastors and other speakers, press communications, etc. A News Bulletin in German and in English shall continue to be issued by the Standing Committee. By this means and others an understanding of conditions of every church, even of those in process of organization, is to be spread among all Lutherans. The energetic support of weak and suffering Churches shall continue to be the most important of all branches of work.

"7. The Large Committee shall not be renewed in the form which it has hitherto had. In its stead there are to be organized within the Churches and Church territories larger and smaller special committees, which, in connection with the Executive Committee, are to be active in the cause sponsored by the World Convention within their respective Churches. Each Church or Church territory shall regulate the extent, composition, order of business, method of operation and name of its special committee, according to its own best judgment, as its own peculiar circumstances may indicate as being appropriate and conducive to the attainment of its objects. The chairman of each special committee shall keep the president of the Executive Committee informed concerning the organization of such special committee and of all important items pertaining to its work.

"8. To the Executive Committees of the various groups shall be entrusted the important duty of doing everything that is possible and necessary within their sphere of influence to give the work of the World Convention and its Standing Committee the support (backing) that is indispensable. The World Convention must secure publicity. Appreciation of its aims and significance must be cultivated, kept alive and deepened, and if the World Convention is to fulfill its great mission, it must enlist the heartfelt interest and the most liberal financial support in all parts of world-wide Lutheranism. Its Standing Committee is unable to accomplish anything without the devoted and continued co-operation of the Executive Committees of the various groups.

"9. It is of the utmost importance that the group Executive Committees work together harmoniously in the three main groups with the representatives of these groups in the standing Executive Committee of the World Convention. Details as to such co-operation, such as the organization of group Executive Committees, is left to the Churches or (and) church organizations which hitherto have assumed the work for the Word Convention in their respective group or will do so in the future.

"10. The co-operating Churches and Church territories should contribute according to their ability to the expenses of the Executive Committee and to the duly approved budget of the Relief Work.

"11. Organization is indispensable. But everything depends on the life manifested by the organization. The World Convention stands and falls with the faith that works through love, the faith that lives in the Lutheran Churches.

"Rule of Transition

"The delegates to the second World Convention are within their own Churches and Church territories, responsible for the organization of the special committees (vide 7-9). Until the organization of the committees, they are personally responsible for the work to be entrusted to these."

The Committee on Nominations presented the following names for the Executive Committee for Continuation Work: Dr. John A. Morehead and Dr. L. W. Boe, for America; Bishop L. Ihmels and Baron von Pechmann, for Germany; and Dr. A. Th. Joergensen and Dr. Per Pehrsson, for the Scandinavian lands. This report was adopted by the Convention and the men named were elected the Executive Committee. The Executive Committee as thus re-elected met at Orobro Sweden, a few days later and organized as follows:

President—Dr. John A. Morehead
First Vice-President—Bishop Ludwig Ihmels
Second Vice-President—Dr. Per Pehrsson
Treasurer—Dr. Alfred Th. Joergensen
Assistant Treasurer—Dr. L. W. Boe
Recording Secretary—Baron Wilhelm v. Pechmann

E. General Observations

In general we observe that

1. The Copenhagen Convention was constituted of more official and more complete representation of the Lutheran Churches of the world than the Eisenach Convention was. One of the perplexing problems with which the Executive Committee had to deal after Eisenach was the dual character of the representation of the Lutheran Churches in the World Convention movement. At Eisenach the Churches of North America were represented by official delegates chosen by the Churches themselves. These bodies afterwards approved the recommendation of the Eisenach Convention and rendered a high degree of material and moral support to the entire move-

ment. The Churches of Europe, on the other hand, were represented at Eisenach indirectly and unofficially by men who were not selected by the Churches themselves but were "designated" by the European Committee on Arrangements because they were Church scholars and leaders and well known for their devotion to the positive faith of the Church. In preparation for the Copenhagen Convention the Executive Committee encouraged all the Lutheran Churches to select their own delegates, with the proviso that they accept the doctrinal statement adopted at Eisenach. These efforts succeeded so well that at Copenhagen official delegates were present from all the Lutheran free Churches and the Lutheran territorial Churches of Germany and from the Lutheran Churches of France, Hungary, Jugo-Slavia, China, India and Japan. In Sweden the delegates were chosen by the House of Bishops and the Pastoral Association. Thus it is clear that decided progress has been achieved in making the World Convention the official representative of the Lutheran Churches of the world.

2. The Second Lutheran World Convention also gave some indications of progress in unity of doctrine. The doctrinal declaration at Eisenach in 1923 (see Minuntes 1924, p. 91) had been reached after much searching. Not only was that declaration heartily reaffirmed by Copenhagen in 1929, but it was taken for granted by all who participated. No uncertain note was ever sounded. The smaller Churches have clearly been strengthened in their confessional attitude during the past six years. The larger Churches have come to understand and trust one another. So manifest was the doctrinal unity of the Convention in all its actions and discussions that it has been made a point of criticism by the liberalist press that the delegates were so unanimously faithful to the heritage of historic Lutheranism.

3. It was noticeable, too, that the Copenhagen Convention registered progress in the work of promoting the ecumenical spirit among the Lutherans of the world. The efforts of the Executive Committee by visitation and publication to cultivate acquaintance and common interest among the various groups of Lutherans has borne rich fruit. It was clear at Copenhagen that Lutherans are moving towards a unified intelligence and a consciousness of Lutheran solidarity and in consequence of that are lifting their eyes above the limitations of language and nation and ecclesiastical organization. In addition to the official delegates hundreds of visitors from all over the world attended one or more of the sessions and sectional meetings, while thousands crowded the Cathedral for the open meetings there. The Convention not only manifested this world-wide interest among the delegates and visitors, but itself helped to promote more intimate fellowship than hitherto by furnishing many fine opportunities for valuable personal intercourse. Thus Lutheranism is slowly, very slowly, being liberated from the narrowing bonds of the external and the particularistic and is moving out into the broad plains of the ecumenical and the truly evangelical.

4. The World Convention movement is fraught with great possibilities

for good to the Kingdom of God as represented by the Lutheran Churches:

a) Through the exchange of ideas. The program at Copenhagen was full and varied, and the papers presented were so lengthy that many of the delegates wished that there had been more time for impromptu discussion. The papers as a whole were not new, but they showed a salutary effort to find new points of view, and no one who followed the presentation of the addresses and the discussions that ensued could fail to gain new light on these familiar topics. And even more important than the exchange of ideas that takes place during the sessions of the conventions is the exchange of literature and visits that take place between the conventions. This is of great practical value for the cause of the Gospel.

b) Through co-operation in practical tasks. The large volume of work achieved by the Executive Committee during the past six years in the face of tremendous difficulties has established a definite function and sphere for this ecumenical movement. One of the general principles adopted at Copenhagen is that the World Convention shall not become a complicated organization but shall definitely continue as a simple servant of the Churches. The action of the Copenhagen Convention on the reports of its special committees clearly shows that the Lutheran Churches of the world today recognize in the Executive Committee of the World Convention an effective clearing-house for international Lutheran activities of various kinds. A mere glance at the report of the Committee on Resolutions will serve to indicate that Copenhagen greatly enlarged the range of possibilities and opportunities for world-wide co-operation among Lutherans through the agency of the Executive Committee. In this respect the Convention manifested a surprising degree of enterprise and vigor.

c) Through the cultivating of fellowship and understanding. That imponderable influence that emanates from personality and often makes itself felt without the medium of words is no small factor in promoting the interests of the Kingdom of God where earnest Christian men from such varied nationalities, lay and clergy, young and old, meet and mingle freely for so many days in succession. The personal contacts on the floor of the convention, in the meetings of special committees and of the continuing committee, at social occasions, in deputation work and the exchange of visits, and in numerous other ways, gradually produce a warmth of fellow feeling in which polemic and misunderstanding and isolation melt down into irenic and common interest and cooperation. This was keenly felt by those who entered into the spirit of the Copenhagen Convention. It is not the smallest factor in helping the Lutherans of the world to discharge their responsibility concerning the Gospel.

It will be observed that under item 7 of the report of the Committee on Organization a slight change is made in organization. The Large Standing Committee (see Minutes 1924, p. 92), hitherto existing gives way to Special Committees chosen by the Church bodies themselves.

F.　Recommendations

As delegates we unanimously recommend

(a)　That the Lutheran World Convention be the designated agency of the United Lutheran Church in America for such purposes as are contemplated in the Resolutions of the Copenhagen Convention, recorded under C, without interference, however, with the prerogatives of the other agencies of The United Lutheran Church in America.

(b)　That The United Lutheran Church in America approve the change in organization planned by the Copenhagen Convention (see Item 7 in report of Committee on Organization).

(c)　That the Executive Board be asked to act as our Special Committee for the Lutheran World Convention.

(d)　That the Executive Board be authorized to act upon the budget when submitted by the Executive Committee of the Lutheran World Convention.

> F. H. KNUBEL,
> A. R. WENTZ,
> E. C. J. KRAELING,
> E. CLARENCE MILLER,
> J. A. MOREHEAD,
> J. J. SCHERER, JR.,
> N. WILLISON,
> PAUL W. KOLLER,
> J. A. W. HAAS,
> F. P. MANHART.

XI.　WORLD CONFERENCE ON FAITH AND ORDER

Report of Commissioners:

The Reports which have been submitted to us embody the "findings" of the World Conference on Faith and Order held at Lausanne, Switzerland, August 3-21, 1927. (See Minutes, U. L. C. A., 1928, pp. 81 ff.)

We deem it important that our Church should bear in mind what is said in the Preamble to the Reports, which was unanimously adopted by the full Conference at its session on August 20th, relative to the object of the Conference. "It is emphatically *not* attempting to define the conditions of future reunion. Its object is to register the apparent level of fundamental agreements within the Conference and the grave points of disagreement remaining; also to suggest certain lines of thought which may in the future tend to a fuller measure of agreement." The Preamble further says: "Though we recognize the reports to be neither exhaustive nor in all details satisfactory to every member of the Conference, we submit them to the churches for that deliberate consideration which could not be given in the brief period of our sessions."

Your delegates to the Conference, all of whom are likewise members of the Commission now reporting, voted for the reports in the sense indicated in these excerpts taken from the Preamble, and with the definite understanding that the Church which they represented was not bound by any of the statements contained in the reports.

The members of your Commission are agreed that a constructive criticism of the Reports and an honest effort to be helpful in search of truth, require that ambiguities and inadequacies be noted and that suggestions be offered showing how, in our judgment, progress might be made toward a common understanding. We are quite in accord with the following action of the Continuation Committee adopted at its meeting at Prague in September, 1929:

Resolved, that the Continuation Committee reaffirms the foundation principle of the World Conference on Faith and Order that the ultimate union of the Churches requires "the clear statement and full consideration of those things in which we differ as well as of those things in which we are at one."

We therefore proceed to record for your information and consideration the results of our careful study of the Reports.

I

The statement of the Conference in regard to *The Call to Unity* begins with the words: "God wills unity." This is the one basic declaration upon this subject and upon it we have concentrated our attention.

We believe that our United Lutheran Church is ready to endorse this proposition so qualified as to make clear the difference between unity and union.

The statement in the Report under consideration refers to the unity of the Church. This is a unity involving the relationship of personalities. It is therefore in its very nature spiritual, the unity of the Spirit and a unity in spirit. The unity of the Church in this sense exists even now. Certainly God wills such unity; and He wills that such unity be manifest in appropriate dispositions and acts.

Whether God wills the union of all Christians here on earth in one visible body, without regard to the existence or non-existence of the spiritual unity, is quite another question. We believe that the way to the union of the Churches is through the inner spiritual unity of a common faith, and that the union should be as comprehensive as this unity will permit. We believe also that the conditions of these times call for a new study, detached as far as possible from traditional predilections, of the relative importance of the hitherto divergent views about unity. Perhaps by such a study we might find more of value in organization and Order than we have in the past;

and others might learn to appreciate more the importance of unity in Faith and Confession.

II

Your Commissioners discover in the report on *The Church's Message to the World—the Gospel*—a most significant and inspiring phenomenon in the realm of Christian thought and belief. In its final form, as submitted to us, the report was unanimously received by the representatives of the Eastern Orthodox Church, as well as by those of the Lutheran, Anglican, Presbyterian, Methodist, Baptist, and other groups. This report stands out alone among the six as the one for which all the members of the Conference felt that they could vote, even those to whom it was not in every respect satisfactory. Perhaps no other document purporting to define the Gospel has ever been so widely received even for submission to the Churches for their consideration. It should be noted also that this statement was embodied practically in full in the Message of the International Missionary Council held in Jerusalem in 1928. No one can thoroughly appreciate these facts without recognizing that here is a testimony approaching ecumenical significance and value.

Under these circumstances it might seem a profanation to suggest that the Message is not all that is to be desired and not all that is possible in the way of a full, clear and unincumbered statement of what the Gospel of Christ is. Yet this was quite manifest in the plenary session of the Conference which received the report for transmission to the Churches.[*] We deem it proper, therefore, to point out how, in our judgment, the statement might be improved; and this we would do without in any way abating the joy we have that so valuable a testimony was given out by the Conference.

Passing by for the present any obscurities that may appear in words and phrases, any and all references to the effects of the Gospel, and all that is descriptive rather than definitive, we believe that the statement should give adequate recognition to the pedagogical values of the Law as the background for the Gospel of redemption. This would lead to a more definite pronouncement concerning Atonement and the necessity of faith in Christ for justification and newness of life.

III

In regard to the report on *The Nature of the Church,* we find it very difficult to disentangle that which belongs to the very nature of the Church from things which pertain rather to the work of the Church and its manifestation in the world. This is to be explained by the differences pointed out at (b) in the *Notes.* These "differences" enter in at the very beginning of the report and their influence is discernible in one way or another in almost every paragraph. Indeed, the differences pointed out in the report on *The Ministry of the Church* appear also in this report, (see Notes (b), 4), and cast doubt upon the meaning of the word "ministry" at 5 under the fifth paragraph of the report.

---

[*] See Faith and Order, p. 414f.

As a result of the "differences" the report gives no clear and altogether consistent definition of what the Church is. Now it is conceived of "as the communion of believers in Christ Jesus," to which all would doubtless subscribe; and now, in the same sentence, as "the people of the New Covenant, the Body of Christ, and the Temple of God." To this likewise all would subscribe, but with varying interpretations of these several scriptural phrases; some taking them .(as they do also the appellation, the Bride of Christ) in a mystical sense, others insisting that they were intended to teach the visible character of the Church as determined by Christ Himself. Again, all could subscribe to the statement that "there is and can be but one Church, holy, catholic, and apostolic;" but with different interpretations of the terms, especially of the word Church; some using it inclusively so as to embrace all who believe in Christ, others exclusively, as embracing only those who belong to a particular Church.

We believe that the questions, whether the Church be visible or invisible, or whether it be both visible and invisible, require further study; and that such study should lead to a better understanding. The Church here on earth may be spoken of as invisible or visible accordingly as it is thought of from the point of view of its essential being, comprising those who are the living members of Christ's body, or from the point of view of temporal organization and administration. We believe that from the one point of view it is truly said that the Church is invisible, and that from the other the Church may be spoken of as visible. In the congregation, for instance, we have the Church visible, in which are included all those who have been baptized according to Christ's command and who hear the Gospel, hypocrites and wicked men as well as true believers and godly persons; but within the congregation there are those who are in union with Christ Jesus by faith and who are "sealed with that Holy Spirit of promise." These are the Church invisible, the true Body of Christ. The same is true of the general organization of the Church. Yet there are not two Churches, the one visible and the other invisible, but only one Church. These seemingly contradictory predicables are but the ways of expressing two different aspects of the Church as it presents itself to thought. And we believe that there may be, and probably in the course of development has been, undue emphasis laid now on the one side and now on the other.

As regards the paragraphs on "characteristics," or marks of the Church, we believe that here also further study is necessary for the sake of clarity and sufficiency of statement. If these paragraphs are to be taken as an enumeration of the marks (nota) of the Church, we would suggest that it is sufficient to name the preaching of the Gospel and the Administration of the Sacrament of Baptism and the Lord's Supper as such marks. Moreover, we would emphasize that the Word and Sacraments are not only marks by which the Church "can be known of men," but that they are also and above all means of grace whereby men learn truly to know Jesus Christ and in Him to have fellowship in the eternal gifts and blessings which He bestows through Word and Sacrament.

We believe that it will be agreed that God "has appointed His Church to witness" by word and life to the redemption that is in Christ Jesus; and we add that it can do this only as it proclaims the truth as it is in Jesus.

IV

That which we have said in regard to Report III is true also with reference to the report on the *Church's Common Confession of Faith;* namely, that the differences stated in the *Notes* have left their marks upon the report from the beginning. This appears particularly in the very guarded expression concerning the Holy Scriptures and the two ancient Creeds of the Church. Differences in doctrine are admitted. Yet, notwithstanding these, it is said that "we are united in a common Christian Faith." It is further said that this common faith is "proclaimed in the Holy Scriptures;" yet by this formula the question as to whether or not tradition is to be conjoined with the Scriptures as a source from which articles of faith may be drawn and a rule or standard by which they may be judged is carefully avoided. Though tradition is not mentioned here, there is nothing that excludes it. And nothing more is said about the Holy Scriptures in this statement on the Church's Common Confession of Faith.

It is also declared that this common Christian Faith "is witnessed to and safeguarded in the Ecumenical Creed, commonly called the Nicene, and in the Apostles' Creed." Yet there is no indication here that the members of the Conference agreed to recommend these Creeds for use in their respective communions. On the contrary, the Notes say that some of the Churches "make no use of Creeds," and that "it is understood that the use of these Creeds will be determined by the competent authority in each Church."

Nevertheless, we believe that there is a common faith that is shared by living members in all of the Churches "which accept our Lord Jesus Christ as God and Saviour;"* and we believe that this is all that the Conference meant at that time to say.

Our Church acknowledges the prophetic and apostolic Scriptures of the Old and of the New Testament as the only rule and standard according to which all dogmas and teachers should be esteemed and judged; and we would respectfully request all who are interested in Christian unity to consider anew whether it is possible to say more or less.

We accept the Apostles', the Nicene, and the Athanasian Creeds "as important testimonies drawn from the Holy Scriptures, and reject all errors which they condemn."

We believe, however, that while the quest for Christian unity must be conducted "in the direction pointed out by the Ecumenical Creeds,"** due

---

* The original Call for a Conference. See Faith and Order p. vii.
** See Declaration of Lutherans. Faith and Order p. 374.

regard must also be given to that which the Church has attained in the way of doctrinal development and confessional statement since the formulation of the ancient creeds, c. may attain in the future. Thus very important articles of faith not included, at least not adequately stated, in the earlier creeds, will come into consideration.

V

Report V treats of *The Ministry of the Church*. It is difficult, if not impossible, to decide whether, in any one of the five propositions concerning which the members of the Conference say "we find ourselves in substantial accord," the word "ministry" is used of an office and function or as a collective term denoting an order of ministers, the clergy as distinct from the laity. The latter seems to be the meaning. The obscurity here arises again out of the "differences" which are pointed out in the subsequent paragraphs and especially in the *Notes*.

We believe that the first necessity for a united church, so far as the ministry is concerned, is a definition of the ministry that leaves nothing obscure and in which all can heartily agree. And this ought not to be impossible. Yet we can see no way to reach such agreement except by patient and prayerful study of the whole question of the ministry in the light of the Word of God, of history and of the present conditions and needs of the Church and of the world. For instance, on the one hand, it might be found by such study that there is nothing in episcopacy, as a form of Church government and administration pure and simple, that makes its universal acceptance impossible; and on the other, that certain doctrines which have been long associated with episcopacy might well be given up as not consonant with the whole New Testament idea of priesthood.

Without attempting here to define what we understand by the Ministry of the Church, we would say that the ministration of the Word and Sacraments "is essential to the being and well-being of the Church;" and that the orderly ministration of the Word and Sacraments requires that there should be a ministry or ministers.

VI

In the Report on *The Sacraments* we find several statements which are of sufficient interest and importance to justify us in bringing them again to the special attention of our Church. We note with interest that the Conference testifies "to the fact that the Christian world gives evidence of an increasing sense of the significance and value of Sacraments." We cordially assent to the following propositions: "We agree that Sacraments are of divine appoin'ment." "We hold . . . . that the Sacraments are means of grace through which God works invisibly in us. We recognize also that in the gifts of His grace God is not limited by His own Sacraments." "We believe that in Baptism administered with water in the name of the Father, the Son and the Holy Spirit, for the remission of sins, we are baptized by one Spirit into one body." "We believe that in the Holy Communion our Lord is present." "We agree that the Sacrament of the Lord's Supper is the Church's most sacred act of worship." We enter into the prayer with which the statement closes, "that the differences which prevent full communion at the present time may be removed."

Like the other reports this one recognizes and frankly points out "differences in conception and interpretation;" and these were sufficient to convince the Conference that it "should not go into detail in considering Sacraments."

We deem it proper to add the following suggestions in reference to the subject now under consideration.

A Sacrament is a means of bringing and conferring grace, life, salvation, assurance and consolation to the believer. In this it does not differ from the Word of the Gospel itself. It is, as St. Augustine said, a *verbum invisibile*. It is the Word of God in Baptism that makes it a gracious water of life. In the Sacrament of the Altar the chief things, besides the bodily eating and drinking, are the words: "This is My body, which is given for you;" "This is the New Testament in My blood, which is shed for you, for the remission of sins."

Christ is in His Word; Christ is in His Sacraments. In the preached Word He is set forth audibly, and to all the hearers collectively. In the Sacrament He gives Himself individually to the recipients. In either case faith is necessary to a worthy and profitable reception.

The chief "differences" which we note here grow out of the following questions: Are Sacraments necessary? How many Sacraments are there? What have we in a Sacrament? What benefits does a Sacrament confer? Who can administer a Sacrament validly? We believe that all these questions can and must be answered only from the Holy Scriptures.

Nothing is said in the Report concerning the proper subjects of baptism.

VII

Report VII, on *The Unity of Christendom and the Relation thereto of Existing Churches,* stands in a class by itself. In the form in which it finally came before the Conference it was referred to the Continuation Committee. The report was amended and revised by a committee of six appointed by the Continuation Committee, and as so revised was presented to the Business Committee and by it "submitted to the Churches for such consideration as they may desire to give it." (See Minutes of the U. L. C. A., 1928, p. 90.)

In view of the Declaration of the United Lutheran Church made at Washington, D. C., in 1920, Concerning the Organic Union of Protestant Churches and Concerning Cooperative Movements Among the Protestant

Churches (see Minutes of the U. L. C. A., 1920, pp. 96-99), your Commission deemed it unnecessary to consider this report at length.

We find, however, at least two suggestions in the report to which we would give our full endorsement.

A. 1. The first of these appears in Section IV, paragraph 2, where it is said: "In the meantime, we welcome the movement already under way for the union of bodies of similar doctrine, polity and worship, and trust that it may continue with ever greater success." In line with this suggestion and with the present situation in mind,

We recommend that the United Lutheran Church reaffirm its Declaration Concerning the Relation of the Evangelical Lutheran Church Bodies to One Another, as follows:

"In the case of those Church Bodies calling themselves Evangelical Lutheran, and subscribing the Confessions which have always been regarded as the standards of Evangelical Lutheran doctrine, the United Lutheran Church in America recognizes no doctrinal reasons against complete cooperation and organic union with such bodies." (Minutes U. L. C. A., 1920, p. 96.)

2. The other suggestion is found in Section VI of the report under consideration, in the first paragraph. It is as follows: "Ambiguous statements and hasty measures may hinder rather than hasten the work of unification." This appears in the first and second drafts of the report as well as in the final. It seems to have been the sifted judgment of the Conference. It is ours, too. We believe that a true, harmonious and lasting union of Churches cannot be achieved except it be with full understanding and upon a basis that is free from equivocations and ambiguities. We believe also that much damage is done to the cause of Christian unity by that undiscerning spirit which sees in the present divided condition of the Church the one cause of the slow coming of the Kingdom of God on earth. There are other causes which are, perhaps, more potent and which would work with little less power, if not with more, against a monstrous ecclesiastical organization seething with internal divisions. We believe that the movement for union should proceed along lines which recognize ecclesiastical order, and we deprecate any impatience which would force the issue without regard to the development of the Church as a whole, led, as we firmly believe, by the Holy Spirit, for whose continued guidance in this as in all other movements in the Church we fervently pray.

We recommend that this be adopted as the expression of the United Lutheran Church.

B. With reference to the work of the World Conference on Faith and Order in the future and our relation thereto we recommend

1. That the United Lutheran Church continue its Commission on the World Conference on Faith and Order, to keep in touch with the Continuation Committee and to advise the United Lutheran Church of its plans and purposes.

2. That the United Lutheran Church note with approval the action of the Continuation Committee in appointing at its meeting in August 1929, at Maloja, Engadine, Switzerland, a Theological Committee in accordance with a recommendation of the Committee of Reference, which had reported that "from many quarters the suggestion had come . . . . that the difficulties revealed at Lausanne should be referred to Commissions of theological experts." The Chairman of the Theological Committee is the Rt. Rev., the Bishop of Gloucester.

3. That this Commission be prepared to present at the proper time to the Theological Committee of the World Conference on Faith and Order, a more ample and specific statement of our position than is possible in this report on all questions which may properly come before the said Theological Committee.

4. That this Commission be charged with the duty of carrying out the instruction of the United Lutheran Church given at the Erie Convention, namely, "That this Commission be instructed to keep in touch with other Lutherans, especially those now related or hereafter to be related to the Conference on Faith and Order, and to frame its recommendations with a view to the maintenance and furtherance of Lutheran unity."

5. That copies of this report be forwarded to the members of the Theological Committee of the World Conference on Faith and Order. Also that copies of the concluding portion of our report to the 1928 convention be sent to the Committee. (See Minutes U. L. C. A., 1928, p. 96.)

6. That for the year 1930 the Executive Board be authorized to make an appropriation of $250.00 to the treasury of the World Conference on Faith and Order, and the same amount for the year following, if needed.

(Signed) M. G. G. SCHERER,
HOLMES DYSINGER,
W. H. GREEVER,
A. STEIMLE,
JOHN ABERLY.

It will be noted that the Commission made two series of recommendations, noted below as A. and B.

A. Recommendations referring to Report VII.

Recommendation 1. The Executive Board approved this recommendation and referred it favorably to the Milwaukee Convention.

Recommendation 2. Similar action was taken with regard to Recommendation 2. It is therefore, likewise submitted.

B. Recommendations in regard to the future.

In reference to the work of the World Conference on Faith and Order in the future and our relation thereto the Commission presented six recommendations. These recommendations as shown in the report were adopted by the Executive Board and are submitted for the action of the Convention.

XII. MISCELLANEOUS

1. Census of Religious Bodies—"Lutherans":

The Reverend Dr. George L. Kieffer, Statistical Secretary of the United Lutheran Church, called attention in February, 1929, to the fact that the Bureau of the Census had issued, as a part of the Census of Religious Bodies for 1926, a consolidated report on "Lutherans" No. 89, which could be purchased from the Government Printing Office at $130 for the first thousand reprints and $61 for each additional thousand. The Executive Board authorized the Statistical Secretary to order two thousand reprints of this Bulletin for distribution throughout the Constituent Synods.

2. Copyright of Common Service Book:

Upon suggestion of the President that it seemed desirable to arrange that the copyright of the Common Service Book be placed in the name of The United Lutheran Church in America, the Executive Board took action directing the President and Secretary of each of the Three General Bodies to execute the necessary papers and that the proper course be taken to effect the change of copyright. A letter from Dr. Grant Hultberg, Business Manager of the Board of Publication, to the Secretary, under date of August 26, 1929, says "The assignment of the copyright of the Common Service Book with Music and the Occasional Services from the three General Bodies to the United Lutheran Church has been received and properly placed on record with the Register of Copyrights, in Washington, D. C."

3. Seals of General Bodies:

Likewise upon the suggestion of the President, the official seals of the General Synod, the General Council and the United Synod in the South were gathered and placed in the fireproof vault at the Lutheran Church House, 39 East 35th Street, New York City.

4. National Lutheran Commission for Soldiers' and Sailors' Welfare:

At the meeting of the Executive Board on December 12, 1929, the President submitted the following letter which is the final report of the National Lutheran Commission for Soldiers' and Sailors' Welfare.

November 14, 1929.
To the Presidents of the General Bodies participating in the National
Lutheran Commission for Soldiers' and Sailors' Welfare—
Dear Mr. President:
Enclosed herewith I am sending to you officially that which constitutes a final report from the National Lutheran Commission for Soldiers' and Sailors' Welfare. It consists only of a financial statement from the auditor concerning the receipts and disbursements of cash by the Commission.
When last the Commission met as a whole and decided upon the dis-

tribution of a surplus such disposition was made to the two Lutheran bodies entitled to the same in accordance with agreements reached earlier in the life of the Commission. All of the affairs of the Commission had not been settled at that time so that a small remainder of cash was held by the treasurer. The Executive Committee of the Commission was given full authority to bring to a conclusion the remaining business. The Executive Committee transferred this full authority to the four officers of the Commission, namely, F. H. Knubel, *Chairman;* C. M. Jacobs, *Vice-Chairman;* O. C. Mees, *Secretary* and E. F. Eilert, *Treasurer.*

All of the records of the Commission have been sorted and everything of any importance whatsoever has been placed in the fireproof vaults of the Library of the Mt. Airy Theological Seminary, Philadelphia, Pa. These records are contained in twenty-seven labeled transfer cases, properly numbered with the contents of each box indicated in a prepared statement. A copy of this statement is to be found in Case No. 1, other copies being also contained appropriately in Cases No. 4 and No. 5.

It will not be difficult for any proper investigator to examine these files upon application made to the officers of the Commission. Even in the far future historical students will have opportunity to examine them by application at the Library.

After payment of all expenses there remained a final balance of $1,610.78. This has been distributed to the same two bodies which received amounts from the first distribution. The Norwegian Lutheran Church in America receives $1,487.82. The United Danish Lutheran Church in America receives $122.96. Vouchers and checks for these amounts are enclosed with the copy of this letter which is being sent to the presidents of the two bodies mentioned. They are asked to arrange so that the vouchers be properly executed and returned to the Rev. Dr. Wm. Freas, the Lutheran Church House, 39 East 35th Street, New York City. These two vouchers will then be filed with all others at Philadelphia constituting the final papers for the records. The auditor's account, as sent herewith, includes these two disbursements.

It is hoped that you will submit this report to your body in such form as seems desirable to you and thus secure on the records of all General Bodies official statement that the work of the National Lutheran Commission for Soldiers' and Sailors' Welfare has been closed.

I am confident that with this final letter of mine you unite with me in thanksgiving to our Lord Who alone enabled us all to perform this service.

With truest greeting, I am

Faithfully,

F. H. KNUBEL,
Chairman.

NATIONAL LUTHERAN COMMISSION FOR SOLDIERS' AND SAILORS' WELFARE

Final report of E. F. Eilert, Treasurer; October 31, 1929

RECEIPTS

Contributions $1,335,704.47
Interest 42,341.05

Our Lutheran Boys 425.03
Sale of Literature 1,838.41
Women's Committee (Donations)............ 6,465.41
                                              _____
                                                            $1,386,774.37

EXPENDITURES

Books $28,651.40
Brotherhood $341,530.73
Brotherhood S. A. T. C. 8,145.42
                                              _____
                                                            349,676.15
Buildings 22,479.72
Chaplains' Emergency 9,233.85
Chaplains' C. P. Loans 6 650.00
Chaplains' Equipment 27,432.94
Chaplains' Expense 25,388.16
                                              _____
                                                            68,704.95
Camp Pastors' Equipment 30,103.08
Camp Pastors' Expense 160,298.46
Camp Pastors' Traveling 8,920.06
Camp Pastors' Salaries 170,669.22
                                              _____
                                                            369,990.82
Direct Service 14,673.38
Executive Salaries 34,011.52
Executive Traveling 21,574.79
Executive Expense 19,537.31
                                              _____
                                                            75,123.62
Furniture and Fixtures 5,692.27
Financial Campaign Committee
Expense 36,876.16
Postage 1,875.54
Salaries 10,357.28
                                              _____
                                                            49,108.98
France and European Commission 85,295.26
Industrial Work 5,128.62
Our Lutheran Boys 4,872.26
National Lutheran Commission—Canada 1,500.00
Norwegian Synod 2,500.00
Norwegian Church of N. W. 3,500.00
National Lutheran Free Church 500.00
Office Salaries 27,294.03
Office Expenses 23,199.48
Office Postage 7,317.59
                                              _____
                                                            57,811.10

Printing	14,837.37
Publicity	1,911.18
Reserves	900.00
Service Clubs	56,302.89
Sundry Contributions	19,006.70
Synodical Conference	1,201.04
Washington Office	2,720.25
Women's Committee	43,506.76
Sundries—Division of Surplus	96,171.15
National Lutheran Council—France	5,008.50

$1,386,774.37 $1,386,774.37

I have audited the books of the National Lutheran Commission for Soldiers' and Sailors' Welfare and hereby certify that the above is a true statement of the receipts and disbursements to October 31, 1929.

(Signed) HENRY CRAEMER,

Public Accountant and Auditor.

E. F. EILERT, *Treasurer*   F. H. KNUBEL, *Chairman.*

5. Invitations for Next Convention:

The Executive Board recommends to the United Lutheran Church, that a special commi tee be appointed, consisting of the Chairmen of the several synodical delegations, to which shall be referred all invitations for the next convention of the United Lutheran Church, this Committee to report before a vote is taken.

6. Arrangements for the 1930 Convention of the United Lutheran Church:

Early in the biennium the Executive Board decided upon Tuesday evening, October 7th, 1930, as the date for the opening of the Seventh Biennial Convention of The United Lutheran Church in America. Later it was determined that the Hotel Schroeder in Milwaukee be chosen as the place of meeting with evening services at one or more churches.

7. Reservation of Space for Delegates to the Convention:

Upon petition of the Ministerium of Pennsylvania, it was resolved by the Executive Board that for this convention a definite reservation of space be made for delegates alone and that separate space be assigned to visitors.

F. H. KNUBEL

E. CLARENCE MILLER

M. G. G. SCHERER

The recommendation (III, B, 1, (a)) concerning the enrollment of the United Lutheran Synod of New York was adopted.

The item (III, B, 6) concerning the change of name of the Synod of Georgia and Adjacent States was read and received as information.

Pending further consideration of the Report of the Executive Board, the Rev. A. A. Zinck presented a block and gavel made from the furniture of the First Church of the Redeemer, organized by the Rev. Dr. W. K. Frick, and expressed the hope that the love and zeal and consecration to the missionary enterprise which characterized Dr. Frick may be with the convention. The President received this gift with expression of thanks and with appreciative reference to the work of Dr. Frick.

Mr. J. W. Jouno of Milwaukee introduced Mr. L. L. Smith, Secretary to Governor Kohler, who welcomed the convention on behalf of the Governor. Mr. Robbin B. Wolf responded to the words of welcome.

A printed copy of the Minutes of the Erie Convention, certified by the Secretary and President, under seal, was submitted and approved. The President thereupon declared it to be the official protocol of the proceedings of the Sixth Biennial Convention of The United Lutheran Church in America.

The President presented his report which was referred to the Committee on President's Report.

PRESIDENT'S REPORT

Recently a Yale professor prepared a questionnaire for the children of the junior high schools in Norwalk, Conn. One indirect query read: "_____ Protestant ministers are below the average in intelligence." The young pupils were asked to insert "Some," "All" or "No" in the blank. The fact is cited, not in order to criticize the professor's folly, but in order to remind our pastors that the world is watching and testing them as much as ever. Even children are invited to be our judges. Adverse criticism of the ministry is always a ready topic for shallow minds, but during the last few years some careful analyses have appeared which deserve attention. For instance, a tabulation was made of the educational preparation of American clergymen, and it was revealed that Lutheran pastors are college and seminary graduates in far higher percentage than others. A book was also published entitled, "The Beliefs of 700 Ministers." Here again the consistent fidelity of Lutheran pastors to evangelical faith was the outstanding manifestation. Neither of these investigations was conducted under Lutheran auspices. They are mentioned here, not primarily to emphasize the advantage shown in our favor, but as examples of a growing tendency to study intensely the facts concerning the Christian ministry. In connection therewith every reader of current religious literature knows the cry for a different kind of minister, claiming that the minister of the past with his set task and his set beliefs is not fitted for present conditions and that we need men who have a changed faith and a changed conception of their task.

It is required in our by-laws that these presidential reports shall summarize the general situation of the Church. They have been prepared each biennium on the basis of many facts and observations jotted down as the months passed by. On each occasion when the time came to study these notes one recurring and prevailing element in the Church's life has emerged as an outstanding theme for a discussion of the state of the Church. The topic has been a different one with each biennium. The gathered notes of the past two years reiterated predominantly the ministry of the Church, and this report aims to study the Church from that point of view. Some of the accumulated notes, of a general character, were condensed in the previous paragraph. Others refer particularly to our own Church. For instance, one can never attend any meeting where some plan for the Church's advance (spiritually, educationally, financially) is considered without hearing the statement, "the pastors are the key-men." Unless the pastors can be won to it, the plan is conceived to be hopeless. The repetition grows somewhat wearisome, because the remark is not altogether true, having something of a priest-ridden flavor. It is of chief importance as concerns our ministers that the sentence is usually uttered in a dejected tone, or sometimes the added remark is openly made that it is useless to attempt to gain the support of more than a portion of the pastors; the many others are then characterized with shameful adjectives. All of these things are usually said by the laity. This leads us to another series of accumulated observations. It is an undeniable fact that the laity of our Church has been steadily growing stronger. No conclusion as to our Church is more gratifying than that which develops from a careful consideration of the advances in every respect on the part of our men and women and young people. The serious question is as to whether the ministry is progressing as fast as the laity. No answer to the question is possible, but we ministers would do well to ask it of ourselves and of our Lord while in prayer. There are strong letters from laymen in the president's files during the past biennium revealing the spiritual hunger of the laity. Indeed there are instances there also where in the consideration of the same problem a pastor proposes a very materialistic course of procedure while a layman advocates a deeply spiritual method. In how far has secularism infected the ministry?

Yet another series of gathered observations may itself seem at first to be a grossly materialistic one. It is impressive to consider the very number of our pastors—several hundred over three thousand. Placed side by side they would form an unbroken line of men two miles long—behind them, the million and more of our members. This far flung line indicates the possibilities for our Church, since there is no priest-ridden flavor to the realization that this magnificent aggregation of men constitutes the God-given leadership of the Church. In a day like the present when the opportunities are so thrillingly portrayed by our Boards and other agencies, when the necessity for a vigorous prosecution of our work is acute, when it would seem that our failure to make greater advances than we do cannot be laid chiefly upon the laity, are we forced to the conclusion that some things are amiss in the ranks of these 3,400 leaders?

Let no reader of this report class it with the frequent railings against the ministry, based usually upon limited knowledge. The writer personally knows hundreds of these 3,400 men, and is persuaded that many hundreds of them deserve the thanks of the Church and the State. They are powerful, patient builders of America's strength. To them God is powerfully living amid the contrary ways of men and of nations. Truth to their conviction will ultimately prevail, whether it be the truth revealed by religion or the truth discovered by the research of science. They proclaim religion as something which is not only to be believed and discussed, but also thoroughly to be lived. They regard the Church as the temple of truth, not as a place of sensational sideshows. To them the home is the sacred center of social life, and the modern assaults upon marriage (trial marriage, companionate marriage, easy divorce, birth control, etc.) strike at the very heart of social welfare. These ministers know Jesus Christ to be the Ruler of the universe, the revelation of God, and the reconciliation of man with God. As I speak of these men I wish my voice might reach far abroad to call upon the people of the Church first of all, but then also upon all the clean press, all the clean public men, all the educators of the land, to uphold this host of ministers to the utmost. They are the salt of the earth.

When, however, such truthful praise has been uttered, the facts and questions preceding it in this report lay a demand upon all of us included in the 3,400 that we re-examine ourselves as to inspirations for the ministry which once fired our souls. Have we fallen from those ideals? What are the ideals? What are the true responsibilities of a pastor? What are the essentials of a successful ministry? What are the tests whereby to determine our fidelity? If we need and are to have a stronger ministry one method for its attainment will be through self-examination by the pastors. The chief essential is not a preparatory college and seminary education. Fidelity to the evangelical faith is not the only test of a true pastor. As a guide in self-appraisement I propose the answer of the Psalmist to his own question, "Who shall ascend into the hill of the Lord? Or who shall stand in His holy place?" The reply reads, "He that hath clean hands, and a pure heart; who hath not lifted up his soul unto vanity, nor sworn deceitfully."

Clean Hands. In ordination a man pledges himself not only to preach and teach the Word of God in accordance with the Confession of the Evangelical Lutheran Church, but he is also asked, "Will you adorn the doctrine of our Savior by a holy life and conversation?" His answer is "Yes, with my whole heart, the Lord helping me through the power and grace of His Holy Spirit. Amen." He is obligated to godliness. His "whole heart" is set upon purity and piety.

Here then is one ideal to which we ministers do well to recall ourselves again and again. The beautiful Old Testament description thereof is, "The Lord hath set apart him that is godly for Himself." The beautiful New Testament description is, "Separated unto the Gospel of God." "Set apart," "separated." How terrible is the descent from such titles to the description which calls some ministers "good fellows," "good mixers." Some even gamble in Wall Street, and swap vile stories in the clubs of the town. They are ultimately and properly despised. The reputation of a true minister is that he is manifestly "a man sent from God."

Here, also, is a responsibility, a responsibility to his calling. It is true that the same obligations for godliness rest upon all Christians, but the minister is an official representative of religion. Where is the pastor who has not at some time contemplated Paul's words with salutary trembling: "Lest when I have preached to others, I myself should be a castaway."

We recognize also in that call for "clean hands" one essential for a true pastorate. These are times of peculiar lawlessness and moral carelessness. It is fitting that ministers listen often to the words, "Keep thy garments always white." There are sins peculiar to the ministry, which are to be guarded against. Such are vanity and envy and jealousy, which go hand in hand; hypocrisy, especially in the form of cant, which Jowett describes as "deadening familiarity with the sublime"; compromise with the world's thoughts and ways. Indolence and its associated disorderliness need also be watched. Slipshod and indifferent workmanship are common facts, and we need the vigor with which Paul worked. He says, transliterating his Greek words, that he labored, agonizing according to Christ's energy, which energized in him with dynamite (Col. 1:29). Finally, a pastor should beware of impatience, the sin of Moses, the servant of the Lord. Patience is not weakness, but power, its component parts being confidence, perseverance and endurance.

The security for purity is piety. Piety is a test of a minister's fidelity. What portion of our daily life is spent in meditation and prayer? Do we ever read a prayer book while seated in a train? Is it true as stated that in some of our theological seminaries the atmosphere for the cultivation of piety does not exist? Unfortunately we do not possess in the English language a satisfactory book of devotions peculiarly for pastors. The nearest to it is Strodach's "Oremus." In German there exists the old, but extremely valuable, "Evangelisches Brevier" of Dieffenbach-Mueller. It prescribes and gives directions for a pastor's six periods of prayer daily. Constant use thereof might not be helpful, but it would be well for every minister to follow it occasionally in life throughout an entire year. The very suggestion of six daily devotions reveals to most of us our shortcomings in pious practices. Likeness to Jesus is our destiny, "and every man that hath this hope in him, purifieth himself, even as he is pure."

A Pure Heart. What is purity of heart? Wherein consisted the purity of the heart of Jesus? Perhaps we can describe it at once as unselfishness, and know the description to be true. There are, however, beautiful angles for a vision of such a heart. An examination of the Hebrew word for pure reveals that it means first "beloved," "chosen," and then because it has been so favored and has also been showered with mercies becomes "pure." Perhaps our English adjectives "lovely" and "choice" best describe such a heart. To describe it fully, a pure heart is a beloved, lovely, and loving heart.

We recognize thus the second ideal for a true minister, in that he has laid deep hold upon the idea that he has been separated, set apart, because he has been beloved and chosen, that he is God's picked and endowed man, that every power he possesses is a mercy obtained from God because he was chosen. Such an idea, such an ideal, inevitably produces an unselfish heart, a pure heart.

We come also to the minister's second responsibility. He has been chosen to serve. The richness of God with which he has been endowed must be shared. The purity of his heart, like that of Jesus, is rooted in unselfishness; he is here, not to be ministered unto, but to minister. The first responsibility was to his calling, while this is a responsibility to his fellowmen. He knows himself definitely as their debtor. In this respect also he is a man sent from God.

The second essential of a true pastorate develops clearly, namely, that there must exist a genuine love for the people of the congregation. How can a pastor deal with the mystery of human souls unless he loves them? Love is a minister's second source of power, patience having been the first. As Paul expresses it in I Corinthians 13, love is more powerful than eloquence, wisdom, or heroic sacrifice; it never fails. Though unexpressed in the written document, a pastor's call from a congregation is a call to love them. Recognizing the unsuccessful, incomplete, fragmentary, warped condition of all human lives without Christ; realizing the woeful ignorance of the great mass of his congregation as to the Bible, the story of the Church, the faith of the Church, and the work of the Church; conscious of the provincial narrowness of even the large majority of Christians, without any world-view of humanity or concern for it;—with all of this constantly in mind, a pastor must wisely, patiently, lovingly lead his people unto "the unity of the faith, and of the knowledge of the Son of God, unto a perfect man, unto the measure of the stature of the fulness of Christ."

Here, then, is the second test of our fidelity as ministers. Have we merely coddled our congregations or have we developed strong men in Christ? Have we imbued them with anything of the universality of Christ? Have we known how to inspire and direct them individually and collectively unto definite work for Christ's sake? Failure in this last item is probably all too common among us.

Who hath not lifted up his soul unto vanity. Moffatt's rendition of this phase is illuminating: "Who never sets his mind on what is false." Only one who is a minister can appreciate the hugeness of a minister's task today, and can know the dismay of a minister's heart as he thinks of the mass of teaching agencies and mouthpieces in the world, which proclaim falsities and attractively counsel that which is empty and vain. It is quite natural that many a pastor is at least sometimes tempted to methods of operation which appear captivating, calculated to draw and to hold the people. It is supremely necessary therefore that as pastors we return ever and again to the realization that Jesus Christ is intensely earnest to save men and that He alone "is able also to save them to the uttermost." It is supremely necessary furthermore that we "set our minds" upon the fact that His saving power inheres within and is imparted through the means of grace, the Word and the Sacraments. All else is vanity. Even our patience and love, powerful though they be, accomplish nothing without these channels of divine, dynamic energy. The office of the ministry exists only for the sake of the means of grace.

We realize, therefore, the minister's third ideal, which is his supreme ideal. He has been called to be the administrator on earth of the saving power of God. In the majestic vision of Jesus Christ in the first chapter of Revelation the ministers are the stars in His right hand. He is a true minister who knows that the pastorate is the ideal task of life and who lives its ideal.

This is his third responsibility, a responsibility to himself, that he learn how to choose between the false and the vain on the one hand and the true and the powerful on the other, knowing with Paul, "Woe is unto me, if I preach not the gospel." Every life is a series of choices, and to no man is the bewilderment greater than to a minister. How difficult, for instance, is the choice of reading, that the mind be not glutted with vain things. He must, therefore, lift up his soul, set his mind unswervingly to divine methods, determined that herein also he shall be a man sent from God. It seems fitting to suggest that we, as ministers of the United Lutheran Church in America, in our need of choices, study once more the entire Washington Declaration of our Church.

Another essential for us becomes manifest, and a most comforting one. If we have become assured that Christ is in earnest to save men, we may know definitely that He is more interested in our true success than are we ourselves. We may know also that as He desires our trust in Him, so also He trusts us in our choices of true things, taking us absolutely at our word.

We are provided now with another test of our fidelity. Is the work of the congregation organized entirely for the faithful administration of the means of grace? Do the works of evangelization, of education, and of mercy receive full attention? No one of these is false and vain.

Nor Sworn Deceitfully. The previous topics emphasized the minister's hands and heart and soul or mind. Here our tongue, sure indicator of both physical and spiritual health, becomes involved. The words "sworn deceitfully" must be applied primarily to the minister's ordination vow, but his tongue is busy continually in his sermons. Let us recognize that our sermons are properly nothing but variegated developments of our vow. The solemnity of the latter should constantly permeate the former. It is common belief "that the influence of the pulpit is by no means so great as it once was." This may be a fact in so far as the pulpit was once the center of intellectual preeminence in many communities. Since, however, the means of grace are the sure channels of divine grace, the essential power of preaching has not changed and will not change.

We gain, therefore, our final ideal for the minister. He is the exalted mouthpiece of God and of the Church which accepted his vow and ordained him. Both have taken him at his word, trusting that he did not swear deceitfully. In the pulpit he is only a voice, yet a voice dedicated to eternal truth as known by a widespread communion of saints. The pulpit is not his, but is a place for the proclamation of the faith confessed by that communion. In the highest sense the minister is a churchman, appreciative of and loyal to his Church, both in his own community and at large. We sometimes hear that there are ministers in the churches, unfaithful at heart to the faith of their churches, uncertain in their utterances, afraid to disavow their vows and even selfish enough to wish merely to keep their jobs. Where there are such men who have sworn deceitfully, it is a matter of wonder that they are not afraid of the Lord.

A final and tremendous responsibility for the minister becomes manifest also. Though he be but a voice in the pulpit, nevertheless that voice possesses individuality. He stands there as an individual witness for the truth, and the Bible lays great stress upon this element of witnessing in preaching. All of the Scriptures he knows, all the doctrine of his church, all of his study and meditation are ultimately fused into and illuminated by his personal living experiences of God. Our sermons when true are thus revelations of our lives. It is in this way that our sermons become individual testimonies. Indeed a sermonic utterance of ours, thus conceived, becomes a definite burden upon us, as the prophets felt it, and there is no relief from the burden until the sermon has been preached. It is when preaching in this way that a man knows he is sent from God. This also is the highest joy of preaching, that a man can give voice to his personal experience of delight in the Lord and in the faith of his Church.

Another essential must be emphasized. As ministers our sermons must be the result of the hardest kind of work. Primarily we must be constant and intense students of the Bible; at least an hour thereof daily will not be too much. We must also be close students of the confessions of the Church. Our voices will gain authority only in this way. Somebody has said that when best concentrated a man is not using more than one fifth of his brain power. Let us use the reserve forces on God's truth. The great preachers of all times have been great students all their lives, above all of the Scriptures. We preach, we swear deceitfully, if we have not been students.

This is the final test of our fidelity, that we know our preaching to be centered on vital truth, that we do not proclaim our own vain imaginations, but "all the counsel of God."

This report in its introduction emphasized the desire for an even stronger ministry than we now possess. Several pages have been devoted to one method for the attainment thereof, namely self-examination by the pastors. A brief guide in self-appraisement has been suggested. There is a second method, which must also be used. The statement thereof will not occupy much space, but its importance cannot be overestimated for the sake of the Church's good. We need an improvement in our arrangements for the training of our pastors and other workers. Attention is asked to the following facts:

Theological education in America has developed in haphazard fashion. Like Topsy, it just grew. Only of late has there been any tendency towards a thorough examination thereof. We of the United Lutheran Church in America have inherited this haphazard development. It is a marvel that the churches have prospered as well as has been the case, under these circumstances. The results bear strong testimony to the fidelity of theological schools and of the thousands of ministers themselves.

As a second fact, it is undeniable that unanimous dissatisfaction with our present conditions exists in our Church today. Nowhere is the topic mentioned without instant expression from every individual present that important changes ought to be made. Wide differences of view are to be found as to the character of such changes, but unanimity exists as to the need. It is probable that every delegate to this convention would so express himself.

In the third place the Church is prevented from accomplishing her constitutional objects. The constitution provides that she is "to conserve the unity of the true faith, to guard against any departure therefrom, and to strengthen the Church in faith and confession." It also says she is "to awaken, coordinate and effectively direct the energies of the Church in such operations as the following: (a) the training of ministers and teachers to be witnesses of the Word." Under present arrangements for theological education, including the synodical educational policy, it is doubtful whether she can effec ively attain these objects.

As a fourth consideration literally many of our Church's servants now seek portions of their training in institutions here in America which are entirely outside of our Church.

Finally we have had a Commission on Theological Education for a number of years. It has done enduring work and has initiated a number of valuable conferences among the authorities of theological seminaries. Some of its recommendations have been gladly followed by those institutions. A recommendation will come before this convention which would bind the Commission closely to our Board of Education. The plans initiated by the Commission continue to operate. Conferences of seminary authorities continue to be in prospect. Nevertheless an atmosphere of hopelessness or of long waiting has developed throughout the Church.

In view of all these facts the president is undertaking to submit a recommendation to the convention, without urging its adoption. He is himself not fully persuaded of its wisdom, but believes that a discussion by the convention will have value.

Recommended that the Executive Board, in consultation with the Conference of Synodical Presidents and with the Board of Education, study the Church's arrangements for the training of ministers and teachers and bring recommendations for changes therein to the next convention. (See Minutes, Tuesday, October 14th.—Secretary.)

———

This report is expected to include a summary of the president's own work. It has been his continued policy to act in important matters only upon consultation with the Executive Board. Thus the report of that Board contains all such items. A statistical mention of travels to meetings of synods and boards and committees, of surveys and conferences, of sermons and addresses, of interviews and correspondence, etc., could be prepared, but is probably not desired.

All specific instructions of the last convention were followed. Elections of that convention resulted in a number of conflicts with our Constitution and By-Laws, in that individuals were chosen for agencies beyond the prescribed possibilities. These men made their own choices of membership, resulting as follows: The Rev. Dr. H. Anstadt, on the Board of Publication and the Board of the Home for the Aged; the Rev. Dr. G. Gebert on the Commission of Adjudication; the Dev. Dr. W. H. Greever on the Executive Board; the Hon. H. W. Harter on the Board of Ministerial Pensions and Relief; Dr. W. J. Showalter on the Board of Education and the Church Paper Committee.

The name of Mr. Ross Young on the standing committee for Young People's Association was a mistake; the intended name was that of Mr. Ross E. Smith. The Rev. Dr. Arthur Smith resigned, for worthy reasons, as chairman of the Committee on Women's Work. The Rev. Dr. F. M. Urich was appointed in his place In the place of Mr. A. A. Ritcher, deceased, on the Committee on Church Architecture, Mr. Howard I. Eiler was appointed.

As representatives to meetings of other Lutheran bodies the following were appointed: Augustana Synod (1929), the Rev. Dr. M. G. G. Scherer; Suomi Synod (1929), the Rev. Drs. M. G. G. Scherer and F. F. Fry; Augustana Synod (1930), the Rev. Dr. P. Scherer; Suomi Synod (1930), the Rev. Dr. F. F. Fry; Icelandic Synod (1930), the Rev. Dr. N. J. G. Wickey.

The Secretary's Report was then presented and the memorials from Constituent Synods were referred to the Committee on Memorials.

REPORT OF THE SECRETARY

The Secretary begs leave to report, for the consideration of the Convention, the following

Memorials: 1 from the Pittsburgh Synod; 1 from the Synod of New York; 1 from the Wartburg Synod; 1 from the West Pennsylvania Synod; 2 from the Synod of Canada; 1 from the Synod of Nebraska; 1 from the Nova Scotia Synod; 3 from the Texas Synod; 5 from the Ministerium of Pennsylvania.   M. G. G. Scherer.

The Secretary announced that the Rev. Paul A. Kirsch had been appointed assistant secretary for this Convention.

The Convention proceeded to the election of a President under the direction of Tellers' Committee No. 1.

Treasurer E. Clarence Miller presented his report.

REPORT OF THE TREASURER OF THE UNITED LUTHERAN CHURCH IN AMERICA

For the Two Years Ended June 30, 1930

APPORTIONMENT AND SPECIALLY DESIGNATED FUNDS
For the Year Ended June 30, 1929

Synods	Apportionment for Calendar Year 1929	Received on Apportionment	Received on Specials
Ministerium of Pennsylvania	$463,756	$257,418.91	$242,271.40
United Synod of New York	326,518	167,058.06	219,423.73
United Synod of North Carolina..	52,019	30,906.18	25,203.69
Synod of Maryland	103,803	61,529.94	48,419.67
Synod of South Carolina	42,942	23,550.00	15,895.46
Synod of West Pennsylvania.....	116,679	93,545.59	74,627.09
Synod of Virginia	39,653	17,329.55	26,013.51
Synod of Ohio	157,146	121,000.00	137,012.41
Synod of East Pennsylvania	112,000	103,825.00	138,135.23

Allegheny Synod	71,258	61,264.00	49,184.00
Pittsburgh Synod	165,167	128,956.84	107,761.11
Indiana Synod	28,893	22,858.80	18,253.89
Illinois Synod	80,249	61,000.00	53,213.12
Texas Synod	8,967	2,906.98	5,278.09
Susquehanna Synod of Central Pennsylvania	87,160	68,715.51	44,439.09
Mississippi Synod	843	585.07	561.39
Synod of Iowa	19,340	7,200.00	6,351.75
Michigan Synod	30,697	21,799.94	15,712.73
Synod of Georgia	8,663	7,970.91	6,868.80
Synod of Canada	42,101	6,195.13	8,048.65
Synod of Kansas	16,674	11,745.13	9,002.95
Synod of Nebraska	26,935	23,258.10	26,485.03
Wartburg Synod	28,774	3,000.00	7,917.25
German Nebraska Synod	21,419	2,570.00	4,682.90
California Synod	13,198	10,261.55	8,131.68
Rocky Mountain Synod	5,161	4,002.26	4,540.77
Synod of the Northwest	70,902	34,527.86	39,646.37
Manitoba Synod	13,840	1,400.00	1,298.01
Pacific Synod	6,756	7,892.00	6,515.04
Nova Scotia Synod	4,521	1,722.57	2,345.59
Synod of West Virginia	10,721	5,000.00	13,011.92
Slovak "Zion" Synod	19,771	200.00	901.74
Florida Synod	3,466	415.66	449.99
Miscellaneous	......	....	1,002.00
Women's Missionary Society	......	....	343,922.59
	$2,199,992	$1,371,611.54	$1,712,528.64

Received on apportionment $1,371,611.54
Undistributed balance of July 1, 1928 .... 8,900.84

1,380,512.38

Distributed in accordance with the basis of the
United Lutheran Church Budget 1,360,000.00

Undistributed apportionment, June 30, 1929 .... $20,512.38

CASH ACCOUNT, GENERAL FUND
For the Year Ended June 30, 1929
RECEIPTS

Proportion of apportionment........................ $54,400.00
Interest 3,796.52
$58,196.52

DISBURSEMENTS

Salaries: President $7,500.00
      Secretary 6,000.00
      Clerks 4,087.50
Traveling expenses: President 193.65
            Secretary 121.53
Committee on Constituent Synods 15.00

General expense 426.53
Printing and stationery 26.39
Postage 160.91
Rent, New York 3,030.00
Treasurer's expense 150.85
Telephone 143.51
Luther League 7,542.76
Erie Convention expense 17,233.56
Auditing 450.00
Committee on Evangelism 200.31
Women's Work Committee 69.02
Committee on Joint Catechism 107.50
Executive Board 1,296.53
Common Service Book Committee 486.13
Necrology Committee 371.80
Laymen's Movement Committee 148.75
World Convention expense 8,843.42
Church Paper Committee 131.02
Committee of Adjudication 694.70
Church Music Committee 69.03
Committee on Moral and Social Welfare 114.25
Church Architecture Committee 135.72
Publication of Minutes 4,969.63
Committee on Army and Navy Work 6.70
Young People's Association Committee 13.90
Federal Council of Churches 3,042.86
Publicity 2,599.20
Committee on German Interests 253.94
Committee on Theological Education 445.19
Committee on Transportation 13.48
Statistical and Year Book Committee 907.72
Statistical Secretary's expense 219.68
Committee of Fifteen 61.00
Synodical delegates 44.00
Committee on Lutheran Church Unity 192.83
                                                ————— 72,520.50

Excess of disbursements over receipts $14,323.98
Overdrawn, July 1, 1928 ....$ 2,452.17

Overdrawn, June 30, 1929 ....$16,776.15

APPORTIONMENT AND SPECIALLY DESIGNATED FUNDS
For the Year Ended June 30, 1930

Synods	Apportionment for Calendar Year 1930	Received on Apportionment	Received on Specials
Ministerium of Pennsylvania	$511,329	$270,962.19	$191,476.34
United Synod of New York	339,117	148,842.33	130,068.80
United Synod of North Carolina ..	66,996	34,927.03	15,101.11
Synod of Maryland	115,399	87,994.04	68,390.74
Synod of South Carolina	48,364	18,129.60	13,408.18
Synod of West Pennsylvania	124,322	102,279.17	42,141.83
Synod of Virginia	42,727	19,167.38	19,603.63

Synod of Ohio	173,037	123,000.00	91,191.80
Synod of Eastern Pennsylvania	123,763	92,375.00	74,415.00
Alleghany Synod	77,172	55,099.00	27,430.00
Pittsburgh Synod	185,736	136,834.83	79,246.47
Indiana Synod	31,744	24,332.41	15,327.54
Illinois Synod	88,212	70,000.00	36,381.55
Texas Synod	9,967	3,150.12	1,368.66
Susquehanna Synod of Central Pennsylvania	96,472	72,909.14	27,300.68
Mississippi Snyod	976	755.38	945.40
Synod of Iowa	23,020	10,100.00	6,770.83
Michigan Synod	33,724	20,857.87	11,116.27
Synod of Georgia	9,434	8,945.21	5,854.37
Synod of Canada	42,302.00	6,395.73	13,166.57
Synod of Kansas	18,957	13,200.00	5,665.24
Synod of Nebraska	29,877	20,040.52	13,084.09
Wartburg Synod	16,238	5,100.00	5,004.71
German Nebraska Synod	22,936	3,330.00	2,345.70
California Synod	15,098	9,693.55	6,871.15
Rocky Mountain Synod	5,875	3,575.78	2,666.60
Synod of the Northwest	77,505	40,159.48	32,865.91
Manitoba Synod	16,101	1,300.00	1,620.31
Pacific Synod	7,888	6,506.00	2,688.26
Nova Scotia Synod	4,927	1,937.17	2,192.58
Synod of West Virginia	11,925	7,700.00	6,043.48
Slovak "Zion" Synod	25,137	350.00	597.42
Florida Synod	3,708	2,790.17	715.54
Miscellaneous		180.00	10,425.04
Women's Missionary Society			356,671.66
	$2,399,985	$1.422,919.10	$1,320,163.46

Received on apportionment $1,422,919.10
Undistributed balance, July 1, 1929 .... 20,512.38

$1,443,431.48

Distributed in accordance with the basis of the
    United Lutheran Church Budget 1,440,000.00

Undistributed apportionment, June 30, 1930 .... $3,431.48

CASH ACCOUNT, GENERAL FUND
For the Year Ended June 30, 1930
RECEIPTS

Proportion of apportionment $59,664.00
Interest 2,454.13
                                              ————— $62,118.13

DISBURSEMENTS

Salaries: President $7,500.00
          Secretary 6,000.00
          Clerks 3,825.00
Traveling expenses: President 360.88
                    Secretary 90.40
General expense 711.05
Printing and stationery 111.75

Postage	121.70
Rent, New York	3,030.00
Treasurer's expense	142.25
Telephone, New York	146.47
Luther League	4,500.00
Auditing	450.00
Committee on Evangelism	109.85
Executive Board	1,198.68
Common Service Book Committee	85.30
Statistical and Year Book Committee	993.09
Laymen's Movement Literature	77.49
Church Paper Committee	111.70
Special Commission	6.84
Committee on Moral and Social Welfare	141.43
Church Architecture Committee	105.57
Committee on Army and Navy Work	25.63
Federal Council of Churches	3,000.00
Publicity	1,172.30
Committee on German Interests	69.62
Committee on Theological Education	114.66
Committee on Transportation	19.16
World Committee on Faith and Order	420.81
Milwaukee Convention expense	4.64
Statistical Secretary's expense	44.58
Synodical Delegate	58.76
Committee on Lutheran Church Unity	403.97
International Inner Mission Conference	200.00
Committee on Investments	66.70
Inter-Church Conference	30.00

		35,450.28
Balance		$26,667.85
Overdrawn, July 1, 1929		16,776.15
Balance United Lutheran Church Treasury, June 30, 1930		$9,891.70

SUMMARY OF CASH BALANCES AT JUNE 30, 1930

Balance, Apportionment Fund		$3,431.48
" United Lutheran Church Treasury		9,891.70
" General Bequests		2,572.71
" Sotter Trust		271.25
		16,167.14
Overdrawn, Hoffman Trust, principal	$20.00	
Overdrawn, Hoffman Trust, income	56.25	
		76.25
Balance on hand, June 30, 1930		$16,090.89
In hands of Treasurer	$15,590.89	
In hands of Secretary	500.00	
		$16,090.89

RECAPITULATION OF APPORTIONMENT RECEIPTS
For the Years ended July 31, 1919 to 1924, inclusive,
the Eleven Months ended June 30, 1925, and the
Years ended June 30, 1926 to 1930, inclusive

1919	$223,687*
1920	877,995
1921	1,014,567
1922	1,026,672
1923	1,074,187
1924	1,167,115
1925	1,104,403**
1926	1,258,381
1927	1,270,977
1928	1,408,113
1929	1,371,611
1930	1,422,919

*Partial year.
**Eleven months.

TRUST INVESTMENTS AT JUNE 30, 1930

EMMA KIRMSE SOTTER TRUST
Income for Home Missions and Church Extension:
$3,000 Altoona & Logan Valley 1st 4½s, 1933.
  500 U. S. Fourth Liberty 4¼s.
3,000 Appalachian Elec. Power 1st and Ref. 5s, 1956.
3,000 Georgia Power Co. 1st and Ref. 5s, 1967.

W. P. HUFFMAN TRUST
Income one-third each to: Lutheran Orphans' Home at Salem, Va.
                       Home Missions.
                       Foreign Missions.
$2000 American Gas & Electric 5s, 2028.
3,000 Georgia Power & Light 1st 5s, 1967.
2,500 Mortgage, 5407 Vine St., Philadelphia (Principal and interest at 5½% guaranteed by Integrity Mortgage Guarantee Co.)

M. S. HOTTENSTEIN TRUST
Income as determined by the United Lutheran Church in America,
$1,000 Hotel Chelsea 1st mortgage 6s, 1945.

CHRISTIAN PFLAUM, JR., TRUST
Income for Mission purposes:
$5000 Times Square 46th St. Bldg. 1st 6s, 1953.

R. A. HAFER TRUST
Income: Three-fifths to Missions.
        Two-fifths to Education and Ministerial Pensions.
40 shares Northern Pacific R. R. Co. C/D.
10 shares Public Service Co. of N. J. 7 pct. pfd. stock.
Respectfully submitted,
E. CLARENCE MILLER, *Treasurer.*

Philadelphia, August 1, 1930.

We have audited the accounts of the Treasurer of the United Lutheran Church in America for the two years ended June 30, 1930, and we certify that, in our opinion, the foregoing statements of

Apportionment and Specially Designated Funds,
> for the years ended June 30, 1929,
> and June 30, 1930,

Cash Accounts, General Fund,
> for the years ended June 30, 1929,
> and June 30, 1930,

Summary of Cash Balances at June 30, 1930,

Recapitulation of Apportionment Receipts
> for the years ended July 31, 1919 to 1924, inclusive, the eleven months ended June 30, 1925, and the years ended June 30, 1926 to 1930, inclusive, and

Trust Investments at June 30, 1930

are in accordance with the books of account and are correct.

LYBRAND, ROSS BROS. & MONTGOMERY,
Accountants and Auditors.

It was moved and carried that the report of the auditors be accepted.

The Convention proceeded to the election of a Treasurer under the direction of Tellers' Committee No. 2.

Tellers' Committee No. 1 reported that the Rev. F. H. Knubel had received 429 votes for President out of a total of 481 cast. The Secretary declared that Dr. Knubel, having received more than a three-fourths majority of the votes cast, had been elected President of The United Lutheran Church in America.

The Convention proceeded to the election of a Secretary under Tellers' Committee No. 1.

The Convention then resumed consideration of the report of the Executive Board.

The item concerning the use of asterisks (II, 6) was adopted.

The item concerning Convention Calendar (II, 7) was adopted.

The item concerning the proposed merger of the Board of American Missions and Inner Mission Board and concerning work for deaf mutes (II, 8 (a) and (b)) was adopted.

Action on the report of the Executive Board was suspended to hear the report of the Tellers.

Tellers Committee No. 2 reported that Dr. E. Clarence Miller had received 465 votes out of a total of 468 cast. The President declared Dr. Miller elected as Treasurer.

Consideration of the Executive Board's report was resumed.

The President ruled that the item concerning the removal of Hartwick Seminary to Brooklyn (III, B, 1 (b)) can be ready for action only after the Commission of Adjudication has made its report. (See Afternoon Session, Wednesday, October 8th; Afternoon Session, Thursday, October 9th; also Evening Session, Saturday, October 11th—Secretary.)

The item concerning the Pacific Synod and the School of Religion of the University of Oregon (III, B, 4) was adopted.

Action on the proposed Constitution of the Evangelical Lutheran Church in Japan (IV, B, 2 (f)) was postponed until the report of the Board of Foreign Missions is before the Convention. (See Morning Session, Friday, Oct. 10th.—Secretary.)

The action of the Executive Board in granting the petition of the Board of American Missions relative to the establishment of a Council of Lutheran Home Mission Boards (IV, B, 3 (a)) was approved.

Action on the Executive Board's report was suspended to hear the report of the Tellers.

Tellers' Committee No. 1 reported that the Rev. M. G. G. Scherer had received 407 votes out of a total of 440 votes cast. The President declared Dr. Scherer elected as Secretary.

Consideration of the Executive Board's report was resumed.

The item concerning the Siebenburger Saxons (IV, B, 3 (b)) was adopted.

The recommendation concerning the establishment on the part of the Board of American Missions of relations with the International Missionary Council (IV, B, 3 (c)) was approved.

The item concerning the policy of bi-lingual education (IV, B, 6 (b)) was deferred until the report of the Board of Education is under consideration. (See Afternoon Session, Saturday, October 11th.—Secretary.)

The recommendations (A), (B), (C) and (D) concerning

the relationship of our Inner Mission Board with the International Inner Mission Federation (IV, B, 7 (c)) were adopted.

Consideration of the item concerning the forming of a holding corporation by the Parish and Church School Board (IV, B, 8) was deferred until the report of the Parish and Church School Board is presented to the Convention. (See Tuesday's Session, October 14th.—Secretary.)

The budget for the years 1932 and 1933 as recommended by the Executive Board (VI, 6) was adopted.

The report of the Committee of Fifteen (Item VI, 7, of the Executive Board's report) was presented by the chairman of the committee, Mr. Peter P. Hagan.

Treasurer Miller addressed the Convention and introduced Mr. J. K. Jensen who explained to the Convention the various charts prepared by him for the use of the Synod of the Northwest.

Pending consideration of Item VI, 7, the convention adjourned at twelve o'clock with prayer by the Rev. John Weidley.

Afternoon Session

Wednesday, October 8, 1930, 2:00 o'clock.

Devotions were conducted by the Rev. John Schmieder and the President called the Convention to order.

The Convention resumed consideration of the report of the Executive Board item VI, 7.

A resolution presented by Mr. W. H. Hager was referred to the Committee on Memorials from Constituent Synods. (See item 10 of the report of the Committee, Afternoon Session, Thursday, October 9th—Secretary.)

On motion the entire course of action of the Committee of Fifteen was approved and the President announced, with the general consent of the Convention, that the committee goes out of existence, having completed its work. Item VI, 7, of the Executive Board's report was thus disposed of.

The item (VIII, 4) concerning the Intersynodical Hymnal Committee was adopted.

The report of the delegation to the Second Lutheran World Convention (X, 4) was presented by the Rev. A. R. Wentz. In connection with this report the Rev. J. A. Morehead, President of the Executive Committee of the Lutheran World Convention, addressed the convention. Thereupon recommendations (a), (b), (c) and (d) of the report were adopted, and the item (X, 4) of the Executive Board's report was thus disposed of.

The Rev. M. G. G. Scherer, chairman of the Commission on World Conference on Faith and Order, presented the report of that Commission. (See item XI of the report of the Executive Board.)

The first series of recommendations (A. 1 and 2) were adopted, carrying with them the adoption of suggestions 1 and 2, based respectively upon Sections IV and VI of the Lausanne Report No. VII concerning The Unity of Christendom and the Relation Thereto of Existing Churches.

Recommendations 1, 2, 3, 4, 5 and 6 concerning the future work of the World Conference on Faith and Order and our relation thereto (series B) were adopted.

The recommendation of the Executive Board concerning invitations for the next convention (XII, 5) was adopted and the Rev. E. P. Pfatteicher, President of the Ministerium of Pennsylvania, was appointed convener of the committee.

Consideration of the item concerning the establishment of a Bureau of Architecture (IV, C, 5) was deferred until the report of the Committee on Church Architecture is brought before the Convention. (See Morning Session, Monday, Oct. 13th—Secy.)

The Rev. Paul Koller, Executive Secretary of the Board of Foreign Missions, introduced Mr. V. Ch. John and the Rev. C. H. Swavely, delegates from the Evangelical ·Lutheran Church in the Andhra Country, India. Mr. John spoke of the organization, of the numerical strength and the work of the Andhra Lutheran Church and brought greetings of that body to The United Lutheran Church in America. Mr. Swavely spoke of the Andhra Lutheran Church as a church of Luther's Small Catechism, a church of devotion and a church with a burden, referring to the millions of souls among whom it labors to bring to them the light of the Gospel. These delegates were welcomed by the President.

By common consent a Supplementary Report of the Commission of Adjudication was presented by the Rev. R. E. Tulloss.

SUPPLEMENTARY REPORT OF THE COMMISSION OF ADJUDICATION

At a meeting of the Commission held in Milwaukee on Tuesday afternoon, October 7, 1930, there was presented for consideration a communication from the Secretary of The United Lutheran Church in America, quoting from the minutes of a meeting of the Executive Board items regarding a certain matter relating to the location of a theological seminary, and in accordance with an action of the Board requesting from the Commission a decision upon two questions, as follows:

(a) Whether The United Lutheran Church in America has any authority at all in the matter of organization or location or relocation of theological seminaries.

(b) Whether The United Lutheran Church in America has definitely stated that no Synod shall have authority to locate or change a location without the approval of The United Lutheran Church in America.

It was duly voted to receive the communication, and to proceed to consider whether such an inquiry can, under the Constitution of The United Lutheran Church in America and the existing Rules of Procedure of the Commission, be accepted for consideration and decision.

After discussion the following resolution was unanimously adopted:

Whereas, the Constitution of The United Lutheran Church in America (Article XII, Section 1) provides that "this Commission shall constitute a court for the decision of all questions of principle or action arising within the United Lutheran Church in America, which have been properly referred to it by resolution or by appeal from any of the Synods," And

Whereas, the Rules of Procedure of the Commission, duly adopted by the Commission and approved by The United Lutheran Church in America, provide, relating to this matter, as follows:

(a) "The Commission . . . . . . concludes that a fair and liberal interpretation of the Constitution provides two sources from which disputed questions may arise, ... namely

First: by resolution of the Convention of The United Lutheran Church in America.

Second: by appeal of any of the Synods."

—Page 6, Rules of Procedure, under Questions, Presentation."

(b) "All disputed questions concerning doctrine, practice, principle or action which may be referred to this Commission for decision shall be by resolution duly adopted by a Convention of The United Lutheran Church in America or by a Constituent Synod."

—Page 9, Rules of Procedure, under "Practice, Resolutions."

Therefore, be it

Resolved, That the inquiry now before us, not having been presented by resolution of a Convention of The United Lutheran Church in America or of a Constituent Synod, may not properly come before the Commission for consideration or action.

The question of the advisability of a change in the Rules of Procedure was thereupon discussed. The following resolution was unanimously adopted:

Whereas, it appears that at times during the interim between conventions of The United Lutheran Church in America it may be desirable for the Executive Board to seek a decision upon some disputed question concerning doctrine, practice, principle or action, at the hands of the Commission, Be it

Resolved, That the Rules of Procedure of the Commission be amended, changing the first sentence on page 9 of the printed Rules, under the heading "Practice, Resolutions," from the form above quoted (see [b] under previous resolution), to read as follows:

"All disputed questions concerning doctrine, practice, principle or action which may be referred to this Commission for decision shall be by resolution duly adopted (a) by a Convention of The United Lutheran Church in America; or, (b) during the interim between conventions of The United Lutheran Church in America, by the Executive Board; or, (c) by a Constituent Synod."

The attention of the Convention is directed to the fact that since the resolution immediately preceding involves a change in the Rules of Procedure of the Commission, action of the Convention upon this section of the report is called for.

LUTHER KUHLMAN, *Vice President.*
REES EDGAR TULLOSS, *Secretary.*

The President stated that the report, in so far as it is a ruling, was not subject to action. He stated further that the suggested amendment to its Rules of Procedure, brought in by the Commission, might be acted upon by the Convention.

It was moved and carried, that action on the suggested amendment be deferred until the regular time for the report of the Commission of Adjudication. (See Afternoon Session, Thursday, October 9th—Secretary.)

By common consent the Rev. E. P. Pfatteicher at this time presented the report of the Church Papers Committee.

REPORT OF THE CHURCH PAPERS COMMITTEE

The religious press faces great difficulties! It has before it even greater opportunities! The difficulties are brought about by the attitude of the secular press on religious matters! The opportunities are there to set forth fallacies in thought and statement, conserving and extending the work of the Christian Church.

We shall touch first upon the difficulties introduced by the injection of religion into the secular press. Even an apparently unreligious age is at times "very religious"—somewhat superstitiously religious. The secular press, whether we think of it as the newspaper or the magazine, caters to a cosmopolitan group. It is true that great changes have taken place in this group. The vocal element in it in times past has, with certain well-known exceptions, been conservative. Today, it is radical. Yesterday it was national and provincial. Today it is international and apparently merged along radical lines. Neither the newspaper nor the magazine are interested in delving to the bottom of doctrinal differences because they have never fully appraised the close connection between doctrine and life. The newspaper and the magazines are just as standpat in their religious program; there are exceptions of course, as the denominational sheet. The *Christian Century* some time ago spoke about the amateurs in religion who are flooding our book market. We can speak likewise of the amateurs in religion who occupy editorial chairs in the offices of secular publications. The news of the average convention usually misses the inner spirit of the thing by a mile. The day dreams of near theologians, who have become embittered by some unfortunate experience, fill our magazines.

If these things be true it will be seen that the religious press has greater opportunities than ever simply because the need is greater than ever. However, the religious press, and we refer to the denominational press, can not hope to win out in our day and generation by copying its ancestor in taking a shot here and a shot there and filling up its editorial page with expressions of pharisaic self righteousness. It must evaluate the work of its neighbor in kindly yet accurate way and must ever be ready to give to its readers and those whom they can reach a reason of the hope that is its own. Its whole policy must be constructive not destructive, a re-formation and not a de-formation.

A single sheet, be it daily, weekly, monthly or quarterly, will not answer the purpose, for our constituency is a multiple group. There are groups within groups, interests within the one great joint interest.

We are committed to a weekly, or rather to as many weeklies as are absolutely needed to meet the requirements of our members. The United Lutheran Church is seeking to develop an informed membership through two semi-news, semi-didactic sheets, *The Lutheran* and *Lutherischer Herold*. It rejoices in having two capable editors, The Rev. Dr. Nathan R. Melhorn of *The Lutheran* and the Rev. Dr. C. R. Tappert of the German weekly. These weeklies have not grown over night. They have been subject to much care and nurture. We are unwilling to be caught in the present-day craze constantly to change both policies and make-up. We have discussed with the editor of *The Lutheran* certain minor changes which we believe would make for present-day cravings of a proper sort. Among other things we have suggested that the cover page contain an index after the fashion of many magazines. Many of us have been prompted to pick up a magazine and turn to page —— because of our interest in the subject there discussed. Dr. Melhorn is peculiarly gifted in writing headlines and suggesting subjects to writers. We can no longer assume that our constituency will read a weekly from cover to cover and we must not take that for granted. Unless readers readily find some one, to them, worth-while article without looking through the whole weekly they will soon put the paper aside without even a cursory examination. Another suggestion made by us deals with the shifting of that most readable section, "Across the Desk," to the editorial pages. "Across the Desk" was born when we had two editors. Now that we have one we believe that the two pages sometimes assigned to editorials might profitably be assigned, one to editorials written in serious vein, the other to the delightful intimacies of which the editor is capable. We have further suggested that instead of devoting two pages to daily devotions, one page, in smaller type if need be, be set aside for these devotions, and the other page be used for a sermon by preachers of the church.

The committee on personnel, a subcommittee of our committee, reports that "in view of the large responsibility involved in editing *The Lutheran* and *Lutherischer Herold* and in order to provide for any emergencies that may arise, steps should be taken to appoint an assistant editor for each as soon as feasible." Adopted by the Committee.

In the the field of monthlies, our mission interests have three journals, *The Foreign Missionary, der Missionsbote* and *Woman's Work*. The Committee has had under discussion the possibility of a single great missionary magazine prepared and published conjointly by the Board of Foreign Missions, the Board of American Missions, the Board of Inner Missions, and the Women's Missionary Society with editors representing each of these groups. A subcommittee has been appointed and a meeting is contemplated with representatives of these groups to ascertain the sentiment within the groups.

The merger of two important quarterlies, *The Lutheran Quarterly* and *The Lutheran Church Review,* sponsored by the Church Papers Committee, has been carried to a happy consummation in the publication of *The Lutheran Church Quarterly.* We believe that there are great possibilities in this merger if our theologians and the masses will stand back of it—our theologians with worth-while contributions of mind and spirit, our masses with contributions of subscriptions.

Your committee respectfully recommends:

(1)   The observance of the centennial of *The Lutheran* (Lutheran Observer, 1831) in 1931 and the preparation of plans for this observance.

(2)   The re-election of the Rev. Dr. Nathan R. Melhorn as editor of *The Lutheran* and the Rev. Dr. C. R. Tappert as editor of *Lutherischer Herold.*

It nominates the Rev. Drs. John Aberly and Joseph Sittler, and Dr. Showalter for full terms.

Respectfully submitted,

The Committee,

H. OFFERMANN, *Chairman.*

E. P. PFATTEICHER, *Secretary.*

Recommendations 1 and 2 were adopted.

The President declared that in the adoption of recommendation 2, the Rev. N. R. Melhorn had been elected as editor of *The Lutheran* and the Rev. C. R. Tappert as editor of the *Lutherischer Herold.*

At five o'clock the Convention adjourned with prayer by the Rev. Wm. M. Horn.

Evening Service

Celebration of the Quadricentennial of the Augsburg Confession

The Vesper Service was conducted by the Reverends Paul H. Krauss and S. W. Herman.

Music by the combined Lutheran choirs of Milwaukee.

Address: "The Augsburg Confession in the Light of Modern Tendencies" by the Rev. J. A. W. Haas, President of Muhlenberg College.

Address: "Why I Love the Augsburg Confession" by the Rev. Ralph H. Long, Executive Director of the National Lutheran Council.

SECOND MEETING
Morning Session

HOTEL SCHROEDER
Milwaukee, Wisconsin
Thursday, October 9, 1930, 8:45 o'clock.

Matins were conducted by the Rev. F. K. Fretz.

The Convention was called to order by the President.

The Minutes of the Wednesday morning and afternoon sessions were read by the assistant secretary and declared approved.

The Rev. Chalmers E. Frontz, Chairman of the Nominating Committee, reported nominations as follows:

For the *Executive Board*:

Rev. Marion J. Kline; Rev. J. L. Morgan; Rev. Joseph Sittler; Mr. John Greiner, Jr.; Mr. B. B. Miller; Mr. Wm. H. Stackel; Rev. Charles J. Smith; Rev. Rees Edgar Tulloss; Rev. A. J. Turkle; Mr. A. H. Durborow; Mr George Hemsing; Mr. Frederick W. Kakel.

For the *Commission of Adjudication*:

Rev. Ellis B. Burgess; Rev. H. C. Roehner; Mr. Robbin B. Wolf; Rev. W. H. Greever; Rev. Augustus Steimle; Hon. C. F. Ribble.

For the *Committee on Church Papers*:

Rev John Aberly; Rev. Joseph Sittler; Mr. Wm. J. Showalter; Rev. Robert D. Clare; Rev. J. W. Horine; Hon. Benj. F. Apple.

The Rev. David R. Huber reported the nominations for members of the Executive Committee of the Laymen's Movement as follows:

Mr. F. W. Albrecht; Mr. A. Raymond Bard; Mr. C. J. Driever; Mr. John Greiner, Jr.; Hon. Henry W. Harter; Mr. E. G. Hoover; Mr. J. P. Hovland; Mr. P. A. Myers; Mr. Heiby W. Ungerer; Hon. John L. Zimmerman; Mr. J. L. Clark; Mr. P. H. Glatfelter; Mr. Peter P. Hagan; Mr. Wm. H. Hager; Mr. Thomas P. Hickman; Mr. E. Clarence Miller; Mr. Harvey C. Miller; Mr. George E. Neff; Mr. Fred W. Wefer; Mr. E. J. Young.

The Rev. E. E. Fischer presented the report of the Committee on Moral and Social Welfare as follows:

REPORT OF THE COMMITTEE ON MORAL AND SOCIAL WELFARE

The Committee organized with Dr. E. E. Fischer as chairman and Dr. E. C. Dinwiddie as secretary.

The following report is submitted in two parts. In the first part the committee re-submits that portion of its report to the Erie Convention upon which consideration was postponed until this Convention. The second part consists of a statement prepared in response to the Memorial of the Alleghany Synod, requesting an interpretation of the phrases "to engage in just wars" and "to serve as soldiers", found in Article XVI of the Augsburg Confession. (Minutes, 1928, pp. 135-6).

PART I

MARRIAGE AND DIVORCE

The instability of the modern family is clearly revealed in the mounting divorce rate. At present the rate in the United States is about one divorce to every seven marriages. (In Canada it is one to 109). This fact is in itself startling, but it does not fully indicate the gravity of the situation. What is even more threatening is the fact that great numbers at the present day, including some of the teachers of our youth, have ceased to regard divorce as in any way an evil. On the contrary, it is now accepted in large circles as a necessary and salutary expedient of modern life, affording a convenient means of escape when the continuance in the marriage relationship has ceased for any reason to be desirable.

It is this attitude which bodes ill for the future and renders it exceedingly difficult to cope with the situation in a large way. Marriage and divorce, so far as their legal aspects are concerned, are controlled and regulated by the State. Without stricter marriage and divorce laws it is futile to expect a general improvement in the situation. And yet public opinion in its present state seems unwilling or unprepared to alter the existing laws in favor of a stricter code.

But whatever may be the situation from the legislative point of view, there are Christian convictions on the subject of marriage which are binding on the Christian conscience and which the Church must maintain. It is true that when a minister performs a marriage he acts as an official of the State, and is amenable to the laws of the State according to which he performs the marriage. But this does not exempt him from his Christian obligation. Unless he is convinced that he can sanction a marriage from the Christian point of view, he should have the courage to refuse to perform it. This applies not only to cases in which one or both parties may be divorced persons, but to all cases where the blessing of God cannot be invoked with a good conscience. The rite of Christian marriage constitutes one of the services of the Church, and it is always with this idea in mind that the minister of the Gospel should perform it. As long as there is laxity in this respect, it will be impossible for the Church to testify as it should to the sanctity of the marriage bond.

There is another duty devolving upon the Church; namely, to safeguard its own membership against the pernicious influence of the low standards which now prevail so generally. Happy marriages are still the rule and not the exception among Christians; but there is little reason to expect that this condition will continue unless the Church seeks deliberately and aggressively to overcome the effects of the modern trend. Without a system of education which is not only intent upon pointing out the evils of the present situation, but aims to inculcate right standards, the future of even our Christian youth is problematical. Protest is necessary but more is required. Our youth must be taught the positive obligations of marriage from the Christian point of view. Without education there is no guarantee that the rising Christian generation will remain unaffected.

The Meaning of Marriage

With respect to the meaning and purpose of marriage the Christian teaching is explicit. Marriage performs a twofold function. In the first place, it is the divinely appointed way for the establishment and maintenance of the family. This factor has already been dealt with in another section of this report and need not be enlarged upon. Its significance here is to point out the value which marriage has for society as a whole, and the reason why it needs to be protected against the capriciousness of individualism. Only upon the basis of a stable marriage relationship can the family prosper and accomplish its indispensable task. And in the second place, marriage is intended by God to assist the individual to realize the highest ends of being, not only from the temporal, but also from the spiritual point of view. In a very real sense it is one of life's great schools. The discipline which it involves and the opportunities which it offers can be made to develop character according to the will of God. But the fulfillment of this purpose also demands a rigid form of marriage. To esteem the relationship lightly is not only to miss its spiritual blessings but to deprive life of one of its most helpful forms of discipline.

The idea of marriage as divinely instituted involves, therefore, by its very nature the principles of monogamy and indissolubility. Where it is regarded as only a temporary union, having as its end the attainment of a merely selfish happiness and so to be formed and broken at will, its true purpose is frustrated. Only a life-long union between one man and one woman, involving complete self-impartation, is compatible with social as well as with individual well-being. Any other view of marriage as an institution would not only be contrary to the will of God but a distinct menace to the social order.

For the Christian marriage has still another significance. It is a type of the mystical union of Christ with His Bride the Church. Husbands are to love their wives as Christ loved the Church and gave Himself for it, and wives are to submit themselves to their own husbands as unto the Lord. Where marriage is thus consummated "in the Lord", the oneness of husband and wife will be established upon a firm spiritual foundation. Together they will become heirs of the grace of God. All carnal and purely human considerations will fall into the background and the union will be maintained in perfect freedom. This constitutes the unique characteristic of a Christian marriage, and should be made prominent in any effort to instruct the young with respect to the meaning and obligations of the marriage estate.

DIVORCE

On the question of divorce the teaching of the Church is not uniform. Not only is there a divergence of opinion between Protestants and Romanists, but Protestants themselves are not of one mind on the subject. Among the latter there is general agreement on the question of adultery as a justifiable cause for divorce. The statement of our Lord in Matt. 5:32, and repeated in 19:9, is regarded as final on this subject. But on the question of desertion there is no unanimity, one group maintaining that when it is "malicious," it may be regarded as a justifiable cause, another refusing to recognize it as a justifiable cause under any circumstances.

Until recently this difference was accepted as a fact and each group was content to conform its practice to its conscientious convictions. Of late, however, there has appeared a tendency on the part of some whose churches recognize the validity of divorce for desertion to question the propriety of this attitude. The large increase in the number of divorces granted each year for desertion, and especially the abuse to which this cause is being subjected in modern divorce proceedings, have raised the question of the moral right of the Church to sanction the remarriage of any persons divorced for desertion. This fact, together with the situation itself, makes it expedient that the whole matter be re-examined in the light of the Scriptures and of modern conditions. The following statement is therefore submitted for consideration to the United Lutheran Church.

DIVORCE FOR DESERTION

The passage upon which the Scriptural justification for divorce for the cause of desertion is grounded is I Cor. 7:15, where Paul writes, "But if the unbelieving depart, let him depart. A brother or a sister is not under bondage in such cases; but God has called us to peace." The context is as follows: Paul has been answering a series of questions which had been submitted to him by the Corinthian congregation. Among these evidently was one which inquired what attitude the believer should take toward the marriage relationship in the case of mixed marriages, that is, where the other party was a heathen or a Jew; and more especially, what his attitude should be in those instances in which the other party to a mixed marriage deserted.

The first question Paul answers by asserting that mixed marriages are binding. Religious differences in themselves do not constitute a justifiable cause for divorce. "If any brother hath a wife that believeth not, and she be pleased to dwell with him, let him not put her away. And the woman that hath an husband that believeth not, and if he be pleased to dwell with her, let her not put him away."—I Cor. 7:12, 13. The question at issue here, it should be noted, was not one simply of separation but of actual divorce. This is indicated by the apostle's use in both clauses of the verb "aphienai"—to put away—which was one of the technical words to signify divorce. In these instances, therefore, divorce was not to be thought of.

The second question, concerning the attitude of the believer when the unbeliever deserted, Paul answers by declaring that "a brother or a sister is not under bondage in such cases." The apostle is evidently drawing a contrast. In the former cases, where the believer was not deserted, he maintains that he continued to be under bondage. In the latter case, where the unbeliever deserted, the brother or sister was no longer under bondage.

It is the meaning of this expression "not under bondage," therefore, which is the crucial question. The interpretation which has been given to it by those who have found in it a justification for divorce has been "not under bondage to the marriage relation." This was the meaning which Luther, Calvin and Zwingli gave to it, which has since been followed by the majority of Lutheran and Reformed dogmaticians and exegetes, and which has been widely accepted among Protestant Christians. When so interpreted its import is that the marriage bond is effectually severed by desertion, enabling the deserted one to secure a legal divorce, and permitting him, when so divorced, to marry again without violating any Christian principles. Over against this view is the view of those who maintain that the expression justifies separation but carries with it no right of remarriage.

The objections which are now being offered to the former interpretation are in the main three. It is maintained, in the first place, that it reads too much into the words "ou dedoulotai"—is not under bondage. All that the apostle meant to imply, it is argued, was that the brother or sister, in such cases was not bound to continue to live with the deserting one or to continue to seek reconciliation. It should be noted, however, that the cases of which the apostle was speaking were cases where the separation had already been put into force. There could have been no question of the believer living any longer with the deserter or of seeking reconciliation with him. The latter had gone with the avowed purpose of never returning. Had the slightest hope of reconciliation remained we may rest assured that the apostle would not have released the believer from the obligation of pursuing it. His advice then would have been for such a one to remain unmarried or to become reconciled. But here it is simply "let him depart. A brother or a sister is not under bondage in such cases." An inference, therefore, is that he wanted the brother or sister to know that the marriage had been dissolved and that the believer was no more bound by it. Of the right to remarry nothing is said. This follows only if it is assumed that it is actual divorce which the apostle had in mind.

This interpretation appears to be substantiated by the literal meaning of "ou dedoulotai"—"is not bound like a slave." A slave's status remained unchanged, however outward circumstances changed. Even the death of his master did not essentially change his status; he remained a slave. But Paul contends that the Christian did not bear this relation to the marriage covenant—he was not bound to it like a slave. The desertion changed his status. Just as death freed the surviving party and opened the way for another marriage—Romans 7:2—so desertion freed the deserted one, and likewise opened the way for another marriage.

One fact ought not to be lost sight of in the whole discussion; namely, that the desertion must be final and complete. This probably was in the apostle's mind when he added the warning, "But God has called us to peace." It is true, the peace to which he referred was the inner peace—not even marital infelicity was to rob the Christian of that, for to that he had been called by God. But this inner peace could be morally maintained only where every effort had been made to maintain the outward peace. In other words, nothing humanly possible should be left undone to prevent the desertion, or, if this occurred, to bring about a reconciliation. Only after these efforts failed was the marriage to be considered dissolved. The Church, at any rate, has felt the necessity of safeguarding itself in this particular by so interpreting the mind of the apostle. It has insisted that desertion must be "malicious" in order to be a justifiable cause for divorce, and that only those who have been deserted in this way can be married again with the sanction of the Church.

In every other instance it has insisted upon separation without the right of remarriage.

The second objection is that, in interpreting the meaning of Paul's words as sanctioning divorce for desertion, the apostle is made to teach a doctrine which is contrary to a specific teaching of our Lord. Our Lord permitted divorce for the one reason of adultery. By permitting divorce for the additional reason of desertion, Paul, it is held, would be guilty of modifying our Lord's teaching in an essential particular, and this would destroy the unity of the Scriptures.

That Paul knew what he was doing is evident from the fact that he does not claim to have a command of Christ on which to ground his advice with respect to mixed marriages. He introduces this advice with the words, "But to the rest speak I, not the Lord." His meaning is not that on this subject he cannot speak as an inspired apostle He knows himself to have "the Spirit of God," as he claims at the close of the chapter, even when he is speaking by permission and not by commandment. What he means is that he had no specific word of Christ with which to answer the question which had been raised. For the answer to this question he had to draw on the mind of Christ as that mind had been formed within him by the Holy Spirit.

There is something in this very attitude which should make us pause. Had Paul desired to impress upon those who had been deserted nothing more than the necessity of living separately, he would not have been at a loss for a specific command of Christ. Then Christ's words which apparently make adultery the only justifiable cause for divorce and so permit remarriage under no other circumstances would have been literally applicable. But evidently Paul did not regard these words as applicable to the circumstances under discussion. Jesus had answered the question, "Is it lawful for a man to put away his wife for every cause?" It was a question which involved the interpretation of the Jewish law on divorce. According to Moses, divorce was permitted the husband if he discovered some uncleanness in his wife. Did this mean that a man could put his wife away on the slightest pretext, as some claimed, or only for adultery, as others claimed? Jesus answered that a man had no right to put away his wife for every cause. The "uncleanness" must be adultery in order to justify divorce with the right to remarry.

It should be noticed, however, that Jesus did not answer the specific question which had been asked Him until He had called attention to the fact that the law of Moses, however interpreted, did not represent the original will of God. What the law of Moses permitted with respect to divorce was a condescension to a sinful humanity because of the hardness of man's heart. According to the will of God marriage was to be regarded as indissoluble. So it was established by the Creation narrative which antedated the Mosaic legislation and which Jesus reaffirmed as embodying the original will of God. Even though adultery, therefore, could be regarded as severing the marriage bond, thus permitting divorce, the divorce itself should not be regarded as in accordance with God's will. It might be inescapable, but only because of man's sinfulness. This is the natural inference from Jesus' argument in Matt. 19:3-9, and justifies the attitude which condemns all divorce as contrary to the will of God, demanding that even the "innocent" party to a divorce give evidence of suitable repentance before he be married again with the sanction of the Church.

Paul, in answering the question which had been proposed to him, follows the method of his Lord. He first makes sure that the will of God as reaffirmed by Christ is understood. Marriage according to the will of God is to be regarded as indissoluble: husbands are not to put away their wives and wives are not to depart from their husbands.— I Cor. 7:10, 11. This is the will of God and therefore constitutes the ideal in His Kingdom; and it is according to this ideal that marriages between Christians are to be maintained. Should circumstances arise which would make separation expedient, there is to be no re marriage. In the Kingdom of God reconciliation is in order and nothing should be done to hinder it.

Having said this, Paul proceeds to answer the specific question which had been asked him concerning the status of mixed marriages after the unbeliever had deserted. His verdict is that a brother or a sister is not under bondage in such cases. It appears that even as adultery severs the bond so does desertion when it is complete and final. In the latter case no less than in the former, man by the hardness of his heart makes the fulfillment of the will of God impossible. Crime, sickness, cruelty, incompatibility of temper may make temporary separation expedient or necessary, but none of these causes in itself destroys the possibility of reconciliation. In the complex life of the early Church these causes were no less operative than they are today. But there is nothing in the New Testament even to hint that they were regarded as justifiable causes for divorce. But malicious desertion differs from these. It destroys the essence of the marriage relationship.

Whether or not Paul altered in an essential way the teaching of Christ depends on whether we regard the saying in Matt. 19:9 as exhaustive legislation on the subject of divorce, which Christ intended to be binding upon the Church for all time, or merely an answer to a specific question which had been asked Him, and therefore only as an illustration of the way in which His teaching with respect to the indissolubility of marriage would have to be applied in a sinful world. If it is legislation then it represents a unique divergence from Jesus' ordinary way of teaching; for nowhere else does He legislate. His method is always to lay down the principles of His Kingdom and then to allow men to make the necessary applications as circumstances arise.

Indeed, so fixed is this method of teaching that many scholars have come to regard the clause, "saving for the cause of fornication" as an interpolation. The original saying of Jesus they maintain, is found in Mark 10:11 (Cf. Luke 16:18) where marriage is declared to be indissoluble without any modifying clause whatsoever. What we have in Matthew is an attempt on the part of the evangelist, not without some justification, to apply Jesus' original saying to actual circumstances.

But be that as it may, Paul apparently knew Jesus' saying on divorce only as it is found in Mark.

In the seventh chapter of I Corinthians no mention is made anywhere of any excepting clause. The apostle knows only the principle of an indissoluble marriage as embodying the mind of Christ. The application of this principle to the peculiar circumstances which Christianity met in the heathen world had to be worked out, as was the case with other principles. This Paul does in the case of desertion. He simply carries forward the application of the principle of Christ's teaching to the circumstances as they arose in the early Church. A similar task awaits the Church of this as of every age. The problem today is to determine what constitutes desertion, not merely from the legal but from the spiritual point of view. When may it be said that one has utterly forsaken the marriage bond to which one had been a party?

The third objection is the practical one that, by admitting desertion as a justifiable cause for divorce, the Church is found in the position of fostering the very laxity which it ought so much to deplore and combat. That this cause is being notoriously abused at the present day is patent to every one. But the wisdom, to say nothing of the right, of the Church of barring it entirely must be seriously questioned. Adultery as a justifiable cause for divorce may also be, and is, abused. But the way in which to combat the abuse is not by refusing to recognize the effects of adultery upon the marriage relation. Those who are guilty of the crime and remain unrepentant should be punished. The State for its part should be more zealous in enforcing the law which makes adultery a punishable offense; while the Church should be more conscientious in the way in which it carries out the rule not to sanction the remarriage of the guilty party to a divorce under any circumstances.

The abuse of the cause of desertion should be remedied in a similar way. To refuse to recognize the effects of malicious desertion upon the marriage relation would be mistaken zeal. The Church can and should protect itself by requiring a stricter adherence on the part of both clergy and laity to the principles which govern its attitude toward the remarriage of those who have been divorced for desertion. How this can best be done remains to be determined. To demand that the officiating pastor guide his conduct by what the divorce papers set forth will not suffice. With the present lax conscience on divorce it often occurs that the guilty party, especially if it is the wife, is permitted to secure the divorce, while the innocent party, out of a perverted sense of honor or of sportsmanship, will take the blame and legal guilt. Perhaps the safest course to pursue is to investigate, so far as is possible, each individual case, and by personal conference to determine where the guilt lies, and above all whether the divorced person who desires to remarry truly understands the meaning of the rite and the serious obligations which it involves. It is in this direction probably that the Church's effort to reform must move, for along this line abundant opportunity will be found, not only to testify to the Christian ideal of marriage, but also to oppose the present abuse without surrendering an essential principle.

These are the reasons why the Committee hesitates to suggest any change in the traditional attitude of the Lutheran Church on the question of the scriptural grounds for divorce. While it believes that the convictions of those who hold to only one ground for divorce should be respected and that the Church should do nothing to coerce their consciences in the matter, it feels that it would be neither wise nor expedient to abandon a doctrine or practice which has the authority of the Word of God, simply because of the abuse to which it may be subjected by the world. What the United Lutheran Church is now asked to do is to endorse as a Church substantially what the former General Synod declared to be its position at its meeting in 1907 and what the former General Council declared to be its position at its meeting in 1903, and what is declared to be the teaching of the Scriptures in the "Lutheran Commentary"—*Matthew,* by C. F. Schaeffer; *Mark,* by J. A. W. Haas; and *I Corinthians,* by H. E. Jacobs.

STATEMENT ON MARRIAGE AND DIVORCE

1. The United Lutheran Church, in accordance with the teaching of the Scriptures, holds that marriage is a holy estate, ordained of God, and to be held in honor by all. It deeply deplores the increasing disregard of the sanctity of the marriage tie, and solemnly protests against all teaching and practice which violates this sanctity and are therefore contrary to the revealed will of God.

2. It urges its pastors to instruct their people regularly and systematically in the meaning and responsibilities of marriage; to seek to maintain among them a Christian conscience on divorce; to be ready, whenever conditions demand it and opportunity offers, to bring the gospel of reconciliation to bear upon those who may be in serious danger of estrangement; and in general to minister through Word and Sacrament to that growth in grace which is the only effectual safeguard against the moral laxity of the times.

3. While it is indispensable that a pastor in performing a marriage

comply with every civil requirement, we maintain that he is also accountable to God, and that he therefore not only has the right, but should feel constrained, to refuse to perform any marriage which, so far as he has had the opportunity of discovering after earnest endeavor to ascertain the facts, is not in accordance with the divine requirements. The rite of Christian marriage is a service of the Church and its distinctively religious character when performed by a minister of the Church should never be subordinated to other considerations.

4. With respect to divorce we hold that marriage according to the will of God is indissoluble and is normally terminated only by the death of either party. When it is otherwise dissolved the will of God is frustrated. In general, therefore, all divorce is to be condemned, and, whenever possible, avoided.

5. A great body of the leading thinkers of the Lutheran Church in the past have taught that the marriage bond is effectually dissolved by the sins of adultery and malicious desertion, and that, when a divorce has been legally granted for either of these causes, the innocent party is free to marry again. This position we now reaffirm.

6. With respect to the remarriage of divorced persons, the United Lutheran Church recommends to its constituent synods that they insist that their pastors abide by the rule that only the innocent party to a divorce which has been granted on scriptural grounds can be remarried under the auspices of the Lutheran Church during the lifetime of the other party, and then not until the expiration of a year after the divorce shall have been granted.

7. The matter of retaining within, or admitting to, the membership of the Church persons who have been divorced on other than scriptural grounds and who have remarried during the lifetime of the former husband or wife falls under the rule of discipline provided for by the constitution of the congregation. In all such instances pastors and church councils are exhorted to proceed with care and true spiritual wisdom, having proper regard for the Church's purity and honor, but also mindful of her mission to minister the means of grace so that sinners may be converted, restored and saved.

PART II
STATEMENT ON ARTICLE XVI OF THE AUGSBURG CONFESSION

Article XVI was included in the Augsburg Confession to refute the Anabaptists and others who taught that civil righteousness fell outside the scope of the Christian's duty. The State, according to their view, was an alien institution from which the Christian must hold himself strictly aloof. He must not take an oath, hold civil office, bear arms, or in any way serve the State as an end in itself. To do so involved the compromise of Christian convictions.

In a similar way some denied the right of the Family to its own existence as a divine institution. Christian righteousness, they held, was an exclusive thing and owed no obligation to marriage or the Family as institutions having value for the race and existing by divine appointment.

Over against this attitude toward the State and the Family, Article XVI of the Augsburg Confession simply reiterates the teaching of the New Testament. "The Gospel," it maintains, "teaches an eternal righteousness of the heart," which "does not destroy the State or the Family, but requires their preservation as ordinances of God, and in such ordinances the exercise of charity." That is, the State and the Family have each a necessary function to fulfill in God's economy for the race. Together with the Church they constitute the three divine institutions within whico the Christian life must realize itself. The duties which belong to each institution are different, but they all alike have divine sanction, and each group forms an essential part of the Christian conception of ethical righteousness, according to which the Christian is to endeavor to live.

With this general statement of the Christian's relation to the State and the Family there can be no disagreement. The only questions which can arise are those suggested by the Memorial under consideration. These are two: (1) Does the inclusion of the phrases "to engage in just wars" and "to serve as soldiers" among the duties owed the State commit our Church irrevocably to the war-system as a means for settling international disputes? (2) Can the duty "to serve as soldiers" continue to be regarded as a Christian duty, in view of the new conscience on war?

With respect to the first question the answer is no: our Church is not committed by its Confession to the war-system as necessary in itself. When the Confession was written, the state of civilization was such as to make war appear to be an inescapable necessity of mankind. It was the only method available for the settling of international disputes. To have repudiated its use would have meant the repudiation of the integrity of the State; and this the reformers were unwilling to do, even though it meant the deliberate sanctioning of armed conflict.

However, it should be observed that the phrases "to engage in just wars," and "to serve as soldiers" were used only as illustrations of the way in which citizens of that day could help preserve the integrity of the State. They were not intended as absolute but only relative obligations. The end in view was the preservation of the State, and only as they contributed to this end could they be regarded as having validity. But, under the providence of God and through the preaching of the Gospel, the time must come when armed conflict will no longer be necessary to safeguard the integrity of the State; when other means and agencies better adapted to this end will have been devised. It thus becomes the duty of the Christian citizen to oppose the war-spirit and support the efforts for a permanent peace. By so doing he will not be acting contrary to Article XVI of the Augsburg Confession but fulfilling the spirit of its teaching.

It should be remembered, however, that the whole subject belongs to the ethics of the State. With the specific form which the agencies for peace shall assume the Church as a Church has nothing to do. It is the Church's function to teach its members that Christian righteousness includes within its scope civil righteousness, and that the Christian is bound to fulfill the requirements of this righteousness in the most effective way that the circumstances permit. The support of the movement for peace by arbitration and adjudication now seems to be the most effective way. To this extent the Church should enlighten the Christian, and to this end it should instruct and quicken his conscience. But the manner in which his support shall be given belongs to the realm of Christian freedom, and therefore lies beyond the right of the Church to determine for the individual.

The second question, "Can the duty 'to serve as soldiers' continue to be regarded as a Christian duty in view of the new conscience on war," cannot be so easily answered. Inasmuch as the question itself has become a matter of conscience it has ceased to be a matter on which the Church can legislate with authority for the individual. It may lay down the general principle that the State is a divine institution, and that under certain circumstances it may become the duty of the Christian to defend the State even at the cost of human life. But what these circumstances must be, or in what way one is to lay down his life, cannot be determined by the Church. Here the individual conscience can alone serve as sufficient guide.

Article XVI of the Augsburg Confession recognizes this limitation. Christians, it asserts, are justified in engaging only in "just" wars. Beyond this broad statement of principle it does not presume to go. For the rest it invokes the conscience. "Christians," it adds as a concluding word, "are necessarily bound to obey their own magistrates and laws, save only when commanded to sin, for then they ought to obey God rather than men." And this is as far as the Church can go. It cannot coerce the conscience. When a Christian refuses to take up arms for conscientious reasons the Church is bound to respect his convictions. On the other hand, it has no right to condemn him who, for reasons which are no less conscientious, feels impelled under certain circumstances to serve as a soldier. The only limiting circumstance is that the war be a "just" war, that is, a war, which so far as the human reason and understanding are able to discern, is waged in behalf of a just cause.

The distinction between a "just" war and an "unjust" war is sometimes criticised as an impossible distinction and therefore unwarranted. No war, it is maintained, can be justified from the point of view of the

Kingdom of God, for in the Kingdom only love can be the constraining power to regulate the conduct of men. That is true. But the ethics of war does not fall within the ethics of the Kingdom, but of the State. It is the State's function to administer justice in a sinful world, and to this end it bears the sword. In the use of the sword it is to be governed by the principle of legal justice, and in that sense it is possible to speak of a "just" war.

Legal justice, however, is a relative thing, and man's sense of it can be deepened and purified. Here lies the opportunity of the Church. Without any radical modification of its teaching with respect to the ethics of the State, it can so guide the development of man's sense of justice that it will become more and more difficult to justify a war at the bar of public opinion. And when public opinion refuses to sanction a war, the most telling victory for peace will have been won.

In view of this statement, the Committee recommends the adoption of the following resolution as a substitute for the resolution presented at the Erie Convention by the Rev. Edwin Heyl Delk, D.D., and referred to this Committee for consideration.

RESOLUTIONS

1. The United Lutheran Church in America in Convention assembled at Milwaukee, Wis., hereby declares its profound gratitude to Almighty God for every advance which is being made toward the realization of a permanent peace among the nations of the earth.

2. We believe that the material losses of war, the fears engendered, the consequent hatreds and immeasurable suffering and sorrow resultant from international conflicts make war a devastating calamity for both victor and vanquished.

3. We further believe that through the growth of public confidence in the agencies and instruments for international peace the way can be opened, under the providence of God, for the substitution of the peaceful processes of adjudication and arbitration in place of armed conflict in the settlement of international disputes.

4. We therefore resolve to call upon the whole Christian Church to further the realization of this great hope by bringing the Gospel of our Lord Jesus Christ to bear upon the hearts of men, that they may learn to love peace and pursue it in a spirit of patient forgiveness and willing self-sacrifice after the example of our Lord Jesus Christ.

5. We further resolve to call upon all men as citizens of their respective lands to regard it as a solemn obligation of their citizenship to support in every way the forces which are working for a permanent peace among the nations of the world.

For the Committee.

E. E. FISCHER, *Chairman.*

The time for debate upon the first part of the report was limited to one hour. The seven items of the "Statement on Marriage and Divorce" were first considered.

Item 1 was adopted.

Item 2 was adopted.

Item 3 was adopted.

Item 4 was adopted.

Item 5 was adopted.

Item 6 was adopted.

Item 7 was adopted.

A motion to adopt the preliminary statement was made and carried.

Upon the request of Dr. Fischer that the portion of the report adopted at the Erie Convention (Minutes pp. 582ff) be considered a part of this report, the President responded that it was a statement of the United Lutheran Church on a topic which is directly related to this.

The second part of the report, "Statement on Article XVI of the Augsburg Confession," was then taken up.

Again the time for debate was limited to one hour.

On motion of the Rev. F. R. Knubel the first resolution was amended by striking out the words "the steady" and inserting in place thereof the word "every."

On motion of the Rev. Paul E. Scherer the third resolution was amended by striking out the words "is being" and inserting in place thereof the words "can be."

After the adoption of the foregoing amendments a motion for the adoption of resolutions 1, 2, 3, 4, and 5 was carried.

The President stated that the introductory statement had been received under the order for the reception of reports.

The Secretary presented the report of the Commissioners to the National Lutheran Council as follows:

REPORT OF THE COMMISSIONERS TO THE NATIONAL LUTHERAN COUNCIL

Your Commissioners have the honor to submit their report of the work of the National Lutheran Council for the past biennium of the United Lutheran Church in America:

Under the gracious guidance of God, the National Lutheran Council from year to year is extending its sphere of usefulness and service as the general agency of the Lutheran Church Bodies officially uniting in this common work. Through this agency a common Lutheran representation has been established in part before other branches of the Christian Church, the Government and the American people in matters properly belonging to its work as defined in the regulations drawn up by its Commissioners.   In the eleven years of its existence, the National Lutheran Council has fostered a better and broader understanding of common Lutheran problems and indirectly therefore has played its part in the encouragement and in some instances the formation of a number of intersynodical committees and conferences, such as the American Lutheran Statistical Association, the American Federation of Lutheran Brotherhoods, the National Lutheran Educational Conference, the Lutheran Student Association of America, the Lutheran Foreign Missions Conference of America, the National Lutheran Inner Mission Conference, the National Lutheran Editors' Association and the Lutheran Home Missions Council of America.

The Commissioners' report on the National Lutheran Council's work for the period beginning July 1, 1928 up to and including June 30, 1930 covers the following: I. Regular Work; II. Emergency Work; III. Personnel and Budget.

I. REGULAR WORK

1. Representation. The opportunities in this branch of the service of the National Lutheran Council increase with the passing of every year. During the past biennium representation has been exercised in the American Committee on the Rights of Religious Minorities affecting the Magyar and German Lutherans in Roumania, and the Lutherans in Lithuania, Jugoslavia, Poland, etc. The problems of immigration quotas, regulations for the securing of Communion wine under the prohibition regulations, the carrying forward of the census of the "Lutherans" for 1926 by the U. S. Census Bureau rather than the "Lutheran Church Bodies," and the securing of the acceptance of a general statement of the origin and history of "American Lutherans" and doctrine, position, and polity, were among the items of representation before the U. S. Government by the National Lutheran Council. The Lutherans were also represented before general organizations such as the International Missionary Council, the American Bible Society, the Congregationalist Church as to their proselyting activities in the Lutheran parishes of Volga Valley of Russia, the China Famine Re-

lief, etc.   The representation work of the National Lutheran Council also rendered personal service to persons and families in their relation to governments; as an example, the securing of the release of captured Chinese missionaries.

2. Statistical and Reference Library Service. This branch of the National Lutheran Council's work, in charge of Rev. G. L. Kieffer, D.D., Litt.D., as reference librarian and statistician, with the co-operation of Dr. O. M. Norlie as librarian, has grown during the past biennium. The Statistical and Reference Library has been at the disposal of the National Lutheran Council's Editorial Committee in the preparation of the Lutheran World Almanac and Encyclopedia, furnishing all of the statistical matter, the directories, and helping in many other ways. The Lutheran World Almanac and Encyclopedia is at least one enterprise by and through which a common front, a common testimony, and a common source of information is supplied, covering all Lutheran Church Bodies and Synods in the United States and Canada.   In a very true sense it sets forth the American Lutheran Church as a whole. The reference service of this department is rendered to individuals, churches, synods, and the several departments of the National Lutheran Council on many and varied subjects: and annually the statistics of the Lutherans and encyclopedia articles on the Lutherans are supplied to various reference books and magazines such as "The International Encyclopedia," the "Americana Year Book and Encyclopedia," Dr. H. K. Carroll of the "Christian Herald," and almanacs like the Eagle, World, etc. In addition, annually with the co-operation of many leading Lutherans, an article of achievements and projects of the Lutheran Church in the United States and Canada, is released. These articles form the basis for the article on "Trends and Events" in Section V. of the 1930 edition of the Lutheran World Almanac and Encyclopedia. Perhaps the outstanding achievement of the Statistical and Reference Department was the co-operation with the United States Bureau of Census in the taking of the 1926 U. S. census of "Lutherans," the result of which has been published in the United States Government Bulletin entitled "Lutherans—1926."   The Department also secured a special rate from the Government Printer which enabled a wide distribution of this Bulletin to the number of 6,000 copies.

The service of the Department also involves preparation of various articles, book reviews, surveys, etc., that appeared in the Lutheran periodicals and magazines from time to time. During the eleven years of the statistical and reference work of the National Lutheran Council there has been developed a great appreciation of the value of Lutheran statistics and a greater interest in facts concerning the Lutheran Church of the United States and Canada, and of the World. When the work was started eleven years ago there was great difficulty in finding very many Lutheran people who understood the ramifications of the organization of the Lutheran

Church in America. Statistics were almost unobtainable. Since then there have been published six volumes of the Lutheran World Almanac. Not only Lutherans are able to understand themselves, but the standard reference shelves contain these volumes, and the students in the universities and the libraries are coming to an understanding of the importance and the influence of the Lutheran Church. Encyclopedias eleven years ago had little or nothing concerning the Lutheran Church. Some even grouped the Lutheran Church as a part of the Reformed Church of Germany (see the Dewey Decimal System of Classification). Today no encyclopedia wants to go to press unless they have some authoritative statement concerning the work of the Lutheran Church. An altogether different state of mind exists today from what existed eleven years ago. The Lutheran Church today is regarded as an important factor in the very life of the United States and Canada. This change has been gradual and has come about by careful plodding and releasing of accurate facts in an unchangeable way.

3. Publicity Service. The publicity service of the National Lutheran Council has been carried forward by the News Bureau, Mr. W. P. Elson, secretary for publicity. There has been intensive development of the science and art of church publicity, especially through the religious press, general periodicals, magazines, and newspapers, both for the Lutheran Church as a whole and for the co-ordinated assistance of publicity committees or bureaus of individual synods or church bodies. Successful newspaper publicity has been achieved through this general Lutheran agency by promptly reporting occurrences, achievements, and programs having news value within the life of the Church; and by the aid of influential laymen, pastors, and committees on church publicity establishing contacts with editors of the daily and weekly press, thereby creating a receptivity for Lutheran news. The News Bureau made releases to approximately 1,400 newspapers. In addition to the service rendered the Lutheran, general, and religious press the News Bureau also rendered special publicity service to religious organizations, General Lutheran Church bodies, districts, synods, and general organizations. It publishes weekly a news bulletin which is sent to the religious press, and from time to time news bulletin specials are released on subjects of more than passing importance. The achievement of the News Bureau, of course, is the fact that the press in general today does publish many items of Lutheran news. The commendation of the Lutheran Editors' Association has been won by the service rendered by the News Bulletin.

Another publicity accomplishment of the National Lutheran Council has been the Lutheran Exhibit, a collection of maps, charts, mottoes, etc. telling the story of the work of the Lutheran Church, which has traveled from place to place, and wherever shown has told the story.

The National Lutheran Council, through its News Bureau as the American channel of publicity for the second Lutheran World Convention held at Copenhagen in the summer of 1929, released the program and many of the speeches and papers in advance to the secular and religious press of America.

4. Quadricentennials.

A. Quadricentennial Celebration of Luther's Small Catechism. An article on this subject giving in detail an account of the remarkable world-wide celebration of the Catechism anniversary is found in the 1930 edition of the Lutheran World Almanac. The National Lutheran Council contributed to the celebration by reference material on Luther's Catechism offered in the 1928 edition of the Lutheran World Almanac; by securing and offering to Lutheran editors a quadricentennial memorial series of ten articles on the Catechism, which were widely published and quoted in the church press of this country and Europe; by the production and distribution of 3,000,000 Catechism poster stamps; by the release of news stories concerning the celebration to the church and secular press and by securing publicity for the many Catechism anniversary celebrations throughout the Lutheran world and by furnishing speakers on call so far as possible for celebrations.

B. Quadricentennial Celebration of the Augsburg Confession. The National Lutheran Council's contribution to this celebration includes:

a. The fifty-seven pages of the new 1930 Lutheran World Almanac devoted to the Augsburg Confession. Articles on the confession, accurate and informing, prepared by some of the foremost authors of the church, are thus offered for the encouragement of the re-study of this primary confession of the church.

b. A syndicated memorial series of fifteen articles on the Augsburg Confession by outstanding Lutheran authors of America and Europe are now being published in the Lutheran periodicals of the United States and Canada.

c. The securing and distributing of the serial story "A Daughter of Old Augsburg," now appearing in a number of the church papers.

d. Favorable editorial comment on the Augsburg Confession and its quadricentennial celebration was inspired by the feature stories sent to the secular press. News items covering celebrations by local Lutheran groups throughout the country were supplied to the press by the publicity department.

e. The distributing of the official German Augsburg Confession Medal as well as the "Augsburg Anniversary Poster Stamp" of the American Lutheran Publicity Bureau.

5. The Public Celebration of the Tenth Anniversary of the Organization of the National Lutheran Council.

The tenth anniversary of the organization of the National Lutheran Council was held in Grace Lutheran Church, Columbus, Ohio. (For a report in detail of this celebration see the Lutheran World Almanac for 1930, page No. 36).

II. EMERGENCY WORK

The National Lutheran Council has been working in complete harmony with the Executive Committee for continuation work of the Lutheran World Convention and has supported to the utmost its program for Lutheran Church relief and conservation. The fact that actual economic recovery from impoverishment and distress of the greatest war of history can come to the people of the countries of Europe only after generations of privation and toil has necessitated continued contributions for World Service by the Lutherans of America. Lutheran minorities have been aided, Lutheran students have been assisted in order that the ranks of the ministry might be supplied, and the martyr church of Russia has received such aid as was possible.

From July 1, 1928 to June 30, 1930 the moneys expended for European relief are as follows: In Russia, $30,372.22; in Germany, $1,355.58; in Poland, $2,171.25; in Austria, $1,540.00; in Roumania, $1,300.00; in Czecho-Slovakia, $800.00; in Jugo-Slavia, $800.00; in France, $1,000.00; in Latvia, $1,000.00; in Spain, $100.00; in Esthonia, $100.00; in Jerusalem, $65.68; in Lithuania, $346.50; in Mesopotamia, $25.00; in Switzerland, $500.00; in Hungary, $500.00; in Bohemia, $200.00; in China for famine relief, $515.45; Near East Relief, $20.01; West Indies Hurricane relief, $48.50; in India, Gossner Mission, $20,308.27; Lutheran World Convention for European relief (Feb. 1, 1930 to June 30, 1930) $9,373.88; making a total of $72,442.34.

WORLD SERVICE PROGRAM FOR 1930

At the meeting of the Council held in New York January 16, 1930, a new policy in regard to the administration of Lutheran World Service funds was inaugurated. So long as the emergency continues or other arrangements shall have been made, the Council will continue the ingathering of funds for Lutheran World Service but will entrust emergency relief work and the distribution of such funds to the Executive Committee for Continuation Work of the Lutheran World Convention under the personal direction of Dr. John A. Morehead, its president. The Council thus joins similar relief agencies of the Lutheran Churches in Europe and other continents in administering relief funds through the Lutheran World Convention's Executive Committee. The knowledge that they are being supported by the various Lutheran World agencies and relief societies through the Lutheran World Convention, is inspiring weak and endangered Lutheran Churches overseas to new joy and hope. At the meeting of the Council it became evident that emergency relief work must be continued. Upon careful estimates of amounts needed for specific purposes especially in continuance of work that the Council had already begun in the past, an appeal for contributions amounting to $69,000 to be devoted to the following causes was authorized:

1. Repayment of loans:
   (a) To Dr. E. Clarence Miller ....$ 6,000
   (b) To United Lutheran Church Foreign Mission Bd. 1,200
   (c) To balance of pledge to Gossner Mission.... 1,800
                                                ————— $ 9,000
2. For celebration of Augsburg Confession anniversary   2,500
3. For Lutheran World Convention:
   (a) Administration expense for World Service.. 7,500
   (b) To provide for Russian relief, other European
   relief, and Gossner Mission 50,000
                                                ————— 57,500
                                                  $69,000

That the Russian Lutheran Church, suffering together with other Christian Churches of that unhappy land, as perhaps no other church since the beginning of Christianity, must receive the major part of the help the Lutherans of America can give, should be evident to all. The most effectual help the Church in America can offer is to make possible by adequate financial aid the continuance of the Leningrad Seminary for the training of future spiritual leaders. Financial aid must be given also to the pastors still at work, the majority of whom, aside from their mental and spiritual distress which at times becomes almost unbearable, being deprived of almost all the necessities of life, must suffer actual physical want. The Lutheran Church in America dare not forsake these brethren in the faith nor refuse to come to their assistance.

III. PERSONNEL AND BUDGET

The membership of the Council is as follows: Church Bodies officially participating and their commissioners: United Lutheran Church, Rev. J. A. W. Haas, D.D., LL.D., Rev. Charles M. Jacobs, D.D., LL.D, L.H.D., Rev. L. W. Steckel, D.D., Rev. M. G. G. Scherer, D.D., Rev. C. A. Freed, D.D., Rev. P. W. Koller, D.D., Hon. E. F. Eilert, C. S. D., Mr. G. F. Greiner; Norwegian Lutheran Church, Rev. J. A. Aasgaard, D.D., Rev. L. W. Boe, D.D., LL.D., Rev. J. A. O. Stub, D.D.; Augustana Synod, Rev. G. A. Brandelle, D.D., LL.D., Rev. Peter Peterson, D.D., Joint Synod of Ohio, Rev. C. C. Hein, D.D., Rev. E. Poppen, D.D.; United Danish Church, Rev. N. C. Carlsen; Lutheran Free Church, Rev. H. J. Urdahl; Icelandic Synod, Rev. K. K. Olafson. Other Church bodies unofficially participating in Lutheran World Service programs: Buffalo Synod, Danish Lutheran Church, Eielsen Synod, Iowa Synod, Suomi Synod and the Finnish Apostolic Church.

The officers are as follows: President, Rev. G. A. Brandelle; vice president, Rev. C. C. Hein; secretary, Rev. N. C. Carlsen; treasurer, Hon. E. F. Eilert.

Executive Committee: Rev. G. A. Brandelle, Rev. C. C. Hein, Rev. N. C. Carlsen, Hon. E. F. Eilert, Rev. M. G. G. Scherer, Rev. Charles M. Jacobs, Rev. H. J. Urdahl, Rev. L. W. Boe and Rev. E. Poppen.

The Rev. John A. Morehead, D.D., LL.D., Th.D., S.T.D., who for eleven years served the National Lutheran Council as its Executive Director and by the wise and consecrated administration of his office fashioned the Council into an agency, unique in the history of the church, for the service of the Lutheran Church at home and abroad, felt constrained to resign his office at the January 1930 meeting in order to devote all of his time and energy to the administration of the work of the Lutheran World Convention. The Commissioners recognizing the fact that the work of the National Lutheran Council and of the Lutheran World Convention has grown to such an extent that it is beyond the ability of any one man to have charge of both, regretfully accepted Dr. Morehead's resignation, thus separating the office of Executive Director of the National Lutheran Council and that of the President of the Executive Committee for Continuation Work of the Lutheran World Convention. As a temporary arrangement to make the separation of these two offices financially possible, a resolution was passed providing for a reduction of the Council's clerical expense by $5,900. This sum taken from the Council's annual budget account shall be devoted to the payment of the Lutheran World Convention's administration expense. The balance required for this purpose to be included in the World Service Appeal.

All the work of the National Lutheran Council was, until February 1, 1930, under the direction of Dr. Morehead, as Executive Director. Since February 1, 1930, Rev. Frederick H. Meyer, pastor of Fordham Lutheran Church, New York City, has served as Acting Executive Director. He will serve until Rev. Ralph H. Long, newly elected Executive Director, assumes charge. The Rev. O. C. Mees, Canton, Ohio, served as Appeal Manager for the year 1929.

The annual budget of the National Lutheran Council is $33,896.66, apportioned on a per capita basis to the officially participating Church Bodies as follows: United Lutheran Church, $18,488.87; Norwegian Lutheran Church, $6,066.89; Augustana Synod, $4,678.36; Joint Synod of Ohio, $3,466.44; United Danish Church, $374.82; Lutheran Free Church, $700.87; Icelandic Synod, $120.41.

The amount paid on its quota by the United Lutheran Church in the year 1929 was $16,790.00; in 1930, to June 30th, $9,890.00.

RECOMMENDATIONS

Your Commissioners offer the following recommendations:

1. That the United Lutheran Church in America continue to pay its share of the budget for the maintenance of the National Lutheran Council.

2. That the 1930 World Service Program for $69,000 be approved and that the pastors and parishes of all constituent synods be encouraged and urged to contribute their proportionate part of $37,967.52 which is expected of the United Lutheran Church.

Section IV. by G. L. K. in the 1929-1930 Lutheran World Almanac extensively quoted in this report.

Respectfully submitted,

CHARLES M. JACOBS,

For the Commissioners.

REPORT OF THE NATIONAL LUTHERAN COUNCIL ON SPECIAL PUBLICITY SERVICE

With the biennium, July 1st, 1928 to June 30th, 1930, the News Bureau of the National Lutheran Council has completed five years of special publicity for the United Lutheran Church, whereby the secular press of the United States and Canada has been served with news stories relating to the aims and special interests of the United Lutheran Church in America. All service in this connection has been rendered by the News Bureau without cost, charges being made only for the postage, stationery and other items of extra expense.

During the biennium lists of daily newspapers varying from 468 to 2,460 in number have been served with fifty-two general news stories concerning the work of the Church. Eighty-one news items of varying sectional importance were mailed to local lists of dailies and weeklies ranging from 2 to 463 in number. Fourteen of the general articles for United States and Canadian dailies were translated and mailed to 154 German newspapers.

During the twenty-four months, 36 special news stories were released through wire and news agencies, 126 "news tips" were delivered by telephone, telegraph, messenger or mail to news and wire agencies, news photo services and individually selected newspapers, and 8 photographs were delivered to various newspapers.

In addition to the above, in preparation for the Erie convention of the Church, one letter enclosing news material was sent to 538 convention delegates, and six pictures of news personages in matrix form were supplied to mat-using newspapers throughout the country.

The special publicity during the biennium includes service rendered to various boards and committees of the Church, and conventions of constituent synods.

An attempt has been made throughout the biennium to keep the wire and news agencies serving the newspapers informed in advance about the approaching conventions and special meetings which may prove of general news interest Thus in numerous cases it has been possible to secure adequate newspaper coverage of such events taking place in cities distant from New York without incurring any extra expense for the mailing of news stories and arranging to report the meeting. This type of service has an added advantage through the fact that mailed news stories from every conceivable source ,largely commercial, (termed "free handouts"), are reaching the editors of newspapers, large and small, in such quantities as to make it impractical to spend the time necessary to edit and re-write those which would be most useful. One editor of a small newspaper friendly to Lutheran news informed the secretary of the News Bureau recently that he receives an average of one peck of such news stories a day. Included in this quantity, of course, is the Lutheran material which may not always get attention on a busy day. One advantage of serving newspapers through the Associated Press, United Press, International News, and like agencies, is that the news material need not be lost in the vast amount of free publicity which commercial concerns are mailing to the editors.

There is increasing necessity for notifying wire news agencies of important events in advance of their occurrence rather than after they have taken place. It is at this point that the agencies of the Church can assist very materially in improving the character and nature of our publicity service. If there is any weak place in the present system it is that reporting news events to the News Bureau of the National Lutheran Council is not carried out systematically save by a few of the boards or individuals connected with them. It has been the hope of the Bureau that a system would be evolved by which each board and committee would appoint one responsible member to devote considerable attention to the securing of publicity on all matters of vital importance to the Church through the adequate reporting of news, both to the News Bureau and to newspapers in any locality where the board happens to meet. As a part of the same program adequate news reporting should be set up for all constituent synods at time of convention and between conventions to serve the newspapers and wire agencies directly and to call upon the News Bureau of the National Lutheran Council for co-operation and aid wherever it may be advisable.

Considerable progress in the development of this program and the more rapid service to the newspapers of church news has been made during the biennium. It is hoped that the active co-operation of the whole Church will do much to provide both more voluminous and effective publicity.

Respectfully submitted,

W. P. ELSON, *Secretary*.

FREDERICK H. MEYER, *Acting Executive Director*.

The Secretary then introduced the Rev. Ralph H. Long, Executive Secretary of the National Lutheran Council, who addressed the Convention.

Recommendation 1 was referred to the Executive Board.

Recommendation 2 was adopted.

At 11:45 o'clock the convention adjourned with prayer by the Rev. W. H. Blancke.

Afternoon Session

Thursday, October 9, 1930, 2:00 o'clock.

Devotions were conducted by the Rev. Stephen M. Paulson and the President called the Convention to order.

The Rev. J. A. Leas, Chairman of the Committee of Reference and Counsel, reported as follows:

1. The attention of your committee having been directed to a poem entitled, "Thou, Luther's Church," written by a devoted layman, Mr. John W. Hahn, as a prayerful appeal to the Lutheran Church at large and in "Christian love dedicated to The United Lutheran Church in America, assembled at Milwaukee, Wisconsin," we would, therefore, recommend that this convention accord recognition of the said dedication and that a letter of thanks be sent to the author.

2. Information of the serious illness of the Rev. J. F. Ohl, Mus.D., D.D., having reached your committee, we recommend that the committee be authorized to send him a telegram of sympathetic greeting on behalf of the convention.

3. A letter of greeting has been received from the American Lutheran Mission of Shantung, China, and the committee recommends that the chairman of the committee be permitted to read it to the convention.

4. We recommend that the first order of business on Thursday afternoon be the hearing of the Rev. President G. A. Brandelle, D.D., LL.D., the representative of the Augustana Synod.

5. The committee recommends that, immediately following the address of Dr. Brandelle on Thursday afternoon, the Rev. L. W. Boe, D.D., President of St. Olaf College and the representative of the Norwegian Lutheran Church of America, be presented.

6. Since a form for the installation of the Presidents of Synods and of the United Lutheran Church has been published, we, therefore, recommend

(a) That this form be now introduced and that it be used at the installation of the president elected at this convention.

(b) That the time for the installation be Friday evening of this week.

Item 1 was adopted.

Item 2 was adopted by a rising vote.

Item 3. The recommendation was adopted and it was moved and carried that the greetings be acknowledged and authority given the committee to send a suitable response.

Item 4. The recommendation was adopted. Dr. Leas then introduced Dr. Brandelle who addressed the Convention. At the request of the President, the Rev. Charles M. Jacobs responded to Dr. Brandelle's message of greeting from the Augustana Synod.

Item 5. The recommendation was adopted. Dr. Boe was then introduced and addressed the Convention. At the request of the President, the Rev. S. W. Herman responded to the address of Dr. Boe.

Item 6. Recommendation (a) was adopted. It was voted to amend recommendation (b) so that the installation be held in connection with the services on Sunday evening. The recommendation as amended was adopted.

Dr. Leas then read the following resolution offered by Mr. Peter P. Hagan:

Resolved, That this convention express its appreciation to Mr. Harvey C. Miller, Chairman of the Transportation Committee, for his able and untiring efforts to insure the comfort and safety of delegates coming to this biennial meeting and especial thanks to the Pennsylvania Railroad for the special train with its unique stationery, menus and conveniences provided, as well as the club and observation cars. The electric lighted emblem on the rear of the train announced to all the meeting of the convention and destination of the fourteen cars composing it.

Resolved, That a copy of this resolution of appreciation be sent to General W. W. Atterbury, President, and Mr. J. S. Eysmans, Vice President, and the Board of Directors of the Pennsylvania Railroad.

The resolution was adopted.

The Rev. Luther Kuhlman presented the report of the Commission of Adjudication as follows:

REPORT OF COMMISSION OF ADJUDICATION

The Commission held its organization meeting at Erie, Pa., on Friday, October 12th. The following officers were elected for the biennium:

President—Dr. Henry E. Jacobs.
Vice-President—Dr. Luther Kuhlman.
Secretary—Dr. R. E. Tulloss.
Clerk—Judge E. K. Strong.

Meetings of the Commission were held at Mt. Airy, on January 4, 1929, and on April 12, 1929.

The resignation of Judge Henry W. Harter, made necessary by his election to membership on another board of the United Lutheran Church, was presented at the January meeting and was accepted with regret.

Upon nomination by the Commission, the Executive Board of the United Lutheran Church elected Mr. Robbin Wolf, of Pittsburgh, Pa., to succeed Judge Harter.

An appeal from the Evangelical Lutheran Synod of California dated November 22, 1928, came before the Commission and was considered. It constituted the chief item of business during the biennium.

The following is a copy of the Opinion rendered by the Commission upon this Appeal.

OPINION OF THE COMMISSION OF ADJUDICATION OF THE UNITED LUTHERAN CHURCH IN AMERICA, IN REPLY TO AN APPEAL FROM THE EVANGELICAL LUTHERAN SYNOD OF CALIFORNIA, DATED NOVEMBER 28, 1928

At a meeting of the Commission of Adjudication of the United Lutheran Church in America, held at Mt. Airy, Pa., Friday, January 4th, 1929, the Commission had before it an Appeal from the Synod of California, adopted by that body at a special session held in Riverside, California, November 22nd, 1928; and a letter from the Council of the "First Lutheran Church" of Los Angeles, Calif., signed by the Rev. W. S. Dysinger, President, and Mr. M. B. Wiseman, Secretary, with reference to the Appeal.

After due consideration of the form of the Appeal and the manner of its submission, the Commission determined that the Appeal was in proper form and had been presented in the proper manner. The Appeal was, therefore, officially received for consideration by the Commission.

In order that the writers of the letter above referred to might have ample opportunity for supporting the statements made therein, the Commission provided for the submission of briefs, and set Friday, April 12th, 1929, at Mt. Airy, Pa., as the date and place for a meeting for final consideration of the Appeal.

In accordance with this action the Commission convened at Mt. Airy, on Friday, April 12th, having before it, in addition to the original Appeal and the letter above referred to, the following papers:

1. A Brief submitted by Dr. W. S. Dysinger and his associates, dated February 12, 1929.
2. An additional document entitled "Some Observations on Legal Questions" in support of the foregoing brief, prepared by attorneys associated with Dr. Dysinger, dated February 12, 1929.
3. A Brief submitted by the Evangelical Lutheran Synod of California, dated March 8, 1929.
4. A document entitled, "Some Observations on Legal Questions," prepared by an attorney associated with the officers of the Synod, dated March 12, 1929.

Copies of these documents had been sent in advance to all members of the Commission.

After ample consideration of the original Appeal, the letters referred to, and the briefs submitted, it was decided that no procedure was open to the Commission other than to give direct answers to the questions proposed in the Appeal. The following statement was thereupon unanimously adopted as the action of the Commission.

The Commission of Adjudication recognizes that the whole matter here involved is one having both civil and ecclesiastical aspects and implications, and that the province of the Commission is to decide the strictly ecclesiastical phases of the question submitted. This it is the purpose and desire of the Commission to do, without intrusion into the realm of a civil court.

The Commission, therefore, proceeds to make reply to the questions in the appeal, regarding them as inquiries from a synod with reference to matters within its jurisdiction and control.

Question 1. Were the amendments to the Constitution of said congregation, as set forth above, legally made?

Reply: The Commission is not clear whether the matter here involved is a civil or ecclesiastical question, or whether the civil or ecclesiastical implications are not so closely related as to be practically inseparable.

If it be a civil question, it is beyond the jurisdiction of the Commission, and has already been decided by the Court; although, with full respect to the judgment of the court, we believe that the basis of the decision is none too well grounded in law.

In so far as it is an ecclesiastical question, we are convinced that the plain intent of the framers of the congregational constitution involved, was to make it impossible to amend certain sections thereof except by *unanimous consent;* and that the amendment of Article XII, while technically a seeming possibility, was actually and morally violative of the clear spirit and intent of the document as a whole, and in this sense an amendment not permissible under the Constitution; and hence an action clearly contrary to sound ecclesiastical law and polity.

Question 2. Did the majority group in said congregation under the congregational constitution as it existed prior to the alleged amendments, have

the right and power to withdraw the congregation from membership in said synod despite the protest of the minority group against such action?
Reply: No.

Article II, Section 1, of the congregational constitution provides: "This Church . . . . shall always be connected with a district synod of the General Synod of the Evangelical Lutheran Church in the United States."

Article XII, Section 1, of the Constitution provides: "No alteration or amendment of Article II . . . . shall ever be made so long as any member of the Church is opposed to such alteration or amendment."

It is clear that under the congregational constitution as it existed prior to the alleged amendments, withdrawal from the synod could be accomplished only by a unanimous vote of the membership of the Church.

Question 3. Did the said synod have the right and power under its constitution to recognize the minority group as the lawful congregation?

Reply: Article X, Section 4, of the Synodical Constitution involved reads as follows:

"In cases of strife and division, should any part of a congregation belonging to the synod reject the faith as set forth in Article I, Section II, or revolt against the constitutional provisions or its obligations as a member of the synod, that part of the congregation whether majority or minority of its members, which continues in unity with the synod and its faith shall be recognized as the lawful congregation."

From this it is unmistakably clear that the synod had the right and power to recognize the minority group as the lawful congregation.

Question 4. Was the action of the synod recognizing the minority group as the true Church, as set forth in the statement of facts, legal and in accordance with its synodical constitution?

Reply: In so far as ecclesiastical questions are here involved, such action was legal and in accordance with the Synodical Constitution.

Questions relating to the name and property of the congregation and any other matters in the fourth item of the Synodical Action (page 42, Proceedings of the Thirty-sixth Annual Convention of the Evangelical Lutheran Synod of California) which are clearly civil in character and import, are recognized as lying beyond the jurisdiction of the Commission.

Question 5. Is the seceding group a congregation in organic or any connection with the United Lutheran Church in America?

Reply: In accordance with the Constitution of the United Lutheran Church in America (Article IV) a congregation can be an integral part of the United Lutheran Church in America only through its association with other congregations in a synodical organization.

Done at Mount Airy, Pennsylvania, Friday, April 12, 1929, by the Commission of Adjudication of the United Lutheran Church in America.

Respectfully submitted,

R. E. TULLOSS, *Secretary.*
H. E. JACOBS, *President.*

The President stated that the report was received as an authoritative decision of the Church through its Commission of Adjudication.

The President then called for the reading of that portion of the Commission's Supplementary Report pertaining to a change in its Rules of Procedure.

Moved and carried, That the recommendation of the Commission be adopted.

The President then called attention to the portion of the Executive Board's report referring to the removal of Hartwick Seminary. (See Executive Board's Report, III, B. 1 (b)).

The two questions of the Executive Board were reworded so that the first shall read;

"Has The United Lutheran Church in America any authority at all in the matter of organization or location or relocation of theological seminaries," and the second;

"Has the United Lutheran Church definitely stated that no Synod shall have authority to locate or change a location without the approval of The United Lutheran Church in America."

In the amended form the two questions were referred to the Commission of Adjudication. (See Evening Session, Saturday, October 11th.—Secretary.)

Mr. Arthur P. Black addressed the Convention and presented the report of the Laymen's Movement as follows:

REPORT OF LUTHERAN LAYMEN'S MOVEMENT FOR STEWARDSHIP

The program of the Lutheran Laymen's Movement for Stewardship during the past biennium has been advanced along the same lines followed in previous bienniums, but with a changed emphasis. The Every Member Canvass and Stewardship have been given more attention, and Student Aid less attention. Distinct changes in methods of procedure have resulted.

A BRAND NEW PROGRAM

The principle change involves the relation of the Every Member Canvass to the benevolent program of our United Lutheran Church, and came about naturally when the Special Committee of Fifteen created by the Erie Convention to devise ways and means to raise the apportionment 100%, turned that work over to the Laymen's Movement.

REPORT OF THE COMMITTEE OF FIFTEEN

The report of the Committee of Fifteen has been made a part of the report of the Executive Board. (See Report of Executive Board, Item VI, 7) It includes, in full, the Proposed Plan outlining the method of procedure as approved by both the Executive Committee of the Laymen's Movement and the Committee of Fifteen. Read in connection with this report it will give a clear understanding of what our Church is doing to advance its benevolent program. This Proposed Plan is being worked out on the theory that no financial plan, however well conceived, can succeed unless and until it is promoted along informational and educational lines. Other features are emphasized in the report of the Committee of Fifteen. This report explains, as a matter of information, the method of procedure being followed. **(See Recommendation 1.)**

THE PERSONAL EQUATION

The supreme value of the personal equation has been stressed, and will continue to be stressed constantly by those engaged in the organization work in the different synods. It was with this thought in mind that Mr. J. L. Clark and Mr. E. J. Young, President and Vice President, respectively, of the Laymen's Movement, volunteered their services, and as much of their time as might be required, to put the Proposed Plan in operation in each Conference in every synod.

WORKING OUT THE PLAN

The Ohio Synod was the first to be set up (September, 1929). It has four Conferences. A set-up meeting was held in each Conference. The average attendance was around fifteen. The President of Synod attended all four meetings. The President of Conference attended the meeting in his Conference. The men who attended the meetings were selected by the President of Synod and President of Conference in each instance. All were laymen, one of whom, in each Conference, was designated as the key man. The time and place of each meeting were designated by the President of Synod, or the President of Conference, or both.

METHOD OF PROCEDURE IN MEETINGS

At each meeting a detailed explanation, step by step, of the origin, purpose, and working out of the Proposed Plan, was made by Mr. Clark and Mr. Young. Major emphasis was placed on the educational significance and the practical importance of the annual Every Member Canvass and its four aides (a) the Duplex Envelope (b) the Budget (c) the Pledge Card and (d) the Quarterly Statement. Illustrations showing how a real Every Member Canvass works were cited. A copy of the Proposed Plan, copies of Every Member Canvass folders, copies of all letters mailed to pastors, were given to each man present; *also, a list of all congregations in the Conference represented, showing in parallel columns the amount of each congregation's deficit for each of the past three years.* The President of Synod and President of Conference made whatever explanatory statements their judgment dictated. A general appeal, *in the name of our Church,* to support its benevolent program, was made, and the men invited to volunteer to take up personally with the pastors and their councilmen (and their congregations when invited to do so), the question of raising the apportionment 100 per cent. The men were given the privilege of selecting their assignments in so far as possible, and counselled to make their approach first through the pastor, he being the key-man in his congregation, and then through the Council. The number assigned to each congregation varied from two to four or five. In every instance the men were counselled to introduce the Every Member Canvass—including its four aides—into those congregations not using it, and to give all personal assistance possible. Special emphasis was laid on the fact that in working out this proposed plan we are entering upon a campaign rather than a drive, and that it will take years to reach our goal—a 100 per cent apportionment in every synod.

NINE SYNODS SET UP

At the time this report was written (June, 1930) nine synods had been set up. The same method of procedure followed in the Ohio Synod was followed in all the others. These nine synods represent thirty-three conferences. All told, four hundred and ninety-seven men were assigned to work in the deficit congregations in these synods. The following tabulated statement tells the story from the standpoint of statistics:

Name of Synod	Number of Conferences	Number of Workers Assigned
Ohio	4	39
West Pennsylvania	3	28
Pittsburgh	7	94
Alleghany	3	25
East Pennsylvania	4	59
Susquehanna	4	45
Maryland	4	103
Michigan	2	57
Indiana	2	47
	33	497

This number of lay workers enlisted for personal work will be at least quadrupled by the time the last set-up meeting has been held. There is a place in this program for every layman who will work.

A Paragraph of Significant Facts

In connection with the set-up meetings several significant facts stand out. The attendance in practically every instance approximated 100 per cent of those invited. In several meetings there were more present than had been invited. In more than half the meetings there were a number of local pastors who made helpful suggestions. In every meeting the interest manifested was marked. In not a single instance did a man decline to co-operate. The presidents of synod, the presidents of conference, and the key men, rendered the finest kind of service, and in a way that was inspiring to behold. Pastors and laymen got together on common ground, with a common goal in view, did real team work, and came to understand each other better. With few exceptions the pastors of deficit congregations to be visited showed a willingness to co-operate. The great majority welcomed the proffered aid.

Reasons for Wholehearted Co-operation

This proposed plan has the authority of the United Lutheran Church in America back of it—in fact, it is our Church program. It is worked strictly through official channels—the president of the Church, the president of synod, the president of conference, the pastor, the council, the congregation. There is nothing in it that in any way interferes with any synodical program or conference program or congregational program. It brings pastors and laymen together in a truly co-operative way, and helps congregations to help themselves. It ties the practical and the spiritual together in a simple, definite, constructive way. It is a standing challenge to pastors and laymen alike to raise their apportionment—not as an unpleasant duty or a hard obligation, but as a high privilege.

The Follow-Up Program

From time to time the Washington office of the Laymen's Movement supplies all workers with specific information about our Church activities, to be used as talking points in their meetings with pastors, councils, and congregations. Several of the key men call their co-workers in their respective conferences together, at intervals of a month or six weeks, for round-table discussions and to make reports. All key men are urged to follow this plan. The president of synod, president of conference, key man, and synodical stewardship secretary, where there is one, constitute a standing committee to supervise the follow-up in their respective conferences. When assignments are accepted every effort is made to impress the men with the importance of the follow-up. Much remains to be desired along this line. But a start has been made and it is planned to make the follow-up as satisfactory as the original set-up.

Some Well-Defined Conclusions

It is planned further to organize every conference in every synod. The degree of success attained in those synods yet to be organized will depend upon the co-operation given by the synodical officials and enlisted laymen. We have already gone far enough to justify these conclusions:

(a) There are consecrated laymen of ability in every conference who stand ready to answer the call to definite, constructive, personal service.

(b) Presidents of synod, presidents of conference, outstanding laymen, the majority of pastors of deficit congregations, and the majority of councilmen, will co-operate to raise the United Lutheran Church in America apportionment 100 per cent.

(c) Business and professional men will take time for Church work if they are given something definite to do, provided they are convinced it will help advance the program of our great Church.

(d) The average pastor of a deficit congregation welcomes help from outstanding laymen from other congregations in his conference, when convinced they are motivated by the desire to render a real service. The same is true of the average councilman.

(e) The uniting of the official agencies of our Church into a co-operative, working organization, strikes a responsive chord in the hearts of pastors and laymen alike. We all are coming to realize more fully the truth of Mr. Roger Babson's observation that *"We are all in the same boat."*

What Others Say

Indorsements of the proposed plan, and generous offers of co-operation, have come, unsolicited, from the Board of American Missions, the Board of Education, the Board of Secretaries, the executive secretary of the Board of Foreign Missions. Several synods have officially approved it in their printed minutes. A number of synodical bulletins have carried statements approving it. Several presidents of synod have written letters indorsing it, both officially and personally.

Change in Personnel

Those sponsoring the proposed plan have such faith in their ability to enlist the laymen of our Church for volunteer service that the services of our two associate secretaries, Mr. C. W. Herman Hess, and Mr. George L. Rinkliff, were dispensed with December 1st, 1929, by the unanimous vote of the Administrative Committee at a meeting in Philadelphia the last week in August. Mr. Hess had been with the Laymen's Movement more than five years, Mr. Rinkliff a few months less than three years. Both made many friends for the Laymen's Movement and for themselves through their contacts with pastors, councils and congregations in the various synods.

Distinctive Features of the Every Member Canvass

The Every Member Canvass has filled a larger place in our Church program this biennium than ever before. Several distinctive features may be mentioned:

(a) *Its universality.* It is in use in thirty-two of our thirty-three synods, and in an increasing number of congregations.

(b) *More and better publicity.* It is being given more attention each year in synodical publications, church bulletins, the *Parish School Magazine, Lutheran Men,* and *The Lutheran.*

(c) *More and better co-operation.* Perhaps the outstanding feature of the past year's work has been the fine spirit of co-operation everywhere evident.

(d) *Increased attention by conferences.* It is being given a place in conference programs heretofore denied it. The Adams County Conference in the West Pennsylvania Synod devoted an entire day and evening to discussions of the Every Member Canvass from (a) the standpoint of the pastor, (b) the standpoint of the Council, (c) the standpoint of the congregation, (d) the standpoint of our United Lutheran Church. We commend this type of program to every conference in every synod.

(e) *Making Stewardship the Basis.* There has been a growing tendency along this line. More and more pastors and councilmen are coming to understand that in a real Every Member Canvass the major emphasis is on the informational and the spiritual rather than the financial. To that end they are seeking to develop a stewardship consciousness in their congregations. The Juniata Conference in the Susquehanna Synod made stewardship its theme at one of its meetings, covering three-day sessions and one evening session. The theme was presented under the following heads: (a) Bible Teachings on Stewardship, (b) Meaning of Stewardship Applied to Money, (c) Meaning of Stewardship Applied to Time and Talent, (d) Purpose of Stewardship, (e) Promotion of Stewardship, (f) Applied Stewardship in the Home, (g) Fundamental Principles of Stewardship. We commend this type of program to every conference in every synod.

(f) *Tieing the Practical and Spiritual Together.* In its Every Member Canvass promotion and publicity work the Laymen's Movement aims to tie the practical and spiritual together. To this end the constant emphasis placed on the fundamental principles of stewardship is supplemented by an equally constant empasis on such practical suggestions as these:

(1) The Every Member Canvass should be an every *member* canvass, not an every *family* canvass.

(2) Every member should be a *pledged* member, and should make his contributions *weekly* through the duplex envelope.

(3) Make offerings for benevolences and payments for current expenses on a more nearly 50-50 basis, without reducing the pledge to current expenses.

(4) Make the regular apportionment of our United Lutheran Church the *minimum,* not the maximum amount to be raised.

(5) Make Paul's Four-Fold Plan for giving (I Cor. 16:2) our plan, and make his motive for giving (II Cor. 9:6-7), our motive.

(6) Loyalty to our United Lutheran Church program, as well as loyalty to Christ's program, demands that every congregational treasurer forward to the synodical treasurer all offerings for benevolences *monthly.*

(7) The two-treasurer system is recommended for those congregations where the officials forget the Commandment " Thou shalt not steal," and use benevolence money to pay current expense bills.

(8) Talk *causes* rather than *money* when promoting the benevolent program of the Church at large, the synod, or the congregation.

(9) Substitute "God can" for "I can't." .... "Paul may plant; Apollos water; but God gives the increase." .... "Attempt great things for God, expect great things from God."

(10) Objectives of the Every Member Canvass, in their proper order, are: (a) to promote the spirit of Church loyalty, (b) to build up the congregation, (c) to finance the budget. The surest way to realize these three objectives is through the use of the budget, the duplex envelope, the pledge card, and the quarterly statement.

EVERY MEMBER CANVASS DATA

Number of orders for literature received from pastors, 1,420.
Estimated number of congregations reached, 2,000.
Number of folders issued during the campaign, 7.
Total number of copies distributed, upon request, 1,374,000.
Number copies Annual Church Booklet for 1930-31 total, 400,000.

This booklet was issued by twelve boards and agencies of our Church. The cost of printing was prorated on a space basis. As in the past the cost of distribution is being borne by our Laymen's Movement. Heretofore the annual church booklet was issued in the fall. This year it was issued in the spring so as to give pastors the benefit of its use in their congregations during the summer months. It is designed as an educational aid in the preparatory campaign for the Every Member Canvass.

A goodly number of pastors make the canvass independently of outside help, and prepare their own literature, but there is no way of ascertaining how many. **(See Recommendation 2.)**

STUDENT AID

As the result of a survey made during January and February, 1929, the Laymen's Movement is confining its activities in the field of student aid to those synods requesting its help. This has resulted in a general curtailment of its student aid program, as is shown by the following data:

140 students were aided in 1928-9 in the total sum of $27,275.
106 students were aided in 1929-30 in the total sum of $20,360.
90 students (estimated) in 1930-31 will receive the sum of $16,000.
The number of students on our rolls graduated from our seminaries last May was 17.
The number who will be graduated from our seminaries next May will be 17.

The total number aided to prepare for the ministry to date is 90.
The total amount disbursed for student aid to date is $123,387. (See
Recommendation 4.)

In Memoriam

The Grim Reaper took heavy tolls from our Laymen's Movement the
past biennium. Between the time of the Erie Convention and the time
this report was filed no fewer than seventeen of our loyal members transferred from the Church Militant to the Church Triumphant. One of the
number was our beloved treasurer, Mr. William L. Glatfelter, of Spring
Grove, Pa., who departed this life Easter Sunday evening, 1930. He served
us in an official capacity for more than a decade, was one of our most generous financial supporters, never missed a committee meeting when it
was physically possible for him to attend, and his sound advice and
wise counsels were an invaluable aid to our work.   He was a faithful
Christian steward in the true scriptural sense.

New Treasurer Elected

The Laymen's Movement was particularly fortunate to secure the services
of Mr. Glatfelter's son, Mr. Philip H. Glatfelter, also of Spring Grove,
Pa., as treasurer. He was elected at a meeting of the Executive Committee in Philadelphia, May 15th. His election as treasurer was followed by
his election to membership on both the Executive Committee and the
Administrative Committee.

An Appreciation

On behalf of the loyal membership of the Laymen's Movement, whose
continued support year in and year out makes our program possible, the
undersigned express warmest thanks to the distinguished president of our
United Lutheran Church in America, the presidents of our synod, the
presidents of conference, local pastors and their official families, and the
officials of our colleges and seminaries, for their fine co-operation in the
promotion of our work. Their sympathetic attitude and wise counsels have
been a constant help and a never-failing source of encouragement and inspiration.

Recommendations

1. That the proposed plan to raise the apportionment 100 per cent, in-
dorsed by the Executive Committee of the Laymen's Movement and the
Committee of Fifteen, as explained in this report and in the report of the
Executive Board, be approved.

2. That the annual, simultaneous Every Member Canvass be re-indorsed,
that in the preparatory work leading up to it the major emphasis be placed
on the educational and the spiritual values, and that pastors and councils
be urged to talk more about causes and less about money.

3. That the month preceding the Every Member Canvass be devoted
to the special consideration of the fundamental principles of stewardship,

and that pastors and their official families be requested to promote a definite program of stewardship in their congregations throughout the year.

4. That the student aid program of the Laymen's Movement, as being worked out in co-operation with the president of our Church and the presidents of synod, be approved.   J. L. CLARK, *President.*

ARTHUR P. BLACK, *Secretary.*

Mr. J. L. Clark, President of the Laymen's Movement, was introduced and after he had addressed the Convention recommendations 1, 2, 3 and 4 were adopted.

The hearing of the report of the Commission on Lutheran Church Unity was deferred. (See Evening Session, Saturday, October 11th.—Secretary.)

The Rev. M. L. Stirewalt presented the report of the Committee on Memorials from Constituent Synods as follows:

REPORT OF COMMITTEE ON MEMORIALS FROM CONSTITUENT SYNODS

The following memorials, received from various synods, have been considered by your committee and are herewith submitted with suggestions and recommendations.

1. From the Pittsburgh Synod:

"Believing that the best interests of the Church will be served by having the same rule apply to standing committees which the United Lutheran Church in its wisdom has seen fit to apply to all elective boards and committees, the Pittsburgh Synod hereby memorializes The United Lutheran Church in America to include the following addition to its By-Laws: In Section V, Division B, after Item 9 add Item 10 to read as follows:

"'No member of any standing committee shall be eligible for appointment for more than four successive terms of two years each and no person shall be a member of more than two standing committees at one and the same time.'"

ELLIS B. BURGESS, *President*
PHILIP H. R. MULLEN, *Secretary.*

Reply: We recommend that the memorial be divided into two parts.

Investigation reveals that more than fifty per cent of the total membership of the standing committees has been changed since the organization of The United Lutheran Church in America. The work of certain standing committees requires the continued attention of those who are specially gifted and trained for such work. We therefore suggest, with reference to the first part of the memorial, that no change be made at present in the method of making these appointments.

On the second part of the proposed By-Law we recommend the adoption of the following:

No person shall be a member of more than two appointive standing committees at one and the same time.

2. From the Synod of New York:
"That we memorialize The United Lutheran Church in America to use voluntary pledges secured in advance from the constituent synods as the basis for its annual budget." PAUL ANDREW KIRSCH, *Secretary.*

Reply: We recommend that this memorial be referred to a special committee on a plan for laying the apportionment for study and report to the next convention.

3. From the Wartburg Synod:
"The Wartburg Synod of the Evangelical Lutheran Church memorializes the United Lutheran Church to direct the Board of Education to assign Kropp candidates to our colleges in the future, being convinced that the affiliations in a college and regular English work likewise will be a better help for their work in the Church." R. NEUMANN, *President.*

Reply: Information received from the Board of Education concerning certain changed conditions relating to the reception and assignment of Kropp candidates leads the committee to report that action on this memorial is unnecessary.

4. From the West Pennsylvania Synod:
"That the West Pennsylvania Synod memorializes The United Lutheran Church in America at its next biennial convention to instruct its Committee on Evangelism to prepare definite evangelistic literature to be used in evangelistic work."

HENRY ANSTADT, *President.*
M. R. HAMSCHER, *Secretary.*

Reply: The committee recommends that this memorial be approved.

5. From the Evangelical Lutheran Synod of Canada:
"In view of the approaching convention of 'The American Lutheran Conference,' the Evangelical Lutheran Synod of Canada respectfully requests that The United Lutheran Church in America at the present convention give their opinion of this new body, and asks whether the unity of the

Lutheran Church in America would not be furthered by the joining of The United Lutheran Church in America in this movement.

"The Evangelical Lutheran Synod of Canada respectfully memorializes The United Lutheran Church in America to declare itself as opposed to all divorces except such as are granted on the sole Scriptural ground of adultery."

J. REBLE, *President.*

H. SCHORTEN, *German Secretary.*

C. H. LITTLE, *English Secretary.*

Reply: (a) After a conference with the delegation here present from the Synod of Canada and by their action, we are authorized to withdraw for them this memorial.

(b) This item has been acted upon by the convention in the report of the Committee on Moral and Social Welfare.

6. **From the Synod of Nebraska:**
"That we request The United Lutheran Church in America to prepare a list of subjects in which all candidates for the Lutheran ministry shall pass a satisfactory examination before the Synod Examining Committee to which they apply for ordination."

W. I. GUSS, *President.*

F. C. WIEGMAN, *Secretary.*

Reply: The committee recommends that the request herein presented be referred to the Conference of Presidents of Synods for consideration.

7. **From the Nova Scotia Synod:**
"We beg leave to call attention to the action of the Nova Scotia Synod taken at its last convention:

"'That synod memorialize the United Lutheran Church on the question of Lutheran immigrant work at the port of Halifax.' (1929 minutes p. 22).

"May we further connect this memorial with the action of the Executive Board of the United Lutheran Church relative to the seeking for co-operation of other general Lutheran bodies in immigrant work? (United Lutheran Church, 1928 minutes, p. 62).

"Respectfully submitted for the Nova Scotia Synod,"

GEO. P. ENDY

L. F. HARTZELL

FRISBY SMITH

Committee.

Reply: The committee recommends that the memorial be referred to the Inner Mission Board.

8. From the Texas Synod:

1930

" (1)   That we memorialize The United Lutheran Church in America in the matter of women delegates to meetings of synod to determine whether or not such procedure is unscriptural.

" (2)   That synod memorialize The United Lutheran Church in America that its policy with the Inner Mission Board be changed so that this board be empowered to start work in its own name.

" (3)   To the convention of The United Lutheran Church in America concerning the distribution of the apportionment obligation to the constituent synods.

"We believe that the apportionment method by which the United Lutheran Church now for several years has endeavored to raise the funds needed for its benevolent operations has demonstrated the wisdom of such a method sufficiently to warrant its retention by the church. We, furthermore, believe that the failure to raise a sufficient amount to satisfy the annual budget is due to a wrong principle of distribution.

"The Word of God (I Cor. 16:2) requires that the collection for benevolent purposes be made through freewill offerings from every Christian in the measure with which God has prospered him. This biblical principle, we believe, has not been adhered to in the distribution of the apportionment to the several synods affiliated with the United Lutheran Church, but contrariwise, without regard for the peculiar ability of the individual synod, each synod has been assessed the same per communing member though it is evident that there is a marked difference in ability of each synod, as is evidenced by the value of congregational property described in the annual statistical reports of congregations and synods. The question before us, then, brethren, is how we may measure the relative ability of the synods. This, it seems to us, could be accomplished on the basis of property valuation as shown in the last reports, less the indebtedness of each synod. Allowance should also be made in some equitable manner for the support which the individual synod must give to its charitable and educational institutions.

"We believe that by such a method the weaker synods and congregations who are much behind in meeting this obligation would rather be encouraged when the amount is more within their reach, while congregations and synods who have heretofore raised the full amount would according to Christian principle not slacken their endeavor in this exercise of their Christian privilege and duty. "

J. C. A. PFENNINGER, *President.*
FRED W. KERN, *Secretary.*

1929

"Beschlossen, dass wir, die Texas Synode, die Vereinigte Lutherische Kirche von Amerika ersuchen, ein Gutachten ueber diese Frage zu geben: Ist die Gemeinde vertretung seitens der Frauen der Gemeinde schriftwidrig?

Achtungsvoll,

PAUL KUEHNER, *Sekretaer.*

Reply: (1) Inasmuch as this memorial involves a study and summary of biblical teachings and interpretation and questions of church polity, we recommend that a special committee be appointed to prepare a statement on the subject for consideration at the next convention. This also includes the similar memorial prepared by the same synod in 1929 and included in the group of memorials from that synod.

(2) This request is answered in the third resolution in the report of the Inner Mission Board to this convention.

(3) We recommend reference to a special committee on a plan for laying apportionments for study and report to the next convention.

9. From the Ministerium of Pennsylvania:

" (1) (a) We recommend that the Ministerium request the United Lutheran Church to instruct its Board of Publication to set aside a certain sum from its profits, each year, till a fund be established of sufficient size to warrant the translation and publication of at least two outstanding books each year from the interest of the fund.

" (b) We approve the suggestion that an editorial committee be appointed by the proper authorities to make the necessary selection, that at least one be an outstanding book of the day, and that such classics of the past as may be most valuable be included from time to time."

Reply: We recommend the approval of the objectives mentioned in these memorials and their reference to the Board of Publication for consideration.

" (2) By motion this Conference (Allentown) requests the Ministerium of Pennsylvania to memorialize The United Lutheran Church in America to retain the budget at the same amount for the next biennium as for the present one."

Reply: This matter has already been determined by action of this convention.

" (3) We further endorse the recommendation that the Ministerium of Pennsylvania memorialize the United Lutheran Church to adopt the two-fold basis of laying apportionment; viz, communing members and current expenses."

Reply: We recommend reference to a special committee on a plan for laying apportionments for study and report to the next convention.

"(4) *Resolved,* That the Ministerium memorialize the United Lutheran Church to adopt a schedule whereby United Lutheran Church campaigns be given the right of way every ten years with the right of way for synodical campaigns five years after each United Lutheran Church campaign."

Reply: Being unable to forecast what cause or crises may confront the Church we deem it inexpedient to attempt to regulate campaigns so closely and for the future, but we would urge that they be co-ordinated as far as possible by the supervision and co-operation of general and synodical agencies.

"(5) *Resolved,* That the Ministerium memorialize the United Lutheran Church to request the Laymen's Movement for Stewardship to co-ordinate the educational work on stewardship in the various departments of the Church."

Reply: The committee recommends the adoption of this memorial and its reference to the Parish and Church School Board.

10. Resolution referred by the Convention to this committee:

"*Be it further resolved,* That all of the constituent synods shall accept this principle and shall meet their obligation to pay in *full* the annual budget for benevolence, it being understood that in fixing the basis of synodical apportionment for the budget of benevolence, due consideration be given to the financial ability of the smaller synods of the United Lutheran Church."

Reply: We recommend the approval of the principle contained in this resolution and that, inasmuch as it involves a method of procedure in connection with the apportionment, it be referred to a special committee on a plan for laying apportionments for study and report to the next convention.

Memorial No. 1. The President ruled that the recommendations of the committee amounted to amendments to the By-Laws and therefore would require for adoption a two-thirds vote.

The recommendation of the committee concerning the first part of Memorial No. 1 was adopted: to wit, "that no change be made at present in the method of making these appointments."

To the second part of the memorial the recommendation of the committee was adopted as follows: "No person shall be a member of more than two appointive standing committees at one and the same time."

Memorial No. 2. The reply to Memorial No. 2 was adopted.

Memorial No. 3. Action on the reply to Memorial No. 3 was postponed until the report of the Board of Education is presented. (See Afternoon Session, Saturday, October 11th.—Secretary.)

Memorial No. 4.   The reply to Memorial No. 4 was approved.

Memorial No. 5.   The reply to Memorial No. 5 was received as information.

Memorial No. 6.   The reply to Memorial No. 6 was adopted.

Memorial No. 7.   The reply to Memorial No. 7 was adopted.

Memorial No. 8.   Reply (1) to the memorial from the Texas Synod was adopted.

Reply (2) was received as information.

Reply (3) was adopted.

Memorial No. 9.   Reply (1) (a) and (b) was approved.

Reply (2) was received as information.

Reply (3) was approved.

Reply (4) was approved.

Reply (5) Action postponed until the report of the Parish and Church School Board is presented to the Convention. (See Tuesday's Session, Oct. 14th.—Secretary.)

Memorial No. 10.   The reply to item 10 of the report was adopted.

The Rev. Theo. O. Posselt presented the report of the Committee on German Interests as follows:

REPORT OF THE COMMITTEE ON GERMAN INTERESTS

The Committee held three meetings during the biennium, January 28, 1929, at Baltimore; May 8, 1929, at New York; November 19, 1929, at Philadelphia. Prof. Henry Offermann, D.D., served as chairman, and Pastor Fritz O. Evers as secretary of the committee.

Until failing health had compelled him to decline a reappointment to membership in this committee, the Rev. John J. Heischmann, D.D., of Brooklyn, N. Y., had been a most valuable and beloved member of this committee and the similar organization which preceded it. From the memorial resolution adopted upon his death the following may be quoted: "In the death of Dr. Heischmann the German element of the Church and of the country loses one of its most lovable characters, a leader of vision and ideals, a friend proven and true. In many important fields of labor has he given himself to the service of the Church, in conference, synod and the general boards and conventions of the Church. May it be given to many of his co-workers and followers to be as instant in the cultivation and preservation of the beautiful heritage of the German in the American Lutheran Church as John J. Heischmann was to the day of his death!"

The committee obtained the approval of the Executive Board for the convening of the Sixth General German Conference of the United Lutheran Church on October 9 and 10, 1929, in St. Johannis Church, Reading, Pa., the Rev. Robert Ischinger, pastor. The Conference was attended by 138 pastors and 21 lay delegates. The following synods were represented in this voluntary attendance: Ministerium of Pennsylvania, United Synod of New York, Canada, Pittsburgh, Maryland, Wartburg, German Nebraska and Manitoba. The officers elected by the Conference are: President, Rev. C. Reinhold Tappert, D.D.; Vice President, Pastor Robert Ischinger; Secretary, Pastor H. P. Hassen; Treasurer, Mr. William Moennig.

The theme of the Conference was "The place and mission of the German constituency in the U. L. C. A." Three papers dealt with the outstanding problems of the present-day situation. They were excellently prepared, and evoked earnest discussion. Pastor Siegmund G. von Bosse spoke on "The Language Question;" Pastor Ernst A. Tappert, D.D., treated the subject, "Our Share in the Work of the Church;" Pastor Paul A. Kirsch offered a paper on "Representation of German Interests." Every one of these problems is vital for German pastors and congregations. The discussion strengthened the conviction of the worth-whileness of our work, of its divinely ordained place in the history and development of the Lutheran Church in America, and of its special opportunity at this time, and with the sympathetic understanding and help of the other sections of the Church to foster all things essential to its life and growth in such a manner as they may never before have been recognized and cared for. The Linguistic Policy of the United Lutheran Church and the organization of the Linguistic Division of the Board of American Missions, with its German department, are harbingers of the fact that the Church of this generation intends to serve this strong and valuable element with all diligence and understanding care.

These conferences, which were held bi-annually since the organization of the United Lutheran Church, have offered a welcome opportunity to pastors and interested laymen facing the same general problems in different and far distant fields to form contacts with one another, exchange ideas and to strengthen the bonds of union between them, thereby intensifying their common interest and love for the United Lutheran Church. For this reason the social parts of a conference's program carry special significance. A pilgrimage to the Old Trappe Church, and to Valley Forge, as well as a banquet one evening, contributed largely to the harmony and success of the conference.

Your committee occupied itself with the consideration of the proposed form of constitution for German congregations, which was afterwards approved by the Executive Board, and subsequently published.

The work on a revised form of the Occasional Services in German, carried on in conjunction with the Committee on Common Service Book, is making progress.

Your committee devoted the major part of its meetings and deliberations to a thorough study of the entire question of an adequately prepared ministry for our German and German-English congregations. The conclusions arrived at in these discussions were presented by the chairman, Prof. Offermann, to the special group organized in connection with the Board of Education, to deal with this problem and reappear largely in the findings of this commission which are being submitted to this convention by the Board of Education.

Your committee observed the many new avenues of exchange of thought and personalities inaugurated recently between America and Germany. A clearer knowledge and a truer appreciation of each other will be of greatest benefit to the coming generations of these two nations. Its Lutheran history and background, and its great achievements in the field of theology seem to make Germany stand out as the most desirable place where gifted students of our seminaries could enlarge their vision, deepen their faith, gain an ecumenical view of the Lutheran Church, and enrich their theological training.

The Committee, therefore, presents the following recommendation to the United Lutheran Church in convention:

Resolved, that this convention instruct the Executive Board to consider the inauguration of a regular exchange of students and members of our seminary faculties between our institutions and Lutheran universities in Europe, especially in Germany.

Your Committee, in accordance with the policy outlined at Chicago, at the time of its creation six years ago, stands ready, as heretofore, to assist any board or agency of the Church in the working out of problems affecting the German portion of the United Lutheran Church.

Respectfully submitted,
HENRY OFFERMANN, *Chairman.*
FRITZ O. EVERS, *Secretary.*

Action on the recommendation was postponed until the report of the Board of Education is before the Convention. (Afternoon Session, Saturday; October 11th.—Secretary.)

Mr. Wm. H. Hager, Chairman of Tellers' Committee No. 1, reported elections as follows:

For the *Executive Board* each of the following received a majority of the votes cast:

Rev. Marion J. Kline	Mr. John Greiner, Jr.
Rev. J. L. Morgan	Mr. B. B. Miller
Rev. Rees Edgar Tulloss	Mr. Wm. H. Stackel

The President declared them elected.

For the *Commission of Adjudication* each of the following received a majority of the votes cast:

Rev. Ellis B. Burgess	Rev. H. C. Roehner
Mr. Robbin B. Wolf	

The President declared them elected.

For the *Committee on Church Papers* each of the following received a majority of the votes cast:

Rev. John Aberly	Rev. J. W. Horine
Dr. Wm. J. Showalter	

The President declared them elected.

For the *Executive Committee of the Laymen's Movement* each of the following received a majority of the votes cast:

Mr. F. W. Albrecht	Mr. E. G. Hoover
Mr. J. L. Clark	Mr. E. Clarence Miller
Mr. C. J. Driever	Mr. Harvey C. Miller
Mr. Peter P. Hagan	Mr. George E. Neff
Mr. Henry W. Harter	Mr. John L. Zimmerman

The President declared them elected.

The Rev. D. G. M. Bach, the delegate from the Japan Mission and the Evangelical Lutheran Church in Japan, addressed the Convention, bringing greetings and speaking of the needs and hopes of the Japan Mission.

At five o'clock the Convention adjourned with prayer by the Rev. E. K. Counts.

Thursday Evening

A banquet of the Laymen's Movement for Stewardship was held at the Hotel Schroeder, Milwaukee, Wis., on Thursday evening, October 9, 1930. Approximately 280 were in attendance.

Invocation by the Rev. Paul A. Kirsch.

Toastmaster: Mr. Fred H. Wefer.

Song Leader: Rev. Ross H. Stover.

Soloist: Mrs. Olsen (Choir of First Lutheran Church).

Speakers: Rev. Frederick H. Knubel.

"How Can the Laymen's Movement Help to Energize and Advance the Work of Our Church?"

Rev. N. R. Melhorn,

, "The Plan of *The Lutheran* in Our Church Program."

George E. Neff, Esq.

"The Laymen's Movement.

"(a)   What Is Its Value?

"(b)   Is It Worth While?"

Mr. Jesse L. Clark, President of the Laymen's Movement.

THIRD MEETING

Morning Session

HOTEL SCHROEDER
Milwaukee, Wisconsin.
Friday, October 10, 1930, 8:45 o'clock.

Matins were conducted by the Rev. F. C. Schuldt.

The President called the Convention to order.

The Minutes of the Thursday morning and afternoon sessions were read by the assistant secretary and approved.

The Rev. C. Theo. Benze, President of the Board of Foreign Missions, addressed the Convention and introduced the Rev. Paul W. Koller, Executive Secretary, who presented the report of the Board.

REPORT OF THE BOARD OF FOREIGN MISSIONS

The Board of Foreign Missions submits herewith to the United Lutheran Church in America its Seventh Biennial Report. In making this report we endeavor to set forth in a concise way the work of the Board at home and abroad. We are making every effort to make the report exact in every detail—but we ask that the Convention remember the constant shifting in the missionary personnel and also in the conditions under which the work in the field is done. The two years under review have not seemingly shown much change in the conditions under which the work is carried on, but both at home and abroad there are under currents which affect the work and add new difficulties to the service we are trying to render. In our Church we have not been disturbed much by matters of doctrine. It is a wonderful thing that the world round our missions teach the simple Gospel of Jesus Christ the Saviour of men and the need of a life lived in allegiance to Him. However, attacks on Foreign Missions and a growing materialism at home have not been without evil effect. On the other hand these difficulties have called out a more determined restatement of the purpose and motive of Foreign Missions. In the fields the growing spirit of nationalism has brought new problems and calls for the finest and best in missionary activity. This matter will be reported more fully as each mission's work is set before you in the report. We must note with reference to these matters the influence of the Jerusalem message upon the whole world of missions. The decided stand for Jesus Christ and a life lived in Him has had great influence during these last two years in turning the face of the Church to the need of Foreign Missions, a vital factor in a full-rounded Christian program.

REORGANIZATION OF THE HOME OFFICE

Ever since the death of Dr. Brown the work of the home office has been carried on with a staff of two general secretaries and a field secretary. In the fall of 1928 the Board in answer to the growing requirements of the work reorganized the home office by the appointment of an Executive Secretary, setting up of the work according to departments and the election of a layman as treasurer. The actual working of the new plan was begun with the appointment of Rev. Paul W. Koller, D.D., as Executive Secretary, who took charge on the first of December, 1928. The following is the allocation of the work under the new plan of operation:

1. The Executive Secretary, Dr. Paul W. Koller, has general supervision of all of the departments and for the present is responsible for the work of the Candidate Department and the Foreign Fields Department with a division of the work of the Foreign Fields Department among the secretaries.

2. Secretary Dr. L. B. Wolf has charge of the Home Base Department which includes cultivation of the Home Church, supervision of missionaries on furlough, transportation, purchasing, the care of the Mission House, and for the present he also conducts the correspondence with the missions in China and South America and the missionaries on these fields.

3. Secretary Dr. George Drach has charge of the Literature Department which includes the editing of the publications of the Board, and the publicity and stereopticon departments, the preparation of literature and the printing of all books, pamphlets and literature authorized by the Board. For the present he also conducts the correspondence with the missions in India and Japan and the missionaries on these fields.

4. Secretary Dr. M. Edwin Thomas has charge of the Department of Special Gifts, and for the present conducts the correspondence with the mission in Africa and the missionaries on this field.

5. Treasurer Mr. George Weitzel has charge of the work of the Finance Department and pays all bills and drafts authorized by the Board. All orders are to be signed by the respective departmental secretary and countersigned by the Executive Secretary.

THE COUNCIL OF SECRETARIES

The Executive Secretary with the Departmental Secretaries and the Treasurer constitute an Executive Council. This Council meets at least once every week and considers all matters that pertain to the departments and require consideration and action. The Executive Secretary is the chairman. In his absence the Secretary of the Home Base Department shall act. The Council elects its own recording secretary.

THE EPIPHANY APPEALS FOR THE DEBT

The United Lutheran Church at its last convention gave permission to the Board of Foreign Missions during the Epiphany Seasons of 1929 and 1930 to make an appeal to both congregations and Sunday schools for the Foreign Mission debt. The Board through its secretaries made these appeals and the Church has responded in a very encouraging manner. In 1929 $51,000 was given for the debt and in 1930 $92,000 was given. With this money and other contributions the Board has been able to pay $189,000 on its debt. This with a balanced budget for the last year is doing very much to put our finances on a firm basis. The Board, however, respectfully reminds the Convention and the Church that we cannot do very much aggressive work until the entire debt is paid. **(See Recommendation 1.)**

THE WOMEN'S MISSIONARY SOCIETY

The co-operation of the Women's Missionary Society is a great and valued factor in the work of Foreign Missions. The society carries on work in all fields except British Guiana and at the same time provides the salaries of all women missionaries. In addition it erects many buildings and furnishes the equipment. The money so contributed by the Women's Society is sent to the field through the Foreign Mission Board. There are two regular representatives of the Women's Society who meet with the Foreign Board and whose presence is greatly appreciated. The Women's Society also does splendid work through its Literature Department and its educational work is most valuable. During the biennium the Women's Missionary Society sent through our Board to all fields a total of about $383,000. We are profoundly thankful for what the society is doing. However, your Board wishes to say frankly that in their estimation the best service in missions cannot be done until the idea of separate women's work and men's work is eliminated and there be here at home one board of management and control.

CO-OPERATING SYNODS

Three general bodies co-operate with us in our foreign work. The

Augustana Synod, the United Danish Church and the Icelandic Synod. With fine spirit they have merged their efforts with ours and make regular contributions to the cause of Foreign Missions. Augustana Synod co-operates in India, the United Danish Church and the Icelandic Synod in Japan. Just what is contributed is shown in the treasurer's report and the reports concerning the fields. The United Danish Church has two representatives, the Augustana Synod has one full voting member on the Board and two representatives, and the Icelandic Synod should be asked to name a representative. The value of this co-operation cannot be meas-ured in figures but it means a great deal not only in work done on the field but in making the ties closer here in America. Your Board would express its appreciation of the co-operation on the part of the synods named above. **(See Resolution 2.)**

LUTHER LEAGUE OF AMERICA

During the biennium the Board of Foreign Missions received from the Luther League of America $12,000 in full payment of their objective in the Argentine, viz., the educational building in connection with our Church in Villa Del Parque; a bronze tablet in the vestibule of the Church in-dicates the source of this fine gift. The Board of Foreign Missions ap-preciates greatly the co-operation of the Luther League and especially are we happy that this gift came just when we were celaring up our obliga-tions in South America. During the biennium we also received from the Luther League of Pennsylvania $1,000 for the proposed hospital in China. The Luther League of New York supports Missionary Heins in Japan and the Luther League of North Carolina Rev. A. H. Kaitschuk in Africa. There are many other gifts from the Luther League, including the Inter-mediate and Junior Departments. All these make us greatly appreciative of the Luther League of America.

GREAT NEEDS

We do not desire to report at length about needs at home and abroad, but underlying all we have said and even our encouraging figures is the great fact that we do not have sufficient resources to carry on the great Foreign Mission work of our Church. In our largest fields where the Church is already established, the future is bound up with our ability to grasp the opportunity that is ours. We have presented a good face but our hearts are heavy with the inability to carry on as we should. We would like in this paragraph to say to the Convention and the Church that we are in great need of money and co-operation in order that we go forward. God seems to have opened the way and we cannot take the opportunities unless the Church enlarges its missionary heart. This state-ment is simple but it goes deep in our duty and privilege before God.

THE MISSIONARY STAFF

Space will not permit us to report at length concerning our missionary staff of 185 missionaries. However, we desire to bear witness before the Convention and the Church to the efficiency and loyal devotion of our missionaries. They have many trials to face and the strain of doing more than one person's work, made necessary by our reduced budgets, is very great. They never falter, however, and seldom complain. We want to pay our respects to our missionaries and bear testimony that no church has a more loyal, consecrated and efficient staff of missionaries than our own. In every country in which they work our missionaries and their mission field stands high in the missionary world. All honor to our missionaries not only of the past but of the present.

PORT SERVICE FOR OUR MISSIONARIES

In New York and San Francisco, we have groups of splendid men and women who take the time to meet our incoming missionaries, and for those who depart special farewell services are held. Steamer boxes with a memento for each day of the voyage, prepared by the missionary societies of churches of New York and San Francisco, are presented to the missionaries and their families. This kindly service is greatly appreciated by all of our missionaries and by the Board as well. In New York the chairman is Rev. E. R. Jaxheimer and in San Francisco, Rev. E. A. Trabert has served during the biennium.

CANDIDATES

During this biennium on account of a shortage in funds not very many men missionaries have been sent to the fields. We have endeavored, however, to fill the vacancies caused by missionaries resigning either on account of ill health or for reason over which they had no control. Those who have been sent we believe to be of a high type and every effort has been made to assure ourselves of their physical fitness. This last year all candidates have been required to pass the tests of Johns Hopkins Diagnostic Clinic. It is no easy task to secure missionaries and when secured no one can tell how they will stand the strain of service in our fields.

The new missionaries called, commissioned, and sent out during the biennium are as follows:

India: Dr. and Mrs. V. E. Zigler, Rev. and Mrs. E. G. Wood, Miss Nellie Cassell, M.D., Miss Grace L. Moyer, M.D., Miss Mabel H. Meyer, R.N., Miss Hilda Kaercher, Miss Susan Glatz, Miss Ada Kron.

Africa: Dr. George Gulck, Rev. George Gesler, D.D.S., and Mrs. George Gesler, M.D.

China: Dr. and Mrs. Taylor Beagle, Miss Clara Sullivan.

British Guiana: Rev. and Mrs. Paul M. Counts (short term).

RESIGNATIONS

The following missionaries have resigned:

India: Rev. and Mrs. C. P. Tranberg, Miss Helen Brenneman, Miss Christine Eriksson, Miss Rose Brummer.

Japan: Miss Amy Thoren, Dr. and Mrs. C. K. Lippard.

British Guiana: Rev. and Mrs. H. E. Haas.

China: Dr. and Mrs. Paul Loudenslager, Dr. and Mrs. Taylor Beagle.

Africa: Rev. K. R. Jensen, Rev. and Mrs. F. H. Bloch, Dr. and Mrs. E. A. Lape, Rev. and Mrs. O. E. Bluehdorn, Rev. and Mrs. Paul M. Counts.

HOME BASE

Under the new organization the Home Base department is especially intrusted with the cultivation of the home churches, the supervision of the missionaries on furlough, the purchase of goods and supplies for office and the missions, the care of property owned by the Board and the transportation or travel arrangements to and from the fields, in consultation with the travel arrangement committee of the fields. Undoubtedly of these functions, the chief is the cultivation of the churches in a knowledge of our foreign fields in a considered plan by which they may more fully do their part in world evangelization.

Synodical Committees of Foreign Missions, which have been set up in our Synods, were found so helpful in our past efforts. These must be enlisted in organizing conferences within the synods which with the synodical officers and especially the Presidents of Synods can greatly aid in arousing a new spirit and promote a new faith-filled endeavor in our churches' congregational life. The aim is not to place a financial objective before the churches, but to stir up zeal and an intelligent conception of what Christ would have His Church do to realize the purpose of His redemptive plan for all men in all lands. The heart of such work is to impress the churches with the missionary message and the place this should have in a congregation's life.

There is considerable detail connected with travel arrangements to and from the foreign fields. To new missionaries, who have never traveled it seems best to make all arrangements for the first journey, and follow more or less past experience. Travel on the Atlantic is rapidly undergoing change. Every large steamer presents first, second and tourist classes, at a great variety of expense, and with ideas of comfort that should suit all. The Board is working out some plan with its missionaries that may suit all and be satisfactory as to cost to meet the Board's income and ideas. Missionaries are consulted as to routes and steamers and classes of boats and passage. The utmost endeavor is being made out of past experience to come to the best workable plan.

Committees on the fields are ready to give help to missionaries, returning home, and rules have been drawn up in consultation with other foreign boards to administer this department in the best manner.

No Board at the Home Base has a more perplexing task than to see that the health of its missionaries is what it ought to be when they start on their missionary career, and when they return after their service in a tropical climate. We have always had the help of good doctors as medical advisers. Lately the Board is availing itself of a Diagnostic Clinic at Johns Hopkins Hospital, which it is hoped will render this part of the home administration both more satisfactory to the missionary body and more helpful to the Board.

It must not be forgotten that after every effort of the Board there must precede and follow a sympathetic and praying Church, so that under the good hand of our Father in heaven this part of our Church's work may go forward and meet the approval of our Lord Jesus Christ, whose Kingdom we seek to establish in all the earth.

The outgoing and incoming of our missionaries for the biennium indicates that it is a considerable task that is involved in making arrangements for their travel. During this period it has cost the sum of $82,312. Great care is shown in choosing passages by good steamers and in every way doing all for the comfort and health of the missionaries.

The Transportation Department of the Board sent out and returned the following missionaries:

INCOMING MISSIONARIES

Name	Field	Date of Arrival
Rev. and Mrs. J. A. Linn	Japan	October 11, 1928
Rev. and Mrs. J. D. Curran	Africa	October 21, 1928
Rev. and Mrs. F. H. Bloch	Africa	October 22, 1928
Miss Christina Eriksson	India	November 25, 1930
Miss Clara Leaman	India	November 27, 1928
Rev. and Mrs. L. A. Gotwald	India	February 1, 1929
Rev. and Mrs. A. F. A. Schmitthenner	India	May 12, 1929
Rev. and Mrs. J. F. Fiedler	India	May 21, 1929
Miss Verna Lofgren	India	May 31, 1929
Rev. and Mrs. C. P. Tranberg	India	June 11, 1929
Rev. O. V. Werner	India	June 8, 1929
Miss C. Hollerbach	India	June 22, 1929
Dr. Arline Beale	India	July 12, 1929
Sister L. Gilliland	Africa	July 15, 1920
Miss Mabel Dysinger	Africa	July 15, 1929
Miss Elsie Otto	Africa	July 15, 1929
Dr. E. A. Lape	Africa	July 15, 1929
Miss Amy Thoren	Japan	July 29, 1929
Rev. Harvey J. Currens	Africa	September 1, 1929
Rev. and Mrs. H. Heilman	Africa	September 10, 1929
Miss Annie Powlas	Japan	September 13, 1929
Mr. and Mrs. W. J. Miller	Africa	September 23, 1929
Rev. K. R. Jensen	Africa	October 27, 1929
Miss Agnes Christenson	India	October 28, 1929
Rev. and Mrs. C. B. Caughman	India	December 11, 1929
Miss Lottie L. Martin	India	December 13, 1929
Miss Emma Johnson	India	March 4, 1930
Rev. C. Swavely and Family	India	March 8, 1930
Rev. L. E. Irschick and Family	India	April 2, 1930
Miss Martha Akard	Japan	April 30, 1930
Miss Edith Eykamp	India	May 12, 1930
Rev. and Mrs. J. E. Graefe	India	May 16, 1930
Mr. and Mrs. Wm. Bembower	India	May 19, 1930

Name	Field	Date of Arrival
Miss Jessie Thomas	India	May 19, 1930
Rev. and Mrs. F. W. Heins	Japan	June 19, 1930
Miss Ruth Swanson	India	June 25, 1930
Dr. Jacob R. Jensen	Africa	July 12, 1930
Miss Maud Powlas	Japan	July 10, 1930
Miss Faith Lippard	Japan	July 12, 1930
Rev. P. O. Machetzki	South America	July 19, 1930
Rev. and Mrs. D. M. G. Bach	Japan	July 12, 1930

OUTGOING MISSIONARIES

Name	Field	Date of Departure
Dr. Nellie S. Cassell	India	October 3, 1928
Miss Hilda Kaercher	India	October 3, 1928
Dr. Grace L. Moyer	India	October 3, 1928
Miss Mabel H. Myer	India	October 3, 1928
Miss Florence Welty	India	October 3, 1928
Miss Selma Anderson	India	October 12, 1928
Miss Helen Shirk	Japan	October 12, 1928
Rev. and Mrs. A. C. Knudten	Japan	October 24, 1928
Rev. and Mrs. E. T. Horn	Japan	October 24, 1928
Dr. and Mrs. V. Zigler	India	January 12, 1929
Miss Maida Meissner	India	February 12, 1929
Mrs. C. E. Buschman	Africa	May 22, 1929
Dr. and Mrs. J. D. Curran	Africa	May 22, 1929
Rev. J. C. Finefrock and Boys	India	June 1, 1929
Rev. and Mrs. W. C. Hepner	Japan	June 8, 1929
Mr. and Mrs. J. Haltiwanger	Africa	June 12, 1929
Miss P. Whitteker	India	June 15, 1929
Dr. and Mrs. I. Cannaday	India	June 15, 1929
Miss Hilma Levine	India	August 7, 1929
Miss Ada Kron	India	August 7, 1929
Miss Freda Strecker	China	August 15, 1929
Rev. and Mrs. W. Matzat	China	August 24, 1929
Rev. and Mrs. E. G. Wood	India	August 5, 1929
Rev. and Mrs. J. R. Fink	India	September 4, 1929
Dr. George K. Gulck	Africa	September 18, 1929
Miss M. C. Sullivan	China	September 20, 1929
Dr. and Mrs. M. T. Beagle	China	September 20, 1929
Rev. and Mrs. J. A. Linn	Japan	September 25, 1929
Mrs. J. C. Finefrock and Children	India	September 27, 1929
Rev. and Mrs. A. J. Stirewalt	Japan	October 3, 1929
Rev. and Mrs. G. K. Gesler	Africa	October 9, 1929
Miss Agatha Tatge	India	October 19, 1929
Rev. and Mrs. H. H. Sipes	India	October 30, 1929
Rev. and Mrs. A. F. A. Neudoerffer	India	November 15, 1929
Dr. Mary Baer	India	November 19, 1929
Rev. and Mrs. M. L. Dolbeer	India	February 6, 1930
Rev. and Mrs. H. H. Moyer	India	February 22, 1930
Rev. and Mrs. P. M. Counts	South America	April 4, 1930
Miss Clara Leaman	India	April 14, 1930
Miss Elsie Otto	Africa	May 21, 1930
Rev. and Mrs. J. D. Curran	Africa	May 21, 1930
Rev. and Mrs. H. Heilman	Africa	July 12, 1930
Mr. and Mrs. J. W. Miller	Africa	July 18, 1930
Rev. and Mrs. L. A. Gotwald	India	August 8, 1930
Miss Verna Lofgren	India	September 5, 1930
Miss C. Hollerbach	India	September 5, 1930
Rev. A. F. A. Schmitthenner	India	October 17, 1930

LITERATURE

The Literature Department has received for each year of the biennium only $4,900. This amount has been expended for *The Foreign Missionary* and *Der Missionsbote,* the Board's Quarterly Bulletin, the Annual Report of the Foreign Missions, advertising, occasional pamphlets and leaflets, the stereopticon department, new books and curios.

The Foreign Missionary and *Der Missionsbote* are indispensable English and German monthly missionary magazines for all pastors, teachers and societies which wish to keep in constant touch with all our foreign missionaries and their work. The number of subscribers in singles and clubs fluctuates as subscriptions are discontinued and new ones are added. The present circulation is about 7,000 for *The Foreign Missionary* and over 3,000 for *Der Missionsbote.*

The Annual Report of the Foreign Missions of the United Lutheran Church for the year 1928 has been highly praised in our own and in other churches. The report for the year 1929 is ready for distribution at this convention of the United Lutheran Church. It is intended to be the voice of our foreign missionaries in all fields, telling us about their work, experiences, discouragements, achievements and opportunities. Supplementing this report with the specific thought of enlisting definite prayers and supplications, is the new plan originated in India, called "Helpers Through Prayer," whereby monthly leaflets printed in India are mailed to groups in America who will read them and pray over them. Some hundreds of people in our Church through their group leaders have indicated their desire to read the leaflets and help through prayer. New names may be added at any time.

The Epiphany Season literature usually includes a circular appeal and return postal cards for ordering supplies, sent to all pastors, a Foreign Mission Day service for Sunday schools and churches and offering envelopes, sent free to all who will use them for the missionary education of their people.

The occasional pamphlets and leaflets on our missions, on the Board's work, on rules for missions and missionaries, on the parish abroad plan, and on more general foreign missionary matters, are all published for free distribution. The Board as a rule publishes no literature for sale.

In the conduct of the stereopticon department it has been found advisable to make a nominal rental charge of $2.50 for each use of a lecture with slides, in order that the necessary repair of slides may be made and the equipment of the department may be provided. When at a lecture an offering is taken and sent for foreign missions, no rental charge is made. During the past two years the slides and lectures have been in constant use in all parts of the United States and Canada, and have given very good satisfaction. The twenty-seven lectures of the Board are kept up to date by missionaries on furlough.

By special arrangement with the Women's Missionary Society certain types of missionary literature are to bear the joint imprint of the Board and the Society. Thus the joint imprint will appear on the "Facts Series" of leaflets and also on the supplementary mission study book on India prepared by Mrs. J. F. Seebach and published by the Women's Missionary Society. The general mission study books to which Mrs. Seebach's book is supplementary are those of the Missionary Education Movement on: "India Looks to the Future" by Oscar McMillan Buck, for adults and young and seniors; "The Star of India" by Isabel Brown Rose for intermediates, and the other study books of this year published by the movement and sold by the United Lutheran Publication House and the Lutheran Literature Headquarters of the Women's Missionary Society. It is hoped and expected that during the coming fall and winter months an unusually large number of mission study classes to study India will be formed not only in the women's societies but also in the Sunday and weekday schools, the Luther Leagues, the Brotherhoods and other societies of the Church.

DEPARTMENT OF SPECIAL GIFTS

The work of this department is carried on under three heads, namely, Foreign Mission Pastors, Parishes Abroad and Proteges.

FOREIGN MISSION PASTORS
$1,200 or more annually

It is worthy of note that all of our missionaries are supported by individuals, organizations, or congregations. Could the Board afford budgets for more missionaries and secure the men, there are at present congregations willing to assume their support.

We deem this the best kind of evidence that the "missionary spirit" still lives in our Church.

Space does not permit the recounting of methods employed to raise the missionary pastor's support on the part of congregations. We show, two, however, to illustrate how the work was done. One pastor wrote inquiring cost of supporting a missionary. He stated that it was his feeling that if the loose odds and ends could be gathered together, work for which the congregation gets no credit, they could support a missionary. Later, when the final total was made, they found there was sufficient not only for a foreign missionary but a home missionary as well.

The other instance was on this wise. A manufacturer whose product is marketed throughout the entire east informed his pastor that he would like to do some foreign mission work. The reason for this was that he was living, at least partly, from sales in the Orient, and being a Christian gentleman he chose to do something for the moral and spiritual uplift of those people. The result was that a comparatively small congregation has its missionary in China. The support comes chiefly from this Christian manufacturer and his firm. The purpose of this department is not only to augment the income of the Board but also to educate church members in missionary thought and co-operation.

Congregations Supporting Missionaries

Supporters	Pastor	Missionary	Field
1. Allenton, Pa., Christ's	G. H. Kinard	H. H. Moyer	India
2. Allentown, Pa., St. John's	W. C. Schaeffer, Jr.	Oscar V. Werner	India
3. Altoona, Pa., Second	G. N. Lauffer	Harry Goedeke	India
4. Ashland, Ohio, Trinity	A. H. Smith	J. M. Armbruster	Argentine
5. Baltimore, Md., St. Paul's	J. B. Rupley	J. D. Curran	Africa
6. Baltimore, Md., St. Mark's	R. D. Clare	I. Cannaday	India
7. Baltimore, Md., Second Eng.	J. E. Grubb	L. W. Slifer	India
8. Boyertown, Pa., St. John's	D. F. Longacre	Clarence E. Swavely	India
9. Brooklyn, N. Y., Redeemer	H. T. Weiskotten	A. F. A. Neudoerffer	India
10. Canton, Ohio, Trinity	Earl C. Herman	Geo. Rupley	India
11. Canton, Ohio, Trinity	Earl C. Herman	A. C. Knudten	Japan
12. Canton, Ohio, Trinity	Earl C. Herman	Harvey J. Currens	Africa
13. Chambersburg, Pa., First	Henry Anstadt,	James W. Miller	Africa
14. Charleston, S. C., St. Andrew	Chas. B. Foelsch	C. K. Lippard	Japan
15. Dayton, Ohio, First	Chas. L. Venable	George R. Schillinger	Japan
16. Dayton, Ohio, First	Chas. L. Venable	Victor McCauley	India
17. Dixon, Ill., St. Paul's	Lloyd W. Walter	Carl B. Caughman	India
18. Ft. Wayne, Ind., Trinity	Paul H. Krauss	J. Ira Haltiwanger	Africa
19. Ft. Wayne, Ind., Trinity	Paul H. Krauss	Luther A. Gotwald	India
20. Grand Rapids, Mich. Trinity	R. J. White	Robt. H. Daube	Argentine
21. Greensburg Pa., First	B. C. Ritz	G. K. Gesler	Africa
22. Greensburg, Pa., Zion	A. W. Steinfurth	August Schmitthenner	India
23. Hanover, Pa., St. Mark's	John S. Tome	Theo. Scholz	China
24. Harrisburg, Pa., Memorial	L. C. Manges	G. R. Haaf	India
25. Harrisburg, Pa., Zion	S. W. Herman	John K. Linn	Japan
26. Harrisburg, Pa., Zion	S. W. Herman	L. Grady Cooper	China
27. Harrisburg, Pa., Zion	S. W. Herman	R. M. Dunkelberger	India
28. Hummelstown, Pa., Zion	C. G. Leatherman	P. O. Machetzki	Argentine
29. Huntingdon, Pa., St. James'	E. L. Manges	Geo. K. Gulck, M.D.	Africa
30. Johnstown, Pa., First	G. W. Nicely	A. J. Stirewalt	Japan
31. Lititz, Pa., St. Paul's	W R. Sammel	Rajah B. Manikam	India
32. Mansfield, Ohio, First	H. C. Roehner	J. C. Finefrock	India
33. Mansfield, Ohio, First	H. C. Roehner	C. E. Norman	Japan
34. Norristown, Pa., Holy Trinity	P. L. Yount	Leon Irschick	India
35. Brooklyn, N. Y. State L. L.		F. W. Heins	Japan
36. Concord, N. C., N. C. State Luther League		Arnold H. Kaitschuk	Africa
37. Oregon, Ill., St. Paul's	J. E. Dale	Wm. Matzat	China
38. Perkasie, Pa., S. Perkasie and Hilltown	Chas. F. Brobst	Chas. H. Reinbrecht	China
39. Phila., Pa., Messiah	Ross H. Stover	J. E. Graefe	India
40. Phila., Pa., Ch. of Nativity	J. C. Fisher	H. H. Sipes	India
41. Phila., Pa., St. John's S. S.	Chas. J. Gabel	W. Theo. Benze	India
42. Phila., Pa., St. Matthew's	E. H. Delk	C. J. Voskamp	China
43. Phila., Pa., Tabernacle	W. J. Miller,	M. L. Dolbeer	India
44. Phila., Pa., Temple	A. Pohlman	N. R. Sloan, M.D.	Africa
45. Pittsburgh, Pa., First	A. J. Holl	Fred L. Coleman	India
46. Pittsburgh, Pa., Mt. Zion	G. Elmer Swoyer	J. Arthur Linn	Japan
47. Pottstown, Pa., Emmanuel	I. B. Kurtz	Fred J. Fiedler	India
48. Reading, Pa., Trinity	Herman F. Miller	Edward T. Horn	Japan
49. Richmond, Va., First	J. J. Scherer	Robt. S. Oberly	Africa
50. Rochester, Pa., Grace	H. Reed Shepfer	Edmund G. Wood	India
51. Rockford, Ill., Trinity	H. H. Banner	C. W. Hepner	Japan
52. Rockford, Ill., Trinity	H. H. Banner	V. Ch. John, M.A.	India
53. Shelby, Ohio, First	D. Bruce Young	P. P. Anspach	China
54. Shippensburg, Pa., Memorial	W. W. Barkley	J. Roy Strock	India
55. Sterling, Ill., St. John's	E. C. Harris	S. C. Burger	India
56. Toledo, Ohio, Glenwood	A. E. Bell	Virgil E. Zigler, M.D.	India
57. Wilkinsburg, Pa., Calvary	L. A. Krouse	David D. Dagle	Africa
58. Wilmington, Del.,	Dr. C. S. Stine	Ray Cunningham	India
59. Winchester, Va., Grace	N. E. Cooper	L. S. G. Miller	Japan
60. York, Pa., Radiant Cross Prayer Meeting, St. Matthew's	J. B. Baker	Harry Heilman	Africa
61. York, Pa., Zion	G. A. Getty	J. Russell Fink	India

PARISHES ABROAD

Next in importance to supporting a missionary is supporting a parish abroad. These are almost unlimited in number, of various kinds, available at $50.00 and upwards per year. One hundred and eighty-five have been assigned. The advantages to the patron are many. Not the least is the privilege of corresponding with the missionary in charge of the parish. When he comes on furlough his visitation is a red letter day, particularly to the young people supporting the parish. To have one's own objective and to learn at first hand what is being accomplished stimulates missionary zeal and giving. "Information begets inspiration."

SUPPORT OF PROTEGES

This plan, too, has its appeal to a patron. If one cannot go himself, for the command includes all, then the next best step is to have a substitute. The patron and protege plan offers this opportunity. Four hundred and seventy individuals, Sunday school classes, Luther Leagues and other organizations are now supporting proteges. As far as possible and our rules permit, this department has kept the patron in touch with his or her protege. While the number is not as large as it might be, especially when one considers that 2,500 workers are employed in our mission fields, and there are many appeals for more, still we rejoice in the 470 now assigned. Some of these are supported at real sacrifice. Letters reach us, coming from pastors and others, depicting real self denial on the part of certain members, that a "substitute" may be maintained. It would be grounds for great rejoicing if double the number of assignments could be reported two years hence. Workers can be supported from $35.00 and upwards per year, boy's scholarships at $25.00 and upwards.

The list is too long to record names of all patrons. For your information we append data on missionaries, parishes abroad and proteges, according to synods.

SUPPORTERS OF SPECIAL GIFTS BY SYNODS

	Alleghany	California	Canada	East Penn.	Eng. Neb.	Georgia	Ger. Neb.	Illinois	Indiana	Iowa
Missionaries	3			11				5		
Parishes Abroad	8		1	26	6			2	4	1
Proteges	15	4	7	42	11	1	10	30	4	2

	Kansas	Maryland	Michigan	Min. of Pa.	New York	N. Carolina	Northwest	Ohio	Pacific	Pittsburgh
Missionaries		3	3	9	2	1		10		6
Parishes Abroad		3	2	30	31		2	20		26
Proteges	1	42	5	66	51	2	5	40	1	42

	Rocky Mount.	S. Carolina	Susquehanna	Virginia	West Penn.	West Virginia	Augustana	United Danish	Luther League of America	Totals
Missionaries		1		2	5					61
Parishes Abroad		1	5	1	7	2		1	1	183
Proteges	2	5	21	5	37	1	13	2	3	470

THE TREASURER'S STATEMENT
THE DEFICIT

The following comments are made to bring to the attention of the United Lutheran Church in America the important changes in the finances of the Board during the past two years

The deficit, as of the date of this report, is $254,484.48. The deficit of the General Fund as of the date of the last United Lutheran Church in America Convention on June 30, 1928, was $335,042.16; the decrease in deficit over a period of two years is $80,557.68.

It must be understood that this deficit does not include liabilities incurred in purchases of properties in foreign fields, nor investments made in properties.

This deficit has fluctuated considerably in the past two years as the following figures show:

General Fund Deficit June 30, 1928 .... $335,042.16
General Fund Deficit December 31, 1928 .... 443,119.81
General Fund Deficit June 30, 1929 .... $366,405.58
General Fund Deficit December 31, 1929 .... 412,016.91
General Fund Deficit June 30, 1930 .... $254,484.48

The cause of this fluctuation is the irregularity of receipts. The first six months of the church year, from July 1st to December 31st, always suffer on account of uncertain receipts on apportionment. To further illustrate this the following table is made.

Year Ending	Per cent Received First 6 Mos.	Per cent Received Last 6 Mos.
June 30, 1927	39%	61%
June 30, 1928	41%	59%
June 30, 1929	35%	65%
June 30, 1930	40%	60%

It can be easily seen from these figures why the Board is in distress these first six months. For those who do not know, it is well to say that the disbursements vary little during the year. The budget is made on a certain basis and one-twelfth of it is forwarded every month to the fields; if the budget could be sent to the fields according to proportion of receipts, there would be no distress during the lean months, but this cannot be done as the fields must have a definite amount with which to plan work.

The Board was reorganized as of January 1, 1929, and at this time the Board's debt had reached its peak and was $443,119.81.

This explanation is also made to show the cause of the increase in deficit the first six months of every year.

The deficit as of the date of this report, June 30, 1930, was $254,484.48, a net decrease in deficit of $188,635.33.

This decrease is the result of the following:

Two years' receipts on Epiphany Appeal..........	$143,929.60	
Less expenses	9,008.55	
Net result of appeal		$134,921.05
Credit on operating fund January 1, 1929, to June 30, 1930		53,714.28
		$188,635.33

PROPERTY, INVESTMENTS AND LIABILITIES

It has always been the practice of the Board never to include investments in properties on fields, as assets.

The same practice has always prevailed as to liabilities. Within the past two years all of the unpaid notes of Buenos Aires have been cancelled. The Shantung Mission property is being paid off at the rate of $4,375 every quarter. When payments are made they are charged to Land and Building Fund, which Fund is replenished with receipts on undesignated legacies.

TRUST AND ANNUITY FUNDS

Trust Funds during the biennium have increased $26,815.58 and Annuity Funds have increased $16,750 for the same period

ANDHRA CHRISTIAN COLLEGE FUND

This fund has increased $31,657.36 in the past two years. There are still some unpaid pledges. The receipts consisted of unpaid pledges and interest received on investments. Interest is also credited to this fund every year from the general fund for use of moneys belonging to Andhra Christian College. Some of the interest is sent to India to help operate the present Andhra College.

LOANS AT BANK

Moneys received as the result of the Epiphany Appeal were used to reduce borrowings. These borrowings amounted to $191,500 as of December 31, 1928, and at the time of this report were reduced to $70,000. There is still $13,000 in this Epiphany Appeal money which will be also paid at bank on loans.

BALANCED BUDGET

The Board is thankful to report that the budget balanced this year with a credit of $25,617.83.

Percentage of disbursements for year ending June 30, 1930

Fields	48.09%
Literature	.80%
Finance	1.99%
Intermissionary	.33%
Office Expenses and Overhead	4.10%
Miscellaneous Allowances and Pensions	1.68%
Specials and Gifts to Fields	1.32%
Board Debt Expenses	.70%
Funds and Women's Missionary Society	40.99%
	100.00%

The Board appreciates the efforts of the Special Committee of fifteen to raise 100% apportionment and asks that their efforts be continued.

INDIA

MISSIONARIES

Name	Residence	Arrival
Rev. L. L. Uhl, D.D.	Emeritus	1873
Miss Anna S. Kugler, M.D.	Guntur	1883
Miss Agnes I. Schade	Emeritus	1890
Miss Katherine Fahs	Emeritus	1894
Miss Mary Baer, M.D.	Chirala	1895
Miss Annie E. Sanford	Guntur	1895
Rev. S. C. Burger	Narsapur	1898
Rev. Dr. and Mrs. Victor McCauley	Tenali	1898
Miss Ellen B. Schuff	On Furlough	1900
Miss Emilie L. Weiskotten	On Furlough	1900
Rev. Dr. and Mrs. Isaac Cannaday	Guntur	1902
Rev. Dr. and Mrs. J. Roy Strock	College, Guntur	1908
Miss Jessie S. Thomas	On Furlough	1908
Miss Betty A. Nilsson, M.D.	Rajahmundry	1908
Rev. Dr. and Mrs. R. M. Dunkelberger	Rajahmundry	1909
Rev. and Mrs. J. C. Finefrock	Tanuku	1911
Mr. and Mrs. William Bembower	On Furlough	1911
Rev. and Mrs. Oscar V. Werner	On Furlough	1911
Miss Agatha Tatge	Rajahmundry	1911
Rev. and Mrs. A. F. A. Neudoerffer	Tallapudi	1912
Rev. and Mrs. G. R. Haaf	On Furlough	1912
Rev. and Mrs. T. A. Holmer	Dowlaishwaram	1912
Miss Florence M. Welty	Guntur	1912
Miss Mary S. Borthwick	Bhimawaram	1912
Rev. and Mrs. H. H. Sipes	High School, Guntur	1913
Miss Louise A. Miller	Repalle	1913
Rev. and Mrs. Fred L. Coleman	Theol. Sem., Rajahmundry	1914
Rev. and Mrs. J. E. Graefe	On Furlough	1915
Rev. and Mrs. George A. Rupley	Tarlupad	1915
Miss Charlotte B. Hollerbach	On Furlough	1915

Name	Residence	Arrival
Miss Hilma Levine	Guntur	1915
Miss Agnes C. Christenson	On Furlough	1915
Rev. and Mrs. Harry Goedeke	Rentichintala	1919
Miss Emma K. Baer	Chirala	1919
Rev. and Mrs. J. R. Fink	Satenapalli	1921
Rev. and Mrs. H. H. Moyer	Peddapur	1921
Rev. and Mrs. Fred J. Fiedler	On Furlough	1921
Rev. and Mrs. A. F. Schmitthenner	On Furlough	1921
Rev. and Mrs. L. A. Gotwald	On Furlough	1921
Rev. and Mrs. M. L. Dolbeer	Narsaravupet	1921
Miss Lilith Schwab	Rajahmundry	1921
Miss Alice J. Nickel	Narsaravupet	1921
Miss Selma Anderson	Rajahmundry	1921
Miss Metta K. Blair	Rentichintala	1921
Miss Pauline Whitteker	Samulkot	1921
Miss Maida S. Meissner	Rajahmundry	1921
Miss Edna Engle	Guntur	1921
Rev. and Mrs. C. B. Caughman	On Furlough	1922
Rev. and Mrs. Clarence H. Swavely	On Furlough	1922
Rev. and Mrs. Leon E. L. Irschick	On Furlough	1922
Miss Clara Leaman	Rentichintala	1923
Miss Verna Lofgren	On Furlough	1923
Miss Lottie Martin	On Furlough	1923
Miss Ruth H. Swanson	On Furlough	1924
Miss Edith Eykamp	On Furlough	1924
Miss Emma Johnson	On Furlough	1924
Rev. and Mrs. W. Theodore Benze	Yelleshwaram	1925
Mr. and Mrs. R. L. Cunningham	Guntur	1925
Rev. and Mrs. L. W. Slifer	Repalle	1925
Miss Arline Beal, M.D.	On Furlough	1925
Miss Frances M. Segner	Guntur	1927
Dr. and Mrs. Virgil E. Zigler	Rentichintala	1928
Miss Nellie S. Cassell, M.D.	Guntur	1928
Miss Grace L. Moyer, M.D.	Rajahmundry	1928
Miss Mabel H. Meyer	Chirala	1928
Miss Hilda M. Kaercher	Rajahmundry	1928
Rev. and Mrs. E. G. Wood	Rajahmundry	1929
Miss Susan Glatz	Kodaikanal	1929
Miss Ada Kron	Rajahmundry	1929
Dr. and Mrs. James Bradley	Under Appointment	1930

28 ordained, 4 unordained missionaries, 30 wives, 38 single women. Total missionaries, 100.

The two outstanding problems of our mission in India which are before the Church today are the development of the Andhra Evangelical Lutheran Church and the establishment of the Andhra Christian College.

The Andhra Lutheran Church

Our hearts rejoice over the progress made by the Andhra Evangelical Lutheran Church since its organization in 1927. The former Guntur and Rajahmundry synods have been entirely absorbed into the new organization and the fields have been divided into conferences, two in the Rajahmundry or North Field, three in the Guntur or South Field. For the first time an Indian Lutheran, Mr. V. Ch. John, a layman and a leader in the Church, appears before the United Lutheran Church in America in convention assembled, as a delegate of the Andhra Lutheran Church in India, now enrolled as an associate synod of this body.

The more recent developments in the Andhra Lutheran Church are the enlargement of the delegations at the annual conventions by making all ordained men, Indian and American, full delegates. A small executive committee has been given power to transact *ad interim* business and serve as a court of final appeal against action taken by the other standing committees. A ministerium consisting of fifteen Indian and eighteen American ordained ministers, has the same functions as ministeriums in our American synods. A committee on pastoral charges has large powers of assignment to parishes. The system of calls by congregations as practiced in America is not adapted to the present stage of development in India, but parishes may indicate their preferences to the committee and the committee carefully considers them along with the other factors involved, including the pastor's own wishes. Changes in parishes automatically come at the end of five years, except in the case of the few self-supporting parishes, where upon request the pastor may remain a maximum of ten years. Salaries are fixed by the committee in accordance with definite rules and the committee also decides the time of each pastor's retirement from active work.

The Committee on Finance and Budget decides what appropriations are to be made to the parishes, but a self-supporting parish has a high degree of autonomy. The President of the Church is ex-officio the chairman of the Executive Committee, the committee on pastors and the budget committee and is a member of every other standing committee.

In general the Andhra Church manages the evangelistic work among the non-Christians, the parochial work of the congregations and their schools and the village prayer houses with the simple houses of the workers. It also manages the institutions which train catechists, evangelists and Bible women, and now desires to add also the theological seminary at Luthergiri.

The mission for the present retains the boarding schools, the higher elementary schools, the training school for teachers, the high schools and the college. It also manages the medical work. Sooner or later most if not all of these departments will be transferred to the church as leaders are developed in sufficient number and with experience to manage them. The missionaries are of course members of the Andhra Church and bear their share of its activities but they naturally form a small minority. The whole process of the transfer of responsibility will take many years. In 1929 the mission proposed the transfer of some additional departments but the Church requested further time to assimilate what it had already received—a wise decision.

In addition to a missionary, Rev. Isaac Cannaday, D.D., the Andhra

Lutheran Church was represented by an Indian Lutheran, Dr. Samuel John, at the Lutheran World Convention in 1929 at Copenhagen.

ANDHRA CHRISTIAN COLLEGE

The Board of Foreign Missions is not prepared to make any definite proposals at this time concerning the location and character of Andhra Christian College. It forwarded through our mission an invitation to all other Protestant missions in the Telugu country to co-operate in a united college at Guntur but all except one of them expressed preference for Bezwada as the permanent location.

The Board of Foreign Missions approved the approach through the Andhra Christian Council to the other Protestant missions concerning the location at Bezwada on the following conditions: 1. That not fewer than five other missions of the Andhra country co-operate in the united college. 2. That the other missions collectively give assurance to contribute towards capital expenditure rupee for rupee with our mission a sum not less than Rs. 250,000 (about $83,000) which may extend to Rs. 400,000. 3. That the other missions give definite assurance to contribute collectively not less than the equivalent of Rs. 25,000 per annum (about $8,500) towards recurring expenditure. 4. That the other missions or the home boards give these assurances by February 1, 1931.

There is a disposition on the part of all interested bodies to wait until the special education commission from the Foreign Missions Conferences in America and England has studied the problem of Christian higher education on the field. This commission is expected to be in the Telugu country in December. Meanwhile Andhra Christian College continues to be conducted temporarily at Guntur, where it has an enrollment of about 800 students, in addition to 700 in the Guntur High School and branches. With an increased number of teachers among whom are four ordained missionaries and Dr. R. B. Manikam, with additional courses of study, with good results in the government examinations and under the able management of the principal, Dr. J. Roy Strock, Andhra Christian College already has become the leading college in the Telugu country. Some of the Andhra College Fund, as the report of the treasurer of the Board will show, has been sent to India for permanent scientific equipment but the bulk of the fund remains in the treasury of the Board awaiting the final decision concerning location and co-operation. A committee in our mission is working on a revision of the constitution for the college which will be considered by the Board of Foreign Missions after it has passed through the hands of the council of missionaries. The mission pleads for patience until the vexing political, educational and inter-mission problems connected with the permanent establishment of the college, can be solved.

The Sudras Are Coming

Members of the middle or Sudra classes are coming in increasing number into the Christian Church. The day of complete self-support awaits their ingathering. Already in some parts of South India there are clear indications of Sudra mass movements. Preparation for such a movement which seems inevitable in our own field, depends upon an increase in missionaries, money and the training of Sudra Christian workers. Recently two Christians of Sudra origin have received training in the Luthergiri Training School in a class of thirty-nine men, who finished their course this year and are now employed as catechists and evangelists. In addition twenty-three men are being prepared for ordination and will be graduated next year. The wives of the married students at Luthergiri receive special Bible training under Mrs. Paradesi. Quite a number of changes have occurred recently in the staff of teachers at the seminary and Bible Training School, both among the missionaries and Indian professors, but an earnest effort is being made to preserve a permanent staff of professors. During the past year an Indian professor's house and two lines of dormitory rooms were added to the equipment of this institution.

Missionaries

We rejoice that a good proportion of those who have spent furloughs in America have returned to the field. Our India mission has an enviable record for continuity of the service of missionaries. On account of its financial embarrassment the Board has not been able to send as many new missionaries to India as are required and those in the field have been obliged in a number of instances to do double work by taking charge of more than one district or department. No special reference is made in this connection to the work of the women missionaries concerning which the usual report of the Women's Missionary Society will contain definite information. The Augustana Synod has one ordained missionary and six women missionaries in our field and has been making an annual appropriation of $25,000 for the India mission.

Among the more important events of the past two years is the transfer of station headquarters from Tadepalligudem to Tanuku at no additional cost to the Board. The proceeds of the sale of the property at Tadepalligudem for Rs. 40,000 or about $14,000, sufficed to cover the expense of purchasing a site at Tanuku and of erecting a missionary's bungalow and other necessary buildings there, as well as of purchasing a new site and providing a small church and school building for the Tadepalligudem congregation.

The Federation of Lutheran Churches and Missions

The Gandhi movement in India, which is a wide-spread movement of non-co-operation or passive resistence to the British Government in the interest of self-government, is undoubtedly one of profound and permanent significance, which is having its influence also upon the government of the churches established in the mission fields. In line with the tendency of this movement towards independence is the transformation of the All-India Lutheran Conference, which was composed almost entirely of missionaries, into a Federation of Lutheran Churches, composed largely of Indian delegates, representing the churches established in our own field, the Andhra Evangelical Lutheran Church and those established in Chota Nagpur, known as the Gossner Evangelical Lutheran Church, in the Tamil country, known as the Tamil Evangelical Lutheran Church, in the fields of the Santal mission, the Schleswig Holstein and East Jeypore missions, the Swedish mission in the Central Provinces, the Danish mission in the Madras Presidency and the Ohio Mission in the Telugu country.

The second convention of this federation was held in April, 1930, at Ranchi, Bihar, where the delegates were the guests of the Gossner Evangelical Lutheran Church, next to our own Andhra Church, the largest Lutheran body in India. It is very gratifying to be able to report that the Federation elected as its president one of our own missionaries, Rev. R. M. Dunkelberger, D.D., of Rajahmundry, who also is the president of the Andhra Evangelical Lutheran Church.

INDIA MISSION—GENERAL WORK

Stations or Charges	Missionaries in the Field	Workers	Congregations	Baptized Members	Communicants	Added During Year	Inquirers	Sunday School Pupils	Field Contributions	Schools	Pupils	Hospitals	In-Patients	Dispensaries	Out-Patients Visits
Guntur Field	0														
Baratla-Chirala	0	146	116	17,617	7,003	1,927	1,811	5,791	Rs. 20,303	62	2,087	0	0	0	0
Guntur Taluk	2	123	95	12,156	5,487	995	1,311	5,029	8,584	66	1,522	1	163	1	5,678
Guntur Town	2	29	1	2,100	1,044	396	182	823	7,325	7	704	1	314	1	1,187
Markapur-Cumbum	0	73	94	3,565	1,353	367	645	577	16,558	24	600	0	0	0	0
Narsaravupet	5	136	148	12,676	4,955	1,264	1,317	2,247	17,119	64	1,701	0	0	0	5,045
Palnad	2	164	84	13,054	3,099	1,087	1,119	4,168	16,993	57	1,665	0	0	0	0
Repalle	2	141	134	10,722	4,515	1,345	1,055	2,613	17,972	84	1,803	0	0	0	0
Sattenapalli	2	147	126	12,484	4,950	1,409	1,650	4,128	17,834	68	1,775	0	0	0	0
Tenali	2	150	120	17,991	7,174	1,570	1,570	4,401	26,203	83	2,717	0	0	0	0
Tripurantakam	4	29	21	1,055	325	366	280	318	1,260	17	361	0	0	0	0
Andhra College	0	71	0	0	0	0	0	0	81,337	1	804	0	0	0	0
High School	2	36	0	0	0	0	0	0	28,503	1	712	0	0	0	0
Industrial Work	0	45	0	0	0	0	0	0	1,231	1	18	0	0	0	0
Rural School, Lam.	0	10	0	0	0	0	0	45	3,109	1	62	0	0	0	0
Rajahmundry Field	2														
Bhimawaram	0	142	100	13,627	5,354	1,047	322	2,398	29,426	91	2,435	0	0	0	0
Dowlaishwaram	1	132	76	3,526	2,042	238	470	2,158	13,985	60	2,291	0	0	0	0
Korukonda	1	43	38	2,626	1,041	142	470	543	3,897	28	572	0	0	0	0
Narsapur	2	127	96	8,572	3,705	804	766	2,449	14,011	69	2,564	0	0	0	0
Peddapur	4	17	2	415	161	40	160	279	41	5	789	1	78	1	0
Rajahmundry Town	0	56	3	1,625	845	186	198	721	28,985	37	562	0	0	0	0
Samulkot	2	59	43	1,795	694	149	454	802	4,806	77	808	1	153	1	7,665
Tanuku	0	119	91	6,060	3,497	412	367	2,052	16,512	24	1,964	0	0	0	0
Yelleswaram	2	43	38	1,321	487	205	247	580	2,642	1	855	0	0	0	0
Bhim. High School	0	42	0	0	0	0	0	258	21,900		833	0	0	0	0
Luthergiri	2	14	4	261	109	77	9	301	1,309	6	327	0	0	0	0
Gallapudi	2	79	66	2,874	1,155	482	931	1,045	6,653	43	1,126	0	0	0	1,250
Totals	40	2,181	1,496	146,122	58,995	14,354	15,361	45,580	498,274	984	31,657	4	708	4	30,825
Women's Work	30	514		0	0	0	0	2,795	45,176	41	3,517	4	4,694	4	54,423
On Furlough	30														
Grand Totals	100	2,695	1,496	146,122	58,995	14,354	15,361	48,375	543,450	1,025	35,174	8	5,402	8	85,248

JAPAN
MISSIONARIES

Name	Residence	Arrival
Rev. and Mrs. J. M. T. Winther	Kurume	1898
Rev. Dr. and Mrs. A. J. Stirewalt	Tokyo	1905
Rev. Dr. and Mrs. L. S. G. Miller	Kyushu Gakuin, Kumamoto	1907
Rev. Dr. and Mrs. Edward T. Horn	Theological Sem., Tokyo	1912
Rev. and Mrs. Charles W. Hepner	Osaka	1912
Miss Martha B. Akard	On Furlough	1913
Rev. and Mrs. John K. Linn	Theological Sem., Tokyo	1915
Rev. and Mrs. S. O. Thorlaksson	Kobe	1916
Rev. and Mrs. D. G. M. Bach	On Furlough	1916
Rev. and Mrs. Clarence E. Norman	Fukuoka	1917
Miss Maude O. Powlas	Ji Ai En, Kumamoto	1918
Miss Annie P. Powlas	On Furlough	1919
Rev. and Mrs. George N. Schillinger	Kyushu Gakuin, Kumamoto	1920
Rev. and Mrs. Arthur C. Knudten	Nagoya	1920
Miss Marion E. Potts	Kyushu Jo Gakuin, Kumamoto	1921
Rev. and Mrs. Arthur J. Linn	Moji	1922
Miss Helen Shirk	Hakata-Fukuoka	1922
Rev. and Mrs. F. W. Heins	On Furlough	1924
Miss Faith Lippard	Ogi	1925
Miss Grace M. Beers	Ji Ai En, Kumamoto	1926
Miss Martha B. Harder	Kyushu Jo Gakuin, Kumamoto	1926
Miss Mary E. Heltibridle	Ji Ai En, Kumamoto	1927
Miss Helene Harder	Tokyo	1927
Miss Maya Winther	Saga	1927

Thirteen ordained missionaries, 13 wives, 11 single women. Total missionaries, 37.

With the rest of the Lutheran world our mission in Japan celebrated last year the 400th anniversary of Luther's Small Catechism and this year the 400th anniversary of the Augsburg Confession, as well as the 1900th anniversary of Pentecost. To mark these anniversaries new Japanese translations of the Small Catechism and of the Augsburg Confession have been published and are being used in an intensive evangelistic effort which is contemporaneous with a nation-wide Christian movement under the leadership of Rev. Toyohiko Kagawa, the outstanding Christian evangelist of Japan. This movement, called the Kingdom of God Movement, seeks immediately to increase the number of Christians and within the next few years to win a million souls for Christ in the land of the rising sun.

The Japanese Christian Church is still young as church history goes. It is adding to other celebrations this year that of the seventieth anniversary of the landing of the first Protestant missionaries in Japan. The seed sown through seventy years has found lodgment in hundreds of thousands of hearts and has borne fruit to the glory of God in Christ Jesus, but the need is for a more deeply prepared soil and a more thorough rooting out of weeds that hinder growth.

Our Lutheran mission in Japan is one of the younger ones and has a history of only thirty-eight years. It is still a comparatively small mission and yet, when compared with missions in our own and other churches not only in Japan but also in India and other countries, it shows as good and even better results than many of them for the first thirty-five years of effort. The Lutheran Church has been planted in twenty-three cities, towns and villages in the southern large island of Kyushu and in the main island of Hondo. Besides our thirty-six foreign missionaries, including wives, there is now a well qualified and devoted group of twenty-five ordained Japanese pastors, seven of whom have studied theology in America, and five unordained evangelists. They are serving a baptized membership of 3,160. Our unexcelled middle school for boys, Kyushu Gakuin, at Kumamoto, has been a conspicuous feature of the mission work for twenty years and has an enrollment of nearly 700 students. The institution on which we must chiefly rely for the more rapid development of the whole work is the theological seminary at Tokyo, where sixteen young Japanese are now in training for the gospel ministry and for leadership in the Church. Two congregations have become self-supporting, first the one at Kurume and then the one at Fukuoka.

The more recent advance in material equipment may be summarized as follows: A parsonage on the church lot in Kobe, to be used also as a place of worship until the church is built, has been completed and in use since February, 1930. Many will remember the strenuous and successful efforts of Dr. C. K. Lippard for this undertaking. At the expense of the local congregation a parsonage for the Japanese pastor has been built at Kurume. A well-located site has been purchased at Nagoya costing about $5,000. The small frame church building which stands on rented land, will be moved to the new site and used until the proposed church can be financed. In Amagi the congregation with the help of the missionary bought a tract of land for a church building and has appealed to the Board for money to help build it. At Naogata the congregation will contribute $500 towards a church building if a balance of about $1,750 can be provided from other sources. Two kindergarten buildings have been erected, the Cronk Memorial at the Kumamoto Colony of Mercy, and the Midori, adjoining the missionary's home in Shinyashiki, Kumamoto.

To celebrate the twentieth anniversary of Kyushu Gakuin in 1931, the Board has appropriated $12,500 of the Frank Ritter legacy, held in the Land, Property and Building Fund, for a Ritter Memorial Library Building, with the understanding that at least a similar amount will be raised by the institution itself in Japan for a gymnasium and other needed equipment.

The mission reports that the next most imperative need is a main building for the theological seminary at Tokyo. The present plant, consisting of a dormitory and four professors' houses, is inadequate. With students, class rooms, library, chapel, dining room and offices all housed in one building the question is how long the government will permit such a state of things to continue in an institution which has been recognized by the Educational Department as an institution of higher education.

Next year Kyushu Jo Gakuin, also known as the Janice James School for Girls, will graduate its first class. It is admirably fulfilling its designated purpose. Increased attendance made the erection of a second dormitory unit necessary and now the school is appealing for funds for further expansion in every direction.

The philanthropic or inner mission work of the mission includes the home for aged people and the home for widows and their children in Tokyo, which will be in charge of Miss Anna Powlas on her return to Japan this fall after furlough in America, and the rapidly expanding Colony of Mercy at Kumamoto, which includes the departments of kindergarten work, children's work, from which department this year three girls were sent to Kyushu Jo Gakuin, Rescue Home and Old People's Home, the work being divided between three single women missionaries.

Internationally the outstanding event of the year for the Japan mission relates itself to the Lutheran World Convention at Copenhagen. It meant a good deal to our young Church in Japan to be represented in that convention not only by a missionary, Rev. C. W. Hepner, but also by a Japanese, Rev. H. Inadomi. It was the first time our Church in Japan was represented in a world Lutheran convention and thus was put on the world map of Lutheranism.

Two of our missionaries, Rev. J. M. T. Winther of Kurume and Rev. A. J. Stirewalt of Tokyo, this year completed twenty-five years of service. For these missionaries and their work we give thanks and pray that they may be spared for many more years of service in Japan. A real loss to the mission was the resignation of Rev. and Mrs. C. K. Lippard, D.D., who first went to Japan in 1900. The long continued illness of their second daughter, Lois, made their return to Japan impossible. Another resignation was that of Miss Amy Thoren, after a term of service in Japan.

We now come to what is most certainly the most important matter in the history of our mission in Japan. Convinced that the time is ripe for the organization of the Lutheran Church in Japan, we are presenting a constitution which together with a form of special agreement were written in Japan and then amended by the Board in conference with Rev. H. Inadomi, who stopped over in Baltimore for this purpose on his way to Copenhagen. Only a few slight changes were made at the eleventh annual convention of the church and mission in Japan on March 25-29, 1930, at Kobe, and at its meeting on May 28-29, the Board of Foreign Missions approved the final draft and now submits it to this convention of the United Lutheran Church in America for consideration and action, after which it will be reported to the co-operating United Danish and Icelandic Synods. It is very likely that if approved a special meeting of the mission and church in Japan will be called before the close of this year to put the constitution into effect and thus to establish our second daughter church in the mission field, the first being the Andhra Evangelical Lutheran Church in India, constituted in a similar manner in 1927.

At the same time a modified form of constitution for the organization of missionaries in Japan, approved by the mission and the board, is herewith appended, for the consideration and action of this convention of the United Lutheran Church in America.

By-laws for both the church and the missionaries' organization are in the course of preparation, and the board will see that they conform with the articles of the proposed constitutions and special agreement. And now we commend again our growing and blessed mission in Japan to the parent Church in America for earnest, unceasing prayer and supplication and for zealous, self-sacrificing and increasing missionary effort.

JAPAN MISSION STATISTICS

Stations	Missionaries	National Workers	Baptized Members	Communicants	Added During Year	Sunday School Pupils	Field Contributions	Kindergarten Schools	Kindergarten Pupils	Middle School or Theological Students
Tokyo (Okubo)	8	10	209	110	26	215	954	11	28	16
Tokyo (Ebara)	0	1	38	24	5	51	285	0	0	0
Nagoya	2	2	38	29	10	56	181	1	22	0
Kyoto	0	1	107	63	13	113	448	0	0	0
Osaka	2	2	137	51	19	53	222	0	0	0
Osaka (West)	0	2	37	14	3	25	122	0	0	0
Kobe	2	1	43	28	4	30	228	0	0	0
Hiroshima	0	1	9	5	4	25	37	0	0	0
Shimonoseki	0	1	94	27	4	23	343	0	0	0
Moji	2	1	68	19	10	60	135	0	0	0
Yawata	0	1	62	42	13	60	192	0	0	0
Naogata	0	1	117	55	22	52	275	0	0	0
Kanezaki	0	1	38	10	2	80	11	0	0	0
Hakata	3	4	190	79	18	330	845	1	37	0
Saga	2	1	192	36	15	35	342	1	18	0
Ogi	2	5	36	10	1	76	149	1	37	0
Karatsu	0	1	44	13	5	48	75	0	0	0
Amagi	0	1	43	21	4	38	84	0	0	0
Hida	0	1	87	33	9	95	145	0	0	0
Kurume	2	4	325	122	34	96	897	1	40	0
Omuta	0	1	154	49	16	72	208	0	0	0
Kumamoto	8	15	564	133	30	280	711	1	75	300
Kyushu Gakuin	4	3	440	157	10	75	420	0	0	700
Minamata	0	1	95	30	8	85	395	0	0	0
Totals	37	62	3167	1160	285	2073	$7716	17	257	1016

PROPOSED CONSTITUTION OF THE EVANGELICAL LUTHERAN CHURCH IN JAPAN

Adopted by the Japan Mission at its eleventh annual convention at Kobe, March 25-29, 1930, and by the Board of Foreign Missions at its meeting on May 28-29, 1930.

THE CONSTITUTION

PREAMBLE

In the Name of the Father, and of the Son, and of the Holy Spirit. Amen.

Having been called by the Gospel and made partakers of the grace of God, and by faith, members of our Lord and Saviour Jesus Christ, and through Him, of one another.

We, members of Evangelical Lutheran congregations in the Empire of Japan.

Recognizing that all power in the church belongs primarily and exclusively to our Lord Jesus Christ, the Head of the Church; and all just duties and powers exercised by the Church are committed to her for the furtherance of the Gospel through the Word and Sacraments; and that congregations are the primary bodies through which power committed by Christ to the Church is normally exercised.

Acknowledging it to be the duty of all Christians to labor for the extension of the Kingdom of God not only in this country, but in the whole world by proclaiming the truth of His Word, preaching the Gospel of His grace and by the administration of the Sacraments in accordance with His commands, relying upon the promise of the divine Word that He who began this good work will perfect it until the day of Christ Jesus.

Do hereby adopt this Constitution and thereby organize the Evangelical Lutheran Church in Japan, in order to fulfill the divine will by our united efforts and through mutual encouragement; and we invite all congregations having the same faith and purpose to unite with us upon the terms of this Constitution in one organization to be known as the Evangelical Lutheran Church in Japan.

ARTICLE I. NAME

The name and title of the Church organized under this constitution shall be the Evangelical Lutheran Church in Japan.

ARTICLE II. DOCTRINAL BASIS

1. The Evangelical Lutheran Church in Japan receives and holds the canonical Scriptures of the Old and New Testaments as the inspired Word of God, and as the only infallible rule and standard of faith and practice, according to which all doctrines and teachers are to be judged.

2. The Evangelical Lutheran Church in Japan accepts the three ecumenical creeds, namely, the Apostles', the Nicene, and the Athanasian, as important testimonies drawn from the Holy Scriptures, and rejects all errors which they condemn.

3. The Evangelical Lutheran Church in Japan received and holds the Unaltered Augsburg Confession as a correct exhibition of the faith and doctrine of the Evangelical Lutheran Church, founded upon the Word of God; and acknowledges all churches that sincerely hold and faithfully

confess the doctrines of the Unaltered Augsburg Confession to be entitled to the name of Evangelical Lutheran.

4. The Evangelical Lutheran Church in Japan recognizes the Apology of the Augsburg Confession, the Smalkald Articles, the Large and Small Catechisms of Luther, and the Formula of Concord, as in the harmony of one and the same pure Scriptural faith.

ARTICLE III. OBJECTS AND FUNCTIONS

This Church is organized:

1. To promote and extend the Kingdom of God.

2. To preserve the pure teaching of the Gospel and the right administration of the sacraments.

3. To strengthen the Church in the confession of true faith and in the ministry of love.

4. To direct effectively the united efforts of this Church.

5. To solicit and disburse the funds necessary for these and other purposes defined in this Constitution.

ARTICLE IV. MEMBERSHIP

Anyone may become a member of this Church by Holy Baptism or, if already baptized elsewhere, by Confirmation, administered in conformity with the faith and practice of this Church.

ARTICLE V. LOCAL CONGREGATION

A body of believers confessing the faith as set forth in Article II of this Constitution and organized on the basis of this Constitution and by By-laws of this Church, shall be designated a local congregation.

ARTICLE VI. (KYOSHOKU) MINISTERS AND EVANGELISTS

Section 1. Those who are regularly engaged in the official work of this Church, as defined in the By-laws, shall be designated as Kyoshoku, i. e., a. Ministers, b. Evangelists.

Section 2. A minister is one who is ordained. An evangelist is one who, though not ordained, is engaged in the work of the Church, as defined in the By-laws.

ARTICLE VII. GOVERNMENT

Section 1. The government of this Church shall be administered by a General Convention or *ad interim* by its representative organ, an Executive Board, duly elected by the Convention.

Section 2. The General Convention shall consist of the ministers and evangelists (Kyoshoku) ex-officio, and lay delegates elected by the local congregations, as determined in the By-laws.

Section 3. The General Convention shall meet regularly at such time and place as may be determined in the By-laws. Special meetings may be called as determined in the By-laws.

Section 4. Two-thirds of the voting members of the General Convention shall constitute a quorum.

Section 5. The officers of this Church shall be a President, a Vice-President, a Secretary, and a Treasurer, elected by the General Convention.

Section 6. The Executive Board shall be composed of the President, Vice-President, Secretary and Treasurer of the Church, and four other members elected by the Convention.

Section 7. The ordained ministers of this Church shall constitute a Ministerium, which shall function as a committee of the convention. The duties of the Ministerium shall be: 1. The cultivation of the ministerial life. 2. The examination of candidates for the ministry and their recommendation to the convention for ordination. 3. The examination of ministers who desire to unite with this Church and their recommendation to the convention. 4. Recommendations to the convention concerning the discipline of ministers and evangelists.

ARTICLE VIII. DISCIPLINE

Section 1. The members, ministers and evangelists (Kyoshoku) of this Church shall be liable to discipline for the following offences: 1. Denial of the faith or dissemination of doctrine in conflict with the confession of faith as set forth in Article II; 2. Disregard of the Constitution and By-laws of this Church or of the decisions of the General Convention; 3. Conduct that brings disgrace to the Christian name.

Section 2. (Kyoshoku) Ministers and evangelists shall be disciplined by the General Convention on the recommendation of the Ministerium. Temporary discipline *ad interim* may be administered by the Executive Board.

Section 3. Members of local congregations shall be disciplined by the Council of the local congregation.

ARTICLE IX. FINANCES

Section 1. This Church may give and receive donations.

Section 2. Property owned by this Church or transferred to it shall be held by a Board of Trustees (Shadan), elected by the General Convention.

ARTICLE X. BY-LAWS

The Convention may adopt such By-Laws as shall be necessary, provided they are not in conflict with this Constitution.

ARTICLE XI. AMENDMENTS

This Constitution, except Article II, may be amended in the following manner: More than ten members of the General Convention must present the amendment in writing to the convention in session. Final action shall be taken at the next General Convention. A two-thirds vote of all the regular members of the convention is necessary for adoption.

SPECIAL AGREEMENT

Section 1. All matters, including financial appropriations, which require the sanction of the Board of Foreign Missions of the United Lutheran

Church in America, shall have the approval of the constituted organization of missionaries on the field; and all official correspondence of the Church with the Board of Foreign Missions shall pass through the official channel of the constituted organization of missionaries.

Section 2. The Executive Board shall prepare and present to the General Convention for its adoption an annual budget in which shall be indicated the amount of money desired as an appropriation from the Board of Foreign Missions. This budget shall be reported to the organization of missionaries which shall recommend to the Board the amount of the annual appropriation.

Section 3. As a rule financial aid to all local congregations and the budget of the Church shall be decreased annually at the rate of five per cent. Rents, taxes, repairs, and travel of missionaries for the present shall be included under the mission budget.

The annual budget shall include an item for new work and new workers, for which an appropriation is desired from the Board.

Section 4. (a) Ordained missionaries who have been in Japan for at least two years shall be regular members of the General Convention. Those who have resided in Japan for less than two years shall be associate members.

(b) Single women missionaries shall be associate members of the General Convention; but to the Chairman and the Secretary of the Women's Work Committee shall be extended the courtesy of full membership.

(c) Women evangelists under regular appointment by the Executive Board shall be associate members of the General Convention.

(d) Women evangelists working with single women missionaries shall be under the direction of the women's work committee, and when appointed to work approved by Executive Board shall become associate members of the General Convention.

Section 5. The President of the Convention shall be a Japanese, the Vice-President a missionary, the Secretary a Japanese, the Treasurer a missionary. For the time being, there shall be an English Secretary who shall be a missionary, and an Assistant Treasurer who shall be a Japanese. All of these shall be elected by the General Convention.

Section 6. Of the four elected members of the Executive Board, two shall be Japanese and two shall be missionaries.

Section 7. For the time being one-half of the members of the Board of Trustees (Shadan) shall be missionaries. All members of the Board of Trustees shall be nominated by ballot at the annual convention.

Section 8. One-half of the members of the Examining Committee shall be missionaries, who have been regular members of the Mission for at least five years.

Section 9. Any alteration in this special agreement shall be made only by action of the General Convention and of the constituted organization of missionaries.

PROPOSED REVISION OF THE CONSTITUTION OF THE JAPAN MISSION OF THE UNITED LUTHERAN CHURCH IN AMERICA

ARTICLE I. NAME

The name of this Mission shall be the Japan Mission of the United Lutheran Church in America.

ARTICLE II. OBJECTS

This Mission has as its objects:

(1) The extension of the Kingdom of God in the Empire of Japan, through the teaching of the Gospel and the administration of the Sacraments.

(2) The establishment of an indigenous Japanese Lutheran Church.

In accordance with these objects, it conducts direct evangelism, educational work, and the ministry of mercy.

ARTICLE III. FUNCTIONS

This Mission shall function:

(1) As the agent of the Board of Foreign Missions of the United Lutheran Church in America in all matters pertaining to the conduct of the Board's work in Japan.

(2) As the agent of the Board of Foreign Missions in its relations with the Evangelical Lutheran Church in Japan.

(3) Through its constituent missionaries, as members of the Evangelical Lutheran Church in Japan, in furthering its establishment and extension.

(4) As the organization having control and oversight of the work of missionaries belonging to this Mission.

ARTICLE IV. MEMBERS

All missionaries commissioned, sent to Japan and supported by the Board of Foreign Missions of the United Lutheran Church in America shall be members of this mission. No member, however, shall be entitled to vote until he has spent two (2) years in Japan.

ARTICLE V. OFFICERS

(1) Elections: The officers of this Mission shall be President, Vice-President, Secretary and Treasurer, who shall be elected by ballot and shall serve for a term of one year. They shall enter upon the duties of their respective offices at the close of the convention at which they are elected.

(2) Duties of Officers: (a) The duties of the President shall be those usually pertaining to that office. He shall call and preside at all meetings.

He shall countersign all official communications from the Mission to the Board. He shall sign all orders made on the Treasurer, and shall keep a neat and permanent record of all such orders.

(b) The Vice-President shall act for the President in his absence or at his request. He shall be the chairman of the Budget and Finance Committee.

(c) The duties of the Secretary shall be those usually pertaining to the office of a recording and corresponding secretary. He shall record the minutes of each meeting and shall be the official correspondent of the Mission with the Board.

(d) The Treasurer shall receive and disburse all funds according to the conditions laid down by the Board.

Article VI. Executive Committee

The President, Vice-President, Secretary and Treasurer, and ône other to be elected annually, shall constitute the Executive Committee of the Mission.

Article VII. Meetings

(a) Regular: There shall be one regular annual meeting.

(b) Special: A special meeting may be called at any time when there is business of such a nature as to make it necessary.

Quorum: Two-thirds of the voting members on the field shall constitute a quorum.

Article VIII. Reports to the Board

Immediately after each meeting of the Mission an official copy of the minutes, written by the Secretary and countersigned by the President, shall be sent to the Board.

Article IX. Finances of the Mission

(1) The Mission shall submit an annual itemized estimate of the general work of the Mission to the Board for its approval.

(2) The Mission shall recommend to the Board the amount of the annual appropriation for the work of the Evangelical Lutheran Church in Japan.

Article X. Amendments

This Constitution may be amended, subject to the approval of the Board, by a three-fourths majority vote of the voting members on the field at any regular meeting, provided a resolution to consider such amendment shall have been adopted at the preceding regular annual meeting.

Article XI. By-Laws

The Mission may adopt necessary by-laws in harmony with this Constitution, subject to the approval of the Board.

CHINA

Our missionaries on the field were the following during the biennium:

Missionaries	Residence	Arrived
Rev. and Mrs. C. J. Voskamp	Retired	1884
Rev. and Mrs. Theo. Scholz	Kiaochow	1904
Rev. and Mrs. Wm. Matzat	Tsimo	1922
Miss Kate Voget	Kiaochow	1906
Miss Freda Strecker	Kiaochow	1908
Rev. and Mrs. P. P. Anspach	Tsingtao	1925
Miss Erva Moody	Tsingtao	1925
Miss Elvira Strunk	Tsimo	1925
Miss Lydia F. Reich	Tsingtao	1927
Rev. L. G. Cooper	Tsimo	1928
Rev. and Mrs. C. H. Reinbrecht	Kiaochow	1928
Miss M. Clara Sullivan	Peking	1929
Dr. and Mrs. Taylor M. Beagle	Peking	1929

China presents a great study in matters political, social, governmental and religious.

Our missionary staff has suffered from the following changes: Dr. and Mrs. Voskamp have moved from Tsingtao to Hankow, where our retired missionary will find congenial work in helping to prepare Chinese literature for our Lutheran Church and in preaching to his fellow countrymen in Hankow. He has retired after a long and distinguished service in China since 1884. His work was done both in Canton and in Shantung, and as a linguist, he has made a place for himself among scholars.

After a short term in China, Dr. and Mrs. Taylor M. Beagle returned home. His leaving the field was most unfortunate, as it set back our medical work considerably, but under the circumstances the board was inclined to accept his resignation as the only thing to be done.

The other members of the missionary body have shown great fidelity in their management of the different parts of the work.

The property purchase account has been happily adjusted by the action of the Convention at Erie, and there remains due on the purchase price only $79,133.

NATIONAL WORKERS

The Bible school at Kiaochow known as Our Wittenberg in China, has sent six Chinese Evangelists into the field. The President of our Chinese Church has just retired as President and has gone to our Lutheran Seminary at Shekow to continue his theological studies, and in the last summer one of our Chinese preachers has also come back to work after a period of study. Our mission has engaged a young Lutheran preacher from the Norwegian Lutheran Church of America, and an evangelistic worker of fine spirit has joined our mission in the medical department. He is a Korean by nationality and a graduate of our Lutheran Theological Seminary.

On the general work of our mission at the conference held Dr. Mott, the delegate sent to "sit in" was Rev. and Mrs. Theodore Scholz. The purpose of this series of conferences was to agree on a five-year period of evangelism, looking especially to the strengthening of the spiritual life of church members, and setting a goal to double church membership in five years.

Our own Lutheran Church has adopted the slogan: "O God revive thy Church beginning with me."

SELF SUPPORT

A self-supporting National Church is the ultimate goal of mission work in every land. Each year should show increased contributions from the congregations and a decrease from the mission. The Tsingtao Church has raised half its budget last year.

Two other steps are noted: the churches have given to famine relief and toward the publication of Chinese literature for the work among all classes.

OUR ORGANIZATION

Our Lutheran Church is supported by ten different synods or Lutheran boards or societies in Europe and America. Our mission has its own synod—the Shantung Synod—with district conferences at Tsingtao, Tsimo and Kiaochow.

Evangelistic work is carried on in thirty-eight congregations and at sixty-two preaching points. Every effort is being made to strengthen the work of the laymen of the Church. The mission reports with great appreciation the help of Rev. Olson, who came to our mission to carry on Rev. Matzat's work. While absent on furlough, he organized Bible classes among the laymen. All our congregations have shown deep interest in the Church's spiritual growth.

The colporteur work, selling of Bibles and tracts, has been most helpful in preparing the way for the preacher and missionary. At one place the people ask for a chapel to meet for worship.

Our Bible women also report a good year, as they sow the seed and conduct Bible classes in the centers of our mission and among the villages.

SUNDAY SCHOOLS

Our Sunday schools have increased numbers in attendance and effective as an evangelistic agency, and a vacation Bible school brought together ninety delegates to an annual conference of preachers and laymen. For six weeks the number of pupils continued, both in Tsingtao, and at other places schools were conducted.

EDUCATIONAL

Our mission tries to meet the Government requirement of registration. Our Chinese Synod has charge of most schools, members in the school being largely Chinese. A Chinese school inspector was appointed to meet all requirements of the Government.

In our middle schools, now reduced to two, the work has been unhindered. The educational work largely depends on securing good teachers, but the mission has pressed on in its school work and sees no immediate need to change its policy.

It is very significant that though the mission has complied with all the details of Government registration, as yet the latter has taken no action. The Bible work is put in a separate time table and classes are held before regular school hours. Only a few pupils remain at home. At the Sunday services almost 100% attend.

MEDICAL

Our dispensary work had to close in March at Tsimo and all was consolidated. Mrs. Matzat's absence from the field limited the medical work at Tsimo. Her return to the field resulted in reopening the dispensary and the end of the year she reported one hundred and sixty patients. Briefly our medical work in the mission:

	Tsimo	Tai Tung Chen
Patients	163	240
Receipts	$16.97	$13.80
Cost of work	$118.55	$103.26

No doubt exists in the mind of the mission as expressed: "There was a time in China when mission hospitals were more needed."

STATISTICS

Stations	Missionaries	National Workers	Congregations	Baptized Members	Com. Members	Additions	Inquirers	Sunday School Scholars	Contributions	Number Schools	Number Pupils
Tsingtao..........	5	44	10	416	291	62	98	188	$2052	16	397
Tsimo............	4	52	37	495	317	26	96	394	482	18	470
Kiaochow........	5	74	24	702	690	102	148	72	597	28	669
Total.........	14	170	71	1613	1298	190	342	854	$3131	62	1536

LIBERIA, AFRICA

MISSIONARIES

Name	Residence	Arrival
Rev. and Mrs. J. D. Curran	Muhlenberg	1911
Sister Laura Gilliland	Furlough	1915
Mrs. C. E. Buschman	Muhlenberg	1915
Bertha Koenig	Zorzor	1916
Mabel A. Dysinger	Furlough	1917

Mr. and Mrs. James W. Miller .... Furlough 1920
Miss Elsie Otto .... Muhlenberg 1920
Rev. and Mrs. J. Ira Haltiwanger ...... Monrovia 1925
Revfl and Mrs. David D. Dagle ..:.... Sanoyea 1925
Rev. and Mrs. Robert S. Oberly .... Zorzor 1925
Rev. and Mrs. H. J. Currens .... Zorzor 1927
Rev. and Mrs. Harry Heilman .... Furlough 1927
Jacob R. Jensen, M.D. .... Furlough 1927
Rev. A. H. Kaitschuk .... Muhlenberg 1928
Miss Irene Bloch .... Muhlenberg 1928
Miss K. Marie Jensen .... Muhlenberg 1928
Norman R. Sloan, M.D. .... Zorzor 1928
George Gulck, M.D. .... Muhlenberg 1929
Rev. George Gesler .... Muhlenberg 1929
Mrs. George Gesler .... Muhlenberg 1929

Seven ordained, 5 unordained, 7 single ladies, 8 wives of missionaries. As we review the work of this field we find there are many gratifying results.

During the biennium the lives of all our missionaries have been spared. There were only a few cases of serious illness. Except in one or two instances missionaries remained their full time on the field. Resignations have been few, and for these replacements have been sent, except in one instance.

As to the progress of the work let us consider it: First, from the standpoint of evangelism. The mission is giving this a very prominent place. Plans for intensifying this program were adopted at a recent meeting of the Missions Conference. Additional evangelists were employed with the aim of cultivating the communities where there were established congregations. The importance of the Bible school was frequently mentioned to the boys in our boarding schools.

Plans were formulated for printing the catechism, hymns and prayers in the dialects in which our misssionaries work. A survey of all the half-towns located within a day's journey of Zorzor has been completed and two additional evangelists have been employed to assist the missionary in regular visitations.

As to definite results, inquirers, aside from mission employees, have been enrolled in ten or twelve villages. At Sanoyea a number of people, many of them in no way connected with the mission, have been received into the Church. These plan to build their own village, with their own head man, subject to all the laws and obligations of the State.

Second, Congregational Work.

The mission has five established congregations in which the Gospel is regularly preached and the sacraments duly administered. It is a source of deep gratification to report that fifty-one individuals were added to the Church during 1929. The majority of these were adults.

At the Main Station, some disaffected families at the Day Memorial Church withdrew. The faithful ones are supporting their own evangelist, which means that there is a stable nucleus. We believe that this church is now in condition to show better results than formerly.

While the contributions were small as compared with the total cost, still, when missionaries report that all the members are tithers, as in the case in one of the congregations in the interior, there are grounds for rejoicing and hope even along this line.

Another matter worthy of notice is that Christian young men connected with our stations are assisting our evangelists in preaching the Gospel in nearby half-towns.

Third, School Work.

There is work along this line for boys and girls in all three of our stations. Boarding schools are maintained in Muhlenberg and Zorzor, while a day school is in operation at Sanoyea. Very commendable results have been achieved. Recently several fine words of praise have come to us. One from a former United States Government official to Liberia. He stated that the Lutherans have made a worthy contribution to education in Liberia. The other comes from a missionary of another denomination. In a letter to his board he wrote that "the Lutherans have a school that is a school." He was referring to our Muhlenberg Girls' School.

As to maintaining schools in the interior, it is very difficult to obtain Government permission, and where such is secured the instruction must be in English. This makes the task very discouraging. Within the last year the District Commissioner at Zorzor has expressed himself as favoring day schools in the community. This is an advance step and one that gives promise of better things to come. A village school in the midst of inquirers, or a village congregation, is a tremendous asset in building up the Kingdom of God.

Fourth, Medical Work.

Two hospitals are maintained. One at Muhlenberg and the other at Zorzor. Dr. Jensen has done a very valuable piece of work at the main station. As many as 25,000 cases have been treated in the time under review. Nurses' training classes have been maintained.

The Evangelistic program has been given a prominent place. Personal work has been carried on both with patients and visitors. A few have received baptism.

At Zorzor Dr. Lape, and later Dr. Sloan, directed the medical work. While the progress here is not as marked as at the main station, still there are no grounds to feel discouraged. Among these primitive people a doctor must win his way. Successful major operations require better equipment in both buildings and instruments.

Fifth, Industrial Work.

Agricultural and industrial work is taught in connection with our boarding schools. In addition to gardens, in which many vegetables are grown for use in the schools, both boys and girls are taught to make baskets and mats. Sewing and cooking are enjoyed by groups of the Emma V. Day Girls' School, while the boys are instructed in carpentry.

HEALTH MATTERS

During the spring of 1929 a very virulent type of yellow fever took a number of lives, both European and Liberian. Among them were the American Consul and the director of the Advisory Committee on Education in Liberia. As a result, the American Government, at the request of the Advisory Committee, arranged with the Liberian Government for the employment of a Sanitary Engineer in Monrovia. Dr. Smith, recommended by the Public Health Department of the United States Government, is now on the field. It is an understanding with the Liberian Government that a Sanitary Engineer is to be employed in Monrovia, as long as there is any danger from yellow fever. This matter is of tremendous importance for the health of our missionaries as well as others.

In conclusion, the general outlook for the establishment of the Church is hopeful. The new spirit of the East has reached Africa and Liberia. The mission is appointing more evangelists and teachers. These understand their own people and are working for their spiritual deliverance. At the same time we would not forget our missionaries who are laboring so faithfully in our behalf. Let us give them our loyal support and our daily prayers.

STATISTICS

Stations	American Missionaries	National Workers	Congregations	Baptized Members	Added During Year	Inquirers	Aver. Att. Sunday School	Contributions	No. of Schools	Pupils in School	Hospitals
Muhlenberg	17	15	2	75	14	16	140	227.48	2	160	1
Sanoyea	4	5	1	26	15	48	40	112.28	1	28	....
Zorzor	6	10	1	57	12	8	136	87.49	3	115	1
Teh, Mt. Coffee, Kpolopele, etc.	....	....	1	192	10	37	61	....	3	33	....
Total	27	30	5	350	51	109	377	427.50	9	336	2

Note: The total communicant membership is 183.

STATISTICS

Stations	In Patients	Dispensaries	Out Patient Visits
Muhlenberg	355	2	12,902
Sanoyea	......	1	207
Zorzor	15	1	900
Total	370	4	14,009

British Guiana

Missionaries   *Residence*   *Arrived*
Rev. and Mrs. Robert H. Daube ....New Amsterdam 1927
Rev. and Mrs. Paul M. Counts .... New Amsterdam,1930 (short term)

Our New Amsterdam congregation ranks with the oldest Lutheran churches in North America. This congregation is the leader of a vigorous mission work in the Colony. It has, since its being taken over by our Foreign Board, in 1915, made good progress. In the past biennium it has pushed work among all classes of the very mixed population in the city and outlying country. Among Hindus, Mohammedans, and native born of a great variety of nationality and race, work was carried. Negroes, East Indians, Chinese, and aboriginal Indians offer an attractive and responsive field for mission work.

Our congregations are Ebenezer Church in New Amsterdam, Maria Henrietta, St. Lust, Ituni, among the Arawack Indians and during the last two years new churches of Fearn and Germania, with membership of thirty-five and nineteen respectively.

Our missionary must depend on the Christian unordained workers to carry forward this large evangelistic endeavor. The following men are in charge: at Marie Henrietta, Catechist William A. Blair, with a congregation of eighty communicants and a flourishing Sunday school and a Luther League; at St. Lust, Catechist Alfred T. Williams and thirty-nine communicants and a good Sunday school; at Ituni among the Indians, Catechist Stephen Hartman with eight communicants and a Sunday school. In the churches at Fearn and Germania, Mr. J. E. Daphness and Mr. Henry Christian conduct services regularly.

Besides this, Catechists Paul Masih Das and T. C. Menzies do evangelistic work in New Amsterdam, Canje, Lochaber, and Mara Districts among the East Indians. By way of explanation, in British Guiana, East Indians means those who have come from India speaking different languages.

Schools of an elementary grade are conducted by the catechists, assisted by nine other teachers. These schools are supported by the Educational Department, and only cost the mission about five per cent.

INDUSTRIAL WORK

This work was organized in 1925 and has first completed a successful year. The missionary reports:

During the year, courses were offered in woodworking, mechanical drawing, gardening, printing, sewing, English and arithmetic, and the total enrollment reached 132. In addition to these several young men have been receiving full-time training as apprentices in cabinet making. The boys received this training very enthusiastically, and the Department of Education is planning to add several additional features to the work during the present year.

The group of dormitory boys, who had been under the training of the mission for the last two or three years, completed their course during 1929, and returned to their homes up the river well equipped for employment as tradesmen. It is regretted that the courses offered in gardening, sewing, English and arithmetic had to be discontinued because of the board's reduction in the mission budget. At present the industrial school is entirely self-supporting, due to the grant received from the Educational Department, and the profits received from the work of the mission print shop, which is also connected with the industrial school.

The statistics of this active mission show most substantial progress for the biennium.

STATISTICS

Stations	Missionaries	National Workers	Communicants	Baptized Members	Additions	Inquirers	Sunday School Scholars	Contributions	Number Schools	Number of Pupils
British Guiana & New Amsterdam & River Congregations and Schools..............	4	21	400	400	44	50	470	1913	5	259

ARGENTINE

Missionaries	Residence	Arrived
Rev. Paul O. Machetzki	Buenos Aires	1922
Rev. and Mrs. John M. Armbruster ...Buenos	Aires	1924
Miss Corinne M. Manges	Buenos Aires	1925
Miss Myrtle Wilke	Buenos Aires	1927

After ten years under our board's direction, we can make a most hopeful report to the General Convention of the United Lutheran Church. The past history of our work in Argentine, in and around the capital city, Buenos Aires, is full of evidence of God's leading and favor. This last biennium has been marked by signal progress.

For the first time since 1923 the mission which for the last seven years struggled on under a burdensome debt, was free of all debts on its land and buildings. The Luther League's contribution was the final payment on debts, which in 1923 on the death of Dr. Mueller, amounted to Pesos 249,123 or about $100,000. The Board rejoices with the mission in this and is glad to make this report to our Church Convention. This gives our mission a most valuable property, both in Buenos Aires and in the nearby towns. Our work is rooted in the soil of this great sister republic. The total value of all mission property amounts to Pesos 438,547, or about $175,000.

The organization of the mission, which was approved by the board in May, 1925, has continued to function efficiently. It works under the conference of the American missionaries and divides the administration of the mission under three committees, namely (a) Finances, (b) Educational and (c) Evangelistic. The two latter committees are composed of equal numbers of missionaries and nationals. The departments have had a successful year.

The finances of the mission were, due to the board's financial condition, rather cramped. The visit of Rev. Armbruster to the United States was made under Board approval to settle the needs of the field, before its friends, and resulted in an offering of over $4,000. This enabled the mission to carry on all its work without making any severe cuts in its appropriations, or closing of any part of the work.

The Colegio Nacional continued all its classes. At the end of the school year the staff was informed that on financial grounds it was deemed wise to close the fourth and fifth grades. The college teachers volunteered to continue to teach the fourth college class subjects free of charge. This self-sacrifice and co-operation were gladly accepted. All felt it would impede the progress of the college to close this class.

EDUCATION

The financial report made for the two years passed was very satisfactory. The income of the schools in Buenos Aires was in 1928 Pesos 31,027 and 1929 Pesos 34,031. Our enrollment of students in all branches of our mission schools is as follows:

National College (boys only) 74
Commercial School, boys and girls respectively, 53 and 13 69

In our elementary schools in mission there are 316 of whom 227 are boys and 89 girls. Adding special course students numbering 39, our total boys and girls reaches 734, taught by 44 teachers,—a strong force among the young. Our school is in Villa del Parque, a suburb of Buenos Aires and in all its departments is the largest in the Argentina.

EVANGELISM

We report five American missionaries, two ordained and three unordained and ten national workers, three ordained, two unordained and five wives. With this staff of workers, our evangelical movement is pushed forward among all classes and has shown progress. We should name our national workers: Rev. Guzman, Rev. Resa and Rev. Requenas and sub-pastor Estrada and Luciutiata Hotz. In this connection, we must mention the director of our Colegio Nacional, Mr. Viera.

Our evangelical movement has spread and is now firmly established in Villa del Parque, with a flourishing congregation of 189 members. Outside of the city of Buenos Aires churches and Sunday schools carry on work in Caseros and Santos, Lugares, at San Miguel and Jose C. Pas at San Martin Ituzaingo and at Villa Progresso and Calle San Blas.

Our congregations have a membership of 440 communicant and 708 baptized members with Sunday schools having 517 scholars and Luther League and girls' and women's and men's organizations.

ARGENTINE STATISTICS

Stations	Missionaries	National Workers	Congregations	Baptized Members	Com. Members	Additions	Inquirers	Sunday School Scholars	Contributions	Number of Schools	Number of Pupils
Buenos Aires	5	44	1	247	185	27	55	145	5370	1	461
Caseros			1	86	50	3		64	222	1	136
San Miguel			1	160	88	1	11	43	132	1	82
Jose C. Paz			1	102	54	3	11	34	290	1	55
San Martin			1	57	40		3	19	652	1	
Villa Progresso			1	25	15			57	186		
Ituzaingo			1	16			1		5		
Santos Lugares			1	15	8			15	12		
San Blas								139	68		
Total	5	44	8	708	440	34	81	516	6937 Pes.	5	734

OFFICERS AND BOARD MEMBERS

During the past biennium the Board of Foreign Missions has met regularly every two months with an average attendance of fourteen voting and four co-operating and advisory members. Dr. S. T. Nicholas was elected to fill the unexpired term of Dr. J. T. Huddle. Rev. J. P. Nielsen and Rev. I. M. Andersen were elected by the United Danish Synod to succeed Rev. V. W. Bondo and Rev. E. R. Andersen as co-operating members. The list of all officers, secretaries and members during the past biennium is as follows:

OFFICERS

President: Rev. Prof. C. Theodore Benze, D.D., 7304 Boyer Street, Mt. Airy, Philadelphia, Pa.

Vice-President: Rev. J. E. Byers, D.D., 2900 Guilford Ave., Baltimore, Maryland.

Recording Secretary: Rev. George Drach, D.D., 18 East Mt. Vernon Place, Baltimore, Md.

Treasurer: Mr. George R. Weitzel, 18 East Mt. Vernon Place, Baltimore, Maryland.

SECRETARIES

Rev. Paul W. Koller, D.D., Executive, Candidates, Foreign Fields.

Rev. L. B. Wolf, D.D., Home Base Secretary, Corresponding Secretary for South America and China.

Rev. George Drach, D.D., Literature Secretary, Corresponding Secretary for India and Japan.

Rev. M. Edwin Thomas, D.D., Special Gifts Secretary, Corresponding Secretary for Africa.

MEMBERS OF THE BOARD
TERMS EXPIRE IN 1930

Rev. Prof. C. Theodore Benze, D.D., 7304 Boyer Street, Mt. Airy, Philadelphia, Pa.

Rev. R. C. G. Bielinski, Delanco, N. J.

Rev. J. L. Morgan, D.D., 612 S. Main Street, Salisbury, N. C.

Rev. H. W. Snyder, D.D., 5131 Chevy Chase Parkway, Washington, D. C.

Rev. G. Albert Getty, D.D., 40 S. Duke Street, York, Pa.

Mr. James M. Snyder, 1515 Fidelity Bldg., 123 S. Broad St., Phila., Pa.

Prof. C. W. Foss, Ph.D., 3808 8th Ave., Rockford, Ill.

TERMS EXPIRE IN 1932

Rev. J. L. Sieber, D.D., 352 Church Ave., Roanoke, Va.

Rev. S. W. Herman, D.D., 121 State Street, Harrisburg, Pa.

Rev. Charles A. Dennig, 211 East Street, Warren, Pa.

Rev. S. T. Nicholas, D.D., 917 Maryland Ave., N. E., Washington, D. C.

Mr. William H. Menges, Menges Mills, Pa.

Mr. Martin H. Buehler, 1327 Glenn Street, Glenns Falls, N. Y.

Mr. Charles Dahmer, 5th Avenue Bank, 44th St. and 5th Ave., New York, N. Y.

TERMS EXPIRE IN 1934

Rev. J. E. Byers, D.D., 2900 Guilford Ave., Baltimore, Md.

Rev. George Greiss, D.D., 38 S. 8th Street, Allentown, Pa.

Rev. H. C. Brillhart, D.D., 19 Spruce Street, Leetonia, Ohio.

Rev. E. R. Jaxheimer, 8068 87th Road, Woodhaven, N. Y.

Mr. Paul Van Reed Miller, 642 Widener Bldg., Philadelphia, Pa.

Mr. A. Y. Leech, Jr., 1731 "K" Street, N. W., Washington, D. C.
Mr. W. A. Rast, Cameron, S. C.

CO-OPERATING MEMBERS
REPRESENTING THE AUGUSTANA SYNOD
Rev. L. G. Abrahamson, D.D., 3449 7th Street, Rock Island, Ill.
Rev. G. A. Brandelle, D.D., 708 21st Street, Rock Island, Ill.

REPRESENTING THE UNITED DANISH CHURCH
Rev. J. P. Nielsen, Dana College, Blair, Nebr.
Rev. I. M. Andersen, 6533 22d Ave., Kenosha, Wis.

ADVISORY MEMBERS
REPRESENTING THE WOMEN'S MISSIONARY SOCIETY
Mrs. W. F. Morehead, 151 High Street, Salem, Va.
Mrs. S. R. Kepner, 122 3d Street, Pottstown, Pa.

NOMINATIONS
When the foreign mission boards of the three general bodies were
merged to form the Board of Foreign Missions of the United Lutheran
Church one group was elected for six years and then re-elected for a
similar term. Those who thus have served the longest and who are not
eligible for re-election are Rev. Prof. Benze, D.D., who has served as
President of the Board since 1926 and before that back to the merger year
as vice-president, and whose continuous service as a member of the Board
goes back twenty-one years; Rev. R. C. G. Bielinski, who has been a
member of the Board of Missions for twenty-nine years, since 1901;
Mr. James M. Snyder, who also has served for twenty-nine years, who
has been the chairman of the Board's finance committee since its reorganization two years ago and who served both as recording secretary and
treasurer of the General Council's Board; and Prof. C. W. Foss, Ph.D.,
who has been the elected representative of the Augustana Synod. The
other members whose terms expire but who are eligible for re-election are
Rev. J. L. Morgan, D.D., Rev. H. W. Snyder, D.D., and Rev. G. Albert
Getty, D.D.

The Board now makes the following nominations for the election of
members whose terms are to expire in 1936:

Rev. J. L. Morgan, D.D., President of the North Carolina Synod,
Salisbury, N. C.

Rev. H. W. Snyder, D.D., member of the Maryland Synod, Washington,
D. C.

Rev. G. Albert Getty, D.D., member of the West Pennsylvania Synod,
York, Pa.

Rev. Prof. E. E. Fischer, D.D., member of the Ministerium of Pennsylvania, Theological Seminary, Philadelphia, Pa.

Rev. Clarence M. Snyder, member of the Ministerium of Pennsylvania, Norristown, Pa.

Mr. H. Torrey Walker, Ministerium of Pennsylvania, West Collings-wood, N. J.

Rev. Oscar A. Benson, nominated on recommendation of the Augustana Synod, 224 South Street, Ridgway, Pa.

THE DEATH OF DR. JOHN EDWARD BYERS

The Board of Foreign Missions of the United Lutheran Church in America enters the following minute in memory of the Rev. John Edward Byers, D.D., pastor of Grace Lutheran Church, Baltimore, Md., and honored Vice-President of the Board, elected 1928. He was a member of the General Synod Board of Foreign Missions, and then of the first elected Board of Foreign Missions of the United Lutheran Church. He departed this life on Sunday, July 20th, in the Union Memorial Hospital, Baltimore, where he had undergone a serious operation.

Dr. Byers, who combined in a singularly happy combination the virtues which are to be found in a gracious and unselfish personality; the gifts which are evidenced in a sympathetic and untiring pastor; the wisdom and experience of a born administrator and executive; and the blessings of a devoted and self-sacrificing servant of our Lord Jesus and His Kingdom, has left a vacancy in our list of friends, of faithful ministers, of the Board members and dedicated servants of our Lutheran Church, which will be difficult to fill.

We herewith record our deep regard for him as a beloved brother, and efficient workman of his Master; as an unusually able and intelligent member of the Board of Foreign Missions, the objectives of which were most precious to his consecrated understanding, and were centered in his prayer life.

The Board would offer to his bereaved family its Christian sympathy and would enter with them into the rich heritage of faith in his Lord, zeal for the Church and of an abundance of good works which were the wealth of this good minister of Jesus Christ.

LYDIA WOERNER

The Board of Foreign Missions enters the following minute in memory of Lydia Woerner. M.D., who was born on September 28, 1860, and died at Interlaken, Florida, on July 3, 1930. She devoted thirteen years to medical work at Rajahmundry, India, and the hospital for women and children in that city is the abiding monument of her ability and zeal as a medical missionary.

ANNA S. KUGLER

The Board of Foreign Missions enters the following minute in memory of Anna S. Kugler, M.D., born April 19, 1856, who died of pernicious anemia in the hospital at Guntur on July 26, 1930. She went to India in 1883 and served at Guntur for over forty-six years as a medical missionary. The mission hospital at Guntur is the creation of her devoted service and the enduring monument of her missionary achievement. The Board of Foreign Missions and the Church, whose missionary she was, honor her memory by this expression of appreciation for the eminent services she rendered, the value of her Christian life, the achievements of her missionary efforts and the strength and beauty of her loving, loyal devotion to Him Who gave her and all of us His great commission to disciple all nations.

RECOMMENDATIONS

The Board of Foreign Missions bows in deep gratitude before the Divine Head of the Church, acknowledges His favor in the past and prays that His blessing may continue to abide with this work and that the Church may be inspired with an increasing zeal to do the great task committed to it.

1. *Foreign Mission Season—Epiphany.*

Resolved, That the Board of Foreign Missions be permitted during the Epiphany Season of 1931 and 1932 to continue its appeal for offerings to cancel the remainder of the foreign mission debt, the conditions to be the same under which this authority was granted at the Erie Convention, namely, "that the appeal might be made to all congregations and individuals as well as to Sunday schools for offerings on Foreign Mission Day to cancel the indebtedness of the Board of Foreign Missions."

2. *Co-operating Synods.*

Resolved, That we express our deep appreciation to the Augustana Synod for its co-operation in India and to the United Danish Church and the Icelandic Synod for co-operation in Japan.

3. *Icelandic Representation.*

Resolved, That the Icelandic Synod be asked to appoint a representative as a co-operating member of the Board of Foreign Missions.

4. *Special Gifts.*

Resolved, That all congregations in addition to meeting their full apportionment be urged to make special foreign mission contributions for assigned purposes such as Foreign Missionaries, Parishes Abroad and Proteges.

5. *Japan.*

Resolved, That the proposed constitution of the Evangelical Lutheran

Church in Japan, the Special Agreement and the revised constitution of the mission in Japan, be approved.

6. Resolved, That the Board of Foreign Missions be permitted to append to its report a brief minute regarding the death of Dr. Anna S. Kugler and Dr. Lydia Woerner.

7. Resolved, That this convention hear the Rev. J. K. Linn and the Rev. S. O. Thorlaksson at such time as the convention may designate.

C. THEODORE BENZE, *President.*
GEORGE DRACH, *Recording Secretary.*
PAUL W. KOLLER, *Executive Secretary.*

REPORT OF THE TREASURER OF THE BOARD OF FOREIGN MISSIONS
BALANCE SHEET
June 30, 1930
ASSETS:

Cash in banks:

General	$ 85,459.06	
Investment fund	18,018.97	
		$103,478.03

Investments at book values, as annexed:
Bonds and stocks:

Free	$150,330.05		
Pledged as collateral to secure loans payable	93,343.76		
		243,673.81	
Local real estate, mortgages, ground rents, etc.		54,891.08	
Property located at Kodikanal, India		13,000.00	
			311,564.89
			$415,042.92

LIABILITIES:

Loans payable to Union Trust Company of Maryland, secured by b o n d s aggregating, at book values, $93,343.76	$ 70,000.00
	$345,042.92

FUNDS:

Trust funds	$185,558.21
Annuity funds	84,502.81
Andhra Christian College fund	239,844.48
Land and Building fund	40,280.60
Reformation Diamond Jubilee Advance fund	21,303.63
Kobe Equipment fund	5,898.40
Pohlman fund	1,600.00
China Hospital fund	1,000.00
China Famine Relief fund	344.66
Luther League Educational Building fund	18.00
J. M. Armbruster fund	105.22

J. C. Finefrock Automobile fund...................................... 80.00
Women's Missionary Society fund.............................. 18,991.39

                                                           $599,527.40
    Less, General fund overdraft 254,484.48
                                                                            $345,042.92

Note.—The above balance sheet does not include:
    Liabilities incurred in the purchase of properties in foreign mission
    fields not definitely ascertainable at June 30, 1930, but known to
    exceed $91,000, or
    Any investment in such properties (other than that located at Kodi-
    kanal, India) the value of which is also unknown at this date.

BALANCE SHEET
June 30, 1929
Assets:

Cash in banks:
    General ....$ 54,530.52
    Investment fund 300.00
                                                                            $ 54,830.52

Investments at book values:
    Bonds and stocks:
        Free ....$ 79,614.00
        Pledged as collateral to secure
            loans payable 129,814.81
                                                           $209,428.81
    Local real estate, mortgages, ground rent, etc..... 50,591.08
    Property located at Kodikanal, India.................... 13,000.00
                                                                       273,019.89

                                                                       $327,850.41

Liabilities:

Loans payable to the National Bank of Baltimore:
    Secured by bonds aggregating, at b o o k values,
        $129,814.81 ....$115,000.00
    Unsecured 45,000.00
                                                                       160,000.00

                                                                       $167,850.41

Funds:

Trust funds $172,922.77
Annuity funds 68,402.81
Andhra Christian College fund 226,241.48
Land and Building fund 28,689.11
Reformation Diamond Jubilee Advance fund............ 27,224.63
Kobe Equipment fund 6,144.98
Pohlman fund 1,400.00
Nagoya fund 2,178.18

China Famine Relief fund	....	153.67
Luther League Educational Building fund	....	18.00
J. M. Armbruster fund	....	448.85
Susan K. Chester fund	....	351.51
J. C. Finefrock Automobile fund	....	80.00

$534,255.99

Less: General fund overdraft............$365,458.57
      Women's Missionary Society
        fund overdraft 947.01
                            366,405.58
                                      $167,850.41

Note.—The above balance sheet does not include:
    Liabilities incurred in the purchase of properties in foreign mission fields not definitely ascertainable at June 30, 1929, but known to exceed $105,000, or any investment in such properties (other than that located at Kodikanal, India) the value of which is also unknown at this date.

RECEIPTS AND DISBURSEMENTS
For the year ended June 30, 1930
RECEIPTS

	General Fund	Women's Missionary Society Fund	Other Funds
United Church on apportionment............	$432,000.00		
Women's Missionary Society		$247,185.40	
Augustana Synod	14,645.00		
Danish Synod	9,452.40		
Icelandic Synod	1,200.00		
Luther League of America.....................	12,500.00		
Donations received through board treasurer and general treasurer for general fund current work	119,178.47		
Bequests			$ 34,980.90
Donations for specific funds...................			27,619.43
Annuities			16,100.00
Interest on investments	7,938.21		5,443.15
"The Foreign Missionary," and "Der Missionsbote"	4,116.37		
Rental of slides	304.70		
Rental of properties	80.00		
Profit on sales of bonds	127.50		
Total fund receipts for current work	$601,542.65	$247,185.40	$ 84,143.48
Donations for board's debt.....................	92,269.05		
	$693,811.70	$247,185.40	$ 84,143.48
Total fund receipts		$1,025,140.58	
Investments sold		13,087.50	
Bank loans received		15,000.00	
Total receipts		$1,053,228.08	

Less, investments at par or face value included in receipts 20,220.00

Total cash receipts $1,033,008.08

DISBURSEMENTS

	General Fund	Women's Missionary Society Fund	Other Funds
Budgets paid to missions	$312,669.36	$122,767.05	
Specials paid to missions	8,031.14	27,948.58	
Salaries of missionaries	123,236.61	59,865.70	
Traveling expenses of missionaries to and from fields	37,844.66	12,731.56	
Expenses of missionaries in training and on furlough	10,063.51	234.11	
Salaries of secretaries and treasurer....	23,499.96		
Salaries of clerks, stenographers, etc.	7,301.98		
Expenses of treasurer, secretaries and board representatives	4,401.71		
Expenses of candidates and students	2,213.46		
Outfit allowances for missionaries	1,000.00	200.00	
Special allowances and pensions	4,410.20		
Disbursements from specific funds			$ 37,713.46
Contributions to inter-mission organizations	3,278.03		
Partial payment on purchases of Shantung Mission		3,500.00	5,250.00
Partial payments on Buenos Aires property	5,026.91		
"The Foreign Missionary" and "Der Missionsbote"	5,441.31		
Annual report	1,415.85		
Expenses of slides	211.71		
Publicity	832.69		
Office supplies and expenses	2,492.36		
Telephone, telegraph and cables	922.23		
Postage and expressage	531.07		
General office expenses	396.28		
Audit expenses	500.00		
Expenses of local properties	1,016.01		
Interest on bank loans	8,485.67		
Annuities	5,602.11		
Total fund disbursements for current work	$570,824.82	$227,247.00	$ 42,963.46
Expenses of securing donations for Board's debt	6,912.79		
	$577,737.61	$227,247.00	$ 42,963.46
Total fund disbursements		$847,948.07	
Investments purchased		31,412.50	
Bank loans repaid		105,000.00	
Total cash disbursements		$984,360.57	

SUMMARY:

Fund receipts for current work	$601,542.65	$247,185.40	$ 84,143.48
Fund disbursements for current work	570,824.82	227,247.00	42,963.46
Excess of fund receipts for current work	$ 30,717.83	$ 19,938.40	$ 41,180.02

RECEIPTS AND DISBURSEMENTS
For the year ended June 30, 1929

RECEIPTS

	General Fund	Women's Missionary Society Fund	Other Funds
United Church on apportionment	$408,000.00		
Women's Missionary Society		$245,052.03	
Augustana Synod	9,714.72		
Danish Synod	10,030.84		
Icelandic Synod	1,000.00		
Donations received through board treasurer and general treasurer for general fund current work	113,645.59		
Bequests	650.00		$41,462.08
Donations for specific funds			21,176.77
Annuities			2,150.00
Interest on investments	6,769.19		4,978.47
"The Foreign Missionary"	1,771.30		
"Der Missionsbote"	1,474.77		
Rental of slides	169.85		
Rental of properties	558.00		
Profit on sales of bonds	1,157.50		
Total fund receipts for current work	$554,941.76	$245,052.03	$ 69,767.32
Donations for Board's debt	51,660.55		
	$606,602.31	$245,052.03	$ 69,767.32
Total fund receipts		$921,421.66	
Investments sold		15,302.50	
Bank loans received		15,000.00	
Total receipts		$951,724.16	
Less, bonds at par value included in receipts		1,350.00	
Total cash receipts		$950,374.16	

DISBURSEMENTS

	General Fund	Women's Missionary Society Fund	Other Funds
Budgets paid to missions	$340,872.55	$121,683.32	
Specials paid to missions	6,507.66	46,364.99	
Salaries of missionaries	135,467.93	58,926.79	
Traveling expenses of missionaries to and from fields	42,670.57	12,214.46	

Expenses of missionaries on furlough....	13,024.08	204.46	
Salaries of secretaries and treasurer........	17,349.98		
Salaries of clerks, stenographers, etc....	6,624.64		
Expenses of treasurer, secretaries and Board representatives	5,601.48		
Expenses of candidates and students........	5,637.54		
Outfit allowances for missionaries	1,600.00	800.00	
Special allowances and pensions................	4,514.22		
Disbursements from specific funds..........			$ 24,107.81
Contributions to inter-mission organizations	3,030.00	500.00	
Partial payment on purchases of Shantung Mission	875.00	3,500.00	8,750.00
Partial payment on Buenos Aires property	2,964.08		
"The Foreign Missionary"	3,227.97		
"Der Missionsbote"	2,409.00		
Expenses of slides	205.16		
Publicity	832.51		
Office supplies and expenses	2,487.06		
Telephone, telegraph and cables............	649.85		
Postage and expressage	604.05		
General office expenses	817.33		
Legal and audit expenses	2,125.00		74.81
Expenses of local properties	1,667.49		
Interest on bank loans	12,529.56		
Annuities	4,403.10		
Total fund disbursements for current work	$618,697.81	$244,194.02	$ 32,932.62
Expenses of securing donations for Board's debt	2,095.76		
	$620,793.57	$244,194.02	$ 32,932.62
Total fund disbursements......................		$897,920.21	
Investments purchased		22,413.50	
Bank loans repaid		31,500.00	
Total cash disbursements		$951,833.71	

SUMMARY:

Fund receipts for current work............	$554,941.76	$245,052.03	$ 69,767.32
Fund disbursements for current work	618,697.81	244,194.02	32,932.62
Excess or deficiency of fund receipts for current work	$ 63,756.05	$ 858.01	$ 36,834.70

RECONCILEMENT OF ACCOUNTS
For the year ended June 30, 1930

	Balances, June 30, 1929	Receipts	Disbursements	Transfers	Balances, June 30, 1930
ASSETS:					
Cash	$ 54,830.52	$1,033,008.08 / 13,087.50	$984,360.57 / 31,412.50		$103,478.03
Investments	273,019.89	*20,220.00			311,564.89
	$327,850.41	$1,040,140.58	$952,948.07		$415,042.92
LIABILITIES:					
Loans payable to bank	160,000.00	15,000.00	105,000.00		70,000.00
	$167,850.41	$1,025,140.58	$847,948.07		$345,042.92
FUNDS:					
Trust funds	$172,922.77	$ 12,635.44			$185,558.21
Annuity funds	68,402.81	16,100.00			84,502.81
Andhra Christian College fund	226,241.48	16,108.42	$ 7,605.42	$ 5,100.00	239,844.48
Land and Building fund	28,689.11	29,320.19	16,881.88	846.82	40,280.60
Reformation Diamond Jubilee fund	27,224.63	1,354.67	7,275.67		21,303.63
Kobe Equipment fund	6,144.98	1,253.42	1,500.00		5,898.40
Pohlman fund	1,400.00	200.00			1,600.00
China Hospital fund		1,000.00			1,000.00
Nagoya fund	2,178.18	1,850.00	4,875.00	846.82	
China Famine Relief fund	153.67	1,065.39	874.40		344.66
Luther League Educational Building fund	18.00				18.00
Susan K. Chester fund	351.51		351.51		
J. M. Armbruster fund	448.85	3,255.95	3,599.58		105.22
J. C. Finefrock Automobile fund	80.00				80.00
Women's Missionary Society fund (overdraft)	947.01	247,185.40	227,247.00		18,991.39
General fund (overdraft)	365,458.57	693,811.70	577,737.61	5,100.00	254,484.48
	$167,850.41	$1,025,140.58	$847,948.07		$345,042.92

* Represents par or face value of investments received as contributions.

RECONCILEMENT OF ACCOUNTS
For the year ended June 30, 1929

	Balances, June 30, 1928	Receipts	Disbursements	Transfers	Balances, June 30, 1929
ASSETS:					
Cash	$ 56,290.07	$ 950,374.16 / 15,302.50 / *1,350.00	$951,833.71		$ 54,830.52
Investments	264,558.89		22,413.50		273,019.89
	$320,848.96	$ 936,421.66	$929,420.21		$327,850.41
LIABILITIES					
Loans payable to bank	176,500.00	15,000.00	31,500.00		160,000.00
	$144,348.96	$ 921,421.66	$897,920.21		$167,850.41
FUNDS:					
Trust funds	$158,742.63	$ 13,180.14		$ 1,000.00	$172,922.77
Annuity funds	67,752.81	2,150.00		1,500.00	68,402.81
Andhra Christian College fund	208,187.12	16,704.36		4,800.00	226,241.48
Reformation Diamond Jubilee fund	33,569.16	1,464.00	$3,450.00		27,224.63
Kobe Equipment fund	13,581.80	4,563.18	7,808.53		6,144.98
India Industrial fund	797.52		12,000.00	47.52	
Pohlman fund	1,400.00		750.00		1,400.00
Land and Building fund	8,681.98	28,831.94	8,824.81		28,689.11
Nagoya fund		2,178.18			2,178.18
China Famine Relief fund		153.67			153.67
Luther League Educational Building fund	104.28	13.00	99.28		18.00
Susan K. Chester fund	351.51				351.51
J. M. Armbruster fund		448.85			448.85
J. C. Finefrock Automobile fund		80.00			80.00
Women's Missionary Society fund (overdraft)	1,805.02	245,052.03	244,194.02	11,972.67	947.01
Foreign Missions forward fund (overdraft)	11,972.67			11,972.67	
General fund (overdraft)	335,042.16	606,602.31	620,793.57	16,225.15	365,458.57
	$144,348.96	$ 921,421.66	$897,920.21		$167,850.41

* Represents $1,350 U. S. Fourth Liberty Loan 4¼'s received as contributions.

INVESTMENTS, June 30, 1930

Bonds:		Book Values
$1,500	Altoona and Logan Valley Elec. Ry. 4½s, 1933..............$	1,500.00
3,000	American and Foreign Power Co. Inc. Deb. 5s, 2030........	2,692.50
1,000	American Utilities Co. 6s, 1945, Series "A"....................	1,000.00
6,000	Associated Electric Co. 4½s, 1953.....................	5,655.00
5,000	Atlantic Coast Line 4s, 1952 (L. and N. Div.)...................	4,293.75
4,000	Baltimore and Ohio R. R. Co. 1-4s, 1948....................	3,050.00
3,000	Baltimore and Ohio R. R. Co. equip. 4½s, 1940 "D"......	2,969.40
2,000	Baltimore and Ohio R. R. Co., S. W. Div., 5s, 1950........	1,985.00
4,000	Bonded Mortgage Co. of Baltimore 5½s, 1936, Series "E"	3,856.00
3,620	British Guiana Government (Church Endowment) 5s, 1946	3,620.00
500	Center Court Apartment, S. F., 1-6s, 1936.	500.00
8,000	City of Baltimore, New Sewerage Imp., 4s, 1961............	7,200.00
4,000	Central Illinois Public Service Co., 1-4½s, 1967............	3,790.00
2,000	Central Indiana Gas Co. 1-5s, 1931......................	2,000.00
1,000	Central Indiana Power Co. 1-6s, 1947....................	1,000.00
5,000	Central States Electric Corp. Conv. Deb. 5s, 1948............	4,825.00
1,000	Cespedes Sugar Co. 1-7½s, 1939......................	1,000.00
2,000	Chesapeake Mortgage Co. 6s, 1931, Series "C".............	2,000.00
4,000	Chesapeake and Ohio Rwy. Ref. and Imp. 4½s, 1995 Series "B"......................	3,760.00
2,000	Consolidated Cities Lt., Pwr. and Trac. Co. 1-5s, 1962....	1,659.90
2,000	Continental Bond and Investment Co., 6s, 1936, Series "A"	2,000.00
3,000	Continental Mortgage Co. of Baltimore 1st Mtge. Coll. Tr. 1-6s, 1931, Series "A"	3,000.00
3,000	Kingdom of Denmark 5½s, 1955.......................	2,985.00
1,000	Detroit Edison Co. 5s, 1933.........................	1,000.00
3,000	Duquesne Gas Corp. 1-6s, 1945......................	2,925.00
1,000	Edison Electric Co. 1-5s, 1943.......................	1,000.00
3,000	Electric Power and Light Corp. Deb. 5s, 2030............	2,790.00
2,500	Elec. and Peoples Trac. Stock Trust Ctfs. 4s, 1945............	2,500.00
1,000	Elk Horn Coal Corp. Deb. 7s, 1931....................	1,000.00
1,000	Erie Electric Motor Co. 1-5s, 1941....................	1,000.00
1,500	Federal Mortgage Co. 6s, 1940, Series "J"..............	1,500.00
2,000	Federal Mortgage Co. 6s, 1935, Series "J"..............	2,000.00
5,000	Federated Utilities, Inc., 1-5½s, 1957....................	4,737.50
5,000	Florida East Coast Ry. Co. 1-4½s, 1959....................	3,950.00
4,000	Florida Power and Light Co. 1-5s, 1954....................	3,814.00
3,000	No. 40 Wall Street Corp. 1-6s, 1958.....................	2,940.00
4,500	Hughesville School Assn. 1-5s, 1966.....................	4,500.00
5,000	Illinois Central R. R. Co. 4¾s, 1966.....................	4,825.00
2,000	Illinois Power and Light Corp. 5s, 1956....................	1,960.00
2,000	Indiana Ice and Fuel Co. 1-6½s, 1947....................	2,000.00
4,000	Interstate Power Co. 5s, 1957.......................	3,900.00
1,000	Johnstown Passenger Ry. Co. 4s, 1931....................	1,000.00
1,000	Lehigh Valley R. R. Co. 4s, 2003.....................	1,000.00
19,000	Maryland Electric Ry. Co. 1-5s, 1931....................	19,000.00
4,000	Mechanics Investment Trust 1-5½s, 1938....................	4,000.00
6,000	Medical Arts Building 5s, 1938........................	6,000.00
5,000	National Capital Mortgage Co. } Sixteenth St. 1-6s, 1939... Highlands of Maryland, Inc. }	5,000.00
500	Nassau and Suffolk Lighting Co. 1-5s, 1945....................	500.00

5,000	National Union Mortgage Co. 6s, 1931	5,000.00
5,000	National Union Mortgage Co. 6s, 1936	5,000.00
1,000	North Carolina Gas Co. 1-6s, 1948	970.00
1,000	Oklahoma Ry. Co. 1st and Ref. 5s, 1941	1,000.00
5,000	Penn Central Light and Power Co. 4½s, 1977	4,725.00
4,000	Peoples Light and Power Corp. 1-5½s, 1941	3,880.00
3,000	Phila. Co. secured 5s, 1967, Series "A"	3,032.25
1,400	Phila. Elect. Co. 1st S. F. 5s, 1966	1,400.00
1,000	Phila. Suburban Gas and Elec. Co. 1st and Ref. 5s, 1960	1,000.00
8,000	Potomac Mtge. Co. 1-6s, 1935	8,000.00
1,000	Quaker City Tank Line, Inc. Equip. Trust 5½s, 1930	1,000.00
2,000	Rawson Realty and Construction Co., Inc., Boston Postal Service Station 1-5½s, 1938	2,000.00
1,000	St. Louis County Gas Co. 1-5s, 1951	1,000.00
1,000	Scranton Ry. Co. 1st Cons. Mtge. 5s, 1932	1,000.00
4,000	Seaboard Air Line 1-4s, 1950	3,392.61
3,000	Seaboard Air Line R. R., Seaboard and Roanoke, 1st Extended 5s, 1931	3,022.50
1,000	No. 79 Madison Avenue Corp. 1-6s, 1937	1,000.00
3,000	Southern Pacific Co. 4½s, 1968	2,992.50
4,000	S. W. Missouri R. R. Co. Genl. and Ref. 5s, 1931	4,080.00
1,500	Standard Power and Light Co. 6s, 1957	1,492.50
3,000	The Sun Mortgage Co. 1-5½s, 1932, Registered, Series "AA"	3,000.00
2,000	Texarkana and Fort Smith Ry. Co. 1-5½s, 1950, Series "A"	2,010.00
1,000	Tri City Ry. and Lt. Co. 1st and Ref. 5s, 1930	1,000.00
8,000	United Rys. and Elec. Co. of Baltimore 4s, 1949	5,760.00
1,000	United Rys. and Elec. Co. of Baltimore Funding 5s, 1936	1,000.00
1,600	U. S. First Liberty Loan Conv. 4¼s, 1932-1947	1,600
16,450	U. S. Fourth Liberty Loan 4¼s, 1933-1938	15,013.40
2,000	West Penn Rys. Co. 1-5s, 1931	2,000.00

$237,553.81

Stocks:

30 Shares Mutual Bldg. and Loan Assn. of Baltimore City, par $100	$ 3,000.00
24 Shares West Baltimore Bldg. Assn. of Baltimore, par $130	3,120.00

$ 6,120.00

Book
Values

Real estate, mortgages, ground rents, and notes:

Ground rents on properties at 920, 924, 1040 and 1042 W. Fayette St., Baltimore, Md.	$ 4,959.88
Mortgage on 2511 N. Calvert St., Baltimore, Md., at 5 per cent	5,000.00
Mortgage on 5716 Hegerman St., Philadelphia, Penna., at 6 per cent	2,500.00
Mortgage on 5849 Coleman St., Philadelphia, Penna., at 6 per cent	4,500.00
Mortgage on 1019 S. Randolph St., Philadelphia, Penna., at 6 per cent	1,500.00
Note of L. B. Wolf and Alice B. Wolf, due June 29, 1929, at 5 per cent	5,000.00

Notes of Charles R. Fisher, guaranteed by C. B. Morehead, at
  6 per cent:
      Due September 10, 1928 (extended indefinitely) $2,250.00
      Due September 10, 1929.. 2,215.00
      Due September 10, 1930... 715.00

                                                                   5,180.00
Note of Mrs. W. J. Harper (now Mrs. Hattie K. Hogg), due
  December 31, 1921, at 8 per cent.. 1,000.00
Property at 18 E. Mt. Vernon Place, Baltimore, Md.................... 16,000.00
Equity in property at 2900 E. Woodland Ave. Baltimore, Md........ 9,251.20

                                                        $ 54,891.08

Property located at Kodikanal, India..$ 13,000.00

SUMMARY:

Bonds $237,553.81
Stocks 6,120.00

                                                        $243,673.81
Real estate, mortgages, ground rents and notes....................... 54,891.08
Property located at Kodikanal, India 13,000.00

    Total book values ....:...$311,564.89

Respectfully submitted,
GEORGE R. WEITZEL, *Treasurer.*

Baltimore, Md., July 15, 1930.
  We have audited the accounts of the Board of Foreign Missions of the
United Lutheran Church in America for the two years ended June 30, 1930,
and we certify that, in our opinion, the foregoing statements submitted by
its treasurer are correct.
LYBRAND, ROSS BROS. & MONTGOMERY,
Accountants and Auditors.

    Mr. George R. Weitzel, Treasurer of the Board of Foreign
Missions, spoke in regard to the improved financial condition of
the Board.

    Secretary Koller then introduced the following missionaries:

From India:
                Rev. and Mrs. A. F. Schmitthenner
                Rev. and Mrs. C. H. Swavely
                Agnes Christensen
                Jessie Thomas
                Edith Eykamp
                Emilie Weiskotten
                Rev. L. L. Uhl (retired)

From Japan:
> Rev. John K. Linn
> Rev. S. O. Thorlaksson
> Rev. F. W. Heins
> Rev. D. G. M. Bach
> Faith Lippard
> Martha Akard
> Maude Powlas

From South America:
> Rev. Paul O. Machetzki
> Rev. R. H. Daube
> Corinne M. Menges

From Africa:
> Rev. David D. Dagle
> Dr. Norman Sloan
> Bertha Koenig
> K. Marie Jensen

From China:
> Rev. Theo. Scholz

New Missionaries to India:
> Jessie Cronk
> Christie Zimmerman

The Rev. Theo. Scholz brought greetings from China; the Rev. R. H. Daube from British Guiana; the Rev. David D. Dagle from Liberia; and Miss Emilie Weiskotten from India.

The President read a cablegram from Africa as follows:

"Convention United Lutheran Church,
 Schroeder Hotel,
 Milwaukee, Wis.

 "Greetings from Africa.   Council."

Dr. Benze then presented the recommendations of the Board.

The Convention, by a standing vote, joined in the expression of thanksgiving and prayer.

Recommendations 1, 2 and 3 adopted.

Recommendation 4 was adopted after the Rev. M. Edwin Thomas, Secretary for Special Gifts, had addressed the Convention upon the subject.

On motion to approve item 5 the Rev. George Drach, Recording Secretary of the Board, addressed the Convention.

Recommendation 5 approved.

Item IV, B, 2 (f) of the report of the Executive Board, concerning the proposed Constitution for the Japan Church, which item had been deferred, was adopted.

Recommendation 6 was adopted by a rising vote.

Recommendation 7 was adopted.

The report of the auditors was accepted.

Secretary Koller introduced the Rev. J. K. Linn who read a message from the Japan Mission and addressed the Convention.

He was followed by the Rev. S. O. Thorlaksson, the other representative from the Japan Mission in attendance upon this Convention.

At twelve o'clock the Convention adjourned with prayer by the Rev. Charles S. Bream.

Afternoon Session

Friday, October 10, 1930, 2:00 o'clock.

Devotions were conducted by the Rev. David R. Huber.

The President called the Convention to order.

The Secretary reported on the Roll of Delegates as follows:

Number of delegates elected:

Clergymen: 277;   Laymen: 272;

Total: 549

Number of delegates in attendance:

Clergymen: 277;   Laymen: 255;

Total: 532

Twenty-five synods have 100 per cent attendance of their congregations.

All clergymen elected are present; 17 laymen are absent.

Two delegates from the Evangelical Lutheran Church in the Andhra Country, India, and one delegate from the Japan Mission and Church are present.

The report was received as information.

The Rev. J. A. Leas, Chairman of the Committee of Reference and Counsel, presented the following report:

1. We recommend that the Rev. L. L. Uhl, veteran missionary, be allowed five minutes to speak in connection with the report of the Committee on Lutheran Brotherhoods on Saturday morning.

2. We recommend that the committee on place of the next convention be given the privilege to report at once.

3. The following communication having come from Dr. C. H. Little, we recommend that the protest be entered on the Minutes. (Note: Constitution, Article VIII, Section 5).

"To the United Lutheran Church in Convention assembled:

"As a matter of conscience I desire to enter protest against the action of the convention yesterday in including malicious desertion as a ground for divorce (and in adopting the preamble containing the exegetical reasoning on which this decision was reached) and I respectfully ask that my dissent be recorded in the printed minutes of this convention.

"Signed: C. H. LITTLE."

Milwaukee, Wis.
October 10, 1930.

4. We recommend that the Rev. Howard Gold be permitted to present certain resolutions relative to publicity work and that the resolutions be approved.

5. We recommend that President Haapanen of the Suomi Synod be heard at this time and that he be permitted to present his two associates, Dr. Wargelin, President of the Suomi College, and Missionary Superintendent, the Rev. J. F. Saarinen.

Recommendation 1 was adopted.

Recommendation 2 was adopted.

The Rev. E. P. Pfatteicher then presented the report of the committee on place of the next convention, as follows:

To the President and members of the United Lutheran Church in convention assembled:

Having been designated a committee to assemble and pass upon the various invitations extended to the United Lutheran Church for future conventions, we would respectfully report as follows:

Invitations have been received from Asbury Park, N. J.; La Crosse, Wis.; Nashville, Tenn.; Philadelphia, Pa.; and St. Louis, Mo., for 1932, and for Rochester, N. Y., and Savannah, Ga., for 1934.

Your committee in its recommendations for 1932 decided to eliminate La Crosse, Wisconsin, because that would impose an unjust burden on the Synod of the Northwest, which is so graciously entertaining us this year through the courtesy of its Milwaukee churches. Your committee decided to eliminate Asbury Park from consideration because of inadequate church facilities.

Having reduced the consideration of invitations to those from Nashville, Tenn., Philadelphia, Pa., and St. Louis, Mo., your committee heard representatives from these centers.

The plea of the representative from Nashville was heard after the reading of an invitation from Savannah, Ga., for 1934 because of the celebration in 1934 of the 200th anniversary of the arrival of the Saltzburgers. This latter important occasion, though no action was taken by your committee binding the United Lutheran Church for 1934, was in the minds of your committee in eliminating Nashville by way of recommendation for 1932.

The plea of the representatives from St. Louis was strong and urgent, it being the opinion of the local committee and the President of the Illinois Synod that Missouri could profitably both teach and learn in a closer contact with the United Lutheran Church. The committee, though deeply impressed by the representations made, was swayed in its final judgment by the fact that both Milwaukee and St. Louis are in the middle west. It expressed the hope that St. Louis would at some future time renew its invitation.

In deciding to recommend Philadelphia as the place in which the next convention is to be held, your committee was swayed by the following reasons :

(1)   The consistent, persistent and courteous manner in which Philadelphia has kept its door open in spite of the gale that has been blowing from the outside since the formation of the United Lutheran Church.

(2)   The fact that Philadelphia is not simply the cradle of Lutheranism but also a present day home and workshop of Lutheranism with important Inner Mission and Home Mission activities, the home of the Publication Board and of the Treasurer of the United Lutheran Church.

(3)   The fact that Philadelphia is ready to learn some of the things which the United Lutheran Church can teach it.

These considerations and others presented by representatives of the East Pennsylvania Synod and the Ministerium prompted your committee to recommend, first, that the 1932 convention be held in Philadelphia and second, that the convention of 1932 determine the place for the holding of the 1934 convention.

The report was adopted.

Recommendation 3 of the Committee of Reference and Counsel was unanimously adopted.

Recommendation 4 was adopted.

The Rev. Howard R. Gold offered the following resolutions :

Whereas the rapid secularization of life shows that the time has come for the organization of the Church for adequate and worthy publicity as a matter of educating the public in things for which the Church stands ; and

Whereas it is important to co-ordinate the publicity activities of the various synods, boards and auxiliaries of the United Lutheran Church with those of the United Lutheran Church itself; and

Whereas this need calls for the systemization of newspaper publicity and internal promotion on the part of the United Lutheran Church and of synods, boards and auxiliaries,

Therefore be it

Resolved, (1)   That we request The United Lutheran Church in America to authorize its Committee on Publicity to arrange for a "Conference on Church Publicity" by representatives of its constituent synods and of its boards and auxiliaries at as early a date as feasible and be it further

Resolved, (2)   That we request The United Lutheran Church in America to authorize its Publicity Committee to prepare and publish a practical "Publicity Manual" for distribution to its pastors; and be it finally

Resolved, (3)   That we request The United Lutheran Church in America to include in its budget for publicity an amount not exceeding $3,000 to finance these two projects.

Resolution 1 was adopted.

Resolution 2 was adopted.

Resolution 3 was referred to the Finance Committee of the Executive Board.

Recommendation 5 of the Committee of Reference and Counsel was adopted by unanimous consent.

Dr. A. Haapanen, President of the Suomi Synod, addressed the Convention and introduced Dr. J. Wargelin, President of the Suomi College, and the Rev. J. F. Saarinen, Missionary Superintendent of the Suomi Synod, each of whom addressed the Convention.

At the request of the President, the newly elected President of the Pittsburgh Synod, the Rev. Henry H. Bagger, responded to this address.

The Rev. J. Bradley Markward, President of the Board of American Missions, addressed the Convention; and the Rev. F. F. Fry, Executive Secretary, presented the report of the Board.

REPORT OF BOARD OF AMERICAN MISSIONS

The Board of American Missions has been doing big business in Kingdom building during another biennium.

It helped to establish 87 new missions—one for every eight days. A Church Extension loan was granted every two weeks.

These new missions are distributed through twenty Synods, and minister to different linguistic groups: English, German, Italian, Hungarian, Siebenbuerger, Slovak and Finnish.

Their contributions to congregational support and benevolences of the Church merit comment and commendation. They averaged $50 per confirmed member. The stress and strain of the times have not halted the progress of American Missions.

The Board entered the State of Arkansas and started its first mission at Fort Smith.

It administered $1,500,000 of the Church's mission funds, conscious of its obligation of stewardship.

It aids in the support of 603 mission congregations and 85 preaching points.

Work is done in 14 tongues: English, German, Siebenbuerger, Magyar, Slovak, Lettish Windish, Lithuanian, Italian, Finnish, Spanish, Danish, Cree, Yiddish. The Gospel is one; the languages are many .

More than 32,000 souls were added to our Home Mission congregations of the United Lutheran Church.

During this period 42 mission congregations assumed self-support; 6 were merged and 14 were discontinued.

Fewer mission congregations are vacant than at any previous time.

Humbly and gratefully the Board acknowledges the unfailing guidance of the Holy Spirit without which it could not have carried on.

HOME MISSIONS

The missionary enterprise is the thermometer of the Church. The acid test is its missionary passion. When the fires on the home altars burn brightly we know that the light is shining far and clear. If missionary enthusiasm is low, it is because the Church has lost its zeal.

The people of our churches can always be trusted to give generously to causes which command their interest and confidence. When the Church hears from the lips of missionary prophets the story of lives redeemed and sins forgiven through the power of the conquering Christ, there will be no lack of enthusiasm in money or life.

All missionary history is the story of heroic messengers who have brought the Gospel message to those to whom they were sent regardless of the hazards on the way. It is a story of high adventure, of partnership with God and the stewardship of life. It records steady advance from the lone pioneer in the days which tried men's souls. Although there is variety of methods, the purpose is always one, to get the message through. They helped to put the "angel" into evangelism. They did not shrink from the lonely task, the solitary road. They gloried in it.

With experience and the march of years has come enlarged vision of the significance and magnitude of Home Missions. It requires trained minds, broad sympathies and comprehensive outlook. It underscores Muhlenberg's motto, "Ecclesia plantanda." This involves individual as well as corporate responsibility.

Our Lord did not establish churches merely to provide centers of worship and religious training, important as these are. Every true church is a spiritual powerhouse. From it should radiate influences which establish the Kingdom of God in the hearts of men. So the Church from the beginning has been a missionary church. Its Founder was a missionary. Its spirit is missionary—giving, sending, sharing. Remove the missionary quality from the Church and you weaken its very life. Beginning at Jerusalem, it has reached unto the uttermost parts of the earth, ever seeking to proclaim the Christian message to all men.

THE AMERICAN CITY AND SUBURBS

The Church in America faces a new frontier which calls for the same devotion and consecration as were demanded by the frontier of old. This new frontier is "The American City and Its Suburbs." The recent federal census proclaims it from the housetops. Many American cities show growth in population of surprising dimensions and often in unexpected quarters.

The United States began as a rural nation; it has become an urban nation. Our rural parishes and their needs must not be neglected. No relaxation of effort dare be thought of in ministering to racial groups and underprivileged people. We must look well to our outposts. Above all confusing and conflicting appeals sounds the challenge of the cities and their suburbs.

The American city dominates the country and dictates its policies. It is therefore strategic. If the city is to control the Nation, Christianity must control the city. Here it is that religion is put to the test and has its greatest opportunities for permeating not only the city but through the city the entire Nation.

This is the question of the hour: Is Christianity sufficiently vital to maintain itself as a dominant factor in the great centers of population? Pleasure, profit, luxury, lust and a multitude of like powers and passions have eaten the heart of the Gospel challenge for sacrificial living and service. Men hear and heed every other call rather than the call of the Infinite.

The Church in America needs to re-emphasize the truth that the Gospel of Jesus is supreme and final. Many things have transpired to weaken this conviction and to slacken the step of the messengers.

The Gospel of Christ is still the power of God unto salvation to communities and individuals alike. Notable victories have been won. The cause of Christ has been advanced in America. Thanks to God, unceasing thanks, for what has been done. Churches and individuals have given liberally of their means. A few of us have attempted to administer the task, but the real work has been done by the Synods and the missionaries. What a group they are, counting it all joy to have a share in making America Christian.

PROGRAM OF AMERICAN MISSIONS

The program of the Board of America Missions is a varied one. It conducts schools, trains children in kindergartens, supports students in colleges and theological seminaries, establishes missions, builds churches, furnishes missionary pastors for preaching points and mission congregations. It does many things, but it does them all for one purpose, to bring men and women, boys and girls, under the dominion of Jesus Christ. That is the motif that runs through all the work. This is the final test of American Missions.

In reviewing the accomplishments of the biennium, we are vividly conscious that it is not by might nor by power but by the Spirit of God that these things have been and will be done. If we are to capture America for Christ, there must be a revival of prayer and consecration on the part of pastors and people.

No standard of measurement can compute the vibrant influence exerted by the United Lutheran Church in all parts of North America. Flaws, faults, imperfections are recognized clearly. Our ideals are far in advance of our limited achievements. The shining goal is at a distance, but we are heading toward it. If adequate means were forthcoming, we could do so much more that is in our hearts. Nevertheless we are quickening the conscience of America. We hold high the flaming torch of truth. We teach and proclaim the glorious Gospel of the blessed God. Only eternity can reveal the radiant light, the transforming power, the abiding inspiration under the guidance and blessing of the Spirit of God.

No Board of the Church can be successful in the full sense of the word unless all who are associated with it share in its record of progress. This Board is changing human lives, moulding personalities and multiplying witnesses in its endeavor to expand the Kingdom of Christ in America.

COMPREHENSIVE SURVEY

Study the map of North America and you will discover that certain fields have been overlooked and other fields overloaded with Lutheran Churches. The new policy aims to change this condition and distribute our forces and funds to greater advantage. The slogan of "more missions" is changed to "better missions."

The Survey Commission has dealt resolutely with duplication of effort and aims at the truest economy and use of the Church's funds. The conduct of Home Missions in co-operation with synodical initiative called for the formulation of principles and policy which has received the endorse-

ment of the Church. It involved a revision of methods and re-arrange-
ment of programs. It is the Board's firm conviction that the only
adequate basis for establishing a new mission is the need of more adequate evangelization of the community.

The salary schedule has been raised in many missions so that with
capable leadership and more modern equipment, a marked improvement
in results can be noted. All of the Synods have responded to the Board's
appeals with wholehearted co-operation. A balanced budget has been
maintained at all times.

LUTHERAN HOME MISSIONS COUNCIL OF AMERICA

The newest development in American Missions is the Lutheran Home
Missions Council of America. With the consent of the Executive Board,
an invitation was sent to five other Lutheran bodies belonging to the
National Lutheran Council to consider the possibility of fuller co-operation
in Home Missions. These various Lutheran bodies sent representatives
to the first meeting in Hotel Sherman, Chicago, March 27, 1930.

Our approach to comity prepared the way for the Articles of Agreement adopted without a dissenting vote at a later meeting in Edgewater
Beach Hotel, Chicago, July 2. These Articles of Agreement are as
follows:

1. The *name* of this organization shall be: LUTHERAN HOME
MISSIONS COUNCIL OF AMERICA.
2. The *object* of this organization shall be: Mutual encouragement and
edification in Home Mission work and methods; the study and survey
of Home Mission fields; the approval and adoption of principles according to which Home Mission fields may be occupied and worked without
duplication of effort and expense and without the practice of unfriendly
competition. The Council shall also offer its services as a body of arbitration in cases of controversy between any of the participating bodies
in matters connected with work in Home Mission fields. The powers
of the Council shall be advisory only.
3. Lutheran General bodies shall be entitled to elect the voting *membership* of this Council as follows: bodies with a confirmed membership
of 50,000 or less, two members; bodies with a confirmed membership of
100,000, three members; bodies with a confirmed membership of 200,000,
four members; bodies with a confirmed membership of more than 200,000,
one additional member for every additional 200,000 confirmed members,
as also for a remaining fraction thereof in excess of 100,000. Each duly
elected member of the Council shall be entitled to one vote. Members
of the Council shall be elected by the respective Home Mission Boards
or by the respective General bodies. Meetings shall be open, and the
privilege of the floor, but not the right to vote, may be extended to
visitors.
4. The *officers* of the Council shall be: a President, a Vice President,
a Secretary, a Treasurer. Their term of office shall be one year. Election of officers shall be by ballot. The duties of the officers shall be
those usually attaching to their respective offices.
5. Regular *meetings* of the Council shall be held annually, on the

fourth Tuesday of January. Special meeting may be called by the officers.

6. The officers of the Council shall constitute its *Executive Committee*. This committee shall arrange the programs of the annual meeting, and shall preform whatever other duties may be assigned to it by the Council.

7. In case of *controversy* involving Home Mission agencies of any two bodies represented in the Council, the president shall appoint a committee consisting of representatives of three bodies not directly involved in the controversy. This committee shall endeavor to effect a settlement satisfactory to both parties. Controversies to receive the attention of the Council must be presented in writing. When a Committee on Controversy reports failure of its efforts, the Council itself shall consider the case and shall render an advisory decision, with recommendations.

Our united aim is the cessation of competition and the dawn of a new day in American Missions. To find ways to co-operate in the conquest of a continent is the quest of the Lutheran Home Missions Council. Rivalry and competition discredit our standing in the eyes of the Church and the world. We need a better understanding in extending the Kingdom of our Lord in this western land. This applies to the planting of new missions and relocation of self-supporting congregations. Its powers are advisory and consultative, not legislative. The Lutheran Home Missions Council of America sounds the call for simplicity of organization, economy of operation, efficiency in service, adequate returns for the funds expended and harmony within Lutheran groups doing Home Mission work.

The Kingdom of God will certainly be established in America, but its coming will be sadly retarded if we are not wise enough, brave enough and resourceful enough to advance together in brotherly co-operation. We should chant in unison a stirring processional as we march forward to possess the land for Christ.

RELATIONSHIP TO SYNODS

The Board's record during the biennium has been encouraging in its relationship to the Synods. A new departure was introduced in lending men of the Staff to Synods for emergency work. Superintendent Hillerman gave considerable time to such calls from the Rocky Mountain and Pacific Synods. Superintendent Ludwig responded to similar calls from the Pittsburgh Synod, the Ministerium of Pennsylvania and the Canada Synod. Superintendent Hoffman has been giving his major attention to missions in Manhattan and Long Island in compliance with the request of the United Synod of New York. Here is a demonstration of active co-operation between Synods and the Board of American Missions.

Upon their own initiative, several Synods have discontinued the services of their Missionary Superintendent or Field Missionaries. Synodical presidents have assumed extra demands upon their time because of limited funds. Among them may be cited the Pacific Synod and the Indiana Synod.

THE STAFF

The Board welcomed to its Staff the Rev. Dr. Ernst A. Tappert as its first Divisional Secretary of Linguistic Interests. He brings to the work a wealth of experience and wisdom and an intimate knowledge of linguistic groups, their history, tradition and customs, which already are bearing fruit. He took charge of the Linguistic Department January 1, 1930, and was installed in St. John's Church, Christopher Street, New York City, January 16.

The Staff consists of an Executive Secretary, two Divisional Secretaries, three Superintendents of English Missions and a Superintendent of the German Department. Responsibility has been distributed so that definite spheres and tasks are assigned to each.

While there must be a check up on routine work, the chief emphasis is not on the statistical but the spiritual. The more the machinery of the Church can be mastered and kept in the background, and the more spiritual values are kept in the foreground, the more vital Christianity we can expect to produce. Unless this is the fruitage of all Church leadership, nothing else can matter much. While the men of the Staff are only human and their work is for people who are very human, something divine enters into the building and expansion of the Kingdom when the workers toil for God.

INTERNATIONAL MISSIONARY COUNCIL

The International Missionary Council is making plans to carry forward its responsibility in connection with work among the Jews. This responsibility was accepted by them at the Jerusalem meeting. It recognizes the necessity of obtaining the full time service of some well qualified man. Such a secretary would strengthen greatly the work of all the different churches as they are seeking to bring the Gospel to the Jews. The work must be international in scope, for the problems are much the same, and it is evident that whatever may be done in New York will have great influence upon such work in Eastern Europe.

Dr. John R. Mott, Chairman of the Council, approached Dr. A. C. Hoffman, of Geneva, Switzerland, to become Executive Secretary of the Council and he has accepted. He is a great favorite among students, and expects to take on this new work September 1, 1930.

One reason for the desirability of such a bureau here in America is found in the existence of so much sentiment among Christian denominations that missionary work among the Jews should be abandoned. Through this bureau also our work would be in touch with the vital Jewish Mission Work carried on in Europe. It is their conviction that something more than good will should exist between Jews and Christians. Missionary Henry Einspruch is now on an important committee since he represented the United Lutheran Church in America at the conference in Budapest and Warsaw.

Two hundred and fifty dollars was appropriated by the Board for one year. The Executive Secretary was elected as its representative.

DIVISION OF ENGLISH MISSIONS
DR. JOHN F. SEIBERT, *Divisional Secretary*

The United Lutheran Church has met upon Mission territory. It does not seem so long a time since the lamented Dr. Frick uttered the expression that has become classic. "The whole English Lutheran Church of Milwaukee went downtown under one umbrella." Yet within the memory of many of the delegates to this convention the English Lutheran Church of Milwaukee has expanded from Dr. Frick and his wife to twelve congregations numbering 6503 confirmed members, and instead of the "one umbrella" has a property value of $1,063,726, and each year contributes $56,957.00 for the benevolent operations of the church. The notable thing, brethren of the convention, is that this expansion was due to Home Missions. With but one or two exceptions every Church has received Home Mission aid. We trust you will look at Redeemer, Dr. Frick's mother church, Epiphany, Reformation, Lake Park, Ressurection, Incarnation, Washington Park, Redeemer, southside and Wauwatosa churches as notable illustrations of the fine work of the Home Mission Board. We then urge you to go to Pentecost, West Allis and Bay Shore to see the type of work that the Board is now doing.

Most of the delegates, too, in getting to Milwaukee, passed through Chicago, where upwards of sixty churches have received Home Mission aid and many of them have developed into strong congregations. Then, too, look at Racine, where they have just entertained the Women's Missionary Society, and at Kenosha, where the mother church, itself a product of Home Missions, has so splendidly been fostering the mission recently organized and you will see visible demonstrations of some Class A missions and will be encouraged to continue in the great work of making America Christian.

NEW MISSIONS AND SELF-SUPPORTING CONGREGATIONS

We have prepared a table showing the exact mission situation in each of the twenty-nine Synods through which the Division operates. From this report it will be seen that thirty-four missions were organized and that thirty-three congregations became self-supporting. Each one of the new missions seems to have been organized only after careful consideration by the Synodical authorities involved, and all give promise of developing into strength. A few illustrations will suffice. We are particularly happy to report that through the organization at Fort Smith, by Superintendent McConnell, we were able to enter the great State of

Arkansas, and where through the merger of two congregations we have been permitted to secure a property easily worth $25,000 for the modest sum of $8,300.

At Westwood, Elmwood Park, Field Missionary Gerberding has been permitted to witness one of the finest demonstrations of Home Mission progress, having been successful, through the Board's Church Extension loan, the Synod of Illinois' fine co-operation and through personal gifts in securing the choicest location and in erecting a beautiful chapel and parsonage. This mission will be supported by Christ Church, Rev. Geo. P. Lottich, pastor, itself a former Mission of the Women's Missionary Society. We wish some of the convention could visit this plant. We are sure you would get a new vision of Home Missions. At Bayshore, this city, Field Missionary Baughman has gathered a congregation of a hundred representative people, and has erected a church building that is a model for young mission congregations.

Field Missionary Strobel, of Toledo, Ohio, in harmony with a well developed plan, has organized a congregation in the choicest section of that city of United Lutheran Churches. At St. Louis Park, Minneapolis, Field Missionary Shellhart organized a church that numbers nearly a hundred members and that gives promise of developing into a splendid congregation. Superintendent Myers is very happy at the organization of Mt. Calvary, Erie, and takes delight in showing it as a Class A Mission. For the detailed statement of new missions, we refer to Appendix A, and we invite your earnest attention to the splendid list of missions that now have joined the ranks of self-supporting congregations as found in Appendix B.

New Church Buildings

The biennium has been an era marked by the erection of good church buildings. However, we hesitate to speak of these for somehow the feeling seems to have spread that congregations cannot prosper as they ought without fine churches, and that they occasionally make the mistake of building beyond their ability to the sorrow of the congregation and of the Board also. St. Stephen's, Chicago; Calvary, Louisville; Barnitz Memorial in Denver, and Trinity, Boulder, Colo.; Westwood, Elmwood Park; Phoenix, Arizona; Trinity, Kalamazoo, Mich.; Olivet, Detroit; West Palm Beach, Florida; Incarnation, Washington, D. C.; St. John's, Rutherford, N. J., and others, some of them after years of effort, now have buildings that are a credit to our church.

Accessions

The accessions have been surprisingly large. The percentage for the biennium has been twenty-six. Thus the goal of ten per cent per year has been more than reached. You can count on our mission churches. Look at the record: East Pennsylvania Synod, twenty-six per cent; Illinois, thirty; Maryland, thirty-nine; Michigan, thirty-two; Ministerium of Pennsylvania, twenty-three; Northwest, thirty-two; Ohio, forty-seven; Pittsburgh, twenty-five, and United Synod of New York, thirty-one. A total of 16,520 adults were received into membership. The losses were 5,266. A net gain therefore of 11,352 to the confirmed membership of the Church. All honor to our faithful missionaries for so creditable a record.

THEY PAY TOO

According to the Statistical Secretary, the per capita giving for 1926, the highest year since the merger, was $23.31 for the entire United Lutheran Church. The per capita of our mission congregations, as shown by our table, for the biennium was $69.15 or $34.57 per annum. The significance of these figures becomes apparent when it is recalled that should the entire Church do as well for one biennium the Boards would have no indebtedness, the Pension Fund could be paid up in full, and the Campaign for Endowment for Colleges and Seminaries would reach one hundred per cent. It is startling but it is true. We hope this truth will register. The average church member does not appreciate how the Mission Churches must give to secure property and pay current expenses. They lead the churches. Instead of criticizing them, let us emulate them! All honor to them!

REPORT OF SURVEY COMMITTEE

The Survey Committee literally has devoted days to a consideration of our missions. They were considered and discussed from every possible angle. All the information from the applications, the reports, and from the Staff in the field was used. As a result, they formulated four general principles that were unanimously adopted by the Board for its guidance. They have been sympathetically considered and adopted by many Synods. They are:

1. We recommend that the Board adopt, and recommend to the Synodical Home Mission Boards for their consideration the principle that the only adequate justification for the establishment of a mission is the urgent need for an adequate evangelization of the community concerned.

2. We recommend that the Board adopt and commend to the Synodical Home Mission Boards for consideration the principle that the measure of success for home mission work by Boards, Secretaries or Synods, should never be the number of missions established or supported, but the extent to which an increasing service is rendered by the missions established to the work of Christ at home and abroad.

3. We recommend that the Board request the several Synods to make a comprehensive survey and careful study of the Home Missions within their jurisdiction, with a view to relieving the Board of American Missions of the continued support of those Missions that give little or no hope of progress or which seem to be filling no pressing need; and that within a reasonable time appropriations for such Missions be discontinued, and

that the funds so released be devoted to more promising Mission enterprises.

4. We recommend to the Board for its adoption as an educational principle that with the universal use of the automobile and the promise of ever-improving transportation facilities in twentieth-century America, churches may be expected to serve successfully areas many times as large as in former periods, thus encouraging larger congregations, less overhead to our members per capita for current support and more funds released for benevolence, and greater efficiency generally.

You will notice that in harmony with the report of this committee, the Synods have been carefully reviewing the missions on their territory with the result that fifteen missions have been withdrawn from the budget. The practice of comity was put into effect before the Home Missions Council was organized. Thus at Ottumwa, Iowa, our mission was closed and practically our entire membership was received into the Augustana Synod Church, the Rev. P. O. Bersell, pastor. At Astoria, Washington, the Augustana Synod and the United Lutheran Church were conducting missions that, with the language question being practically settled, were really competitive. The Augustana Synod has a modern hospital at Astoria, and after conference it was decided that the United Lutheran Church should withdraw and recommended that our membership unite with that Church. At Williston, N. D., the Northwest Synod recommended that we withdraw and use its offices to have the membership unite with the Norwegian Church. At Fordson, Michigan, there was an Independent Church organized by the Missouri Synod, that with its pastor came into the Michigan Synod and that rendered it unnecessary for us to continue the mission that had been served by Field Missionary Lentz. At Salinas, California, the discontinuance of the mission resulted in the sale of the property, the money being used to splendid advantage in strengthening another mission. At Fairbanks, Alaska, a number of the prominent charter members had left the territory, and when the Divisional Secretary visited the field, with President Frederick of the Pacific Synod, it was felt best to discontinue the work, and the young man taken with them, to be the missionary pastor, was brought back to the States and placed in another mission. In several instances the missions were found to be of the self-sustentation order, and were taken over by the Synods. Some further work along this line will probably have to be done to get our roster of missions up to date. For a complete list of congregations discontinued from the budget see Appendix C.

CHURCH EXTENSION FUNDS NEEDED

Our chief difficulty is to secure sufficient Church Extension Funds to provide the buildings for the new missions that can be organized. The United Synod of New York, for example, has approximately fifteen missions that are worshipping in halls, storerooms, portable chapels and houses. The missionaries are diligently striving to pay for lots preparatory to building. But what a loss of energy and how discouraging at times to the missionary! Synods everywhere are sensing the need and are doing what they can to meet the situation. Here in Milwaukee, in Detroit, Chicago, New York, Philadelphia, Pittsburgh, Minneapolis, Baltimore, the North Carolina Synod, the Kansas Synod, the Ohio Synod and elsewhere, either through Field Days, Church Extension Societies, Church Financing Corporations of various kinds, efforts are being made to meet the situation. The Indiana Synod has decided that they will organize no more missions until those that are on the funds are thoroughly equipped and to this end has voted temporarily to abolish the office of Missionary Superintendent and use the funds for this purpose.

CONGREGATIONS SUPPORTING MISSIONS DURING BIENNIUM

The list of congregations and of individuals supporting American Missions shows an appreciable addition over the report of two years ago. Then we had seven congregations that had their own Home Mission areas. Now we can report twenty-one. Besides a number are supporting several missionaries. All but two of the appended list are for the English Division. Adult Classes, Brotherhoods and congregations can get a real thrill out of what the Board of American Missions is doing by supporting a congregation and watching it grow. Assignments can be made for the congregation of average means. Correspondence is solicited.

First Church, Altoona, Pa., M. J. Kline, D.D., pastor.
    Emmanuel, Rochester, N. Y., F. E. Reissig, missionary.
    St. John's, East Juniata, Pa., H. W. Bender, missionary.

Zion Church, Harrisburg, Pa., S. W. Herman, D.D., pastor.
    Shoop's, Colonial Park, Pa., T. W. Eshenauer, missionary.
    St. Paul's, Harrisburg, Pa., F. H. Shimer, missionary.

Memorial Church, Harrisburg, Pa., L. C. Manges, D.D., pastor.
    First, Valley Junction, Pa., F. C. Maurer, missionary.

Zion, Hummelstown, Pa., C. G. Leatherman, D.D., pastor.
    Messiah, Merchantville, N. J., Roy L. Yund, missionary.

St. Pauls, Gordon, Pa., A. C. Harris, pastor.
    St. John's, Westville, N. J., J. Harold Mumper, missionary.

Trinity, Germantown, Philadelphia, Pa., H. F. Baughman, pastor.
    Trinity, Woodbury, N. J., Roy V. Derr, missionary.

S. S. of Resurrection Church, Buffalo, N. Y., W. A. G. Schmidt, pastor.
    Messiah, Denver, Colo., Wilson P. Ard, missionary.

St. Paul's, Columbia, S. C., H. A. McCullough, D.D., pastor.
    Trinity, Everett, Wash., D. D. Kistler, missionary.

Grace, Rochester, Pa., H. R. Shepfer, pastor.
    Holy Trinity, Beaver, Pa., George L. Ulrich, missionary.

Redeemer, Brooklyn, N. Y., H. T. Weiskotten, Ph.D., pastor.
    St. Thomas, Locust Manor, L. I., W. F. Frey, missionary.
    Jamaica So., Rich Hill Circle Parish, L. I., E. H. Lehr, missionary.
    Bethany, Springfield Gardens, L. I., J. S. Bousum, missionary.
    Bellmore Parish, L. I., A. E. Deitz, D.D., missionary.

St. Johannis, Reading, Pa., R. H. Ischinger, pastor.
    Field Missionary E. Rosenquist, Manitoba Synod.

Trinity, Akron, Ohio, Franklin C. Fry, pastor.
    First Hungarian, Akron, Ohio, Ralph Zimmerman, missionary.

First, Mansfield, Ohio, H. C. Roehner, D.D., pastor.
    Westwood, Dayton, Ohio, H. T. Pospesel, missionary.

First, Dayton, Ohio, C. L. Venable, pastor.
    Westwood, Dayton, Ohio, H. T. Pospesel, missionary.
    North Riverdale, Dayton, Ohio, D. T. Holland, missionary.

Trinity, Canton, Ohio, E. C. Herman, D.D., pastor.
    Trinity, Niles, Ohio, J. W. Bressler, missionary.

First, Springfield, Ohio, J. B. Markward, D.D., pastor.
    Auburn, Springfield, Ohio.

Keller Memorial, Washington, D. C., S. T. Nicholas. D.D., pastor.
    Grace, Eugene, Oregon, Frank S. Beistel, missionary.

Calvary, Wilkinsburg, Pa., L. A. Krouse, pastor.
    Advent, Wilkinsburg Manor, Pa., J. E. Slater, missionary.

Mt. Zion, Pittsburgh, Pa., N. S., G. E. Swoyer, pastor.
    Calvary, Arnold, Pa., Paul J. Trout, missionary.

Christ, Chicago, Ill., George P. Lottich, pastor.
    Westwood, Chicago, Ill., F. L. Schreckenberg, missionary.

Miss Julia Wattles, Pittsburgh, Pa.
    Grace, Houston, Texas, William J. Hoebel, missionary.

CO-OPERATION OF SYNODICAL SUPERINTENDENTS AND MISSION COMMITTEES

    Sometimes we wonder if the Church really grasps the care and attention given to its mission work. Each one of the twenty-nine Synods has a committee of at least five men who meet monthly or quarterly to hear reports and to plan for the best interests of the missions within their Synod. Our experience is that they conscientiously fulfill their duties. Most of these have full time Missionary Superintendents or Presidents of Synods to furnish information, to carry into effect decisions reached and to see that vacancies are supplied. The Board of American Missions, therefore, gets the exact situation as it exists in the whole field, and is able to plan for the good of all. We record our appreciation of the unfailing courtesy and co-operation received from all these men entrusted with the oversight of the missions in their Synods.

The Work of Dr. Hancher and Dr. Hillerman

The Division of English Missions at present has two men who serve as General Superintendents. The Rev. A. D. R. Hancher, D.D., has been located at Jacksonville, Florida, to give assistance particularly to Synods that are too weak to have full time Presidents or Missionary Superintendents. As such he meets with the Mission Committees, makes personal investigation of proposed fields, gives sympathetic attention to missionary pastors in their many problems, and is ready at the call of the Board to take charge of such mission fields as may need his expert service. Superintendent Hancher, during the biennium, has submitted to an operation, that due to the love of a kind Heavenly Father and expert surgical care has spared him to us and will enable him effectively to perform his work. The Board is thankful indeed that he has so completely recovered. His report of his activities is as follows:

"The President of the Board and the Executive Secretary, together with Dr. C. A. Freed, a member of the Board, visited the State of Florida and the following Missions: Tampa, Lakeland, St. Petersburg, Miami, Hollywood, West Palm Beach. This visit was almost immediately followed by the worst hurricane the state has ever known—September 16, 1928. It was particularly severe at West Palm Beach. Fortunately for the Mission, it had no property at that time, but the individual members suffered severely. Clothing and groceries valued at more than $500, together with $450 contributed by the Board for relief work, were handled through this office.

"During the Lenten Period many churches were visited in the interest of Church Extension, and private contributions solicited.

"During the period the mission at Miami has secured a lot and worked out plans for a Church. West Palm Beach Mission has built and paid for a completely equipped Church. The mission at Tampa has secured an excellent property on which services are held in a remodeled dwelling. St. Augustine has been canvassed, and also DeSota City, Sebring and Avon Park.

"In North Carolina the organization of a mission at Alamance with fine prospects was authorized.

"In the Virginia Synod a special survey of all the missions is now being made.

"In the South Carolina Synod the towns of Anderson, Blacksburg, Darlington, Gaffney, Hartsville, Greer and Union were canvassed. Organization of a mission at Union was authorized.

"In the Georgia Synod, Columbus and a part of Atlanta have been canvassed, and the canvass of Mobile, Alabama, is now in progress.

"The various Synods have been visited as far as possible. Meetings with pastors and Church Councils of the various missions have been held and their situation discussed. The meetings of the Synodical Home Mission Committees have been attended, together with the Women's Missionary Convention, and addresses made.

"Monthly and quarterly reports have been made to the Board, and correspondence of the office carried on. One very happy feature is that only one mission is vacant at the present moment."

The Rev. George H. Hillerman, D.D., in addition to meeting the Mission Committees of the California and Pacific Synods and keeping the Board thoroughly informed of developments on the West Coast, has spent the major part of his time in rehabilitating two important missions, staying by them until the crisis had passed and pastors had been secured. Barnitz Memorial, at Denver, Colo., and Longview, Wash., will remember his self-sacrificing service for years. At the former place the pastor had suddenly been called home, with his church half-completed, and in the latter field the church was vacant and in serious financial difficulties. Both are now going missions, with Rev. W. A. Drahn and Rev. A. M. Knudsen as the missionaries.

WHAT OF THE FUTURE

Are there fields of surpassing importance to which the Board of American Missions is called? Every observer of the United States census for 1930 must be impressed with the thought as to where the major emphasis should be placed in the matter of organizing missions. I have before me a list of ninety-three cities of 100,000 to 6,958,792 inhabitants, showing the percentage of increase since 1920. The roll of the cities is challenging. Nearly 27,000,000 people live in them; with their suburbs there must be 35,000,000. It is to the credit of the United Lutheran Church that she has representation in eighty of them. It should be our goal to plant the church in the other thirteen. The New York and Chicago metropolitan areas have larger populations than the rest of the states combined. These are simply illustrations. Wherever there is a metropolitan center we find all denominations at work, and it becomes us carefully to study the situation. It is thrilling to note the way Synodical Boards are awake to the situation. On every hand surveys are being undertaken to learn the facts. The Board must be placed in position to heed the call, Occupy! Occupy!! Occupy!!!

IN MEMORIAM

It is our painful duty to record the death of two fine missionaries. The Rev. F. Ross Shirck, graduated from Midland College and the Western Theological Seminary, and successfully had served several pastorates at Stella, Neb., Nevada, Iowa, Grace Church, Omaha, Ottumwa, Iowa and at Dundalk, Md. He had entered upon his work at Dundalk with his customary energy, and was having remarkable success in finishing the church and in adult catechetical work when he was stricken.

The Rev. Hans B. Lundh, a graduate of Augustana College and of the Chicago Seminary of the Class of '29, had accepted a call to the mission at Missouri Valley, Iowa, and had just been ordained by the Iowa Synod. He was very happy and anticipated his work with pleasure. His father was a prominent pastor in Sweden, and he, on his way to Sweden to come in under the quota, stopped at Chicago over Sunday, attended services at Trinity Church, Rev. Gottfried Nelson, pastor, and was stricken with cerebral hemmorrhage while reading the service. He died shortly afterwards. Rev. Mr. Lundh was a vocalist of superior ability. "Blessed are the dead who die in the Lord."

DIVISION OF LINGUISTIC INTERESTS
Dr. E. A. Tappert, *Divisional Secretary*

When Paul had heard the Macedonian cry: Come over and help us, he had set foot on European soil and begun that great work, as the result of which we are Christians today. From Philippi he had gone to Berea and Thessalonica, and finally to Athens, the capital of Greece. Here certain philosophers of the Epicureans and Stoics encountered him, the most exclusive and undemocratic people of the earth. They sneered at his queer preaching, and said: What will this babbler say? Then Paul, standing on Mars Hill, addressed them and in a fiery speech crashed into all their prejudices by declaring in words of convincing power: That God has made of one blood all nations.

A famous preacher once remarked that if an Englishman, a Scotchman, an Irishman, a German, a Frenchman, a Scandinavian and representatives of all other nations were placed in a row, and a lancet were struck in their bared arm, the blood let out would show the same characteristics: It would be red, complex, fibrin, globulin, chlorin, containing sulphuric acid, potassium, phosphate of magnesia, and so on, and all scientific doctors, no matter what their school, would agree with St. Paul that God has made of one blood all nations. The countenance of the five races of the human family may be different as the result of climate, education and habit, but the blood is the same, indicating that they all belong to the same human family, and that they all come under the gracious will of God, who wants all men to be saved and to come to the knowledge of the truth.

The United Lutheran Church is recognizing these facts in its wide scope of missions. Without race prejudice she is trying to bring the Gospel to all nations, no matter what their race or language may be, and it is with those of foreign tongues that she has the most promising and blessed work. The Linguistic Interests of the Board of American Missions are assuming ever increasing importance. Many thousands of Lutherans, chiefly from the diaspora, people with a decided Lutheran consciousness, are coming to the Western Hemisphere, especially into Canada, crying for the Bread of Life. German colonists from Poland and Russia form the larger part of the new immigration; Siebenbuerger Saxons are coming over in surprising numbers, Magyars and Slovaks abound in all the industrial centers; Finnlanders outnumber all other immigrants, and Letts and Esthonians present a pressing missionary problem. Among all these nationalities the Board of American Missions is trying to do the work which the Church has committed to it, hampered on all sides by lack of men and means. Even if we could double our missionary forces in Canada today, we could not hope to cope with the situation, and we wish we could cry out into the Church with a thousand tongues: Send laborers into the vineyard!

One of the most pressing problems that confronts our Church today is how to supply the Church with pastors who can minister in more than one language. It is an old problem, resulting from the Reformation principle that the Church must preach the Gospel in the language of the people. In Europe the problem is comparatively simple. It has language problems in all the many places where different races mingle. But inasmuch as the races do not mix, the situation remains unchanged through centuries, and there is no need of frequent adjustments in order to cope with it.

Here in America conditions are entirely different. There is a constant state of transition, a continuous amalgamation, assimilation, absorption. Racial distinctions are preserved for a limited time only; complete assimilation in the great melting pot of America is only a question of time. Here lies the root of our difficulties. Since the training of pastors is within the province of the Synods, it is natural that the Synods have considered their immediate needs rather than the constant need of the church. A review of the past clearly shows that each generation has taken care of its own needs, and that their educational institutions have gone through the same process of transition as the constituency of the Synods to which they belonged. Colleges and seminaries which were founded for the distinct purpose of preparing men for the bilingual ministry, have gradually become exclusively English in the same measure as the Synodical body became anglicized. The pioneer church of our country received its ministry from Europe. In a few decades the originally almost exclusively German church had become almost exclusively English. By the middle of the last century when the great German immigration set in we had no native ministry able to cope with the situation, and no institution in which to prepare such a ministry. It was during this period that our Church suffered the greatest losses. Belated efforts were made to provide for the shepherding of those teeming millions. New institutions were opened for the training of a bilingual ministry which served their purpose well for a time. But as the Synods changed their complexion, so did these institutions of learning; today again they are purely English institutions. This is the natural course of events. With our linguistic problem we are again where we were before, and it is as acute as ever. Thus in the course of years and experience it has become increasingly evident that for a successful and harmonious ministry in the linguistic service of the Church the uniform and sympathetic training of a native ministry is essential. While by the grace of

God and many sacrifices on the part of the pioneers in this diversified field of the Church's activity the present efficient and commendable staff of faithful workers has been won, the percentage of failures nevertheless has been unduly large, and many difficulties have arisen, due to the necessity of employing workers indiscriminately. Some lacked in things American, others failed because they were not sufficiently familiar with the language, customs and traditions of the groups they endeavored to serve. So there we are, trying to preach the Gospel to the people in their own language, and being continually handicapped by the lack of an adequate ministry.

We are convinced that one central institution devoted primarily to the permanent and exclusive training of men for service in this specific extraordinary field would go a long way to alleviate the situation and would assure the Church of a constant, sufficient and adequately prepared linguistic ministry.

Such an institution should provide for a complete Liberal Arts course, with special regard to the language, literature and history of the races for which pastors are to be trained. It should furthermore provide for a complete theological course, with special regard to the homiletical and liturgical training in the language of those foreign groups. We must get rid of the notion that any kind of training will be good enough for these people. On the contrary, we need the very best. Slovaks and Magyars particularly are very discriminating when it comes to a pastor, and nothing would hurt our cause in their eyes more than if we would try to satisfy them with a half-baked, short-cut ministry.

Again, such an institution must have the proper environment. Look where the prophets of old were trained: in the wilderness. Training these men in our big cities with their fine churches and commodious parsonages would spoil them for the primitiveness and simplicity of our mission fields. Only pioneer surroundings make for pioneer missionaries.

Again, such an institution must be a model in economy and discipline. Some of our Colleges have developed a tendency to create a rather expensive taste in the student, which is a decided detriment to efficient mission service. On the other hand: the rather lavish support, which some of our beneficiaries have received, has made them contemptuous of menial labor and prone to rely on others rather than to strain every effort to help themselves.

It is evident that none of our English speaking colleges and seminaries could be preempted for such a purpose. They are mostly Synod-owned, and serve their particular Synodical purposes; they also fear the stigma which is attached to the word "foreign." They want to remain purely American, that is, English speaking institutions.

The only permanent solution of this problem, which has vexed the Church for more than a century seems to be the establishment of some such central institutions in which all our bilingual pastors could be trained. With such an institution at our service we would no longer need to rely on any supply that may come to us from Europe, but we could recruit our ministerial supply from our own Churches and train them in our own school, as a Church under normal conditions should do.

When at the convention at Washington, in 1920, a linguistic policy was adopted by the United Lutheran Church, the foundations were laid for a work which is bound to increase in importance from year to year, and to yield fruit beyond all expectations. The lack of such a policy in the past is responsible for untold losses in membership and resources. An intelligest application of this policy, especially with regard to Canada, will let us in on the ground floor through a door which is wide open, inviting us to do our utmost in looking up and gathering in those who are of our household of faith, irrespective of race and language. In accordance with the Plan of Operation a Divisional Secretary has been placed in charge of all the linguistic interests, so that it is now possible to co-ordinate the work and to approach the different problems from a new angle. There is now a larger outlook, and the diversified mission propositions with their necessities and possibilities can be presented with greater force than ever.

We can group our linguistic work under seven captions: 1, German; 2, Slovak; 3, Magyar; 4, Finnish; 5, Lettish-Esthonian-Lithuanian; 6, Italian; 7, Jewish. There are some scattered Scandinavian groups, Swedish and Danish, which, however, are being served in connection with our German and Finnish work. Our Syrian work was discontinued; in the same measure as conditions in the homeland improved, the colony became smaller and smaller, so that finally only a few members remained. The Ministerium and the Board helped Pastor Jaure Abraham to return to his homeland, where he is to continue his work under the auspices of the Herrmannsburg Mission, aided by gifts from some of the Philadelphia German Churches.

1. GERMAN MISSIONS

The fact that more than half of the Lutherans of the world are of the German race makes it appear natural that by far the largest group under our care are German. One thing, however, must be noted which perhaps is not universally known. Only a very small percentage of the material which we gather into our German congregations and missions comes from the former German Empire. That is a fact which gives the whole situation a different aspect. In former years the bulk of our German congregations came from the different states of the German Empire, with a little sprinkling from Switzerland, Austria-Hungary and Poland. In spite of the fact that many thousands of nominal Lutherans have immigrated since the war, our German Churches in the U. S.

have received only an infinitesimal part of that immigration; most of their additions come from non-German countries. In the West and in Canada the immigration comes almost exclusively from Poland and Russia. The only material exceptions are the Siebenbuergers and Banater Suabians, who hail from the former kingdom of Hungary. These Germans are mostly of the farming class, and as such considered desirable immigrants. Some 175 years ago their fathers were colonized by Empress Katherine II in the Wolga region, and later, after the partitioning of Poland, in Volhynia and Podolia. Here they turned the wilderness into a veritable paradise. Their descendants prospered greatly until the war changed their status and made them homeless. Since the war some 300,000 of the Wolga Germans have come to America, most of them to the United States. They are scattered all over the Western States down to the Pacific. Only a few of them have been gathered into our Churches; the Wartburg, the German Nebraska and the Texas Synods each have a few congregations, but they are negligible in comparison to what the Congregationalists and the Evangelische Synod von Nordamerika have succeeded in gathering. There is a vast host yet to be gathered in. Being highly emotional they are not easy to handle, and other than the customary measures have to be employed in dealing with them. However, we have examples which show that an energetic, determined, yet tactful pastor can achieve wonderful results among them. They are very faithful in Church attendance, liberal givers for benevolences, with a strong pietistic trend. They warrant our interest and closest attention.

The Canadian immigration is of more recent date. Those coming from Poland are not quite as destitute as those who have escaped from Soviet Russia only with their bare lives. They are poor, desperately poor, in worldly goods, but they are also poor in spirit, and hand in hand with their longing for a home of their own goes the longing for a Church home, be it ever so modest and small. Our Church is doing a great work among these people. Untiring are the efforts of Pastor Wahl in advising and helping them to settle where they can be regularly supplied with Word and sacrament. Invaluable are the services of our field missionaries who have to live under conditions and wrestle with problems of which most people have no idea. Think of that young graduate of Saskatoon Seminary, who on a borrowed Indian pony rode 160 miles into the wilderness until he reached his field of labor; think of him with the aid of Missionary Weidenhammer, building himself a house at a total cost of $37.50. It is refreshing to witness in this age of selfishness and materialism the unselfish and sacrificing spirit of our missionaries in the Canadian Northwest; their indomitable will to brave the rigors of climate, the discomfort of the most primitive living conditions, the heart-breaking task of serving their widely scattered flock on impossible roads, and all that at a mere pittance for a living; it is a spectacle that fills the heart with pride and great hope for the future; these men are Empire builders, and if we as a Church had no reason to be grateful for anything, we should be grateful for our missionaries.

We have 116 missions and preaching points in the German Department, 55 of which are located on the territory of the Manitoba Synod. That in itself shows the magnitude and importance of this field. Our possibilities are limited only by our means. The ripeness of this tremendous field is a challenge to our Church to strain every effort in the gathering of this great harvest. What in other mission fields we may gather drop by drop, we are apt to lose here by buckets. We need not do any proselyting with such an enormous reservoir of Lutheran strength, ready to be tapped. If the present situation is wisely handled and the work adequately supported it will result in a strong, loyal and active Lutheran Church in this great Dominion, and will prove one of the finest investments that the Church has ever made. For this reason Saskatoon College and Seminary should receive all possible support. The Manitoba Synod is altogether too weak and too poor to support such an institution from its own meagre funds. The strengthening of this Seminary is all the more important as it prepares men for bilingual work, and indications are not lacking that the demand for English services is about to make itself felt in this heretofore purely German Synod. The first congregation to request English services was St. Johannes, Edmonton, Alberta, where Pastor Joern will begin regular English services in the Fall. President Hartig has expressed his conviction that Edmonton needs a purely English congregation. In Saskatoon steps have been taken to acquire a beautiful site, adjoining the University grounds, for the purpose of erecting an English Lutheran Church. Our brethren up there are wide-awake, and will not neglect to provide for the future.

The territory of the Canada Synod is not nearly so large, and fairly well covered. It has not received very much German immigration, if we except the Siebenbuergers, but quite some Scandinavian and Finnish. Nevertheless there are some mission possibilities, and a field missionary, whom they have desired for some time, could be used to advantage. New mission fields have been opened at Brantwood and Chatham. Montreal offers great possibilities, which Pastor Ischinger, of Reading, has graciously offered to explore, free of charge, during his vacation. (St. Johannes, of Reading, Pa., has agreed to support one of the field missionaries in Manitoba). Kitchener is likely to become an important missionary centre; it has received an increase of almost 2000 during the past year, mostly Lutherans. Waterloo Seminary is providing the Synod with able men for its mostly bilingual congregations. A thorough survey of Northern Ontario by General Superintendent Ludwig revealed the presence of many Lutherans of Finnish and Scandinavian extraction, but few Germans, and only the larger cities seem to offer any prospect for a successful mission enterprise. The Canada Synod has 16 missions and preaching stations.

The Wartburg Synod has only six missions at this time. St. Paul's and Stephen Ludwig Roth Missions, Chicago, were merged and became self-supporting. Mt. Clare was transferred to the English Department; Good Shepherd, Breitung, was dissolved, and Friedens, Iron Mountain, was transferred to the Augustana Synod. There are quite a number of Wolga Germans on the territory of this Synod, and if opportunity offers these people may prove fertile ground for successful mission operations.

The German Nebraska Synod has 15 missions and preaching stations. One mission became self-supporting; one was transferred to the Synod of the Northwest; one was dropped. Much work is still to be done among Russian immigrants. The Synod receives its ministerial supply from the Martin Luther Seminary, which has undergone remarkable changes, both in spirit and scholarship, and which promises to become a real asset and a big factor in the solution of our Home Mission problems. This year it sent three able men into the ministry who can handle both languages with ease.

The Texas Synod has 8 German missions and preaching points, aside from a number of English missions. Miles, Texas, became self-supporting; Alice and Falfurrias were dropped as hopeless. The Texas Synod is handicapped by its weakness over against the enormous expanse of its territory. There should be a promising field in the rapidly growing, large towns of the State, for which a field missionary has been suggested.

In the California Synod the transfer of St. John's, Oakland, to the English Department, the loss of Dinuba to Missouri, and the congregation at Sanger becoming self-supporting, leaves us but one mission, Bethel Church, San Jose, Cal.

Our missions in the East are of a different character. Some are older congregations, too weak to stand on their own feet, others are an attempt to gather some of the newer immigration from the German Republic; all are bilingual, with English predominating.

The United Synod of New York has five missions in which German is used. Erloeser, Buffalo, became self-sustaining again. Immanuel, Webster, Mass., united with an Augustana Synod Church. The prospects are that the remaining congregations will become English before long.

The Ministerium of Pennsylvania has 4 German-English missions. A Reiseprediger has been engaged in the person of Pastor Otto Kleine, who holds occasional services in different towns in Eastern Pennsylvania and New Jersey, exploring the field and looking for an opportunity where he might establish some permanent work. His services at times are attended by large crowds, made up by Pennsylvania Germans and immigrants. But he realizes that most of his hearers are members of established Churches, who like to hear an occasional German sermon, and that many of the newer immigration can be depended upon for a Christmas or an Easter service, but not for the permanent organization of a congregation. Nevertheless his endeavors are not without success. Not only has he drawn many to divine services who otherwise would scarcely have come, but at some places he has laid what would seem the foundation of permanent organizations. Princeton, N. J., in particular, seems to be the point in which Christian sentiment is likely to crystalize which may result in the establishment of a long-needed Lutheran Church in this important educational centre. It is hard work, and Pastor Kleine needs the prayers and sympathetic co-operation of his brethren.

We have one more group in the German Department, which is of particular interest, the Siebenbuerger Saxons, who are being cared for by the Pittsburgh Synod. They have shown the most remarkable response to our missionary efforts. Though German in speech and culture, they do not mix well in German congregations on account of certain racial peculiarities which have been developed in them through centuries of separation and seclusion. Around the year 1150 King Geisha II of Hungary induced a number of German peasants from Flanders and the lower Rhine to settle in the uninhabited regions at the foot of the Carpathian Mountains. In 1211 another batch of settlers were brought into the Burgenland by Andrew II. The country was known as Transylvania; among the inhabitants it was called Siebenbuergen, probably on account of the seven fortified castles, where courts of law were established. As early as 1520 the doctrines of Martin Luther took root among these people. Honterus, inspired by Luther's teaching at Wittenberg, became the Reformer of his homeland; he organized the Church on evangelical principles, and Martin Luther himself provided him with a constitution for the Church.

These sturdy Germans soon became the outpost of civilization in the East. Hun, Turk and Tartar battled against this small band and tried to overwhelm them by sheer force of numbers. But through all these centuries they succeeded in preserving their liberty, their culture and their faith. Thus they have lived for 800 years, entirely surrounded by people of different race, language and faith, ever watchful of their independence, ever suspicious of their surroundings. These conditions have made them clannish to the extreme, even to the exclusion of other German speaking people; they have made them suspicious of everything that is foreign to them.

During the past 30 years they have come to this country in large numbers. Some 30,000 settled in Western Pennsylvania and Eastern Ohio. For years our Church was hardly aware of their presence. Ten years ago there was only one weak Saxon congregation at Youngstown, Ohio. Since then they have enjoyed the sheltering care of the German Conference of the Pittsburgh Synod, and the work among them has experienced phenomenal growth and development. The gain in membership has been close to 3300 souls. Lately many Saxons have come to Canada.

Last March, at Kitchener, Ont., a meeting of young Saxon immigrants was called on short notice, at which 124 men and 6 women declared their willingness to unite with the Church. The Pittsburgh Synod has 6 Saxon mission congregations. The latest at Detroit, Mich., and Windsor, Ont., after 6 months numbers almost 500 souls. Our work among these people promises the very best of success.

The United Lutheran Church may well be proud of the work which has been done within the German Department. The missions keenly feel their debt of gratitude for every counsel which is given, for every help which is extended to them by the Board. They feel grateful also for the interest and aid which the Women's Missionary Society has extended in increasing measure. Above all they feel grateful to Almighty God, who has provided them with the Bread of Life, and to all who have been God's helpers in this blessed work.

Only one of our missionaries in the German Department died during the biennium.

Pastor George Gersib, born and educated in Germany, was ordained by the German Nebraska Synod in 1912. He served a number of parishes in that Synod until on December 1, 1928, he became Pastor of St. Johannes Mission, at Lipscomb, Texas. After only eight months of successful missionary service, the Lord called him to his reward on July 18, 1929. He died in the prime of life, leaving a widow and two small children.

SLOVAK MISSIONS

Next in importance to our German work is the work among the Slovaks. It presents particular problems because it is work with an entirely different race, and many of the mistakes which have been made, and the ill-success which has attended some of our efforts, have been due to a lack of understanding, a lack of appreciation of the traits and characteristics of this race.

It is one of the oldest races in Europe. In its two branches it occupies the territory Northwest (Czecho-Slovakia) and Southeast (Jugo-Slavia) of Hungary. The Southern part, known to the ancients as Pannonia Sava, became a Roman province under Cæsar Augustus, but freed itself during the fifth century. In the Holy Roman Empire of the German Nation, under Louis the Pious, it had its own native ruler. It was christianized rather early through the efforts of Methodius and Cyrillus, who also gave the people a unified language by translating Bible and Church literature into a pannonic-slavonic dialect somewhat in the same manner in which Martin Luther made his Saxon dialect the German language. Cyrillus is the inventor of the alphabet, which is named after him, and which is still in use in those regions and all over Russia. Since the death of Methodius, in 885, this language was used extensively in Bulgaria, Croatia, Serbia, Dalmatia and Russia, with all the Slavic people who held to the

Greek Catholic Church; it was the language of Church and school up to the close of the seventeenth century. The northern part was originally settled by a Celt tribe, the Bohers. At the beginning of the Christian era the Germanic tribe of the Marcomanni occupied the land. During the sixth century it was conquered by the Slavic Czechs, who are supposed to have come from Greater Croatia. This was in 623, and Samo, their leader, became their king. Methodius established the Christian church in the land. At the outbreak of the World War a large part of the Northern Slovak population lived within the confines of Hungary. These, among whom our Lutheran Church is particularly strong, had to live under a great handicap. They were not permitted to develop a literature of their own, nor have books printed in their own language. They had to get hymn books and liturgy from Bohemia, and use them in their services, though the Czech language is quite different from the many dialects which are being used by the Slovak people. From all these facts it will appear that work among the Slovaks is not as easy as it would appear on the surface. Due to the lack of a universally recognized language, the lack of proper literature and the almost impossible task of training men capable of coping with this complex language situation, this work is one of the most difficult ever undertaken by the United Lutheran Church.

By the middle of the 16th century three-fourths of the Slovaks were Protestants. Then the counter reformation set in, which drove out the Protestants by the thousands, and ever since the Lutheran Church has had to fight for its existence. It is much to the credit of the Slovaks that they stubbornly resisted all Romanizing attempts, and bravely defended the heritage of the Reformation under the stress and duress of centuries. Nothing is as precious to them as their Lutheran faith. They are staunch Lutherans, and conscientiously so, and that again facilitates the work among them. We do not need to persuade and urge them; we need not be afraid that they will run away from us and unite with non-Lutheran Churches; they are loyal to the core, and they deserve all the attention and guiding care which the Church can give them.

It is almost fifty years ago that the Slovaks began to come to America in ever increasing numbers. Attracted by the comparatively high wages they settled in the coal fields and in the industrial regions. For a long time our American Lutheran Church scarcely took notice of them. They were left to themselves, and they tried to help themselves. They organized their first congregation at Freeland, Pa., in 1884. The first pastor was Cyrill Droppa. This congregation is the mother of all Slovak Lutheran congregations, and belongs to the Ministerium of Pennsylvania. The real founder of the congregation was a layman, Michael Zemany, who is also the founder of the "Slovenska Evangelica Jedusta" (Slovak Evangelical Union) a beneficiary organization in which all Slovaks are interested.

The founding of the Freeland congregation was followed in close succession by similar organizations at Hazelton, Nanticoke, Mahanoy City, Mt. Carmel, St. Clair, Lansford, Northampton, all in Pennsylvania. Their first Synodical contact was with the Missouri Synod. Our Church took up the work only a little more than twenty years ago, after some of the pastors in the hard coal region, among them particularly our lamented Dr. Ramer, had drawn the Church's attention to these people among whom they had done some personal work for years. Since then systematic efforts have been made to build up a Slovak constituency in our Church, and though the work has been handicapped by a chronic lack of workers and other hindrances, yet the efforts of the men engaged in this work, especially the untiring labors of the late Dr. Ramer, have not been without fruit. Of course, if we consider that 100,000 Lutheran Slovaks have come to this country, and that less than 15,000 have been gathered into our Lutheran Churches, we cannot say that our work is done. The immigration is practically at a standstill, but there are still so many of former immigrations to be gathered that we have a great work before us. Our chief difficulty is due to the fluctuation of the Slovak population in consequence of industrial depressions and realignments and to our inability to supply a sufficient number of pastors fast enough to fill the many vacancies, and to take advantage of opportunities for new work. However, the outlook is hopeful. Though we still have quite a number of vacant congregations, we manage to supply them regularly with the help of our students. We have a number of splendid men in preparation for the ministry who, when graduated, will enable us to fill almost all the vacancies. We are now able to tighten the lines and will not permit any student to enter the Seminary without a regular college course. There will be no further discrimination in favor of future Slovak students who will be held to bear part of the expense of their education as other beneficiary students are required to do.

One of the problems with our Slovak congregations is to line them up with Synods. Most of them are still "independents," but the situation shows signs of improvement. Two congregations united with the Ministerium this spring; others are contemplating to unite with the Slovak Synod Zion. Chiefly through the efforts of Pastor F. C. Fry, of Trinity Church, Akron, Ohio, the combined membership of S. S. Peter and Paul Church (Slovak Synod), and Dr. Martin Luther Church (Independent) with the better part of the Missouri Synod Church, organized Holy Trinity Slovak Lutheran Church, a strong self-supporting congregation. The Slovak Holy Trinity Church, of Newark, N. J., is building an $80,000.00 Church plant in a most beautiful location, which will be the high-water mark in Slovak Church construction, and a credit to our work. The congregation lately united with Zion Synod.

The Slovak Synod Zion has decided upon a very important step, namely to send a Slovak missionary into Canada. Thousands of Lutheran Slovaks have settled in Ontario, and practically no work has been done among them. The Board has approved of this decision, and will bear part of the expense. With the help of the Slovak mission committee a plan has been worked out for the regular supply of vacant congregations by our Slovak pastors, with the help of students. Another plan is under consideration, namely, to create strong centres from which the entire surrounding territory is to be supplied with the aid of Assistant Pastors. That would save men and means, and give much greater satisfaction. We have Slovak pastors in the following Synods: Zion, United Synod of New York, Ministerium of Pennsylvania, Pittsburgh Synod, Ohio Synod, Synod of the Northwest. Of our nine students seven are engaged in the supply of vacant congregations; one was transferred to the Maywood Seminary upon the urgent request of the President of Zion Synod, who wants him to assist Dr. Lichner in his large congregation at Chicago; another was transferred to the Northwestern Seminary upon request of President Gerberding, so that he could supply our Western congregations. Two new students have been accepted. Three freshmen in Muhlenberg College were dropped for being deficient in their studies.

Our Slovak work needs the interest and sympathetic help of our American pastors. Where the pastors of our English congregations have played the part of big brother to their neighboring Slovak brethren, the results have been most beneficial. Care should be taken not to be overzealous in anglicizing them; time will take care of that. Our object is to keep them in the Church, to strengthen them in their weakness, to encourage them in their efforts, to guide them in their difficulties, to keep hem from making mistakes. Endeavors along these lines will be richly rewarded, for it is hard to find a more docile, grateful, loyal and devoted people than the Lutheran Slovak.

A word may be said here about the sad and serious loss which our work has suffered through the untimely departure of Dr. Ramer. The Slovak cause never had a more devoted friend. His interest and zeal in behalf of these people were almost an obsession with him. Through the length and breadth of the land he travelled, never tiring, to serve them. As long as there is a Slovak work in our Church, there will stand out in broad letters the name of Dr. A. L. Ramer.

MAGYAR-WENDISH MISSIONS

These missions were formerly grouped with the Slovak for no other reason than that both nationalities were subjects to the former kingdom of Hungary. Racially the Magyar is as far apart from the Slovak as is the German or the Englishman. They differ widely in trait and character. The Magyar is not slavic but of Finnish-Ural extraction, with a slight admixture of Mongolian blood. This race came from the Wolga and the Ural, and at first settled in Bessarabia and Moldavia, around the year 884. Their chieftain was Arpad, who in 889 led them into the valley of the Theiss and the following year added Transylvania to his possessions. For fifty years they were the terror of Europe. Known as Huns, they devastated Germany, Italy and France, until in 955 they were disastrously defeated by King Otto I of Germany. In 994 their King Geisa I was baptized, whose son, Stephen, surnamed the Holy, succeeded in christianizing his entire realm. They had been in possession of their land for 1000 years, when, after the World War, the treaty of Trianon robbed them of three-fourths of their territory and reduced them to a mere shadow of their former importance. They are very proud and aggressive, sociable and hospitable, the men of fierce courage, and the women of rare beauty.

The Wends, or Winds, are a Slavic race. They formerly occupied a large tract between the Carpathian mountains and the Adriatic Sea. From here they extended northward through Saxony and Pomerania to the Baltic Sea. Most of them have been Germanized. They live in a compact body only between the Drau and Kulp. They are also known as Slovenes. While the Slovak and the Magyar were very antagonistic, there has been remarkable harmony between the Magyar and the Wend. This is exemplified by the fact that the Wendish Lutherans in our country are invariably served by Magyar pastors.

Our Magyar-Wendish constituency is not as large as the Slovak, yet it is by no means negligible, and gives sound hope of future growth. While the Slovak Protestants are all Lutherans, the Magyars are divided between Calvinists and Lutherans. This fact has brought the Reformed and Presbyterian Churches into the field who have profited by our inactivity so that today some ten thousand Lutheran Magyars are to be found in these reformed Churches. In spite of the fact that we have no native Magyar ministry, our work has made good progress. We have a splendid body of highly cultured, hard working and self-sacrificing missionaries in the field, men of whom our Church can justly feel proud. Work in New Brunswick, Perth Amboy, Cleveland, Buffalo, Akron, Detroit, Pittsburgh, has made satisfactory progress. In New York the new promising mission is being served in connection with Caldwell, N. J. In Bethlehem Pastor Pottschacher and his brave flock have erected a splendid Church building, which in strongly Catholic surroundings bears visible testimony of Lutheran sacrifices. In Canada we have just made a beginning. Pastor DePapp, with the aid of Student Ruzsa, of Waterloo Seminary, is making a determined effort to establish work at Windsor, Kitchener, Brantford, Galt, Toronto, Welland and Hamilton. Here we should have another man.

At the dedication of Zion Hungarian Lutheran Church of Bethlehem, eight Magyar pastors were present, and there organized the "Hungarian

Lutheran Pastors' Association of America." Pastor Stephen Ruzsa was elected President; Pastor DePapp, Secretary, and Pastor Andor Leffler, Treasurer. This association is intended for mutual fellowship and for the furthering of common interest. It will give these brethren a chance to talk over the particular needs of the field, plan new work and devise ways and means for the upbuilding of God's Kingdom among the Magyar people. This step is highly commendable. As another bond of union, Pastor DePapp has published a Hungarian parish paper, the "Evangelikus Hirado" (The Evangelical Herald). We are very hopeful of the Hungarian situation. It is in the character of our Magyar brethren that they will push to the utmost the work, once begun, and we are satisfied that their sterling qualities will be a welcome asset to the life of our American Lutheran Church.

Of Wendish congregations we have only a few. The largest is that of Bethlehem, Pa., with its beautiful church building and large number of active people so ably served by Dr. Stiegler. Smaller congregations are located at Newark, N. J., and Perth Amboy, with a group of Wendish people at Steelton, Pa., who are being served by one of our Siebenbuerger pastors. As there is only a limited number of Wends in the United States, there is not much hope of a considerable growth of membership from these people, but it will be well worth our while to gather what can be gathered.

FINNISH MISSIONS

There is a close relationship between the Magyar and the Finn. They are of the same Altaic or Turanic race of which one branch settled in Hungary, in the midst of German and Slavish people, another one went north, and forms to this day the racial foundation of the people inhabiting the northernmost part of Scandinavia and Russia from the Baltic to the Ural mountains. The Finn or Suomalaiset as he calls himself (that is, Swamp people) is a straight, faithful, taciturn, goodnatured and industrious character. He dislikes flattery, is adverse to innovations, serious minded and extremely careful and cautious. Suomi is spoken by the common people, while Swedish has been the language of the educated classes, the tradesmen and the city dweller. Since the World War this has been greatly changed; a new national consciousness has been born, and Suomi is gradually taking the place of Swedish everywhere. One of our Finnish missionaries recently had his Swedish name changed into a Finnish one by a Finnish court of law. They are a high-strung nation with a high degree of culture and a fiery spirit of liberty, one of the few newly established nations that made good. In the ninth century the Finns are mentioned as pirates in company with the Normans. In 1156 King Eric of Sweden tried to christianize the land, but with little success. Sweden conquered the land in 1249, and introduced the Reformation in

1528. After many attempts Russia occupied Finland in 1808. During the World War Finland obtained its independence.

During the past twenty-five years, especially since the close of the war, many thousands of Finns have sought a new home in America. The earlier settlers went into the Western States with a few settlements here and there in the East. The newest immigration has gone partly into the far West of the United States, especially, however, into Canada, both East and West. In Ontario they rank first among all immigrants. Toronto is said to have received 7000 Finns during the past few years, as many as the Province of British Columbia. Some 1200 Finnish girls went to Toronto in search of work. There are said to be more than 300,000 Finns in America today. They present, no doubt, the most pressing mission problem which has faced the Church for years. Three general Lutheran bodies are at work among them; the Suomi Synod, the Apostolic and the National Church. All three have not been able to cope with the situation. We have been aiding the Suomi Synod in its work, bearing half of the expense for their missionaries, and giving aid to nine of their students in their Theological Seminary at Hancock, Michigan. The Synod voted to appoint a commission which in consultation with a committee of the United Lutheran Church in America is to find a way to a possible closer co-operation. The proposed opening of a mission in Toronto was deferred to await the outcome of this conference, which is to take place during the Milwaukee convention.

Our Finnish mission work comprises ten districts; Oregon with four stations; California with six stations; Manitoba with three stations; Ontario with six stations; New York State with two stations; Washington with six stations; British Columbia with fifteen stations; Maine with seven stations; Wisconsin with six stations; Montana with five stations. Many of these stations are merely preaching points. A survey of Canada gives the following figures: British Columbia, fifty communities with a population of 1500 Finns. (Missionary Salminen, who is on this field, estimates the Finnish population of British Columbia at 8000, of whom 1000 live in Vancouver); Alberta thirty communities with 3500 people; Saskatchewan 25 communities with 1750 Finns; Manitoba ten communities with 500 Finns; Ontario with more Finns than all other provinces combined; report covers 96 places with 18,750 Finns.

Judging from other reports and observations we consider these figures altogether too low. They show, however, what a tremendous mission opportunity and mission duty are confronting the Lutheran Church in this field, how it challenges the Church, either to go to work or to quit. There are others who will receive these thousands who knock at our door if we do not. The United Church of Canada has a number of missionaries at work among the Finns, and it has the means to put up $10.00 for our $1.00. Yet these people are Lutherans and don't want to be anything but Lutherans, and will leave our Church only if we actively or passively refuse to receive them. There are unholy forces at work among them. Through their contact with Russia they have inherited some of that red communism which is the relentless foe of church and religion. They are like the man on the road to Jericho who had fallen among thieves. God forbid that our United Lutheran Church should be found acting like that priest and Levite, and pass this opportunity of doing good unto those who are of the household of faith. God forbid that we should view this situation with the spirit of Cain and say: Am I my brother's keeper? If we fail our Finnish brethren now in this emergency, what will the future Lutheran Church think of us?

LETTISH-LITHUANIAN-ESTHONIAN MISSIONS

Letts and Lithuanians are of the same race; they are of the Indo-German family, and speak the Letto-Slavish language. Lithuania became known in history when Ryngold defeated his enemies in 1236 and became ruler of his people. Christianity was introduced in 1386. Since 1501 it was united with Poland and when Poland was partitioned it was annexed by Russia. After the World War it became a republic. Confessionally it is largely Roman Catholic. Lettland was subject to the German Knight Order, from which it bought its independence in 1525, when Walter von Plettenburg became its ruler. In 1721 it was surrendered to Russia. After the World War it became a republic. Confessionally it is almost exclusively Lutheran. Esthland, in their own language Wiroma, border-land, was sold to the Schwertbrueder in 1347. For centuries it was the pawn of surrounding nations, and successively occupied by Danes, Swedes, Russians, Lithuanians. It was the convenient battle ground upon which they fought out their differences. In 1721 it came into the possession of Russia. It also became a republic after the World War, and is predominately Lutheran. The inhabitants are of the Finnish race.

There is only a limited number of these people in our country. We are doing work among the Lithuanians in Philadelphia, among the Letts in Philadelphia, New York, Boston, and Manitoba. For lack of men and means we have not been able to begin work among the Esthonians, of whom there is a large colony in New Jersey and some smaller ones in Canada. All we have been able to do was to make a survey of the situation. If we do not want to miss our opportunity altogether we should place a man into the field soon or it will be too late. It will be hard and slow work, but it ought to be worth trying.

ITALIAN MISSIONS

While hitherto we have dealt with missions among our own Lutheran household of faith, it now remains to touch upon what little work we have among non-Lutheran Christians and those who are no Christians at all. It is not much; merely a gesture to indicate that we recognize our Christian duty to bring the light of the Gospel to all who know not the Christ, though we feel, for evident reasons, that for the time being we must confine our efforts chiefly to those who are of the household of faith.

There are many millions of Italians in this country. Though nominally almost exclusively Catholic, only a very small percentage attend the Roman Churches, and it is a general complaint among their priests that no nationality shows so much indifference, if not antagonism to the Church, as the Italian. Historically this is not hard to understand. The old saying that a prophet is not without honor except in his own country applies also to the Pope. Italy is priest-ridden like no other country in Europe, and the abuses and exploitations of centuries have weighed so heavily on the people's mind that, when they come to this country they are very wary, and give the Church a wide berth. That applies especially to the men. In consequence we have that great mass of unchurched Italians in our country, a latent danger to the institutions of our land, beyond the reach of the Roman Church and very difficult to reach by any of the Protestant denominations. We often hear Protestant efforts to win the unchurched Italian called proselyting among Catholics. But if the Italians were loyal Catholics, the Protestant Churches would hardly have missions among them, as little as we think of having Protestant missions among the Irish Catholics. But if we agree that any large body of unchurched people is a danger to our country, our Italian missions are abundantly justified.

Most of the mission work among Italians in our country is done by the Presbyterian Church, which has the best point of contact with these people through its close relationship to the Waldensians, who are the real backbone of its Italian work. These Waldensians are members of that heroic sect which was organized by Petrus Waldus in 1170 for the purpose of Bible study, was ex-communicated by the Pope in 1184, forbidden the use of the Scriptures in 1229, terribly persecuted through centuries, again and again almost annihilated, until in 1859 it received religious liberty. They are Presbyterian in doctrine and practice, and naturally align themselves with that Church here. Our work is chiefly among those who have broken with the Roman Church. It is naturally hard and slow work. Those who look for quick results in membership increases or in material returns must of necessity be sorely disappointed and discouraged. We do not doubt that our missionaries often feel the same way. The fact that even the best among them is not doing much better than the weakest is proof that the difficulty is with the field, not with the men.

Our oldest Italian mission is St. Peter's in Philadelphia. It was started in 1908 by Mrs. E. R. Cassiday, wife of the pastor of St. Peter's English

Lutheran Church. The influx of Italians gradually crowded out the American membership, so that it had to relocate in another part of the town, leaving the Church building to the mission. Later the Martin Luther Neighborhood House was added to the equipment. The Church property has a value of $15,000, with an indebtedness of $2,500. Pastor Renzetti is aided by three women workers.

St. Paul's, Monessen, Pa., was our second venture; organized in 1918 it has made slow progress. It has no property; however, the Pittsburgh Synod has a fund of $5,000 in hand for this mission, which will be available, as soon as the congregation has raised an equal amount for a Church building.

The third and most prosperous of our missions is Holy Trinity, Erie, Pa. Organized in 1920 it has a commodious chapel, acquired with the help of the Erie Church Extension Society, which seats about 200 and has a value of $14,000. It is used every day, and the crowded condition of the building makes the erection of a more spacious and better adapted building a necessity in the near future. An effort will be made to pay off the present indebtedness of $3,500 and then start work on a building fund. An encouraging aspect of the Erie situation is the stable character of the work and the fine spirit among the Italo-American youth.

Fourth in number is Christ Italian Mission, New York. It was begun in 1924 and has no property. The particular difficulties which attend Church work in New York are doubly felt by missions which can use Church buildings only in the afternoon, when everybody is out for recreation. In spite of the manifold hindrances creditable work is being done. The pastor is also supplying an English mission in Long Island.

From the Atlantic we have to go to the Pacific Coast to find our next mission. St. John the Divine, San Francisco, Cal., organized 1924; Italian Lutheran Mission, Fresno, Cal.; Italian Lutheran Mission, Sacramento, Cal.; the latter organized in 1926 and 1927, respectively, are being served by the same pastor. None of these missions have any property. California is a hard field for any Church, and the work among the Italians is no exception.

Our youngest mission is the Church of the Redeemer, Chicago. It is less than three years old and owns no property. It has a large field in South Chicago (Cicero) but it is also a hard field. All these missions need the ardent prayers of the Church. While faithful workers may do the planting and the watering, it is the Lord who must give the increase. It would seem to us that nothing short of a great spiritual awakening must come from the Lord before our work among the Italians of our land will become a success. With God nothing is impossible, and like as He has given our missionaries among the heathen an open door, suddenly and most unexpectedly at times, when the workers had almost given up in despair, so he can do in this branch of our work, and put to shame all our doubts and misgivings, and give us a harvest beyond all expectations.

JEWISH MISSIONS

Among all our mission activities, Jewish Mission is the hardest, the least successful, the least appreciated and the most disputed work of the Church. For centuries the Christian Church had excluded the Jew from her call to make diciples of all nations, and instead of winning the Jew for Christ by word and example she persecuted him. Even the Reformation did not awaken the Church to a realization of its Christian duty to the Jew; theologians decreed and Christian people readily agreed that the Jew was cursed of God; that he was outside the pale of salvation, and that it was wasted energy to try and convert him. Luther himself is supposed to have inclined to this opinion, and there are many today who share it. Only with the gradual awakening of Christian consciousness came the realization of a Christian's duty to the Jew, of the absolute demand of Christian love, which cannot exclude the Jew from the best it has to give, which cannot discriminate, but is held to the rule: There is neither Jew nor Greek. A Church which is guided by the love of Christ cannot let the Jew go on in his blindness; think of the Lord, who considered himself sent to the lost sheep of the house of Israel; think of St. Paul in whom the love of Christ was so powerful that in spite of all the harm the Jews had done him, he nevertheless was willing to give his all for them, and said: "For I could wish that myself were accursed from Christ for my brethren, my kinsmen according to the flesh." Such love which is ready to sacrifice its own salvation for the salvation of others, is needed for a successful mission work among the Jews. The fact that Jews are not converted in larger numbers is easily explained by the failure of so many Christians to live up to their Christian ideals. What an opportunity has the Church missed by not winning over the Jew! What a valuable asset they would have been to the Church with their indomitable spirit, their aggressiveness, their persistance. A race which has survived the greatest catastrophies, and has withstood centuries of persecution and abuse undaunted is worth winning, and not only the Church but the world in general would be benefited through the contributions of men, who like Nathanael, are Israelites indeed, in whom is no guile.

A great change is taking place in the attitude of the modern Jew toward Christ, and the Church should take note of it. Christ is no longer pictured as the Thole, the hanged one, the accursed; the modern Jew is taught to look upon Jesus with just pride, to acclaim Him as the great benefactor and teacher of mankind, the model man, the acclaimed scion of Israel. There is some serious searching of hearts and some honest seeking of truth among them, that cannot pass by Jesus, who claimed: I am the Truth. Quite a few of the highly cultured and idealistic Jews have found in Jesus the answer to the questioning and longing of their heart, and have embraced Christianity, not for the sake of social standing, or because they had become indifferent to the faith of their fathers, but because they had recognized in Jesus the hope of Israel, and in the New Testament the fulfillment of the Old.

It would be ridiculous to expect that our four missionaries should discharge the obligation of the United Lutheran Church to the Jew. What can four men do over against three to four million people? The problem is not so easily solved. Every Christian congregation has the God-given duty to evangelize the Jew. Every pastor is called to be a Jewish missionary, be it even in the reverse order: First to the Gentile, but also to the Jew. Our missionaries are to be only the instructors and leaders in this work. Unless they have the intelligent co-operation of Christian pastors and people they are only a drop in the bucket. Instead of complaining that this work costs money and that the results are scarcely noticeable, every pastor should ask himself: What have I done, what can I do, to bring Israel to Christ? Only if the whole Church organizes as an army of Christian soldiers and with word and example, with love and compassion assails the heart of Israel, will our Jewish mission work be the success, which we all desire it to be, and untold blessings will come to the Church, that has been true to her calling.

Salem Hebrew Mission of Baltimore, organized in 1920, is the only one among our missions which has a mission centre, with office and reading rooms, and connected wi'h a nice chapel. The value is close to $50,000 with a debt of $6,000. Pastor Einspruch and his women workers are untiring in their efforts to bring the Jew to the knowledge of the truth, and the Church to the knowledge of the Jew. Much to our regret, Miss Grace Bredehoft, a most faithful helper, felt herself compelled to give up her work. A successor has not yet been found. Pastor Einspruch is the publisher of two papers—one the "Mediator," with a circulation of 64,200, to bring the message of Christ to the Jew; the other, the "Hebrew Lutheran," to present the cause of the Jew to Christians. Services, instructions and visitations are regularly held. Recently a demand was made for an edition of Martin Luther's Smaller Catechism in Yiddish, and Pastor Einspruch was asked to furnish the translation. Eighteen persons have been baptized; some 12,000 Jews have been approached, and more than 1,000 tracts distributed.

Messiah Hebrew Mission of Philadelphia has no property. The work is that of the individual to the individual, heart to heart talk between the missionary and the prospective convert, instead of public preaching. Preaching is done to the Christian rather than to the Jew, so as to train pastors and congregations to active participation in the conversion of the Jew. For this purpose tracts are freely distributed and the "Messiah Hebrew Lutheran" is mailed in 1,700 copies to pastors and friends. The "Mediator" is regularly mailed to about 2,500 Jews. The missionary is trying to establish personal contacts in services to which special invitations are extended to Jews. During the past biennium 12 Jews were baptized and received into Lutheran Churches as the result of Pastor Morentz's efforts.

Christ Mission to the Jew at Pittsburgh, Pa., after a long vacancy has received a worthy successor to John Legum in the person of Dan Bravin. This mission is also without a home, but the Legum Memorial Fund is slowly growing, and when completed, will be used for the acquisition of a building to serve as an office and also as a dwelling for the missionary. Pastor Bravin's work, like that of Pastor Morentz, is done mostly in the English language. He appeals to the better-class Jew, where he finds less of the fanaticism of the Yiddish element and more willingness to listen to reason. His work consists in personal evangelism, house-to-house visitation, hospital visitation, mail evangelism and efforts to reach the Jew through the Churches. He publishes "The Dawn," which is sent out in 4,500 copies to Jews of all stations of life, also to 700 students of the University of Pittsburgh. During the past year the missionary visited 975 homes and made personal contact with 837 individuals. He baptized one convert.

Emmanuel Hebrew Mission, Toledo, Ohio, is our latest venture. The work done here by missionary Rubenstein is more along the lines of earlier methods. His work is done mostly in Yiddish; he has a great deal of house-to-house visitation, distributing tracts and parts of Scripture. In the absence of a mission centre he invites men to his home, where they will rather go than to a Christian mission centre. He is assisted by an able woman worker, Miss Lucretia Lafer, who is helping by colportage and work among the women and children. Nine persons were baptized, some 2,000 Jews were approached, 10,000 tracts distributed.

All of our Jewish missions are supervised and ably assisted by local mission committees. We are greatly indebted to the Women's Missionary Society for the help extended to our women workers. We commend the cause of Jewish Missions to the prayerful consideration of the Church.

EDUCATION OF MISSIONARIES

The Plan of Operation for the Board of American Missions, adopted at the Richmond Convention, charges the Board with the duty of developing a permanent missionary staff, giving it authority to enlist the help of our educational institutions, the Women's Missionary Society, the Laymen's Movement and others, and to aid or establish schools for the training of missionaries for our Division of Linguistic Interests. Both the Women's Missionary Society and the Laymen's Movement have most loyally and liberally supported our work, and they are assured of our gratitude and appreciation.

Again we have received quite a number of men from Kropp-Breklum; three came to us in 1929 and ten are due this year, some of whom have already set foot on our shores, and others will follow as soon as passage can be secured for them. The American Lutheran Church owes a great debt of gratitude to these institutions, without whose help our Canadian work would have been doomed. Almost all of our losses in Canada are due to the fact that the stream of missionaries did not flow freely enough at a time when they were most needed. It is true that the present arrangemen is not an ideal one. We have no hand in the selection of the men; we get them as a finished product, mostly at an age, when they are set in their convictions, and when they find it rather hard to accommodate themselves to entirely new conditions. Then there is the language question. In the same measure as our congregations become anglicized it becomes increasingly difficult for these men to give our congregations the kind of service which they require. But until the Church gives us an institution which will guarantee us a lasting supply of bilingual pastors, we must keep up this relationship and must be grateful for what we get and make the best of it.

During the last few years Martin Luther Seminary has become a potent factor in the solution of our educational problem. It has forged ahead in rapid strides, and has made such improvements in spirit and scholarship that its former critics would scarcely believe that it is the same institution. The students now receive an excellent training, both in German and English, and a home training which makes them excellent missionaries. Too much credit cannot be given to Dean Huebner, who has worked wonders, and who enjoys the confidence and loyal co-operation of his Synod.

Another veritable school of the prophets is the Seminary at Saskatoon, Sask. Here we train men from the field for the field, as it should be. The particular requirements of the great Canadian Northwest can be best filled by men who have grown up under the exacting conditions which are found there. Men from the East would not last long with 40 degrees below and the most primitive living conditions. It takes hardened men of sterling character to stand the rigors of the climate and the effects of that extreme loneliness which longs for companionship and finds no way to satisfy this longing. Whoever has seen that splendid body of missionaries from our Canadian institutions must say: Thank God for Saskatoon and Waterloo Seminaries!

The Finns have their own Seminary at Hancock,, Michigan, where they train splendid missionaries at less cost than any other institution.

DIVISION OF LATIN AMERICA
Dr. F. F. Fry, *Secretary*

More progress in new buildings and improved physical equipment was made in our West Indies missions during the biennium than at any similar period. Thanks to the prompt response of the United Lutheran Church to the Board's appeal for Hurricane Relief. $31,000 was received. A complete transformation resulted. Our missions rejoice in their new or renovated church plants, and send letters of gratitude and appreciation to the Church in the States.

Porto Rico's Progress

A new Church was built and equipped at Zion, Bayamon. The Sunday school was renovated. Extensive repairs were made to the house at Pajaros, where services are held as part of the parish.

The new Villa Betania, Home for Women Missionaries, is the outstanding improvement. Attractively situated, it provides a home for our regular nurse and a well equipped laboratory.

New Sunday school buildings were dedicated at Santisma Trinidad, Bayamon, and our mission at Catano. The parsonage at Catano was reenforced and substantial improvements were made.

The Church at Toa Baja was thoroughly renovated and restored. An adjacent lot was purchased for $500—the gift of a friend of the mission—and a new parsonage is in the process of construction.

A new lot was bought at Higuillar for $250, and a Sunday school building will be erected.

Much needed repairs were made to the chapel at Juan Domingo.

The San Juan Church, which houses the San Pablo Spanish congregation and the first English congregation, has been beautified with a large new chancel window and other marked improvements.

Virgin Islands

Practically all of our Church properties in the Virgin Islands were reconditioned.

The Queen Louise Home, in Frederiksted, St. Croix, is to all intents a new building.

The Ebenezer Orphanage is practically rebuilt.

The three Churches in the Island, Christiansted, Kingshill and Frederiksted have undergone extensive repairs, and are in first-class condition.

The new parsonage at Frederiksted was altered completely from basement to attic. It is now a commodious and comfortable home.

The parsonage and Queen Louise Home at Christiansted were improved also, as well as the Old People's Homes.

The Church and parsonage at St. Thomas, and the Church at St. John's suffered the least damage, and these were restored to their original beauty.

Our Church properties have arisen out of the wreckage and ruin, and stand as living monuments to the liberality of our people.

Spiritual Advance in the Islands

The spiritual condition of our people in the Islands evidence greater improvement than the physical plants. Attendance at Church and Sunday school has reached a new high standard. Week-day Religious Schools and Confirmation Classes have established new records. The sacrament of the Lord's Supper is administered to increasing numbers.

NATIVE PERSONNEL

Best of all is the dedication of the lives of native workers.

Miss Carmen M. Villarini, a graduate of the University of Porto Rico and a teacher of marked ability, heads up the kindergarten work in Porto Rico. She is the first native to have charge of this Educational Department. She accepted the Board's agreement at a considerably smaller salary than she had been receiving.

A young man of Santisima-Trinidad congregation, Bayamon, is preparing for the Lutheran ministry. He is supported by the United Synod of New York, and is taking academic training at the University of Porto Rico. This is in harmony with the Board's policy that native workers should take their university course in the country which is to be the scene of their future labors.

Three young women have joined the ranks as kindergarten helpers, under the direction of Miss Villarini. Their financial support is provided by the Women's Missionary Society.

Missionaries who resigned during the biennium are: Rev. J. C. Pedersen, of St. Thomas; Rev. Albert Ell, of Toa Baja, Porto Rico; Deaconess Clara Smyre, of the Queen Louise Home, Christiansted, and Rev. Louis G. Gray, of Frederiksted. They have been succeeded by Rev. Herman D. Whitteker, St. Thomas; Rev. Balbino Gonzalez, Toa Baja; Rev. Eugene C. Kreider, Frederiksted, and Mrs. Beatrice Benjamin, at the Christiansted Home.

Miss Mary Markley, of Roanoke, Virginia, was in charge of kindergarten work during part of the biennium, but she returned to the States because of her health.

PRESENT STAFF

The staff of missionaries and workers in Porto Rico is

Rev. Alfred Ostrom, D.D.............Puerta de Tierra, San Juan
Rev. and Mrs. Eduardo Roig ....Puerta de Tierra, San Juan
Rev. and Mrs. William G. Arbaugh....Santurce, San Juan
Rev. and Mrs. Gustav K. Huf ....Bayamon
Rev. S. Hernandez ....Catano
Rev. G. E. Marrero ....Bayamon
Rev. Balbino Gonzalez ....Toa Baja
Mr. Juan Zambrana ....Gandul
Mr. Frank Colon ....Dorado
Miss Frieda M. Hoh, R. N. ....Bayamon
Mrs. Maria Caraballo ....Bayamon
Mrs. Ramona Sotomayor ....Bayamon
Miss Carmen M. Villarini ....Monte Flores
Miss Marina Agostini ....Puerta de Tierra
Miss Berta Casos ....Catano
Miss Ana Luisa Dominquez ....Bayamon

Miss Rosario Ojeda ....Bayamon
Miss Elisa Silva ....Puerta de Tierra
Miss Angilica Martinez..............Puerta de Tierra
Miss Ofelia Baldorioty ....Puerta de Tierra
Miss Clara Rosa ....Catano

VIRGIN ISLANDS
Rev. and Mrs. Herman D. Whitteker. .St. Thomas
Mr. Carl E. Francis ....St. John's
Rev. and Mrs. Ivar O. Iverson ......Christiansted, St. Croix
Rev. and Mrs. Eugene C. Kreider......Frederiksted, St. Croix
Deaconess Maren Knudsen............Queen Louise Home—Frederiksted
Deaconess Emma Francis..............Ebenezer Orphanage—Frederiksted
Deaconess Edith Prince ....Ebenezer Orphanage—Frederiksted
Mrs. Beatrice Benjamin ....Queen Louise Home—Christiansted
Mr. Alexander Creagh ....Christiansted
Mr. Reginald MacFarlane ....Frederiksted

RELIEF WORK
Relief work in the Islands has gone hand and hand with the building program. This was administered by our missionaries with such system and discretion as to win the commendation of Governor Theodore Roosevelt of Porto Rico, and Governor Waldo Evans, of the Virgin Islands. The Board ministered to the necessities of our suffering and impoverished people, and the ministry of mercy and serving love is continued at all times.

This is made possible by the generous appropriations of the Women's Missionary Society, which provides for all women workers. The Light Brigade, under Mrs. C. K. Lippard, makes an annual contribution of $500 for sick and neglected babies. The administration of the funds is guarded with utmost care so as to accomplish the greatest possible good.

Christmas boxes, with their toys, candy and useful gifts are awaited with keen expectancy by the natives, and their distribution is a time of rejoicing. Other boxes are sent to different missions in the West Indies throughout the year, and they add much in the way of encouragement and support.

LUTHER LEAGUE OBJECTIVE
The Luther League of America has made Porto Rico its current objective. A fund of $25,000 is being raised to build a Training School at Monte Flores, the highest point in San Juan, and will be in hand at the Reading Convention in July, 1931. This will open a new field for the preparation of teachers and workers.

When the Island of Enchantment became a possession of the United States, it was almost shattered from the effects of war. Its cities were hotbeds of disease. Its country population had been herded into the larger centers. The story of how the United States Government assisted the Island to work its way out of so wretched a condition is familiar. In one generation the population has doubled. The last census reveals that 43 per cent of the people are fourteen years old and under, creating a serious economic problem to support this large non-productive group. Poverty, hunger, disease, illiteracy and lax morals indicate the present condition of the Islands. This condition produces a vicious circle, poverty producing disease—disease producing poverty.

An organized effort to combat these evils is in progress under the vigorous supervision of Governor Theodore Roosevelt. Porto Ricans are not given to rioting or racketeering, but are law-abiding. They have faith in the ability and integrity of the present administration. Support from the United States Government has been enlisted, along with influential groups in the States.

The fundamental need of the West Indies is a higher standard of Religious Education. The Board follows the method of the Master, and begins with child nurture. Lutheran kindergartens are admittedly the best in the Islands. Other denominations, including Roman Catholics, are modeling their teaching and methods after our kindergartens. This work is taken seriously in our missions six days a week. A systematic course of instruction is given by consecrated teachers under capable supervision.

Our missionary pastors, teachers and visiting nurse are consecrating their lives and efforts to help these people. Much permanent progress has been made. God helping them, they shall not fail.

As a mark of appreciation of the constructive work of the Board of American Missions, practically all of the Missions in Porto Rico and the Virgin Islands have increased their financial pledges to the Board, and they are paid in full.

Women missionaries, acting as heads of departments, were granted voice and vote at the annual meeting of the Missionaries' Conference in Porto Rico, in response to the petition of the Conference.

The Board approved also the publication of a Spanish translation of some authorized edition of Luther's Catechism.

Missionaries' Conference

The following rules governing the Evangelical Lutheran Missionary Conference of Porto Rico were approved by the Board in this modified form:

Name:
The name of the organization shall be The Lutheran Missionaries' Conference in Porto Rico.

Membership:
Membership in this Conference shall be limited to Pastors and Workers called and commissioned by, or under the jurisdiction and supervision of,

the Board of American Missions of the United Lutheran Church in America, and one layman from each and every congregation under the direction and control of the Board of American Missions of the United Lutheran Church in America.

Officers:
There shall be a President, Vice President, Secretary and Treasurer. They shall be elected at the annual meeting of the Conference. Ministers only are eligible to the office of President, Vice President and Secretary.

Meetings:
There shall be a regular annual meeting of the Conference, to be held in January or February, and such special meetings as the Executive Committee may determine.

Purpose:
This Conference shall aim to increase the efficiency of the working staff, and to develop the field most effectively. To this end there shall be discussion of doctrinal and practical questions; the peculiar problems and the possibilities of the field shall be studied and surveyed; the attention of the Board of American Missions shall be directed to matters which may be conducive of the development and growth of the field.

Committees:
There shall be an Executive Committee. It shall consist of the President, Vice President, Secretary and Treasurer, together with one clergyman and two laymen, to be elected annually by the Conference. This Committee shall represent the Conference and act in its behalf when the Conference is not in session. It shall have the right and power, in the name of the Conference, to make recommendations and suggestions for consideration by the Board of American Missions. But in all matters of major importance the Committee shall first ascertain the judgment of the Conference before its recommendations are transmitted to the Board of American Missions. This Conference shall constitute such other standing committees as its judgment may dictate. The President is ex-officio a member of all committees. He shall have the right of voice and vote in all matters under consideration by the Committees.

Limitations:
All actions of this Conference affecting the workers shall receive the approval and authorization of the Board of American Missions before the same can become effective or operative.

WEST INDIES

Our missionary force with its competent, spiritual leadership is the greatest asset in the West Indies. These missionaries numbered 42 during the biennium; a field treasurer, 9 missionary pastors, 13 missionary helpers, 11 kindergarten teachers, 5 deaconesses, and three women workers. These served 19 congregations and 14 mission stations, in addition to the educational work and the care of sick and neglected children. We have 10 parsonages and 4 school buildings. The organizations include 30 Sunday schools, 7 Daily Kindergartens, 8 Luther Leagues, 9 Junior Luther Leagues, 8 Daily Vacation Bible Schools, and 6 Light Brigades.

Rocky Boy Mission

Favorable predictions in taking over Rocky Boy Mission have been justified. New life is demonstrated at every turn. The Board is singularly fortunate in the personnel of its missionaries. They have won the respect and confidence of the Indians on the Reservation.

Rev. William H. Gable is giving able leadership and proper direction. He has shown fine administrative ability. He has developed the mission in a comprehensive way and organized different groups of Indians on a working basis. His wife is doing her full share. She is adapted and equipped for its difficult and varied needs. Their growing sons lend a hand and add to the general efficiency.

Miss Florence M. Buckner was commissioned during the biennium to succeed Miss Ora J. Brookover, resigned, and has taken hold with characteristic energy and zeal. She revels in hard work. Her personality plus magnetism have won many friends. Naturally the mission is giving a good account of itself. The missionaries have strong faith and buoyant optimism. In their capable hands the record is satisfactory. With God as their partner, they have aimed high and worked hard.

The new parsonage on the Reservation has been finished and furnished with the aid of special funds. Visitors are impressed at once with its homelike atmosphere. The Indians are welcome at all times, and their ideals and standards have been elevated.

Religious Training

Particular stress is laid on religious training. Weekday classes for boys and girls are held. The Sunday school has shown marked improvement in attendance, worship and instruction. Missionary Gable has introduced liturgical features into the Sunday services, which had been wholly lacking. Lenten services were held every Friday evening, with gratifying interest.

More Indians on the Reservation were baptized than ever before. The Lord's Supper was administered. The Church is the center of the Reservation, and its spirit pervades all other activities. Malcolm Mitchell has been invaluable as interpreter. Paul Mitchell, his son, matriculated as a freshman at Midland College during the past scholastic year. Its President, Dr. H. F. Martin, became his confidant and testifies to his studious habits as well as his personal popularity with other college students.

Rocky Boy makes a strong appeal to our Missionary Societies and Luther Leagues, as well as to individuals, Sunday School Classes and congregations. It received more gifts during the biennium than any other Lutheran mission in America.

Literally hundreds of bundles, boxes and barrels filled with useful clothing, supplies and gifts were sent to the mission, and were received by the Indians with great joy.

Rocky Boy captures the imagination, and has an urge and lure which win supporters in every section of the Church. The story of Rocky Boy is exhilarating and teems with romance.

The United States Government has taken note of its steady advance, and through the Department of the Interior has written to the Board asking that a doctor be added to the missionary staff.

A new era is dawning for the North American Indian. With larger opportunities for advanced education, Indian young people stand between the Tepee and the City. No one can fail to note the trend of migration to the centers of population. As young Indians attend our schools and colleges, ideas expand and ideals change with the unfolding of their minds. They are entering a new world.

A broader horizon is awakening new possibilities. Instead of taking up agricultural pursuits as formerly, a wider variety of occupation is offered by the Government. All of this emphasizes our responsibility in providing religious training. Our missionaries are keenly aware of their God-given opportunity.

WEST INDIANS IN NEW YORK

Although our West Indian congregation in New York City is a member in good standing of the United Synod of New York, its work is still reported under the Division of Latin America with which it has been so closely connected for the past ten years.

The Church of the Transfiguration is located in the Harlem section of New York City, where in a district of one square mile is found the greatest negro city the world has ever known. Literally from the ends of the earth 150,000 colored people have gathered, constituting a community, the story of which when written will read like the Arabian Nights. In this population are about 30,000 West Indians, among whom there are a goodly number of Lutherans. These were entirely lost to the Church until our work was started among them in 1920.

Today a congregation of more than 700 souls gratefully acknowledges the brotherly care which the Church is giving them. Although the present business depression has been most serious for these people, throwing many, especially servants, out of work, there has been little decrease in Church offerings because these people love the Church so deeply that their gifts have continued to average $5,000 yearly. No bazaars or worldly methods are used to secure these contributions. The congregation maintains all the activities found in the best organized congregations of our Church, including weekday classes for religious instruction.

Naturally a great amount of inner mission work must be done in a parish of this character, and the Pastor, the Rev. Paul E. West, probably visits more prisons, hospitals, asylums and courtrooms in his pastoral duties than any other minister, outside of the brethren who are giving their whole time to inner mission work.

The Church building is in use seven days in the week, with frequently two or three meetings going on at the same time. This is made possible because the building is four stories high. On special days extra services are required to provide for all, and even then hundreds are turned away at certain festivals. The full service and vestments as provided in the Common Service Book are in constant use. In addition there are certain vestments and customs of the Danish National Church still retained, inasmuch as these people are accustomed to these forms, as were their forefathers for three hundred years. Gregorian music is used in the services, and the great chorales of the Church are also rendered most devoutly. So many baptisms, funerals and weddings take place in this Church, which is a small building just around the corner from Lennox, on 126th street, that like another famous Church of the Transfiguration it has become known as "The Little Church Around the Corner."

Work is being carried on among our white Spanish people, the services being held in the same church building. This congregation has encountered many difficulties, and does not have as large a field since there are not so many Protestants among whom to work. Nevertheless, under Student James E. Soler, of Buenos Aires, Argentine, the work has developed remarkably in the last few months. Under the direction of this consecrated brother the congregation will soon be in a position to apply for membership in one of the Constituent Synods. No greater field is open before the Lutheran Church at the present time than the work among the Spanish speaking people. A man of faith with the right qualifications for leadership can readily find a large field among our Spanish brethren both in North and South America.

The greatest appeal from those in the deepest distress, both spiritually and materially, is the call that comes to us from the States that border on Mexico, where hundreds of thousands of Mexicans are dwelling as sheep without a shepherd.

CHURCH EXTENSION AND FINANCE
Dr. Z. M. Corbe, *Secretary*

The objective of the Department of Church Extension is sometimes misunderstood because the term "Church Extension" has many meanings and the religious bodies of this country use it in widely different senses. Before and since the merger the term has been used in the United Lutheran Church in a very restricted sense, and includes only those mission activities which have to do with aiding mission congregations in securing suitable property.

The Department of Church Extension naturally includes all related activities, as it was recognized from the beginning that the most efficient administration would be secured by assigning all similar activities to one department. Therefore, all real estate holdings, the administration of legacies and such other business transactions as are necessary in so large a work as that of the Board of American Missions, are under the management of this department.

While the objective of Church Extension is thus narrowed, its field of operation is not. No greater service can be rendered a mission than aiding it in securing property and a permanent Church building. It has happened that promising missions have been retarded in growth and others made hopeless because funds were not available to provide a Church home when most needed.

Given an adequate Church Extension fund, this Board could double its evangelistic work without asking for an increase in apportionment. A campaign for five million dollars would not end with securing the money since such a fund would put an end to present conditions where our missionaries, like the Hebrews of old, are expected to make bricks without straw. An adequate Church Extension fund would release for soul saving the labors that are now devoted to securing Church buildings, and would, without doubt, result in the United Lutheran Church growing faster than any other Church body.

The fundamental principle of Church Extension is that its resources should constitute a revolving fund to be loaned out for five years without interest, with the possibility of renewal when absolutely necesssary for an additional three years. With our present investment of $1,503,000 we should have $188,000 returns each year, which is about five times the amount realized.

The causes contributing to this deficit are many, but the most outstanding is the tendency of missions to follow the fashion set by established congregations of building beyond their means. A Church burdened with mortgages is not in a position to repay Church Extension loans or contribute to benevolence. This situation is not peculiar to our Church, however. The Methodist Episcopal Church, in their report last year, calls attention to their Book of Discipline, which says:

"In order more effectually to prevent our people from contracting debts which they are not able to discharge, it shall be the duty of the Quarterly Conference of every Charge where it is contemplated to build a house or houses of worship, to see . . . . that one-half of the money required, according to such estimate previously made of the amount necessary to build shall be secured or subscribed before any such building shall be commenced."

The report then goes on to say:

"For a number of years many of this Department's most difficult and perplexing problems have been caused by the submission of a series of financial emergencies, the result of either ignorance of this provision of the Discipline, or its complete disregard. The majority of these cases are in no real sense of the term Missionary projects, yet nearly all of them, when they reach their most desperate condition, are laid on the door-step of the Board of Home Missions and Church Extension."

This describes most accurately the problem of salvaging wrecks which has engaged our Board's serious attention for four years. Recently a policy has been adopted which requires that a congregation to secure a loan must have raised in cash from its own members one-fourth of its requirements before building, and yet this action, lenient when compared with the Methodists, has not been favorably received.

Other causes for the shortage in the return of loans are the rapid changes which occur in communities where a few years can transform a promising mission field into a hopeless task. The placing of men unqualified for missionary service in mission fields, all too frequently without consulting either the Synodical authorities or this Board, is another factor in preventing missions returning their loans promptly.

Other missions founded in the days when it was not unusual for altar to be set up against altar is another factor in retarding the return of Church Extension loans.

In view of these circumstances and realizing that other conditions may develop which make it impossible for missions to repay their obligations in full at one time, arrangements have been made to accept monthly payments, frequently of very small amounts. This has started a steady flow of funds, which it is hoped will in time become a flood of sufficient magnitude to bring refreshment to certain parched sections of our field.

During the past biennium we have aided 54 missions with loans, amounting to $238,880.00. Further aid was extended missions by the payment of interest on first mortgages amounting to $88,797.00 for 166 congregations.

FINANCES

The very full report required of the Treasurer by the Convention will present the essential features of this Department. Since the last convention this Board has operated on a balanced budget without retrogression.

This adjustment was made possible through the loyal co-operation of the Synods, which arranged for the care of unproductive fields by the pastors of the nearest parishes wherever this was possible. There has also been a slight decrease in overhead by the readjustment of our field men. It is confidently expected that this form of retrenchment will be continued during the present biennium.

LEGACIES

Unless otherwise designated legacies are usually placed in the Memorial Loan Fund, where, throughout the ages the gift will play its part in extending the Kingdom. Pastors and devoted Churchmen should bring to the attention of those who have been blessed with this world's goods, this splendid form of service. During the past biennium the following legacies were received:

James Matter		$17,177.45
Martha C. Henson	$8,000.00	
Transmitted to Foreign Board	4,000.00	
		4,000.00
John B. Franke		6,381.43
J. K. Laudermilch		5,000.00
Julia Beck Fromlet		5,000.00
Bransby C. Pentz		5,000.00
Carrie Tremain		5,000.00
Etta M. Harroway		3,987.77
John H. Davy	$3,601.18	
Refund	1,800.59	
		1,800.59
J. E. Cooper		2,500.00
Theo. C. Birnbaum		2,240.61
Fredericka Fennell		1,920.00
Mrs. E. M. Hobbs		1,216.02
Sophia B. Kramlich		1,000.00
Sarah E. Sell		905.00
Weltha Calkins		823.47
Loyetta E. Lark		500.00
Amanda C. Scheurich		456.87
Dr. H. H. Hartman		285.00
David W. Seidler		200.00
Flora B. Sahen	$200.00	
Transmitted to Foreign Board	100.00	
		100.00
George W. Bruner		135.00
Dr. Fred. P. Mayser		128.64
Elizabeth S. Wollenhaupt		90.00
Elizabeth Pfaff		50.00
Mary Schaefer		50.00
Columbia City, Indiana		22.08
Wilson ·F. Lobach		12.50

PROMOTION AND PUBLICITY

Tell it to the Church! Give the facts to the people!

That is the policy of the Board of American Missions in publishing its good news. The entire Staff has been diligent in presenting the cause of Home Missions and Church Extensions in all sections of the Church and to all groups of our constituents. Our advancing cause has been brought home to Synods, Conferences, congregations, Ministerial Associations, student groups, Sunday Schools, Women's Synodical Missionary Societies and local organizations, Luther Leagues and Summer assemblies, while the latest developments have been given from time to time through our Church periodicals.

New Publications:

"In the Land of Unending Summer"—a descriptive booklet well illustrated, of the Board's work in the West Indies.

"Building for Eternity"—a Church Extension booklet giving the latest facts and information. Both of these booklets are distributed and circulated by the Women's Missionary Society, as well as the Board of American Missions.

"We and Our Neighbors"—a study of our challenging opportunities in the North American continent.

"The Place of Denominational Activity in Projecting the Home Mission Enterprise," by John C. Seegers. Published by the Home Missions Council and distributed by the Board of American Missions.

"The New Fact Series"—concise statements in convenient form of the work among Germans, Italians, Hungarians, Slovaks, West Indians and Jews. Also one on Alaska and another on Home Missions. Each of these groups is dealt with in separate leaflets.

Illustrated lecture on Porto Rico, 65 slides.

Illustrated lecture on the Virgin Islands, with 60 slides.

"With the Rocky Boy Indians," an illustrated lecture with 60 slides.

Illustrated lecture on Home Missions.

These lectures are typewritten, and the slides are easily handled. Furnished free of cost to Sunday schools, Missionary Societies, Luther Leagues, Light Brigades, etc.

Field Days For Church Extension:

Toledo, Dayton, Chicago and Minneapolis put on successful Field Days. A two-day program was set up. Men of the Board and the Staff presented the cause of American Missions from the pulpits of our Churches Sunday morning. A union service was held in the afternoon or evening. All missions were visited by the entire group. Conferences were held with Synodical officials and Home Mission Committees together with the local pastors, which led to a better understanding and more active cooperation.

Home Mission Conferences:

The Ministerium of Pennsylvania, the Pittsburgh Synod, the Synod of East Pennsylvania, the Synod of the Northwest and other Synodical bodies arranged conferences of Home Missionaries of the Synod. Mission opportunities and responsibilities were discussed, and many practical questions were answered. The Board of American Missions was represented by a member of its Staff.

Evangelistic Services:

Out on the Pacific Coast, General Superintendent Hillerman was in great demand in hold one week's daily services in many of our missions.

The result has been highly commendable, and stirred our struggling enterprises to renewed faith and consecration. His theme is "Home Missions and Evangelism," which was given to the people in such striking fashion as to arouse the indifferent and quicken missionary fervor and zeal.

Summer Schools:

Summer assemblies at Lakeside, Ohio; Columbia, South Carolina; Mt. Airy, Philadelphia; Hartwick Seminary, New York; Massanetta Springs, Virginia; Lake Wawasee, Indiana; Northwest Synodical, Green Lake, Wisconsin, together with many others, have included American Missions on their program. Representatives of the Board and the Staff gladly accepted invitations from all parts of the United Lutheran Church to present a course of study and give popular addresses on the great cause which has appealed to the imagination and kindled the interest of the whole Church.

CO-OPERATION ALONG ALL LINES

The Board of Education:

A contribution of $2,500 for the biennium was made by our Board to the Board of Education for the support of Kropp-Breklum, in Germany, in preparing students to serve in our mission fields. The Board of Education has asked the Board of American Missions to appoint a committee to consult with a similar committee of the Board of Education in regard to the future support of such students.

The Board of Education assists our Board in the support of pastors at Durham, North Carolina; Lafayette, Indiana; University and St. Mark's, Seattle, Washington; West Chester, Pennsylvania; Boulder, Colorado; Rock Hill and Clemson College, South Carolina.

The Inner Mission Board:

The Board of American Missions is pleased to assist the Inner Mission Board in notifying Home Mission pastors of the arrival of Lutheran immigrants within the bounds of their parishes, requesting that they be visited at an early date and afforded the privileges of a Church home.

It has granted also part time service of the Rev. Fred W. Kern, of Houston, Texas, in caring for Lutheran seamen during their stay in that port.

It assists also in providing a house for the Rev. H. Becker, of Winnipeg. He has charge of the immigrant work at Northwestern Canada, under the supervision of the Board of Inner Missions.

The Women's Missionary Society:

The Board wishes to record its deep gratitude to the Women's Missionary Society for their friendly spirit and substantial support. As a mark of appreciation, Miss Flora Prince and Mrs. Philip M. Rossman were invited to attend the stated meetings of the Board as advisory members. Mrs. T. W. Kretschmann represented the Society in the interests of English Missions. Mrs. W. F. Morehead, President, and Miss Amelia D. Kemp, Executive Secretary, were present at several meetings of the Board as special guests. They were heartily welcomed, and their presence proved helpful.

Thirty-six missions are supported by the Society. Among them may be noted the only mission in Arkansas; Barnitz Memorial, Denver; Boulder, Colorado; University, Seattle, and Longview, Washington; Grace, Casper, and Trinity, Laramie, Wyoming; Elyria, Ohio; Watauga Parish, North Carolina; Great Falls and Rocky Boy Mission, Montana; Westwood and Belmont Park, Chicago; Trinity, Kalamazoo, and many others. Favorable recommendation has been made to assume St. Mark's, Asheville, North Carolina; the only mission in the capital of Alaska, and new work in the Beaver River District, Saskatchewan.

Students preparing for the ministry of our linguistic groups receive aid from them. All women teachers and workers in the West Indies and at Rocky Boy, and those who contribute to the progress of our Italian, Hebrew, Slovak and southern mountain work are made possible by their support; acknowledgement is made also of the grant of Church Extension loans, interest donations and special gifts.

The Laymen's Movement for Stewardship:

Paul Mitchell, of Rocky Boy Mission, is the first North American Indian in preparation for the Lutheran ministry. He was accepted by the Laymen's Movement as a beneficiary student, and receives an appropriation of $250 per year. His first year at Midland College marked definite progress in his educational development.

The Board is grateful also for the financial aid given to seven other students for the ministry who are now in our service.

The Board of Deaconess Work:

The relation of the Deaconess Board to the Board of American Missions has continued to be thoroughly harmonious. Grateful acknowledgement is made of the faithful services of Sister Clara Smyre, of the Baltimore Motherhouse, and Sister Emma Francis and Sister Edith Prince of the Philadelphia Motherhouse. The Board is indebted to the Danish Motherhouse in Copenhagen, for Sister Maren Knudsen, whose ministry of mercy challenges our admiration and awakens gratitude to God. The assistance of these trained workers in the ministry of serving love has been invaluable.

The Augustana Synod:

The Board welcomes this opportunity of acknowledging its debt of gratitude to the Augustana Synod for giving the valued services of Dr. Alfred Ostrom, who recently completed twenty-five years of missionary service in the West Indies. It is grateful also for the gifts received in Christmas boxes, and its support of the industrial work in the West Indies.

IN MEMORIAM

Dr. A. L. Ramer, General Superintendent of Immigrant Missions, met with a fatal accident while in the discharge of his duties. The following minute was entered on the records of the Board.

"Dr. A. L. Ramer passed into the life immortal March 8, 1929. He was a loyal servant of Christ and His Church. He gave his life with rare devotion to the cause he loved and served. He filled a unique place in our work among New Americans, and was a familiar figure in all sections of the land.

"Early in his ministry he dedicated himself as an itinerant missionary to Hungarian and Slovak people. With singleness of purpose he centered his energies upon our fellow Lutherans, who had come to the United States and Canada from southeastern Europe. As proof of his definite choice, he spent two years in Budapest applying himself with unremitting diligence to the study of the language as well as of the customs and life of the people in their homeland.

"The Church was quick to recognize the value of his training and gifts in ministering to these scattered people. In 1908 he was called as Superintendent of the Slav Mission Board of the General Council. After the merger, in 1918, he was continued as Superintendent of the Board of Immigrant Missions of the United Lutheran Church in America. When the Board of American Missions was organized, in January, 1927, he was elected General Superintendent of Slav-Hungarian work.

"While in the discharge of his official duties, he met with a fatal accident in Camden, N. J., March 5, 1929.

"The beauty of his character, the sincerity of his life, and the simplicity of his message endeared him to many. He had a warm, throbbing heart, quick to discern the needs and problems of his missionaries. His patience apparently had no limit. He gave freely of his best to the discouraged and the lonely. Everywhere he brought inspiration, hope and comfort.

"He was an eloquent champion of his cause. His largeness of heart, breadth of sympathy, broad humanity and genuine concern for their spiritual care made him an outstanding figure in his chosen calling. He realized the value of having the supervision of an American over both Magyars and Slovaks. He followed the example of the Great Apostle as a missionary traveler Distance had scant meaning to him if the souls of these people yearned for the Word of God and the Sacraments. An urgent call from them was sure to receive favorable response, if possible, and often he crowded the possibilities. He was ready at any time to journey a thousand miles to minister to five or six humble families and conduct a religious service for them. Dr. Ramer stated he never went on any of these errands of love without administering the Lord's Supper.

"Railroad officials recognized his worth in lifting the morale of these people, many of whom were in their employ, and an annual pass was forthcoming upon his personal asking. A record of 30,000 miles a year for a score of years, crossing the continent sixteen times, is not easily duplicated. In every section of the land saddened homes and stricken hearts mourn the loss of a personal friend and spiritual guide. Such men belong to the company of God's elect.

"Gladly we record our affection and esteem for this servant of God. He has passed through the portals of victory and taken his place with the immortals. We commend his widow and son to the tender mercies of God. He left a rich legacy of fidelity and devotion to duty, and an example of true humility and submission to the perfect will of God.

"Recommended that the Secretary of the Board be instructed to convey to his widow and son this expression of our esteem and sympathy, that a copy of this minute be sent to "The Lutheran," for publication, and be included in our report to the next convention of the United Lutheran Church in America."

Mr. William L. Glatfelter

Another serious loss was sustained in the passing of Mr. William L. Glatfelter, a charter member of the Board, and Chairman of its Finance Committee. The Board's appreciation of his character and work follows:

"A loving Heavenly Father has seen fit to remove from our midst a devoted and wise co-worker. Mr. W. L. Glatfelter, through years of close association endeared himself to this Board by his Christian character, loyal comradeship and wise counsel.

"We desire to record our high appreciation of the services which Mr. Glatfelter rendered as a member of this Board, as well as his outstanding usefulness to the various institutions and activities of the United Lutheran Church.

"The Board of American Missions of the United Lutheran Church, assembled in the city of Baltimore, desires hereby to record its sentiments of love and affection for our deceased Brother, as well as the deepest sympathy for his sorrowing loved ones.

"*Be It Therefore Resolved*: That the Board of American Missions express its faith in all the dispensations of a loving Heavenly Father even in those which bring us deepest sorrow.

"*Be It Resolved*: That we record our esteem and affection for our deceased friend and colleague.

"*Be It Resolved*: That we express our sympathy and affection for the bereaved family of our Brother.

"*Be It Resolved*: That these resolutions be inscribed on our Minutes, that a copy be sent to Mrs. W. L. Glatfelter and Mr. P. II. Glatfelter, and that a copy be sent to the official publication of the United Lutheran Church."

Dr. W. M. Rehrig

Rev. W. M. Rehrig, Ph.D., for many years a member of the Board of Immigrant Missions, and at one time its president, entered into life December 8, 1928. The summoning messenger found him seated at his desk with manuscript before him, but the spirit had fled. He served on the Board of Immigrant Missions from its organization in 1905 until the merging of the Boards in 1927. His interest in the welfare of the immigrants was vital; his policy to carry on the work, wise; his purpose to establish these strangers in the land of their adoption faltered at no obstacle; his devotion to their spiritual ministry, untiring. He willed his estate to Muhlenberg College for the establishment of a lectureship on Evidences of Christianity. The Board of American Missions is cognizant that the cause of missions has lost a staunch friend, and hereby records its high appreciation of the noble service he rendered.

Dr. John Henry Meyer

The Board of American Missions noted with genuine sorrow the passing of the Rev. John Henry Meyer, D.D., pastor of the Church of Our Saviour, Jersey City, N. J. He entered into life July 6, 1929. He was an active member of the Board of West Indies Missions from the time of the merger convention in New York, 1918. He rarely missed a meeting and took a lively interest in its progress. He was a warmhearted, genial, sincere Christian, who cherished the missionary passion. He followed in the way of the Master, copying His spirit and giving full proof of his faith in the ministry of love and service.

Four Missionaries

Four missionaries heard the final summons during the biennium. The Board holds their memory in grateful recognition of their faithful service. They are:

Rev. Fred Ross Shirck, Dundalk, Md.
Rev. George Gersib, Lipscomb, Texas.
Rev. J. C. Miller, Lakeland, Fla.
Rev. Hans B. Lundh, Missouri Valley, Iowa.

ORGANIZATION

Officers:

President—J. B. Markward, D.D.
Vice President—Rev. H. W. A. Hanson, D.D., LL.D.
Recording Secretary—Mr. Grant Hultberg.
Treasurer—Rev. Z. M. Corbe, D.D.

Members:

Terms expiring 1930—Rev. G. A. Benze, D.D., Rev. H. W. A. Hanson, D.D., LL.D., Rev. J. B. Markward, D.D., Rev. J. Maurer, D.D., Mr. Grant Hultberg, Mr. Harry Snyder, Mr. A. Raymond Bard.

Terms expiring 1932—Rev. F. O. Evers, Rev. J. M. Francis, D.D., Rev. Paul H. Krauss, Rev. L. H. Larimer, D.D., LL.D., Mr. H. F. Heuer, Mrs. Charles H. Lehmann.

Terms expiring 1934—Rev. A. E. Bell, D.D., Rev. C. A. Freed, D.D., Rev. G. K. Rubrecht, D.D., Rev. J. C. Seegers, D,D., Mr. A. H. Durboraw, Mr. W. I. Eck, Mr. S. F. Telleen.

Divisional Committee on English Missions: Rev. J. C. Seegers, D.D.,

Rev. A. E. Bell, D.D., Rev. G. K. Rubrecht, D.D., Mr. Grant Hultberg.

Divisional Committee on Linguistic Interests: Rev. F. O. Evers, Rev. G. A. Benze. D.D., Rev. J. Maurer, D.D., Mr. W. I. Eck.

Divisional Committee on Latin America: Rev. J. M. Francis, D.D., Rev. Paul H. Krauss, Rev. L. H. Larimer, D.D., LL.D., Mr. H. L. Snyder.

Divisional Committee on Church Extension: Mr. A. Raymond Bard, Mr. A. H. Durboraw, Mr. H. F. Heuer, Rev. C. A. Freed, D.D.

Divisional Committee on Finance: Mr. S. F. Telleen, Mr. Charles H. Lehmann, Rev. H. W. A. Hanson, D.D., LL.D.

Committee on Conference with Foreign Board: Rev. J. B. Markward, D.D., Rev. J. C. Seegers, D.D., Rev. Paul H. Krauss, Mr. H. F. Heuer.

Committee on Conference with Board of Education: Rev. H. W. A. Hanson, D.D., LL.D., Rev. G. K. Rubrecht, D.D., Mr. Grant Hultberg, Mr. A. H. Durboraw.

Committee on Conference with Inner Mission Board: Rev. F. O. Evers, Rev. C. A. Freed, D.D., Mr. S. F. Telleen, Mr. W. I. Eck.

Committee on Conference with Deaconess Board: Rev. J. M. Francis, D.D., Rev. A. E. Bell, D.D., Mr. A. Raymond Bard.

Committee on Conference with other Lutheran Bodies: Rev. J. B. Markward, D.D., Rev. G. K. Rubrecht, D.D., Rev. J. C. Seegers, D.D., Mr. Grant Hultberg Mr. A. H. Durboraw.

Sub-Committee, Comity Conference: Rev. J. B. Markward, D.D., Mr. Grant Hultberg, Rev. F. F. Fry, D.D.

Committee on Beneficiary Education: Rev. H. W. A. Hanson, D.D., LL.D., Rev. J. C. Seegers, D.D., Rev. L. H. Larimer. D.D., LL.D., Mr. S. F. Telleen, Rev. F. O. Evers.

Committees on Review: Rev. Paul H. Krauss. Rev. J. M. Francis, D.D., Rev. F. O. Evers, Mr. A. Raymond Bard, Mr. H. L. Snyder.

Nominations:

Board of American Missions: Rev. J. B. Markward, D.D., Rev. H. W. A. Hanson, D.D., LL.D., Rev. G. A. Benze, D.D.. Rev. J. Maurer, D.D., Mr. H. L. Snyder, Mr. A. Raymond Bard, Mr. Grant Hultberg.

Board of West Indies Missions: Rev. J. B. Markward, D.D., Rev. H. W. A. Hanson, D.D., LL.D., Rev. J. Maurer, D.D., Mr. H. L. Snyder, Mr. A. Raymond Bard, Mr. Grant Hultberg. To fill a term expiring in 1932, Mr. H. F. Heuer.

Board of Northwestern Missions: Rev. J. B. Markward, D.D., Rev. H. W. A. Hanson, D.D., LL.D., Rev. G. A. Benze, D.D., Rev. J. Maurer, D.D., Mr. H. L. Snyder, Mr. A. Raymond Bard, Mr. Grant Hultberg.

Board of Immigrant Missions: Rev. J. B. Markward, D.D., Rev. H. W. A. Hanson, D.D., LL.D., Mr. A. Raymond Bard, Mr. Grant Hultberg.

Staff:

Executive Secretary—Rev. Franklin F. Fry, D.D.
Divisional Secretary of English Missions—Rev. J. F. Seibert, D.D.
Divisional Secretary of Linguistic Interests—Rev. E. A. Tappert, D.D.
General Superintendents of English Missions: Rev. I. C. Hoffman, D.D.,
Rev. A. D. R. Hancher. D.D., Rev. G. H. Hillerman, D.D.
General Superintendent of German Missions—Rev. Paul Ludwig.
General Superintendent of Finnish Missions—Rev. John F. Saarinen.
Attorney—George E. Neff, Esq.

RECOMMENDATIONS

The Board of American Missions returns humble and heartfelt thanks to the great Head of the Church for His unfailing guidance and favor, and prays that His continued blessing may attend its work and that this Convention may be inspired with renewed zeal and devotion to the winning of America for Christ.

1. Recommended that the cause of Church Extension be commended to congregations and individuals of the United Lutheran Church in America so that they may be encouraged to increase their gifts for the establishment and expansion of the Church in all sections of the Western Hemisphere.

2. Recommended that this Convention will open the heart and conscience of the Church to its duty and privilege of supporting the Russian refugees who have come to this western land, and all other groups from Europe, our brothers in the faith, and that it stir our pastors and all our people to realize the vital fact that its linguistic work is not of secondary value, but is essential to the fulfillment of the Church's call to work on American soil.

3. Recommended that the Board of American Missions ask the United Lutheran Church in America for its approval of the organization of the Lutheran Home Missions Council of America, and the participation of the Board of American Missions under the proposed Articles of Agreement.

4. Recommended that the Board of American Missions petition the United Lutheran Church in America to set apart the year 1938, the Twentieth Anniversary of the organization of the United Lutheran Church in America, for Church Extension.

5. In view of the close relationship which our colonization work bears to the Immigrant Mission work of our Church, it is highly desirable that both be placed under one head. Recommended, that the Board of American Missions memorialize the United Lutheran Church in America to transfer the Immigrant Mission Department from the jurisdiction of the Board of Inner Missions to the Board of American Missions.

J. BRADLEY MARKWARD, *President.*
GRANT HULTBERG, *Secretary.*

FRANKLIN F. FRY, *Executive Secretary.*

APPENDIX A
NEW MISSIONS

California Synod
Beverly Hills—Beverly Hills

East Pennsylvania Synod
Yeadon, Pa.—Trinity

Illinois Synod
Elmwood Park—Westwood
Chicago—Acacia Park
Waukegan—St. Paul's
St. Louis—Unity

Kansas Synod
Fort Smith, Arkansas—United
Lutheran

Ministerium of Pennsylvania
Rhawnhurst—Redemption
Ogontz Avenue—St. Peter's
Tacony—Good Shepherd
Pleasantville—Epiphany
Mountainville—Trinity
Maple Shade—Trinity
Fox Chase—St. Timothy

Nebraska Synod
Spencer—United Lutheran

North Carolina Synod
North Kannapolis
Alamance

Northwest Synod
Minneapolis—St. Louis Park
White Fish Bay—Bayshore
Salem, S. D.—Christ

Ohio Synod
Elyria—Emanuel
Toledo—Hope
Middletown—Zion

Pacific Synod
Seattle—St. Mark's

Pittsburgh Synod
Erie—Mt. Calvary
Homestead Park—Messiah
Dravosburg—St. John's

United Synod of New York
Briarwood—All Saints
Leonia, N. J.—Holy Trinity
Cranford, N. J.—Calvary
Dunellen, N. J.—St. Luke's
Bayside West, N. Y.—Good
Shepherd
Red Bank, N. J.—Holy Trinity

West Pennsylvania Synod
Loganville—Freysville Parish

APPENDIX B
SELF-SUPPORTING MISSIONS

California Synod
San Bernardino—First
Glendale—First
Los Angeles—St. Paul's
Santa Monica—St. Pauls
Sanger—St. Paul's
Redlands—First

East Pennsylvania Synod
Coatesville—Our Saviour
Manoa—Trinity

Illinois Synod
Chicago—Epiphany
St. Louis, Mo.—Advent

Indiana Synod
Indianapolis—Christ
Louisville—Calvary

Michigan Synod
Detroit—Hope
Detroit—Reformation

Ministerium of Pennsylvania
Philadelphia—St. James
West Collingswood—St. Luke's

Northwest Synod
Wauwatosa—St. Matthew's
Milwaukee—Washington Park

Ohio Synod
Cleveland—St. James
Toledo—Olivet

Pittsburgh Synod
Farrell—Grace

Sewickley—St. Paul's
Clairon—Grace
Aliquippa—House of Prayer
Pittsburgh—Epiphany

Rocky Mountain Synod
Trinidad, Colo.—Zion

United Synod of New York
Newark—Advent
Valley Stream—St. Paul's
New Haven, Conn.—First

Virginia Synod
Roanoke, Va.—Emmanuel

West Pennsylvania Synod
Goldsboro—Mt. Zion

APPENDIX C

MISSIONS DISCONTINUED FROM THE BUDGET

California Synod
Monrovia—St. John's
Salinas—Our Saviour

Indiana Synod
Louisville—Bethany
Evansville—Christ

Iowa Synod
Ottumwa—St. Mark's

Michigan Synod
Fordson—Fordson

Northwest Synod
Milwaukee—Redemption

Ohio Synod
Springfield—Trinity

Pacific Synod
Fairbanks, Alaska—St. John's
Astoria, Ore.—Memorial

South Carolina Synod
Mt. Pleasant—St. Paul's

Pittsburgh Synod
Carnegie—St. Andrew's
Coudersport—St. Paul's

Rocky Mountain Synod
Burlington, Colo.

United Synod of New York
Buffalo—Zion

Ministerium of Penna.
Magnolia, N. J.—Trinity

BENEFICIARY STUDENTS

Slovak:

John Balog ....Mt. Airy Seminary
George Billy ....Maywood Seminary
J. Albert Billy ....Mt. Airy Seminary
Joseph W. Billy ....Muhlenberg College
Andrew Brndjar ....Maywood Seminary
George Churlick ....Mt. Airy Seminary
John A. Janisak, Jr. ....Mt. Airy Seminary
Andrew Kanyuch ....Mt. Airy Seminary
Stephen Medved ....Mt. Airy Seminary
John Mikletz ....Mt. Airy Seminary
George Abraham ....Muhlenberg College
Stephen Krasny ....Muhlenberg College
Vlado Ondrejcek ....Muhlenberg College

Two Slovak students will enter college this Fall:

Andrew Mazak ....Roanoke College
John Kanyuch ....Muhlenberg College

Hungarian:

Eugen Ruzsa ....Waterloo Seminary
Andor Leffler ....Mt. Airy Seminary

German:

Warren Churchill ....Martin Luther Seminary
Alfred Duis ....Martin Luther Seminary
Henry J. Goede ....Martin Luther Seminary
Wolfgang Goemmel ....Martin Luther Seminary
Carl Goldenstein ....Martin Luther Seminary
George Herber ....Martin Luther Seminary
Edwin J. Hirsch ....Martin Luther Seminary
Henry Knaub ....Martin Luther Seminary
Alfred Pannbacker ....Martin Luther Seminary
Richard Schipporeit ....Martin Luther Seminary

Finnish:

John E. Hattula ....Suomi College and Seminary
Viljo Ibar Oeiman ....Suomi College and Seminary
Aarne Johaness Juntunen ....Suomi College and Seminary
Antti Kopra ....Suomi College and Seminary
Wallace Korpi ....Suomi College and Seminary
Frans Koski ....Suomi College and Seminary
Douglas Ollila ....Suomi College and Seminary
Edward Puumalainen ....Suomi College and Seminary
Carl M. Jervinen ....Suomi College and Seminary
Arvid E. Kuitunen ....Suomi College and Seminary
Einar W. Lehte ....Suomi College and Seminary
Matti N. Lepista ....Suomi College and Seminary
Alex. Tamminen ....Suomi College and Seminary

Spanish:

Leopoldo Caban—also aided by Laymen's Movement and New York
    and New England Synod.
Balbino Gonzalez—also aided by New York and New England Synod.
Francisco Agnostini—approved by the United Synod of New York for aid.

Indian:

Paul Mitchell—Midland College—also aided by Laymen's Movement and
    individuals.

STATISTICAL REPORT
GERMAN MISSIONS
CANADA SYNOD

Name	Place	Organized	Bapt. Memb.	Val.	Indebted
St. Johannes	Arnprior, Ont.	1891	211	$7,000	
St. Jacobus	Northcote, Ont.	1891	120	1,500	
St. Marcus	Chesley, Ont.	1894	260	5,800	
Zion (Town)	Massey, Ont.	1904	60	4,000	
Zion (Country)	Massey, Ont.	1904	103		
Chalk River	Chalk River, Ont.	1904	66	1,000	
St. Paulus	Denbigh	1868	59	2,000	
St. Stephanus	Raglan	1887	161	4,850	300
Preaching Point	Quadeville				
Christus	Maynooth, Ont.		188	2,925	1,400
St. Matthaus	East Zorra, Ont.	1853	115	7,400	
St. Matthaus	Plattsville		15	500	

Name	Place	Or-ganized	Bapt. Memb.	Val.	In-debted
St. Petri.........Wiarton, Ont.		1888	155	15,000	75
Preaching Point...Owen Sound					
Brantford			50		
Chatham, Ont.			60		
			1,621	$51,975	$1,775

MANITOBA SYNOD

Name	Place	Or-ganized	Bapt. Memb.	Val.	In-debted
St. Johannes.......	Dresden, N. D.	1896	165	$9,000	$120
St. Johannes.......	Snowflake, Man.	1927	110	250	
Preaching Station..	Osnabrock, N. D.				
	Thalberg, Man.	1911	288	5,000	
St. Johannes.......	Gruenwald		108		
Preaching Station..	Jackfish Lake		43		
Bethanien	Inglis	1901	165	11,500	
Immanuel	New Cana	1901	75	400	
St. Paulus........	Elbourne, Sask.	1907	144		
St. Paulus........	Serath	1907	92		
Dreieinigkeit	Esk, Sask.	1907	291	3,850	372
St. Johannes	Brightholme, Sask.	1916	248	6,000	300
St. Paulus........	Silvergrove	1902	120	1,500	
St. Johannes.......	Luseland, Sask.	1910	139	4,000	350
Preaching Station..	Luselandtown				
St. Johannes......	Laird (Stony Hill)	1901	159	8,000	200
Immanuel	Hubbard	1917	90	1,000	
Petri	Goodeve	1907		1,060	
St. Johannes.......	Edmonton, Alta.	1903	327	20,000	6,350
St. Johannes.......	New Sarepta	1911	212	7,000	1,100
Preaching Station..	Rosenthal	1929			
	Barrhead	1929	132	1,500	1,168
	Lunford	1929	32		
	Manola	1929	47		
Preaching Station..	Mellowdale		37		
	Camper	1911	61	1,400	
St. Paulus........	Gretna	1897	102	3,000	
St. Johannes......	Niverville	1900	56	800	
St. Johannes.......	Friedensfeld	1925	156	8,000	1,000
Christus	Ruciman	1925	88	500	
St John's.........	Shellbrook	1924	41	100	
St. Paulus........	Sturgeon River	1930	60	100	
Preaching Station..	Kandahar	1928	36	50	
	Leask	1929	48		
	Fox Dale	1925	33		
	Blue Heron	1929	46		
	Boro Green	1928	43		
	Shell Lake	1928	38		
	Big River	1929	11		
	Makwa	1929	80		
	Meadow Lake	1929	18		
	Loon Forks	1929	11		
	Beaver River	1930	16		
	Fawcett	1927	60		
St. Johannes......	Flatbush	1930	58		
	Busby	1929	58		
	Alcomdale	1927	44		

Name	Place	Or-ganized	Bapt. Memb.	Val.	In-debted
Preaching Station..	Portobello	1924	53		
	Rosevear	1929	50		
—	Wolf Creek	1928	31		
	Sunnybrook		69	500	125
	Strawberry Creek		57		
	Stettler		52		
	Watrous, Sask.		50		
Preaching Station..	Prince Albert		19		
Dreieinigkeit	Saskatoon		140	5,000	2,100
			4,709	$99,460	$11,085

GERMAN NEBRASKA SYNOD

Name	Place	Or-ganized	Bapt. Memb.	Val.	In-debted
St. Johannes......	Lincoln, Neb.	1912	94	$12,000	$4,450
Christus	Pierce, Neb.	1903	115	14,600	
St. Johannes.......	Norfolk, Neb.	1902	86	19,000	5,650
	Winside				
Zion	Sutton, Neb.	1896	170	6,500	
	Lodge Pole, Neb.		51	3,000	900
St. Paulus........	Rocky Ford	1911	94	3,000	
St. Paulus........	La Junta	1915	150	3,500	
St. Paul's.........	Lamar, Colo.	1925	80	5,000	
St. Paul's.........	Linn, Kansas	1916	97	6,000	1,700
Friedens	Stillwater	1911	90	4,000	
Zion	Perry	1907	140	1,500	
St. Petri	Creston, Neb.	1909	187	11,000	4,000
St. Petri	Howells, Neb.	1900	141	2,000	
Pilger	Howells, Neb.	1891	57	2,000	
			1,652	$93,100	$16,700

WARTBURG SYNOD

Name	Place	Or-ganized	Bapt. Memb.	Val.	In-debted
	Chicago, Ill.	1914	206	$20,000	$2,575
St. John's.........	Cudahy, Wis.	1928	231	15,000	12,000
Tabor	West Allis, Wis.	1927	272	5,500	3,600
St. Johannes.......	Chicago, Ill.	1909	389	30,000	16,600
Martin Luther Mission	Chicago, Ill.	1918	203	37,000	6,500
Wartburg Mission	Berwyn, Chicago, Ill. ..	1917	141	8,000	235
			1,442	$115,500	$41,510

TEXAS SYNOD

Name	Place	Or-ganized	Bapt. Memb.	Val.	In-debted
First Luth........	Tivoli	1922	67	$3,500	$350
Emanuel	Inez		65		
Friedensgemeinde..	Vernon	1922	202	6,200	750
Martin Luther.....	Coletteville	1918	152	5,100	
St. Johannes......	Goliad				
St. Michael.......	Ray Point	1925	73	2,000	400
Kreuz	Pawnee	1926	62	3,000	1,000
St. Paul's.........	George-West (Town)..	1924	20	1,000	800
			641	$20,800	$3,300

UNITED SYNOD OF NEW YORK

Name	Place	Or-ganized	Bapt. Memb.	Val.	In-debted
First	Jeffersonville	1852	196	$25,000	$6,000
Immanuel	Madison, Conn.	1895	73	1,800	
St. Paul's	Linden, N. J.	1928	106	8,700	5,300
Zion	Ridgefield, N. J.	1926	140	15,000	7,300
St. John's	Mamaroneck, N. Y.	1913	350	60,000	23,500
			865	$110,500	$42,100

MINISTERIUM OF PENNSYLVANIA

Name	Place	Organized	Bapt. Memb.	Val.	In-debted
Immanuel	Lakewood, N. J.		200	$3,000	$400
St. Johannes	Williamstown, N. J.		45	16,000	6,000
Dreieinigkeit	Maple Shade, N. J.	1927	75	2,250	1,550
St. Timotheus	Phila.-Fox Chase	1927	100		
			420	$21,250	$7,950

PITTSBURGH SYNOD

Name	Place	Organized	Bapt. Memb.	Val.	In-debted
St. Johannes	Cleveland, Ohio	1922	667	$57,000	$27,625
Teutsch	Cleveland, Ohio	1926	560	32,500	18,500
Honterus	Gary, Ind.	1925	140	44,000	32,500
Christus	Canton, Ohio	1927	72	11,000	9,200
St. Petrus	Detroit, Mich.	1930	275		
St. Paulus	Windsor, Ont.	1930	196		
			1,910	$144,500	$87,825

CALIFORNIA SYNOD

Name	Place	Organized	Bapt. Memb.	Val.	In-debted
St. John's	Oakland, Calif.	1921	145	$12,000	$5,850

SUMMARY

Name	Bapt. Memb.	Val.	In-debted
Canada Synod	1,621	$51,975	$1,775
Manitoba Synod	4,709	99,460	11,085
German Nebraska Synod	1,552	93,100	16,700
Wartburg Synod	1,442	115,500	41,510
Texas Synod	641	20,800	3,300
United Synod of New York	865	110,500	42.100
Ministerium of Pennsylvania	420	21,500	7,950
Pittsburgh Synod	1,910	144,500	87,825
California Synod	145	12,000	5,850
	13,305	$669,085	$218,095

SLOVAK MISSIONS

Name	Place	Organized	Bapt. Memb.	Val.	In-debted
St. Paul's	New York	1927	258	$15,000	$11,000
St. John's	Trenton, N. J.	1907	154	14,000	4,500
Holy Trinity	Philadelphia, Pa.	1900	170	11,000	
St. John the Baptist	Camden, N. J.	1911	95	15,000	6,500
Holy Trinity	Newark	1893	900	40,000	
Zion	Garfield, N. J.	1919	175	16,000	5,300

Name	Place	Organized	Bapt. Memb.	Val.	Indebted
St. Emmanuel	Mahanoy City, Pa.	1893	199	3,000	400
Dr. Martin Luther	Jessup, Pa.	1895	130	11,000	2,700
Holy Trinity	E. Pittsburgh, Pa.	1922	200	40,000	20,000
	Cairnbrook, Pa.		35	1,000	
St. Paul's	Port Clinton, O.	1913		11,000	200
	Proctor, Vt.		70		
	Guttenberg, N. J.				
	Northampton, Pa.				
	Palmerton, Pa.				
	Bethlehem, Pa.				
	Grassflat, Pa.				
	Shepptown, Pa.				
	Pottstown, Pa.				
	Cannonsburg, Pa.				
	Saltsburg, Pa.				
	Buffalo, N. Y.				
	Akron, O.				
	Byesville, O.				
	Crainsville, O.				
	Dover, O.				
	Dayton, O.				
	Barton, O.				
	Philipsburg, Pa.				
	Wheeling, W. Va.				
	Muskegon Hghts, Mich.				
	Phillips, Wis.				
	Cudahy, Wis.				
	Tabor, Minn.				
	Holdingsford, Minn.				

Note: There are a large number of smaller Slovak settlements which cannot be regularly supplied; the above named are more or less regularly visited by our pastors and students.

MAGYAR MISSIONS

Name	Place	Organized	Bapt. Memb.	Val.	Indebted
Zion	Bethlehem, Pa.		300	$45,000	$31,800
	Allentown, Pa.		100	5,500	
	Palmerton, Pa.				
First	New Brunswick, N. J..	1808	387	36,000	5,700
Holy Trinity	Caldwell, N. J.	1928	127		
Holy Trinity	New York City	1930	190		
	Buffalo, N. Y.				
First	Pittsburgh, Pa.	1925	70	30,000	20,000
First	Akron, O.	1926	209	22,000	14,590
	Windsor, Ont.	1928	132	1,900	1,200
Preaching Station	Montreal				
	Kitchener				
	Brantfort				
	Galt				
	Hamilton				
	Welland				

WENDISH MISSIONS

Name	Place	Organized	Bapt. Memb.	Val.	Indebted
First Magyar-Wendish	Perth Amboy, N. J.	1918	175	$26,000	$8,000
St. John's	Newark, N. J.		150	8.000	3.000

LETTISH MISSIONS

Name	Place	Organized	Bapt. Memb.	Val.	Indebted
St. Mark's	Philadelphia, Pa.		65		
St. Mark's	New York City		60		
Preaching Station.	Manitoba		139		
	Sifton, Man.				
	Fork River				
	Borketon				
	Dauphin				
	Winnipeg				
	West Selkirk				
	Libau				
	Bird River				
	Le Pas				
	Boston, Mass.				

LITHUANIAN MISSIONS

Name	Place	Organized	Bapt. Memb.	Val.	Indebted
St. John's	Philadelphia, Pa.		70	$15,000	$5,000

ITALIAN MISSIONS

Name	Place	Organized	Bapt. Memb.	Val.	Indebted
Christ	New York City	1924	120		
St. Peter's	Philadelphia, Pa.	1908	98	$15,000	$2,500
Neighborhood House	Philadelphia, Pa.				
Holy Trinity	Erie, Pa.	1920	200	14,000	3,500
St. Paul's	Monessen, Pa.	1918	77		
St. John the Div.	San Francisco, Cal.	1924	34		
Italian Mission	Fresno, Cal.	1926	31		
Italian Mission	Sacramento, Cal.	1927	25		
Redeemer	Chicago, Ill.	1927	38		

FINNISH MISSIONS

		Value	Indebtedness
Oregon District	202 confirmed members		
	Portland	$8,000	$3,700
	Carleton	2,000	200
	Hockinson		
	Vader		
California District	85 confirmed members		
	Los Angeles		
	Reedley	8,000	2,200
	San Pedra		
	San Diego		
	Pasadena		
	Hollywood		
Manitoba District	100 confirmed members		
	New Finnland, Sask.	3,000	1,520
	Winnipeg		
	Elmo		
Ontario District	87 confirmed members		
	Copper Cliff, Ont.	2,500	350
	Naughton, Ont.		
	Pyrylanmaki		
	Sault Ste Marie, Mich.		
	Newberry, Mich.		

		Value	Indebted-ness
New York District......182 confirmed members			
	North Van Etten		
	Spencer		
Washington District.....117 confirmed members			
	Seattle	2,000	
	Aberdeen		
	Independence		
	Kent		
	Issaquah		
	East Stanwood		
British Columbia Dist....Vancouver			
	Nanaino		
	Ladysmith		
	Victoria		
	Salmon Arms		
	Webster Corner		
	Chase River		
	Fraser Arms		
	Nelson		
	New Westminster		
	Lulu Island		
	Yennhandon		
	Falkland		
	Mara		
Maine District..........492 confirmed members			
	South Paris	3,000	
	Harrison	2,000	
	West Barnstable	5,500	
	Hyannis		
	Sagamore		
	No. Brookline		
	Proctor		
Wisconsin District......163 confirmed members			
	Superior	6,000	800
	Oulu-Vaino	2,200	
	Marango		
	Brabtwood	1,000	
	Westboro		
	Suomi, Minn.		
Montana District........100 confirmed members			
	Butte		
	Milltown		
	Hamilton		
	San Coule		
	Great Falls		

GENERAL SUMMARY

German Missions	117
Slovak Missions	35
Magyar Missions	16
Wendish Missions	2
Lettish Missions	13
Lithuanian Missions	1
Finnish Missions	58
Italian Missions	9
Jewish Missions	4

255

CHURCH EXTENSION LOANS
1928-1930

Synod	Church	Location	Amount
California	Grace	Phoenix, Arizona	$10,000
California	St. Paul's	Santa Monica	5,000
North Carolina	St. Mark's	Asheville	5,000
Florida	Holy Trinity	Miami	3,000
Florida	First	West Palm Beach	7,600
Illinois	Acacia Park	Chicago	2,000
Illinois	Westwood	Elmwood Park	10,000
Illinois	Trinity	Macomb	3,000
Illinois	Grace	Villa Park	2,000
Illinois	English	Wilmette	10,000
Iowa	Central	Mason City	2,500
Maryland	Luther Memorial	Baltimore	3,500
Maryland	St. John's, Brooklyn	Baltimore	5,000
Maryland	Our Saviour	Lansdowne	4,000
Maryland	Incarnation	Washington, D. C.	5,000
Michigan	Nativity	Detroit	2,000
Michigan Synod for	Olivet	Detroit	5,000
New York	St. Luke's	Bay Shore, L. I.	10,000
New York	Calvary	New York City	5,000
New York	St. Paul's, Slovak	New York City	5,000
New York	Zion	Ridgefield, N. J.	5,000
New York	St. John's	Rutherford, N. J.	5,000
Northwest	Trinity	Glenburn, N. D.	2,000
Northwest	Pentecost	Milwaukee, Wisconsin	5,000
Northwest	First English	West Allis, Wisconsin	1,000
Ohio	Redeemer, Parma	Cleveland	4,000
Ohio	Trinity	Niles	5,000
Pacific	Trinity	Longview, Washington	3,000
Pacific	Zion	Medford, Oregon	2,500
Pacific	American	Salem, Oregon	5,000
Pacific	St. Mark's	Seattle, Washington	3,500
Pacific	University	Seattle, Washington	1,500

Synod	Church	Location	Amount
East Pennsylvania Synod for Temple		Delaware Gardens, N. J.	10,000
East Pennsylvania	Trinity	Yeadon	5,000
Ministerium of Pennsylvania	First Hungarian	Bethlehem	2,500
Ministerium of Pennsylvania	Trinity	Clarks Summit	4,000
Ministerium of Pennsylvania	Calvary	Laureldale	5,000
Ministerium of Pennsylvania	Advent	West Lawn	5,000
Pittsburgh	Trinity	Clairton, Pa.	5,000
Pittsburgh	Teutsch	Cleveland, Ohio	5,000
Pittsburgh	Holy Trinity, Italian	Erie, Pa.	3,375
Pittsburgh	St. Mark's	Trafford, Pa.	3,000
Rocky Mountain	Trinity	Boulder, Colorado	10,000
Rocky Mountain	Grace	Casper, Wyoming	3,000
Rocky Mountain	First	Colorado Springs, Colo.	2,105
Rocky Mountain	Trinity	Denver, Colorado	10,700
Rocky Mountain	St. Paul's	El Paso, Texas	1,000
Slovak Zion	Holy Trinity	Newark, N. J.	10,000
Texas	St. Luke's	San Antonio	1,100
Virginia	Holy Trinity	Kingsport, Tenn.	2,500
Wartburg	First	Cudahy, Wisconsin	3,000
Wartburg	St. John's	West Allis, Wisconsin	2,000
			$240,380

REPAYMENT OF CHURCH EXTENSION LOANS

Synod	Church	Location	Amount
Alleghany	Mt. Olivet	Bushman, Pa.	$125.00
California	St. Michael's	Berkeley	350.00
California	St. Paul's	Sanger	40.00
California	Grace	San Jose	250.00
Canada	St. Paul's	Galt, Ont.	250.00
Canada	First	Kitchener, Ont.	250.00
Illinois	Mt. Zion	Chicago	2,625.00
Illinois	North Austin	Chicago	8,000.00
Illinois	Norwood Park	Chicago	5,000.00
Illinois	St. Paul's	Evanston	150.00
Illinois	Reen Memorial	St. Louis, Mo.	200.00
Iowa	St. Mark's	Ottumwa	587.81
Iowa	First	Valley Junction	100.00
Manitoba	St. Paul's	Friedensfeld, Sask.	50.00
Manitoba	Holy Cross	Golden Bay, Man.	200.00
Manitoba	Trinity	Saskatoon, Sask.	550.00
Maryland	Luther Memorial	Baltimore	3,000.00
Michigan	East Jefferson	Detroit	2,000.00
Mississippi	St. Mark's	Goodman	100.00
Mississippi	Grace	Laurel	400.00
Nebraska	Salem	Fremont	500.00
German Nebraska	First St. Paul's	Burlington, Colo.	500.00
German Nebraska	St. Johannes	Norfolk	325.00
United New York	St. Peter's	Albany	2,000.00
United New York	Messiah	Flushing, L. I.	5,000.00
United New York	St. Andrew's	Glen Morris, L. I.	1,600.00
United New York	Calvary	Jersey City, N. J.	1,000.00
United New York	Advent (East Orange)	Newark, N. J.	400.00
United New York	First	New Haven, Conn.	2,000.00
United New York	First	Schenectady	350.00
United New York	St. Paul's	Valley Stream, L. I.	500.00
Northwest	St. John's	Killdeer, N. Dakota	93.00

Synod	Church	Location	Amount
Northwest	Trinity	Lansford, N. Dakota	100.00
Northwest	Holy Trinity	New London, Wisconsin	2,500.00
Northwest	Faith	Winona, Minn.	350.00
East Pennsylvania	Tinicum Memorial	Essington	150.00
East Pennsylvania	St. Paul's	Harrisburg	75.00
East Pennsylvania	Holy Trinity	Narberth	375.00
East Pennsylvania	Bethany (Memorial)	Philadelphia	500.00
East Pennsylvania	St. Andrew's	Philadelphia	50.00
East Pennsylvania	Our Saviour	Stone Harbor, N. J.	1,000.00
East Pennsylvania	Calvary	West Chester	37.50
East Pennsylvania	Ascension	Haddon Heights, N. J.	100.00
Min. of Pennsylvania	Trinity	Mountainville	500.00
Min. of Pennsylvania	Gloria Dei	Philadelphia	750.00
Min. of Pennsylvania	Grace, Roxborough	Philadelphia	2,400.00
Min. of Pennsylvania	Mediator	Philadelphia	700.00
Min. of Pennsylvania	St. Stephen's	Philadelphia	5,000.00
Min. of Pennsylvania	St. Luke's	West Collingswood, N. J.	75.00
Min. of Pennsylvania	Holy Trinity (Wilkes-Barre)	Kingston	200.00
Min. of Pennsylvania	Atonement	Wyomissing	5,000.00
Pacific	St. John's (Trinity)	North Yakima, Wash.	3,496.50
Pittsburgh	Calvary	Arnold, Pa.	435.00
Pittsburgh	St. John's	East McKeesport, Pa.	50.00
Rocky Mountain	First	Colorado Springs, Colo.	87.58
Texas	First	Dallas	320.70
Virginia	Emmanuel	Roanoke	1,650.00
West Virginia	Edgewood	Wheeling	500.00
Wartburg	St. Johannes	Chicago, Illinois	200.00
Wartburg	Tabor	Chicago, Illinois	1,000.00
Wartburg	St. Paul's	Guttenberg, Iowa	400.00

$66,498.09

Synod	Mission Parishes June 30, 1930	New Missions Since June 30, 1928	Self-Supporting Since June 30, 1928	Missions Discontinued from Budget	Accessions During Biennium	Losses During Biennium	Confirmed Membership June 30, 1930	Sunday School Enrollment	Congregational Expenses	Contributed Benevolences	Valuation of Church Property	Total Indebtedness	Vacancies 1928	Vacancies 1930
Alleghany	2	2	0	0	23	12	200	136	$2,476	$839	$16,000	0	1	0
California	12	0	6	0	483	217	1,091	1,249	152,708	10,781	218,800	71,462	4	2
Canada	6	1	0	2	230	100	582	398	42,714	4,046	106,500	46,174	1	1
East Pennsylvania	23	0	2	0	1,399	358	3,961	3,014	356,864	21,216	1,052,942	501,003	1	1
Florida	8	4	0	0	184	84	535	428	15,854	3,398	149,523	76,675	0	0
Georgia	4	0	0	2	206	12	469	308	22,965	3,199	108,400	49,325	3	1
Illinois	21	0	2	1	1,164	340	2,713	3,489	208,213	15,108	649,062	322,508	0	0
Indiana	12	1	2	0	439	148	1,167	1,238	54,457	7,391	199,000	93,529	2	0
Iowa	6	0	0	1	199	76	698	556	21,836	3,305	94,000	26,929	0	0
Kansas	6	7	0	0	226	106	762	797	34,463	6,603	170,160	77,938	1	2
Maryland	12	0	2	0	508	69	1,118	1,335	128,023	7,267	287,000	157,800	0	2
Michigan	14	1	8	0	701	237	1,419	1,459	95,151	10,658	363,150	195,874	1	1
Min. of Pennsylvania	22	2	0	1	1,244	379	3,670	4,069	231,032	15,247	772,762	422,466	0	0
Mississippi	5	0	0	0	83	29	644	402	2,541	1,271	38,300	4,150	2	0
Nebraska	4	3	0	0	176	52	132	222	9,182	2,320	17,000	10,281	0	1
North Carolina	22	8	2	0	352	124	2,305	2,634	71,283	7,818	312,700	35,887	0	0
Nova Scotia	2	3	0	0	19	19	90	50	3,687	542	26,000	12,150	3	0
Northwest	28	8	2	1	1,853	632	3,865	2,801	174,935	23,807	572,200	301,718	0	1
Ohio	19	0	0	1	1,036	374	1,402	1,801	136,660	14,820	351,000	193,907	0	0
Pacific	21	0	5	2	872	340	1,859	1,970	109,292	11,273	328,000	196,169	1	0
Pittsburgh	21	0	1	1	1,190	444	2,921	2,530	198,712	20,709	533,400	279,009	0	0
Rocky Mountain	10	8	0	1	331	192	1,176	1,048	112,509	7,204	256,350	132,687	2	1
South Carolina	7	0	0	1	109	40	411	361	12,329	2,392	41,200	3,342	1	3
Sus. of Central Penna.	1	0	0	1	42	7	244	234	3,425	862	22,000	1,075	0	1
Texas	5	0	0	0	107	82	317	343	9,925	1,725	42,000	19,479	1	0
United Synod of New York	44	6	8	1	2,946	708	7,198	5,914	421,616	22,464	1,214,954	647,980	1	0
Virginia	9	0	1	0	252	57	832	677	24,438	13,247	77,250	13,513	1	0
West Pennsylvania	5	0	0	0	89	62	765	1,079	16,128	3,654	94,500	8,550	1	0
West Virginia	5	0	1	0	57	16	191	679	33,966	3,186	187,000	35,040	1	0
Total English Missions	356	34	33	15	16,520	5,266	42,732	41,227	$2,707,275	$246,352	$8,122,053	$3,936,620	28	14

REPORT OF THE TREASURER OF THE BOARD OF AMERICAN MISSIONS

CERTIFICATE OF AUDIT

We have audited the accounts of The Board of American Missions of the United Lutheran Church in America for the year ended June 30, 1929, and we certify that in our opinion the annexed balance sheet at June 30, 1929, correctly sets forth the financial position of The Board of American Missions at that date, and that the annexed Consolidated Statement of Receipts and Disbursements of The Board of American Missions for the year ended June 30, 1929, contains all contributions and other income appearing in the records which were duly accounted for, and that all disbursements appearing therein were supported by proper vouchers.

LYBRAND, ROSS BROS. AND MONTGOMERY.

August 28, 1929.

BALANCE SHEET, June 30, 1929
ASSETS

*Cash		$112,460.26
Securities Owned, at Ledger Values:		
Bonds	$148,391.25	
Stocks	10,258.80	
Investment Mortgages	10,000.00	
Investment Note	10,000.00	
		178,650.05
Advanced Expense Accounts		825.00
Advanced for Women's Missionary Society.		3,453.48
Loans to Churches:		
Board Loans	1,251,558.46	
Agency Loans	150,010.53	
		1,401,568.99
Equipment, Furniture and Fixtures		8,904.38
Real Estate:		
Owned by Board	405,064.00	
Held as Agent	25,670.00	
		430,734.00
		$2,136,596.16

LIABILITIES

Loan Payable	$10,200.00	
Mortgage Payable	20,000.00	
		30,200.00
Net Assets		$2,106,396.16

FUNDS

General Funds:		
Missions	$12,427.79	
Church Extension	361,763.17	
		$374,190.96
Endowment Funds:		
Missions	41,599.03	
Church Extension	20,632.21	
		62,231.24
Permanent Loan Fund		1,231,558.46
Memorial Loan Fund		45,155.43
McMurray Trust Fund		37,525.21
Annuity Funds		73,150.00
Special Funds:		
Missions—Special Funds	22,383.94	
Missions—Designated Gifts	491.63	
		22,875.57
Church Extension:		
Designated Gifts	190.00	
Church Extension:		
Special Funds	32,380.00	
Church Extension:		
Omnibus Investment Fund	49,958.76	
		82,528.76
Agency Accounts:		
Women's Missionary Society	149,310.53	
Northwest Synod	2,200.00	
Sundry	25,670.00	
		177,180.53
Total Funds		$2,106,396.16

*Cash includes investments in temporary loans and securities made through the Fifth Avenue Bank of New York, subject to call by the Treasurer.

CONSOLIDATED STATEMENT
RECEIPTS AND DISBURSEMENTS
Year Ending June 30, 1929

Balance July 1, 1928		$66,874.68

RECEIPTS

United Lutheran Church on Apportionment.	$517,480.00
Women's Missionary Society	77,197.16
Women's Missionary Society, Designated Gifts	2,100.74
Synods, Churches, Societies, Individuals	15,339.17
Returned Loans	29,667.20
Interest and Dividends on Securities and Investments	15,222.72
Income on Trusts not held by Board	922.35
Annuities	1,500.00
Bequests	42,387.16

Designated Gifts and Specials	41,132.47	
Proceeds of Sale of Securities	50,307.96	
Account Sales Contract and Real Estate....	3,100.00	
Refunds	794.92	
Loans, Fifth Avenue Bank, New York	30,000.00	
Total Receipts		$827,151.85
		$894,026.53

DISBURSEMENTS

Loans to Churches	$94,200.00	
Interest Grants to Churches	44,329.83	
Salaries:		
Missionaries	431,878.06	
Secretaries, Superintendents, Etc.	33,380.00	
Expenses:		
Missionaries	15,231.14	
Secretaries, Superintendents, Etc.	13,847.79	
Board Meeting and Members' Expenses..	5,671.21	
Seminary and Student Aid	15,818.91	
Upkeep of Charitable Institutions in Virgin Islands	5,924.50	
Transmission of Designated Gifts and Specials	18,307.50	
Payments to Annuitants	5,373.75	
Interest on Loans and Mortgage	2,028.50	
Real Estate and Buildings	13,307.00	
Equipment and Furniture	1,730.38	
Maintenance, Repairs, Insurance and Taxes..	3,614.12	
Legal Expenses, etc., Account Estates......	970.63	
Payment to Foreign Board, Account Henson Bequest	1,000.00	
Repayment of Loans	30,000.00	
Securities Purchased ..,..................	35,762.29	
Accrued Interest on Securities Purchased...	1,906.26	
Maintenance Contribution to Lutheran Church House, New York City	2,190.00	
Office Supplies and Expenses	519.54	
Telephone and Telegraph	253.73	
Sundry Expenses, Postage, etc.	534.78	
Publicity	1,991.91	
Auditing	794.44	
Contribution to Home Missions Council.....	1,000.00	
Total Disbursements		$781,566.27
*Cash on hand on June 30, 1929, includes investments in temporary loans and securities made through The Fifth Avenue Bank, New York, subject to call by the Treasurer		112,460.26
		$894,026.53

ZENAN M. CORBE, *Treasurer.*

REPORT OF THE TREASURER OF THE BOARD OF AMERICAN MISSIONS

July 28, 1930.

CERTIFICATE OF AUDIT

We have audited the accounts of the Board of American Missions of the United Lutheran Church in America for the year ended June 30, 1930, and we certify that in our opinion the annexed balance sheet at June 30, 1930, sets forth correctly the financial position of the Board of American Missions at that date and that the annexed Consolidated Statement of Receipts and Disbursements for the year ended June 30, 1930, contains all contributions and other income appearing in the records which were duly accounted for, and that all disbursements appearing therein were supported by proper vouchers.

LYBRAND, ROSS BROS. & MONTGOMERY,

BALANCE SHEET, June 30, 1930
ASSETS

Cash		$ 19,674.94
Accounts Receivable (Synods)		4,407.51
Securities owned at ledger values:		
Bonds	$ 243,091.25	
Stocks	10,381.39	
Investment Mortgages	10,000.00	
Investment Notes	10,340.00	
		273,812.64
Accrued Interest Purchased		591.54
Advanced Expense Accounts		943.38
Loans to Churches:		
Board Loans	$1,333,777.61	
Agency Loans	169,185.53	
		1,502,963.14
Equipment and Furniture		9,185.88
Real Estate:		
Owned by Board	380,114.00	
Held as Agent	25,670.00	
		405,784.00
		$2,217,363.03

LIABILITIES

Loans Payable	$ 17,200.00	
Women's Missionary Society	2,397.32	
Mortgage Payable	20,000.00	
		39,597.32
		$2,177,765.71

FUNDS

General Funds:		
Missions	$ 42,109.97	
Church Extension	343,699.05	
		$ 385,809.02

Salaries:
Endowment Funds:
Missions	43,760.97	
Church Extension	13,819.08	
		57,580.05
Permanent Loan Fund		1,278,827.61
Memorial Loan Fund		77,314.43
McMurray Trust Fund		27,004.46
Annuity Funds		71,062.93

Special Funds:
Missions—Designated Gifts	490.75	
Missions—Special Funds	24,471.38	
Church Extension—Designated Gifts	583.83	
Church Extension—Special Funds	59,765.72	
		85,311.68

Agency Accounts:
Women's Missionary Society	169,185.53	
Churches	25,670.00	
		194,855.53
		$2,177,765.71

CONSOLIDATED STATEMENT OF RECEIPTS AND DISBURSEMENTS
For the year ended June 30, 1930

Balance, July 1, 1929		$ 112,460.26

RECEIPTS:
United Lutheran Church, on apportionment	$ 547,490.00	
Women's Missionary Society	75,547.73	
Women's Missionary Society:		
Designated Gifts and Specials	14,556.25	
Synods, Churches, Societies and Individuals	12,970.30	
Returned Loans	37,094.31	
Interest and Dividends on Securities	18,262.65	
Income on Trusts (not held by the Board)	959.53	
Contributions to Memorial Loan Fund	2,587.73	
Bequests	29,495.86	
Refunds and Proceeds Class B Securities	3,988.73	
Interest on Church Loans	1,865.00	
Proceeds Sale of Real Estate and Account Sales Contract	391.07	
Proceeds Sale of Equipment	400.00	
Proceeds Sale of Securities	81,900.00	
Loans from Bank, etc.	65,500.00	
Designated Gifts and Specials	13,717.22	
		906,726.38
Total receipts		$1,019,186.64

DISBURSEMENTS:
Loans to Churches	$ 144,680.00	
Interest Grants to Churches	43,927.50	

Missionaries	427,016.81
Secretaries, Superintendents, etc.	35,121.66
Expenses:	
Missionaries	22,276.55
Secretaries, Superintendents, etc.	12,619.97
Board Meetings and Members	4,652.23
Seminary and Student Aid	12,402.23
Upkeep of Charitable Institutions:	
Virgin Islands	5,783.86
Transmission of Designated Gifts and Specials....	24,641.81
Payments to Annuitants	5,432.90
Interest on Loans and Mortgage	3,074.96
Real Estate and Buildings	250.00
Equipment and Furniture	911.75
Maintenance, Repairs, Insurance, Taxes, etc.	2,800.42
Legal Expenses, etc.	930.40
Refunds, Account Bequests and Estates..................	5,182.92
Repayment of Loans	58,500.00
Securities Purchased	175,462.59
Accrued Interest on Securities Purchased...........	6,657.03
Contribution to Lutheran Church House, New York	2,277.50
Office Supplies and Expenses	507.42
Telephone and Telegrams	278.18
Sundry Expenses, Postage, etc.	638.09
Publicity	1,752.59
Auditing	732.33
Contribution to Home Missions' Council..............	1,000.00

Total disbursements	999,511.70
Cash on hand, June 30, 1930	$ 19,674.94

ZENAN M. CORBE, *Treasurer.*

MISSIONS ACCOUNT
Balance Sheet at June 30, 1930

ASSETS		LIABILITIES AND FUNDS	
Available Cash — General Fund	$ 11,457.54	Designated Gifts ....$	490.75
Home Mission Endowment	977.59	Special Funds	5,118.07
Designated Gifts	490.75	Due Women's Missionary Society	3,172.57
Harroway Fund	341.95	General Fund	42,109.97
Kaercher Fund	238.86	Home Missions Endowment	43,760.97
Special Funds	2,118.07	Harroway Fund	9,439.45
		Kaercher Fund	9,913.86
Total cash	$ 15,624.76		
Bonds	94,035.00		
Stocks	3,520.88		
Advanced Expenses	825.00		
	$114,005.64		$114,005.64

SECURITIES IN MISSION FUND ACCOUNTS

Bonds — Book Value

1,500 B. and O. R. R., 4%, due 1948	$ 1,500.00
6,000 Detroit Edison, 5%, due 1933	6,175.00
4,000 L. V. R. R., 4½%, due 2003	4,000.00
4,000 Memphis P. and L., 5%, due 1948	4,000.00
5,000 N. Y. Tel. Co., 6%, due 1941	5,450.00
1,000 Consumers' Power Co., 5%, due 1936	1,000.00
2,000 St. Louis Co. Gas, 5%, due 1951	2,000.00
5,000 Union E. and Pr. Co., 5%, due 1932	5,137.50
7,000 C. B. and Q. R. R., 4%, due 1958	6,597.50
5,000 Pac. G. and El., 4½%, due 1957	4,900.00
4,000 D. and H. Co., 4%, due 1943	3,775.00
43,000 N. Y. C., 4½%, due 1930	43,000.00
6,500 B. and O. Equipment, 4½%, due 1930	6,500.00
	$94,035.00

Stocks

88 Shares, York Trust Co. .... $ 3,520.88

CHURCH EXTENSION ACCOUNTS
Balance Sheet at June 30, 1930

ASSETS

Cash—General Fund ....$	483.92
Memorial Loan Fund....	68.51
Church Extension Endowment Fund	444.08
McMurray Trust Fund	260.71
Annuity Funds	528.56
Designated Gifts	583.83
Special Funds	1,680.57
Total cash ....$	4,050.18
Bonds ....$	149,056.25
Investment Mortgages ..	10,000.00
Investment Notes	10,340.00
Stocks	6,860.51
Loans to Churches	1,333,777.61
Due from Synods	4,407.51
Real Estate	380,114.00
Equipment	9,185.88
Agency:	
Loans to Churches	169,185.53
Real Estate	25,670.00
Due from Women's Missionary Society—Interest Grants	775.25
Accrued Interest Purchased	591.54
Advanced Expenses—Account Estates	118.38
	$2,104,132.64

LIABILITIES AND FUNDS

Loan Payable ....$	17,200.00
Mortgage Payable (Harlem, N. Y.)	20,000.00
General Fund	343,699.05
Permanent Loan Fund..	1,278,827.61
Church Extension Endowment Fund	13,819.08
McMurray Trust Fund	27,004.46
Memorial Loan Fund	77,314.43
Annuity Funds	71,062.93
Special Funds	59,765.72
Designated Gifts	583.83
Agency:	
Women's Missionary Society	169,185.53
St. Luke's, York, Pa..	25,000.00
Harmony Grove, Pa.	500.00
Cly, Pa.	170.00
	$2,104,132.64

Securities owned at June 30, 1930   Book Values

BONDS

In Church Extension Endowment Fund

3,000 El. and Peoples Traction Co., 4%, due 1945.........................$	1,875.00
1,000 Howard Gas Co., 6%, due 1937...	1,000.00
2,000 St. Louis, Springfield and Peoria, 5%, due 1939................	2,000.00
2,000 West Penn. Ry., 5%, due 1931...	2,000.00
6,500 B. and O., 4½%, due 1930..	6,500.00

In Memorial Loan Fund

5,000 Louisville and Nashville, 4%, due 1940.................................	4,855.00
5,000 Louisville and Nashville, 4½%, due 2003.............................	5,100.00
30,000 N. Y. Central, 4½%, due 1930...	30,000.00
1,000 Crew Levick and Co., 6%, due 1931.....................................	1,000.00

In McMurray Trust Fund

5,000 Illinois Central, 4%, due 1955..	4,743.75
2,000 B. and O., 4½%, 1930..	2,000.00

In Annuity Funds Account

600 Liberty Loan, 4¼%, due 1932-34........................	600.00
5,000 West Penn. Power Co., 5%, due 1956....................................	5,243.75
1,000 Public Service Newark Terminal, 5%, due 1955..................	952.50
5,000 Alabama Power Co., 5%, due 1956..	5,131.25
1,000 Gallitzin School District, 5%, due 1936..............................	1,000.00
5,000 N. O. Texas and Mex. Ry., 5%, due 1943............................	5,012.50
5,000 Penna. Ry. Gen. Mtge., 4½%, due 1965...............................	5,043.75
1,000 L. V. Gen. Cons. Mtge, 4%, due 2003.................................	1,000.00
1,000 Erie El. Motor Co., 5%, due 1941..	1,000.00
27,000 N. Y. Central, 4½%, due 1930...	27,000.00
500 B. and O., 4%, due 1948	500.00
500 502 Park Ave., 6%, due 1941	500.00

In Special Funds

5,000 B. and O. R. R. Co., 5%, due 1948......................................	5,285.00
5,000 C. and N. W. R. R. Co., 5%, due 2037..............................	5,303.75
1,000 Jefferson and Placquemine Drain. Dist., 5%, due 1949........	1,000.00
7,000 Public Service El. and G. Co., 4½%, due 1967....................	6,947.50
6,000 Southern Pacific, 4%, due 1955..	5,692.50
1,000 Riverside Traction Co., 5%, due 1960.................................	770.00
10,000 N. Y. C., 4½%, due 1930...	10,000.00

Total bonds ....$	149,056.25

In Special Funds

4 Shares Riverside Traction Co. ....$	96.00
40 Shares Fidelity Trust Co., Pittsburgh, Pa.	3,250.00
52 Shares Integrity Trust Co., Philadelphia, Pa.	3,514.51

Total stocks ....$	6,860.51

LOANS TO CHURCHES

Location and Names of Debtors	Dates of Loans	Maturities	Amounts
CALIFORNIA SYNOD			
Alhambra, Calif.:			
Grace	1925	1930	$ 4,000.00*
Berkeley, Calif.:			
St. Michael's	1920	1929	2,150.00
Gardena, Calif.:			
St. John's	1926	1931	3,000.00
Glendale, Calif.:			
First	1917	1928	500.00
Huntington Park, Calif.:			
St. Luke's	1925	1932	1,000.00
Los Angeles, Calif.:			
Hollywood	1924	1932	5,000.00
St. Paul's	1925	1930	3,000.00
Oakland, Calif.:			
St. Johannis	1922	1930	2,500.00
Phoenix, Ariz.:			
Grace	1928	1933	10,000.00
Richmond, Calif.:			
Grace	1926	1931	5,000.00
San Jose, Calif.:			
Grace	1895	1900	1,750.00
Sanger, Calif.:			
St. Paul's	1908	1913	320.00*
Santa Monica, Calif.:			
St. Paul's	1926-29	1931-34	15,000.00
			$53,220.00
CANADA SYNOD			
Brantford, Ont.:			
St. Matthew's	1919	1931	5,000.00
Galt, Ont.:			
St. Paul's	1913	1933	750.00
Guelph, Ont.:			
St. Paul's	1915	1931	2,000.00
Hamilton, Ont.:			
Trinity	1915-23	1928-30	7,080.00
Kitchener, Ont.:			
First	1913	1930	3,864.59
Montreal, Que.:			
Redeemer	1910	1930	4,000.00
Ottawa, Ont.:			
St. Peter's	1913	1930	4,000.00
			$26,694.59
NORTH CAROLINA SYNOD			
Asheville, N. C.:			
St. Mark's	1928	1933	5,000.00
Durham, N. C.:			
St. Paul's	1925	1930	5,000.00

Hendersonville, N. C.:

Grace 1922	1933	2,000.00
Highland, N. C.:		
Good Hope 1927	1932	2,000.00
Raleigh, N. C.:		
Holy Trinity 1922	1930	5,000.00
Rocky Mount, N. C.:		
Trinity 1925	1931	5,000.00
		$24,000.00

SOUTH CAROLINA SYNOD
Batesburg, S. C.:

Faith 1912	1932	1,500.00
Clinton, S. C.:		
St. John's 1925	1930	2,500.00
Columbia, S. C.:		
Reformation 1926	1931	3,000.00
		$7,000.00

FLORIDA SYNOD
Daytona, Fla.:

Resurrection 1925-27	1930-32	10,000.00
Hollywood, Fla.:		
St. John's 1927	1932	7,500.00
Miami, Fla.:		
Trinity 1929	1934	3,000.00
St. Augustine, Fla.:		
Memorial 1926-27	1931-32	5,000.00
St. Petersburg, Fla.:		
Trinity 1921	1931	15,000.00
West Palm Beach, Fla.:		
First 1927-30	1935	10,000.00
		$50,500.00

GEORGIA SYNOD
Birmingham, Ala.:

Christ 1921	1932	25,800.00
Macon, Ga.:		
Redeemer 1924	1929	5,000.00
		$30,800.00

ILLINOIS SYNOD

Acacia Park 1929	1934	2,000.00
Aurora, Ill.:		
Our Redeemer 1907-08	1910-13	2,500.00
Centralia, Ill.:		
Redeemer 1920	1927	5,000.00
Champaign, Ill.:		
Grace 1916	1929	2,000.00*
Chicago, Ill.:		
Belmont Park 1922	1930	3,500.00*

Epiphany 1916	1928	5,000.00
Oak Park 1926	1929	2,750.00
Reformation 1918	1923	1,500.00
Our Saviour (Riverdale)...............1913	1918	1,000.00
St. Andrew's 1924	1929	2,500.00
St. Luke's 1907	1931	2,500.00
Westwood (Elmwood Park) 1929	1934	10,000.00*
Woodlawn Memorial 1923	1928	9,000.00*
Elmhurt, Ill.:		
Elmhurst 1923	1928	3,000.00
Epiphany 1926	1931	3,500.00
Evanston, Ill.:		
St. Paul's 1922-25-26-27	1932-33-34	28,350.00
Macomb, Ill.:		
Trinity 1929	1934	3,000.00
Maywood, Ill.:		
Broadview 1926	1931	6,000.00
Murphysboro, Ill.:		
First 1926	1931	5,000.00
St. Louis, Mo.:		
Advent 1924	1929	5,000.00*
Faith 1926	1931	6,500.00
Reen Memorial 1915	1916	3,300.00
St. Mark's 1881	1884	961.17
Villa Park, Ill.:		
Grace 1930	1935	2,000.00
Wheaton, Ill.:		
St. Paul's 1928	1933	4,000.00
Wilmette, Ill.:		
English 1921-30	1935	15,000.00
		$134,861.17

INDIANA SYNOD

Batesville, Ind.:		
Bethany 1912	1914	1,400.00
Evansville, Ind.:		
Christ 1923	1928	2,000.00*
Indianapolis, Ind.:		
Bethany 1926	1931	4,000.00
Bethlehem 1924	1931	5,000.00
Gethsemane 1921	1926	3,000.00
Lafayette, Ind.:		
Holy Trinity 1900	1931	9,500.00
Memphis, Tenn.:		
First 1926	1931-32	7,500.00
Terre Haute, Ind.:		
Unity 1924	1929	4,000.00
		$36,400.00

IOWA SYNOD

Council Bluffs, Ia.:		
St. John's 1919	1924	2,000.00

Des Moines, Ia.:			
Unity	1924	1929	3,000.00
Iowa Falls, Ia.:			
English	1918	1931	1,000.00
Mason City, Ia.:			
Central	1928	1935	7,500.00
Missouri Valley, Ia.:			
St. Paul's	1926	1931	2,000.00
Muscatine, Ia.:			
Grace	1900-01-23	1905-28	4,000.00
Princeton, Ia.:			
Zion	1898	1903	300.00
Valley Junction, Ia.:			
First	1920	1931	600.00
Waterloo, Ia.:			
St. Luke's	1917-20	1922-25	1,300.00
Trinity	1928	1933	15,000.00
			$36,700.00

KANSAS SYNOD

Fairmount, Mo.:			
Fairmount	1926	1931	5,000.00
Hutchinson, Ks.:			
Zion	1921	1929	1,500.00
Kansas City, Ks.:			
Trinity	1926	1931	10,000.00*
Kansas City, Mo.:			
St. John's	1926	Demand	10,000.00
Sedalia, Mo.:			
Trinity	1895	1930	1,800.00
Tulsa, Okla.:			
First	1914	1919	1,500.00
Valley Falls, Ks.:			
St. Paul's	1891	1891-96	1,200.00
			$31,000.00

MANITOBA SYNOD

Edmonton, Alta.:			
St. John's	1923	1926	1,500.00
So. Edmonton, Alta.:			
St. John's	1921		1,500.00
Brightholme, Sask.	1921	1921-29	450.00
Esk, Sask.:			
Gartenland	1923	1927	146.00
Golden Bay, Man.:			
Holy Cross	1922	1928-30	300.00
Golden Spike, Alta.:			
St. John's	1927	1932	5,000.00
Friedensfeld, Alta.:			
St. Paul's	1922	1929	50.00
Harts Hill, Alta.:			
St. John's	1914	1928	30.00

Kinderley, Alta.:
Friedens	1914	1927	75.00

Leduc, Alta.:
Rosenthal	1922	1927	75.00

Saskatoon, Sask.:
Saskatoon College	1915-20	1924	6,475.00
Trinity	1922		1,550.00

Steinbach, Man.:
St. John's	1925		1,000.00

$18,151.00

MARYLAND SYNOD
Baltimore, Md.:
All Saints	1922-24	1932	7,000.00
Luther Memorial	1930	Demand	3,500.00
Redeemer	1928	1933	5,000.00
St. John's (Brooklyn)	1928	1933	5,000.00
St. John's (East Riverdale	1923	1928	1,000.00
Maryland Synod	1928	1930-31	10,000.00

Lansdowne, Md.:
Our Saviour	1930	1935	4,000.00

Washington, D. C.:
Incarnation	1928	1933	5,000.00
St. Stephen's	1927	1931	5,000.00

$45,500.00

MICHIGAN SYNOD
Ann Arbor, Mich.:
Trinity	1893	1898	2,000.00

Butler, Ind.:
Evangelical	1866	1869-73	500.00

Detroit, Mich.:
Augsburg	1926	1931	3,800.00
Hope	1926	1930	7,000.00
Luther Memorial	1926	1931	7,000.00
Nativity	1927-28	Demand	5,500.00
Michigan Synod	1929	1934	5,000.00
Reformation	1926	1931	10,000.00
St. Paul's	1920	1925	5,000.00
Unity	1924	1927	11,567.05

Flint, Mich.:
Trinity	1922	1927	5,000.00

Fort Wayne, Ind.:
Christ	1917-26	1918-27	2,000.00

Gary, Ind.:
Grace	1924	1929	10,000.00*

Jackson, Mich.:
Reformation	1926	1931	4,000.00

Kalamazoo, Mich.:
Trinity	1928	1933	5,000.00*

Lansing, Mich.:
Redeemer	1923	1928	4,000.00

Pontiac, Mich.:
　Ascension ....1926　　　1931　　　6,000.00
Saginaw, Mich.:
　Resurrection ....1925　　　1930　　　2,500.00
Windsor, Ont., Can.:
　Trinity ....1924　　　1929　　　6,000.00

　　　　　　　　　　　　　　　　　　　　　　　　　　　$101,867.05

MISSISSIPPI SYNOD
Goodman, Miss.:
　St. Mark's ....1924　　　1927-29　　　200.00
Laurel, Miss.:
　Grace ....1923　　　1928　　　2,100.00

　　　　　　　　　　　　　　　　　　　　　　　　　　　$2,300.00

NEBRASKA SYNOD
Benson, Neb.:
　First ....1908　　　1913　　　1,200.00
Ericson, Neb.:
　First ....1899　　　1904　　　150.00
Fremont, Neb.:
　Salem ....1924　　　1932　　　14,500.00
Hooper, Neb.:
　Grace ....1916　　　·1927　　　600.00
Omaha, Neb.:
　Grace ....1896　　　1901　　　3,000.00
　St. Luke's ....1909-10　　1914-15　　2,625.00*
Lincoln, Neb.:
　Grace ....1893　　　1898　　　4,000.00
　St. James' ....1925　　　1933　　　3,500.00
South Sioux City, Neb.:
　First English ....1925　　　1931　　　5,000.00
York, Neb.:
　First ....1908-22　　1913-27　　800.00

　　　　　　　　　　　　　　　　　　　　　　　　　　　$35,375.00

GERMAN NEBRASKA SYNOD
Havelock, Neb.:
　Zoar ....1916　　　1921　　　600.00
Lincoln, Neb.:
　Martin Luther ....1926　　　1929-37　　　900.00
　St. John's ....1916　　　1919　　　750.00
Lodge Pole, Neb.:
　Immanuel ....1922　　　1927-34　　　900.00
Norfolk, Neb.:
　St. Johannis ....1920　　　1925　　　425.00

　　　　　　　　　　　　　　　　　　　　　　　　　　　$3,575.00

UNITED SYNOD OF NEW YORK:
Baldwin, N. Y.:
　St. Peter's ....1924　　　Demand　　　5,000.00

Bellaire, N. Y.:		
Good Shepherd 1925	1930	2,000.00
Blasdell, N. Y.:		
First 1926	1931	2,000.00
Bronx, N. Y.:		
St. Paul's (Slovak) 1929	1935	5,000.00
Brooklyn, N. Y.:		
St. Andrew's 1916	1921	8,000.00
Calvary 1905	1910	2,500.00
St. Philips 1921-26	1929-30	5,000.00
Buffalo, N. Y.:		
Zion 1896	1901	2,000.00
Bay Shore, L. I.:		
St. Luke's 1930	1935	10,000.00
Endicott, N. Y.:		
Nativity 1926	1931	2,000.00
Forest Hills, N. Y.:		
Grace 1927	1932	4,000.00
Franklin Square, N. Y.:		
Ascension 1925	1930	3,000.00
Gerritsen Beach, N. Y.:		
St. James' 1926	1931	5,000.00
Gloversville, N. Y.:		
St. James' 1893	1895	200.00
Hartford, Conn.:		
St. Paul's 1924	Demand	3,700.00
Hasbrouck Heights, N. J.:		
Trinity 1923	1928	2,000.00
Hillside, N. J.:		
Calvary 1925	1930	5,000.00
Hoboken, N. J.:		
Trinity 1911	1916	2,000.00
Howard Beach:		
St. Barnabas 1924	1929	3,000.00
Jamaica, N. Y.:		
Our Saviour 1924	1929	5,000.00
Jamaica, Baisley Park, L. I., N. Y.:		
Incarnation 1925	1927	3,000.00
Jersey City, N. J.:		
Calvary 1919	1924	1,500.00
Little Neck, L. I., N. Y.:		
Christ 1926	1931	3,000.00
Newark, N. J.:		
Grace 1906	1933	6,000.00
East Orange, N. J.:		
Advent 1924	Demand	400.00
New Britain, Conn.:		
Reformation 1926	1929	4,900.00
Nutley, N. J.:		
Trinity 1927	1932	4,000.00
Oswego, N. Y.:		
St. Matthew's 1888	1893-1900	2,150.00
Paterson, N. J.:		
First 1907-27	1912-32	5,960.90

Pelham Park, Bronx, N. Y.:			
Calvary	1925	Demand	5,000.00
Queens (Dunton), N. Y.:			
St. Paul's	1925	1930	5,000.00
Ridgefield, N. J.:			
Zion	1930	1935	5,000.00
Richmond Hill Circle, N. Y.:			
Holy Comforter	1926	1931	1,000.00
River Edge, N. J.:			
Grace	1923	1928	3,000.00
Rochester, N. Y.:			
Emmanuel	1924	1927	5,000.00
Rutherford, N. J.:			
St. John's	1930	1935	5,000.00
Schenectady, N. Y.:			
First	1922	Demand	3,150.00
Second	1928	1933	5,000.00
Snyder, N. Y.:			
Ascension	1927	1932	5,000.00
Springfield Gardens, N. Y.:			
Bethany	1925	1933	5,000.00
Syracuse, N. Y.:			
Atonement	1918	Demand	5,000.00
Teaneck, N. J.:			
St. Paul's	1928	1933	5,000.00
Union Township, N. J.:			
Christ	1927	1932	3,000.00
Valley Stream, N. Y.:			
St. Paul's	1925	1933	2,500.00
Woodhaven, N. Y.:			
St. James'	1924	1929	5,000.00
			$174,960.90

NORTHWEST SYNOD

Appleton, Wis.:			
Trinity	1924	1929	5,000.00
Beloit, Wis.:			
Atonement	1908-18	1913-23	8,000.00
Billings, Mont.:			
First English	1920	1925-28	6,200.00
Fond du Lac, Wis.:			
Our Saviour	1926	1931	5,000.00
Grand Forks, N. D.:			
St. Mark's	1915	1929	900.00
Great Falls, Mont.:			
St. John's	1927	1932	10,000.00*
Glenburn, N. D.:			
Trinity	1929	1934	2,000.00
Jefferson, Wis.:			
St. Mark's	1926	1931	1,000.00
Killdeer, N. D.:			
St. John's	1920	1925	2,000.00
Lansford, N. D.:			
Trinity	1920	1925	900.00

Lincolnton, Minn.:			
St. Andrews	1925	1930	3,000.00
Livingston, Mont.:			
Redeemer	1912	1932	5,000.00
Madison, Wis.:			
Luther Memorial	1921-22-24-27	1932	39,300.00
Marinette, Wis.:			
St. James'	1922	1927	5,000.00
Marshfield, Wis.:			
Trinity	1924	1929	3,000.00
Milwaukee, Wis.:			
Pentecost	1924-28	1933	6,500.00
Resurrection	1913	1920	700.00
Washington Park	1921	1929	15,000.00
Minneapolis, Minn.:			
Epiphany	1926-27	1931-32	5,000.00
Holy Communion	1910-13	1915-18	2,000.00
Mt. Carmel	1926	1931	4,000.00
Resurrection	1923	1928	2,000.00
St. James'	1916	1921	2,000.00
Oshkosh, Wis.:			
St. John's	1924	1927	3,000.00
Oxboro, Minn.:			
St. Luke's	1927	1932	2,000.00
St. Paul, Minn.:			
Ascension	1925	1933	5,500.00
Superior, Wis.:			
Holy Trinity	1926	1929	5,000.00
Walters, Minn.:			
Faith	1923	1926	1,500.00
Waukesha, Wis.:			
St. Luke's	1926	1928-31	8,000.00*
Wauwatosa, Wis.:			
St. Matthew's	1921	1929	15,000.00
West Bend, Wis.:			
Trinity	1926	1931	3,000.00
West Allis, Wis.:			
First	1929	1934	1,000.00
Williston, N. D.:			
Trinity	1925	1928	8,200.00
Winnipeg, Man., Can.:			
First English	1912-21	1915-26	26,288.38
			$211,988.38

NOVA SCOTIA SYNOD

Halifax, N. S.:			
Resurrection	1915	1930	5,000.00

OHIO SYNOD

Akron, O.:			
First Hungarian	1927	1932	5,000.00
Bowling Green, O.:			
First	1923	1928	3,000.00

Cambridge, O.:

Christ	1913	1918	1,000.00

Cleveland, O.:

Emmaus	1912	1916	1,150.00
Parma, Redeemer	1928	1933	4,000.00

Cleveland Heights, O.:

Messiah	1924	1929	5,000.00

Columbus, O.:

Hilltop	1919	1924	2,000.00
Immanuel	1891-96	1893-1906	4,250.00
Indianola		Demand	3,333.33*
Redeemer	1923	1928	3,000.00

Continental, O.:

Christ		1897	300.00

Covington, Ky.:

First	1920	1931	5,000.00

Dayton, O.:

Grace	1912	1917	1,700.00
No. Riverdale	1914	1919	1,500.00
Westwood	1916	1921	1,500.00

East Cleveland, O.:

St. James'	1919	1924	2,000.00*

Fremont, O.:

St. Mark's	1921	1926	3,000.00

Kent, O.:

First	1908	1913	1,000.00

Lakewood, O.:

Trinity	1921	1926	10,000.00

Marion, O.:

St. Paul's	1917	1922	1,000.00

Niles, O.:

Trinity	1924-28	1930-33	10,000.00

Sebring, O.:

Trinity	1915	1918	1,000.00

Springfield, O.:

Fifth	1902	1904	2,000.00

Toledo, O.:

Augsburg	1925	1929	5,000.00
Bethany	1927	1932	5,000.00
Home Acres	1922	1927	1,000.00
Messiah	1925	1930	2,000.00
Redeemer	1925	1930	5,000.00

			$89,733.33

PACIFIC SYNOD

Bellingham, Wash.:

St. Mark's	1924	1929	1,000.00*

Everett, Wash.:

Trinity	1920	1929	5,000.00

Longview, Wash.:

Trinity	1926-30	1931-33	13,000.00*

Medford, Ore.:

Zion	1926-28	1933	5,500.00

Portland, Ore.:			
Redeemer	1925	1932	1,200.00 .
Salem, Ore.:			
American	1928	1933	5,000.00
Seattle, Wash.:			
Holy Trinity	1901-03	1902-06	3,500.00
St. James'	1923	1928	2,500.00
St. Mark's	1929	1934	3,500.00
University	1926-27-30	1931-32-33	18,500.00*
Spokane, Wash.:			
St. Paul's	1924	1929	3,000.00
Vancouver, B. C.:			
Redeemer	1913	1918	5,000.00
Victoria, B. C.:			
Grace	1910	1913-25	5,967.50*
			$72,667.50

East Pennsylvania Synod

Bristol, Pa.:			
Zion	1920	1932	3,000.00
Collingdale, Pa.:			
First	1926	1931	5,000.00
Drexel Hill, Pa.:			
Grace	1925	1930	5,000.00
Essington, Pa.:			
Tinicum Memorial	1922	1930	2,850.00
Harrisburg, Pa.:			
St. Paul's	1924	1932	2,925.00
Merchantville, N. J.:			
Messiah	1927	1932	2,500.00
Narberth, Pa.:			
Trinity	1921-24	1932	7,125.00
Palmyra, N. J.:			
First	1925	1930	5,000.00
Philadelphia, Pa.:			
Luther Memorial	1921	1932	5,000.00
St. Andrew's	1904	1932	1,950.00
Runnemede, N. J.:			
Trinity	1928	1933	2,500.00
Sea Isle City, N. J.:			
Messiah	1918	1919	500.00
Trenton, N. J.:			
Bethel	1924	1932	10,000.00
West Chester, Pa.:			
Calvary	1925	1932	1,462.50
Yeadon, Pa.:			
Trinity	1930	1935	5,000.00
East Pennsylvania Synod	1930	1935	10,000.00
			$69,812.50

Ministerium of Pennsylvania

Allentown, Pa.:			
Redeemer	1926	1931	3,000.00

Attleboro, Pa.:			
Redeemer	1906	1930	800.00
Bethlehem, Pa.:			
First Hungarian	1929	1934	2,500.00
Chester, Pa.:			
Nativity	1920	1933	2,500.00
Clark's Summit, Pa.:			
Trinity	1930	1935	4,000.00
Haddonfield, N. J.:			
Our Saviour	1928	1931	2,500.00
Haddon Heights, N. J.:			
Ascension	1916	1932	1,900.00
Laureldale, Pa.:			
Calvary	1930	1935	5,000.00
Mountainville, Pa.:			
Trinity	1924	1933	4,500.00
Oaklyn, N. J.:			
St. Mark's	1928	1931	2,500.00
Philadelphia, Pa.:			
Gloria Dei	1924	1934	14,250.00
Grace (Roxboro)	1926	1932	600.00
Mediator	1923	1930	6,300.00
Reading, Pa.:			
Nativity	1928	1933	5,000.00
Shavertown, Pa.:			
St. Paul's	1927	1932	2,500.00
Somers Point, Pa.:			
Grace	1927	1932	2,500.00
West Collingswood, N. J.:			
St. Luke's	1917	1930	2,925.00
West Lawn, Pa.:			
Advent	1929	1932	5,000.00
			$68,275.00

SUSQUEHANNA SYNOD OF CENTRAL PENNSYLVANIA			
Jersey Shore, Pa.:			
Grace	1908	1911	500.00
Scranton, Pa.:			
Grace	1902	1907	1,300.00
			$1,800.00

PITTSBURGH SYNOD			
Arnold, Pa.:			
Calvary	1923	1928	2,565.00
Ashtabula, Pa.:			
First	1912	1917	1,000.00
Butler, Pa.:			
Trinity	1923	1928	8,000.00*
Cleveland, O.:			
St. Johannis	1924	1929	5,000.00
Teutsch	1929	1934	5,000.00
Clairton, Pa.:			
Trinity	1929	Demand	5,000.00

East McKeesport, Pa.:

St. John's	1911	1933	450.00

Garfield (Blair Co.), Pa.:

English		1907	500.00

Gary, Ind.:

Honterus	1927	1932	5,000.00

Farrell, Pa.:

St. John's	1928	1933	4,000.00

Monessen, Pa.:

St. Paul's	1910	1915	1,000.00

Pittsburgh, Pa.:

First Hungarian	1926	1931	5,000.00
St. James'	1907	1932	2,000.00
St. Paul's	1906	1909	700.00
Messiah	1915	1930	2,000.00*
Pittsburgh Synod	1930	1935	3,375.00

Sharon, Pa.:

Trinity	1926	1933	3,000.00

Swissvale, Pa.:

St. John's	1908	1913	2,000.00

Wesleyville, Pa.:

Messiah	1920	1933	3,000.00
Pittsburgh Synod	1927	Demand	5,000.00

Trafford, Pa.:

St. Mark's	1930	1935	3,000.00

$66,590.00

ROCKY MOUNTAIN SYNOD

Boulder, Colo.:

Trinity	1929	1934	10,000.00*

Casper, Wyo.:

Grace	1924-29	1934	8,000.00*

Colorado Springs, Colo.:

First	1894-1929	1934	4,912.42

Denver, Colo.:

Trinity	1908-28-29	1933-Demand	13,000.00*
Messiah	1924	1927	2,000.00

El Paso, Texas:

St. Paul's	1929	1933	1,000.00

Laramie, Wyo.:

First Scandinavian	1925	1930	4,000.00*

Pueblo, Colo.:

St. Mark's	1906	1929	1,500.00

$44,412.42

SLOVAK ZION SYNOD

Camden, N. J.:

St. John the Baptist	1927	1932	2,000.00

East Pittsburgh, Pa.:

Trinity	1924	1932	3,000.00

Newark, N. J.:
Holy Trinity 1930   1935   10,000.00

$15,000.00

TEXAS SYNOD
Dallas, Tx.:
First 1923   1928   2,679.30
Pawnee, Tx.:
Holy Cross 1927   1932   1,000.00
San Antonio, Tx.:
St. Luke's 1926-30   1931-35   6,100.00

$9,779.30

VIRGINIA SYNOD
Kingsport, Tenn.:
Trinity 1928   1933   2,500.00
Lynchburg, Va.:
Trinity 1922   1929   5,300.00*

$7,800.00

WEST VIRGINIA SYNOD
Charleston, W. Va.:
Trinity 1925   1930   5,000.00
Clarksburg, W. Va.:
St. Mark's 1926   1929   1,400.00*

$6,400.00

WARTBURG SYNOD
Breitung, Mich.:
Good Shepherd 1925   1930   1,500.00
Chicago, Ill.:
Friedens 1923   1928   3,000.00
Martin Luther 1926   1931   2,000.00
Mont Clare 1921   1924-34   2,200.00
St. Johannis 1916   1921   600.00
Tabor 1927   1932   2,000.00
Cudahy, Wis. 1930   1935   3,000.00
Guttenberg, Ia.:
St. Paul's 1923   1931   4,500.00
West Allis, Wis.:
St. John's 1929   1933   2,000.00

$20,800.00

RECAPITULATION OF LOANS TO CHURCHES

At June 30, 1930

Synod	Amount
California Synod	$ 53,220.00
Canada Synod	26,694.59
North Carolina Synod	24,000.00
South Carolina Synod	7,000.00
Florida Synod	50,500.00
Georgia Synod	30,800.00
Illinois Synod	134,861.17
Indiana Synod	36,400.00
Iowa Synod	36,700.00
Kansas Synod	31,000.00
Manitoba Synod	18,151.00
Maryland Synod	45,500.00
Michigan Synod	101,867.05
Mississippi Synod	2,300.00
Nebraska Synod	35,375.00
German Nebraska Synod	3,575.00
United Synod of New York	174,960.90
Northwest Synod	211,988.38
Nova Scotia Synod	5,000.00
Ohio Synod	89,733.33
Pacific Synod	72,667.50
East Pennsylvania Synod	69,812.50
Ministerium of Pennsylvania	68,275.00
Susquehanna Synod of Central Pennsylvania	1,800.00
Pittsburgh Synod	66,590.00
Rocky Mountain Synod	44,412.42
Slovak Zion Synod	15,000.00
Texas Synod	9,779.30
Virginia Synod	7,800.00
West Virginia Synod	6,400.00
Wartburg Synod	20,800.00
	$1,502,963.14

Board Loans	$1,333,777.61
Agency Loans—Women's Missionary Society	169,185.53
	$1,502,963.14

The Rev. Z. M. Corbe, Treasurer of the Board of American Missions, also addressed the Convention.

Secretary Fry introduced the Rev. Fedor Ruppeldt, official representative of the Lutheran Church of Czechoslovakia, with which the United Lutheran Church has established relations. The Rev. Mr. Ruppeldt bore the greetings of the Church in Czechoslovakia, and the President responded thereto.

Secretary Fry introduced Malcolm Mitchell, Indian Chief and interpreter of the Rocky Boy Mission, who offered a prayer in the Cree language. Dr. Fry also introduced the Rev. William H. Gable of the same mission who briefly addressed the Convention.

The Rev. William G. Arbaugh spoke of the work in Porto Rica. The Rev. George C. Weidenhammer reported on his work among the Russian refugees in Western Canada; the Rev. D. D. Kistler, President of the Pacific Synod, addressed the Convention as did also the Rev. S. N. Carpenter of Birmingham, Alabama, and the Rev. Oscar Krauch of Texas.

Dr. Markward then presented the recommendations of the Board.

The Convention, by a standing vote, joined in the expression of thanksgiving and prayer.

Recommendations 1, 2 and 3 adopted.

Recommendation 4 was referred to the Executive Board to report at the next Convention.

Recommendation 5 referred to the Executive Board.

The report of the auditors was accepted.

The Rev. A. Pohlman presented the report of the Committee on Evangelism as follows:

REPORT OF THE COMMITTEE ON EVANGELISM

During the past biennium, the program, recommended by your committee and adopted by you at Erie, was carried out by a large number of the constituent synods of the United Lutheran Church. Institutes on evangelism were held in many parts of the country, and, although the results are necessarily of a kind that cannot be readily tabulated, we are encouraged to believe that they are fully commensurate with the efforts put forth by those who directed and attended the institutes.

Your committee, by a pamphlet on "Setting Up Institutes on Evangelism," and another on "The Practical Possibilities of Luther's Small Catechism," by correspondence, and by personal contacts, did what it could to promote an effective evangelism throughout the Church.

We recommend that synods which have not held such institutes do so during the coming year. A complete program will be found in the minutes of the Erie convention, page 288f.

We suggest to synods which have had such institutes the advisability of following these by similar meetings within their conferences in order that the information and inspiration may be carried down to the local congregations.

Though the results during the last ten years have been increasingly encouraging, we feel there is need of constantly emphasizing and re-emphasizing the duty and privilege of carrying on evangelistic work. In this work both machinery and method are important, but it is our deep conviction that spirit is of prime importance. No program of evangelism will be successful unless there is behind it a church membership that is quickened by the Holy Spirit to a real appreciation of God's grace on the one hand and of sinful man's utter need on the other. We believe it would be of incalculable value to our enterprise of evangelism to have our pastors stress anew the great basic truths of our faith both in their preaching and in their pastoral visitations. The members of our churches must be inspired to vital Christian living, and this vital Christian living must be personally directed into channels of witnessing for Christ.

Your committee has no new principles and no new methods to offer. We believe that the principles and methods laid before you during the last ten years are sound and of permanent value. In order to obviate the necessity of reading through our former reports for this material, we are giving herewith a brief summary of the major points in those reports:

For an effective evangelism that is true to the peculiar genius of our Church, the congregation must be the center of activity. It is the congregation that is responsible for those in the community who are not of the Church. Evangelism to be successful must be the outgoing of the congregation's life. It must be the constant and uninterrupted program of every congregation.

Three things should always be in the mind of every congregation: Retention of those who are in the Church; reclamation of those who have lapsed from the Church; recruiting of those who have not been in the Church. These three are mutually complementary and together constitute the whole program of evangelism.

For the purpose of retaining our present members, these factors should be fully utilized: The home; the Sunday school; the catechetical class. The congregation must use its influence to keep these spiritually effective.

For the purpose of reclaiming those who have lapsed, these factors are important: Personal work on the part of every member of the congregation; special congregational services with a distinctly evangelistic aim; the regular services with sermons that carry an evangelistic appeal.

For the purpose of recruiting those who are entirely outside Christ and His Church, the above factors will again be used, and to these will be added special literature that can be put into the hands of the un-churched and also the adult catechetical class. Instruction of new converts, both before and after confirmation, is highly important and the only adequate means of securing a faithful and intelligently informed church membership.

A good motto for every congregation is: "The Whole Congregation at Work All the Year for Souls." Pastors and Church Councils should give repeated study to this matter of evangelism. Personal workers should be taught and trained for their work in special classes organized for this purpose. The entire congregation should be inspired to witness for Christ.

We have celebrated the nineteen-hundredth anniversary of Pentecost. What we need to do now is to use the Spirit given to the Church as the disciples of old used Him. We need to apply the divine power that abides in the Church to the deep spiritual needs of men. Advent, Epiphany, Lent, Post-Easter, Post-Pentecost—these are the special seasons in which the Church's divine Spirit and power must go forth to the saving of souls.

Respectfully submitted,

PAUL J. HOH,
Secretary of the Committee.

The Revs. E. E. Flack and Carroll J. Rockey addressed the Convention.

The recommendation of the committee was adopted.

At five o'clock the Convention adjourned with prayer by the Rev. J. Kent Rizer.

------◆------

Evening Service

The Evening Service was held under the auspices of the Board of Education.

The Rev. A. Steimle presided and the Rev. G. Morris Smith conducted the Service.

Addresses: "Challenge of Christian Education"
    by Dean Luther A. Weigle, Ph.D., D.D.
"The Answer to the Challenge of Christian Education"
    by the Rev. Gould Wickey.

------◆------

FOURTH MEETING
Morning Session

HOTEL SCHROEDER
Milwaukee, Wisconsin.
Saturday, October 11, 1930, 8:45 o'clock.

Matins were conducted by the Rev. Thos. B. Uber.

The Convention was called to order by the President.

The Minutes of the Friday morning and afternoon sessions were read by the assistant secretary and approved.

The Rev. Theo. O. Posselt, Chairman of the Nominating Committee, reported nominations as follows:

For the Board of Foreign Missions:

Rev. Oscar A. Benson; Rev. E. E. Fischer; Rev. G. Albert Getty; Rev. J. L. Morgan; Rev. Clarence M. Snyder; Rev. H. W. Snyder; Mr. H. Torrey Walker; Rev. E. Neudoerffer; Rev. Geo. G. Parker; Rev. Theo. O. Posselt; Rev. J. H. Reble; Rev. Walter H. Traub; Mr. Virgil W. Doub; Mr. Jacob Wagner.

For the Board of American Missions:

Rev. G. A. Benze; Rev. H. W. A. Hanson; Rev. J. B. Markward; Rev. Jacob Maurer; Mr. A. Raymond Bard; Mr. Grant Hultberg; Mr. H. L. Snyder; Rev. R. H. Benting; Rev. John Body; Rev. Frederick A. Bowers; Rev. E. C. J. Kraeling; Mr. B. B. Slifer; Mr. James M. Snyder; Mr. Henry Walter.

For the Board of Northwestern Missions:

Rev. G. A. Benze; Rev. H. W. A. Hanson; Rev. J. B. Markward; Rev. Jacob Maurer; Mr. A. Raymond Bard; Mr. Grant Hultberg; Mr. H. L. Snyder; Rev. R. H. Benting; Rev. John Body; Rev. Frederick A. Bowers; Rev. E. C. J. Kraeling; Mr. B. B. Slifer; Mr. James M. Snyder; Mr. Henry Walter.

For the Immigrants Mission Board:

Rev. H. W. A. Hanson; Rev. J. B. Markward; Mr. A. Raymond Bard; Mr. Grant Hultberg; Rev. John Body; Rev. E. C. J. Kraeling; Mr. B. B. Slifer; Mr. Henry Walter.

For the West Indies Mission Board:

Rev. G. A. Benze; Rev. H. W. A. Hanson; Rev. J. B. Markward; Rev. Jacob Maurer; Mr. A. Raymond Bard; Mr. Grant Hultberg; Mr. H. L. Snyder; Rev. R. H. Benting; Rev. John Body; Rev. Frederick A. Bowers; Rev. E. C. J. Kraeling; Mr. B. B. Slifer; Mr. James M. Snyder; Mr. Henry Walter.

For the Board of Education:

Rev. H. J. Black; Rev. Franklin K. Fretz; Rev. Howard R. Gold; Rev. C. H. Stein; Mr. Henry Wolf Bikle; Mr. Frederick Henrich; Prof. R. S. Saby; Rev. S. G. von Bosse; Rev. W. H. Greever; Rev. Albert H. Keck; Rev. Henry Moehling, Jr.; Mr. Geo. A. W. Achenbach; Prof. H. T. Deininger; Mr. A. G. Renau.

For the Inner Mission Board:
Rev. G. H. Bechtold; Rev. Herman Brezing; Rev. P. D. Brown; Mr. Carl M. Distler; Mr. T. C. Rohrbaugh; Rev. David A. Davy; Rev. Ira R. Ladd; Rev. Harold S. Miller; Mr. Fred W. Bauers; Mr. Fred Stussy, Jr.

For the Board of Publication:
Rev. Oscar F. Blackwelder; Rev. S. W. Herman; Rev. Emil W. Weber; Mr. L. Russell Alden; Mr. F. Wm. Cappellmann; Mr. Einar Schatvet; Mr. W. G. Semisch; Rev. J. J. Scherer, Jr.; Rev. C. R. Tappert; Rev. R. E. Tulloss; Mr. E. G. Hoover; Mr. John George Kurzenknabe; Mr. John N. Landenberger; Mr. William Thornton Whitsett.

For the Board of Ministerial Pensions and Relief:
Rev. J. H. Reble; Rev. Ross H. Stover; Mr. Wm. A. Granville; Mr. H. J. Herbst; Mr. W. T. Stauffer; Rev. C. Brown Cox; Rev. P. A. Kirsch; Rev. C. P. Swank; Mr. John Martin; Mr. Wm. H. Steinkamp.

For the Parish and Church School Board:
Rev. Paul H. Heisey; Rev. George H. Rhodes; Rev. Wm. C. Schaeffer, Jr.; Mr. Dan Smith; Rev. E. H. Klotsche; Rev. J. F. Lambert; Rev. Earl S. Rudisill; Mr. Clarence C. Dittmer.

For the Board of Deaconess Work:
Rev. Allen L. Benner; Rev. C. T. Benze; Rev. L. A. Thomas; Mr. E. S. Gerberich; Mr. Frederick J. Singley; Rev. O. D. Baltzly; Rev. R. D. Clare; Rev. Paul R. Siebert; Mr. Karl F. Berger; Mr. W. L. Kinney.

For the National Lutheran Home for the Aged:
Rev. Henry Anstadt; Rev. Oscar F. Blackwelder; Rev. J. L. Frantz; Rev. J. E. Harms; Rev. J. T. Huddle; Rev. Richard Schmidt; Rev. H. E. Snyder; Rev. F. Wagner; Rev. John Weidley; Mr. L. Russell Alden; Dr. W. M. Butler; Mr. F. E. Cunningham; Mr. Harry T. Domer; Mr. W. H. Finckel; Mr. John H. Jones; Mr. F. W. Kakel; Mr. H. L. Snyder; Rev. J. B. Baker; Rev. J. M. Francis; Rev. S. T. Nicholas; Rev. Carl C. Rasmussen; Rev. J. B. Rupley; Rev. Simon Snyder; Rev. Chas. F. Steck; Rev. Chas. M. Teufel; Rev. John S. Tome; Mr. Paul Brindle; Mr. Virgil W. Doub; Mr. M. Haller Frey; Mr. W. O. Hiltabidle; Dr. Croll Keller; Mr. Paul F. Myers; Mr. M. P. Moller, Jr.; Mr. Jacob Umlauf.

The Rev. David A. Davy presented the report of the Committee on Lutheran Brotherhoods and introduced Mr. H. E. Isenhour, the newly elected President, who addressed the Convention.

REPORT OF THE COMMITTEE ON LUTHERAN BROTHERHOODS

"Of all things beautiful and good,
The kingliest is brotherhood."
—*Edwin Markham.*

Through its efficient and untiring Executive Secretary, and its able President,

THE BROTHERHOOD REPORTS

A RISING TIDE OF INTEREST

Year by year there has been a growing knowledge of the purpose and program of the Brotherhood, and as a consequence a rising tide of interest in the work of the Church among men. There is an increasing conviction that men must return to leadership in carrying forward the work of the Kingdom. The evidences multiply that there is a real awakening among men as to their privilege and responsibility in their relation to Christ. This means a gradual organization of the men for definite, positive service.

It is evident that we can only capitalize this interest by organization with a definite program, looking toward the conquering of the world for Christ. Simply getting men together and urging action, accomplishes little or nothing. In order to get things done we must organize our forces. This is constantly brought home to us by achievements in every field of activity. Explain the power of the men in the Labor Unions, of employers' associations, of industrial concerns, and we say at once the power lies in the fact of the organization. This results in co-operation, in the blending of individual force into a great conquering power for the accomplishment of the end in view. This important fact we have been slow to learn in securing the power of the men in the work of the Kingdom. This great work will not be done by banquets and speeches. It will never be done until we are organized and given definite tasks to do.

This the Brotherhood is doing. It is not organization alone that we are seeking, but in each case the adopting of and operation of a definite, positive program. We regard the introduction of secular addresses and trifles, for a program, utterly out of harmony with the Church and the purpose of the Brotherhood. The Brotherhood is concerned with the task Christ gave us, "Go ye into all the world and preach the Gospel to every creature." This by all means is the most important and greatest program that can engage an organization. Therefore to use the time and possibilities of the Brotherhood for other purposes is to prostrate a great and virile power from service to Christ to secular, worldly, selfish ends.

We beg pastors and others. if they want an organization of that kind, not to call it a "Brotherhood." We are brethren in Christ and bound heart and soul to accomplish the triumphs of the Kingdom, and to crown

Him Lord of all. Any other purpose we regard as an insult to the spiritual aspirations of men, and false to our obligation to Christ.

FOUR OBJECTIVES

In order that this devotion to Christ may find expression, we have divided the command of Christ, "Go ye into all the world, and preach the Gospel to every creature," into four parts. The Four Objectives are:

First—Win the outside man.
Second—Bring back the lapsed members.
Third—Develop the church life of the boys.
Fourth—Increase the attendance of men at the services of the Church.
(See Recommendation 2.)

This is the distinct and positive task of the Brotherhood. This must be done. The progress of the Church depends on this achievement. No one but the men can do this in any large way. The men can do it. The men will do it if organized and set at the task. We do not propose to let anything displace or overshadow these objectives. We shall press their acceptance and operation unrelentingly, as a definite program of the Brotherhood.

This is truly a man's job. The doing of these objectives will not only result in large additions to the Church, but also in overcoming some of the most serious defects in the life of the Church. They have now been adopted by Synods, Synodical Brotherhoods, and many congregational Brotherhoods, and fine results are being obtained.

In addition to this fundamental program, it has been the expressed desire of many men to determine on some material objective to which we might devote our energies. In answer to this desire, in the Providence of God, two such objectives have come before the Brotherhood, both of which have now been made a part of our work.

THE MULBERRY HOME

In the central states we have no general Home for our aged people. Our churches there have stood by, while other denominations and organizations have made provision for their aged fellowmembers, and in some cases have cared for our own. Now in the Providence and Mercy of God, an unusual opportunity has come to us to remedy this situation.

The Weidner Institute at Mulberry, Indiana, was closed about three years ago. The property consists of twenty acres of land and three buildings. The ownership was lodged in the Synod of Indiana. This Synod offered to turn this entire property over to us in consideration of the payment of the debt outstanding against it. This amounts to approximately twelve thousand dollars. Adding the cost of repairs and alteration, then for about thirty thousand dollars we will have a property that to produce would cost us well over one hundred thousand dollars. We will be able to care for about forty-five people in this Home. The Brotherhood felt the need, saw the opportunity, and thankfully has taken the responsibility of leadership in this work of serving love.

The Brotherhoods and Synods of Ohio, Indiana and Michigan have endorsed the project, and have equal representation on the Board of Trustees. Arrangements have been made also to operate the Home in closest affiliation with the Board of Inner Missions of our Church. (See Recommendation 4.)

The Home was opened August 1, 1930. The need of this work has been shown by many inquiries received, asking for membership in this Home. The men of the central states are thus given the opportunity to do a greatly needed work, one that will bring happiness to many of our beloved fellow-Christians in their declining years.

THE IRON MOUNTAIN LUTHERAN SCHOOL
FOR BOYS AND YOUNG MEN

More than a year ago the Brotherhood was asked by the Inner Mission Board to establish a mountain school for boys and young men, at Konnarock, Va. While the girls' school, which is maintained there by our Women's Missionary Society, has been doing a good work, it became evident that to redeem the mountain districts not only the girls, but the boys and young men must be given a Christian training.

After carefully investigating the matter, the Brotherhood Executive Committee has decided to make this the second of its important material objectives. Here again in a wonderful way the Lord has made it possible for us to come into possession of a property well adapted for this purpose, at a comparatively small sum. We found available a two hundred acre farm with complete equipment and a number of buildings, including a hotel, an assembly building, that can now be purchased. Two years ago this property was not available, nor will it be available two years hence. The property is so arranged that we can accommodate at least one hundred students. The purpose is to establish a distinctly Christian Trade School. The students are to be taught all branches of farming, manual training work, and all other things that go to make it possible to help them to establish normal Christian homes.

A Lutheran congregation will be organized and a special effort will be made to lead every student to Christ and into membership in the Church. When these students return to their homes, it is our hope that they will at once affiliate themselves with one of the Lutheran Churches in their community or establish such a church. In this way we purpose to conserve the training they have received in our school, for Christ and our Church. We design to give them only enough English education to help them transact the business on the farm. It is our aim to so train them that they will go back to their homes and establish productive farms and prosperous Christian homes, and thus redeem the mountain districts. We are persuaded, after investigation, that there is no other way in which the distressing conditions in the mountain regions can be overcome.

To this end we purpose to work in the closest affiliation with Rev. Kenneth Killinger, the mountain missionary of the Virginia Synod, whose work is immediately adjacent to this school. We hope not only to strengthen his work, but also to extend his territory through the training we will be able to give these young men. We expect, therefore, first of all to receive the young men from the territory in which Mr. Killinger is now operating. We deem this arrangement wise for the reason that when these young men return to their homes, they will then have training that will enable them to render important service in the Church. Otherwise, gradually we will lose our contact with the students, and as a consequence lose the value of the training which we have given them. The school operated by the Women's Missionary Society, is two miles distant from the property here spoken of. It is the purpose therefore to operate these two schools as a unit, and arrangements looking to that end are now under way.

There is no question concerning the need of this work. Clearly God has opened the way for us to do a notable work for Him, and it is our confident belief that the men of our Church will respond to the support of this institution to the extent that will enable us not only to purchase this fine property, but also to conduct the school for the years to come. **(See Recommendation 5.)**

"LUTHERAN MEN"

At the Convention of the Brotherhood two years ago at Erie, we formally united with the American Federation of Lutheran Brotherhoods. The first convention of this organization was held in October, 1929, in Chicago.

It was agreed at that time on the part of our committee, to permit "Lutheran Men" to become the organ of the American Federation of Lutheran Brotherhoods. The ownership and editorship of the paper is retained by us and our own interests are fully featured, but in this way we come to have contact with Lutheran men generally. It is the first time, so far as we know, in the history of Lutheranism in America that the same paper has been operated and read by Lutherans of the various Lutheran Bodies. **(See Recommendation 3.)**

PRESENT STATUS ENCOURAGING

The Brotherhood faces great difficulties: Lack of interest in the Kingdom; the fact that other organizations than the Church are placed first; years of inactivity; lack of leadership; indifference on the part of some pastors.

All these and others stand in the way of our progress. We have faced this situation with full confidence, that through Him we shall conquer. We are sowing the seed year by year that will result in rich fruitage. It is not the work of a day, or of a year, but a continuous service we must render for a long time to come.

Along the lines of winning the good will and of increased interest and wide spread information, we have made decided progress. The actual increase in membership is not as rapid as we earnestly desire, but it is not slower than that of other agencies of the Church dealing with similar conditions. Never in our history has the prospect for progress been so encouraging as at this time. There is no question that we shall be able to organize the men of our Church and carry forward the Four Objectives and many important projects that may develop for the advancement of our Church and the glory of our Lord.

JACOB W. KAPP, *Executive Secretary.*
C. J. DRIEVER, *President.*

RECOMMENDATIONS

Prompted by this splendid report of the Brotherhood which was amplified and stressed throughout its Seventh Biennial Convention, October 5 to 7, your Committee respectfully presents the following recommendations for consideration and action:

1. That the Church commend its Brotherhood leaders for the adoption of such a forward looking program, and for the advanced steps that are being undertaken in full harmony with the world-wide comprehensive program and plans of the Church.

2. That the four objectives as promulgated by the Brotherhood be urgently called to the attention of every United Lutheran man for prayerful consideration and enthusiastic co-operation.

3. That the agreement of the Brotherhood whereby "Lutheran Men" became the organ of the American Federation of Lutheran Brotherhoods, be approved on the basis reported.

.4. That the action of the Brotherhoods of Ohio, Indiana and Michigan, as authorized by their respective Synods, in establishing a Home for the Aged at Mulberry, Indiana, be heartily commended, and that this worthy project be recommended to good stewards of God's gold.

5. That the Iron Mountain Lutheran School for Boys and Young Men especially be commended as an object for general benevolence and prayers on the part of the men of the Church.

6. That the Church-wide development of the Brotherhood, through congregational, conference and Synodical organizations, be urged upon local, conference and Synodical leaders, as an effective means for the co-ordination and extension of service for Christ and His Kingdom by the men of the Church.

Respectfully submitted,

JOHN L. ZIMMERMAN,   H. E. ISENHOUR,
W. C. SCHAEFFER,   A. E. ALBRIGHT,
J. E. HEINDEL,   W. O. HILTABIDLE,
H. A. KINGSBURY,   WILLIAM B. AHLGREN,
G. DALTON MYERS   C. OBENHACK,
RODNEY T. MARTINSEN,   R. G. WALTER,
G. M. JONES,   D. A. DAVY, *Chairman.*
WILLIAM J. BAUERLE,

Recommendation 1 adopted.

Under recommendation 2 the Rev. W. C. Schaeffer, Jr., addressed the Convention. Recommendation 2 adopted.

Recommendation 3 adopted.

Mr. A. F. Sittloh spoke concerning the claims of Mulberry Home.

Recommendation 4 adopted.

The Rev. A. E. Bell presented the claims of the Iron Mountain Lutheran School for boys and young men.

Recommendation 5 adopted.

Recommendation 6 adopted.

In accordance with a special order, the Rev. L. L. Uhl addressed the Convention on the work of men in the Church.

The Rev. Frank M. Urich presented the report of the Committee on Women's Work and introduced the newly elected president of the Women's Missionary Society, Miss Flora Prince, who addressed the Convention.

REPORT OF THE COMMITTEE ON WOMEN'S WORK

Since his appointment under date of March 10, 1929, the Chairman of the Committee on Women's Work has attended the meetings of the Executive Board of the Women's Missionary Society and observed the efficient manner in which the multiform operations of this consecrated group of women are carried on.

During the biennium considerable progress in the expansion and development of a more effective program of missionary effort has been made.

The large volume of business which confronts the stated meetings of the Executive Board of the Women's Missionary Society receives most attentive treatment. Business details are carefully transacted and our women display amazing aptitude in adapting their program to the requirements of sound missionary policy.

An important characteristic of all their deliberations is the conscious effort to co-ordinate their activities with the work of the various Boards of the Church.

A mere perusal of the agenda of each meeting of the Executive Board is a liberal education in missionary culture and bears eloquent testimony to the diplomatic insight, wise administration and statesmanlike quality of this competent body of women.

Should circumstances so shape themselves in the future that a combination of our women's missionary work with that of the work of the several mission boards of the United Lutheran Church would appear advisable, we venture the prediction that under such an arrangement our women would bring to the consolidation both executive skill and wide experience in the promotion of the great missionary imperatives.

The Report herewith appended is more than a mere cursory statement of what has been accomplished during the past two years. It is a compendium of missionary information that reflects the breadth and scope of the work to which the women of the United Lutheran Church are devoting themselves with such conspicuous fidelity and sucess.

Pastors and church workers in general will find the Report an invaluable aid in planning congregational missionary programs and in seeking to develop deeper appreciation and greater interest in this branch of the work committed to the Church.

Respectfully submitted,
The Committee on Women's Work,
FRANK M. URICH, <i>Chairman.</i></div>

Report of the Executive Board of the Women's Missionary Society
July 1, 1928 to July 1, 1930

It is with much gratitude that we face another biennium of the Women's Missionary Society. Our missionaries have been particularly blessed with good health and strength; their work has been of an unusually high order. The work of the Society has had a corresponding record. We can only thank God for these gifts in service which we lay at His feet, and ask for a continued share in the opportunity to carry on.

We have set down the catalogue of information which is needed for help in knowing just where we stand, and where we can advance.

SYNODICAL SOCIETIES

We note our strength in the Synodical Societies, which bound together are the Women's Missionary Society of the United Lutheran Church in America. From this strength has come the renewed efforts which have given the causes for gratitude for the work we have been permitted to do. The thirty-one Synodical Societies are Alleghany, California, Canada, East Pennsylvania, Florida**, Georgia, Illinois, Indiana, Iowa, Kansas, Maryland, Michigan, Mississippi, Nebraska (English), Nebraska (German), New York***, North Carolina, Northwest, Nova Scotia, Ohio, Pacific,

---

Note: **Florida organized in 1929.

***The New York Society was organized in 1929 by the merging of the three Societies in New York: The New York, The New York and New England, and The Ministerium of New York.

Ministerium of Pennsylvania, Pittsburgh, Rocky Mountain, South Carolina, Susquehanna Central, Texas, Virginia, Wartburg, West Pennsylvania, West Virginia.

EXECUTIVE BOARD, BOARD OF TRUSTEES

The twenty members of the Executive Board are also the members of the Board of Trustees.

Executive Board:

The officers of the Executive Board are:

President, Mrs. W. F. Morehead, elected 1926, re-elected 1928; Vice President, Miss Flora Prince, elected 1926, re-elected 1928; Recording Secretary, Mrs. P. M. Rossman, elected 1926, re-elected 1928; Treasurer, Mrs. John M. Cook, elected 1928; Statistical Secretary, Mrs. J. M. Bramkamp, elected 1928.

The Members of the Executive Board are:

Mrs. M. J. Bieber, elected 1924, term expires 1930; Mrs. W. S. Dysinger, elected 1924, term expires 1930; Miss Eleanora E. Demmler, elected 1924, term expires 1930; Mrs. James P. Reese, elected 1924, term expires 1930; Mrs. T. W. Kretschmann, elected 1924, term expires 1930; Mrs. O. D. Baltzly*, elected 1926, term expires 1932; Mrs. S. R. Kepner, elected 1926, term expires 1932; Mrs. A. V. Pohlman, elected 1926, term expires 1932; Mrs. A. B. Leamer, elected 1926, term expires 1932. Mrs. A. O. Mullen, elected 1926, term expires 1932; Mrs. Thomas Frack, elected 1928, term expires 1934; Mrs. Theodor Kemnitz, elected 1928, term expires 1934; Mrs. R. N. McMichael, elected 1928, term expires 1934; Mrs. A. M. Obenauf, elected 1928, term expires 1934; Mrs. W. M. Snyder, elected 1928, term expires 1934.

Board of Trustees:

President, Vice President and Recording Secretary are the same as for the Executive Board. Treasurer, Miss Flora Prince. The members are the same as for the Executive Board.

The 1930 biennial convention is charged with the responsibility of electing a President, Vice President, Recording Secretary, Statistical Secretary, Treasurer and five members of the Executive Board to fill vacancies of those whose terms expire, and one member to fill unexpired term for Mrs. O. D. Baltzly, who resigned July, 1930. The present Treasurer and Statistical Secretary are eligible for re-election.

BOARD MEETINGS

The Executive Board has held six meetings during the biennium. The first meeting was held in the First Church in Johnstown, Pa., the day

---

*Resigned July, 1930.

following the close of the 1928 biennial convention, and the other meetings have been held in the Muhlenberg Building, Philadelphia, Pa. The dates of the meetings were September, 1928, February, June and October of 1929; and February and June, 1930.

ADMINISTRATIVE COMMITTEE

The Administrative Committee consists of the five officers of the Executive Board. There have been eight meetings, one in December, 1928, in Pittsburgh, and seven in the Muhlenberg Building, Philadelphia. 1929: February, April, October and December; 1930: February, April and June. July, 1930, the committee met in New York.

STAFF

The Staff appointed is as follows: Executive Secretary, Amelia D. Kemp; Executive Secretary of Literature, Mrs. Charles L. Fry; Field Secretary, Mrs. Herbert C. Bell; Secretary for Young Women, Nona M. Diehl; Light Brigade Superintendent, Mrs. C. K. Lippard; Secretaries for Women Students, Mary E. Markley and Mildred E. Winston.

DEPARTMENTS

The following department secretaries were appointed: Annuity, Mrs. David A. Davy; Box Work, Mrs. F. F. Fry; Deaconess, Mrs. W. P. M. Braun; Extension, Mrs. A. C. Schenck; India Lace, Mrs. A. S. Woll; Life Membership and In Memoriam, Mrs. L. K. Sanford; Mission Study, Mrs. C. P. Wiles; Patron and Protege, Eleanor M. Robinson; Thank Offering, Mrs. C. E. Gardner; West Indies, Mrs. F. F. Fry, later resigned, and Miss Beulah Weiser appointed to fill vacancy.

LITERATURE COMMITTEE

Appointed by the Executive Board: Mrs. B. E. Copenhaver, Chairman; Mrs. Charles L. Fry, Executive Secretary of Literature; Mrs. D. Burt Smith, Mrs. Virgil B. Sease, Mrs. E. S. Lewars, Mrs. C. T. Benze, Mrs. H. C. Bechtolt, Mrs. C. F. Kuder. Ex-officio by virtue of office: Mrs. M. F. Altof, Mrs. J. F. Seebach, Mrs. C. P. Wiles, Doctor Mary E. Markley, Mrs. W. P. M. Braun, Mrs. A. C. Schenck, Miss Nona M. Diehl, Mrs. C. K. Lippard.

CANDIDATE COMMITTEE

Doctor Mary E. Markley was appointed chairman, with Miss Flora Prince and Amelia D. Kemp.

COMMITTEE ON INTERDENOMINATIONAL RELATIONSHIPS

This Committee is: Mrs. P. M. Rossman, chairman; Mrs. F. F. Fry, Mrs. A. V. Pohlman and Amelia D. Kemp.

ADVISERS TO THE BOARDS OF THE CHURCH

By appointment the following served as advisers to the Boards of the Church: Board of American Missions: Miss Flora Prince, Mrs. P. M. Rossman and Mrs. T. W. Kretchmann; Board of Foreign Missions: Mrs. W. F. Morehead and Mrs. S. R. Kepner; Board of Education: Mrs. A. V. Pohlman and Miss Dorothea Hess; Deaconess Board: Mrs. J. P. Reese and Mrs. W. P. M. Braun; Board of Ministerial Pensions and Relief: Mrs. A. O. Mullen and Mrs. Oscar C. Schmidt; Inner Mission Board, Mrs. W. A. Snyder and Mrs. M. J. Bieber.

MISSIONS AND THE MISSIONARIES

Our missionaries serve under the Boards of the Church in the regular fields of the Church. There is an increasing interest in the support of missionaries and of the missions. The distribution of such support is as follows:

UNDER THE BOARD OF AMERICAN MISSIONS

MISSIONS IN THE UNITED STATES

Women Missionaries	Supported By
Ft. Smith	
California	
Alhambra, Grace	California Synodical
Sanger, St. Paul's	
Santa Barbara, Grace	
Colorado	
Boulder, Trinity	
Denver, Barnitz Memorial	
Pueblo, St. Mark's	
Illinois	
Chicago, Belmont Park	
Tabor Mission	
Westwood, Elmwood Park	Christ Church, Chicago
Indiana	
Gary, Grace	
Kansas	
Kansas City, Trinity	
Michigan	
Kalamazoo, Trinity	Michigan Synodical
Montana	
Great Falls, St. John's	Alleghany Synodical
New Jersey	
Vineland, Redeemer	Ministerium of Pa. Synodical
New York	
Endicott, Holy Trinity	
North Carolina	
Asheville, St. Mark's	North Carolina Synodical
Watauga Parish	
Ohio	
Ellyria, Emanuel	Ohio Synodical

Pennsylvania
  Butler, Trinity .... Pittsburgh Synodical
  Pittsburgh, Messiah
South Carolina
  Rock Hill
Tennessee
  Nashville, St. Paul's .... Indiana Synodical
Washington
  Bellingham, St. Mark's
  Longview, Trinity
  Seattle, University
Wisconsin
  Waukesha, St. Luke's .... Northwest Synodical
Wyoming
  Casper, Grace
  Laramie, Trinity

In Canada
  Quebec, Montreal, Redeemer
  British Columbia, Victoria, Grace

Women Missionaries	*Supported By*
Miss Florence Buckner	
at Rocky Boy, Indian Reservation	Northwest Synodical
Miss Cora Pearl Jeffcoat	
at Watauga Parish, N. C.	Light Brigades
Miss Lucretia Lafer	
at Jewish Mission, Toledo, Ohio..	Ohio Synodical
**Miss Frieda Bredehoft	
at Jewish Mission, Baltimore, Md.	
Miss Frieda Hoh	
at Porto Rico, West Indies	
**Miss Mary Markley	
at Porto Rico	
Sister Maren Knudsen	
at Frederikstead, Virgin Islands	
**Sister Clara Smyre	
at Virgin Islands (Christiansted)	
Sister Emma Francis	
at Frederiksted, Virgin Islands	
Sister Edith Prince	
at Frederiksted, Virgin Islands	

UNDER THE INNER MISSION BOARD
The Faculty at the Konnarock Training School, Konnarock, Virginia
*Mrs. Catharine Cox Umbarger,
  Principal .... Maryland Synodical
Miss Helen Dyer, teacher .... Washington, D. C., Missionary Union
Miss Eleanor Smith, teacher ...... New York Conference, N. Y. Synod
Miss Sarah Leonard, teacher
Miss Katrina Umbarger, teacher
Miss Ida Twedten, nurse

Note: The Wisconsin Conference of the Northwest Synodical Society
contributes toward the support of one of the teachers.
  *Resigned September 1, 1930.
  **Resigned.

UNDER THE BOARD OF FOREIGN MISSIONS
WOMEN MISSIONARIES

In Africa: *Supported By*
Sister Laura Gilliland ....Alleghany Synodical
Mrs. C. E. Buschmann ....Temple, Philadelphia
Miss Marie Jensen ....Messiah, Williamsport, Pa.
Miss Mabel Dysinger ....Pittsburgh, Synodical
Miss Elsie Otto ....West Virginia, Synodical
Miss Irene Block
Miss Bertha Koenig

In China:
Miss Erva Moody ....Illinois Synodical
Miss Lydia Reich ....Epiphany, Milwaukee, Wis.
Miss Frieda Strecker
Miss Elvira Strunk
Miss M. Clara Sullivan ....North Carolina Synodical
Miss Kathe Voget

In India:
Miss Selma Anderson ....Emanuel, Souderton, Pa.
Miss Emma Baer
Doctor Mary Baer ....Maryland Synodical
Doctor Arline Beal ....Young Women, Pittsburgh Synodical
Miss Mette K. Blair ....Kountze Memorial, Omaha, Nebraska
Miss Mary S. Borthwick ....Holy Communion, Phila., Pa.
Doctor Nellie S. Cassell ....Christ, Baltimore, Md.
Miss Agnes Christensen ....Kansas Conference, Augustana
Miss M. Edna Engle
**Miss Christina Erickson ....Light Brigades
Miss Edith Eykamp ....Unity, Chicago, Ill.
Miss Katherine Fahs ....Retired
Miss Susan Glatz ....Kodaikanal School Board
Miss Charlotte Hollerbach
Miss Emma Johnson ....Young Women, Trinity, Rockford, Ill.
Miss Hilda Kaercher
Miss Ada Kron ....Augustana Synodical
****Doctor Anna S. Kugler .....East Pennsylvania Synodical
Miss Clara J. Leaman ....St. Paul's, Carlisle, Pa.
Miss Hilma Levine ....District Luther League, Augustana,
                                    Galesburg, Illinois
Miss Verna Lofgren ....Augustana Synodical
Miss Lottie Martin
Miss Maida Meissner
Miss Mabel H. Meyer ....New York Synodical
Miss Louisa A. Miller
***Doctor Grace L. Moyer ......Light Brigades
Miss Alice J. Nickel ....Good Shepherd, Brooklyn, N. Y.
Doctor Betty A. Nilsson ....Augustana Synodical
Miss Annie E. Sanford
Miss Agnes I. Schade ....Retired
Miss Ellen Schuff
Miss Lilith Schwab ....Kansas Synodical
***Miss Frances Segner ....West Pennsylvania Synodical
Miss Hildegrade Swanson

In India   *Supported By*
  Miss Agathe Tatge .... Advent, New York City, N. Y.
  Miss Jessie Thomas .... Ohio Synodical
  Miss Emilie S. Weiskotten .... Ministerium of Pa. Synodical
  Miss Florence M. Welty.......... Indiana Synodical
  Miss E. Pauline Whitteker .... Trinity, Lancaster
  *Doctor Lydia Woerner .... Retired

In Japan:
  Miss Martha B. Akard
  Miss Grace M. Beers
  Miss Helene H. Harder .... German Nebraska Synodical
  Miss Martha M. Harder ;....... East Penna. Synodical
  ***Miss Mary E. Heltibridle ..... Maryland Young Women
  Miss Faith G. Lippard .... Northwest Synodical
  Miss Marion E. Potts
  Miss Maude Powlas
  Miss Annie Powlas .... Light Brigades
  ***Miss Helen M. Shirk......... Ministerium of Pa. Synodical
  **Miss Amy J. Thoren .... Northwest Synodical
  Miss Maya Winther .... Danish United Lutheran Church

In South America:
  Miss Corinne M. Menges
  Miss Myrtle S. Wilke

      *Died July 3, 1930.
      **Resigned.
      ***Assumed May, 1930.
      ****Died July 26, 1930.

MISSIONARIES SENT OUT SINCE OCTOBER, 1928

To Porto Rico we sent in September, 1929, Miss Mary Markley, who gave promise of becoming a valuable missionary kindergartner. There was keen disappointment in the fact that because of her health it was necessary for Miss Markley to return to her home in Roanoke, Virginia. Her health will not permit her to live on a mission field.

To China we sent in September, 1929, Miss Clara Sullivan, from Wilmington, North Carolina. Miss Sullivan is a graduate of Lenoir-Rhyne College, and is a well equipped teacher, whose success in the classroom has been proved. Miss Sullivan has completed one year of the study of the Chinese language. As soon as she has learned the language the Mission in Shantung will assign her to a definite post.

To Rocky Boy, Montana Indian Reservation, we sent in September, 1929, Miss Florence Buckner, from Dublin, Pennsylvania. Miss Buckner is a graduate of State Teachers' College, at Indiana, Pennsylvania, and has taught successfully in Philadelphia and New Jersey.

To India we sent in August, 1929, Miss Ada Kron, of Bertrand, Nebraska, and she is a registered nurse, having received her training at Emmanuel Hospital, Omaha, Nebraska, where she served on the staff, following her graduation. Miss Kron is a member of the Augustana Synod, who support her on the field.

DOCTOR LYDIA WOERNER

Our human tributes to Doctor Lydia Woerner are not adequate to measure her life. Her medical skill was whole-heartedly given for India from 1899 to 1912. It was in 1910 that the Rajahmundry Hospital was built and started under Doctor Woerner and Doctor Betty Nilsson. Within two years, in 1912, Doctor Woerner contracted an infection in performing an operation, and it was necessary to come to America, and she was never able to return to India. In 1906, about midway of the thirteen years in India, Doctor Woerner came to America for a furlough. She became the "good angel" of the community in Interlaken, Florida, where she lived when India was no longer possible. In India today, hearts have been brighter for many years because Doctor Woerner ministered to bodily ills when she lived and served there. In America, wherever she was, and suffering was made known to her, her skilled hand in healing was used.

NEW MISSIONARIES, 1930

To India we will send, in October, 1930, two missionaries whose promise for usefulness is great.

Miss Jessie Mae Cronk, of Salem, Virginia, graduate of Marion College, Marion, Virginia, and of Gettysburg College.

Miss Christie Eleanor Zimmerman, of Selinsgrove, Pennsylvania, first honor student of Selingsgrove high school, and holder of Snyder County Scholarship in Susquehanna University.

Both of these young women have had experience in the classroom. Miss Cronk taught in Darlington School, Chester, Pennsylvania, for the academic year 1929-30. Miss Zimmerman taught at Derry, Pennsylvania, for four years, and spent the academic year, 1929-30, at the Biblical Seminary, New York. Both candidates were students at the summer term 1930 of the Biblical Seminary in New York. Miss Cronk and Miss Zimmerman will be commissioned at the 1930 convention by the Board of Foreign Missions.

NEW BUILDINGS

In Japan a second unit was added to the Janice James School dormitory. In Japan, at the Colony of Mercy, the Katherine Scherer Cronk Kindergarten was built. The School and the Colony are both in Kumamoto.

In Porto Rico a residence for the women missionaries was built at Bayomon.

KONNAROCK TRAINING SCHOOL BOARD

On the Board of the Konnarock Training School the following are from the Women's Missionary Society: Mrs. W. F. Morehead, term expires December, 1930; Mrs. G. W. McClanahan, term expires 1932; Mrs. S. R. Kepner, term expires 1934; Miss Flora Prince, term expires 1934.

INCREASE IN DUES

At the 1928 biennial convention it was recommended that "an increase in the regular dues of the Society be considered. The Convention voted that each Synodical Society should bring the result of the deliberations to this Convention in 1930. The result is as follows:

Voted To Increase—8

Illinois, suggest to 15 cents; Northwest, Virginia, 15; Florida, 25; Georgia, 15; New York, 15; West Virginia, California, "Provided *all* do."

Voted Not To Increase—10

Texas, stress membership; Rocky Mountain, new members; Canada, 25 per cent increase in members; Ohio, special efforts in thankoffering and specials; Kansas, members, life members and patron and protege; English Nebraska, 20 per cent increase in members; West Pennsylvania, each individual give as able; Pacific, each individual try to increase; Wartburg, North Carolina, increase offerings.

No Action, Sentiment Expressed—13

East Pennsylvania, "Prefer more members to money. Perhaps education needed in that line, specials accepted willingly;" Indiana, stress thankoffering; Ministerium of Pennsylvania, "Sentiment overwhelmingly against;" South Carolina, "We are stressing membership and extension to the unattached woman as a much bigger item than the veteran of many battles, however, *we* will step in line;" Pittsburgh, discussed in executive meeting and decided not to bring to convention; Alleghany, Susquehanna Central, Maryland, Michigan, Mississippi, German Nebraska, Nova Scotia, Iowa.

All of the 31 Synodicals reported.

HEADQUARTERS ESTABLISHED IN PHILADELPHIA

In 1918, when the merger brought about the organization of the Women's Missionary Society of the United Lutheran Church, the executive office of the Women's Missionary Society was fixed at Pittsburgh, Pennsylvania. The Treasurer carried her work at her home. The Secretary for Young Women and the Superintendent of the Light Brigade, when they were appointed, carried on their work from their homes. The Life Membership and In Memoriam work was done by the department secretary at her home, and a part of the detail carried in the Pittsburgh office. The Literature Committee, in 1918, had its office and rooms in the Drexel Building, Philadelphia. In 1923 the Muhlenberg Building was built in Philadelphia, at 13th and Spruce streets, by the Lutheran Publication Society, and the Literature Committee moved into rooms in the new building. The Light Brigade Superintendent also opened an office in the new building.

By action of the biennial convention of 1928 the headquarters were fixed in the Muhlenberg Building, Philadelphia. The action was that the headquarters should provide offices for the general treasurer, the secretary for young women, the superintendent of the Light Brigade, the Literature Secretary and the executive secretary.

In January, 1929, the Executive Office was moved from the Fulton Building, Pittsburgh, Pennsylvania, to the Muhlenberg Building, Philadelphia. The Treasurer opened an office in the Muhlenberg Building. Provision was made for that part of the detail of the Life Membership department which had been carried in Pittsburgh. The Secretary for Young Women came to the Muhlenberg Building. These offices were opened on the seventh floor, where the Literature rooms and the Light Brigade Superintendent were already established.

Work Of The Executive Secretary

The record in part is: Regular office routine, correspondence with the missionaries and the constituency, issuing annuity bonds, agenda for Executive Board and Administrative Committee meetings, monthly notes from headquarters for *Lutheran Woman's Work,* monthly Prayer Calendar for *Lutheran Woman's Work,* candidate correspondence and interviews, interviews with missionaries upon arrival from the fields, and answering calls for representation of the Women's Missionary Society.

In representing the Society these

Meetings Have Been Attended	*and*	*Addresses Made*
2 Annual Council of Women for Home Missions		
1 Annual Federation Women's Boards Foreign Missions		
7 Board of Foreign Missions		
5 Board of American Missions		
1 Board of Education		
1 Synod		
5 Synodical Conventions, Women's Missionary Society		2
11 Conferences, Women's Missionary Society		9
6 Executive Committees (by invitation only)		
10 Local Women's Missionary Society		10
6 Young Women's Missionary Society		6
24 Thank Offering		24
1 Week of Prayer		1
1 World Day of Prayer		1
2 All Day Mission Study Class		1
1 School of Missions		1
1 Summer Assembly		6
1 Young People's Conference		1
1 College Y. W. C. A.		1
2 College Student Dinners		2
Church Services		7
Sunday Schools		8
2 Mother and Daughters Banquets		2

Total Public Addresses.... 82

Departments

Every department has felt the need for increasing effort in order to meet the calls from the fields because of the cut budgets. The secretaries redoubled and worked harder than ever. Within one year, from the

October, 1928, biennial convention, when the cut was made, we were able to restore the budgets. The gifts came in willingly, and in many instances following sacrifice and prayer.

NEW HOME MISSIONS

The list under the Board of American Missions has been maintained. With the addition of Miss Florence Buckner to the roster of missionaries we have a picturesque and challenging new mission field at home—Rocky Boy, Indian Reservation in Montana.

STAFF

The outstanding contribution of the Staff during this biennium was the visit to the Orient of Doctor Mary Markley, chairman of the candidate committee. Dr. Markley, who went at her own expense, was given official appointment to represent the Women's Missionary Society. She left America July, 1929, to visit our Missions in China, Japan and India. The missionaries from all three missions report most gratefully on Doctor Markley's visit, because of the wise counsel she was able to give, and because of her open minded attitude toward the work on the fields—she went to learn. Since her return to America, in March, 1930, Doctor Markley has given expression to her appreciation of the courtesy and kindness of the missionaries through whom she was given every possible opportunity to see the missions at work. In Japan Doctor Markley was honor guest at the Woman's Convention. In India the missionaries painstakingly prepared for and held an all-day conference, at which formal presentation was made of the mission in its varied phases—schools, hospitals and churches.

THE OUTLOOK

The debt, consisting of a $50,000 bank note, has given much concern. Gifts have been received which have reduced the note considerably. At the time these reports were assmbled the balance yet to pay was $16,000. The outlook will be clear concerning our future if we can meet the balance due.

RECOMMENDATIONS

Recognizing the responsibility for the task to which we have set our hand, and relying on the promises of the Father of all, the Executive Board make the following recommendations:

1. That the plans be launched at the 1932 biennial convention for the celebration of Doctor Anna S. Kugler's fifty years in the mission in India.
2. That the special for the biennium be the American Memorial to Mrs. E. C. Cronk, plans to be presented to this convention by the special committee.
3. That in order to preserve the early history of the Women's Missionary Society each Synodical Society be requested to prepare an historical

sketch of the work of the Synodical Society from the beginnings, these sketches to be kept on file in the Executive Office.

4. That the 1930 Christmas offering and the 1931 undesignated Lenten Self Denial offering be given for southern mountain work.

5. That the 1931 Christmas offering and the undesignated 1932 Lenten Self Denial offering be given for the Bhimavaram Hostel in India.

6. That a study of the status and work of the women in the United Lutheran Church be made by the following committee: Mrs. W. F. Morehead, Doctor Mary E. Markley, Miss Jessie S. Thomas, Mrs. Carl Eggers, Mrs. H. C. Bell. This survey to be presented to the Executive Board of the United Lutheran Church before being presented to the Woman's Missionary Society biennial convention.

7. That we request invitations for the entertainment of future biennial conventions be in the hands of the Executive Board at least four months prior to the convention at which the invitation is to be accepted.

8. That the budget to be adopted at this convention become operative January 1, 1931. The proposed budget is as follows:

BUDGET
January 1, 1931, to January 1, 1933

Board of American Missions ....'		$177,684
Salaries: Home Mission Pastors	$65,384	
Parish Workers:		
Watauga, N. C., and Rocky Boy	4,800	
Jewish Missionaries:		
Toledo, O., and Baltimore, Md.	4,800	
West Indies Missionaries	12,600	
Total Salaries	$87,584	
West Indies	7,700	
Travel	$1,500	
Children's Homes	5,200	
Milk Fund	1,000	
	7,700	
Linguistic Division	12,400	
Interest Requirements Based on Present Claims ..	15,000	
Loans to Churches	25,000	
New Work	30,000	
	177,684	
Board of Education		6,000
Board of Ministerial Pensions and Relief		10,000
Inner Mission Board		22,000
Salaries at Konnarock Training School, Va.	$10,920	
Health Work	2,000	
Maintenance	9,080	
	$22,000	
Board of Foreign Missions		432,716
Africa:		
Maintenance, Including Restoration....	$13,200	
Medical	4,000	

Travel of Missionaries 4,400
Salaries, Present, Possible New...... 4,200

$35,800

China:
Maintenance, Including Restoration.... 17,400
Travel of Missionaries 1,500
Salaries 10,200
Share of Purchase Price of Property. 7,000

36,100

India:
Maintenance, Including Restoration.... 152,256
Travel ....; 22,000
Salaries, Present and Possible New.. 62,800
Exchange on Salaries 6,300

243,356

Japan:
Maintenance, Including Restoration.... 55,560
Travel 5,000
Salaries 26,500
Endowment, Janice James School, final. 2,300

89,360

South America:
Maintenance, Including Restoration.... 20,000
Travel 1,500
Salaries and Exchange 6,600

28,100

$432,716

Total to Boards in the United Lutheran Church $648,400
Interdenominational Missionary Boards and Committees 6,300
Council of Women for Home Missions Migrant
 Work $200
Council of Women for Home Mission Committee
 Work 500
Federation of Women's Boards, Foreign Mis-
 sions, Christian Literature Committee 100
Union Christian Colleges in the Orient 5,500

$6,300

Scholarships for Candidates 1,000
Specials 60,000
American Memorial to Mrs. E. C. Cronk, to be
 Raised by Special Contributions $50,000
Hostel at Bhimavaram 10,000

$60,000

General Appropriations 22,870
Literature Committee, Including Promotional Lit-
 erature $20,000
Interdenominational:
 Missionary Education Movement..... $400
 Council of Women for Home Mis-
  sions Dues 220
 Federation Women's Boards of For-
  eign Missions Dues 150

Missionary Review of the World...	100	
Foreign Missions Conference of North America	1,000	
Summer Schools	1,000	
		2,870

		$22,870
Specific Appropriations		69,200
Lutheran Women's Work Life Membership Supplement	$7,000	
Biennial Convention, 1932	20,000	
Interest to Annuitants	25,000	
Repayment Balance on Loan	15,000	
Interest on Loan	1,800	
Miscellaneous	400	
	$69,200	
Administration		85,994
Travel Representatives to Meetings	$1,000	
Rent, Offices and Literature Rooms	9,264	
Office Expenses	1,700	
Expenses, officers, staff, parish worker, Watauga, field secretary, board and committee meetings, insurance treasurer's bonds	10,525	
Departments	2,605	
Printing and Stationery	800	
Salaries, Executive and Clerical Staff, 19 people.	60,100	
	$85,994	
Emergencies		11,000
Total		$904,764

SUMMARY

Boards of the United Lutheran Church	$648,400	
Interdenominational Boards and Committees	6,300	
Scholarships for Candidates	1,000	
Specials	60,000	
General and Specific Appropriations	92,070	
Administration—Departments, Rent, Meetings, Insurance, Treasurer's Bond, 19 Salaries	85,994	
Emergencies	11,000	
		$904,764

Respectfully submitted,
THE EXECUTIVE BOARD,
By AMELIA D. KEMP,
Executive Secretary.

Philadelphia, Pa., July 16, 1930.

Miss Prince introduced Miss Amelia D. Kemp, Executive Secretary; Mrs. John M. Cook, treasurer; and Miss Nona M. Diehl, Secretary of Young Women's Work.

The Rev. A. Pohlman responded to the address of Miss Prince.

The Rev. H. C. Roehner presented the report of the Committee on Associations of Young People and introduced the Rev. Amos J. Traver, General Secretary of the Luther League; Mr. Clarence C. Dittmer, President of the Luther League, and Miss Brenda Mehlhouse, Junior Secretary. The report follows:

REPORT OF THE COMMITEE ON ASSOCIATIONS OF YOUNG PEOPLE

The Luther League of America, the official young people's organization of the United Lutheran Church, has continued to make excellent progress and advancement in its work during the last biennium.

Throughout the Church, increasingly young folks who have been members of the Luther League and have received the fine training which all who sincerely take a part in its work receive, are being found in positions of service and leadership in the local congregations, as teachers in Sunday schools, active workers in missionary societies, members of the Church Councils, officers in the Sunday schools, members of boards in district Synods, as well as in the United Lutheran Church. Their training is evident. Such young folks who have reached maturity, and are now so active in the work of the church, are alone worth all the efforts of the Luther League. But they are only a small portion of the hundreds who are receiving the training in preparation for leadership and service.

ONE HUNDRED PER CENT ON APPORTIONMENT

It is of interest indeed to note that the Luther League of America was able to report last year that all the Synodical and State leagues had paid their dues, their apportionment, for the support of the work in full, 100 per cent. That manifests not only a fine spirit but is an indication of the kind of training which the young folks are receiving in the way of inculcating the sense of obligation to support the work and to support it in full as determined by the Luther League of America.

Anyone can visage the influence of such young people in later years in respect to the apportionments of Synods and the United Lutheran Church. It might be that the final raising of the full apportionment, 100 per cent, of which we have been hearing so much for so many years, by the congregations and Synods of the United Lutheran Church, will have to come by having all the future members of the church come up through a course of training in the Luther League.

MISSIONARY OBJECTIVES

The Luther League of America during the last three bienniums has had three great missionary objectives, namely, Andhra Christian College in

India, where the Luther League furnished the funds to build the administration building; the Parish Hall in the Buenos Aires Mission, and this biennium the Luther League is gathering funds for a building for the Training School for Christian Workers in Porto Rico.

The objective for Andhra Christian College was $25,000 The Luther League paid to the Board of Foreign Missions $30,000 for that cause. The Buenos Aires goal was $12,000. The Luther League raised an over-subscription of $2000. The present goal for Porto Rico is $25,000.

These Missionary objectives have not only been of considerable financial assistance to the work of foreign missions, but even of more value has been the intelligent interest which has been aroused in the hearts and lives of the young people in missions. The missionary objectives have been a great blessing to the Luther League. The concrete objectives have made the missionary fields and their needs more real. The constructive training in missions which the young people have received, will be reflected later in our church life. In these days especially, when in many sections there has been much of criticism of foreign missions, our young people have had their intelligent and hearty interest aroused as at no other time.

We would, therefore, heartily commend the principle that the Luther League each biennium have some missionary objective, and that it be permitted to select such an objective subject to the approval of the Executive Board of the United Lutheran Church, which has endorsed each of the objectives thus far.

INCREASED FINANCIAL HELP NEEDED

The Luther League has been handicapped by the lack of funds. It has been doing excellent work. It has enlarged its work, but on all sides and at all times, it has been hampered and restrained from doing all that it could have done, because sufficient funds have not been available.

Denominations increasingly have given financial assistance to their young people's work, some supporting the work in its entirety. They recognize the primary importance of the work among their young people and foster it generously.

Assistance has been given to the Luther League, but to date it has not been sufficient to take care of what is needed beyond what the Leagues themselves can raise. Only lack of funds, we are confident, has kept the Finance Committee from apportioning a larger amount up to this time. The work among our young people is being handicapped and measurably crippled by the lack of funds.

Your committee brings in the same recommendation which it did at the last convention of the United Lutheran Church. We again recommend that $10,000 per annum be given to the Luther League for carrying on the work among the young people of the church.

It is not necessary for us to go into detail as to the work and accomplishments of the Luther League during the biennium. The report of the General Secretary, the Rev. Amos T. Traver, which will follow this report, will do that.

Respectfully submitted,

THE COMMITTEE.

Report of the General Secretary of the Luther League of America

If it were possible to visit a thousand of our United Lutheran Churches on a single Sunday evening before Vespers, the values of the Luther League devotional would be unescapable. Thousands of young folks bound together by a consecrated, intelligent loyalty to Christ, meet weekly to worship together and to discuss problems vital to the experience of Christian youth. On every meeting night somewhere a boy or girl is faltering a first public prayer, speaking with unaccustomed lips on a religious subject or leading a first devotional program. This army of youth, training in the Luther League, challenges the imagination. The church of tomorrow will be infinitely richer in spiritual power and effective leadership because the Luther League is training "the youth of today, for the church of tomorrow." Our devotional, educational, missionary and practical program has won general support and produced confidence in a coming leadership for the church.

EXTENSION

There is little unoccupied territory in the United Lutheran Church today. With the reception during the biennium of the Luther Leagues of Alabama, Mississippi and Porto Rico the extension of our organization seems practically complete. There is still a field for intensive work within territories generally organized. Every parish without a League is an opportunity.

EFFECTIVE ORGANIZATION

The Luther League seeks consciously to train its leaders for their responsibilities as leaders in the Church of tomorrow. It purposes to correct the recognized organization faults in the church by efficient methods in its own organization. The Church is hampered by a failure to respect apportionments and quotas. Every constituent League paid its 1929 dues in full to the Luther League of America before the 15th of December. In the last biennium every constituent League paid or overpaid its quota for the Buenos Aires objective before the Omaha Convention. There was an over-subscription of $2,000. Quotas set for other League projects such as subscriptions for the Luther League Review are undertaken with serious purpose. Treasurers are instructed to send monthly checks and to hold benevolent monies inviolate. Correspondence is also taken seriously and answered. Organization methods are taught at scores of conventions and summer assemblies. Every Luther League officer trained in efficient organization principles is a promise of a more efficient church leadership in coming years.

SYNODICAL LEAGUES

The policy of the Luther League conforms to the policy of the United Lutheran Church in its recommendation for the Synodical rather than the State form of organization. As swiftly as the Constituent Synods adjust their boundaries to exclusive territories, the State Leagues will seek the status of Synodical Auxiliaries. Where Synodical territories overlap, the State form of organization will be one of the important factors in preparing the way for mergers. In such instances we believe the State organizations should be maintained until the territorial problem is solved.

IN INDIA

The development of young people's work in our India Church has followed the general program of the Luther League. All three departments, Junior, Intermediate and Senior are authorized by the Andhra Synod. The all-Lutheran Conference is considering a Luther League that will unite all the Lutheran Young People in India. Rev. R. D. Philip Augustus has been called as full time Secretary for the A. E. L. C., with additional responsibility for Sunday School work and Stewartship. The selection of Pastor Augustus is a most happy one, and promises large returns for the India Church. An appropriation toward his salary is made by the Luther League of America.

PERSONNEL

The Officers and Executive Committee for 1929-31 are as follows:

Honorary Members: Rev. L. M. Kuhns, D.D., Litt.D.; Hon. E. F. Eilert, C. S. D.; Secretary, Harry Hodges; Officers: President, Mr. C. C. Dittmer; First Vice President, Mr. Herbert W. Fischer; Second Vice President, Mr. Alvin H. Schaediger; Recording Secretary, Miss Eva Peeler; Treasurer, Mr. Charles W. Fuhr; General Secretary, Rev. A. J. Traver; Educational Secretary, Rev. A. J. Traver; Missionary Secretary, Dean May Scherer; Life Service Secretary, Rev. C. A. Portz; Intermediate Secretary, Rev. R. J. Wolf; Junior Secretary, Miss Brenda L. Mehlhouse. Members at Large: Mrs. S. T. Peterson, Mr. Paul Brindle, Miss Winnie Butt, Rev. M. J. Bieber, D.D., Rev. C. M. Teufel, D.D., Mr. John G. Kurzenknabe, Rev. W. A. Mehlenbacher, Rev. Rudolph G. Schulz, Jr., and Chairman of the Committee on Associations of Young People, Rev. H. C. Roehner, D. D.

FIELD SECRETARIES

At the present time only three Synods provide for full time Secretaries, Ohio, New York, and Virginia. Part-time secretaries are maintained by North and South Carolina, Illinois, Pennsylvania, Canada Synod and the States of the Central West co-operatively. The experience of the Synod of Ohio alone would justify the addition of a full time Luther League Secretary to the Synodical staff wherever possible.

WORK LITERATURE

Ample provision is made for the guidance of local workers. "A Worker's Handbook," in loose-leaf form, with all literature published in standard size, is proving effective. Over 225,000 separate pieces of literature were distributed by the six departments of the League in the last biennium.

THE REVIEW AND TOPICS

The Monthly Review is gaining subscribers in an encouraging number. The 1930 spring campaign resulted in nearly 3000 subscriptions notwithstanding a raise in price at $1.25 per year (90c in clubs). *The Topics Quarterly,* edited by Rev. C. P. Harry, D.D., is distributed in quantities of 13,000 per quarter and is gaining steadily. These two publications are practically self-supporting, due to the fact that there is no charge against them for editorial service.

AGE GROUPINGS

The age grouping for which the Luther League provides is as follows: Junior, 9 to 12 years, with a supplementary program for Little Leaguers under 9; Intermediate, 13 to 16 years; Senior, 17 plus. Miss Brenda L. Mehlhouse is in charge of the Junior Department, Rev. Robert J. Wolf, of the Intermediate Department, and the General Secretary of the Senior Department. Careful study is being given to the problem of age groupings, and as soon as deemed practical adjustments will be made to conform to better educational theory.

The Junior League bands together over 13,000 children in 570 Leagues. 116 Leagues were added in 1929. A four-year program of topics "Preparing for Church Membership," has been in progress since 1927, and has been most effective. The missionary topics are selected and the leader's helps prepared under direction of the Light Brigade. A popular feature of the Junior program is "The Good Neighbor Club." By this plan over 30 Junior Leagues in institutions and missions have been adopted and aided by strong organizations. A native Junior Secretary has recently been appointed for our India Mission.

The Intermediate Department has grown from 130 Leagues in 1927 to 350 in 1930. 79 new Intermediate Leagues were added in 1929. The Department does not insist on a particular form of organization, although it offers a model constitution for a combination boy and girl society. Where the local congregation desires separate organizations there is no objection. In some cases organized Sunday school classes are affiliated. An important feature of the program is the development of District Intermediate Organizations, holding conventions and carrying out their program independent of the Senior District League. The Department of Boys' Work is also growing. Contacts with the Boy Scout Organization are maintained. A valuable consultative service is also offered committees projecting summer camps.

PROGRAM DEPARTMENTS

Education, Missions and Life Service are the three program departments. Secretaries for these departments should be in every local, district and synodical League. Many of our constituent organizations now report the three secretaries in every local. No better suggestion could be offered the indifferently successful local than the appointment of these secretaries and the promotion of the full League program.

The Educational Department stresses Weekly Devotionals, Daily Bible reading, the Reading Course, the Discussion and Study Groups, Pageantry and Better Organization methods.

The Missionary Department stresses the Monthly Missionary Devotional, the Mission Study Class and Missionary Objective. Each biennial objective has been over-subscribed. The present objective is $25,000 for a Training School for Christian Workers in Porto Rico under The Board of American Missions. Service objectives are suggested for the local and district Leagues.

The Life Service Department stresses The Stewardship of all of Life, Study Groups in Vocational Guidance, Recruiting for Full and Part-time Church Service, the Celebration of Life Service Day, and the Holding of Life Service Rallies.

SPECIAL DAYS

Three special days are authorized in the Luther League, and orders for services prepared for use either in the League Devotional or at Vespers: Missionary Objective Day the last Sunday in January; Life Service Day the first Sunday in May, and Luther League Day the last Sunday in September. February and March are also designated for Mission Study Classes for Young People.

PERSONAL EVANGELISM

The Luther League offers the locals a plan for personal evangelism. Pamphlets have been prepared giving complete directions. The aim of the program is to capitalize youth friendships for Christ. It is not ex-

pected that the average Luther Leaguer will be prepared at first to
evangelize directly. His first opportunities will be in bringing his friends
within the circle of influence of the pastor and the Church. As an indirect
outcome of this program it is expected that 10,000 new members will be
added to the Luther League of America in this biennium.

CORRELATION

The problem of a correlated educational program for the parish is
still unsolved. Various conferences have been held at the call of the
Parish and Church School Board. Perhaps the most valuable outcome
of these conferences has been a growing appreciation of the chaotic organization of the educational agencies in the average parish. The selection of organizations in many parishes is not the result of thoughtful
planning. A survey of our parishes will discover by the side of the
Junior, Intermediate and Senior Luther Leagues, the Light Brigade, the
Young Women's Missionary Society, organized Sunday School Classes,
Social and Athletic Clubs, Boy and Girl Scouts, Camp Fire Girls and
many other national or local organizations. Before satisfactory correlation is possible with the Church School, there should be an authorized plan
of organizations. One organization should be authorized for each age
group as provided in the departmentalized Church School.

The program of these authorized organizations should prepare our children and youth for membership in the Women's Missionary Society and
the Brotherhood. With a consecutive plan of organizations it would be
possible to correlate the programs definitely with the departmentalized
program of the Church School. The educational program of the parish
then would become a unified whole. The organizations themselves by
conference are now making marked progress in the solution of this
problem. The Luther League believes that it has a program that with
some adjustments would meet the needs of the church below the age
groups comprising the Women's Missionary Society and Brotherhood. It
seeks supremely to know and conform to the will of the church.

FINANCES

With opportunities for service constantly increasing, the income of the
Luther League is static. The United Lutheran Church appropriates $6,000
per year to the Luther League. Dues paid by the Senior Luther Leagues
produce approximately $7,000. The Sustaining Membership Fund must
carry the remainder of the budget, of $20,000. This is by far the smallest
budget of any of the young people's organizations in the larger communions. In view of the evident lack of training in benevolent giving in
the Church at large, our young people should be encouraged to give to
benevolent objectives. The Methodist Episcopal Church, North, provides
for the Epworth League over-head and the entire giving of their young

folks beyond the local Church demands, is directed toward benevolent objectives. We believe a somewhat similar plan, if adopted by the United Lutheran Church, would materially better the attitude of the church of the coming years toward benevolent giving. The Luther League desires to be a young people's society. Therefore, it must be dependent.

CONVENTIONS

July 5-10, 1929, the Eighteenth Biennial Convention was held in Omaha, Nebraska. More delegates came by way of Chicago on one special train than the entire membership of the York, Pa., Convention, in 1922. In point of attendance, careful preparation, inspiration and good fellowship, the Omaha convention was a high mark in League history. The Nineteenth Biennial Convention will be held in Reading, Pa., July 2-6, 1931. Plans for the convention are already under way, and widespread interest promises the largest gathering of Lutheran youth ever held in America.

APPRECIATION

The confidence expressed in the Luther League by leaders of the United Lutheran Church is a constant source of appreciation. The Luther League is an adopted child of the United Lutheran Church. It played an important part in preparing the church for the merger of 1918. It was most natural that it should become the official young people's organization of the church it had helped to found. The Luther League belongs to the United Lutheran Church. Its place in the church family is accepted, and Luther League workers everywhere are received with consideration. The Luther League is correspondingly grateful and pledges itself in the words of its historic motto to be "Of the Church, By the Church, and For the Church."

Respectfully submitted,
AMOS JOHN TRAVER.

The recommendation concerning missionary objectives was adopted.

The recommendation concerning annual appropriation was referred to the Finance Committee of the Executive Board.

Mr. Wm. H. Stackel presented the report of the Committee on Investment of Endowments and moved the adoption of the recommendations.

REPORT OF COMMISSION ON METHOD OF INVESTING ENDOWMENT FUNDS

1. The following resolution adopted at the last biennial convention (see minutes, page 332) outlines the specific task of your Comission:

"RESOLVED, That a special Commission of seven men be appointed by the Executive Board to consider the advisability and method of having all trust and endowment funds belonging to the Church and its various Boards managed and invested by a common agency of the Church, report of said commission to be made at the next Convention."

2. The following persons were appointed by the Executive Board in conformity with the foregoing resolution:

G. A. Achenbach, Carl M. Distler, Peter P. Hagan, E. Clarence Miller, P. A. Myers, William H. Stackel and Robbin B. Wolf.

At the first meeting of the Commission the following officers were elected:

Chairman, William H. Stackel; secretary, Carl M. Distler.

3. We have made an intensive study of all phases of this question, have held two meetings and through extended correspondence and personal interviews have reached a unanimous judgment on the report and recommendations herewith presented.

4. We commend in the highest terms the conscientious control which the several endowed agencies of the Church have exercised over their respective endowments but we believe that the ever-increasing funds entrusted to them suggest the advisability of adopting without delay a new method surrounded by all possible safeguards for the control and supervision of all trust and endowment funds. A new stimulus in the accumulation of such funds should result from the inauguration of such a policy.

5. We believe a standing Investment Commission with full authority to deal with all investment problems is essential to any improved plan and in favor thereof we cite the following points:

(a) Men especially qualified by training and experience may then be selected for this specific responsibility.

(b) Uniformity in the handling of investment problems for all endowed agencies would be assured.

(c) Meetings of an Investment Commission would be given wholly to financial and investment problems thus assuring even greater care and consideration of such matters than is possible under present plans.

(d) Collective judgment on each investment problem would be assured.

(e) Income from endowments would be available to each endowed agency as soon as received thus involving no delay or inconvenience.

6. We furthermore believe that best results would be achieved if all trust and endowment funds, unrestricted as to investment, were merged into one common fund. Under this plan each endowed agency would have an undivided interest in each investment corresponding to its proportionate interest in the whole fund and the common income would be divided among

the several endowed agencies in the same proportion.

The advantages of a common fund may be summarized as follows.

(a) Each agency's unrestricted investment would represent the same type and quality of security and yield the same rate of income.

(b) In case of loss on any investment, the loss would be charged against income and the capital of all endowments would be kept unimpaired.

(c) Each agency would share proportionately in gains and appreciation of investments.

(d) Closer investment of funds would be rendered possible by pooling all uninvested cash.

(e) Bookkeeping would be simplified and expense reduced.

(f) Periodic certification to the several agencies of their unrestricted investment accounts would be simplified because each would be furnished the same statement. This would take the form of a list of investments held, on one side of the balance sheet, and amounts credited to the several endowed agencies on the other side. The two sides would balance and the share of each participating agency could be readily established.

7. Committing of all endowment and trust funds into the safekeeping of responsible banks or trust companies is an essential part of our recommendation as we believe such funds should be safeguarded to the fullest possible extent.

8. It should be carefully noted that our recommendations involve the working out of all details with each endowed agency or with its duly authorized Committee in order that due attention may be given to special situations and maximum benefits to all be assured. The plan also provides for competent legal counsel on each step proposed so as to avoid any legal complications.

9. It is not proposed to interfere in any manner with the gathering ot endowments or with the disposition of its separate income by each of the several agencies as heretofore.

10. It is not proposed that the Investment Commission be incorporated or that it actually handle or take custody of funds.

RECOMMENDATIONS

We recommend that in order to effect the foregoing purposes the Church adopt the following resolutions:

1. *Name.* That a standing commission to be known as the Investment Commission of the United Lutheran Church in America be formed.

2. *Members.* That such Commission be composed of the following:

(a) Five men possessing the necessary qualifications elected by the Executive Board of the Church.

(b) The President and Treasurer of the Church as ex-officio members.

(c) A fully authorized and empowered representative of each Board or Agency of the United Lutheran Church in America holding endowment and/or trust funds in excess of $25,000.00 and electing such representative from its own membership.

(d) A fully authorized and empowered representative of the governing board of each endowed Lutheran institution to which the Commission may at any time grant the privilege of representation, elected from its own membership.

3. *Terms of Members.* That the members elected by the Executive Board shall hold office for five years or until their successors are chosen, provided that the terms of those first elected shall be so arranged that the term of one member of this class shall expire annually. That the terms of all other elected members shall be fixed by the electing Board or Agency but shall not exceed the term of five years.

4. *Organization.* That as soon as the President of the Church deems practicable, he shall convene the Commission which shall then proceed to organize (a) by the adoption of Rules and Regulations to be submitted to the Executive Board for its approval and (b) by the election and/or appointment of such officers and committees as shall be provided in such approved Rules and Regulations. Changes in the Rules and Regulations shall be effective only when approved by the Church or, ad interim, by the Executive Board. Included in the Rules of the Commission shall be a provision that no investment or re-investment shall be made except upon the approval of at least three members.

5. That the Investment Commission, in co-operation with all Agencies of the Church holding endowment and/or trust funds is hereby instructed as soon as practicable to perfect and put into operation a plan for bringing under its supervision all endowment and trust funds of such Boards and Agencies and any other funds that they may have for investment, and to that end is hereby given all necessary authority upon its organization to direct the investment and re-investment of such funds and to transact all business necessary and incident thereto.

6. That such plan for the control and supervision of investments shall include provision for committing endowment and trust funds for safekeeping with banks and/or trust companies under arrangements that will furnish the largest possible protection to such funds.

7. That such plan shall include provision approved by competent counsel for merging all endowment and trust funds into one common fund in which each endowment and trust shall have a proportionate interest.

8. That the income from endowment and trust funds shall be made available to the Boards and Agencies as received.

9. That the commission shall make full report to each endowed Board and Agency at least semi-annually and comprehensive report of its proceedings at each biennial convention of the Church.

10. That the books and records of the Commission shall be open for exam-

ination at all reasonable times by duly authorized representatives of the several Boards and Agencies whose funds are invested under the direction of the said Commission.

11. That the books and accounts of the Commission and of all endowments held by custodian banks and trust companies shall be audited annually.

12. That all Boards and Agencies are hereby instructed under proper legal advice to co-operate with the Commission in perfecting these plans and putting them into operation as soon as practicable and to conform their by-laws to the procedure herein outlined.

Respectfully submitted,

WILLIAM H. STACKEL, *Chairman*
CARL M. DISTLER, *Secretary*.

Treasurer E. Clarence Miller and Mr. Peter Hagan addressed the Convention.

Pending further consideration of the report of the Committee on Investment of Endowments, the Convention adjourned at 11:45 o'clock with prayer by the Rev. George N. Lauffer.

————————◆————————

Afternoon Session

Saturday, October 11, 1930, 2.00 o'clock.

Devotions were conducted by the Rev. C. F. Stickles.

The President called the Convention to order.

The Rev. J. A. Leas presented the recommendations of the Committee of Reference and Counsel as follows:

1. Your committee would recommend the adoption of the following resolution:

Resolved, That this convention gratefully acknowledges with sincere and hearty appreciation, the gracious hospitality of the city of Milwaukee. and of the Lutheran Churches of the city; the generous co-operation of the press in the publication of the proceedings of the convention; the pastors and congregations who have extended courteous and unsparing effort in our service; the choirs of local churches which have assisted so acceptably in the public meetings and services; and lastly, but most particularly, the unstinted, untiring labors of the Milwaukee Committee for this Seventh Biennial Convention of The United Lutheran Church in America, the gracious ladies, the General Chairman of that Committee, and the chairmen and members of its various divisions, to whom the convention is so greatly indebted.

2. The congregation of the First Lutheran Church at Findlay, Ohio. sends greetings to The United Lutheran Church in America in convention assembled. We recommend that the greetings be received with thanks and suitably acknowledged.

3. In the issue of the *American Lutheran* of September 10th, there appears an appreciation from His Excellency, President Herbert C. Hoover, of the history and influence of the Lutheran Church of this country. Believing that this appreciation is intended for the entire Lutheran Church of America, we recommend that it be read and that suitable recognition be given by the President and Secretary of the Convention.

4. The following communication has come to your committee:

"In the interest of further effectiveness in the administration of the work of Inner Mission in the United Lutheran Church, we recommend that the convention requests the Executive Board to consider the advisability of merging the Inner Mission Board, the Board of Deaconess Work, the Committee on Evangelism and the Committee on Moral and Social Welfare."

"Signed:

CLARENCE E. KRUMBHOLZ
JAMES OOSTERLING
G. W. BECHTOLD."

We recommend that it be referred to the Executive Board for consideration.

5. We recommend that the Rev. J. C. Kunzmann be given five minutes in connection with the report of the Board of Education to present the cause of the Pacific Seminary.

6. We recommend that Mr. E. Clarence Miller be given an opportunity at this time to present, and we recommend for adoption, a certain resolution bearing upon the work of congregational treasurers.

7. The Rev. K. K. Olafson, of Seattle, Wash., President of the Icelandic Synod, is present as fraternal delegate from that body. Your committee recommends that he be heard at this time.

Recommendation 1 was adopted.

Recommendation 2 was adopted.

Recommendation 3 was adopted by a rising vote.

Recommendation 4 was adopted.

Recommendation 5 was adopted.

Recommendation 6 was adopted.

Treasurer Miller submitted the following resolution which was adopted:

Resolved, That the constituent synods of this body be requested to advise each of their congregations to require its treasurers to bank all church funds in the corporate name of the church, to keep the offerings of the church for current expenses and for benevolence in separate bank accounts and under no circumstances to draw on the benevolence account for current expenses, and to remit all receipts for benevolence monthly to the synodical treasurer.

Recommendation 7 was adopted and the Rev. K. K. Olafson, President of the Icelandic Synod, was introduced and addressed the Convention, bringing greetings from his synod and expressing the hope that some day the Icelandic Synod may become officially a member of The United Lutheran Church in America.

By request of the President, the Rev. Samuel G. Trexler, President of the United Synod of New York, responded to President Olafson.

The President read the following cablegram from the Evangelical Lutheran Church in the Andhra Country, India:

"President Knubel,
United Lutheran Church Convention,
Milwaukee, Wisconsin.

"Andhra Lutheran Church Convention sends grateful thanks to Mother Church. Praying for Divine guidance in furthering advances in Master's Kingdom." "Dunkelberger."

The Convention requested the President to respond to the cablegram.

Moved and carried, That the Convention hold a session at eight o'clock this evening.

The Rev. A. Steimle presented the report of the Board of Education.

REPORT OF THE BOARD OF EDUCATION

The Board of Education of the United Lutheran Church in America submits its Seventh Biennial Report herewith.

This report is a record of the stewardship which we have accepted and prayerfully undertaken. It is an exhibit of the efforts of the Church to leaven higher education with the spirit of Christ. It is a statement of reasoned convictions and measured judgments with respect to the future development of the Church's work in the field of higher education along positive and constructive lines. It is the expression of a prayer that the Church will be conscious, always, of the vital part which the schools play in the welfare and progress of Church and State.

I. MATTERS OF ADMINISTRATION

1. Board Personnel

The following constituted the officers and membership of the Board for the biennium:

> President, The Rev. Augustus Steimle, D.D.
> Vice-President, Prof. Hugo C. M. Wendel, Ph.D.
> Secretary, The Rev. William M. Horn, D.D.
> Treasurer, Prof. Ralph D. Owen, Ph.D.

The Executive Committee is constituted of the officers and of the following members:

> The Rev. Robert D. Clare, D.D.
> The Rev. E. P. Pfatteicher, Ph.D., D.D.
> Mr. W. J. Showalter, Sc.D., LL.D.

Besides the above, the following constituted the membership:

> Mr. J. L. Clark
> Glenn M. Cummings, Esq.
> Prof. R. S. Saby, Ph.D.
> The Rev. C. F. Hoppe, D.D.
> The Rev. C. R. Bowers, D.D.
> Dean Adelaide Burge
> The Rev. A. J. Holl, D.D.
> Mr. C. J. Driever
> Mr. J. H. Dingle
> The Rev. Paul Krauss
> The Rev. G. M. Diffenderfer, D.D.
> Hon. Charles Steele
> The Rev. A. A. Zinck, D.D., S.T.D.
> The Rev. E. C. Herman, D.D.

The Advisory Members are:

> From the Women's Missionary Society:
> Mrs. A. V. Pohlman
> Prof. Dorothea C. Hess, M.A.

From the Evangelical Lutheran Augustana Synod of North America:

> President, G. A. Brandelle, D.D., LL.D.

2. An Appreciation

The membership of this Board, which continues over into the next biennium, wishes to record its appreciation of the fellowship, cooperation, and untiring service given by the following retiring members of the Board, who have been with the Board for twelve years and therefore cannot be re-nominated:

> The Rev. A. Steimle, D.D.
> The Rev. R. D. Clare, D.D.
> The Rev. E. P. Pfatteicher, Ph.D., D.D.
> The Rev. C. F. Hoppe, D.D

We also include

> Mr. Glenn M. Cummings, Esq.,

who was first elected to fill an unexpired term and now completes his second term of service.

In addition to these, the terms of Prof. R. S. Saby, Ph.D., and Mr. J. L. Clark, expire. The resignation of the latter was received some time ago and was not filled in order that the one replacing him could serve the whole term by election of this convention.

3. Nominations

The nominations of the Board for the terms which expire at this Convention are the following:

Clergy	Synod
The Rev. Franklin Fretz, Ph.D., Easton, Pa..	Ministerium of Pennsylvania
The Rev. H. J. Black, D.D., Savannah, Ga.	Georgia
The Rev. C. H. Stein, D.D., Lock Haven, Pa.	Susquehanna
The Rev. H. R. Gold, New Rochelle, N. Y.	New York

Lay

*Prof. R. S. Saby, Ph.D., Gettysburg, Pa.	West Pennsylvania
Mr. Frederick Henrich, Buffalo, N. Y.	New York
Henry Wolf Bikle, Esq., Philadelphia, Pa.	East Pennsylvania

* Nominated to succeed himself.

The nominations of the Board for the unexpired terms, to be approved by the Executive Board, are the following:

The Rev. H. H. Bagger, Butler, Pa., to fill the unexpired term of the Rev. A. J. Holl, D.D., resigned.

The Rev. M. L. Stirewalt, D.D., Salisbury, N. C., to fill the unexpired term of the Rev. W. M. Horn, D.D., resigned.

4. The Secretarial Staff

The following were the secretarial staff for the biennium:

> The Rev. C. S. Bauslin, D.D.
> Miss Mary E. Markley, Litt.D.
> The Rev. C. P. Harry, D.D.
> Miss Mildred E. Winston, A.M.

Miss Markley was on leave of absence from July, 1929, to March, 1930. During that time she visited the missions of the United Lutheran Church in Japan, China, India.

The Board filled the position of Executive Secretary, vacant since the death of the Rev. Frederick G. Gotwald, D.D., in February, 1926. They elected the Rev. N. J. Gould Wickey, Ph.D., D.D., president of Carthage College, Carthage, Ill., Dr. Wickey took charge of the work July 1, 1929.

5. The Resignation of Dr. C. S. Bauslin

After serving the Church for sixteen years in the educational field, Dr. Charles S. Bauslin has resigned as College Secretary of our Board in order to accept a call to the St. Mark's Parish, St. Louis, Missouri. Dr. Bauslin was especially interested in stimulating the thought and conviction of the Church with respect to the Gospel Ministry, serving first as the Secretary of the General Synod's Committee on Ministerial Education, then as the General Secretary of the Board of Education of the same body, and finally as College Secretary of the Board of Education of the United Lutheran Church in America.

As an evidence of appreciation of the services rendered, the Board adopted the following:

The Board of Education has received with regret the resignation of the Rev. Charles S. Bauslin, D.D., as a Departmental Secretary of the Board. It accepts it with profound appreciation of the splendid service he has rendered in the long years of his work, and with deep regret that the ties which the years have made are to be severed.

He has given the best years of his life to the cause of religious education. Even before the organization of the United Lutheran Church, in America, he was laboring in the same field on behalf of the General Synod.

His travels have brought him into contact with the membership of the United Lutheran Church in nearly every state in the union. He has left an impress upon the cause of Christian Education and upon the ministry. The honored name he bears is a household word throughout the Church.

As he goes forth into his new duties in an active pastorate, he carries with him the love and affection of every member of the Board and of every member of the Secretariat.

The Board directs that an engrossed copy of this resolution, with the signature of the President and Secretary, be prepared and presented to Dr. Bauslin as a testimonial of its appreciation and esteem.

6. The Re-organization of the Work

In accordance with the recommendation of the Survey Commission for the concentration of the secretarial staff at a central headquarters, and in harmony with the action of the Church for the distribution of Boards, all offices have been centralized at 1415 K Street, N. W., Washington, D. C.

Following suggestions of the Survey Commission, the work of the Board has been re-organized in order that the whole program of the Church in the realm of higher education may be advanced. The work of the Board is now divided according to the functions of Public Relations, Research, Student Work, and Institutional Service. Committees corresponding to these functions constitute the main standing committees of the Board. By Public Relations is meant the developing of interest in the work of the Board through information to the public in general, which may be called publicity; through information to the Church in general and the individual Church in particular, which may be called promotion; and through assisting institutions and student centers in their financial campaigns and also through interesting individuals to contribute to the funds of the Board both indirectly in the benevolent offerings of the Church and directly in the form of loan funds, scholarships, and endowment fund, which may be called finance. Thus, the aim of this division of work is the arousing of interest in higher Christian Education, the spreading of information about our institutions, and the developing of a sense of responsibility for and a willingness to contribute to such work. This work shall be carried on through addresses, news items, literature, exhibits and numerous conferences.

The function of Research has to do with the carrying out of projects authorized by the Board, such as surveying institutions, studying the possibilities of expansion in any given area, gathering and systematizing data from records and reports.

The Student Work deals primarily with the Lutheran students at both Lutheran and non-Lutheran institutions. All the work formerly conducted by the departments of university work, women students and recruiting is included in this division, and none of it shall be neglected. In fact, it is believed that this plan will effect a more efficient and economical system of work. Here we shall endeavor to direct the spiritual growth of students, develop their Lutheran loyalty and give vocational guidance with special reference to service to the Church either clerical or lay. Such work will be accomplished by appointing and directing student pastors and workers, individual and group conferences, loans and scholarships, addresses and literature.

The function of Institutional Service aims to render assistance to our educational institutions in the various aspects of educational administration. The problems of location and expansion, instruction, business management, grounds and buildings, registration records, publicity, etc., are to be studied and service rendered where desired and possible. This work will be carried out through personal visits and conferences, research and surveys, regular and special grants.

It is our conviction that the most important service which we may render our colleges and seminaries is through advice and counsel regarding their educational problems. Too much stress has been placed upon the financial grant which has been given in the past but which after all is a temporary aid. We want to render a service which will have permanent value. This we are prepared to do.

7. Our Budget

Our Budget is woefully small considering the tremendous importance of the work which is attempted. We have operated on an annual budget of less than $135,000 for the biennium. Our administrative expense is less than eight per cent, which is remarkably low considering the small sum of money handled. A study of the Board of Education of another denomination which handles more than a million dollars annually reveals that their administrative expense per cent is higher than ours. Our Student Work is wholly inadequately supported in many places. Properly equipped buildings functioning as Lutheran Student Centers should be obtained. Our Institutions are crying out for more financial assistance, whereby they may render that service for which they were founded and may meet the necessary standards for efficiency.

Even if the apportionment were paid a hundred per cent, we should not be able to carry on a constructive program in a manner befitting the significance of the work and the prestige of the Church. Lacking the income from apportionment, our only hope is that friends who see that the character of the schools determine the character of the Church and who have been blessed materially will make contributions to the Scholarship and Loan Fund, the Ministerial Education Fund, and the Endowment Fund. **(See Recommendation 2.)**

II. MATTERS OF PUBLIC RELATIONS
1. *Cooperation*

The cooperative efforts of our Board are significant. No Church liveth unto itself, and no board of any Church can succeed by attempting to live unto itself.

We report the most cordial and valuable cooperation with the *Luther League,* the *Women's Missionary Society,* the *Board of Foreign Missions,* the *Board* of *American Missions,* and the *Parish and Church School Board.* (For special reference to these, see IV. Matters of Student Work, sections 2, 3, 4.)

Besides these cooperative efforts within our Church, we record our relations with other Lutheran bodies.

Cooperation with the Lutheran Augustana Synod of North America.

Dr. Brandelle, the President of the Augustana Synod, is a valued advisory member of our Board. He has been faithful in attendance and frank in his advice and counsel. This Synod gives us $2,700.00 annually towards work with Lutheran students on non-Lutheran campuses. This division of our work has been in touch with Augustana students in all parts of the country.

The Executive Secretary accepted the invitation from the Board of Education of Augustana Synod to conduct a round table conference on the Lutheran College. The presidents and representatives of the faculties of their colleges were present besides members of the Board. This was the first time that such a conference had been held in the Augustana Synod.

We record our appreciation for this privilege of service and the courtesies extended to our Secretary.

Cooperation with the Icelandic Lutheran Church in North America.

The cooperation with the Icelandic Synod as it affects the support of the Jon Bjarnason Academy and Junior College in Winnipeg, Manitoba, Canada, has continued during the biennium. We have contributed $2,000 annually.

Upon invitation of the President of the Synod, the Rev. K. K. Olafson, our Executive Secretary, visited the institution for the purpose of studying its place in the educational program of that Synod. This was done and a report was made to the meeting of the Icelandic Synod.

While visiting in Winnipeg, Dr. Wickey was privileged to preach in the beautiful church of the Icelandic Synod, now under the successful guidance of the Rev. B. B. Jonnson, D.D.

This Synod is in greatest sympathy with the ideals of the United Lutheran Church. Most of its pastors have been trained at our own Chicago Lutheran Seminary. In every way these friends exhibited their appreciation for the service which the Secretary rendered and the interest which our Board has manifested.

Cooperation with the Joint Synod of Ohio.

The secretaries for Student Work report that definite approaches have been made to us through the Commission on Student Work of this Synod, and that there is an undersanding between this Commission and our Board to the effect "that where work has already been established, each will respect the other's precedence, and that at any new points where work is to be started, consultation shall be had so that it may be effected to the best advantage of the students whether under the direction of our Board or of the Commission. We have further agreed to publish jointly two series of outlines for students' discussion groups." (See, IV. Matters of Student Work, Sec. 2.)

Cooperation with other Lutheran bodies.

Mention is made also of the confidence and cooperation we have enjoyed with pastors of the *Norwegian Lutheran Church in America*, of the *Iowa Synod*, of the *Missouri Synod*, and of the *Wisconsin Synod* at student centers. We hope that this cooperation may become more extensive so that the welfare of our Lutheran students at non-Lutheran campuses may be enhanced.

Cooperation with the Lutheran Student Association of America.

This Association is not connected with any one synod, but is a tremendous power in the lives of Lutheran youth. Our secretaries are endeavoring to increase the service which they render to this forward looking association of Lutheran young men and women. (See also IV. Matters of Student Work, section 2.)

2. Contacts

Our Secretaries are able to maintain many contacts which have much significance for our own work and for our influence upon the work with students in other bodies. We have been honored by the election of Dr. Mary E. Markley as Vice-President of the Council of Church Boards of Education. Our secretaries are members of the University Committee, and the College Committee of this Council, the Federated Student Committee, the Student Committee of the Council of Women for Home Missions, the Student Committee of the Federation of Women's Boards of Foreign Missions, Student Work Committee of the American Federation of Lutheran Brotherhoods. They cooperate also with the Student Volunteer Movement.

Special mention should be made of Dr. Markley's membership in the American Section of the Board of Governors of the Madras Christian College for Women, India; St. Christopher's College, Madras, India, and the Women's Christian Medical College, Vellore, India.

3. Promotional Efforts

We believe one of the great needs in our Church is to develop an educational consciousness. Our Church has it as far as the confirmation age, but then somehow it ceases. We need to awaken and develop that consciousness so far as it concerns the whole individual throughout his entire life. Only thus will our people understand that the work of the Board of Education for our Lutheran students and institutions is fundamental and vital to all other work of the Church.

Accordingly, definite efforts are being put forth by the secretarial staff to develop such a consciousness. Communications were addressed to all synodical presidents, to presidents of Synodical Brotherhoods, and to presidents of Synodical Women's Missionary Societies, to the effect that some time be given to the consideration of the general problem of Christian Education with any specal reference to local institutions which may be deemed advisable. Through these efforts we hope to reach within a three-year-period every synod with a definite message of Christian Education.

Another form of promotion is the writings of the secretarial staff. During one year of the biennium, the staff prepared articles and pamphlets amounting to more than 100,000 words. The staff has also prepared a set of posters which may be shown at meetings of conferences and synods. These posters show the organization of the Board, the aims of the Board's work, some of the distinctive buildings of our institutions, an exhibit of student work at non-Lutheran centers, and the world-wide influence of our colleges and seminaries. *The Lutheran* has been a very valuable avenue for disseminating promotional information, and has been most receptive to all material sent. We record our appreciation for the cooperation of *The Lutheran* in this regard.

The Reformation Season.

This is another way in which we can promote our educational work. We regret to record a disappointing return on the part of the Church to the appeal of last October. The Board by action decided to make Waterloo College and Seminary the objective of the special financial offering to be solicited from the Sunday Schools of the United Lutheran Church in America. Special literature for the occasion, as customary, was prepared, including a four-page Reformation Day Service, two-color poster for display purposes, a special offering envelope, and an announcement for pastors. The pastors were informed of the Board's plans for the observance of this season and the announcement thereof was made six weeks in advance of the day. The financial returns for last October were only $278, as compared with $350 and $420 the two previous years.

It is evident that the financial appeal is less popular and the vocational feature is increasingly popular with the Church. In the light of this evidence, the Board has decided to make no special financial appeal for any particular institution. It is not the chief purpose of the Board to raise money at that season; but it is our hope that the Church will use that season for bringing emphatically to the attention of its membership the importance of higher Christian education for both the Church and the State.

Literature will be sent out as requested. Offerings will be gladly accepted and will be allotted to the various permanent funds which the Board is developing.

We call earnestly upon the Church to set aside the Reformation Season in the interests of the cause of Christian Education. We do not wish any pastor to set aside any reference to the historical and doctrinal significance of the season. We dare not neglect calling attention to the fundamental principles of the Reformation. The freedom and the privileges of the Reformation were purchased at too great a cost to be neglected or even slighted. Our people need to be reminded constantly of the contribution which the Reformation has made to modern civilization and culture. But we believe that the Reformation emphasis will be incomplete without noting, especially and in much detail, the place of Christian Education in the work of the Church. Let the Church pray that our schools may be loyal to the fundamental truths of the Reformation, that our youth may be inspired thereby to constructive efforts in behalf of mankind, and that the Church of today may be passed on to the generation of the future strong in the faith and freed from anything which tends to weaken, to stultify and to kill. **(See Recommendation 1.)**

4. *Friends and Funds*

During the biennium a prominent Lutheran woman gave the Board $1,000.00 for its Scholarship and Loan Fund for Women. A few other gifts have been received.

While it is the business of this Board to assist our student centers and institutions to gather funds for their work, yet it is becoming increasingly clear that our Board must develop funds for special types and pieces of work for which no other agency is prepared to help. The financial reports of the Boards of Education of other denominations have been examined. One of them has a permanent general fund of more than two million dollars. It has about a million dollars in "designated trust funds," not to mention several hundred thousand dollars in miscellaneous funds for specific objects.

We should have an "Endowment Fund," the income of which could be used wherever it is deemed wise, whether it be in promotional efforts, in research, in student work, or in our colleges and seminaries. Then, too, our Scholarship and Loan Funds and the Ministerial Education Fund should be developed. Our Board ought to be in position to help not only prospective ministers and missionaries but also the large number of worthy and needy students, who will be leaders in the Church. Because there is no agency paying any attention to this group, our Church is losing hundreds of outstanding men and women.

The Board of Education does not covet a financial campaign, but we are anxious to render the service which will result in a stronger and better church. The president of a certain church body has secured in a period of six years more than five million dollars for the educational and missionary activity of his church. It is true most of this is in wills, but it shows what can be done. We pray that the Church will see more clearly the work of our Board in its true perspective. **(See Recommendation 2.)**

5. *Christian Education Year*

The Erie Convention of the United Lutheran Church voted "That the Board of Education give all possible aid in making Educational Year a complete success." Pursuant to this action, our Board called together the presidents of our colleges and seminaries at the December meeting of both 1928 and 1929. The 1928 meeting authorized the appointment of an *Advisory Campaign Committee*, which was constituted as follows:

> The Rev. A. Steimle, D.D.
> The Rev. R. D. Clare, D.D.
> Glenn M. Cummings, Esq.
> President R. E. Tulloss, Ph.D.
> President H. F. Martin, D.D.
> President C. J. Smith, D.D.
> President C. M. Jacobs. D.D.

President Tulloss was selected as chairman of the Committee. The Board agreed to provide for the expenses incidental to the work of the committee a sum of $2,000.00.

The 1929 meeting was conducted in the form of a Round Table, discussing three subjects: The campaign situation in the various territories, the real need of the campaigns, and the ultimate grounds for the justification of the existence of the Church College.

At the request of the Advisory Campaign Committee, our Board agreed to allow the Executive Secretary to supervise the preparation of a campaign booklet and a poster.

At the request of the joint conference of the institutional presidents and the Board of Education, President Knubel very kindly allowed the whole matter of the campaigns to be presented to the meeting of the Synodical Presidents, held at Harrisburg, January 8, 1930. The followng resolutions were unanimously adopted, by a rising vote, by the Synodical Presidents:

Whereas, from the beginnings of the Protestant Church in America, it has been clearly recognized that the churches are dependent for pastoral and lay leadership upon the Christian colleges conducted under their auspices, and

Whereas, at this time, in view of new and perplexing problems the need for these institutions is more urgent than ever before, and

Whereas, in the years to come the strength of the United Lutheran Church in America will inevitably depend upon the manner in which its colleges and seminaries render their basic service, and

Whereas, the revelations of the survey report make it clear that unless the resources of our educational institutions are largely increased, they cannot continue to meet the demands of the day and render their vitally needed service to the church, and

Whereas, the United Lutheran Church in America in its conventions at Richmond and Erie has recognized this situation and has set aside a period for emphasis of our educational needs and for campaigns on behalf of our educational institutions, both colleges and seminaries,

Therefore, Be It Resolved—

1. That we, the presidents of the Synods of the United Lutheran Church in America, assembled in conference in Harrisburg, Pa., on January 8th, 1930, hereby record our deeply felt realization of the urgency of the situation, and hereby express our approval of the plans looking toward campaigns throughout the whole church on behalf of our educational institutions.

2. In the belief that the enlarging usefulness of our church and its continuing testimony to the beliefs which it holds are dependent in large measure on the success of these important projects, we call upon our pastors and people, by wholehearted, loyal and generous cooperation, through prayer and personal effort, to do all in their power to bring these campaigns to a successful culmination.

Due to a series of events over which our institutions had no control it was not possible to have all campaigns conducted during 1930, as had been planned originally. They will be spread from the spring of 1930 to the fall of 1931. The total sum sought in the campaigns will be more than $7,000,000. We are glad to report that Newberry College went over the top in the first campaign for $500,000. Other campaigns are now in process.

The serious attention of the Church is called to the financial needs of our colleges and seminaries. We must not estimate the needs of today in terms of standards of yesterday. Every institution which would serve efficiently and effectively must be increasingly supported by the Church. Within the biennium more than twenty-five American colleges have been closed or combined on account of financial difficulties. Many institutions are today hanging in the financial balance. The financial status of our colleges and seminaries needs the prayerful consideration of the whole Church. **(See Recommendation 3.)**

III. MATTERS OF RESEARCH
1. *Church Scholarships for Students*
One of the problems to which this division directed its attention and study was that of synodical aid to students who are planning to give their lives in service to the Church. Various circumstances revealed the need of such a study. For example, sometimes students rejected by one synod would be accepted by another synod. Some synods had no definite plan and were asking for one. It was deemed wise to undertake a study of all plans now functioning in our synods and to attempt a uniform plan, the fundamental principles of which might be accepted by all synods.

Accordingly, the following questionnaire was sent to all synods:

MINISTERIAL BENEFICIARY EDUCATION
Policies and Practices
of .... Synod or Ministerium.
1. *Eligibility*
    Rules for
    a. Endorsements by pastors, congregations, etc.
    b. Physical, mental and spiritual requirements.
    c. Age restrictions.
    d. Marriage restrictions.

2. *Appropriations*
    a. Loans.
    b. Scholarships.
    c. Outright gifts.
    d. Maximum amount.
    e. Minimum amount.
    f. Total amount annually available.
    g. Average number of appropriations per year.
    h. Total amount annually appropriated.

3. *Administration*
    a. Term of service required in ministry or missionary calling.

    b. Spiritual standards.
    c. Moral standards.
    d. Religious activities.

4. *Terms of Repayment*
    a. Notes.
    b. Term.
    c. Interest rates.
    d. Promissory agreements.
    e. Follow-up system.
    f. Losses on repayment.

5. *Supervision of Beneficiaries*
    a. Meetings of Synodical representatives with beneficiaries.
    b. Other meetings of Synodical representatives with beneficiary.
    c. Reports from pastors.
    d. Reports from College Administration.
    e. Reports from beneficiaries.

6. *Helpful Suggestions*
    ....
    ....
    ....
    ....

On the basis of the data gathered and of experience, the following plan is submitted for the general approval of the United Lutheran Church in America and for adoption by the constituent synods. Perfection is not claimed, but it is believed that the adoption of such a well articulated plan will bring a highly desirable degree of uniformity and efficiency in this important work of the Church. **(See Recommendation 4.)**

THE COMMITTEE ON CHURCH SCHOLARSHIPS
of the ....Synod
of the United Lutheran Church in America.

I. ORGANIZATION

Name.—This Committee established by the   Synod of the United Lutheran Church in America shall be known as the Committee on Church Scholarships.

Object.—This Committee shall assist in the education and preparation of properly qualified young men and women for the ministry and the mission work of the United Lutheran Church by granting scholarships, under specified conditions, to those who need financial assistance.

Membership.—The Committee shall be composed of the President of the Synod, three (3) other clergymen, and three (3) laymen to be elected (appointed) by the Synod (President of the Synod). One clergyman and one layman to be elected (appointed) annually each to serve a term of three years.

Officers.—The Committee shall elect a president, vice-president, and a secretary annually. The treasurer of Synod shall act as the treasurer of the Committee.

Meetings.—The Committee shall meet annually in May and at such other times as may be necessary. The exact dates and places for all meetings are to be decided by the Committee.

Quorum.—Five members shall constitute a quorum.

Vacancies.—All vacancies on the Committee shall be filled by appointment of President of Synod to serve until the next annual meeting of Synod.

II. FUNCTIONS

The Functions of the Committee shall be:

1. To receive and administer Funds for Scholarships.
2. To grant Scholarships to young men and women applying for them, according to the rules adopted by the Synod.
3. To have supervision over a student holding a Scholarship as follows:
   (a) Through a written report twice a year from the proper administrative officer of the institution attended by the student.
   (b) Through written reports at least twice during the college year from the student himself.
   (c) By personal visits of members of the Committee to the institutions attended by students holding Scholarships.
   (d) By advising with a student holding Scholarship concerning his (her) activities in the Christian organizations on the campus and in a local congregation.
   (e) By counselling with a student holding a Scholarship concerning the use of the summer vacation.
4. To make an annual report to Synod.

III. PROCEDURE

1. Rules regulating the granting of Scholarships and the guidance of students holding such scholarships shall be submitted by the Committee and changes in these rules may be submitted by the Committee and must be approved by the Synod.
2. These rules shall be printed and a copy given to the applicant for a Scholarship.
3. Every student receiving a scholarship shall pledge himself (or herself) over his (her) own signature, to submit to these rules. This pledge shall be kept in the permanent files of the Committee.

IV. FUNDS

1. The Committee shall receive and administer all funds granted by Synod or received from any other source designated for Scholarships.
2. The Committee shall receive from Synod annually a definite sum for Scholarships.
3. The Committee shall create and develop a Permanent Scholarship fund, the interest of which shall be used for Scholarships.

V. APPLICATION FOR SCHOLARSHIP

1. The application for a Scholarship must be made on blanks furnished by the Committee.

2. Every application must be accompanied by testimonial letters (on blanks supplied by the Committee) from

    (a) Pastor and Church Council;

    (b) President, Principal, or Registrar of College or School;

    (c) A person (not connected with the family or congregation of the applicant) who knows the financial condition of family of applicant;

and by a Report from a Physician.

3. The application for a Scholarship must be made on blanks furnished by the Committee at least ten (10) days before the annual meeting of the Committee.

4. The application for a Scholarship is for one year only. Application for a Scholarship may be renewed annually.

5. The application for a Scholarship shall be considered only when the student is prepared to enter the freshman or a higher class in college.

6. The application of a student who has not maintained standing in the upper third of his class shall not be considered.

7. The application shall receive preference for a student who

    (a) Stood highest in the personal interview with the Committee.

    (b) Is nearest to the completion of a course.

    (c) Is in greatest need of financial aid.

8. The application of a married person shall be considered only because of special circumstances.

VI. PERSONAL INTERVIEW

1. The Committee shall have a personal interview with every applicant for a Scholarship.

2. The Committee in this interview shall examine the applicant concerning

    (a) Personal and intellectual fitness.

    (b) Earning capacity and need for financial aid.

    (c) Motive for seeking to enter Christian work.

    (d) Personal spiritual life.

    (e) Understanding of and acceptance of the faith of the Evangelical Lutheran Church.

    (f) Willingness to observe the rules of the Committee.

3. The Committee shall interview every student applicant for a Scholarship every year even if, as an applicant for a Scholarship, he may have been interviewed a previous year.

4. The Committee may devise its own examination covering any of the above items subject to the approval of Synod.

VII. RULES FOR THE GUIDANCE OF A STUDENT HOLDING A CHURCH SCHOLARSHIP

1. A student shall study at such institutions and for such periods of time as the Committee shall determine.

2. A student may not relinquish studies or be absent from studies for an extended time without the consent of the Committee.

3. A student shall obey the rules and discipline of the institution in which he is enrolled.

4. A student shall take part in the organized Christian activities of the campus.

5. A student shall attend the services of a Lutheran congregation and as far as possible engage in the normal activities of the congregation.

6. A student while attending a Theological Seminary shall engage in such practical Christian work as the Committee may plan and require, as a condition under which the Scholarship is granted.

7. A student may lose his Scholarship at any time by vote of the Committee for the following causes:

(a) Dropping courses or absence from courses without consent of the Committee.
(b) Unsatisfactory grades in courses.
(c) Development of physical defects disqualifying for work in the ministry or in the Church.
(d) Serious defects in conduct, character, or faith.
(e) Disregard of special rulings of the Committee.
(f) Improved financial condition of student.

(The two rules following can be used by Committees on Church Scholarships which are not granted on a basis of services rendered under the direction of the Committee).

8. A student who has received a Scholarship pledges himself by a Promissory Note to repay to the Treasurer of the Synod the amount of the Scholarship (with interest).

(a) If he (she) does not finish the course of study.
(b) If he is not ordained.
(c) If he (she) does not enter the work of the Church.
(d) If he (she) does not complete five (5) years of service in the Church.

9. A student who has received a Scholarship shall have returned to him (her) cancelled Promissory Note (or notes) upon the completion of five (5) years of service in the Church.

VIII. NOTES

(The four rules following can be used by Committee on Church Scholarships which are not granted on a basis of services rendered under the direction of the Committee.)

1. The Treasurer of the Synod and of this Committee shall obtain a promissory note from every student receiving a Scholarship, covering the

full amount of such Scholarship, unless Scholarship has been granted for services rendered under the direction of the Committee.

2. This promissory note (or notes) shall be cancelled and returned to the maker when he (or she) shall have served in the work of the Church five (5) years.

3. This promissory note is obligatory and binding upon a student granted a Scholarship.

    (a) If he (she) does not finish the course of study.

    (b) If he is not ordained.

    (c) If he (she) does not enter the work of the Church.

    (d) If he (she) does not complete five (5) years of service in the Church.

4. The Committee shall receive all money repaid through Promissory Notes.

IX. FORMS

(The following forms are submitted. Some Synods may have forms which are satisfactory. The Board of Education will be pleased to cooperate with Synods in the preparation of forms to fit special conditions.)

Form 1.

APPLICATION BLANK FOR CHURCH SCHOLARSHIP

A. Please fill out this blank carefully and forward to the secretary of the Board or Committee not later than ....

With the application please include in your own handwriting

1. A brief sketch of your life.

2. A brief statement of your reason for seeking the office of the ministry, or some other full-time Christian service.

The application must be accompanied by

1. Letters of recommendation by

    (a) Your Pastor and Church Council;

    (b) President, Principal, or Registrar of your college or school;

    (c) A person not connected with your family or congregation who knows the financial condition of your family.

2. A report from your physician after he has given you a physical examination.

B. Please be prepared to appear for a personal interview with the Committee at a time and place which it will appoint.

Personal

Full name

Address (a) Home   (b) College

Date and place of birth

Baptized: When?   By whom?

Confirmed: When?   Where?
By whom?
Of which congregation are you at present a member?
Who is the pastor?
How frequently do you attend Church services   Where?
How frequently do you commune   Where?

Family
Full name of father   of mother
Residence of parents
Occupation of father   of mother if employed
What is the approximate yearly income of parents?
How many children of the family are dependent and supported by this
     income?
Are you married or engaged to be married?

Education
What elementary school, high school or preparatory school, and college,
     have you attended?   Give dates.
What institution and class do you expect to enter if you receive Scholar-
     ship?
Were you in the highest, the middle, or the lowest third of your gradua-
     tion class?
What offices did you hold in the student body, clubs, or societies?
What extra curricular activities did you take part in?
Are you a member of a fraternity or secret organization?

Financial
What are your estimated expenses for the coming year?
Tuition $ Board $ Room rent $ Clothes $
Church and Benevolences $
Contingent Fees $ Books $ Miscellaneous $ Total $
How do you expect to meet this amount?
How much do you expect to earn, and how?
How much will your parents give you?
How much will other members of your family give you?
Will you have other scholarship aids?   State the sources and the amounts
Total income from above $
Amount desired from the Committee $
Did you work during the summer?   At what?
How much did you earn?
Do you have a debt or debts?   Why was it incurred?
     Does it bear interest?
Give the name and address of a person who knows your family circum-
     stances.

Reasons for Entering the Ministry or Full Time Christian Service
When did you first think of becoming a minister?
  A missionary?
What led you to the thought?
What are your motives in preparing?
What have you done in Sunday School, Luther League, or other Church work?

General
Have you read the rules of the Committee?
Have you returned a copy over your own signature to the secretary of this Committee?
Do you have a copy for your own permanent files?
Will you, if granted a scholarship, put yourself under the direction of the Committee on Church Scholarships?
Date...................... ....
                                          Signature
Place ....

Form 2.
TESTIMONIAL FROM PASTOR AND CHURCH COUNCIL
For the information of the Committee on Church Scholarships of the Synod of ....
To be mailed to ....
       ....
Mr. (Miss) ....is an
  applicant for scholarship aid from the Church Scholarship Fund of the Synod of ....
Will you kindly give us the following information?
1. How long has the applicant been a member of your congregation?
2. What opportunities have you had to form an estimate of his (her) character?
3. What is his (her) general character and conduct?
4. What reputation does the applicant bear in the community?
5. What is the reputation of the applicant's family?
6. What is the applicant's need of financial assistance?
7. What part does the applicant take in the activities of your congregation?
8. What evidence has the applicant given of special fitness for full-time Christian service?

Date .... Signature ....
Place ....

Form 3.

TESTIMONIAL FROM SCHOOL OR COLLEGE LAST ATTENDED

For the information of the Committee on Church Scholarships of the
Synod of ....
To be mailed to ....
....
....

Mr. (Miss) ....is an applicant
for scholarship aid from the Church Scholarship Fund of the Synod
of ....
Will you kindly give us the following information:

1. During what period was the applicant under your instruction?
2. Was the applicant of the first, middle, or lowest third of his class?
3. Was the applicant an industrious and earnest student?
4. In what school or college activities did the applicant take part?
   Athletics   Debate   Dramatics
   Social Clubs   Religious Organizations
   School Publications
5. What was the applicant's general influence among his (her) fellow
   students?
6. Did the applicant show powers of leadership or initiative?
7. What evidence has applicant given of special fitness for full-time
   Christian service?

Please enclose a transcript of student's grades for the last year he (she)
was in your School (or College).
Date ....   Signature ....
Place...................

Form 4.

TESTIMONIAL OF STANDING

For the information of the Committee on Church Scholarships of the
Synod of ....
To be mailed to ....
....
....

Mr. (Miss) .... who is an applicant
for scholarship aid from the Church Scholarship Fund of the Synod
.... has referred us to you.

Will you kindly give us the following information:

1. How long you have known the applicant?
2. Are you related to him (her)?
3. Are you a member of the same church?

4. What opportunities have you had to form an estimate of the family circumstances?
5. What reputation does the family bear in the community?
6. How many dependents are there in the family?
7. Has the applicant earned money for himself (herself)?
8. Are the family circumstances sucl. that it would be impossible for the applicant to attend College (Theological Seminary) without assistance?

Date ....   Signature ....
Place......................

Form 5.

CHURCH SCHOLARSHIP

............Synod of the United Lutheran Church in America

APPLICANT'S HEALTH REPORT

I. General:

1. Name ....File No............
2. Address ....   3. Previous occupation............
4. Birth date ....   5. Birth place ....
6. Single or married ....7. If you have children give ages......
8. Height in stocking feet .... 9. Weight...........
10. Gain or loss past year ....
11. Was early life spent on farm, in small town, or in city?...........
12. Have you regular habits of exercise?...... 13. Kind and amount....
....
14. Describe any injuries you have suffered, giving dates ....
....
....
15. How many cups of tea and coffee daily? ....
16. Specify any deformities..
17. Any surgical operations? Describe giving dates ....
....
....
18. When was your last successful small-pox vaccination? ....
19. Typhoid inoculation ....
20. During past five years how much has your work been interrupted by ill health? Specify, giving dates ....
....
....
....

II. Heredity:

21. Among your immediate family, or grandparents, uncles or aunts, is there any history of (a) Cancer, (b) Tuberculosis, (c) Epilepsy, (d) Insanity, (e) Nervous breakdown, (f) Goitre, (g) Asthma, (h) Hay fever? Specify relative and his disease:

....
....
....
....

22. Give the following data about your immediate family:

	IF LIVING		IF NOT LIVING					
	Age if Living	Health (Good or Bad) If not good give details	Cause of death	How Long Sick	Year of Death	Age at Death	Details	Health Previous
Father								
Mother								
Sisters Brothers and No. 1								
No. 2								
No. 3								
No. 4								
No. 5 Indicate which B or S								
No. 6								
No. 7								
No. 8								

III. Nervous System:

23. Characterize your temperament—Nervous? Irritable? Impatient? Optimistic? Depressed? Phlegmatic? Timid? Aggressive? etc.....
....
....

24. Any lack of emotional control? Unusually sensitive?..............
....

25. Do you fatigue easily? ....
26. Is sustained mental concentration and application difficult?..........
....
....

27. Have you been, or are you now subject to faintness or dizziness? If so, describe ....
....

28. Have you had recurring headaches? If so describe.................
....

29. Have you ever had partial or complete nervous breakdown?........ If so, specify fully ....
....

30. Do you suffer from wakefulness?........Disturbed sleep?........ Difficulty in falling asleep? ....

IV. Organic Disturbances:

31. Have you ever had any trouble with your heart? If so, what and when? ....
32. Have you ever suffered from anemia?...........................
If so, give details ....
33. Have you had frequent protracted colds or coughs, or been suspected of having tuberculosis? If so, give details ....
....

34. Are you careless in diet as to: (a) Regularity........ (b) Hurried eating........ (c) Good quality........ (d) Sweets or unwholesome food..........
35. Are you troubled with constipation? ....
36. Have you ever suffered from dysentery or recurring diarrhoea?......
37. Have your eyes caused you any trouble? If so, describe..........
....

38. Is hearing sub-normal? ....
39. Any ear discharge past three years? ....
40. If you have had any of the following, give date and severity (severe, moderate, mild)
    (a) Measles .... (b) Mumps ....
    (c) Whooping cough........ (d) Scarlet fever ....
    (e) Diphtheria .... (f) Small pox ....

(g) Malaria ....   (h) Influenza ....
(i) Pneumonia ....   (j) Pleurisy ....
(k) Hemmorrhoids (piles)..   (l) Typhoid Fever ....
(m) Rheumatism ....   (n) Tonsilitis ....
(o) Goitre Trouble ....   (p) St. Vitus Dance ......

V. *Comments:*
Estimate in your own words the condition of your health.

PHYSICIAN'S REPORT

I. *General:*   Name of Examiner.......................................
  1. Weight.......... 2. Height........ 3. Temperature........

II. *Head and Neck:*
  4. (a) By Snellen test type report vision—Without Glasses............
                                     With Glasses ....
     (b) Any other eye abnormality ....
  5. Ears: (a) Hearing...... (b) Pain, discharge, etc.................
  6. Nose: (a) Obstructions .... (b) Other conditions.........
  7. Mouth: (a) Gums .... (b) Tongue ....
     (c) Teeth condition ....
     ....
     (d) Tonsils ....
  8. Lympathic glands ....
  9. Thyroid pathology ....

III. *Chest:*
  10. Deformities ....
  11. Measurement: Expanded .... Contracted ....
  12. Lung findings ....
     ....
  13. Cardio-vascular: (a) Heart: Record size, action under exercise
      test* murmurs, compensation, etc ....
     ....
     ....
     (b) Pulse quality ....   (c) Regularity ....
     (d) Reclining pulse rate.....   (e) Reclining blood pressure.....
     (f) Standing pulse rate ....   (g) Standing blood pressure .....

IV. *Abdomen:*
  14. Tenderness at McBurney's point ....
  15. Other tender areas ....
  16. Hernia ....
  17. Are spleen, liver, or kidneys palpable or tender..............
  18. Evidence of gall-bladder disease ....

V. Cutaneous System:
19. Is there any rash, eruption, or other skin pathology...............
....

VI. Nervous System:
20. Is examinee's nervous system stable and sound? Consider fatigue, excitability, irritability, depression, headaches, insomnia............
....
....
21. Any tremors present ....
22. What is condition of knee jerks ....
23. Corneal or other reflexes, if indicated ....

*VII. Genito-Urinary System:***
24. Any indication of kidney, bladder, or urethral trouble ....
....
25. Size and condition of prostate gland ....
....

* Exercise test suggested is stepping on chair five times in fifteen seconds leaving one foot on the chair throughout the test.
** Note—Examination of a woman applicant by a woman physician if so desired.

VIII. Miscellaneous:
26. Muscular development ....
27. Posture ....
28. Spinal deviation ....
29. Varicose veins ....
30. Do arches of feet show any abnormality—flat feet?...............

IX. Laboratory Findings:
31. Urine—(a) Specific gravity............ (b) Reaction............
   (c) Albumen...... (d) Sugar........ (e) Microscopic findings....
32. Stool report, if indicated ....
33. Blood report, if indicated ....
....
34. Other findings ....
....

X. Summary:

	Physically	*Nervously*
Does the examinee rate:—		
(Put X opposite appropriate rating)	Excellent......	....
	Good..........	....
	Fair...........	....
	Poor..........	....

Do you recommend examinee as physically qualified for Christian service?
....
List favorable and unfavorable points from history and examination:
....
....
....
....
....

XI. *Recommendations:*   ....
....
....
....
....
....
Physician's signature .... Date ....
Address:
....

Form 6.

PROMISSORY NOTE

Name of Synod ....
No............ $............
KNOW ALL MEN BY THESE PRESENTS: That I ....
.... of .... County of ....
State of .... am held firmly bound unto the (Name of
Synod) ....·........ in the sum of ....
Dollars, with interest, to be paid to said Synod, its lawful officers, agents,
attorneys or assigns, to which payment well and truly to be made, I do
hereby bind myself, my heirs, executors, administrators, and each and
every one of them firmly by these presents, and I do hereby waive all
benefit and advantage accruing to me from any exemption law or any Act
relative to executions, now in power or hereafter to be passed, with cost
of suit and release of all errors.

Sealed with my seal. Dated the .... day of .... A. D. 19....
The condition of this obligation is such, that if the above bounden
.... shall at such time, and on such
conditions as the above mentioned Synod shall direct, enter into the
ministry and continue to labor therein in connection with the United Lutheran Church in America, and shall be guilty of no act which in the
judgment of said Synod shall render it improper for him to enter or continue in the ministry, then this obligation to be void, otherwise to remain
in force and virtue. And I further empower any attorney in the United

States or elsewhere to appear for me and confess judgment against me for the above amount with costs of suit and release of errors.

Signed, Sealed and Delivered in

     the presence of

....

.... (SEAL)

Form 7.

APPLICATION FOR RENEWAL OF AID

Applicants must fill this blank carefully and mail to the secretary before

....

Personal

Full Name:

Address:

    Home: School:

Class: College: Seminary:

Are you married?   Are you engaged to be married?

Are you a member of a college fraternity or other secret society?

If so, give name

What is your present Church connection?

Location:

Pastor:

How do you maintain connection with this congregation?

State the name of the church you attend while at college:

                                        Seminary:

How frequently do you attend church service?   Where:

Do you attend the daily chapel service?

What specific line of Christian work were you active in while at college-seminary during the past year?

Answer in full.

Has your attitude towards full-time Christian service changed?

Explain.

Educational

According to general standing for the past year, were you in the first, middle, or lowest, third of your class?

Did you fail in any subjects?   Why?

What subjects do you expect to take in your course in the coming year?

Are you planning to take any educational work this year in addition to your college-seminary course?

If so, what courses?   How many hours?   Where?

Have you received the faculty's permission to take this work?

                 The Committee's permission?

In what ways did you engage in student activities (college-seminary) in past year?

What office in clubs or societies did you hold?
Has your course at college-seminary been interrupted during the past year?
If so, what was the cause?   The length of absence?

Financial

Has there been any change since your last application in the ability of your parents or friends to aid you financially?   ,
To what extent can parents and friends aid you for the coming school year?

Did you work during last summer?   At what?
Do you earn money while at school?   How?   How much per week?
Have you any indebtedness?   How much?
To whom are you indebted?   Is it interest bearing?
Have you a scholarship from college-seminary?   Value?
Are you receiving aid from any other source?
What is your estimate of your expenses for the coming school year?

Tuition $ Board $ Room rent $ Clothes $ Church and
Benevolences $ Contingent Fees $ Books $ Miscellaneous $
Total $

How do you expect to meet this amount?
Personal cash $
Assistance of parents
Assistance of others
Scholarship
Other sources
Earnings
Amount desired from Committee
                              Total $

State any information not covered by these questions that you think the Committee should know in order to understand better your financial need.
Signature of applicant:
Date:

2. Future Projects

As stated elsewhere, we believe that this Board can be of special aid to our institutions and to the Church in other ways than by giving grants. One is the carrying out of research projects which will have constructive value. Accordingly, the Board has approved its secretarial staff working on the following problems:

A Study of the Location of Lutheran Colleges.
A Study of the Atmosphere of our Lutheran Colleges.
A Study of the Departments of Bible and Religious Education at our Lutheran Colleges.
A Study of the Effect of Attendance at State Universities on Students' Christian Faith.

IV. MATTERS OF STUDENT WORK
1. FOLLOWING OUR STUDENTS

The re-organization of the work of the Board of Education has been completed comparatively recently so that it has seemed wise to report the activities of the Student Division under the former departments:

Religious Work in State Universities and Other Schools.
Women Students.
Recruiting.

The *extent* of the work of these three departments in following the students from our Lutheran homes wherever they be studying—in Lutheran colleges and seminaries, state universities and colleges, professional and technical schools—may be briefly summarized. The Department of Religious Work in State Universities has through visits been in touch with 145 different institutions in forty-one states of the United States and with seven different institutions in four provinces of Canada. By personal correspondence with pastors, faculty, or students, 194 other institutions have been reached and work among Lutheran students directed or assisted. Following our Lutheran women students as such began in the academic year of 1919-20 when visits were made to forty-nine groups. By June, 1922, 147 campuses had been reached. By June, 1930, 345. These student groups were limited to twenty-three states, the largest numbers being in New York and Pennsylvania.

Recruiting for the Gospel Ministry and for Christian life service on the part of women students has been a function of all three departments. But especial emphasis upon the Gospel Ministry has been given on all Lutheran college campuses by the Department of Recruiting.

The *intent* of the work of these departments has been "to endeavor to conserve the faith, to develop the loyalty, and to increase the spiritual life of all Lutheran students wherever found; and to discover, develop, and direct future leaders of the Church and to secure an adequate ministry." (By-laws, Art. III, Sec. 9.)   The increasing number of young people from our congregations who are attending universities, colleges, and technical schools demand constant and constructive spiritual guidance on the part of the Church.

A. *On Lutheran College and Theological Seminary Campuses.*

The secretaries function by co-operating with Presidents, Deans, faculty members, Y. M. & Y. W. C. A., Student Volunteers, Luther League, Lutheran Students Association of America, and local pastors; in counseling with students as individuals and in groups.

B. *At Non-Lutheran Institutions*

The secretaries minister to students by personal visits, by planning work, by counseling and by co-operating with

1. Student Pastors in student centers—Philadelphia, Ithaca, Boston. (These pastors are supported by Synods and the Board of Education.)

2. Student Pastors, Student Fellows or Student Secretaries in student centers like New York City, Chicago, Lincoln, Nebraska, or at state colleges or universities like State College, Pa.; the Universities of North Carolina, Ohio, Illinois, Michigan, Minnesota, Iowa, Kansas, Colorado, California, Oregon. (These pastors are doing work with students through the co-operation of the Board of Education with the local congregation.)

3. Pastors of local congregations where students in hundreds of educational institutions find a normal Church life during their undergraduate years; for example, State Teachers' Colleges, Normal Schools, Denominational Colleges.

4. Faculty and Students of our Church at institutions where there is no Lutheran congregation.

2. THE UNIVERSITY DEPARTMENT

Under the guidance and blessing of God, the work among Lutheran students in other than Lutheran schools has progressed and prospered in a steady and satisfactory way. During the past biennium the Secretary has visited in all parts of the country excepting the extreme Southwest and the lower Mississippi Valley. It has not been possible, of course, to visit every college and university. Wherever there was specific need, the Secretary has gone and helped to solve the problem. Some of our problems still remain as will be noted later.

Co-operation

We are particularly grateful for the widespread *co-operation* which we have enjoyed and without which the progress of our work would have been much slower than it has been. As in past bienniums, the work with the *Department for Women Students* has been practically one with the work of this department, frequent conferences of the Secretaries, the planning of itineraries so as to cover all important points and meetings to the best advantage, simultaneous visits where that appeared to be wise, and other forms of joint effort, have more than doubled the efficiency of the two departments. We have been in frequent touch with the *Board of Foreign Missions* both with respect to students from other lands studying in this country and in regard to students whom the Board was contemplating calling to service overseas. We have rendered service to *other Boards* in the Church also along their peculiar lines. Intimate co-operation with the *Luther League of America* has helped the work both of the League and of our Board. The University Secretary has continued to be the editor of the Luther League Topics quarterly and has contributed most of the Topics outlines. He is also chairman of the Literature Committee of the Luther

League of America. During the biennium he was chaplain at the Salisbury, N. C., Convention of the Luther League of America and at the state convention of the Luther League at Harrisburg, Pa. In visiting different parts of the country he has been able to seek out League leaders and to strengthen and develop League work wherever he has gone.

The *co-operation of the Synods* of the United Lutheran Church has in most instances been very gratifying. It seems now to be a well recognized custom among the presidents of our synods to consult the Secretary of the University Department when there are vacancies in congregations serving student communities, so that the wide acquaintance with pastors and workers with students which he has may be available in choosing the best man for these strategic centers of the Church's work. Synods have been assuming support for the work in constantly increasing numbers and amounts. The most advanced work in this particular is in the United Synod of New York. Its notable achievement at Cornell is well known. Similar work is rapidly developing at Harvard and in the Boston metropolitan area. Plans are being laid for development in the New York metropolitan area in the near future. Only second to this outstanding piece of work is the work of the Ohio Synod which has established an annual conference of the more than twenty pastors on its territory serving students. This conference is called by the president of the Synod and financed by the Synod, and has proved a most helpful instrument in developing the field.

Outside of the United Lutheran Church we have continued to receive the *co-operation of Augustana.* The president of the Augustana Synod has been a member of our Board representing their interests and they have contributed $2,700.00 a year to the budget of this department. We have been in constant touch with Augustana students in all parts of the United States, not only where their own pastors have been designated as student pastors but at many other points.

The Joint Synod of Ohio has made definite approaches to us through its Commission on Student Work. There is an understanding between the Commission on Student Work of Joint Ohio and our Board to the effect that where work has already been established, each will respect the other's precedence, and that at any new points where work is to be begun, consultation shall be had so that it may be effected to the best advantage of the students whether under the direction of our Board or of the Commission. We have further agreed to publish jointly two series of outlines for student discussion groups. These outlines are nearing completion and the books will be ready by the time the colleges open in September.

We have enjoyed the fine confidence and co-operation of many pastors of the *Norwegian Lutheran Church in America,* a few of the *Iowa* Synod and a few of the *Missouri* and *Wisconsin Synod* pastors working in student communities.

At two points the local work is of a very marked intersynodical character. In the state institutions in Oregon, student work is being done by a general society which receives its support from several synods and numbers members of these synods on its board of directors. The Rev. Wm. Schoeller, Litt.D., is the officient executive secretary. His contacts with our students in the state college, state university, and the state teacher's college have been most happy and helpful. Some of the best student meetings which it has been the good fortune of your secretary to attend, were held in Oregon during his visit there in January, 1930.

At the University of Nebraska, the work is carried on through a Joint Committee also representing five synods. A pastor is about to be called. There are over five hundred Lutheran students at the University of Nebraska.

Outside of the Lutheran Church we have maintained our contacts with the University Secretaries of other *Church Boards of Education* through the University Committee of the Council of Church Boards of Education. We are in constant touch with the secretaries of the Student Department of the Y. M. C. A. and the secretaries of the Student Volunteer Movement. We have also participated in the conferences of Church Workers in State Universities.

The Lutheran Student Association of America

The Lutheran Student Association of Amtrica is an independent association of students which has no direct official relations with any synod. It is a source of great gratification that your secretary has been chosen one of the national advisers of the L. S. A. A. each year from its inception. In consequence he has been privileged to exercise considerable influence in its development. It is gratifying to note that the L. S. A. A. during the past biennium has actually become nation-wide. Lutheran students in Washington and Oregon at a conference held at the University of Washington last January became members of the association, completing its extension to the coast.

The association publishes a paper, *The American Lutheran Student,* subscription price to those who are not students, twenty-five cents a year. It has been issued five times this year, four of the issues being sixteen pages. It was possible to do this through the co-operation of the Augsburg Publishing House, Minneapolis, who placed at the disposal of the association their entire stock of cuts and electros and set up the paper in the same fine style as the *Lutheran Church Herald.*

The conferences of the association, held in all parts of the United States excepting the extreme Southwest, have been unusually large and successful. The secretary of this department was present at four of the conferences. One of the secretaries of the Department for Women Students was present at two of them, and the Executive Secretary of the Board attended another.

Pastors' Conferences

The outstanding feature of the biennium in the work of the Department was the conferences of pastors working with students held the first week in January, 1930, at the Chicago Lutheran Bible School, for pastors in Ohio and westward, and the last week in January at Briar Cliff Lodge, N. Y. for pastors along the Atlantic seaboard and in the South. About half of the pastors connected with our synods who are working with students were present. The program was planned to cover every phase of student work. It began with a consideration of the student's religious life when he appears on the campus as a freshman, the temptations and the strains to which his faith is subjected on the campus, and the best ways to meet them. Then the pastor himself was considered, his educational and personal qualifications, his method of work in dealing with students personally and through the public ministration of the Word and Sacraments. This was followed by the consideration of precise aims that the student pastor should have in ministering to students. Then a program of the best sort of student work was developed and many practical suggestions of just how it should be carried out. The financial support of the work was considered in detail. The pastors who were present went away with much broader information in regard to their work, inspired to put more energy into it, further acquaintance with each other and with the Secretaries, and well acquainted with the way in which the work should be done. The results of the conference were shared with all pastors in the United Lutheran Church and many others through an issue of the Service Bulletin of the department which contained summaries of all that was said and done at each of the conferences together with the Findings adopted.

It appears evident that no other great communion is doing any better student work than the United Lutheran Church in America, and there are few that equal it in program and efficiency. It is a constant source of amazement to other student workers that Lutheran students manifest so much interest in their Church and are so enthusiastic about the program the Church affords on the campus and in the conferences of the Lutheran Student Association of America.

Service Bulletin

Shortly before the last meeting of the United Lutheran Church, the Department began the publishing of a Service Bulletin consisting usually of four pages of four or five thousand words, featuring news by which programs and events of outstanding interest on various campuses are shared with those working on other campuses. Through the medium of the Service Bulletin, a detailed practical guide is given as to what should be done on the average campus during THE MONTH following the issue of the Service Bulletin; BOOKS, a number of books of particular interest to student workers are reviewed each month; a FEATURE ARTICLE deals with some specific phase of work among students. Articles have appeared on "How to Use the Secretaries When They Come," "The Pastor Himself," "Personal Work With Students," etc.; a CALENDAR showing where secretaries of this Department and of the Department of Women Students plan to be during the month, so that pastors nearby, if they have not already done so, may arrange for visits from the secretaries while they are in the neighborhood. This paper has been mailed to all of the pastors in the United Lutheran Church working among students, presidents of synods, colleges, seminaries, the members of the Board, and others interested, making a circulation of about 300. Fifteen issues have appeared in the two years since it was begun.

Correspondence. It must be quite evident that much of the work has to be done by correspondence. It is practical to visit the campus only from the end of September until the end of April and during this period the Christmas and Easter holidays and on many campuses most of January must be omitted, so that the time is extremely short when the secretaries can be of use by a visit on the campus. Correspondence, therefore, is heavy with the vast field and the limited time. The Service Bulletin helps considerably. A very large part of the secretaries' time is taken up in writing and answering letters and in making decisions relative to policy, personnel, and finance on the varous campuses.

The Madison Situation. At the request of President Knubel, representatives were appointed by the Board of American Missions and the Board of Education to consult with representatives of the Synod of the Northwest, the Milwaukee Ministerial Association, and the Luther Memorial Church, Madison, Wisconsin, regarding the financial problem of the latter. President Steimle appointed the Rev. A. A. Zinck, D.D., and the Rev. C. P. Harry, D.D.

The result of the conference between these representatives was that each group be asked to make a special appropriation for the Madison Church. Our Board was asked to appropriate $2,000 for each of the two years, 1930 and 1931.

The Board of Education has agreed to co-operate in helping the Madison Church. Dr. Zinck was made a member of the Advisory Committee who will keep in close touch with the situation.

In concluding, therefore, the report of the work of the Department for Lutheran Students in non-Lutheran institutions, it should be said that during the time this department has existed, the work has become thoroughly established throughout the territory of the United Lutheran Church in America. As changes have taken place in pastorates care has been exercised in the calling of men so that the Church may be very proud of the group of men who are pastors of her churches serving students in non-Lutheran institutions. Not only has the work become established on the campus and in congregations but the synods of the Church have come to realize that when there are students on their territory even if they are not attending Lutheran colleges, they are a responsibility of synod. This is true particularly because more than eighty per cent of the Lutheran students in colleges and universities and professional schools are attending non-Lutheran institutions. During the years in which this department has been functioning through the visits of the secretaries in all parts of the United States and Canada, we have come to know very definitely where our Lutheran students are and approximately in what numbers they attend the various colleges and universities in North America. A program has been developed flexible enough to meet any campus and definite enough to afford a clear guide in the conduct of student work.

Many problems, of course, remain unsolved. Some of these are due to lack of money, some to situations in which it seems impossible to make proper provision for our Lutheran students, such as that for example, at Dartmouth College, Hanover, N. H., where we usually have fifty or sixty Lutheran students and no Lutheran congregation within many miles, or those problems which we have come to call problems of the "Bucknell Type" where there is a considerable body of Lutheran students in attendance upon a college, nearly all of them residing at home or returning home for the week-ends and maintaining fellowship in their home congregation.

3. DEPARTMENT FOR WOMEN STUDENTS
Correlation and Co-operation.

This department functions, so far as possible, wherever women students of our Church are found. On United Lutheran college campuses it has co-operated with the Department of Institutions; on non-Lutheran campuses with the University Department. Only in colleges for women situated at points where there is no local Lutheran Church has this department had no direct connection with other phases of the work of the Board of Education. In such colleges, however, the secretaries can still co-operate with the Lutheran Student Association of America.

With the Women's Missionary Society of the United Lutheran Church, the Board of Education through this department has, since its organization, maintained close co-operation. Two women appointed by the Executive Board of the Women's Missionary Society are valuable advisory members of the Board of Education and of the student committee. The Executive Board of the W. M. S. budgets annually a generous amount of money for the work among women students. The Women's Missionary Society of the United Lutheran Synod of New York and of the Ministerium of Pennsylvania supplement this amount because of the large number of women students on their respective college and university areas.

The department for women students through Miss Winston has maintained a close relationship with the Young Women's Missionary Society. She has been on important committees and has attended conferences and conventions upon special invitation.

Candidate Committee

The Executive Board of the Women's Missionary Society in 1922 appointed the secretary for women students to the Candidate Committee and in 1924 made her chairman. This candidate committee is charged with finding the young women who are qualified to fill specific positions under the various boards of the United Lutheran Church. By this committee young women are recommended through the Executive Board of the Women's Missionary Society for appointments by the Board of American Missions and by the Board of Foreign Missions.

As chairman of the candidate committee Miss Markley, during her leave of absence from the work of the Board of Education from July, 1929, to March, 1930, was the official representative of the Executive Board of the Women's Missionary Society to the missions of the United Lutheran Church in Japan, China, and India.

Requirements educational and professional for successful Christian service are steadily advancing. Our workers must be sought among students or recent graduates. A review of candidates appointed over a series of years will show that they have received their undergraduate training in state universities, denominational colleges, or in state colleges and universities. Professional or graduate work is almost always from necessity taken at non-Lutheran institutions.

Student Secretaries in the Women's Missionary Societies of the Various Synods

Information concerning Christian Education Year has been supplied to all such secretaries and by them has, in many cases, been passed on to their constituencies. Stated addresses on this topic have been given at many of the large missionary conventions by secretaries of the Board of Education and by United Lutheran College faculty members. These student secretaries have since 1919 been gathering the student census from the congregations of their synods. During the past academic year 1329 congregations of the United Lutheran Church have reported 8,063 student members; of these 3,811 were women and 4,192 were men.

The student secretaries are stimulating a most intelligent interest in questions relating to the student and the Church and in the pertinent questions of higher education for the young women of the Church.

Lutheran Student Association of America

Regional conferences of the L. S. A. A. have been attended by Miss Markley and Miss Winston at Lenoir-Rhyne, Wittenberg, Gettysburg, Wagner, and State Teacher's College in Bowling Green, Ohio. The association continued to give a scholarship to a Lutheran student in India for graduate work. The Lutheran Student Association of America contributed to the Russian Seminary in Leningrad during the period from January 1, 1928, until

June 1, 1930, over $4,000.00. With the exception of St. Olaf, Capital Augustana, Bethany and Dana Colleges, those student groups contributing the largest amounts were from the United Lutheran Church.

Teacher Training Schools

Since 1919, the secretaries have visited seventy-one Teacher Training Schools located in eighteen states. Contacts with the students who are preparing to teach children are invaluable to the Church. In September, 1926, a law was passed in Pennsylvania through which additional courses leading to a baccalaureate degree were added to the curricula of the thirteen Normal Schools of the State. This act raised them to the Teachers College status. Each of these institutions is developing a certain phase of education such as Music, Health, Commerce, Library and Kindergarten. Because of the higher rating of the Teacher Training Colleges many students are taking advantage of their proximity and low rate of expense. By far the larger number of students are women. Approximately one-seventh of these students are members of the Lutheran Church. Two of the thirteen Teachers' Colleges are located in towns having no Lutheran Church. Of the 3,300 who were graduated in 1930 from Teachers' Colleges about 450 were Lutheran young women prepared to teach in public school systems.

Women Students and the Church

The value of knowing in an intimate way the women students of our Church can be demonstrated in several different aspects. Probably one of the most striking is the dependence of the Board of Foreign Missions upon students and young alumnæ as candidates for foreign mission service. Questions of no little concern to the Church at large are: Where are our young women receiving their undergraduate education, and is it fitting them for Christian leadership in their communities and in their Church? Where shall our young women receive the professional graduate training necessary for specific forms of Christian service at home and abroad?

4. RECRUITING

Recruiting measures under the direction of the Board of Education have continued throughout the biennium with the same aim and upon the same principles as heretofore. The Church gave a splendid co-operation to the Board's request for an emphasis of the claims of the gospel ministry upon our homes and youth in connection with the observance of the Day for Prayer for Colleges and Universities, in both years.

Upon all Lutheran college campuses representatives of the Board conducted vocational guidance missions in the hope that they might reach those college men of attainments who have not settled the question of their life work and lead them seriously to consider becoming preachers. As a result of these efforts to present the unsurpassed opportunity to live the life offered by the ministry, and the worth to God and man of a preacher of the gospel, a number of commitments to the ministry resulted.

While the enrollment in Seminaries is reassuring for the immediate future, forever it must be said, the church that is not continually recruiting, by prayer and effort, her ministry, is destined to become a decadent church. Any consistent effort of recruiting must frankly confront the quality issue for the ministry of the present-day church. The day of mediocre men is passed.

The leaders of the church of the future will be dependent upon the selective interest manifested by the leaders of the church of today. We believe pastors should have not only a passion for souls, but also a passion for successors. We have read of one New England minister who has turned two hundred men into his profession. If every Lutheran pastor would take an intelligent selective interest in the youth of today, there would be no question as to the supply for the ministry and the influence of the leaders of the Church.

The Luther League has supported the vocational ventures of the Board in a most helpful and constructive manner.

Life Service literature published by this Board has had extensive use.

5. How the Student Division Functions

As a matter of record and for the information of the Church, we submit the plan whereby this division of our work functions:

In General:
1. Scope: The Life of Students
  A. Personal
     a. Religion
     b. Guidance
     c. Culture
  B. Group
     a. The *Organized* group
     b. The *Directed* group
     c. The *Interest* group
     d. The *Spontaneous* group
     e. The *Social* group
2. Field: The Setting of the Life of the Student
  A. The School:
     a. Theological Seminaries
     b. Lutheran Colleges
     c. Universities
     d. State Colleges
     e. Colleges and Schools—Professional and Technical
     f. Colleges, neither Lutheran nor State
     g. Academies and High School—as far as possible
  B. The Church:
     a. The congregation
     b. The Synod, etc.

3. Method: By developing among Lutheran students a program including:
    a. Worship
    b. Study
    c. Service
    d. Friendship
    e. Conferences
A. On Lutheran Campuses through co-operation with the proper administrative officers, faculty members, students and pastors.
B. On other campuses through co-operation with the local pastors, through their congregations, faculty members and students.
    This co-operation is to be effected by:
    a. Visits from the secretaries
    b. Correspondence
    c. Conferences of Pastors
    d. Conferences of Faculty Members
    e. Conferences of Students
    f. A Service Bulletin
    g. Printed matter.

With Special Reference to Guidance

Whereas the former department of recruiting for the ministry has been discontinued in order that the important subject of vocational guidance in religious objectives may be restudied in its newer and wider implications and that this whole subject may be committed to the program of every secretary and member of the Board, we here set down the principles and program carefully formulated by the department in times past as a guide to those charged among other things with prayerful service in behalf of securing worthy servants for the Master's Vineyard:

We recognize

The gospel ministry as a divine calling—Matt. 28:19-20, addressed to individuals—John 15:16, who are to labor through the agency of the Christian Church—Eph. 4:11-12, in the spirit of Christ—Mark 10:42-45, for the salvation of souls—Luke 19:10.

We feel the need of more persistent prayer

For the laborers *now* in the harvest (Col. 4:3);

By the *laborers* now in harvest *for* more laborers who will go forth in the spirit of Christ seeking the salvation of souls—(Luke 10:2);

By our *congregations* and their auxiliaries for their pastors and for a larger consecrated effort in filling up the ranks of the ministry with worthy followers of the Lord Jesus Christ. (Rom. 10:14-15.);

By mothers and at the family altar that sons of prayer and promise may be dedicated to the service of the Lord. (I Sam. 1:27-28.)

We feel the further need

Of proper educational propaganda through every available agency to offset the insidious and false propaganda which has found its way to the stage, the screen, the literature of the day, the lecture platform and the gossip of the street concerning the flabbiness and unworthiness of the ministry as a calling;

Of co-operation on the part of pastors of the United Lutheran Church with the Board of Education of the United Lutheran Church. To this end pastors are requested to correspond freely with the Board through its secretaries.

The Program has been outlined as follows:

In dealing with the home, the Board must act through the local pastor. It must seek to enlist his interest through existing synodical agencies, e.g., Committees on the Family Altar, on Religious Education, young peoples' work, etc.

In dealing with the congregation the Board must supply attractive folders and pamphlets for the literature receptacles to be found in the vestibules of our churches. It should provide material for at least one sermon each year on the ministry to the pastors of our congregations.

In dealing with synods and the conferences belonging thereto the Board is to function through the Executive officers of said synods.

In dealing with colleges and schools directly or indirectly affiliated with the church the Board shall have no one fixed method of approach, e.g., the recruiting mission, but shall adapt its program to the specific field and evolve it in consultation with those in authority.

In dealing with theological seminaries the Board is seeking at least one opportunity during each student generation to present to the students a lecture upon the subject: "The Pastor's Part in Seeking Men for the Ministry."

V. MATTERS OF INSTITUTIONS

The By-Laws of the United Lutheran Church in America says that reports of institutions should be incorporated into the report of the board or committee dealing with the general subject. Accordingly, we have secured reports from the colleges and seminaries. They are incorporated in this section of our report, but in somewhat different form from that in which they were received. This was done in order that the important items of each institution would be more easily noted.

The Statistical Tables are new in this report, and present data never before obtained from our institutions. We believe the church should have this information from its institutions. Our institutions are quite willing that the facts be known.

1. The Turnover in College Presidents

The following changes have taken place in the presidents of our colleges:

Carthage: The Rev. J. Diehl, D.D., succeeded the Rev. N. J. Gould Wickey, Ph.D., D.D., resigning to become the Executive Secretary of the Board of Education.

Hartwick: The Rev. C. H. Leitzell, D.D., succeeded the Rev. C. R. Myers, D.D., resigning to take up a parish.

Newberry: President S. J. Derrick resigned on account of ill health. Prof. Jas. C. Kinard, LL.D., has been elected as his successor.

Waterloo: No president has been secured since the resignation of the Rev. A. A. Zinck, D.D., in January, 1927.

2. PROGRESS THROUGH THE SURVEY

The three volume *Survey of Higher Education for the United Lutheran Church in America* appeared in June, 1929. The Board sent out 835 complimentary sets and sold 227 sets, making a total distribution of 1,062 sets, or 3,186 volumes.

Very distinct progress is being made through the recommendations of the Survey. Our college administrators are endeavoring in every way to fulfill the recommendations of the Survey, so far as time and finance allow. Notwithstanding the lack of money a majority of the major recommendations, dealing with physical plant, government, and faculty, have been carried out at about one half of the colleges.

Your attention is called to the following evidences of progress: five colleges have secured more land; ten institutions have prepared comprehensive campus plans which will direct all future building and development operations; two heating plants have been enlarged; three libraries, two administration halls, two gymnasiums and one President's house have been constructed. At this writing a Chapel, an Astronomical Observatory, a Music and Fine Arts Building, and a Field-House are in process of erection. Seven colleges have increased the number of teachers with the Ph.D. degree. At two institutions more than forty per cent of the faculty hold the degree of Ph.D., or its equivalent. One college was accredited by the regional accrediting association.

3. OUTSTANDING EVENTS

From information sent to the office of the Board and gathered by the Executive Secretary, the following interesting events occurring at our institutions are recorded:

Hartwick Seminary
Removal to Brooklyn, N. Y., with classes held in the Parish House of St. Luke's Church and the Rev. Stephen M. Paulson, D.D., as Dean, effective September 1, 1930.

Gettysburg Seminary
A visit from and lectures by Dr. Adolf Deissman, Berlin, Germany.

Southern Seminary
The addition of an English Bible Course, not requiring Hebrew and Greek for graduation and not leading to the degree of Bachelor of Divinity.

Chicago Seminary
The inauguration of the Rev. L. F. Gruber, D.D., LL.D., as president.
The placing of the seminary under more direct synodical control, the Illinois, the Michigan, and the Wartburg Synods taking action to co-operate in its management.

Martin Luther Seminary
The charter amended so as to receive the right to confer the Bachelor degree, only candidates for the ministry being admitted.

Northwestern Seminary
The gift of $75,000 from Mr. William C. Grunow.

Saskatoon Seminary
The calling of a professor for the Chair of American Lutheran Church Practice and English Bible.

Gettysburg College
The remodeling of Gladfelter Hall at a cost of $110,000.
The dedication of a new Library with capacity for 100,000 volumes and costing $125,000.

Wittenberg College
The completion of a Health and Physical Education Building, costing $400,000. The erection of an Astronomical Observatory, costing $80,000 and donated by Mr. and Mrs. Elgar Weaver.
The holding of the first Youth Conference in the United Lutheran Church with more than 500 young people in attendance.

Carthage College
The enlargement of the heating plant and the remodeling of the heating system.
The erection of a Field House.

Roanoke College
The erection of a gymnasium costing $130,000 equipped.

Newberry College
The successful completion of a campaign for $500,000.

Susquehanna University
The inauguration of the Rev. G. Morris Smith, D.D., as president.
The revision of the curricula and the raising of standards.
The erection of a library building.

Muhlenberg College
The completion of a library building costing $400,000 and the erection of a Chapel, which will cost $250,000.

Wagner College
The dedication of an Administration Building, costing $425,000.
The establishment of a Chair of Biology.
Conducted a campaign for $75,000.

Lenoir-Rhyne College
Conducted a campaign for $80,000.

Waterloo College
Received the State Right to conduct Honor B. A. courses.

Hartwick College
The inauguration of the Rev. C. H. Leitzell, D.D., as President, and
Rev. O. M. Norlie, Ph.D., S.T.D., Litt.D., Pd.D., as Dean.
The dedication of the first building, which will eventually be the Science
Hall. The building cost $300,000.

Grace College
The change of name from Lutheran Woman's College to Grace Lutheran
College for Women, Inc.
The election of Miss Jessie Truman as Dean.

4. THE POSITION OF THE CHURCH COLLEGE

For some time the church college has been weighed in the balance and
in the judgment of many educators, is found wanting. Thirty years ago
President Harper of the University of Chicago prophesied the destruction
of the small college and listed as the menacing agencies the modern high
school, the junior college, the professional school, the state university, the
tendency toward specialization, the decline of the sectarian spirit, and
poverty. More recently, there have been those who declared that the college
of liberal arts is destined to a speedy and inevitable doom. Their judgment
is based upon many of the same grounds as those upon which President
Harper based his opinion. But if we have correctly estimated the opinions
of educators, the college of liberal arts is getting its second breath and will
be more firmly rooted in the American educational system than ever.

However, beneath all these judgments lies a subtle suggestion that the
church college as such is no longer necessary, that it is the college of liberal
arts as seen in the church college which is being weighed in the balance and
found wanting. Accordingly, we read of such questions as follows being
asked: "Is it necessary for the religious bodies to continue the development
of educational institutions in the field of higher education and in the field
of general education, inasmuch as the state, in such a generous fashion is
providing for the instruction in the whole range of general education? Has
not denominationalism vanished to the point where it no longer has an
appeal for a loyalty that should warrant the development of such expensive
and elaborate enterprises as church colleges?"

The judgment of the doom of the church college is not based upon its
inefficiency, for it is recognized that no institution is perfect and that methods
may always be improved. Both friends and foes point to the decreasing
increase in the college enrollments. Whereas from 1890 to 1926 the increase
was fourteen per cent, last year it was only one and one-half per cent. This
is significant for the church college since it means a decrease in income.
Further, it is shown that the Church, especially the Protestant Church, is

apparently withdrawing from the field of higher education. Within the past two years more than twenty-five church educational institutions have been closed or combined with others. The cause of this is the lack of funds. No denomination can compete with private and state institutions on the financial basis. For example, Columbia University, one of the best endowed universities in the world, has recently asked for $34,000,000.00 more endowment. Again, it is common knowledge that when a church college becomes successful it tries to withdraw from the mother who gave it birth and fostered it during the dangerous period of childhood and youth. Further, the unparalleled growth of state colleges and universities seems to be a direct blow at the existence of the church college, especially since they charge little or no tuition and the students think their total expenses will be less. Again, men and women of means are directing their contributions to the large private and state universities. The one hundred most highly endowed institutions have seventy-five per cent of the endowments, but provide instruction for less than thirty per cent of the students enrolled in our American institutions of higher education. Finally, there is the recognition on the part of the universities of the significance of two points which have been the strongest selling points which the church college possessed, namely, the value of the dormitory system and the place of religion in higher education. Harvard University is spending $13,000,000.00 for dormitories alone. Many universities are taking steps to give some attention to the religious side of the student's life. Thus attempts are being made to incorporate the values of the church college in the organization of the university.

Thus, the cry of thirty years ago, "away with the small college," became "away with the liberal arts college," and is now heard as "away with the church college."

The answer to this challenge has been made in the form of the Liberal Arts College Movement, inspired by President Ward of Western Maryland College, Westminster, Maryland. He made a study of the enrollment and endowment resources of four hundred college and universities which was sent to every college president in the United States. Letters of appreciation were received from presidents in all sections of the country, many of whom urged that something be done in the form of an organization "whereby a concerted movement might be launched in behalf of securing the financial resources necessary to qualify all worth-while colleges to their share in providing in the most efficient way possible for the cultural education of the students in the liberal arts colleges in the United States."

After various steps a conference of representatives of two hundred seventy-eight liberal arts colleges was held at the Stevens Hotel in Chicago on March 18-20, 1930.

This conference decided to organize The Liberal Arts College Movement, the objectives of which shall be " to set forth the place of the college of liberal arts in higher education in the United States, and to co-operate with the colleges of liberal arts in securing funds adequate to their needs." A Committee of Five was appointed to select a Committee of Fifteen, whose work will be to develop the work of the movement and to report at a meeting of the movement to be called in connection with the annual meeting of the Association of American Colleges next January at Indianapolis, Indiana.

Our Church is represented on this Committee of Fifteen by President R. E. Tulloss, Ph.D., D.D., Wittenberg College. President Tulloss has also been appointed on the Executive Committee of the Committee of Fifteen. In case President Tulloss cannot be present at any meeting, our Executive Secretary has been asked to substitute.

Although there is no specific reference to the church college, yet those who are in close touch with the developments taking place know that the real leaders are persons connected with church colleges and that the very heart of the movement is the existence of the church college. The time is undoubtedly here when the church college must sell itself to the American mind in a more positive manner than ever. This can be done only through the medium of a new apologetic.

This apologetic, we believe, *must follow at least two lines*. First, there must be a re-emphasis of the individual in the process of higher education. It is quite clear that the interests of the individual are neglected in the efforts exerted by the universities, state and private, to minister to the mass. Quantity is glorified; quality is sacrificed. Even university authorities are conscious of this situation and are urging parents to send their children to the smaller college for their undergraduate, or at least their junior college work. This reaction against mass education is a strong influence in favor of the church college.

A second factor in the new apologetic must be an increasing concern for the moral and religious education of the next generations. The theme, "Religion in Higher Education," has been prominent in educational conferences. It is becoming quite evident that all educational efforts which lack, and do not give due consideration to, the religious element are defective and incomplete.

Our church colleges can no longer play with the problem of religion. They must be distinctively Christian. There must be a definite relation between the profession of faith and the campus activity. There must be the definite conscious attempt to interpret the mind of Christ and to incorporate it in the personalities of all who may be connected with the institution. It dare be no formal matter for the church college to declare that "in Christ we stand face to face with ultimate reality." If the Christian college has faith in that Gospel then it dare not waver in its efforts to bring all its students into the freedom thereof.

But the Church must manifest continued and increased concern for the Church College. With such active and definite interest, our colleges will ever be loyal to the truths founded on the Rock of Ages and will serve the future in greater degree than was possible in the past. **(See Recommendation 3).**

5. THE MINISTRY AND THE SEMINARIES

It is a matter of much pride that the Lutheran ministry in this country has a high scholastic standing. It is reported, that more than eighty per cent of the Lutheran ministry has a college training, and that the denomination nearest the Lutheran is the Presbyterian with a little more than thirty per cent. We should not be satisfied until we have a 100 per cent college-bred ministry.

While four of our seminaries rejected sixteen students on account of inadequate preparation, yet from observations made during the past year, we are disappointed at the ease with which non-college graduates enter some of our seminaries, even after they have been refused entrance at other seminaries. Mature students, with no college degree, could be admitted on examination or by special vote of the faculty. Seminaries receiving grants from this Board should be warned in regard to the violation of the standard of entrance.

In answer to the question, "Is the present-day candidate for the ministry of higher quality, intellectually, than five years ago," three seminaries replied in the affirmative, two said no, and another gave a very discriminating answer: "The situation in the last five years shows little change except in one respect, which, however, is important—there is a steadily decreasing number of poorly prepared men. This, naturally, raises the average of the lower half of the seminary classes. The number of men of the highest grade in any class remains about the same as previously. One college, however, has sent us in 1929 six honor men out of about eight."

One point where our seminaries have not availed themselves of the values of pedagogical procedure is, *they make no or little provision for the student to learn by doing.* The Commission V (American Section) to The Universal Christian Conference on Life and Work, held in Stockholm, Sweden, August 19-30, 1925, commented on this very matter as follows: "Most seminaries fail to make an educational use of the activities in which students are engaged. These activities not only afford to students opportunities to use the truths which they learn from books, and to apply the principles discussed in the class room, but place them in situations within which problems arise which may quicken and motivate the whole of their theological education. It may indeed be possible to reorganize the curriculum, not only with a view to the functions which the young minister is in future to exercise, but with a view to the active functions which he is fulfilling while a student. Such a reorganization would give place in theological education to methods analogous to those of apprenticeship systems in industrial education, or the clinic and the hospital internship in medical education."

We are glad to report that several of our seminaries are attempting something along this line, but there is not as much as should be done. One difficulty is that our seminaries are not manned with individuals who have been trained to organize, supervise and evaluate clinical activities.

Notwithstanding their weaknesses and deficiencies, theological seminaries are fulfilling an important function in the religious life of any nation. Some keen observers of the trend of events in the theological realm are very eager to declare, "In spite of the present confusion of theological education, there are clear signs that the seminaries are moving in the direction of larger Christian fellowship rather than toward the further division and disintegration of Christian forces."

For these signs we are grateful, but we wish our own seminaries might be a little more aggressive towards hastening a united Lutheranism. They are the key to the problem, and should be encouraged in their activity along this line by the enthusiastic attitude expressed by the laymen of the various bodies.

6. THE NECESSITY FOR THE CORRELATION OF ALL EDUCATIONAL AGENCIES OF THE CHURCH

For a number of years the problem of integrating the educational program of the parish has been worked upon by a series of committees including representatives of the Parish and Church School Board and organizations of the Church, the Women's Missionary Society and the Luther League. The task of such integration of Sunday Church School, Week Day Church School, Daily Vacation Bible School, Catechetical Instruction, with the informational, inspirational, and expressional program of the Women's Missionary Society, Luther League and Brotherhood has been a most difficult one.

The problem of integrating the educational program of the parish concerns itself directly with the education and training of the leaders in that parish. Consequently it concerns the institutions of the Church in which such leaders received their education. To be specific the problem raises certain questions: Do the Colleges of our Church give our laity the courses in Bible and Religious Education and the proper motivation to carry on in our parish organizations? Do our parishes avail themselves of full time Religious Education leaders prepared by our colleges? Do the Training Schools and Mother Houses give courses which cover the needs which workers will have to face in the modern parish? Finally, do our Theological Seminaries offer to the future pastor sufficient constructive help for the maintenance and the evolving of a unified educational program for a parish under present-day complex problems? It seems clear that the curricula of all institutions may well be restudied from the viewpoint of the parish both as to content and as to product in lay workers and in full time Christian workers—religious activities directors, deaconesses, pastors. Such a restudy will help solve this problem in the parish.

The Board of Education charged by constitution with promoting the general educational interests of the Church submits to this Convention a recommendation concerning this most important area of the life of our Church. **(See Recommendation 5.)**

7. Kropp-Breklum Seminary

Students from the Kropp Seminary have been supplied to us during the biennium as follows: In the fall of 1928 Berthold Korte and Ernst Schmidt arrived and entered the Chicago Seminary. Last fall and at time of arrival Julius Koehler, Karl Hartwig and Erich Petersen entered Chicago Seminary, and Soenke Friedrichsen, Johannes Schulze and Johannes Hamester entered Waterloo Seminary. Wolfgang Vetter, Johannes Frennsen, Wilhelm Strunk and Walter Wendorf completed their course in Kropp last fall and enter upon further study in our institutions this fall. Strunk and Wendorf are assigned to the Seminary in Saskatoon.

Manfred Mertner, Siegfried Cyrus and August Claus finished in Kropp this June and at this writing await word from our Board when they shall be permitted to come. This permission has been delayed until their support, when here, can be assured. For it means a total of thirteen students from Kropp for whose support the Church is responsible this year, with two others (Gustaf Lehmann and Martin Steffen) making their finals in Kropp during the month of this Convention with expectations of being brought over before Christmas.

The problem of caring for so many students caused an appeal to be made to the German Conference of the United Lutheran Church assembled at Reading, Pa., last fall. The Conference voted $100 for the purpose. A circular letter to the German pastors of the United Lutheran Church in April of this year was responded to with somewhat less than $400. Our Board, in addition to the payment of the passage money, granted aid from its Ministerial Aid Fund to the extent of monies available.

The Wartburg Synod, the Pittsburgh Synod and the United Synod of New York have promised assistance in the ensuing year through their student aid funds. Yet there is not enough support in sight to relieve us from anxiety. Further contributions to this cause are necessary. We cannot bring men to our shores to serve in the ministry of our Church and then leave them to their fate during the period of their preparation here.

The report of Kropp Seminary as of March 1, 1930, states an attendance of sixteen students.

The report of the Pro-Seminary at Breklum for this year has not arrived at this writing. This is doubtless due to the serious illness of Director Petersen. According to the last report received, twenty-four students were enrolled.

8. The Training of Men for a Bi-lingual Ministry

At the call of the Committee on Boards and Committees of the Executive Board of the United Lutheran Church to consider the problem of training men for a bi-lingual ministry, our Board was represented by Dr. Steimle, Dr. Pfatteicher, and Dr. Wickey. Dr. Wickey was selected secretary of the meeting. After due discussion a sub-committee was appointed to prepare a possible policy. Drs. Steimle and Wickey were appointed on this committee and acted as chairman and secretary respectively.

To supply the Church with pastors who can minister in more than one language has always been a problem with the Lutheran Church. This problem arises because of the principle of the Reformation that the church must preach the Gospel in the language of the people. Today the problem concerns more than the training of men to serve German-English parishes. We have people who must be served in other languages.

Members of the Board have given much thought to the matter and were very happy to co-operate in preparing a possible policy, which will be brought to the attention of this Convention by the Executive Board. (See Recommendation 6.)

9. INTERESTING STATISTICS

Because of the increased desire on the part of our educational institutions to let the Church know the facts regarding their operations, and for the sake of those who are seeking to know the financial situation of our schools, especially in the light of Educational Year, we have prepared and incorporated in this report very comprehensive and analytical statistical tables regarding the theological seminaries, the colleges and the junior colleges. These data were secured from the institutions themselves. It should be remarked that in most cases the figures represent the financial status of the institution at the end of their fiscal year 1928-1929. Consequently in some cases the present status is different from that given in the tables.

This is the first time that such detailed information has been gathered. Some of the institutions, not keeping their records according to the plan suggested by the Statistical Blank, could not report. Further, some institutions are connected with other institutions so far as financial operations are concerned. This means that only one report is given for two institutions in a few cases. Because of this incompleteness in the reports we have not given the totals in the tables.

The Church should especially note that every seminary had an operating deficit, that only three colleges did not have deficits, and that each junior college had a deficit. Our institutions need two million dollars as endowment in order that they may not have deficits. Also they need two million dollars more to pay off indebtedness. Thus four million dollars are absolutely necessary if institutions are to be free of debt and current deficits. If the total sum of the campaign goals of Education Year be seven million dollars, it is very evident that the sum is far too small. For there is allowed only three million dollars for new buildings, more equipment, and increased endowments for the maintenance of higher scholastic standards.

Surely the administrative officers are conservative in their demands upon the Church and are limiting themselves to absolute necessities.

Your attention is called to the following figures which are relatively correct and exhibit an interesting picture of the thirteen seminaries, the thirteen colleges and the three junior colleges.

	13 Seminaries	13 Colleges	3 Jr. Colleges	Grand Total
Total Value of Property, including grounds, buildings, equipment	$2,490,041	$10,172,702	$303,536	$12,966,279
Productive Endowment	1,885,490	5,446,214	5,000	7,336,704
Total Assets, including Unproductive Endowment and other Funds	4,797,659	17,394,712	347,964	22,540,335
Total Indebtedness	155,800	1,678,889	65,796	1,900,485
Annual Income for Current Expenses	211,293	1,559,337	65,383	1,836,013
Annual Expenditures for Current Expenses	257,635	1,606,156	67,670	1,931,461
Total Current Deficits	46,342	46,819	2,287	95,448
Total Volumes in Libraries	177,000	287,743	11,450	476,193
Total Faculties	76	418	26	520
Total Student Enrolment, excluding duplicates, in all departments and schools	546	10,781	275	11,602

STATISTICAL TABLES—I. THEOLOGICAL SEMINARIES

THE PROPERTY

Index No.	Founded	Institution	Location	President or Dean	Campus Acre	Campus Value	Bldgs N.	Bldgs Value	Value of Real Property	Library Vol.	Library Val.	Furn. & Fix.	Total Val. of Equip	Total Value of Property
1	1797	Hartwick Seminary	Hartwick Seminary, N. Y.	The Rev. F. Wolford, D. D.	40	$13000	3	$73000	$86000	2000			$12000	$96500
2	1826	Luth. Theo. Seminary	Gettysburg, Pa.	The Rev. J. Aberly, D. D.			9	350000	390000	43000	$50000	$10000	60000	450000
3	1830	Luth. Theo. Southern Sem.	Columbia, S. C.	The Rev. A. G. Voigt, D. D., L. L. D.		23000	5	140000	160000	8000	9000	1500	10500	170500
4	1845	Hamma Divinity School	Springfield, Ohio	The Rev. L. H. Larimer, D.D.,L.L.D.		See Witten		berg College		40000				
5	1858	Susquehanna	Selinsgrove, Pa.	The Rev. F.P.Manhart,D.D.L.L.D		See Susqu		ehanna College	a					
6	1864	Lutheran Theo. Seminary	Mt. Airy, Phila., Pa.	The Rev. C. M. Jacobs,D.D.,L.L.D.	11	300000	11	600000	900000	46000			100000	1000000
7	1891	Chicago Theo. Seminary	Maywood, Ill.	The Rev. L. F. Gruber,D.D.,L.L.D.	15	216000	11	220000	436000	20000	20000	5521	25521	461521
8	1893	Western Theo. Seminary	Fremont, Neb.	The Rev. H. Dysinger, D.D.			1	Waterloo College		5000				23045
9	1911	Luth. Sem. of Canada	Waterloo, Ont., Can.	The Rev. C. H. Little, D.D.		See			loo College					
10	1911	Pacific Theo. Seminary	Seattle, Wash.	The Rev. J.C.Kunzmann.D.D.	14	75000	5	12000	87000	2000	2500	1000	3500	90500
11	1913	Martin Luther Seminary	Lincoln, Neb.	The Rev. J. Huebner,S.T.M.		5000	2	45000	57000	4000	1000	100	1100	58100
12	1913	Lutheran Seminary	Saskatoon, Sask. Can.	The Rev. H. W. Harms.	16	3000	7	62000	67000	3000	5000	5275	10275	77275
13	1921	Northwtn. Luth. Theo. Sem.	Minneapolis, Minn.	The Rev. J. Stump,D.D.L.L.D LHD.		3000	1	50000	53000	4000	6000	3600	9600	62600

Note: Totals omitted because of incomplete reports
   Cents are omitted
   Blanks unless otherwise noted, indicate no report or nothing to report

THE FUNDS: PERMANENT

Index No.	Restricted	Unrestricted	Annuities	Other	Scholarships	Gr. Total End'mnt	Interest Bearing	Non-Int. Bearing	Total Assets
1		30000							
2		525612	28000		67529	621142			621142
3			7100			71100	6700	23500	101300
4	See Witten berg College								
5	See Susque hanna College								
6	64000	503088		25000		690088			957145
7	210323	260242				470565		25059	
8		27000		6000	6000	33000			208500
9	See Waterl oo College								
10	24000	81750	12250			118000			
11	3000			15000		18000			
12			2000	100		2100	800	900	81075
13	2500	91975	2000	200		94675		101987	260702

The Funds: Current Income

Index No.	Additions to Cap. 1928-29	1929-30	In-debtedness	En-dow-ment	Stu-dts.	The Church	Special Gifts Cur. Ex	Msc	Total An.Inc
1				1500					
2	43242	23936		35038	1128	7750		1611	45588
3	17100	12500	800	3446	870	4406	1540		10262
4									
5									
6	25000	45000	25000	16348	2206	32000	3775		54329
7			100000	20673		8384	1716	1197	31970
8	2000		10000	1560	117	1293			2970
9									
10	18226	12991		5841		1667	12378	62	19948
11				180		6800	1500	15	9980
12	50	2000				13781	1940	21	15742
13	54816	27254	20000	3639		15701	1000	165	20505

STATISTICAL TABLES—I. THEOLOGICAL SEMINARIES—Concluded

Number	CURRENT EXPENDITURES — Administration	Instruction	Books, Equipment	Operating	Maintenance	Miscellaneous	Total Expenditures	Surplus or Deficit	THE FACULTY (Degrees—earned only) No.	No.	A. B.	A. M.	B. D.	S. T. M.	Doctor	THE STUDENTS 1st Year	2nd Year	3rd Year	Specials	Grads. in Residence	Grads. in Correspond.	Total Enrolled	COLLEGE GRADUATES 1st Year	2nd Year	3rd Year	Specials	Grads. in Residence	Grads. in Correspond.	Total College Grads.	Non-Luth.	Alumni
1		4500							3							5	3	3				10			No	0	No	No	No report	1	300
2	215	9650		2015	500	600	45766 D	178	6		2	2				4	22	2	6	5		78	22	22	23	6	2		75	2	1450
3		2000			1823		14303 D	4041	4		4					8	22	23	9			33	8	11	14				33		183
4									10							3	22					51									618
5	8852	32000	4914	7439	22407	12193	68168 D	13853	6	10		1				3	6	9	1	5	16	35	30	33	24		32	16	119	2	250
6	5160	21000	700	1657	5513		52005 D	20035	12	3	1	3	5	2		30	34	12	2	32	31	129	11	1		0	re port		75	1	1199
7	400	6684					8741 D	5771	7	2						11	20	1	2	6		81	1	1	N						355
8									5							2	4	4	1		2	9	1			0	re port		3		194
9									4							3	2	2				13	2	1	1	0			0		49
10	3531	6566	427	3710	7133	1356	22723 D	2775	6		3	3	1	1	1	9	4	4	2		2	6			N		No report	3		3	15
11	1100	4430	100	1400	1600		11230 D	1250	4		1	1		1		1	2	3	2			16	2	1	1					1	28
12	1900	7352		2389		3030	18603 D	2861	4							5	3	1	2			11									10
13	989	16350	3307	2304	926	447	21016 D	551	6	4	1	1	1	1	1	5	10	4		21	30	70	3	5	4		No report		75	1	75

STATISTICAL TABLES—II. COLLEGES

THE PROPERTY

No.	Institution	Founded	Location	President	Type	Ac'dited by	Campus Acres	Campus Value	Buildings No.	Buildings Value	Value of Real Property	Library Volumes	Library Value	Furniture fixt res lab.eq Mus'm Value	Total Value of Equip'ment	Total Value of Property
1	Gettysburg	1832	Gettysburg, Pa.	The Rev. H.W.A. Hanson, D.D., L.L.D	M	1,2,3,4	53	338252	11	1047398	1385650	60000	46624	159184	205807	2000000
2	Wittenberg	1845	Springfield, Ohio	The Rev. R.E. Tulloss, D.D, Ph.D. LLD	Co-ed	1,2,3,4	54	34096	7	332698	366794	47864	80748	30598	125690	1591457
3	Roanoke	1853	Salem, Va.	The Rev. C.J. Smith, DD., LLD.	M	2,3,4,	20	50000	18	370000	420000	21470		122250	147250	492484
4	Newberry	1856	Newberry, S. C.	Mr. S. J. Derrick, L. L. D.	Co-ed	2,3,4,	84	123513	18	496119	619632	16000	25000	108405	148525	567250
5	Susquehanna	1858	Selinsgrove, Pa	The Rev. G.M. Smith, D. D.	Co-ed	3	40	551114		1141578	1692692	8000	40120		144000	768157
6	Muhlenberg	1867	Allentown, Pa.	The Rev. J.A.W. Haas, DD, LLD	M	1,2,3,4	72	23347	8	258848	282195	50400	93690	64366		1835782
7	Carthage	1870	Carthage, Ill.	The Rev. J. Diehl, D. D.	Co-ed	1,2,3,4	38	35000	8	352000	387000	19377		84501		366696
8	Thiel	1870	Greenville, Pa.	The Rev. E.C. Xander, D.D.	Co-ed	2,3,4	35		11		387000	20135		70589		458132
9	Wagner Memorial	1883	Staten Island. N.Y.	The Rev. C.F. Dapp, Ph.D., DD.	M	1,2,4	52		11		628626	18000	10000	32000	23996	660625
10	Midland	1887	Fremont, Neb.	The Rev. H.F. Martin, Ph.D., D.D.	Co-ed		12		9		330821	8000		22000		354817
11	Lenoir Rhyne	1891	Hickory, N. C.	The Rev. H.B. Schaeffer, D.D.	Co-ed	2,3,4	37	92000	9	440000	532000	11000	12000	44000	56000	588000
12	Waterloo	1911	Waterloo, Ont., Can	The Rev. W.C. Froats, Dean.	Co-ed	3	16		5			750				122202
13	Hartwick	1928	Oneonta, N. Y.	The Rev. C.W. Leitzell, D.D.	Co-ed	4	112	35000	1	239100	274100	5132	8000	85000	93000	367100

Code: 1. The Association of American Universities.
2. The Regional Accrediting Association.
3. The State University.
4. The Regents (New York).

Note: Blanks unless otherwise stated indicate no report or nothing to report. Cents are omitted. Totals are not given because of incomplete reports.

THE FUNDS: PERMANENT

No.	Productive Restricted	Productive Unrestr'td	Unproductive Ann'ties	Unproductive Other	Scholarships	Grand Total Endowment	Other Assets Int. Brng.	Other Assets Non-intr Bearing	Total Assets	Addit'ns to Cap 28-29	Addit'ns to Cap 29-30
1		850000	50000			930000			2900000		
2	147105	903689	226689		103029	1380222	24996	10000	3244311	46349	200000
3		646113	4000			650113	11017	20110	1173724		
4		165000				165000			732250		
5		348614	38700			387312			1055469	41057	3 57
6		847299							2685692		
7		850464	24400		1000	885864	300	16922	1269026	37195	
8	158173	158173				158173	8109	15234	639026	445	3468
9						356170		300	1016795		
10	33900	109857	6500	8000		158257		119	513193	3320	
11	353000			27000		380000	20000		988000	16000	
12			12000		300				122502		
13	75000					87000		350000	1054000		

THE CURRENT FUNDS: INCOME

No.	Indebtedness	Endowment	Students Tuition	Students Fees	Dorm R'ntals	The Ch'rch	Gifts for C'rrent Exps.	Mi-cell-n-eous	Total mu-nic'al Inc.
1	000	85670	253133	63376	25292	11464	4450	13354	446639
2		38788	36104	2113	5307	3900	9130	7631	102974
3	26400	5717	22739		3795	5744	1016	3471	42481
4	16000	21270	110448	13617	14622	6050	180	44714	210902
5	72350	54863	79734	6200	9050	19075	9075	1760	217442
6	43032	45876	31671	3387	1341	2543	130	1260	86718
7	186452	10281	56840	inc.	inc.	19669		1000	88050
8	300000	17943	26000	inc.	inc.	18000	1000	63943	63943
9	94000	5688	42032	3740	7917	28051	1967	8704	98097
10	207000	22576	35500	5000	9500	3500			116000
11	54655		4371	inc.	inc.	24191	454	75	29091
12	65000		23549	8102		12500	12850	15650	72650

No report.

STATISTICAL TABLES—II. COLLEGES—Concluded

EXPENDITURES / THE FACULTY / College Freshmen

#	Administration	Instruction	Books Equipment Sup.	Operating	Maintenance Educational	Maintenance Non-Educational	Dormitory Main and operating	Miscellaneous	Total Expenditure	Surplus or Deficit	Luth. M	Luth. W	Luth. T	No. Degrees	A.B & B.S. only	Masters Only	Doctors	Fresh. M	Fresh. W	Fresh. T
1	No report								2071	444568 S	54	0	54	3	10	16	22	164	12	176
2	75028	239030	9067	76413	25908	2232	25958	2073	11646	114619 D	72	24	96	6	27	32	37	194	150	344
3	33294	49501	2336	9648	2081	4860	4095	221	3703	46184 S	12	4	16	1	3	21	9	131		131
4	1918	27681	3524	7861	inc. in previous	4011	2157		31957	178945 D	30	11	41		14	18	6	68	42	110
5	37251	106743		22007			9420		6134	216715 D	37		37	2			3	20	21	41
6	Report not in this form								22503	92852 D	18	9	27	1	5	11		156		156
7	24564	50085	7831	6953	3418				4057	111153 D	23	6	29	6	13	11	5	54	40	94
8	15480	53798	3799	8000	500	15051	774		3175	68000 D	23	9	32			8	4	47	32	79
9	13000	30000	1000	22477	2594	1400	8500	3146	4000	101272 D	16	5	21	6	5	4	3	24		24
10	8000	46594	2637	6500					505	120000 D	13	2	15	2	4	1	3	48	41	89
11	10500	50000	32000						9602	29596 D				5	5	1		52	62	114
12										82252 D	21	5	26	7	6	6	7	78	5	12
13	22222	35186	15650	8629	566														67	145

THE STUDENTS / Alumni

Soph M	Soph W	Soph T	Jr M	Jr W	Jr T	Sr M	Sr W	Sr T	Sp M	Sp W	Sp T	Grad M	Grad W	Grad T	Tot M	Tot W	Tot T	Luth M	Luth W	Luth T	SpSch M	SpSch W	SpSch T	Sum M	Sum W	Sum T	Ext M	Ext W	Ext T	GT M	GT W	GT T	Graduates	Ex-Students
136	14	150	127	15	142	133	19	152	6	1	7	38	7	45	604	68	672	272		353	148		148	108	42	150	25	7	32	855	105	960	3700	1800 filed
151	139	290	89	65	154	113	85	298	10	11	21	4	1	5	575	514	1089		253	525	119	165	284	407	458	865	196	511	707	1183	1411	2594	2768	1800
59		59	37		37	32		32	5		5				264		264	44	85	175				69	165					298	96	394	910	2587
39	31	70	45	41	86	24	32	56		5	5		8	8	176	151	326	90	74	174	161	128	289	46	190	230	168	192	360	216	341	557	1200	1600
40	22	62	48	23	71	29	22	51	877						150	90	240	100		242			200	200	187	381	191	486	667	679	1168	1753	
102		102	94		94	88		88	4	6	10				440		440	97	61	158	22	44	66	195	40	382				169	157	1699	1913	4830
39	25	64	28	24	52	28	21	49	6	3	9	29	22	51	153	116	269	76	44	120	48	94	142	20	72	40			114	207	246	326	799	2000
49	25	74	22	21	43	35	27			9	9				159	108	267	63	71	134	47	182	47	44				31		212	389	453	725	
25	28	53	21		21	14		14	9	35	44		8		84		84		1	190	115	22	298	48	203	251	8		469	131	601	240	400	
38	61	99	17	9	26	18	13	31	2	6	8	6			117	126	243	23	17	24	10	3	32			645				54	161	1472	602	63
5		5	21	31		23	34	57	6		6				136	194	330	16		33	26		29				38	105	143	212	202	363	29	112
45	30	75	3	1	4	6		6							28	6	23																	
															123	97	220																	

STATISTICAL TABLES—III. JUNIOR COLLEGES

Number	Name of Institution	Founded	Location	President	Type	Accredited	THE PROPERTY — The Plant				
							Campus Acres	Campus Value	Buildings No.	Buildings Value	Value of Real Prope'y
1	The Collegiate Institute...	1853	Mt. Pleasant, N. C.	Mr. G. F. McAllister, A. M.	M	State Bd.	18	$7500	6	$110000	$117500
2	Marion...	1874	Marion, N. C.	The Rev. E. H. Copenhaver, A.B.	W	State Bd.	7	25000	1	125000	150000
3	Saskatoon...	1913	Saskatoon, Sask., Canada	The Rev. H. W. Harms	Co-ed	Prov.Dpt.	See Sa	skat	oon	Semina	ry

The Equipment / THE FUNDS: Permanent

Library Vol	Library Value	Furn. Fix. Equi.	Total Value of Equipment	Total Value of Property	Prod've Restricted	Prod've Unrestricted	Unproductive	Scholarships	Grand Tot'l of Endowme't	Other Assts	Total Assets	Addition to Capital	Indebtedness	Endowment
6000	$7500	$7500	$15000	$132500	1000	4000		4000	5000	15000	20000	718	20000	
5000	6000	15036	21036	171036				4000	4000	518	20428	718	45796	
450	500				See Sa	l s k	to o	n Se	min	ary				

THE FUNDS: Current Income / Current Expenditures

Tuition	Fees	Rentals	The Church	Gifts for Cur. Exp	Miscellaneous	Total Annual Income	Administration	Instruction	Books, Equipment Operating	Maintenance	Miscellaneous	Total Expenditures	Surplus or Deficit
3442	3983		1041			35436	4735	11750				$35436	1064
692			625	1500		29947		8700				31011	
								3200					

THE STUDENTS

	Academy														Junior College									Special Schools			Grand Total			Lutheran		
	1st Year			2nd Year			3rd Year			4th Yr.			Total			1st Yr.			2nd Yr.			Total											
	M	W	T	M	W	T	M	W	T	M	W	T	M	W	T	M	W	T	M	W	T	M	W	T	M	W	T	M	W	T	M	W	T
1	10		10	20		20	25	2	27	14		14			57	24	1	25	11	2	13	35	3	38				90	5	95			40
2	2	6		6	3		25	3	3		24	31	31	57	24	24	55						137	137	56
3	4	3	7		2		7	3	10	17	8	15	3	18	32	11	43	43

The Faculty

	No. Deg'rs	A. B.	A.M.	Doctor	Lutheran					
					M	W	T	M	W	T
1	3	4	1	2	3		3	7		7
2	10	4	6	6	8	1		2	15	17
3	1	1	1		1	1		1	1	2

VI. CONCLUSION AND RECOMMENDATIONS

As we record the work of the biennium, we recognize the unfailing help of the great Head of the Church. The completion of the Survey and the re-organization of the work of the Board constitute items of tremendous importance for the educational program of the Church.

As we survey the facilities in higher education, we have no small degree of pride in what is being accomplished. Our pastors and workers may not have the proper equipment and buildings for service to Lutheran students at non-Lutheran centers; the buildings of our colleges and seminaries may not be as numerous and large as may be desired; the endowments may be pitifully small; but, nevertheless, influences go out from our institutions and student centers to the remotest parts of the world to instruct, to inspire, and to elevate mankind. Just as the pebble cast into the still water of the lake makes ripples which grow smaller as they pass from sight, but which make the material structure of the universe somehow different from what it was before, so the lives touched by our diligent secretaries, by our earnest student pastors, and by our faithful and sacrificing college and seminary teachers touch and inspire other lives in turn until there flows to the outermost circumference of human interest and abode, a stream of significant influence molding the personalities of the youth of the world. As these youths pass through manhood into age, these influences become more precious and significant. *This is our work invisible.* God grant that we shall be given strength and wisdom to direct it aright.

We submit for your prayerful consideration the following

RECOMMENDATIONS

1. *Resolved,* That all congregations of the United Lutheran Church in America be requested to provide in the calendar of the Church Year for a thorough-going observance of the Day of Prayer for all students and all educational institutions; that the Church pledge itself anew to mark the Reformation season as a period of intercession at the throne of grace on the part of those in the Church of Christ who have the spiritual and material welfare of our Church colleges and seminaries and Lutheran students everywhere at heart. (See II. Matters of Public Relations, Sec. 3.)

2. *Resolved,* That the gratitude of the Church be expressed to those thoughtful donors who have made gifts to the work of the Board during the past biennium, and that the attention of all benevolent persons be called to the significant service rendered through the Scholarship and Loan Fund for Women, the Ministerial Education Fund, and the Endowment Fund now being developed by the Board of Education.

(See I. Matters of Administration, Sec. 7; also II. Matters of Public Relations, Sec. 4.)

3. *Whereas,* the Christian culture, for the perpetuation of which our Colleges and Seminaries were founded, is vital to the life of the Church, and

Whereas, the Survey Report reveals the desperate need of greater resources at our educational institutions, if they are to meet the demands of the day and render that distinctive service to both the church and the state, and

Whereas, our colleges and seminaries, quite conscious of their situation and needs, and in harmony with the actions of the United Lutheran Church in America in its conventions at Richmond and Erie, have started and are projecting campaigns to fulfill in larger degree the purpose for which they were founded,

Therefore, Be It Resolved,

That the United Lutheran Church in America, in convention assembled, does hereby call upon the whole membership of the Church, by loyal and whole-hearted co-operation, through prayer and personal effort, to do all within its power to bring these campaigns to successful culmination.

(See II. Matters of Public Relations, Sec. 5, and V. Matters of Institutions, Sec. 4)

4. *Resolved,* That the uniform plan of giving grants to students by synods, as prepared by the secretarial staff of the Board of Education, be approved by the United Lutheran Church in America and recommended for adoption by the respective synods, with such modifications as may be deemed wise to fit the conditions of the various synods, so that this work of the Church may be continued on a more efficient and effective basis.

(See III. Matters of Research, Section 1.)

5. *Resolved,* That a committee, including the secretarial staff of the Board of Education, be appointed to report on

(a) Data concerning the institutional educational policies, programs, and curricula, as they affect the educational program of the parish; and

(b) The possibility of correlation of such policies, programs and curricula of the higher educational institutions of the United Lutheran Church with the parish educational agencies and program.

(See V. Matters of Institutions, Sec. 6)

6. *Whereas,* the Theological Institutions at Kropp and Breklum for almost half a century have sent many consecrated men into the ministry of our Church in America, who have proved a useful addition to our missionary forces and a valuable asset to the life of our Church, and

Whereas, during the past decade changes have taken place, here and abroad, which have made the placing of foreign-trained men in the American ministry increasingly difficult, and the training of a native ministry for our linguistic work imperative, and

Whereas, this changed status is recognized both here and abroad, overtures having been made by the Directorate of Kropp-Breklum tending to the closing of these institutions, and

Whereas, arrangements are proposed to this convention for the training of men for all our linguistic work here in America,

Therefore, Be It Resolved:

(a) That we return thanks to God for the many blessings which our Church in America has received through the faithful work of Kropp and Breklum and for the faithful and efficient corps of workers, who have come to us from these institutions.

(b) That we recognize with gratitude the great debt which our Church in America owes to the sainted founders of these institutions, Johannes Paulsen and Christian Jensen, and to all who like them have labored and sacrificed so much in our service.

(c) That we empower the Board of Education to take the necessary steps leading to the friendly dissolution of our relationship with Kropp-Breklum.

(d) That a copy of these resolutions be sent to the Board of Directors of Kropp-Breklum.

Respectfully submitted for the Board of Education.
A. STEIMLE, *President,*
GOULD WICKEY, *Secretary.*

REPORT OF THE TREASURER OF THE BOARD OF EDUCATION

For the fiscal year ended June 30, 1929

GENERAL ACCOUNT

Balance on hand, July 1, 1928.. $ 13,679.96

RECEIPTS

Treasurer, United Lutheran Church on Apportionment $119,000.00
Treasurer, United Lutheran Church Woman's Missionary Society 3,110.00
Treasurer, United Lutheran Church, Pacific Sem'r'y 149.72
Treasurer, United Lutheran Church, Martin Luther Seminary 6.00
Treasurer, United Lutheran Church, Philadelphia Seminary 3.77

Treasurer, United Lutheran Church, Chicago Sem.	3.77	
Treasurer, United Lutheran Church, Breklum Kropp Seminary	40.00	
Synod of New York and New England (for Boston work)	2,566.52	
Swedish New England Conf. (Augustana) for Boston work	183.68	
Breklum-Kropp Seminary—Board of American Missions	1,500.00	
Pacific Seminary	35.00	
Postage	1.00	
Augustana Synod (for Religious Work in Universities	2,700.00	
Woman's League (New York and Vicinity)	50.00	
Breklum-Kropp Seminary	5.00	
Income, Estate C. D. McLallen, 1928	5.25	
Income from Annuity Fund	3,051.50	
Interest on deposit	352.49	
		132,763.70
		$146,443.66

DISBURSEMENTS

Secretaries' salaries	$ 10,999.92
Secretaries' traveling expenses	2,548.98
Stenographers	2,095.20
Telephone and telegraph	173.33
Office rent	690.00
Postage	491.50
Office supplies	274.87
Student pastors' salaries	12,734.96
Student pastors' expenses	10,187.22
General expenses	3,545.93
Printing and publications	3,000.20
Annuity payments	3,866.75
Accrued interest on annuity investments	54.08
Woman student workers	2,553.02
Board and executive meetings—Expenses	1,372.40
Pacific Seminary—Budget	2,499.96
Pacific Seminary—Special	269.72
Breklum-Kropp Seminary—Budget	7,000.00
Breklum-Kropp Seminary—Special	1,545.00
Waterloo College and Seminary—Budget	3,499.92
Chicago Seminary—Budget	1,500.00
Chicago Seminary—Special	3.77
Saskatoon College and Seminary—Budget	2,499.96
Saskatoon College and Seminary—Special Appro.	2,684.00
Hartwick Seminary—Budget	1,200.00
Southern Seminary—Budget	3,499.92
Marion College—Budget (to extinguish loan)	2,500.00
Martin Luther Seminary—Budget	499.92
Martin Luther Seminary—Special	6.00
Lutheran Theological Seminary, Phila.—Special	3.77
Midland College—Budget	15,999.96
Midland College—Special	2,000.00

Mt. Pleasant Collegiate Institute—Budget 999.96
Newberry-Summerland College—Budget 4,950.00
Muhlenberg College—Budget 1,500.00
Lenoir-Rhyne College—Budget 1,500.00
Wittenberg College—Budget 1,500.00
Roanoke College—Budget 3,900.00
Susquehanna University—Budget 1,500.00
Wagner College—Budget 1,999.92
Thiel College—Budget 1,500.00
Winnipeg Academy 1,999.92
Gettysburg College 1,500.00
Andhra Christian College 3,000.00
Advisory Committee Educational—Year 1930............ 209.23
                                                                                    $127,859.29

Balance, June 30, 1929 .... $ 18,584.37

SCHOLARSHIP AND LOAN FUND FOR WOMEN
Principal Account
Balance, July 1, 1928 .... $ 89.61

RECEIPTS
Repayment of Loans—Miss Betty O. Mullen.............$ 400.00
Miss Mary E. Markley 90.00
Miss Dorothea C. Hess 5.00
Mrs. L. R. Myer (on special deposit)...................... 1,000.00
Proceeds—Bond, City of Mandan, N. D. 1,000.00
                                                                                    $ 2,495.00

                                                                                    $ 2,584.61
Purchased—1,000 Asso. Gas and Electric 5½'s........   1,000.00

Balance, June 30, 1929 .... $ 1,584.61

Income Account
Balance, July 1, 1928 .... $ 392.47

RECEIPTS
Interest on investments ....$ 332.00
Interest on special deposit to May 1, 1929.............. 6.66
                                                                                    338.66

                                                                                    $ 731.13

DISBURSEMENTS
Loan to Gladys Morgan ....$ 300.00
Collection Fee—City of Mandan 1.00
Loan to Hazel Biederbeck 155.00
Accrued interest on bond purchased 26.43
                                                                                    482.43

Balance, June 30, 1929 .... $ 248.70

CALIFORNIA COLLEGE

Balance, July 1, 1928, and June 30, 1929.................. $ 60.00

LUTHERAN WOMAN'S COLLEGE
RECEIPTS
Special Offerings, Sunday Schools, United Lutheran
Church .... $ 1,918.65

Balance, June 30, 1929 .... $ 1,918.65

ANNUITY PRINCIPAL ACCOUNT
Balance, July 1, 1928 .... $ 781.88

RECEIPTS
Annuity bonds issued ....$ 3,100.00
Marion College, for balance of loan............................ 2,500.00
                                                                                                    ————— 5,600.00

                                                                                                    $ 6,381.88

DISBURSEMENTS
Investments made:
3,000 Georgia Power 1st ref. 5's at 88 ....$ 2,943.75
2,000 Asso. Gas and Electric 5½'s, 1938 .... 2,000.00
                                                                                                    ————— 4,943.75

                                                                                                    $1,438.13

PERMANENT MINISTERIAL EDUCATION FUND
Principal Account
Balance, July 1, 1928 .... $ 1,008.84

RECEIPTS
E. C. Miller, Treasurer .... $ 418.72
                                                                                                    —————
                                                                                                    $1,427.56

DISBURSEMENTS
Purchased—1,000 Chicago Post Office 5½'s, 1932........ $ 1,000.00

Balance, June 30, 1929 .... $ 427.56

Income Account
Balance, July 1, 1928 .... $ 718.06

RECEIPTS
Interest on investments 395.00
                                                                                                    —————
                                                                                                    $ 1,113.06

DISBURSEMENTS
Interest accrued on investment..$ 20.02
Appropriation for Student Board 260.40
Appropriation for Student Board—Breklum-Kropp
Seminary 300.00

Appropriation for Student Board—Wittenberg Col.   200.00
Appropriation for Student Board—R. R. Fare............   20.00
                                                                            ――――――
                                                                                            800.42

Balance, June 30, 1929 .... $ 312.64

PACIFIC SEMINARY AND SASKATOON COLLEGE AND SEMINARY

Special Reformation Day Offerings — Sunday
  Schools, United Lutheran Church
  Balance, July 1, 1928 .... $ 366.43

DISBURSEMENTS
Saskatoon College and Seminary 366.00

Balance, June 30, 1929 .... $ .43

INVESTMENTS
ANNUITY FUND

Par Values	Book Values	
$8,000 Altoona Logan Valley Elec. Ry. 4½s, 1933....$	6,400.00	
2,000 Baltimore and Ohio 5's, 1948.............................	1,975.00	
6,500 Bell Telephone Co. of Pa., 5's, 1948................	6,395.00	
1,000 Chesapeake and Ohio Eq. 5's, 1935................	969.67	
1,000 Penna. R. R. Eq. 5's, 1934	992.26	
2,000 Penna. R. R. Eq. 5's 1935	1,965.60	
3,000 Penna. R. R. Eq. 5's 1938.................................	2,974.80	
1,000 Phila. Elec. 5½'s, 1947	1,030.00	
4,600 Phila. Elec. 5's, 1966..	4,574.37	
2,000 Phila. Suburban Water Co. 5's, 1955.............	1,955.00	
4,000 Baltimore and Ohio S. W. Div. 1st 5's, 1950	4,055.00	
13 Shares Western Union Tel. Co.	1,560.00	
1,000 Chelsea Hotel Co. 6's, 1945............................	1,000.00	
3,500 Phila. Elec. Power 1st 5½'s, 1972....................	3,631.25	
5,000 Quaker City Tank Line Eq. 5½'s, 1934........	5,000.00	
4,000 United Post Office Corp, 1st, 5½'s, 1935........	4,000.00	
5,000 Appalachian Elec. Power 1st 5's, 1956............	4,950.00	
2,000 Lackawanna and Wyoming Valley 1st 5's, 1951	1,935.00	
3,000 Georgia Power 1st 5's, 1967.............................	2,943.75	
2,000 Asso. Gas and Elec. 5½'s, 1938........................	2,000.00	
		$ 60,306.70

SCHOLARSHIP AND LOAN FUND FOR WOMEN

1,000 Chesapeake and Ohio Eq. 5's, 1935................$	969.68	
3,000 West Moreland Water Co. 5's, 1952................	2,970.00	
1,000 Lackawanna and Wyoming Valley R. R. 1st 5's, 1951	967.50	
1,000 Asso. Gas and Electric Co. 5½'s, 1938............	1,000.00	
		$ 5,907.18

PERMANENT MINISTERIAL EDUCATION FUND

1,000	Northern States Power Co. 6's, 1948..............$	1,000.00
500	Fort Spring Mag. Dist. Green Briar Co. W. Va. 5's, 1936	500.00
1,000	Phila. Suburban Water Co. 5's, 1955............	977.50
1,000	Phila. Elec. Power Co. 1st 5½'s, 1972............	1,022.50
1,000	Appalachian Elec. Power 1st 5's, 1956............	990.00
2,000	Lackawanna and Wyoming Valley R. R. 5's, 1951	1,935.00
1,000	Chicago Avenue Station Post Office 5½'s, 1932	1,000.00

7,425.00

$ 73,638.88

Respectfully submitted,
JOHN M. SNYDER, *Treasurer.*

Philadelphia, August 22, 1929.
We have audited the accounts of the treasurer of the Board of Education of the United Lutheran Church in America for the year ended June 30, 1929, and have verified the foregoing treasurer's report, pages 1 to 5, both inclusive, and we certify that all recorded receipts have been accounted for, that all disbursements were authenticated and that, in our opinion, the foregoing report is correct.

LYBRAND, ROSS BROS. & MONTGOMERY,
Accountants and Auditors.

REPORT OF THE TREASURER OF THE BOARD OF EDUCATION

Balance Sheet at June 30, 1930

ASSETS

Cash in Bank	$14,788.87
Bond Interest Coupons	985.00
Investments, As Annexed	74,618.88

$90,392.75

FUNDS

General Fund	$10,821.19
Annuity Fund	61,744.83
Scholarship and Loan Fund for Women	7,635.67
Permanent Ministerial Education Fund	8,137.41
Lutheran Women's College Fund	1,993.65
California College Fund	60.00

$90,392.75

CASH ACCOUNTS, BY FUNDS
For the Year Ended June 30, 1930
GENERAL FUND

Balance, July 1, 1929 .... $18,584.37

RECEIPTS

Through the Treasurer, United Lutheran Church:

Apportionment	$126,000.00	
Women's Missionary Society	3,000.00	
Pittsburgh Synod for Saskatoon College and Seminary	26.00	
Synod of Eastern Pennsylvania	100.00	
United Synod of New York, for Boston Work	3,033.27	
Augustana Synod	2,700.00	
Breklum-Kropp Seminary, Board of American Missions	1,500.00	
Income from Annuity Fund	3,209.00	
Interest on Bank Deposits	363.12	
Sale of Report of Committee on Survey of Higher Education	679.90	
Sale of Furniture	106.00	
Transferred from Pacific Seminary and Saskatoon College Fund	.43	
		140,717.72
		$159,302.09

DISBURSEMENTS

Secretaries' Salaries	$18,933.24	
Secretaries' Traveling Expenses	7,121.79	
Stenographers' Salaries	1,762.31	
Student Pastors' Salaries	12,707.97	
Student Pastors' Expenses	10,640.83	
Student Pastors' Traveling Expenses	1,784.93	
Office Rent	1,477.50	
Rent of Dwelling for Executive Secretary	1,200.00	
Expenses, Board and Executive Meetings	605.43	
Students for Ministry, Board and Expenses	1,580.76	
Printing and Mailing, Report of the Committee for Survey of Higher Education	10 011.83	
Printing and Publications	2,253.45	
Telephone and Telegraph	267.74	
Postage	397.34	
Office Equipment	1,394.38	
Office Supplies	557.31	
Advisory Endowment Campaign Committee Expenses.	106.21	
Council of Church Boards of Education	375.00	
Annuity Interest Payments	4,025.15	
Accrued Interest on Investments purchased	8.25	
Transfers to Other Funds	104.62	
Miscellaneous Expenses	1,517.30	
	$78,833.34	

Transfers to Seminaries and Colleges:

Chicago Seminary, Budget	$2,499.96
Hartwick Seminary, Budget	1,200.00
Martin Luther Seminary, Budget	499.92
Saskatoon College and Seminary, Budget.	6,999.96
Southern Theological Seminary, Budget.	3,499.92
Breklum-Kropp Seminary, Budget	6 000.00
Breklum-Kropp Seminary, Specials	1,540.00

Midland College, Budget	12,000.00
Midland College, Specials	2,000.00
Newberry College, Budget	5,400.00
Roanoke College, Budget	3,499.92
Wagner College, Budget	1,699.92
Waterloo College, Budget	4,999.92
Gettysburg College, Budget	1,200.00
Muhlenberg College, Budget	1,200.00
Susquehanna College, Budget	3.000.00
Thiel College, Budget	1,500.00
Wittenberg College, Budget	1,200.00
Lenoir-Rhyne College, Budget	3,499.92
Andhra College, Budget	3,000.00
Mt. Pleasant Collegiate Institute, Budget.	499.92
Winnipeg Academy	1,999.92
Marion College	708.28

$69,647.56

Budget	$66,107.56	
Specials	3,540.00	
		$148,480.90

Balance, June 30, 1930 .... $10,821.19

ANNUITY FUND

Balance, July 1, 1929 .... $1,438.13

DISBURSEMENTS

Investment in 1M Boston Parcel Post Station 1st 5½s, 1935.. $980.00

Balance, June 30, 1930 .... $458.13

SCHOLARSHIP AND LOAN FUND FOR WOMEN

PRINCIPAL

Balance, July 1, 1929, and June 30, 1930 .... $1,584.61

INCOME

Balance, July 1, 1929 .... $248.70

RECEIPTS

Income from Investments	$305.00	
Interest on Special Deposit	40.18	
		345.18

$593.88

DISBURSEMENTS

Loan to Gladys Morgan	$300.00	
Loan to Hazel Biederbeck	150.00	
		450.00

Balance, June 30, 1930 .... $143.88

PERMANENT MINISTERIAL EDUCATION FUND
PRINCIPAL
Balance, July 1, 1929 .... $427.56

RECEIPTS
Treasurer of the United Lutheran Church 53.41

Balance, June 30, 1930 .... $480.9/

INCOME
Balance, July 1, 1929 .... $312.64

RECEIPTS
Income on Investments $395.00

$707.64

DISBURSEMENTS
Appropriation for Student, Breklum-Kropp Seminary. $150.00
Appropriation for Student, Traveling Expenses......   326.20

$476.20

Balance, June 30, 1930..................................... $231.44

LUTHERAN WOMAN'S COLLEGE FUND
Balance, July 1, 1929 .... $1,918.65

RECEIPTS
Special Offerings, Sunday Schools, United Lutheran Church.. $75.00
Balance, June 30, 1930 .... $1,993.65

WATERLOO COLLEGE AND SEMINARY
SPECIAL REFORMATION DAY OFFERING
RECEIPTS
Sundry Contributions $1,233.58
Transferred from General Fund 41.41

$1,275.00

DISBURSEMENTS
Transfer to Waterloo College and Seminary 1,275.00

Balance, June 30, 1930 .... None

BREKLUM-KROPP STUDENT AID FUND
RECEIPTS
Treasurer of the United Lutheran Church $25.00
Sundry Contributions 482.20
Transferred from General Fund 63.20

$570.40

DISBURSEMENTS
Stationery and Printing $12.00
Board and Expenses of Students 558.40

570.40
Balance, June 30, 1930 .... None

PACIFIC SEMINARY AND SASKATOON COLLEGE AND SEMINARY

Balance, July 1, 1929 .... $0.43
Transferred to General Fund .... .43
                                                              _____
Balance, June 30, 1930 .... None

CALIFORNIA COLLEGE FUND
Balance, July 1, 1929, and June 30, 1930 .... $60.00

SUMMARY OF CASH BALANCES AT JUNE 30, 1930
General Fund $10,821.19
Scholarship and Loan Fund for Women 1,728.49
California College Fund 60.00
Lutheran Women's College Fund 1,993.65
Annuity Fund 458.13
Permanent Ministerial Education Fund 712.41
                                                    _____ $15,773.87
Cash in Bank at June 30, 1930 .... $14,788.87
Bond Coupons, Deposited in Bank July 24, 1930.. 985.00
                                                    _____ $15,773.87

ANNUITY FUND

Par Values		Book Values
$8,000	Altoona & Logan Valley Electric Ry. 4½s, 1933	$6,400.00
5,000	Appalachian Electric Power Co., 1st 5s, 1956.	4,950.00
2,000	Associated Gas & Electric Co. 5½, 1938	2,000.00
4,000	Baltimore & Ohio, S. W. Div. 1st 5s, 1950....	4,055.00
2,000	Baltimore & Ohio, S. W. Div. 5s, 1948	1,975.00
6,500	Bell Telephone Co. of Penna. 5s, 1948.........	6,395.00
1,000	Boston Parcel Post Station 5½s, 1935	980.00
1,000	Chelsea Hotel Co. 6s, 1945	1,000.00
1,000	Chesapeake & Ohio R. R. Equip. 5s, 1935....	969.67
3,000	Georgia Power Co. 1st 5s, 1967	2,943.75
2,000	Lackawanna & Wyoming Valley R. R. 1st 5s, 1951	1,935.00
1,000	Pennsylvania R. R. Equip. 5s, 1934	992.26
2,000	Pennsylvania R. R. Equip. 5s, 1935	1,965.60
3,000	Pennsylvania R. R. Equip. 5s, 1938	2,974.80
1,000	Philadelphia Electric Co. 5½s, 1947	1,030.00
4,600	Philadelphia Electric Co. 5s, 1966	4,574.37
3,500	Philadelphia Electric Power Co. 5½s, 1972 ..	3,631.25
2,000	Philadelphia Suburban Water Co. 5s, 1955 ..	1,955.00
5,000	Quaker City Tank Line Equip. 5½s, 1934...	5,000.00
4,000	United Post Offices Corp. 5½s, 1935	4,000.00
13 shs.	Western Union Telegraph Co.	1,560.00
		_____ $61,286.70

SCHOLARSHIP AND LOAN FUND FOR WOMEN

$1,000	Associated Gas & Electric 5½s, 1938	$1,000.00
1,000	Chesapeake & Ohio R. R. Equip. 5s, 1935 ..	969.68
1,000	Lackawanna & Wyoming Valley R. R. 1st 5s, 1951	967.50
3,000	Westmoreland Water Co. 5s, 1952	2,970.00
		_____ 5,907.18

PERMANENT MINISTERIAL EDUCATION FUND

$1,000 Appalachian Power Co. 5s, 1956	$990.00
1,000 Chicago Ave. Station Post Office 5½s, 1932.	1,000.00
500 Fort Spring Magesterial District Greenbriar Co., W. Va., 5s, 1936	500.00
2,000 Lackawanna & Wyoming Valley R. R. 1st 5s, 1951	1,935.00
1,000 Northern States Power 6s, 1948	1,000.00
1,000 Philadelphia Electric Power Co. 5½s, 1972.	1,022.50
1,000 Philadelphia Suburban Water 5s, 1955.......	977.50
	7,425.00

Total Investments $74,618.88

Respectfully submitted,

RALPH DORNFELD OWEN, *Treasurer.*

Philadelphia, July 31, 1930.

We have audited the accounts of the Treasurer of the Board of Education of the United Lutheran Church in America for the year ended June 30, 1930, and have verified the foregoing balance sheet at June 30, 1930, the cash accounts by funds for the year ended June 30, 1930, and the schedule of investments owned at June 30, 1930, and we certify that all recorded receipts have been accounted for, that the disbursements were properly authorized, and that, in our opinion, the foregoing report is correct.

LYBRAND, ROSS BROS. & MONTGOMERY,

Accountants and Auditors.

In connection with this report the Rev. N. J. Gould Wickey, Executive Secretary of the Board, the Rev. E. P. Pfatteicher, representing the board in the matter of Church scholarships, Dean Jessie Trumann, of Grace College, and the Rev. J. C. Kunzmann, of the Pacific Seminary, addressed the Convention.

Resolution 1 was adopted.

Resolution 2 was adopted.

Resolution 3 was adopted.

Resolution 4 was adopted.

The Rev. R. E. Tulloss moved that, in addition to the action approving Resolution No. 4, we request the Board of Education to study the question still further and to bring up at the Convention two years hence any additional suggestions that seem to be wise and good for the guidance of synodical boards of ministerial education. The motion was adopted.

By common consent and the courtesy of the Board of Education, Dr. Robert E. Speer, representing the Federal Council of the Churches of Christ in America, was presented and addressed the Convention.

By request of the President, the Rev. E. B. Burgess replied on behalf of The United Lutheran Church in America.

The Convention resumed consideration of the report of the Board of Education.

Resolution 5 was postponed until the report of the Parish and Church School Board is before the Convention. (See Tuesday's Session, October 14th.—Secretary.)

The Revs. F. Noeldeke, H. W. Harms and E. A. Tappert spoke in appreciation of the assistance which The United Lutheran Church in America has given to the Kropp-Breklum Institute. They raised the question whether some relief might not be extended to Candidate Boettcher, teacher at Kropp.

With the common consent of the Convention, on suggestion of the President, the Board of Education was authorized to consider the special case of Candidate Boettcher and refer it to the Board of Ministerial Pensions and Relief.

Recommendation 6 was adopted and the Convention was led in prayer by the Rev. J. A. W. Haas.

The report of the auditors was accepted.

Item 3 of the report of the Committee on Memorials, which had been deferred, was now taken up. The recommendation of the Committee on Memorials was referred to the Board of Education with power to act.

The recommendation of the Committee on German Interests, which had been deferred, was adopted.

Item IV, B, 6 (b) of the report of the Executive Board, which had been deferred, was adopted.

At five o'clock the Convention adjourned with prayer by the Rev. M. R. Hamsher.

———————•———————

Evening Session

Saturday, October 11, 1930, 8:00 o'clock.
Devotions were conducted by the Rev. N. J. Gould Wickey.

The President called the Convention to order.

The Rev. A. G. Voigt presented the second supplementary report of the Commission of Adjudication.

Second Supplementary Report of the Commission of Adjudication

OPINION OF THE COMMISSION OF ADJUDICATION

In response to questions submitted by resolution of the Convention as follows:

1. *Has the United Lutheran Church in America any authority at all in the matter of organization or location or relocation of theological seminaries?*

2. *Has the United Lutheran Church definitely stated that no synod shall have authority to locate or change a location without the approval of The United Lutheran Church in America?*

OPINION

The two questions, referred to the Commission of Adjudication by resolution of the Convention on Thursday, October 9th, are not mere academic questions as to the respective rights of the United Lutheran Church and its constituent synods in regard to the government and control of theological seminaries. They grew out of an action of the United Synod of New York, which received consideration, but no decision by the Executive Board. The object of the questions evidently is to arrive at some principle, by which the control of theological seminaries may be so directed that more general interests of the whole Church may be conserved. The particular action of the United Synod of New York which raised the issue, was one pertaining to the re-location of the seminary controlled by that body. The questions involved are not merely those of the legal rights of a constituent synod under the constitution of the United Lutheran Church. It is also a question how the exercise of such rights may affect the general welfare and progress of the entire Church.

The question of the legal rights involved " in the matter of organization or location or re-location of theological seminaries" is not difficult to answer.

I.

The first question is: "Has the United Lutheran Church any authority at all in the organization or location or re-location of theological seminaries?" The word "authority" is here used evidently in the sense of mandatory power. Can the United Lutheran Church declare with mandatory power what shall or shall not be done in the management and control of seminaries?

This question was already definitely decided in the formation of the United Lutheran Church. Before the constitution of this body was adopted, after it had been prepared by the Joint Committee on Ways and Means, an interpretation of the one item that apparently refers to theological seminaries, was given by the said Joint Committee. The item of the constitution referred to specifies among the Objects, "The training of ministers and teachers to be witnesses of the Word." The Joint Committee, in reference to this item, passed this resolution:

"*Resolved,* that it is also the judgment of this Joint Committee that Art. VI, Sec. 4, (a) does not authorize the United Lutheran Church in America to establish and control schools of learning and theological seminaries, except in the Foreign Mission field, but that this is the function of the synods constituting the body." See Minutes of Joint Committee, Baltimore, Feb. 6th, 1918, p. 7.

In consequence of this resolution, the United Synod in the South, which owned and controlled a theological seminary, before it entered the Merger, transferred the ownership and control of its seminary to its constituent synods. See the Minutes of the Convention at Salisbury, N. C., in 1917, p. 14. Neither the General Council nor the General Synod owned a seminary.

If there is any possible doubt in regard to the position that the United Lutheran Church has not mandatory authority over the control of theological seminaries, that doubt must vanish in view of the explicit action, taken by that body in its convention of 1922. (See Minutes, p. 471.) With reference to the re-location of the seminary of the Synod of the Northwest, the Buffalo convention adopted this resolution: "That we recognize that the Synod of the Northwest was acting under its constitutional right in re-locating the seminary, but we deplore the fact that the Synod has seen fit to act contrary to the judgment of the Survey Commission, of the Executive Board and of the Board of Education of the United Lutheran Church in America."

Article VIII of the Constitution, on Powers, is also relevant to the question under consideration. Section 4 of that Article declares: "But each Synod retains every power, right and jurisdiction in its own internal affairs not expressly delegated to the United Lutheran Church in America." Under the Constitution no jurisdiction over seminaries is conferred upon the United Lutheran Church. Therefore, in so far as the first question has reference to mandatory authority, the answer to the question, upon the basis of the existing Constitution and By-laws of the U. L. C. A., must be in the negative.

II.

The second question is: "Has the United Lutheran Church definitely stated that no Synod shall have authority to locate or change a location without the approval of the United Lutheran Church in America?"

The answer to this question is implied in the authoritative statements adduced in reference to the first question. So far from the United Lutheran Church having definitely stated that no Synod shall have authority to locate or change a location without its approval, it has definitely stated the very opposite in the resolution adopted at the 1922 Convention, already quoted. There the United Lutheran Church declared that, in the face of the strongest disapprobation of the general body, a synod is still acting within its constitutional rights when it chooses to follow its own counsel in the matter of the location of a seminary.

The action of the United Lutheran Church, on recommendation of the Commission on Theological Education, which is referred to in the resolution offered in the Executive Board, and all similar actions, do not modify in the least the constitutional provisions explicitly recognized in the Buffalo resolution in reference to the Synod of the Northwest. All such resolutions are only advisory in their character, and not mandatory. The very language used in the particular resolution of the Commission on Theological Education above referred to, cited as if giving the United Lutheran Church power to inhibit the location or re-location of a seminary by a synod, is merely advisory in its form. " That it be *the sense of the convention.*" " No synod or group of synods *should* hereafter organize or locate." That is not the language of mandatory law, but of counsel and advice.

Accordingly the answer to the second question must be in the negative.

III.

But the purely legal aspect of the questions presented is not the only one that should be considered. These questions are evidently expressive of a desire for a definition of the relations between the constituent synods and the general body, which will help to secure harmony between the direction and control of theological seminaries and certain general interests of the Church. Here is where the item of the Constitution, Art. VI, Section 4, (a) becomes important. "The Training of ministers and teachers to be witnesses of the Word." The Constitution imposes upon the United Lutheran Church a general responsibility for the training of ministers of the Word of God. The Constitution nowhere specifices how the body is to effect this. But evidently the interests of the constituent synods and of the whole Church, represented in the general body, should be brought into harmony. In respect to this, the Commission of Adjudication cannot give a formal definition of what the relation is. It can only call attention to a few significant things, that show the trend towards such harmonization of the interests of the synods and of the general body.

At first, the United Lutheran Church concerned itself little with theological seminaries; but after a number of years it realized that it needed a policy in the matter of theological education. Accordingly at the Chicago Convention, 1924, a Commission on Theological Education was created. (See Minutes, p. 336.) This Commission has ever since been working on the policy of theological education, and especially on the problem of correlating the theological seminaries with the general interests of the United Lutheran Church. It is true, the recommendations of the Commission on Theological Education can be only advisory, but they are not on that account futile, or without effect.

This advisory power of the United Lutheran Church is commendable and not to be regarded as insignificant. Synods may not always find a way to conform to the advice and counsel of the general body. Nevertheless, there is great moral weight in the expressed judgment of the entire Church, as represented in the general body. It is manifestly helpful in bringing about a harmony between the spirit and methods of theological education in the seminaries and the spirit and aims of the United Lutheran Church. All the synods and all the theological seminaries will undoubtedly approve the important principle enunciated in the report of the Commission on Theological Education submitted to this Convention, that "our Theological seminaries are engaged in the preparation of ministers for the whole Church and not for any section of it only." There ought to be sympathetic understanding and co-operation between the general body and the constituent synods in the training of ministers for the office of the means of grace.

LUTHER KUHLMAN, *Vice President,*
REES EDGAR TULLOSS, *Secretary.*

The President declared that the decision given in this report stands as the judgment of the Church expressed through its Commission of Adjudication and is so received.

Item III, B, 1 (b) of the Executive Board's report, which had been deferred, was called for. The item was received as information.

The Rev. Paul E. Scherer presented the report of the Commission on Lutheran Church Unity, which was received as information.

THE REPORT OF THE COMMISSION ON LUTHERAN CHURCH UNITY

The first meeting of the Commission was held at the Lutheran Theological Seminary, in Philadelphia, May 22nd, 1929, at which time the following resolutions were unanimously adopted.

Resolved: (a) That this Commission shall secure all possible information regarding the various co-operating agencies now functioning between the general Lutheran bodies in Amer.ca, and (b) ascertain what actions have already been taken by general Lutheran bodies looking to union with other such bodies.

Resolved: That this Commission requests the President of The United Lutheran Church in America to inform the Presidents of all the other general Lutheran bodies having similar Commissions or Committees on Lutheran Church Unity of our readiness to confer with said Commissions or Committees.

On January 17, 1930, at 8 P. M., a joint meeting was held with a like Commission from Augustana Synod at the Lutheran Church House, 39 East 35th Street, New York City. After a full, frank, and free discussion the following resolutions were passed without a dissenting vote:

Whereas, We believe that the next step toward that more complete bringing together of all the general Lutheran bodies in America, which so many deeply long for, should be a closer union of the Augustana Synod and The United Lutheran Church in America, *Be it*

Resolved: That we, in joint session of the Commissions on Lutheran Church Unity of the Augustana Synod and of the United Lutheran Church in America, look with favor upon any measures that look toward and may help forward such closer union or co-operation between these bodies as may upon further study seem feasible. *And be it further*

Resolved: That we ask the Chairmen of the two Commissions to appoint a sub-committee to consider the matter further, and to report to this Joint Committee on a date to be set by them.

The meeting of the sub-committee was held in Chicago, April 8, 1930. It was recommended:

1. That existing lines of co-operation between the two bodies should be strengthened and extended.

2. That the Boards and local organizations of both bodies be instructed to seek such further co-operations as are possible.

3. With regard to the matter of organic union of the two bodies, the Augustana Synod representatives requested the privilege of asking for instructions from their Synod before proceeding to the formulation of definite plans. To this request the United Lutheran Church representatives unanimously agreed.

On Saturday, June 7, 1930, the following action was taken by Augustana:

"1. *Be It Resolved,* That we as a Synod join with the American Lutheran Conference, to go into effect when three or more of the following groups unite, namely, The Norwegian Lutheran Church, The Joint Synod of Ohio, The Lutheran Free Church, The Iowa Synod, The United Danish Church, and the Buffalo Synod.

"2. We also heartily endorse the proposed Constitution and By-Laws of the American Lutheran Conference.

"3. That the Synod declares to the Church Unity Committee: The Synod desires that the Committee should concern itself in the main with methods of closer co-operation of the Augustana Synod and the United Lutheran Church."

Respectfully submitted,
PAUL SCHERER, *Chairman.*
W. A. GRANVILLE, *Secretary.*
R. E. TULLOSS.
C. M. JACOBS.
E. F. EILERT.
J. K. JENSEN.

Dr. Scherer also presented the following:

ADDITIONAL REPORT OF THE COMMISSION ON LUTHERAN CHURCH UNITY

Whereas, certain propositions have come before the Commission on Church Unity with regard to missionary operations among the Finns in Canada looking toward the organization of a Finnish Synod in connection with the United Lutheran Church, and

Whereas, the congregations that would be included in the proposed synod are too few in number and too widely separated to enable such a synod to be efficient, therefore we recommend that

1. The United Lutheran Church through the Board of American Missions offer to finance the Finnish work in Canada on the condition that existing and prospective Finnish congregations unite with the existent synods of the United Lutheran Church on whose territory they are located. In order to provide helpful contact between these Finnish congregations it is recommended also that they be permitted to establish among themselves a Finnish Conference.

2. We recommend further that the Board of American Missions be authorized at its discretion to continue its present support to the Suomi Synod for the coming biennium, thereafter decreasing it annually at the rate of twenty-five per cent for four years unless otherwise instructed by the United Lutheran Church.

3. Meanwhile we recommend that the Boards of Foreign Missions and of Education, and the Committees on Church Papers, Young People's Work and Brotherhoods be requested to seek all possible cooperation with the Suomi Synod.

4. We recommend further that the United Lutheran Church in convention assembled once more put itself on record as frankly desiring and continuing earnestly to invite an ever increasing measure of co-operation with the other general bodies of Lutherans in America, holding itself as cordially ready to welcome approach and eager to make it, wherever there seems to be any disposition to regard either further cooperation or actual organic union as desirable.

5. Finally we recommend that in the event of the acceptance of our invitation to organic union on the part of the Icelandic Synod at any meeting held prior to the next biennial convention of The United Lutheran Church in America, the Executive Board be formally authorized, upon notification of their action, to receive the Icelandic Synod into temporary membership as a constituent synod of The United Lutheran Church in America until the next convention, the Executive Board meanwhile providing such information to the officers of the Icelandic Synod as may be requested, and seeking to develop all possible lines of cooperation.

PAUL SCHERER.

Recommendations 1, 2, 3, 4 and 5 were adopted.

The Convention resumed consideration of the report of the Commission on Investment of Endowments.

Recommendations 1 to 11 were adopted.

Under consideration of Recommendation 12, it was moved and carried that the words "under proper legal advice" be inserted after the word "instructed." Recommendation 12 was adopted as amended.

At this point the President introduced the Rev. J. J. Scherer, Jr., President of the Synod of Virginia, who addressed the Convention in recognition of the centennial of the Virginia Synod.

Tellers Committee No. 2 announced that it was ready to report on elections of the day.

Upon suggestion of the President, it was moved and carried that in cases in which an election had not been consummated, the balloting in a future election be limited to the two men having received the highest number of votes short of a majority.

Mr. Wm. H. Menges, chairman of the committee, then reported elections as follows:

For the *Board of Foreign Missions* each of the following received a majority of the votes cast:

Rev. Oscar A. Benson	Rev. J. L. Morgan
Rev. E. E. Fischer	Rev. Clarence M. Snyder
Rev. G. Albert Getty	Rev. H. W. Snyder

The President declared them elected and stated that there was one layman yet to be elected.

For the *Board of Northwestern Missions* each of the following received a majority of the votes cast:

Rev. G. A. Benze   Rev. Jacob Maurer
Rev. H. W. A. Hanson   Mr. A. Raymond Bard
Rev. J. B. Markward   Mr. Grant Hultberg
Mr. H. L. Snyder

The President declared them elected.

For the *Immigrants Mission Board* each of the following received a majority of the votes cast:

Rev. H. W. A. Hanson   Mr. A. Raymond Bard
Rev. J. B. Markward   Mr. Grant Hultberg

The President declared them elected.

For the *West Indies Mission Board* each of the following received a majority of the votes cast:

Rev. G. A. Benze   Rev. Jacob Maurer
Rev. H. W. A. Hanson   Mr. A. Raymond Bard
Rev. J. B. Markward   Mr. Grant Hultberg
Mr. H. L. Snyder

The President declared them elected.

For the *Board of Education* each of the following received a majority of the votes cast:

Rev. H. J. Black   Rev. W. H. Greever
Rev. Franklin K. Fretz   Mr. Henry Wolf Bikle
Rev. Howard R. Gold   Mr. Frederick Henrich
Prof. R. S. Saby

The President declared them elected.

For the *Inner Mission Board* each of the following received a majority of the votes cast:

Rev. G. H. Bechtold   Rev. P. D. Brown
Rev. Herman Brezing   Mr. Carl M. Distler
Mr. T. C. Rohrbaugh

The President declared them elected.

For the *Board of Publication* each of the following received a majority of the votes cast:

Rev. Oscar F. Blackwelder   Mr. L. Russell Alden
Rev. S. W. Herman   Mr. F. Wm. Cappelmann
Rev. J. J. Scherer, Jr.   Mr. E. G. Hoover

The President declared them elected and stated that there was one layman yet to be elected.

For the *Board of Ministerial Pensions and Relief* each of the following received a majority of the votes cast:

Rev. Ross H. Stover   Mr. H. J. Herbst
Mr. W. A. Granville   Mr. W. T. Stauffer

The President declared them elected and stated that there was one clergyman yet to be elected.

For the *Parish and Church School Board* each of the following received a majority of the votes cast:

Rev. Paul. H. Heisey   Rev. George H. Rhodes
                 Rev. Wm. C. Schaeffer, Jr.

The President declared them elected and stated that there was one layman yet to be elected.

For the *Board of Deaconess Work* each of the following received a majority of the votes cast:

Rev. Allen L. Benner   Rev. L. A. Thomas
Rev. C. T. Benze   Mr. E. S. Gerberich
                 Mr. Frederick J. Singley

The President declared them elected.

At 10:30 o'clock the Convention adjourned with prayer by the Rev. Alvin E. Bell.

SUNDAY SERVICE

A Mission Service under the auspices of the Board of American Missions and the Board of Foreign Missions was held on Sunday evening, October 12, 1930, at 8:00 o'clock in the Evangelical Lutheran Church of the Reformation, Milwaukee, Wis., the Rev. Paul R. Siebert, D.D., pastor.

The Rev. J. Luther Sieber, representing the Board of ,Foreign Missions, introduced the Rev. Paul Koller, D.D., Executive Secretary. Dr. Koller called upon the Rev. Paul Matchetzki from the mission field in South America and Mr. V. Ch. John, from the mission field in India, who addressed the congregation.

The Rev. J. Bradley Markward, D.D., President of the Board of American Missions, introduced the Rev. F. F. Fry, D.D., Executive Secretary, who introduced Mr. Malcolm Mitchell and the Rev. Wm. H. Gable from the Rocky Boy Mission and the

Rev. Wm. G. Arbaugh from the Porto Rican Missions, each of whom addressed the congregation.

Following these addresses the Rev. Frederick H. Knubel, D.D., LL.D., S.T.D., elected for the seventh term as President of The United Lutheran Church in America, was inducted into his office. The induction was conducted by the Rev. M. G. G. Scherer, D.D., Secretary of the United Lutheran Church in America. President Knubel was presented by Dr. E. Clarence Miller, Treasurer, and the Rev. P. A. Kirsch, assistant secretary for the Convention.

FIFTH MEETING
Morning Session

HOTEL SCHROEDER
Milwaukee, Wisconsin.
Monday, October 13, 1930, 8:45 o'clock.

Matins were conducted by the Rev. C. J. Shealy.

The Convention was called to order by the President.

The Minutes of the Saturday morning, afternoon and evening sessions were read by the assistant secretary and approved.

The President called attention to the fact that the auditors' reports had not been acted upon in connection with the treasurers' reports. By general consent the Secretary was authorized to insert, at the proper place in connection with each such report, a note to the effect that the report of the auditors was accepted.

The President announced the death of the Rev. W. L. Hunton of the Board of Publication and the Secretary was directed to send expressions of sympathy to Mrs. Hunton.

The Secretary was also instructed to convey to the Rev. A. Homrighaus the sympathy of the Church in his illness.

Mr. Wm. H. Menges reported for Tellers Committee No. 2 as follows:

For the *Board of American Missions* each of the following received a majority of the votes cast:

Rev. G. A. Benze   Rev. Jacob Maurer
Rev. H. W. A. Hanson   Mr. A. Raymond Bard
Rev. J. B. Markward   Mr. Grant Hultberg
          Mr. H. L. Snyder

The President declared them elected.

For the *National Lutheran Home for the Aged* each of the following received a majority of the votes cast:

Rev. Henry Anstadt	Rev. John Weidley
Rev. Oscar F. Blackwelder	Mr. L. Russell Alden
Rev. J. L. Frantz	Dr. W. K. Butler
Rev. J. E. Harms	Mr. F. E. Cunningham
Rev. J. T. Huddle	Mr. Harry T. Domer
Rev. Richard Schmidt	Mr. W. H. Finckel
Rev. H. E. Snyder	Mr. John H. Jones
Rev. F. R. Wagner	Mr. F. W. Kakel

Mr. H. L. Snyder

The President declared them elected.

The Convention then proceeded to elect further members of the Board of Foreign Missions, Board of Publication, Board of Ministerial Pensions and Relief, and the Parish and Church School Board.

The Rev. N. R. Melhorn, Secretary of the Board of Publication, read a letter from Dr. E. F. Eilert, the President, expressing regret at his inability to be present at the Convention. Dr. Melhorn then presented the report of the Board of Publication and introduced Dr. Grant Hultberg, who addressed the Convention.

REPORT OF THE BOARD OF PUBLICATION

The depression, or business readjustment, prevalent throughout the country during the latter portion of the biennium has made itself felt in the publication business of the Board. But because of the constant and generous support of our constituency, the Board's business has suffered only a slight decrease during the period from July 1, 1928, to June 30, 1930.

We, like all the agencies of the Church, are eager to report continuous expansion. This we can do, for while the volume of current business does not show a percentage of increase over previous totals, very favorable general progress has been made in the field of equipment. An opportunity was given us to complete the building program, which has been a part of our policy since 1922, and we took advantage of it. The Muhlenberg Building was planned to serve the Church administrative agencies. Its use for the mechanical operations of printing and publishing was temporary. We are happy to report the realization of our building program. Adequate office space is now available at 13th and Spruce street, Philadelphia, and we have, in addition, a building for printing which is convenient, suitable for the expansion in business that is imminent, and deemed sure to enhance in value.

NEW MANUFACTURING PLANT

The opportunity was offered in the fall of 1928 to acquire a plot of ground in West Philadelphia adequate for the erection of a printing plant that would provide better manufacturing facilities and at the same time release additional space in the Muhlenberg Building for offices, and accommodations for church organizations requiring increased space. Accordingly, a plot of ground known as Nos. 5001-5011 Lancaster avenue, in West Philadelphia, was purchased in January, 1929, for a price of $48,000 This plot has a frontage of 98 feet on Lancaster avenue, and extends 186½ feet along 50th street to Merion avenue in the rear, thus giving a frontage on three streets, one of them the Philadelphia connection with the Lincoln Highway. On the Lancaster avenue frontage there was a one-story factory building, 50 feet in depth. Architects were then engaged to prepare plans for a two-story manufacturing plant, and in December 1929, contract was let for the erection of a building 98 x 135 feet, two stories and basement, concrete, brick and steel construction, at a cost slightly over $136,000. This building was almost completed at the close of the biennium, and is now being used by our printing plant and bindery. A new press and a new folding machine have been added to our equipment to replace old machinery long in use.

NEW BOOKS

A number of new books have been issued during the biennium. Particular attention is called to the following: "The Family Service Book," prepared by the Common Service Book Committee, and issued at the time of the Erie Convention; "Administering God's Gifts," by George L. Rinkliff, a book on Stewardship; "What Ought I to Believe," by the Rev. J. A. W. Haas, D.D., "Light on the Gospels," by the Rev. Abel Ahlquist, Ph.D., a collection of sermon illustrations; "The Christ Who Is All," by the Rev. A. J. Traver, General Secretary of the Luther League; "My Saviour," a series of Lenten Meditations by the Rev. Gerhard E. Lenski; "The Vestryman," a book dealing with the office, duties and privileges of members of the church council, by the Rev. C. P. Swank, S. T. D.; "Lutheran Makers of America," a collection of short biographical sketches of noted men of Colonial times, by the Rev. Ira O. Nothstein, D.D.; and "A Manual on Worship," by the Rev. Paul Z. Strodach, D.D.

The Religious Education Texts series for Vacation and Weekday Church Schools has been completed by the publication of "God's Good Gifts," for the Pupil and Teacher, by Mrs. Mabel B. Fenner, and "God Working Through Mankind," for the Pupil and Teacher, by Miss Eva M. Stilz. The series for the Vacation Church Schools has also been completed by the publication of "Jesus and His Followers," and "Stories of Early Church Heroes," by Mrs. Maude Junkin Baldwin.

A new hymnal for the Primary and Junior Departments, entitled "The Children's Hymnal and Service Book," compiled by the Common Service Book Committee and the Parish and Church School Board, was published at the close of the first year of the biennium, and has been received with enthusiasm.

"The Lesson Commentary," on Uniform Sunday School lessons, has been issued each year. The volume for 1931 is now ready.

"The Year Book," edited by the Rev. George H. Schnur, D.D., has appeared each year, and will soon be ready for 1931.

The fourth volume in the Key Book series, entitled "The Ministry of Love," dealing with the work of the Inner Missions, by the Rev. Foster U. Gift, D.D., has come from our press.

A Christmas pageant entitled "The Prince of Peace," by the Rev. Eilert C. Nielsen, was published in 1928; and another similar pageant entitled "The Angels' Christmas," by the Rev. Wilfried Tappert, was issued in the fall of 1929.

A German edition of the Constitution for Congregations has been made available.

The total of new books published during the biennium amounts to 175,400 copies.

BOOKS REPRINTED

Under this classification may be mentioned "The Way;" "The Pupil and the Teacher," in the new partly revised edition; "Our Home Altar;" "Introduction to the Epistles and Gospels;" "Martin of Mansfeld;" "Introits and Graduals, Part I;" "The Conservative Reformation;" and "Lutheran Landmarks and Pioneers."

"The Common Service Book" and the "Kirchenbuch" have been reprinted in several editions. "The Book of Worship" has also been reissued.

The total number of volumes of reprinted books amounts to 309,150.

PAMPHLETS AND TRACTS

New pamphlets and tracts have been issued in a total number of 452,000, and previously issued similar publications have been reprinted in a quantity of 178,000.

Children's Services for Christmas, Easter, Children's Day and Rally Day have been issued each year; and the Church Year Calendar has been continued as before.

HYMNALS

Work on the new editions of the Common Service Book with music, authorized by the Erie Convention, was started immediately after the close of the Convention. A revised edition, with the words below the music, and also an edition with from one to three stanzas of the hymns between the staves of the music, were ready for distribution early in March, this year. Both editions harmonize with the original issues in every respect, except for the changes authorized at Erie. With the printing of these two new editions, the total number of Common Service Books printed in the various editions, text and music, reached the total figure of 599,000.

An Altar edition of the Common Service was published in April, this year. This book is printed in large type, on heavy white paper, and bound in red as well as black Morocco. It contains the parts of the Common Service Book used at the altar, designated by the Common Service Book Committee, and is virtually a reprint of the Text edition of the Common Service Book up to and including the Psalms, with the exception of the "Sentences for the Seasons," and the "Invitatories, Antiphones, Responsories and Versicles."

The Occasional Services

The additional services and offices, prepared by the Common Service Book Committee, as authorized by the Erie Convention, were included in two new editions of "The Occasional Services," published in the spring of this year—one printed on thin Bible paper and bound in a flexible full Morocco, and another one printed on heavier paper and bound in a semi-flexible Morocco.

Periodicals

The various periodicals mentioned in the previous report have all been continued throughout the biennium. The total circulation was, at the end of the last fiscal year 857,500 copies, showing a slight increase over the previous biennium.

Graded Lessons

The new graded series for our Church Schools, which is being prepared by the Parish and Church School Board, and which is to be known as the Christian Life Series, was expected to be ready for the first of October, this year. Unforeseen difficulties were, however, encountered, which made it impossible for the Parish and Church School Board to furnish the material as early as anticipated. Publication of the series has, therefore, been postponed to the fall of 1931. In the meantime we will be able to continue to furnish the schools the material they have been procuring from us (until October, 1931). After that date the old International Graded Series will no longer be available, and it is anticipated that the Lutheran Graded Series will also be discontinued, except the portion now available in bound form.

Church Papers

The Lutheran and *Lutherischer Herold* have been published regularly each week during the biennium. Unfortunately both of these papers, which serve as the official organs of the Church, have encountered a decrease in circulation, particularly during the latter half of the fiscal year just closed. *The Lutheran,* which has the larger circulation, has suffered more than the *Herold*, with the smaller circulation, although the percentage of loss is about the same for both papers.

On August first, next year, it will be one hundred years since the first number of the *Lutheran Observer* was issued. Published first as a semimonthly, and then as a bi-weekly, the *Observer* became a weekly in its third year, and continued as such until in our day when it was merged with the *Lutheran Church Work* into the *Lutheran Church Work and Observer*, and then in 1919 combined with *The Lutheran* and *The Lutheran Church Visitor* in the present *The Lutheran*. While the *Observer* was not the first Lutheran religious journal published in this country in English, it was the first one to become a weekly, and the only one of those early Lutheran journals to continue publication into the twentieth century.

The Church papers are of such vital importance to the Church and its work that we believe that the Church would serve its own interest well if it were to celebrate this centenary of one of the forerunners of our Church papers by an intensive and concerted effort to increase the circulation of *The Lutheran* and the *Herold*. Both papers ought, in our opinion, to have a much wider circulation than they have today, and than we have been able to secure for them through the efforts of our Circulation Department, and the many untiring supporters of the papers throughout the Church.

LUTHER'S WORKS

This year in which we celebrate the Four-Hundredth Anniversary of the Augsburg Confession will undoubtedly see the completion of Luther's Works in English, which has been under way now many years. The publication of this set, of which two volumes appeared about fifteen years ago, has suffered many interruptions and encountered unusual delays. The manuscript is, however, now nearly completed, and two additional volumes are already in type.

GENERAL BUSINESS

The accompanying reports of the Business Manager, Mr. Grant Hultberg, and the Treasurer, Mr. John M. Snyder, give figures in detail of the business done during the biennium.

ORGANIZATION

Our Board has continued to meet regularly four times each year. The Executive Committee has met monthly with but two exceptions. It is almost needless to repeat that these meetings have been well attended, and that the Board has conducted your business with unanimity and close attention to all its details.

The organization meeting for the biennium was held on October 30, 1928, and the officers have been the following: Hon E. F. Eilert, C.S.D., President; Mr. D. F. Yost, Vice President; the Rev. N. R. Melhorn, D.D., Litt.D., Secretary; and Mr. John M Snyder, Treasurer.

The Board has sustained the loss of one of its members by death during the biennium. Mr. George D. Boschen died on June 30, 1929. He was a member of the General Council Board of Publication at the time of the merger, and has been a member of this Board from its organization. He cheerfully gave of his time to the work of the Board, and his counsels were of inestimable value.

The Rev. William Lee Hunton, Ph.D., D.D., after an illness extending over nearly two years, died October 12, 1930. From the organization of the Board of Publication until May 1, 1930, he occupied the position of Literature Manager.

Dr. Hunton gave his office the benefit of a long period of previous experience. He was diligent in the performance of his duties, consecrated to the Christian faith involved, courteous to his fellow-workers and a valuable factor in the advances made by this Board.

The Board desires to register in the official records of the United Lutheran Church its consciousness of the devoted service rendered by Dr. Hunton.

STANDING COMMITTEES

The various standing committees have been made up as follows:

Executive Committee: E. F. Eilert, D. F. Yost, N. R. Melhorn, John M. Snyder, C. M. Jacobs, Stanley Billheimer, Croll Keller, O. W. Osterlund and Charles Baum.

Religious Literature: C. M. Jacobs, F. P. Manhart and A. H. Holthusen.

Secular Literature: Stanley Billheimer, Charles F. Steck and H. C. Alleman.

Manufacture and Sales: Croll Keller, G. D. Boschen and Kenneth Baker.

Real Estate and Accounting: O. W. Osterlund, F. William Cappelmann and Charles Baum.

TERMS EXPIRING WITH THIS CONVENTION

Those whose terms expire at this time are: The Rev. F. P. Manhart, D.D., the Rev. N. R. Melhorn, D.D., Litt.D., the Rev. Charles F. Steck, D.D., Hon. E. F. Eilert, C. S. D., F. William Cappelmann, Esq., and Mr. Kenneth Baker.

The term of Mr. George D. Boschen would also have expired at this time.

The Board has placed in nomination the following: Rev. Oscar F. Blackwelder, D.D., Rev. S. W. Herman, D.D., Rev. Emil W. Weber, Mr. F. William Cappelmann, Mr. Einar Schatvet, Mr. W. G. Semisch, and L. Russel Alden, Esq.

The Board deeply appreciates the confidence placed in it by the Church, and the support and encouragement given by the pastors, members and organizations of our congregations. This has been a great source of help to us and the employes of the Board in our work.

RECOMMENDATIONS

1. Recommended, that the proposed celebration of the centennial of the *Lutheran Observer* by a concerted effort to increase the circulation of *The Lutheran* and *Lutherischer Herold,* be commended to the synods, pastors, congregations and members of The United Lutheran Church in America for their support and co-operation, so that the influence and circulation of our Church papers may be greatly increased.

2. Recommended, that until the new Christian Life Course for our Church Schools is ready in the fall of 1931, we urge our Schools to make use of the material now issued by the Publication Board, and that when this new course is available in September, 1931, the Sunday Schools of the United Lutheran Church be requested to adopt for use both the Christian Life Graded Course and the Augsburg Uniform Lesson Series.

E. F. EILERT, *President.*
NATHAN R. MELHORN, *Secretary.*

CONSOLIDATED PROFIT AND LOSS ACCOUNT
For the Year Ended June 30, 1929

Gross Sales of Books, Periodicals, etc.	$712,964.41	
Less Returns, Allowances and Discounts	12,640.76	
Net Sales		700,323.65
Cost of Sales:		
Purchases of Materials, Printing and Binding	$303,022.59	
Printing Department Wages and Editorial Salaries	112,185.73	
Authors and Contributors	12,951.27	
Royalties	1,386.47	
Shipping, Freight, Mailing and Postage	45,457.75	
Rent	27,000.00	
General Manufacturing Expenses	3.253.02	
Insurance	1,916.66	
Depreciation on Machinery, etc.	12,007.59	
		519,181.08
Deduct:		
Sales of Waste, etc.	$3.037.08	
Discounts on Purchases	1,091.89	
Increase in Inventories	20,606.06	
	24,735.03	
		494,446.05
Gross Profit on Sales		$205,877.60
Selling, Administrative and General Expenses:		
Executive and Office Salaries	$73,092.54	
Office Supplies and Expenses	2,969.72	
Expenses of Board Meetings, etc.	885.45	

Telephone, Telegraph and Messenger		1,292.27
Advertising		1,293.91
Legal and Auditing		1,730.92
Memberships		1,591.00
Traveling Expenses		3,931.71
Commissions to Agents		557.38
General Expense		6,693.04
Branch Offices:		
Rentals	$5,050.00	
Postage	2,494.04	
Freight, Hauling, Shipping, etc.......	1,765.42	
Insurance	400.93	
Taxes	249.60	
Light	136.70	
		10,096.69
Uncollectible Notes and Accounts Receivable Written Off		847.64
Depreciation of Furniture and Fixtures		3,629.53
Appropriations:		
The United Lutheran Church	$51,573.37	
Ministerial Pensions	20,000.00	
Historical Society	500.00	
		72,073.37
Pensions		1,550.00
Loss of Furniture and Fixtures Sold		188.38
Lancaster Avenue Property Expenses		934.84
		183,358.39
		22,519.21
Other Income:		
Net Income from Buildings	$3,980.22	
Interest on Investments	5,562.64	
Interest on Bank Balances	5,053.73	
		14,596.59
Net Profit		$37,115.80

CONSOLIDATED PROFIT AND LOSS ACCOUNT
For the Year Ended June 30, 1930

Gross Sales of Books, Periodicals, etc.	$707,446.48	
Less Returns, Allowances and Discounts	12,770.40	
Net Sales		$694,676.08
Cost of Sales:		
Purchases of Materials, Printing and Binding ..	284,441.69	
Printing Department Wages and Editorial Salaries.	104,354.01	
Authors and Contributors	12,241.50	
Royalties	1,385.21	
Shipping, Freight, Mailing and Postage	43,347.58	
Rent	27,000.00	
General Manufacturing Expenses	2,718.92	
Insurance	2.174.14	
Depreciation on Machinery, etc.	12,352.34	
		490,015.39

Deduct:
Sales of Waste, etc. $2,794.41
Discounts on Purchases 1,358.31
——————   4,152.72

485,862.67
Decrease in Inventories 9,052.82
——————— 494,915.49

Gross Profit on Sales $199,760.59

Selling, Administrative and General Expenses:
Executive and Office Salaries $72,649.77
Office Supplies and Expenses 2,700.61
Expenses of Board Meetings, etc. 810.35
Telephone, Telegraph and Messenger 1,212.83
Advertising 1,471.50
Legal and Auditing 1,757.46
Memberships 1,295.00
Traveling Expenses 1,968.35
Commissions to Agents 118.97
General Expense 7,662.11
Branch Offices:
Rentals $5,050.00
Postage 2,837.84
Freight, Hauling, Shipping, etc. 1,494.39
Insurance 457.38
Taxes 285.90
Light 131.69
——————   10,257.20
Uncollectible Notes and Accounts Receivable
Written Off 2,051.26
Depreciation of Furniture and Fixtures 3,711.10
"Christian Life Series," Salaries and Expenses.. 8,353.30
Appropriation: Ministerial Pensions 20,000.00
Pensions 1,883.34
Loss on Furniture and Fixtures Sold 169.88
Lancaster Avenue Property Expenses 1,428.75
——————— 139,501.78

60,258.81

Other Income:
Net Income from Buildings 3,574.58
Interest on Investments 6,496.22
Interest on Bank Balances 7,035.78
——————   17,106.58

77,365.39
Adjustment of Prepaid Subscription to Periodicals for the cur-
rent and Prior Years to Amounts Received Therefor 40,238.82
———————
Net Profit, After Adjustment $37,126.57

BUSINESS MANAGER'S REPORT OF ASSETS AND LIABILITIES

As of June 30, 1930

ASSETS

Cash in Banks and on Hand			$167,104.27
Notes Receivable		$93.00	
Accounts Receivable:			
Merchandise	$156,842.37		
Advertising	2,626.66		
Rents	420.00		
		159,889.03	
		159,982.03	
			149,982.03
Less, Allowance for Doubtful Accounts		10,000.00	
Accrued Interest on Investments			1,721.59
Merchandise and Stock on Hand in Philadelphia and Branch Houses			267,055.55
Securities, at Market Values, June 30, 1930			128,968.00
			714,831.44
Legacies and Bequests, with Accumulations (John M. Snyder, Treas.)			8,230.45
Prepaid Insurance			4,117.85
Plant and Equipment:			
Land		$261,859.50	
Buildings, Machinery and Equipment	$851,267.30		
Less, Allowance for Depreciation	189,071.68		
		662,195.62	
			924,055.12
			$1,651,234.86

LIABILITIES

Accounts Payable, net			$40,490.92
Accrued Salaries, Royalties and Taxes			3,351.94
Amount due Subscribers on Subscriptions for Periodicals		$97,910.15	
Prepaid Advertising		84.00	
			97,994.15
Legacies and Bequests, with Accumulations (John M. Snyder, Treas.			8,230.45
Net Assets			1,501,167.40
			$1,651,234.86

Respectfully submitted,

GRANT HULTBERG, *Business Manager*

SUMMARY OF TREASURER'S CASH ACCOUNT

Balance, July 1, 1928 .... $1,786.22

Receipts:

	Year ended June 30, 1929	Year ended June 30, 1930
Income from Investments.......	275.00	$348.89
Interest on Bank Balances.....	85.89	35.86
David W. Beidle bequest.......	200.00	
	$560.89	$384.75

945.64

$2,731.86

	Year ended June 30, 1929	Year ended June 30, 1930

Disbursements:

Investments purchased:

1,000 Illinois Central Eq. 5s, 1933		$996.59
1,000 Chicago, Rock Island and Pacific 5s, 1933		994.82

1,991.41

Balance, June 30, 1930 .... $740.45

SUMMARY OF TREASURER'S PERMANENT FUNDS

June 30, 1930

ASSETS

Cash $740.45

Bonds, at Market Value, June 30, 1930:

1000 Western New York & Penna. 5s, 1937	$1,010.00
1000 Lehigh Valley R. R. Co. 4½s, 2003	990.00
4000 Altoona & Logan Valley Elec. Ry. Co. 4½s, 1933	3,480.00
1000 Chicago, Rock Island and Pacific Eq. Tr. 5s, 1933	1,000.00
1000 Illinois· Central Eq. Tr. 5s, 1933	1,010.00

7,490.00

$8,230.45

LIABILITIES

Funds:

John Rung Legacy	$3,000.00
David W. Beidle Bequest	200.00

3,200.00

Accumulated Profits, Appreciation of Securities and Accumulated Income 5,030.45

$8,230.45

Respectfully submitted,
JOHN M. SNYDER, *Treasurer.*

Philadelphia, July 31, 1930.

We certify that we have examined the accounts of the Board of Publication of The United Lutheran Church in America for the two years ended June 30, 1930, and that the foregoing statements, in our opinion, correctly set forth its financial condition at June 30, 1930, and the results of its operation for the two years ended June 30, 1930.

LYBRAND, ROSS BROS. & MONTGOMERY,
Accountants and Auditors.

Permission was granted the Board of Publication to add to the official minutes a paragraph referring to the services of Dr. Hunton.

Resolution 1 adopted.

Resolution 2 adopted.

The auditors' report was accepted.

The Rev. R. E. Tulloss then moved the following resolution which was adopted:

Resolved: In order to promote among the members of the congregations greater familiarity with the principles and work of the United Lutheran Church, its boards and committees;

In order to assist in spreading knowledge of the truths of the Bible, provide information concerning the Lutheran Church at home and abroad, and news of interest and value;

In order to complement other efforts to increase support of the Christian work in which we are locally and generally engaged;

The United Lutheran Church approves the recommendation of the Board of Publication to mark the centennial of the first issue of the *Lutheran Observer* by a church-wide effort to increase the number of subscribers to *The Lutheran* and the *Lutherischer Herold,* and requests the delegates of this Convention and the synods they represent to commend these journals to the patronage of all their people.

It authorizes the Board of Publication to bring this action to the attention of pastors and church councils and to arrange for the reception of subscriptions.

The Rev. E. E. Fischer presented the report of the Common Service Book Committee.

REPORT OF THE COMMON SERVICE BOOK COMMITTEE

Three meetings of the Common Service Book Committee have been held during the biennium—on January 10th and 11th, 1929, April 30th and May 1st, 1929, and October 8th and 9th, 1929—all in the Muhlenberg Building, Philadelphia, Pennsylvania. At the first meeting Doctor Luther D. Reed was elected Chairman, and Doctor G. Albert Getty, Secretary. A number of subjects of interest to the Church have occupied the attention of the Committee, and a large amount of work involving research and patient study on the part of sub-committees has been accomplished. The detailed reports of these several sub-committees have been thoroughly discussed by the entire Committee, and the final results appear in several works of outstanding importance to the whole Church.

New Music Editions of the Common Service Book

In conformity with the action of the Erie Convention two new editions of the Common Service Book with music have been issued. In one of these the form of the pages in the former edition has been preserved but the Appendix has been omitted and the changes in the tunes recommended two years ago by this Committees and approved by the United Lutheran Church in convention at Erie (see Minutes of 1928, pages 111-113) have been made. The other edition is an entirely new work so far as make-up is concerned. The instructions given to the Committee at Erie have been carried out and one or more stanzas of each hymn have been printed between the staves of the music. In preparing the material for the press a number of serious mechanical difficulties were encountered. These arose chiefly from the fact that the precise order of the hymns had to be maintained. Most of these difficulties were finally overcome, but in several instances it was found necessary to depart from the recommendations approved two years ago at Erie. The deviations were as follows:

(1)   The tune "Faith" remains at number 136.
(2)   The tune "Hanover" remains at number 294 but is placed second.
(3)   The tune "Regnator Orbis" remains at number 324 but is placed second.
(4)   At number 371 the words of the hymn are printed in connection with the first tune only.
(5)   The tune "London New" is dropped at number 380.
(6)   The tune "Denby" is dropped at number 395.
(7)   The tune "Magdalena" is dropped at number 479.
(8)   The tune "Mornington" remains at number 520.

These changes were made necessary by mechanical reasons alone, and the Committee felt justified therefore in making them.

In both the new Music Editions all the Occasional Services from the word edition have been inserted with the exception of the Order for the

Visitation of the Sick, which is a private office. Notwithstanding the additional material included and the many changes made, the new editions have been kept down to fewer pages than the first music edition contained. In their compact and yet more complete form it is hoped that the new editions will meet the needs of the entire Church.

The Church is indebted particularly to the Rev. Doctor Strodach for most of the detailed work in preparing these editions for the press and in carrying them through. As a member of the Committee and at the same time a representative of the Publication House, he bestowed much painstaking and highly technical labor upon these volumes.

Topical Index

In response to numerous requests a topical index to the hymns in the Common Service Book was prepared by a sub-committee consisting of Doctor Hoover, Doctor Strodach, and the Rev. Mr. Hoh, which after careful study by the entire committee was approved and inserted in the Music Edition.

Jubilee Edition of the Catechism

In accordance with the action taken at Erie two years ago representatives of the Common Service Book Committee continued to co-operate with representatives of six other General Lutheran Bodies in the final revision of the new English translation of Luther's Small Catechism. The action of the Common Service Book Committee upon this final revision was as follows:

(1) Resolved that we agree to the publication of the English translation of Luther's Small Catechism adopted by the Joint Committee as "The Jubilee Edition of Luther's Small Catechism," reserving, however, the right of the Common Service Book Committee to make such subsequent alterations as it may deem imperatively necessary before recommending it to the United Lutheran Church for use in its congregations.

(2) That we express our appreciation of the great amount of work done by the Joint Committee and of their courteous consideration of our many suggestions.

(3) Doctor Getty is authorized to continue as a member of the Continuation Committee, and Doctor Mattes is likewise authorized to serve as one of the editors with the full approval of this committee.

(4) The secretary is instructed to convey to the Continuation Committee the foregoing action together with such explanation as he may deem expedient.

The text of the translation together with a large amount of valuable historical material and a number of interesting illustrations has since been published. The successful completion of this book not only provided a valuable contribution to the literature which marked the Four Hundredth Anniversary of Luther's Catechism, but added another accomplishment to the list of co-operative undertakings made by the several General Bodies of Lutherans in America.

Occasional Services

In accordance with the action of the Erie Convention (see Minutes of 1928, pages 109 and 123) a sub-committee consisting of Doctors Strodach, Hoover, and Scherer prepared a number of additional Orders and Offices, which after careful study and revision, were approved by the committee as a whole. These have been included in the new edition of "Occasional Services," issued by the Publication House. They include: The Blessing of a Church Site and Ground-Breaking; The Rededication of a Church; The Dedication of a Church House; The Blessing of a Cemetery; The Consecration of a Deaconess; The Installation of a Parish Deaconess; The Commissioning of a Foreign Missionary; Thanksgiving and Benediction of Women After Childbirth; The Induction of a President; A Service of Commemoration; The Blessing of an Altar; The Blessing of a Pulpit; The Blessing of a Lectern; The Blessing of a Font (Baptistery); The Blessing of an Altar Cross; The Blessing of a Paten or Ciborium; The Blessing of a Chalice; The Blessing of Sacramental Vessels; The Blessing of Altar Ornaments, Paraments and Vestments; The Blessing of an Organ; The Blessing of a Tower Bell; The Blessing of a Memorial Window; The Blessing of a Steeple Cross; A General Office of Benediction; The Dedication of a Hospital; The Reception of Fellow Members of the Household of Faith; the Restoration of One who has Lapsed to Membership in the Church; The Admission of a Congregation into Synod; the Reception of a Minister into Synod; and Regulations for the Ringing of a Tower Bell-Peal-Chimes.

This rather extensive addition to the Occasional Services already included in the Common Service Book has been made in response to repeated requests for proper forms for the many occasions which constantly arise in the life of congregations and in the work of Synods and Boards of the Church. While suggested entirely for voluntary use and printed only in the pastor's Manual, these forms have been prepared upon the basis of a careful study of historical liturgical precedents. It is hoped that their general use by pastors and officers of the Church may contribute to the dignity and impressiveness of these special occasions, which are generally marked by unusual attendance and interest, and to the development of a desirable uniformity of practice throughout the Church.

Altar Edition

The Altar Edition of the Common Service Book, to which reference was made in our report of two years ago, has been issued by the Publication House. It is a handsome book of large size and legible type, and contains such parts of the Liturgy as are needed by the pastor in his ministrations at the Altar. In typographical beauty of each page and in elegance of binding, it compares favorably with similar Altar Books issued by other Communions here and abroad.

ADDITIONAL COLLECTS

The request for additional collects made at the Erie Convention, and expressed also elsewhere, has been carefully considered. The Common Service Book Committee is of the opinion that no changes in the Liturgy of the Church should be made at this time. To provide additional material for use in connection with the Liturgy, a sub-committee consisting of Doctors Reed, Strodach, and E. E. Fischer has been appointed. It is the intention to issue this additional material in leaflet or pamphlet form as soon as it has been completed.

ORDER FOR ORDINATION

The Erie Convention referred to the Common Service Book Committee a request from the Ministerium of Pennsylvania to amend the Formula for Ordination. As it now stands the Order provides that the officiating Minister when laying hands upon the candidate shall say:

"I now commit unto thee the Holy Office of the Word and Sacraments; I ordain and consecrate thee a Minister of the Church; In the Name of the Father, and of the Son, and of the Holy Ghost."

The Ministerium asked that this be changed to read:

"I commit unto thee the office of the Word and Sacraments, according to the faith of the Evangelical Lutheran Church," etc.

After careful consideration the Common Service Book Committee recommends that the change asked for by the Ministerium of Pennsylvania be not made. In connection with the subject of Ordination the Common Service Book Committee further recommends:

"That the United Lutheran Church recommend to its constituent Synods that the practice of the Church be:
"When a minister of another communion applies for reception into a Synod of the Church, he, having first been received as a member of one of its congregations, shall be ordained."

LINGUISTIC MATTERS

During the biennium the Common Service Book Committee learned unofficially of several translations of the Common Service Book into other languages. This work is ordinarily undertaken by the Missionaries of the Church in their zeal for furthering Lutheran ideals of worship. The Common Service Book Committee rejoices in the loyalty to Lutheran practice thus manifested, but inasmuch as the Common Service Book is the official book of the United Lutheran Church in America, feels that such translations should be undertaken only with the full knowledge and consent of the Common Service Book Committee. Letters were addressed to the Board of American Missions and the Board of Foreign Missions, calling attention to this matter, and these Boards replied assuring us of their desire to co-operate with this Committee in its effort to promote unified worship in all parts of the church at home and abroad.

During the biennium contacts have been preserved with those representing the several linguistic interests of the Church, especially those who have expressed a desire for German Editions of the Common Service Book and the Occasional Services. No definite results worthy of report have been achieved up to the present time, but this Committee expresses its willingness to co-operate in these matters at all times.

Respectfully submitted,
LUTHER D. REED, *Chairman.*
G. ALBERT GETTY, *Secretary.*

The changes noted under the heading "The New Music Editions of the Common Service Book" were approved.

Resolution 1 concerning the Jubilee Edition of the Catechism was adopted.

The resolution concerning additional collects was approved.

The Rev. C. M. Jacobs submitted the following resolution concerning the section of the report in regard to the Order for Ordination:

Resolved, That these recommendations be referred to a special committee with instructions that they be studied in the light of the Lutheran doctrine of the ministry and that report be made to a subsequent convention of the Church.

The resolution was adopted, the size and appointing of the committee being left in the hands of the President.

The report of the Committee on Church Music, already received as a report, here follows:

REPORT OF THE COMMITTEE ON CHURCH MUSIC

At no time in the history of America has interest in music been so general as today. Music schools attended by thousands of students are found in all parts of our land; fine symphony orchestras—among them several of the best in the world, are the pride of our larger cities; choral societies in many places produce the choicest works of the masters; and radios found in hundreds of thousands of homes make it possible for millions of people to hear and enjoy the music of the world's greatest composers.

Perhaps much of this interest may be traced to the work done today in the public schools. This work, elementary at first, has now been developed to such an extent that many schools have well-trained choruses, glee clubs, bands and even complete symphony orchestras, the latter in recent times united in a national organization, whose work, as demonstrated in the last few months, is of excellent character.

Better Music in the Church

All these influences, emanating from many sources, are making themselves felt in the Church. As its members grow in musical intelligence and taste they increasingly demand worthy music in the services of God's house. What satisfied many congregations even a quarter century ago no longer satisfies. There is today an awakened sense of worship that must find its expression in the purest and most fitting form of music. Hence to meet this demand Commissions on Church Music are today active in a number of the larger church bodies, forums, institutes and convocations are held by them, organs of large size are installed, chorus choirs are introduced, congregational singing is receiving more attention, and, wherever possible, organists and choirmasters are employed who are not mere mechanical manipulators of the keys, but who, besides technical skill, also have knowledge and understanding, and, above all, the proper feeling as to what constitutes an act of worship in the musical sense. Anyone who has attended a convention of the American Guild of Organists will know that the great majority of the men and women who are today responsible for the music in representative churches take their work seriously.

Training the Organists

In many of our own churches it is of course true that the quality of the music and its rendition are still below the standard. This is chiefly true of the poorer congregations. The organist is possibly of the "home made" kind, with little knowledge and no skill; the choir under his or her imperfect training sings "cheap" anthems in a cheap way; and the service music and hymn tunes, which preeminently belong to the congregation, and to which the *chief* attention should be given receive the least, with the result that they are sung in a most incorrect, indifferent and slovenly manner. Now for all this there is but one remedy. We must train our own organists as we train our own ministers. We need to have schools in which those who wish to qualify themselves for the Church's ministry of music will not only get the necessary technical training, but where they can also acquire an understanding of the meaning and requirements of the Lutheran orders of worship, and become acquainted with the best forms of the Church's music so as to enable them to select intelligently. And to organists so trained congregations must be willing to pay an adequate salary.

At this point the Committee calls attention to the rich treasures of devotion to our Common Service Book. Here is a book to be *studied*. Pastors, choirs and people need to penetrate into the inner meaning of the services in all their parts, and into the contents of the hymns, so that into all that they speak and sing the *heart* will enter as well as the mouth. To sing only notes without having the text in mind is not worship.

THE MUSIC OF THE CHOIR

For anthems in the Anglican sense there is little place in the Lutheran Orders, though there is a distinct place for the choir in the Introit and Gradual of The Service, and in the Responsory of Matins and Vespers, for all of which the music can be had. Nevertheless it has become the usual custom in our churches to sing anthems. This may be done in place of the Gradual in The Service, and of the appointed Responsory in Matins and Vespers. But in every case the words must fit into the thought of the day and occasion, and the music must be of a kind appropriate to God's house. The anthem, as well as the rest of the service, should always be regarded as an act of worship, and should minister to edification; nor should choirs attempt to sing anthems that are beyond their ability. If an anthem is to edify it is far better to sing a simple one well than to mutilate a more difficult one.

Members of the Committee are often asked to name a collection of such compositions, or to recommend some publication issued at regular intervals that provides music within the ability of the average choir. The usual answer is that none of the latter, and few of the former answer our requirements. A better plan is to gather a library out of the octavo publications of the leading music houses suited not only to the ability of the choir, but also to the Church Year. As an aid in this direction Mr. Peery of the Committee, recently awarded a thousand dollar prize in competition with two hundred other composers, has for months published lists of anthems in *The Lutheran,* chosen in harmony with the theme of the day as expressed in the Introit. The entire year's list is completed and means should be found for publishing it in booklet form for the guidance of organists and choirmasters.

CULTIVATION OF HYMN SINGING

In addition to the service music the Committee urges organists and choirs to pay much more attention to the proper preparation of the hymn tunes, and then to devise some plan by which they can be made the familiar property of the congregation. Very many of the finest and most expressive tunes in the Common Service Book, set to the choicest hymns, are never used, simply because no effort is made to learn and teach them. To learn a tune and then sing it as it should be sung, the choir should first *read the entire hymn* to learn its contents, and the organist in playing it, and the choir in singing it, should seek to give these contents their proper interpretation. After the first use of it with the congregation it should be repeated on several successive Sundays, if the hymn fits the season, and by that time the congregation is likely to know it. Many of the unfamiliar tunes in the Common Service Book could also be used in place of unprofitable anthems, and in this way the congregation would likewise learn to know them.

ACTIVITIES OF THE COMMITTEE

During the past biennium the Committee has had no opportunities to hold Convocations, but the Chairman and Dr. Reed held two Institutes on a smaller scale, the one in Bethlehem Church, Harrisburg, Pa., and the other in Bethel Church, Detroit, Mich., both of them attended by many pastors, organists, choir members and other interested persons. Besides his work in music at the Seminary in Mt. Airy, Dr. Reed also gave a course of five lectures at the Gettysburg Seminary, conducted an Institute at Greensburg, Pa., and spoke on the Liturgy and its Music at Little Neck, L. I., Hollis, L. I., Howard Beach, L. I., Kingston, Pa., and Norwood, Pa. The Secretary, Dr. Rees, lectured the last two years at the Summer School of the North Carolina Synod, this year at the Summer School of the Michigan Synod explained and demonstrated the music of the services to a group of Congregations, and spoke to two different Luther Leagues. Mr. Sykes, organist of Trinity Church, Lancaster, Pa., upon whom the degree of Mus. D. has been conferred, and who was recently chosen conductor of the Matinee Musical Club Chorus in Philadelphia, and appointed special lecturer in the Department of Church Music, Union Seminary, New York, has in preparation a study and musical interpretation of the orders in the Common Service Book, and continues his lectures on Church Music in the Seminary of the Reformed Church at Lancaster, Pa. Mr. Marks, now also Mus. D., in his lectures at Muhlenberg College, Allentown, calls the attention of his hearers to the place music occupies in worship, and lays special stress on the kind of music that should be used. In the School of Music, Wittenberg College, directed by Dr. Bach, constant advances are being made, among them the organization of four choirs, one composed of freshmen, another of sophomores, a third of juniors, and the fourth of skilled voices from all classes. Dr. Carl F. Pfatteicher added a fine series of classical anthems, for a *capella* singing, to his former publications, and continues to do good work as the head of the Department of Music at Phillips Academy, Andover, Mass. In many Lutheran and other churches Mr. Seibert played numerous recitals and his experience in differing surroundings leads him to conclude that the quality of music in our churches is below the standard, and to suggest the slogan: "Better music in Lutheran Churches." He also maintains, altogether correctly, that ministers should extend the courtesy of always placing the material to be prepared for a given service in the hands of the organist in good time. Pastor Trabert has continued the good work on the Pacific Coast and reports that the standards are measurably above those of a few years ago.

CHILDREN'S HYMNAL AND SERVICE BOOK

Since the Committee's last report the Publication House has issued the *Children's Hymnal and Service Book,* prepared by a joint committee of the Parish and Church School Board and the Common Service Book Committee. This book is intended for the Primary and Junior Departments of the Sunday School. Together with the *Parish School Hymnal* our schools are now well equipped for teaching the young how to worship. Pastors and Sunday School workers who still think that so-called hymns and tunes of the jumping-jack and jazz band variety are the proper thing for children, should read the chapter on Sunday School Hymnody in *Practical Hymnology,* by Professor Herbert McNeill Poteat, of Wake Forest College, N. C.

THE COMMITTEE,
J. F. OHL, *Chairman.*

GOMER C. REES, *Secretary.*

Mr. Charles A. Scheuringer presented the report of the Committee on Church Architecture.

REPORT OF THE COMMITTEE ON CHURCH ARCHITECTURE

Twenty-four meetings of the Committee, attended chiefly by the members in or near Philadelphia, were held during the biennium. At the organization meeting Dr. Ohl was elected Chairman and Dr. Reed Secretary.

Mr. A. A. Ritcher, of Reading, Pa., a member of the Committee since its organization, died early in the biennium. His long professional career was distinguished chiefly by work in the ecclesiastical field, and an unusually large number of buildings for Lutheran congregations was designed by him. By appointment of President Knubel, his associate, Mr. Howard P. Eiler, of Reading, Pa., succeeded him as a member of the Committee.

Forty-two sets of plans were reviewed by the Committee and reports rendered. These came from sixteen States and Canada. A summary of the opinions rendered is given later.

CONFERENCES AND CORRESPONDENCE

In addition to the reviewing of plans by the Committee itself, many conferences were held and an extensive correspondence carried on with pastors, architects and others by the chairman and the secretary. The chairman reports letters from 64 persons in 16 states, and the secretary letters from

148 persons in 25 states, England and Canada. The secretary also reports personal conferences with 15 pastors and architects in 5 different states.

The Rev. Mr. Kidd, Mr. Scheuringer and the secretary represented the Committee at a meeting of the Bureaus of Architecture of the different Churches, and the Committee of the Home Missions Council, at Atlantic City in the fall of 1928. The secretary represented the Committee at a similar conference held in St. Louis, December 6-7, 1929, and read a paper on "Building for Worship: A Summary of Principles and Practical Requirements" which was subsequently published in the *American Architect* in the issue of February, 1930, and in the *Christian Herald* March, 1929, issue.

The Rev. E. A. Trabert conferred with a number of pastors and Building Committees on the Pacific coast and advised with them concerning building programs. The Rev. George H. Schnur, D.D., was active in a similar way in the Pittsburgh Synod.

At the request of the authorities at Muhlenberg College and the architect, Frank R. Watson, Philadelphia, the secretary prepared a complete scheme of symbolism and decoration for the new Chapel of Muhlenberg College, Allentown, Pa. The plan, which includes ornamental stone work, the treatment of the altar with its reredos and the stained glass windows throughout the building was adopted in its entirety.

LANDSCAPING AND EXTERIOR DECORATION

The following action was taken on the resolution presented to the United Lutheran Church at Erie by Professor E. H. Dreher, and referred to the Committee:

"The Committee commends the effort of Professor Dreher in calling attention to the importance of beautifying the exteriors of church buildings by proper landscaping and the use of massed shrubbery and plants. Too little attention is usually given this subject and the church building or group of buildings would gain immensely if given a proper setting with a well-thought-out treatment of lawns, trees and massed shrubbery. Even if the ground available be small, intelligent planting and care will secure for the building itself much greater beauty and effectiveness."

PUBLICATIONS

Attention is called to the following publications of the Committee which are available without cost, upon request:

"Church Principles in Church Architecture"—A 20-page pamphlet prepared by the secretary, Dr. Reed now in its third printing.

"Practical Suggestions for Building Committees"—a helpful pamphlet which has been freely distributed and recently reprinted.

"Architectural Leaflets"—a series of attractive four-page folders containing cuts of successful Lutheran Church buildings with descriptive write-up.

"Space Requirements for Church Organs"—a valuable statement prepared by the chairman, Dr. Ohl, in collaboration with representatives of one of the large organ-building companies.

Attention is also called to the following recent publications:

"A Manual on Worship" by Paul Zeller Strodach, D.D., with an introduction by President Knubel. This is a volume of 237 pages, profusely illustrated and handsomely bound. The first half treats of the normal chancel and its furnishings; the second part of the Liturgy and details connected with its use. This book by one of the ablest liturgical scholars in the Church, will be of great service in elevating and unifying the practice of the Church in the fields of architecture and the Liturgy. It is published by the United Lutheran Publication House.

"Pittsburgh Synod Manual," 2d edition, 1929. This contains information on Church Building, Altar Vestments, etc., with illustrations showing altars properly vested. This, together with photostatic designs for embroidery, has been prepared by the Committee on Church Architecture of the Pittsburgh Synod.

"Building the House of God" by Elbert M. Conover D.D., Director of the Bureau of Architecture of the Methodist Episcopal Church. This work of 217 pages, fully illustrated, is packed with helpful information concerning all the details of a Church building program, including not only the church building proper but also the religious education and social units. Published by the Methodist Book Concern.

"American Church Building of Today" edited by Ralph Adams Cram, published by the Architectural Book Publishing Company, New York. This is of folio size, 283 pages, and contains a selection of photographs of exteriors and interiors, details and plans of the most important churches recently erected in America. The selection is confined to the work of representative architects, deemed worthy of inclusion by Dr. Cram, himself one of the ablest architects in the country.

"The Significance of the Fine Arts," a worthwhile work prepared by a group of specialists and published under the direction of the Committee on Education of the American Institute by the Marshall Jones Company, Boston. An excellent bibliography is given with each subject.

"College Architecture in America," by Charles Z. Klauder (a member of our Committee) and Herbert C. Wise, Scribners, 1929. An important work by eminent authorities, containing much information of value to those responsible for the development of Theological Seminaries, Church colleges, schools and similar institutions.

It would be well if the above-mentioned books, and others of similar nature, could be placed in the libraries of our Seminaries and Church Colleges and used for reading courses. In the Seminaries, particularly, the subject of Church Architecture should be included in the regular curriculum. Local chapters of the American Institute of Architects would doubtless be willing to help materially in building up such collections of books and in presenting the various phases of the subject to the student body as the Seminary authorities might arrange.

Following is a summary of plans reviewed:

Plans Approved and Commended

The following were approved and commended for general excellence. Minor suggestions were made by the Committee in nearly every case.

St. Peter's Church, Jamaica, L. I., Cherry and Matz, New York, architects.

Final plans for Trinity Church, Clark's Summitt, Pa., the Rev. F. A. Shearer, pastor, the office of George C. Baum, architect. The exterior drawings were paricularly commended as providing an attractive and churchly type of building at modest cost.

Preliminary plans for Emmanuel Church, Lakewood, N. J., the Rev. August Greve, pastor, John B. Thompson, architect, L. DeForrest Emmert, associate architect Philadelphia. An inexpensvie building seating 134, and costing $10,000.

Plans for a complete church plant for St. Luke's Church, Bayshore, L. I., the Rev. Edmund A. Bosch, pastor, Frederick H. Klie, N. Y., architect.

The Congregation only four years old, plans to build a Parish House as the first unit, and later to complete the plant on an excellent lot owned without encumbrance. The plans indicate careful study and good use of the ground.

Trinity Church, Buolder, Col., G. H. Huntington, Boulder architect. Commended as admirable, and a fine study of the problem.

St. Peter's Church, Scranton, the Rev. C. F. Knoll, Ph.D., pastor, Albert H. Ward, Scranton, architect.

St. Paul's Mission, Spokane, Wash., Rev. A. K. Walborn, pastor, Whitehouse and Prie architects.

St. John's Church, Rutherford, N. J., the Rev. E. K. Knudten pastor, Cherry and Matz, New York, architects.

Block plans for Hope Church, Ottawa Hills, O., by Cahill and Becker, Toledo, architects, with plans for a chapel as the first unit of the group, were approved and commended though several important suggestions were offered.

Plans Approved

St. Barnabas Church, Howard Beach, L. I., Cherry and Matz, New York, architects. Approved with minor suggestions concerning chancel plan.

Plans for a building to be used temporarily for church purposes and later as a parsonage for the congregation at Cudahy, Wis., E. R. Liebort, Milwaukee, architect, were approved as a temporary arrangement with suggestions for larger chancel, etc.

Westwood Church at Elmwood Park, Ill., Tyson and Monberg, Chicgo, architects. Plans for a parsonage and a Parish Building to be used temporarily as a Church were approved.

St. Mark's Church, Seattle, Wash., David I. McNicoll, Seattle, architect. Plans for a simple frame church building were approved as having desirable simplicity and churchly character.

Lutheran Church, at Wilmette, Ill., Buckley and Skidmore, Hammond, Ind., architects. The Committee's judgment was given with reference to points raised by the architects, concerning exterior and interior details.

Plans for a two-story Church building with tower for the First Hungarian Church, Bethlehem Pa., F. Negy, Allentown ,architect. Attention was called to a number of details which should be restudied in order to conform to the general arrangement of Lutheran churches in this country.

Plans for Holy Trinity Church, Maple Shade, N, J., John B. Thompson, Philadelphia architect, were cordially approved as promising churchly effect at limited construction cost. Several suggestions were offered.

Preliminary studies for a new Church building for St. John's Church, Richlandtown, Pa., C. M. Talley, Telford, Pa., architect, were approved with suggestions concerning narrowing and elevating the nave so as to dominate the composition and details concerning tower construction.

Grace Church, Steubenville, O., Peterson and Clarke, Steubenville, architects. The general plan was approved, but suggestions were given relating to proportions and details such as exits, stairways, chancel design, elevations, etc.

St. John s Mission, Salisbury, N. C. Plans prepared by E. W. Wagoner, of Salisbury were approved with minor suggestions.

The Committee conferred with Mr. E. W. Wagoner, Salisbury, N. C., concerning plans for enlarging St. Luke's Church and Sunday School building, Bear Poplar, N. C. The Committee advised redesigning the chancel and also the employment of the early American style which is suggested by the present building, rather than the use of Gothic detail. Revised plans were later approved.

PLANS NOT APPROVED

Church of Our Saviour, Lansdowne, Md., John Freund, Baltimore, architect. Not approved because of various features—sloping floor, incorrect chancel design, poor facade, and other features reminiscent of poor Church designing of a generation or more ago. Detailed suggestions were given for restudy.

Trinity Church, Macomb, Ill. The congregation was advised to secure adequate architectural service and to have other plans prepared. Unsigned plans later submitted were not approved because of numerous unsatisfactory details.

Ascension Church, Shelby, N. C., Earl Rhyne, Belmont, N. C., designer. Not approved because of faulty floor plan and minor details in plan and elevations. The congregation was advised to secure a capable architect for its building, on which it proposes to expend $40,000.

Unsigned preliminary plans and pencil drawings for St. Paul's Church, Roseville, O. The Committee felt that this plan, calling for an elaborate building of pier and clerestory type with transepts ,tower ,etc. ,to cost $80,000, and seating 332 persons, though not without merit, was too ambitious in an architectural way without fully meeting the needs of the congregation, numbering 400. Various suggestions were given for designing a simpler type of building which would provide larger capacity for the same expenditure of money.

Plans for alterations in the First Church, Plymouth, O. Alternate plans, both unsigned, were returned as unacceptable, and the congregation urged to secure a capable architect. A number of names of qualified architects within reasonable distance was submitted.

Unsigned plans for a Church and Sunday School building for St. Matthew's Church, Woodlyn, Pa., prepared by a member of the congregation, were not approved because of faulty floor plans and inconsistent and unsatisfactory elevations. Revised plans were accepted as much approved.

Trinity Church, Macomb, Ill. Revised plans prepared by Grant Beadle, of Galesburg, Ill., were regarded as an improvement, but the Committee was still compelled to report them below the standards desired. Various additional suggestions were given.

Parish House for St. John's Church, Bellmore, L. I. Not approved as entirely deficient in churchly character. The congregation was advised to secure an architect of proven ability, and to have a comprehensive plan prepared of which the Parish House would form a unit. Mr. C. A. Scheuringer, a member of the Committee subsequently offered to assist the congregation in a thorough reworking of their plans. The congregation however, later submitted other drawings prepared by Robert Arnold, Freeport, L. I., architect. Regretfully the Committee reported them as unsatisfactory, being of a domesic rather than a churchly character. without proper chancel arrangements, faulty in roof construction, etc.

Second Lutheran Church, Schenectady, N. Y. Unsigned drawings were not approved as lacking essentials of good Church design. Conference with the Rev. Austin E. Stiles, pastor, discussed new proposals for the Church building, and various suggestions were offered. New plans by W. E. Smith, architect, were reviewed, the Committee noting a considerable improvement, though not able to give them unqualified approval.

Plans for an extension to Zion English Mission at Saulte Ste. Marie, Ont., prepared by John Street. The Committee offered suggestions for redesigning the chancel.

Plans for a mission at Yeadon, Pa., prepared by the Asbestos Buildings Company, Philadelphia, and Henry L. Reinbold, Jr., architect, were not approved as deficient in churchly character, having poor proportion, improperly designed chancel and other unsatisfactory details.

Plans for an inexpensive church building at Miami, Fla., H. Hastings Mundy, architect. The floor plan was approved as well thought out, but the elevations were not approved because they provided for a Renaissance type of building with stucco over frame construction and lacked churchly character. The use of the Spanish mission style and of hollow concrete block construction was suggested. Revised plans were later considered and further suggestions given.

Plans for a Chapel and Sunday School rooms for St. Luke's Church, Charlotte, N. C. These were not approved as impracticable, the Sunday School being over-departmentalized and some of the classrooms less than six feet in width. Suggestions were given for simpler treatment of the entire building. Revised plans were later received and returned without approval.

Floor plans for the Hungarian Church, Windsor, Ont., providing for a church on the first floor, a parsonage on the second floor, and a recreation room in the basement were not approved. A number of suggestions were offered. Revised plans were later considered and further suggestions offered.

Preliminary drawings and a perspective of Holy Trinity Church, Salem, O. Richard A. Zenk and Roy T. Campbell, Youngstown, O., architects. The elevations suggested a building reminiscent of the type of work found in certain parts of the country years ago, and not in keeping with the best work of our cities today. Suggestions were given for restudy.

Plans for Emmanuel Church, Elyria, O., Brice, Hayden and Long, Cleveland, architects, were approved so far as general plan and treatment were concerned, but various criticisms and suggestions were offered.

Preliminary plans for Bethesda Church, Yorkville, Ill. John Hanifen, LaSalle, Ill.. architect, were approved with certain exceptions and a restudy was requested. Revised plans were later received and suggestions given concerning the use of a belfry instead of a cupola, rearrangement of the main entrance and of chancel details. etc. Approval was withheld pending further revision.

Sunday School building plans for the First Church, Dallas, Texas, were not approved because of unchurchly character, the plans calling for a long, low, wide structure. twelve feet in height and with a roof almost flat. Submission of other plans was requested, or investigation of the possible use of a portable chapel.

Unity Church, a Mission at Des Moines, Ia., Donald H. McLennan, architect. These plans were not approved as providing social quarters out of all proportion to the religious provisions in the building, and because of impossible arrangements, poor entrances, etc. Suggestions were given for entire restudy.

Church of the Reformation, West Toledo, O. Plans for a simple frame building to cost not more than $15,000 were not approved as deficient in architectural features and in churchly character.

Grace Church, Alden, Minn. Plans by Ernest H. Schmidt, of Mankato, not approved because of poor planning and details of construction.

OTHER OPINIONS RENDERED

Suggestions were given in a personal conference with the Rev. C. E.

Naugle concerning plans for the Parish Building for Roaring Springs, Pa.

The Church of the Redeemer, Earl Hollenbeck, architect, Charles F. Obenhack, associate architect. In conference with Mr. Obenhack various suggestions were given with reference to chancel design, a Parish Building, and location of gymnasium.

Parish Building for Zion Church, Niagara Falls, N. Y., Charles F. Obenhack, architect. Alternate propositions were discussed in a conference with the architect and counsel given concerning various items.

The Committee endorsed the position expressed by Mr. Klauder, one of its members, in correspondence with Professor Graebner of St. Louis, which stated that "because of the requirements of many states with reference to the licensing of architects, it is well, so far as possible, to select architects for a church of small size, from the state in which the building is to be erected, thus avoiding the necessity of an associate architect for a small project, or of an architect in another state having to pass an examination in the state in which the building is to be erected."

ANALYSIS OF REPORTS RENDERED

The forty-two sets of plans reviewed during the past biennium contrast sharply with eighty-seven reported in 1928, and eighty-six in 1926. The reason for the greatly reduced number is unquestionably to be found in the general business depression throughout the country. The volume of correspondence conducted by the officers is but slightly less than previous bienniums. This indicates that many building projects are simply awaiting favorable economic developments in order to be launched.

Of the forty-two plans reviewed, nine were approved and commended, twelve approved, and twenty-one not approved. Thus 50 per cent of all the plans reviewed could not be approved by the committee, a fact which contrasts unfavorably with previous reports, the ratio standing at 33 1-3 per cent in 1928, and at 40 per cent in 1926.,,

The explanation for this increase in poor plans is probably due to the fact that many of the larger projects prepared by able architects have been delayed, and thus an unusually large proportion of plans for mission congregations was considered. In many cases these originated in frontier locations where it was difficult to secure capable architectural service. In other instances poorly qualified architects or even draftsmen and employees in builders' offices were responsible.

One of the regrettable features of present day living in America is the reckless expenditure of vast sums of money for all manner of purposes without regard for permanent values or good taste. The Church does not escape this general procedure, and while there is a gratifying development of taste and higher standards in the field of Church architecture all over our land, many of our pastors and congregations are not yet fully aware of this and are entrusting their church building projects to mediocre architects or partially trained draftsmen.

In so doing they are simply falling behind the general development of their communities and of the country as a whole. For not only is the number of persons who appreciate good architecture constantly increasing, but there has been a vast improvement in the instruction given those preparing for the practice of architecture in the professional schools. There are approximately fifty Schools of Architecture giving degrees in the U. S. Some twenty-five are identified with the Association of Collegiate Schools of Architecture. These schools, recognized by the American Institute of Architects, are well distributed, their graduates are scattered all over the country, and there is little excuse today for not obtaining the services of a competent architect in practically every section of the U. S.

If the entire Church could review the mediocre work submitted to the Committee for approval, the principle of having only trained architects would certainly be insisted upon and the number of rejected plans would be materially reduced. It is false economy to secure any but the best architectural service. An architect with personal sympathy with the work of the Church, and with adequate training and experience in church building, will be able to give a congregation an edifice well adapted to its requirements, attractive and even distinguished, at a total cost not greater than that necessary to erect an utterly commonplace and unimpressive building of equal size designed by a man of inferior ability.

Other things being equal, the congregation with an attractive and churchly building will more truly represent the Church at large in its community, and will make a greater appeal and thus be more successful in its community, than the congregation with a building whose crudities of design and ornament advertise the deficiencies of taste and church-consciousness of the congregation itself.

These things are of importance for the work of established congregations and of missions alike. They probably mean more to the mission struggling for recognition and sympathy in a new community than they do to the average well established congregation.

In order to keep these ideas and ideals constantly before the Church and to bring the experience of the whole Church to bear helpfully upon the building problems of individual congregations, and particularly our missions, the Committee on Church Architecture was established by the United Lutheran Church at its organization in 1918. This Committee, together with an earlier one of the General Council, were among the first agencies established in this field by any Communion. Practically all the other Protestant Churches subsequently appointed similar committees. The prompt recognition of the importance of this work has since led nearly all of them to establish regular Bureaus of Architecture with offices and permanent staffs. Meanwhile our Committee has continued to function as best it could under its limited organization. Depending upon the occasional and voluntary services of a limited number of its members, it has given counsel and criticism, reported upon plans submitted, published a limited amount of literature, etc. It has not been able to render constructive service in the actual preparation of plans, or even in extensive correction of plans submitted.

Report on the Proposed Bureau of Architecture

The United Lutheran Church at the last Convention adopted the following recommendations of the Committee:

1. That the Committee on Church Architecture be authorized to make a thorough study of the advisability of creating a Bureau of Architecture, and, if such a Bureau be decided upon, to present plans to the Executive Board for the establishment of the same January 1, 1930.

2. That the Executive Board be authorized to act upon the report of the Committee, and if it approve the same, to put the new arrangement into effect as of January 1, 1930, and to finance the work of the Bureau by an appropriation not exceeding $8500 per year for the first biennium.

In accordance with the above action, a thorough study of the work of the Architectural Bureaus of other Churches was made by a Sub-Committee consisting of the following: Dr. Reed, Prof. Laird, the Rev. Mr. Kidd, and Messrs. Scheuringer and Schenck. Visits were made to headquarters, and conferences held with the executives of the following:

The Methodist Bureau of Architecture, 1701 Arch St., Philadelphia, founded 1917, under joint control of the Board of Home Missions and Church Extension, and the Board of Education; the Rev. Dr. E. M. Conover, Director; Walter H. Thomas, Philadelphia, Consulting Architect, three other registered architects, and a number of draftsmen and office personnel in the principal office at Philadelphia, and a branch office at Chicago. Expenditures 1928, $54,000, of which amount $22,000 was supplied by Boards and $32,000 came from fees.

The Baptist Department of Architecture, 23 E. 26th St., New York City, organized 1920, C. E. Merrill, Architectural Secretary. The Secretary, an Associate and several draftsmen are regularly employed, and additional architectural service is secured as required. Its budget for 1928 was in the neighborhood of $30,000.

The Presbyterian Department of Architecture at 56 Fifth Avenue, New York City, established 1923, A. G. Lamont, architect in charge, with three draftsmen, a secretary, etc. About $1,000,000 worth of work in the office at this time.

The Architectural Bureau of the Y. M. C. A., 347 Madison Ave., New York City, Neil McMillan, Jr., Director, established 1906, maintains a staff of thirty-two men, nine of whom are field men and twelve draftsmen. An annual budget of approximately $150,000. Practically $20,-000,000 worth of work in the office at this time.

Other Church Bodies maintain Bureaus or Departments of Architecture as follows: Southern Baptist, Nashville, Tenn.; Congregational, New York City; Disciples, Indianapolis, Ind.; Southern Methodist, Louisville, Ky.; Southern Presbyterian, Atlanta, Ga.; United Brethren, Dayton, Ohio; United Presbyterian, Pittsburgh, Pa.

The work of many of these agencies was also studied by our Committee, chiefly by correspondence and occasional personal contacts with executives. The survey yielded much valuable information, and your Committee is convinced that these agencies are not only rendering invaluable service to individual pastors and congregations, but that they are elevating the standards of church building in their respective communions enormously.

As a result of its studies, the Committee unanimously agrees that it would be to the great advantage of the United Lutheran Church if a Bureau of Architecture could be established, primarily for assistance to mission congregations. The following plan of organization is proposed and has been presented to the Executive Board:

I. Organization

1. We recommend that the present Committee on Church Architecture be continued by the United Lutheran Church, and that a Bureau of Architecture be established and conducted by the Committee The Bureau would be responsible to the Committee, and the Committee would be responsible to the Church for the administration of Bureau affairs.

2. We recommend that the work of the Bureau be begun with the following staff: A director, an architect in charge, and a secretary. The director and the architect in charge shall be appointed by the Committee.

The director shall preferably be a clergyman trained in Church affairs and with some knowledge of architectural matters. He shall engage such other members of the staff as may be necessary from time to time, and whose appointment is not otherwise provided for by the Committee. He shall be responsible for all expenditures and for the general management of the Bureau. He shall present a quarterly report of the Committee covering the work of the Bureau, including financial statement, questions of policy, etc.

The architect shall perform the technical work of the Bureau. If possible a man who has shown competence in church design and who has a small but complete organization should be secured for the initial period. The basis for his remuneration might be cost plus personal service.

The secretary shall act as stenographer, clerk, etc.

In the beginning the Committee would meet with the Director of the Bureau and the Architect in charge, to consider plans submitted by other architects. The Director would formulate and record the criticism and attend to correspondence growing out of these reviews. Gradually this work might be left entirely to the Bureau, except that special meetings of the Committee would be held at the request of the Director to consider important or difficult problems.

The hearty and regular cooperation of the Board of American Missions should be sought in the effort to carry out the action of the United Lutheran Church which requires approval of all plans for missions before loans or other Church appropriations are granted.

II. Operation

We recommend that the following services be rendered by the Bureau:

1. General advisory services without cost.

Office conferences, correspondence and criticism of plans submitted by other architects.

Publication from time to time of pamphlets, circulars, survey blanks and similar material for free distribution.

The preparation, as a matter of promotion and publicity, of special exhibits for Synodical and conference meetings, etc., and the presentation by representatives of the Bureau of its work to congregations and general Church gatherings as opportunity offers.

Formation of collections of useful literature, etc., to be placed at the service of visitors to the Bureau. These would include books and pamphlets on Church buildings, files of architectural magazines, photographs and drawings, slides, samples of building materials, etc.

2. Services with fees.

Fees shall be charged for service of the kind usual in architectural practice. Such service and fees to be in accordance with the practice most approved by existing Bureaus and within the limit of our own Bureau's appropriation by the United Lutheran Church.

Where complete architectural service is rendered missions, the approximate cost of preliminary drawings shall be deducted from the full fee usually charged for complete service.

Field visits at the request of congregations to be charged for at the rate of $25 and expenses each. This charge may be deducted if the congregation later enters into a contract with the Bureau.

3. Files, etc.

The Bureau shall maintain files of correspondence, Minutes of Committee meetings, reports of conferences, lectures, correspondence, etc., by the Committee representatives, etc. It shall also secure and file useful information concerning architects, builders, manufacturers, etc. All projects executed by the Bureau shall be properly filed, and a follow-up system covering its own work devised.

III. FINANCE

The estimated budget for the year covering salaries of Director and stenographer, fees for architectural service, office rent and miscellaneous expenses, totals $9900. Inasmuch as fees from congregations would probably only provide a small part of the annual expense for the first year or two, an appropriation of $8,000 per annum for the first biennium, is requested from the Church to establish and maintain the Bureau.

Various matters delayed the presentation of the above plan to the Executive Board. The general business depression of the country also entered as a factor into its consideration. The Finance Committee of the Executive Board has expressed its sympathy with the proposition and its willingness to appropriate $5,000 a year for three years from funds at its disposal. At its suggestion, the Committee has requested the Board of American Missions to consider the possibility of appropriating $3,000 a year for three years from its funds. At the time of writing this report, the Mission Board has not taken final action upon this request.

The Committee requests the approval by the United Lutheran Church of its proposed plan for the establishment of a Bureau, with the further request that provision be made in whatever way the Church may deem best for an appropriation of at least $8,000 a year for the next biennium.

Respectfully submitted,
J. F. OHL, *Chairman,*
LUTHER D. REED, *Secretary.*

The request of the committee concerning a Bureau of Architecture was referred to the Executive Board.

Consideration of Item IV, C, 5, of the Executive Board's report, having been deferred until this time, the President ruled that the item was included in the above reference to the Executive Board.

Mr. Wm. H. Menges, Chairman of Tellers' Committee No. 2, reported the following elections:

For the *Board of Foreign Missions* the majority of the votes cast were for

Mr. H. Torrey Walker

The President declared him elected.

For the *Board of Publication* the majority of the votes cast were for

Mr. Eimar Schatvet

The President declared him elected.

For the *Board of Ministerial Pensions and Relief* the majority of the votes cast were for

Rev. J. H. Reble

The President declared him elected.

For the *Parish and Church School Board* the majority of the votes cast were for

Mr. Clarence C. Dittmer

The President declared him elected.

The Rev. George H. Schnur, Chairman of the Statistical and Church Year Book Committee, presented the report of that committee.

REPORT OF THE STATISTICAL AND CHURCH YEAR BOOK COMMITTEE

The Statistical and Church Year Book Committee of the United Lutheran Church in America, during the years, 1928-1930, throughout all of their work have had the co-operation of the Statistical Secretaries of the Constituent Synods of the United Lutheran Church in America.

At the Conference of the Statistical Secretaries of the United Lutheran Church held at the time of the United Lutheran Church Convention in Erie, Pa., Tuesday, October 9, 1928, representatives from nineteen constituent synods were present.

At this conference the following subjects were discussed: The Standard Parochial Blank, the Standard Assembly Sheet, the Standard State Church Blank, the Standard System of Parish Records and Congregational Auxiliary Blanks. A great deal of the time at the conference was devoted to the subject of graphic methods for presenting statistical facts. A set of resolutions was passed urging the Statistical and Year Book Committee of the United Lutheran Church concerning the importance of adequate provision for statistical work of the United Lutheran Church.

The following constituent synods were represented by their Statistical Secretaries: Ministerium of Pennsylvania, Ministerium of New York, Synod of North Carolina, Synod of Maryland, West Pennsylvania Synod, Virginia Synod, New York Synod, Ohio Synod, East Pennsylvania Synod, Alleghany Synod, Pittsburgh Synod, Iowa Synod, Georgia Synod, Canada Synod, Nebraska Synod, Rocky Mountain Synod, New York and New England Synod, West Virginia Synod, and Slovak Zion Synod.

Another such conference will be held at the time of the United Lutheran Church Convention at Milwaukee, Wis. Announcement of place and time will be made later. These conferences which have been held at Buffalo, Chicago, Richmond and Erie have proven most valuable.

LIST OF STATISTICAL SECRETARIES

The following served as Statistical Secretaries of the Constituent Synods of the United Lutheran Church in America, during the biennium, 1928-1930.

	1929	1930
Ministerium of Pa.	Rev. Ira F. Frankenfield	Rev. Ira F. Frankenfield
Ministerium of N. Y.	Rev. Geo. R. F. Tamke	Rev. Geo. R. F. Tamke
United New York Synod	Rev. A. L. Dillenbeck, D.D.	Rev. A. L. Dillenbeck, D.D.
Synod of North Carolina	Rev. E. H. Kohn, Ph.D.	Rev. E. H. Kohn, Ph.D.
Synod of Maryland	Rev. W. G. Minnick	Rev. W. G. Minnick
Synod of South Carolina	Rev. H. S. Petrea	Rev. H. S. Petrea
Synod of West Pa.	Rev. D. S. Martin, D.D.	Rev. D. S. Martin, D.D.
Synod of Virginia	Mr. Harry E. Pugh, 105 Lancaster Rd., Richmond, Va.	Mr. Harry E. Pugh
Synod of New York	Rev. A. L. Dillenbeck, D.D.	Rev. A. L. Dillenbeck, D.D.
Synod of Ohio	Mr. Armor W. Ulrici, 3747 Elsemere Ave., Cincinnati	Mr. Armor W. Ulrici
East Pa. Synod	Rev. J. D. Krout	Rev. J. D. Krout
Alleghany Synod	Rev. C. P. Bastian	Rev. C. P. Bastian
Pittsburgh Synod	Rev. Geo. H. Schnur, D.D.	Rev. Geo. H. Schnur, D.D.
Indiana Synod	Mr H. D. C. Loemker, 2151 Emerson Ave., Louisville, Ky.	Mr. H. D. C. Loemker
Illinois Synod	Mr. Fred Sachse, 1523 Edgewater Ave., Chicago	Mr. Fred Sachse
Texas Synod	Rev. F. F. Eberhardt	*Rev. F. F. Eberhardt
Susquehanna Synod of Central Penna.	Rev. C. S. Bottiger	Rev. F. W. Henkel Rev. C. S. Bottiger
Mississippi Synod	Rev. E. K. Counts	†Rev. E. K. Counts
Synod of Iowa	Rev. Leland H. Lesher	Rev. Leland H. Lesher
Michigan Synod	Rev. F. L. Gunderman	Rev. F. L. Gunderman
Synod of Georgia	Mr. D. E. Wilson, 324 W. Shadowlawn Ave., Atlanta, Ga.	Mr. D. E. Wilson
Synod of Canada	Rev. O. Stockman	Rev. O. Stockman
Synod of Kansas	Rev. A. L. Groseclose	Rev. A. L. Groseclose
Synod of Nebraska	Rev. T. D. Rinde	Rev. T. D. Rinde
Synod of Wartburg	Rev. H. R. Pontow	Rev. H. R. Pontow
German Nebraska Synod	Rev. P. Waldschmidt	Rev. P. Waldschmidt

	1929	1930
Synod of California	Rev. John E. Hoick	Rev. John E. Hoick
Rocky Mountain Synod	Rev. C. L. Ramme	Rev. O. F. Weaver
Synod of the Northwest	Rev. D. E. Bosserman	Rev. D. E. Bosserman
Manitoba Synod	Rev. W. Magnus	Rev. W. Magnus
Pacific Synod	Rev. M. O. Heller	Rev. Theo. A. Jensen
New York & New England	Rev. Clarence L. Braun	Rev. Clarence L. Braun
Nova Scotia Synod	Rev. E. V. Nonamaker	Rev. E. V. Nonamaker
Synod of West Virginia	Rev. C. E. Butler	Rev. C. E. Butler
Slovak Zion Synod	Rev. Andrew B. Svasko	Rev. Andrew B. Svasko
Florida Synod		Mr. E. R. Sheldon, 2719 13th St., St. Petersburg, Fla.

* Deceased   † Resigned

While time does bring changes in personnel, the specialized field of statistics requires trained and experienced men. This should be emphasized and kept in mind by all of the Constituent Synods.

PRINTED MINUTES: PROGRESS IN UNIFORMITY AND STANDARDIZATION

The latest complete set of available minutes, 1929, of the thirty-three constituent synods of the United Lutheran Church in America showed some progress in uniformity and the meeting of the requirements of standardization. Some of the synods did not use the standard parochial blank in their minutes. Some of the synods did not print totals for their entire synod. Some did not print a comparison of totals. Some exceed two pages in printing the rubrics of the standard parochial blank. Some still print the rubrics across the narrow width of the page. Inserts seem to have disappeared. The size of the printed minutes is now practically uniform, namely, 6x9 inches, which makes it possible to have the minutes bound in a series of volumes. The constituent synods should conform to the standard parochial blank, and print this blank lengthwise on two pages with approximately forty-one lines to a page, and all of the constituent synods should strike a total and compare with the total of the previous year as to increase or decrease.

STATISTICAL AND CHURCH YEAR BOOK COMMITTEE

Your committee held two meetings during the biennium, April 16, 1929, and April 23, 1930, both meetings were held in the Chapel of the Lutheran Church House, 39 East 35th Street, New York, N. Y. At the first meeting, Rev. George H. Schnur, D.D., was elected Chairman of the Committee and Rev. G. L. Kieffer, D.D., Litt.D., was elected Secretary and Treasurer. Rev. George H. Schnur was elected editor of the 1930 United Lutheran Church Year Book and also the 1931 United Lutheran Church Year Book. Rev. W. Chester Hill is the new member of your Committee appointed in place of Rev. W. M. Kopenhaver, who was unable to attend the meetings in 1928 on account of illness.

THE YEAR BOOK OF THE UNITED LUTHERAN CHURCH

Your Committee at both of its meetings in 1929 and 1930 passed upon and approved the contents of the Year Book of the United Lutheran

Church for 1930 and 1931. The statistical material, the alphabetical directory and geographical directory excepting the allocation of the pastors to their congregations in large cities, were provided by the Statistical Secretary of the United Lutheran Church in America, Rev. G. L. Kieffer, D.D., Litt.D. The Statistical and Church Year Book Committee assumes responsibility for the contents of the United Lutheran Church Year Book.

TOOLS FOR PASTORS

1. *The Standard Parochial Blank.* The Standard Parochial Blank used by pastors in submitting the report of the congregation to the Constituent Synod has been repeatedly revised in order to make it more usable and serviceable.

2. *The Parish Registry.* The Parish Registry, which appeared some years ago under the editorship of Dr. George H. Schnur and by the authority of the Statistical and Church Year Book Committee, has found favor everywhere, and is today a necessity both for congregations and pastors.

3. *Auxiliary Blanks.* The annual auxiliary blanks for congregational schools, congregational societies and organizations and Church Councils and Board of Trustees, and also the monthly auxiliary congregational blanks, the report of the pastors, the report of financial secretaries and the report of the congregational treasurers: (a) current and unusual expenses; (b) benevolence; and the report of committees and boards have all had the approval of the Conference of Statistical Secretaries both at Richmond and Erie, and have been repeatedly revised by the Statistical and Church Year Book Committee. They have been held in abeyance until the call for them has become urgent. They will be ready for use in December, 1930.

Another auxiliary blank will be provided for use in house to house canvas and visitation. These blanks will be a great aid in evangelism work.

SERVICE RENDERED

The Statistical Secretary of the United Lutheran Church in America supplied the United Lutheran Church statistics to the National Lutheran Council for the Lutheran World Almanac for 1929-30 and for the National Lutheran Council's annual releases through Dr. H. K. Carroll for his articles on religious denominations in the United States as published in the *Christian Herald,* 1929 and 1930: to Dr. H. S. Myers of the United Stewardship Council for the Benevolence Statistics, 1929-1930, to the editors of the Encyclopedia Americana, the International Year Book in the articles on "The Lutherans"; to the editors of the World Almanac, Eagle Almanac and many others.

INCOMPLETE PAROCHIAL STATISTICAL REPORTS

All synods should conform to using the standard Parochial Blank and the Standard Assembly sheets, as otherwise statistics are incomplete and their rubrics are few. All Statistical Secretaries of Constituent Synods should strike totals of their parochial reports and make comparisons with previous years. All totals should balance. In conforming with the above, all congregations cannot help but feel that they are, even if small, a part of the larger units: The Constituent Synod, the United Lutheran Church, the Lutherans of America and Lutherans of the World.

JUGGLING OF MEMBERSHIP

There seems to be a distinct shifting and juggling of members which is not alone confined to the communing members. Glowing yearly accessions are announced at Easter time. These accessions seem to melt away when the parochial reports are submitted to the constituent synod. When the different membership rubrics of an entire constituent synod show only a gain of a few members, there surely must be something the matter somewhere. After all, it is the business of the church to win members. The increase and decrease for the year, therefore, becomes a picture of the efficiency of the congregations and synods. In view of the fact that the United Lutheran Church in America has reached a period of growth so that achievements may be tabulated over a period of ten or more years, and lines of expectancies be determined, it is now to be hoped that the time will soon arrive that the membership rubrics will be freed entirely from financial or any other entanglements.

END OF FISCAL YEAR

All of the Constituent Synods of the United Lutheran Church excepting the Synod of Ohio have conformed to the standard of ending their fiscal years on December 31st, the end of the calendar year. The Statistical and Church Year Book Committee has been a pioneer here. Other churches and denominations have commended and are inaugurating movements looking to similar uniformity.

UNITED STATES CENSUS OF RELIGIOUS BODIES, 1926

The complete report of the United States Census of Religious Bodies, 1926, has appeared in two volumes: Vol. 1, Summary and Detailed Tables; Vol. II, Separate Denominations. They may be purchased from the Government Printer for $3.50. These volumes contain much information concerning the United Lutheran Church in America. They may also be obtained from your United States Congressman or Senator.

The bulletin, "Lutherans," which was separately printed by the United States Government, is found in Volume II. Two thousand copies of this bulletin were distributed through the constituent synods of the United Lutheran Church in America.

EXPENSES

The expenses of the Statistical and Church Year Book Committee have been met by the Treasurer of the United Lutheran Church, the amount being recorded in the Treasurer's report.

CHARTS AND GRAPHS

The Chairman of the Statistical and Church Year Book Committee, and the Statistical Secretary of the United Lutheran Church beg permission to present such charts and graphs as they may deem advisable at the time of the Convention which may or may not be desired as part of the minutes.

PAROCHIAL STATISTICS OF THE UNITED LUTHERAN CHURCH—1929

Tables showing totals for the Parochial Statistics for the Constituent Synod as well as for the United Lutheran Church for the year 1928 are hereby appended. The tables showing totals for the Parochial Statistics for the Constituent Synod as well as the United Lutheran Church for the year 1929 will be available for the minutes of the convention.

RECOMMENDATIONS

1. That the constituent synods be requested in the printing of their minutes to make the pages after the title page a calendar page, indicating the special days and dates of the United Lutheran Church and the special days and dates of the constitunt synod, and also a table showing the use of the Budget Benevolence Dollar of the United Lutheran Church and one showing the use of the Budget Benevolence Dollar of the Constituent Synod, or a table showing a combination of both.

2. That we request the constituent synods to urge their congregations to use the "Parish Register" prepared by your Committee for use in congregations of the United Lutheran Church.

3. That we request the constituent synods to secure sufficient number of the sets of the Standard Parish Record cards for Statistical Secretaries, so that the Statistical Secretaries of the constituent synods can complete a card file of all the congregations of the synod.

4. That we request the constituent synods to make use of the State of the Church Blank now ready in final form, as provided by the Statistical Committee of the United Lutheran Church in America.

5. That we request the constituent synods to introduce into the congregations of the United Lutheran Church in America the standard auxiliary congregational blanks for monthly and annual reports and such other blanks as the Statistical Committee in conference with the Statistical Secretaries of the constituent synods of the United Lutheran Church may be able to provide in order that accurate and uniform statistics of the United Lutheran Church in America may become possible.

6. That we request that all constituent synods of the United Lutheran Church be again requested to have their minutes printed in uniform size and style; and, to have their Parochial Statistics printed lengthwise on

the page and not crosswise on a vertical page, using only two pages for all the rubrics, and using approximately forty-one lines to the page; all Parochial Statistics to contain a summary in which a total is given for the synod for the year, together with a total for the preceding year, also, a comparative statement under "Increase" and "Decrease" on all rubrics.

7. That we request all constituent synods to use the Standard Parochial Blanks and Standard Assembly sheets not in modified, but in complete form, thereby conforming their practice to the standard of the United Lutheran Church.

8. That the constituent synods be requested to co-operate with the Statistical and Church Year Book Committee of the United Lutheran Church in the production of a Statistical Handbook of the United Lutheran Church once every ten years.

9. That the constituent synods be again requested to make provision for their statistical secretaries at future conventions of the United Lutheran Church in order that they may attend the Conference of Statistical Secretaries which will meet at the time of the Convention.

10. We request that the fiscal years of all congregational organizations, congregations, constituent synods of the United Lutheran Church, be made concurrent with the calendar year ending December 31st each year, and that all published reports and statistics be of the date December 31st of the previous year, thereby aiding the effort for accurate and uniform statistics in the United Lutheran Church.

11. We request that the constituent synods begin the preparation of a statistical and graphic history of their synod and of their congregations.

Respectfully submitted,

Statistical and Church Year Book Committee.

GEORGE H. SCHNUR, *Chairman,*
GEORGE LINN KIEFFER, *Secretary-Treasurer,*
C. W. CASSELL,
J. D. KROUT,
H. E. PUGH,
C. J. ROCKEY,
M. G. L. RIETZ,
W. CHESTER HILL.

The Rev. George L. Kieffer, Statistical Secretary, analyzed the statistics as presented in the report and moved that the statistical table for the year 1929 and also the analysis of the statistics for the years 1919 to 1929 be inserted in the report. The motion was carried.

Recommendations 1 to 7 inclusive were adopted.

Recommendation 8 was adopted after adding the words "once every ten years."

Recommendations 9, 10 and 11 were adopted.

The report of the Statistical Secretary and that of the Editor of the Church Year Book, having been presented, are here inserted.

Report of the Statistical Secretary of the United Lutheran Church in America

The report of the Statistical Secretary of the United Lutheran Church in America is in part embodied in the report of the Statistical and Church Committee Year Book.

Attention is respectfully called to the part of the committee's report referring to the charts and graphs.

The Lutheran Church has been leader in the field of statistics since 1919, but there is a gap prior to this year. A number of books have recently appeared containing statistical histories of different denominations and churches. The Lutheran Church is usually listed as not having such a history. This is to be lamented. Immediate steps should be taken by each constituent synod and congregation to provide such a history.

The salary of the Statistical Secretary during the biennium was $800 per annum.

Respectfully submitted,

G. L. KIEFFER, *Statistical Secretary.*

The Report of the Editor of the United Lutheran Church Year Book

The report of the editor of the United Lutheran Church Year Book is embodied in the report of the Statistical and Church Year Book Committee.

Respectfully submitted,

GEORGE H. SCHNUR, *Editor.*

PAROCHIAL REPORT OF THE UNITED LUTHERAN CHURCH IN AMERICA FOR THE YEAR 1928

PAROCHIAL

Index Number / Nos	SYNOD	When Organized	Pastors	Parishes	Congregations	Membership: Baptized	Membership: Confirmed	Membership: Communing	Accessions Children: Baptism	Accessions Children: Otherwise	Accessions Adult: Baptism	Accessions Adult: Confirmation	Accessions Adult: Certificate	Accessions Adult: Otherwise	Losses Children: Death	Losses Children: Otherwise	Losses: Death	Losses Adult: Certificate	Losses Adult: Otherwise
(col) 1		2	3	4	5	6	7	8	9	10	11	12	13	14	15	16	17	18	19
1	Ministerium of Pennsylvania	Aug. 15, 1748	463	371	585	283486	193563	141229	6933	2913	533	6214	2904	2071	501	2940	3080	1974	3868
2	Ministerium of New York	Oct. 23, 1786	173	140	147	97846	67735	46287	2873	1343	139	2583	478	1577	142	1547	1505	328	2257
3	United Synod of North Carolina	May, 1803	105	95	161	34418	24572	18504	890	798	157	786	579	44	66	168	252	344	361
4	Synod of Maryland	Oct. 11, 1820	123	119	140	64663	46890	30600	1108	191	79	388	323	237	53	322	410	250	485
5	Synod of South Carolina	Jan. 14, 1824	63	70	109	26837	19906	13358	529	188	56	577	505	409	86	126	244	352	116
6	Synod of West Pennsylvania	Sept. 5, 1825	108	92	160	58440	43519	33438	1363	380	242	1299	734	1633	83	208	687	561	425
7	Synod of Virginia	Aug., 1829	88	78	172	23556	18936	11801	393	169	207	376	337	1035	80	52	222	247	120
8	Synod of New York	Oct. 26, 1830	201	144	162	59345	39031	24817	1690	1274	219	1459	833	196	95	1290	566	429	2112
9	Synod of Ohio	Nov. 7, 1836	226	215	283	81292	56900	47793	1843	832	509	1860	1347	1475	64	566	887	1029	2235
10	East Pennsylvania Synod	May 2, 1842	165	132	159	69051	49866	34183	1636	641	377	1447	1182	99	15	426	689	638	878
11	Alleghany Synod	Sept., 1842	83	70	146	40600	30625	20988	802	146	198	602	368	308	74	462	416	401	483
12	Pittsburgh Synod	Jan. 15, 1845	264	219	317	117310		52244	2934	1566	359	2782	1636	246	2	1750	1015	1384	2601
13	Indiana Synod	Oct. 28, 1848	58	59	76	15659	11896	8614	274	140	64	358	221	275	13	84	110	143	162
14	Illinois Synod	Sept. 18, 1851	149	122	122	50319	33364	25336	1521	1464	360	1703	795	181	25	850	371	497	1253
15	Texas Synod	Nov. 10, 1851	20	19	28	5916	3848	3001	139	95	10	163	51	269	35	45	50	31	53
16	Susquehanna Synod of C. Pa	Feb., 1855	111	85	166	51116	38606	26646	1122	320	215	1099	767	272	16	917	486	462	567
17	Mississippi Synod	July 21, 1855	9	6	12	772	620	270	18		10	15	11	248		17	12	6	25
18	Synod of Iowa	Sept. 3, 1855	28	32	33	14019	8861	6356	425	219	140	532	214	260	27	103	88	193	207
19	Michigan Synod	Oct. 27, 1855	64	71	88	20635	15020	9431	496	333	150	517	489	124	45	233	202	140	620
20	Synod of Georgia	July, 1860	28	37	44	8039	5381	3630	156	103	23	156	238	307	28	43	43	98	170
21	Synod of Canada	July 21, 1861	75	64	87	25210	16639	12589	639	164	19	681	140	79	6	252	247	199	684
22	Synod of Kansas	Nov., 1868	50	36	45	9851	7118	5243	263	131	69	279	199		2	110	113	136	192
23	Synod of Nebraska	Sept. 1, 1871	52	42	55	18078	12122	8252	595	220	167	542	308		55	144	88	263	310
24	Wartburg Synod	, 1875	54	44	55	19278	12615	8186	528	67	45	544	55		18	151	191	40	335
25	German Nebraska Synod	July 24, 1890	84	84	89	17225	11283	8937	452	304	46	406	92		64	65	115	43	87
26	Synod of California	Apr. 2, 1891	58	37	37	9042	5704	4193	305	88	48	298	163		25	236	87	116	231
27	Rocky Mountain Synod	May, 1891	24	15	15	3276	2414	1623	118		19	81	129		11	87	30	37	64
28	Synod of the Northwest	Sept. 22, 1891	101	80	81	46112	29117	22194	1598	1353	220	1502	325	1630		1675	202	321	3421
29	Manitoba Synod	July 16, 1897	41	35	30	11967	6777	5037	562			470		221		111	155		
30	Pacific Synod	Sept. 26, 1901	41	35	93	5665	3330	2239	197	282	37	275	155	294	18	1060	52	59	204
31	New York & New England Synod	Sept. 23, 1902	111	93	93	56485	37618	27236	1464	1818	146	1719	1057		64	340	284	429	1250
32	Nova Scotia Synod	July 10, 1903	8	8	31	5778	3009	1512	135			107	32	3	25		62	30	52
33	Synod of West Virginia	Apr. 17, 1912	22	24	37	6281	4091	3229	126	43	26	137	64		11	33	47		
34	Slovak "Zion" Synod	June 10, 1919	22	18	31	12606	8001	6943	403			299		55			176	61	148
35	Totals for U. S. & Canada		3272	2790	3906	1370183	949188	676839	34530	17594	4896	32256	16725	17506	2010	16413	13184	11241	25976
36	Total Outside of U. S. & Canada		141		1609	150279	63119	48858	123	13	8605	4414	11	1424	28	16	2792	22	5486
37	U. L. C. World Total		3413	2790	5515	1520462	1012307	725697	34653	17607	13501	36670	16736	18930	2038	16429	15976	11263	31462

PAROCHIAL REPORT OF THE UNITED LUTHERAN CHURCH IN AMERICA FOR THE YEAR 1928—Continued

Index No.	CHURCH PAPERS 20 No.Sub.to Official Papers	21 No.S.S.Papers Distributed	22 No.Sub.to Oth'r Ch P'rs	CHURCH SCHOOLS — SUNDAY 23 Number	24 Officers & Teachers	25 Scholars	26 HomeDept	27 Cradle Roll	WEEKDAY 28 Number	29 Teachers	30 Scholars	STUDENTS 31 Catechumens Catechetical	32 Ministry	33 Deaconess	34 In Luthera Institutions	35 Ins t ti ns in Non-Luth	CHURCH SOCIETIES — MEN'S 36 Num	37 Members	WOMEN'S 38 Number	39 Members	YOUNG P. 40 Number	41 Members	FINANCIAL 42 Church Edifices	43 Parsonages	44 School & Parish Houses
1	7216	14382	6206	577	11801	117503	5366	12678	137	848	1678	9646	92	11	297	1515	217	10236	736	35025	614	23650	20924287	2321120	1865300
2	2432	6518	1949	166	2540	24527	373	4802	37	137	1992	2901	46		67	244	122	7164	276	17076	247	8267	8620775	1365125	1240800
3	1229	2629	2644	138	2040	22945	74	1004	71	290	5232	2685	40	4	202	281	44	1432	146	4476	201	4842	2802082	374410	85569
4	1878	4733	1849	143	3546	34761	2345	4156	23	157	1600	1325	9	4	83	465	65	2926	217	11086	188	6771	6128560	729800	273600
5	1100	2424	1570	108	1311	13707	293	621	50	336	4370	1660	28	5	209	274	35	1086	135	4232	159	4300	1329936	247849	89000
6	1592	2385	1439	159	3835	42984	1475	3415	27	154	2410	3640	38	1	178	351	47	2106	228	9695	189	7748	4143100	568239	335500
7	1285	2644	2323	135	2513	14308	1072	1072	35	158	1715	819	14			131	24	818	250	4168	116	3944	1750050	382607	105300
8	1368	6250	1165	139	5172	20010	849	3208	34	126	1309	1873	32		80	278	82	2995	250	9466	242	5980	6286300	968100	510000
9	3383	23451	1819	157	3821	52303	1489	3573	34	104	2190	3303	46	2	324	717	130	6249	463	18250	248	6603	9005600	964800	485500
10	2113	6576	1614	157	2562	36822	3933	3577	43	265	3521	2701	47	2	153	521	94	5108	278	12746	263	7343	7523942	1026642	444126
11	1156	7081	5792	132	5606	24057	1214	2327	49	298	5285	1762	25	2	87	375	2	135	172	5392	119	3968	2995100	456331	83060
12	3842	23026	16145	5299	1123	51463	2918	7017	75	393	555	4643	72	1	228	679	140	5489	516	7612	383	11071	10112794	1387142	512500
13	501	4148	359	140	3004	8867	439	855	30	49	1896	571	14		36	13	24	755	116	3443	66	1375	1598375	228100	46000
14	1784	13413	1694	140	224	27513	511	2907	25	172	218	2007	54	2	120	406	71	2964	253	8785	198	5462	4430857	547370	204350
15	173	244	644	38	3233	1890	24	96	1	15	21	221	33	1		13	53	60	31	1949	27	683	133000	49000	26750
16	1000	5567	589	167	65	32523	1670	2705	8	186	2292	1715	35	3	139	391	39	2219	198	7521	128	4436	41889500	493354	45380
17	38	58	78	32	670	437		9			21	41	7			4	1	14	1	118	5	60	32500	3500	
18	469	3494	424	81	1334	5541	74	796	11	41	518	904	7	1	17	148	13	482	64	2270	59	1878	1003472	159400	3000
19	646	5668	763	34	802	10660	74	898	4	50	566	527	5	1	36	149	25	1009	118	4269	87	2067	2728289	225900	98500
20	555	1016	564	77	699	3237	162	206	22	24	279	267	7		22	86	8	258	61	1789	54	1330	997100	99000	106700
21	1416	1789	579	40	935	6300		847	8	24	536	454	16		34	34	8	377	63	2577	60	2131	1013480	197900	70650
22	394	2246	456	44	494	5648	60	626	23	33	571	232	14		22	153	19	553	90	2719	53	1235	1342490	202900	48000
23	722	3527	2863	53	431	7881	292	989	10	53	471	1155	17	1	34	271	11	312	63	2566	63	1578	1213886	161579	16000
24	766	879		41	458	5834	183		18	39	468	701	9		83		22	684	63	684	41	1224			
25	779	1432	153	66	241	4412	79	211	36	7	738	740	2		35	30	1	12	64	1832	34	1277	675000	221500	13900
26	307	1647	188	37	1714	3606	124	460	4	11	180	413	7		5	99	13	387	66	2033	52	1022	1442800	81300	40200
27	192	1090	72	14	128	1610	121	259	3	70	160	74	2	2	9	45	4	117	20	724	20	404	426500	37700	
28	1315	6852	1032	92	316	14504	40	2488	27	45	1195	1913	27		56	433	55	2196	149	5799	158	4199	3882295	324500	174100
29				54	2174	1791			60	8	1766								16	285	25	584			
30	215	1789	244	36	157	2767	47	343	4	235	54	232	2	3	3	96	12	259	15	1210	44	912	419000	64300	3800
31	1316	4167	1021	95	456	18710	662	2998	46		3016	1646	19	3	48	567	73	3917	165	7770	208	5926	5854778	599900	533095
32	235	233	31	18	66	1153				4		152	5	2	6	6			17	646	7	217	189875	31000	200
33	392	156	854	31		3522	90	344	4	13	306	287	3	2	10	56	12	327	45	1105	27	618	710761	114601	2000
34				22		1112			84	149	3044												530000	129000	23500
35	41809	163027	57123	3671	65465	624908	26046	65787	1033	4513	65123	51212	709	44	2678	8967	1436	63646	5322	209318	4385	133105	114446734	14764569	7486380
36	27			1054	2147	49543			114	1783	39716	110	188		3	18			5	78	8	177	2382300	36000	11800
37	41836	163027	57123	4725	67612	674451	26046	65787	1147	6296	104839	51322	897	44	2681	8985	1436	63646	5327	209396	4393	133282	116829034	14800569	7498180

PAROCHIAL REPORT OF THE UNITED LUTHERAN CHURCH

FINANCIAL

Nos.	VALUATION OF CHURCH PROPERTY				CONGREGATIONAL EXPENSES			CONGREGATIONAL BENEVOLENCE — APPORTIONED						UNAPPORTIONED			SUMMARY	
	Endowment 45	Other Property 46	Total Valuation 47	Indebtedness 48	Current 49	Unusual 50	Total 51	Paid 52	Excess 53	Deficit 54	Education 55	Foreign Missions 56	Home Missions 57	Inner Missions 58	Other Benevolence 59	Total Un-apportioned Benevolence 60	Total Benevolence 61	Total Expenditures 62
1	1017102	1101429	27229238	3493886	1663883	1558820	3224703	381444	3327	196957	13861	34114	14943	382627	59299	504844	886288	4108991
2	203592	801168	12231460	3106587	682537	375919	1058456	107383	90	167352	4582	4307	8455	172675	23196	207437	314820	1373276
3	20439	90049	3372549	373668	245748	214117	459865	44402	10		11005	8536	8437	35190	15451	78637	123039	582904
4	95409	421859	7649228	858753	395248	187620	582868	76166	2262	14906	2701	15550	5328	69861	20046	116595	192761	775629
5	66000	125344	18558329	140640	144384	64429	208813	32251	18	9218	14936	4770	9633	21546	7628	54208	86459	295272
6	297216	616321	5960376	281006	434164	220238	654402	122872	6788	26444	5960	17285	2913	82750	25940	141568	264440	918842
7	167958	212549	2482762	1399656	161318	84825	246143	34864	101		4607	7317	3498	30688	7541	53066	87930	334073
8	202782	477335	8179731	1197690	622028	671484	1293512	76905	1217	50183	79125	5867	8461	50152	7408	146050	229955	1554518
9	111699	327744	1044934	1545175	818489	361518	1180007	211636	3081	40039	10181	21745	9035	31374	91114	162875	374511	1524271
10	152563	119771	9475017	285157	686702	477207	1163909	130250	407	23039	13309	31749	4250	143819	32200	230112	360362	589948
11	42600	179951	3695862	1967604	307667	105550	413217	87718	5945	10869	3983	8147	15049	55991	16642	89013	176731	2043229
12	179951	157537	12979876	411531	1008609	560428	1569037	192549		46851	10668	27719	3482	191979	36228	281643	474192	395076
13	76884	154142	2106896	956680	180289	147656	327945	36377	85	10990	1928	2888	9868	19053	3403	30754	67131	972670
14	61918	13079	5398637	41482	493350	209895	703245	94552	165	12577	47092	15743	366	88499	13671	174873	269245	61153
15	150	115950	222579	485180	28502	19173	47675	3863			203	205	1677	7452	1389	9615	13478	709308
16	113295	2000	4956929	3300	362517	162107	524624	94133	1333	19541	8045	6813	32	53982	20034	90551	184684	6900
17		75810	38000	325045	4080	595	4675	991	2	306	114	25	414	531	532	1234	2225	211268
18	5200	22410	1246882	776904	146032	35453	181485	14050	776	14070	3038	986	815	8810	2485	15733	29783	415686
19	10775	52484	3085874	362042	197185	154429	352614	32955		13649	563	3439	857	19710	5590	30117	63072	182921
20	11250	53300	1266534	114184	88801	60449	149250	13922		3896	2254	1440	722	9515	5683	19749	35671	247165
21	37800	23820	1373130	222106	145046	44862	189908	28791	38	49791	2975	1344	388	18409	5016	28466	57257	328366
22	15250	4460	1632460	122647	135965	150412	286317	23606	387	4882	568	965	3223	12022	4440	18383	41989	231230
23	4460		1548572	112705	127348	46237	173585	31066		12050	7323	3967		2285	9781	26579	57645	165758
24			1155677	64809	114891	31890	146781	8305					815		10672	10672	18977	184218
25	5450	38265	935015	309837	88423	64616	153039	6938	21	29938	3957	590	1188	16805	2074	24241	31179	357108
26	800	58999	1624099	210796	117321	207302	324623	14413	181	2611	283	2206	770	9459	4936	18072	32485	86323
27	40	24269	4885509		40066	33347	73413	6553		1508	85	316	4186	3518	1668	6357	12910	609777
28	3000	96775	4480670		372724	180116	552840	63166			8133	2727		37888	22037	74971	38137	65023
29			330480		54382		54382	8999	212	1235					1642	1642	10641	101219
30		12700	500700	196880	54321	26910	81231	9655	11745	239	1577	371	600	4834	2951	10333	19988	1721679
31	127653	1188393	8303819	1620236	727202	774916	1476118	10345		2687	7619	14581	10146	78686	30184	141216	245561	30069
32	2150	2150	223225	16235	19460	4734	24194	2234		4866					3641	3641	5875	123752
33	1050	86100	914512	171631	71832	23415	95247	10478	279		101	1743	412	13600	2171	18027	28505	78479
34		6000	688500	91858	75120	200	75320	1191							1968	1968	3159	
35	2932175	7585846	148701861	19416910	10761252	7261869	18051503	2109023	28470	794562	270776	247455	132640	1673710	498661	2823242	4932265	22983768
36	25000	48500	2503360		171101		171191								31442	31442	31442	202633
37	2957175	7634346	151205461	19416910	10932243	7261869	18222694	2109023	28470	766062	270776	247455	132640	1673710	530103	2854684	4963707	23186401

COMPARATIVE PAROCHIAL REPORT OF THE UNITED LUTHERAN CHURCH IN AMERICA FOR 1919, 1920, 1921, 1922, 1923, 1924, 1925, 1926, 1927, 1928

Nos.	Year	When Organized	Pastors	Parishes	Congregations	Membership: Baptized	Confirmed	Communing	Accessions Children: Baptism	Otherwise	Accessions Adult: Baptism	Confirmation	Certificate	Otherwise	Losses Children: Death	Otherwise	Losses Adult: Death	Certificate	Otherwise	Church Papers: No.Sub.to Official	No.S.S.Papers Distributed	No.Sub.to Oth'r Ch.P'rs
	1	2	3	4	5	6	7	8	9	10	11	12	13	14	15	16	17	18	19	20	21	22
1	1928		3272	2790	3906	1370183	949188	676839	34530	17594	4896	32256	16725	17506	2010	16413	13184	11241	25976	41809	163027	57123
2	1927		3184	2689	3881	1321780	933650	676496	36668	18264	5397	33871	18704	20012	2023	14772	12677	12117	24464	43917	162246	49825
3	1 Year's Gain		88	101	25	48403	15538	343								1641	507		1512		781	7298
4	1 Year's Decrease								2138	670	501	1615	1979	2506	13			876		2108		
5	1928		3272	2790	3906	1370183	949188	676839	34530	17594	4896	32256	16725	17506	2010	16413	13184	11241	25976	41809	163027	57123
6	1926		3127	2706	3876	1315620	916858	677287	34562	17573	5178	25451	16866	19781	1983	12789	11758	11467	22831	50684	167418	38573
7	2 Years' Gain		145	84	30	54563	32330			21		6805			27	3624	1426		3145			18550
8	2 Years' Decrease							448	32		282		141	2275				226		8875	4391	
9	1928		3272	2790	3906	1370183	949188	676839	34530	17594	4896	32256	16725	17506	2010	16413	13184	11241	25976	41809	163027	57123
10	1925		3011	2649	3875	1276176	886840	669695	35307	16658	5536	31071	17366	18504	2004	12335	11454	12111	23935	50735	174407	36101
11	3 Years' Gain		261	141	31	94007	62348	7144		936		1185			6	4078	1730		2041			21022
12	3 Years' Decrease								777		640		641	998				870		8926	11380	
13	1928		3272	2790	3906	1370183	949188	676839	34530	17594	4896	32256	16725	17506	2010	16413	13184	11241	25976	41809	163027	57123
14	1924		2983	2643	3829	1238009	856180	645836	35138	14029	5746	31020	17314	18090	1982	9918	11250	11887	23356	50224	162037	39471
15	4 Years' Gain		289	147	77	132174	93008	31003		3565		1236			28	6495	1934		2620		990	17652
16	4 Years' Decrease								608		850		589	584				646		8415		
17	1928		3272	2790	3906	1370183	949188	676839	34530	17594	4896	32256	16725	17506	2010	16413	13184	11241	25976	41809	163027	57123
18	1923		2924	2566	3812	1201401	839279	633184	33837	12419	4472	28188	15600	16125	2244	9788	11518	11016	25436	47618	152731	34708
19	5 Years' Gain		348	224	94	168782	109909	43655	693	5175	424	4068	1125	1381		6625	1666	225	540		10296	22415
20	5 Years' Decrease														234					5809		
21	1928		3272	2790	3906	1370183	949188	676839	34530	17594	4896	32256	16725	17506	2010	16413	13184	11241	25976	41809	163027	57123
22	1922		2900	2501	3732	1164550	819063	621123	36016	12704	5599	30954	16345	16445	2334	9370	11741	10934	25650	49267	144631	33867
23	6 Years' Gain		372	289	174	205633	130125	55716		4890		1302	380	1061		7043	1443	307	326		18396	23256
24	6 Years' Decrease								1486		703				324					7458		
25	1928		3272	2790	3906	1370183	949188	676839	34530	17594	4896	32256	16725	17506	2010	16413	13184	11241	25976	41809	163027	57123
26	1921		2887	2492	3803	1147007	801250	597768	37403	11773	5302	30467	16456	16500	2392	8921	11051	11475	25485	36969	118139	21454
27	7 Years' Gain		385	298	103	223176	147938	79071		5821		1789	269	1006		7492	2133		491	4840	44888	35669
28	7 Years' Decrease								2873		406				382			234				
29	1928		3272	2790	3906	1370183	949188	676839	34530	17594	4896	32256	16725	17506	2010	16413	13184	11241	25976	41809	163027	57123
30	1920		2812		3775	1117938	791400	580018	36438		4834	29380	15214	14571			11554	11610	26550			
31	8 Years' Gain		460		131	252245	157788	96821			62	2876	1511	2935			1630					
32	8 Years' Decrease								1908									369	574			
33	1928		3272	2790	3906	1370183	949188	676839	34530	17594	4896	32256	16725	17506	2010	16413	13184	11241	25976	41809	163027	57123
34	1919		2843		3473	1094153	776582	474553	34785		4400	27645	13915	9235				10664	23467			

INDEX No.	23 NUMBER	24 Officers & Teachers	25 Scholars	26 Home Dept.	27 Cradle Roll	28 Number (Weekday)	29 Teachers	30 Scholars	31 Catechumens	32 Ministry	33 Deaconess	34 In Lutheran Institutions	35 In Non-Luth. Institutions	36 Number (Men's)	37 Memb'rs	38 Number (Women's)	39 Members	40 Number (Young P.)	41 Members	42 Church Edifices	43 Parsonages	44 School & Parish Houses
1	3671	65465	624908	26046	65787	1033	4513	65123	51212	709	44	2678	8967	1436	63646	5322	209318	4385	133105	114446734	14764569	7486380
2	3651	64212	613863	25826	65544	928	4183	58491	48823	261	52	2626	8338	1383	63146	5181	208003	3986	133682	108956533	14598321	6830516
3	20	1253	11045	220	243	105	330	6632	2389	52	8	52	629	53	500	141	1315	399	577	5490201	166248	655864
4																						
5	3671	65465	624908	26046	65787	1033	4513	65123	51212	709	44	2678	8967	1436	63646	5322	209318	4385	133105	114446734	14764569	7486380
6	3524	62609	608261	27309	65938	647	3157	45366	48272	851	79	2632	7555	1294	59190	4830	199855	3825	130552	99894373	13381748	5198535
7	147	2856	16647	1263	151	386	1356	19757	2940	142	35	46	1412	142	4456	492	9463	560	2553	14552361	882821	2287845
8																						
9	3671	65465	624908	26046	65787	1033	4513	65123	51212	709	44	2678	8967	1436	63646	5322	209318	4385	133105	114446734	14764569	7486380
10	3531	59940	590169	28187	65706	651	2704	42372	49216	826	90	2551	6753	1211	56892	4515	184475	3547	122380	86288340	12532190	3919089
11	140	5525	34739	2141	81	382	1809	22751	1996	117	46	127	2214	225	6754	807	25843	838	10725	28158394	2232379	3567291
12																						
13	3671	65465	624908	26046	65787	1033	4513	65123	51212	709	44	2678	8967	1436	63646	5322	209318	4385	133105	114446734	14764569	7486380
14	3515	59205	571737	28028	63853	557	2051	38824	49310	828	68	2530	5841	1213	56605	4307	181449	3400	120277	78325563	11169150	3136620
15	156	6260	53171	1982	1934	476	2462	26299	1902	19	24	148	3126	223	7041	1015	27869	985	12828	35921171	3595419	4349760
16																						
17	3671	65465	624908	26046	65787	1033	4513	65123	51212	709	44	2678	8967	1436	63646	5322	209318	4385	133105	114446734	14764569	7486380
18	3440	56863	552872	22164	61995	523	1638	28438	45238	746	67	2381	5402	1137	53706	4151	174535	3200	115726	70971368	10415614	2463970
19	231	8602	72036	3882	3792	510	2875	36685	5974	37	23	297	3565	299	9940	1171	34783	1185	17379	43475366	4348955	5022410
20																						
21	3671	65465	624908	26046	65787	1033	4513	65123	51212	709	44	2678	8967	1436	63646	5322	209318	4385	133105	114446734	14764569	7486380
22	3465	55330	555510	28446	59264	490	1453	25149	35311	717	59	2015	4520	1102	52525	4013	173270	3132	115234	65598841	9237584	1584150
23	206	10135	69398	2400	6523	543	3060	39974	15901	8	15	663	4447	334	11121	1309	36048	1253	17871	48847893	5526985	5902230
24																						
25	3671	65465	624908	26046	65787	1033	4513	65123	51212	709	44	2678	8967	1436	63646	5322	209318	4385	133105	114446734	14764569	7486380
26	3682	54268	522691	26142	52148	375	954	17534	34034	582	85	1712	4292	967	47052	3618	154089	2694	106842	63193694	8138433	878400
27	11	11197	102217	96	13639	658	3559	47589	17178	127	41	966	4675	469	16594	1704	55229	1691	26263	51253040	6626136	6607980
28																						
29	3671	65465	624908	26046	65787	1033	4513	65123	51212	709	44	2678	8967	1436	63646	5322	209318	4385	133105	114446734	14764569	7486380
30	3399	52939	515815	23506	46300	190	326	7070	44334	577	46	1838	4316	892	39426	3547	139205	2367	92822		6928456	
31	272	12526	109093	2540	19487	843	4187	58053	6878	132	2	840	4651	544	24220	1775	70113	2018	40283		7836113	
32																						
33	3671	65465	624908	26046	65787	1033	4513	65123	51212	709	44	2678	8967	1436	63646	5322	209318	4385	133105	114446734	14764569	7486380
34	3412	53524	514924	19019	32228	109	130	4779	36689	526	14	223	611	708	32550	2811	104760	2114	81746		2071193	
35	259	11941	109984	7027	33559	924	4383	60344	14523	183	30	2455	8356	728	31096	2511	104558	2271	51359		12693376	

Column group headings: PAROCHIAL — CHURCH SCHOOLS (SUNDAY: 23 Number, 24 Officers & Teachers, 25 Scholars, 26 Home Dept., 27 Cradle Roll; WEEKDAY: 28 Number, 29 Teachers, 30 Scholars), 31 Catechumens; STUDENTS (32 Ministry, 33 Deaconess, 34 In Lutheran Institutions, 35 In Non-Luth. Institutions); CHURCH SCHOOLS (MEN'S: 36 Number, 37 Memb'rs; WOMEN'S: 38 Number, 39 Members; YOUNG P.: 40 Number, 41 Members). FINANCIAL — Valuation Church Property (42 Church Edifices, 43 Parsonages, 44 School & Parish Houses).

COMPARATIVE PAROCHIAL REPORT OF THE UNITED LUTHERAN CHURCH IN AMERICA FOR 1919, 1920, 1921, 1922, 1923, 1924, 1925, 1926, 1927, 1928—Concluded

FINANCIAL

Index Number Nos.	Valuation of Church Property				Congregational Expenses			Congregational Benevolences									Summary	
								Apportioned			Unapportioned							
	Endowment	Other Property	Total Valuation	Indebtedness	Current	Unusual	Total	Paid	Excess	Deficit	Education	Foreign Missions	Home Missions	Inner Missions	Other Benevolence	Total unapportioned Benevolence	Total Benevolence	Total Expenditures
	45	46	47	48	49	50	51	52	53	54	55	56	57	58	59	60	61	62
1	2932175	7585846	148701861	19416910	10761252	7261869	18051503	2109023	28470	794562	270776	247455	132640	1673710	482380	2823242	4932265	22983768
2	2757866	7523560	140609870	17883930	10487001	8034224	18521226	2156391	31925	623483	434917	320647	129359	480531	515817	1881271	4037662	22558888
3	174309	62286	8091991	1532980	274251	772355	469723	47368	3455	171079	......	......	3281	......	33437	941971	894603	424880
4	......	......	......	......	......	......	......	......	......	......	164141	73192	......	119179	......	......	......	......
5	2932175	7585846	148701861	19416910	10761252	7261869	18051503	2109023	28470	794562	270776	247455	132640	1673710	482380	2823242	4932265	22983768
6	2547063	7441745	128964264	15300109	9443178	8651013	18094191	1853225	30138	460334	300820	268875	100063	314697	441606	1426061	3279286	21373477
7	385112	144101	19737597	4116801	1318074	1389144	42688	255798	1668	334228	30044	21420	32577	1359013	40774	1397181	1652979	1610291
8	......	......	......	......	......	......	......	......	......	......	......	......	......	......	......	......	......	......
9	2932175	7585846	148701861	19416910	10761252	7261869	18051503	2109023	28470	794562	270776	247455	132640	1673710	482380	2823242	4932265	22983768
10	2383469	6733780	118856868	11457989	8676760	7014663	15691423	1828761	41395	458335	623116	218881	110766	403638	526722	188323	3711884	19403307
11	548706	852066	36844993	7958921	2084492	247206	2360080	280262	12925	336227	352340	28574	21874	1270072	44342	940119	1220831	3580461
12	......	......	......	......	......	......	......	......	......	......	......	......	......	......	......	......	......	......
13	2932175	7585846	148701861	19416910	10761252	7261869	18051503	2109023	28470	794562	270776	247455	132640	1673710	482380	2823242	4932265	22983768
14	2281248	5806395	101368976	9265083	8041334	6818421	14859760	1748347	44595	390112	320448	256587	160597	354336	672022	1763990	3512337	18370097
15	650927	1779451	47332885	10151827	271993	443448	319173	360676	16125	404450	49672	9132	27957	1319374	189642	1059252	1419928	4611671
16	......	......	......	......	......	......	......	......	......	......	45280	......	......	......	......	......	......	......
17	2932175	7585846	148701861	19416910	10761252	7261869	18051503	2109023	28470	794562	270776	247455	132640	1673710	482380	2823242	4932265	22983768
18	2007007	4973232	90831211	7441246	7387593	4635721	12023314	1605290	48060	378486	316056	227718	86762	261050	596888	1488474	3093764	15117078
19	925148	2612614	57870050	11975664	3373659	2626148	6028189	503733	19950	416076	45280	19737	45878	1412660	114508	1334768	1838501	7866690
20	......	......	......	......	......	......	......	......	......	......	21906	......	......	......	......	......	......	......
21	2932175	7585846	148701861	19416910	10761252	7261869	18051503	2109023	28470	794562	270776	247455	132640	1673710	482380	2823242	4932265	22983768
22	1851134	3701544	81973253	7047140	6816399	8009146	10825545	1513077	45328	368687	292682	155599	72287	233324	777002	1530894	3043971	13869516
23	1081041	3884302	66728608	12369770	3944853	747277	7225958	595946	16858	425875	21906	91856	60353	1440386	294622	1292348	1888294	9114252
24	......	......	......	......	......	......	......	......	......	......	......	......	......	......	......	......	......	......
25	2932175	7585846	148701861	19416910	10761252	7261869	18051503	2109023	28470	794562	270776	247455	132640	1673710	482380	2823242	4932265	22983768
26	1895798	2400790	76507115	6011472	6621268	3835135	10456403	1440132	62601	342307	569521	140190	66369	240927	884653	1901660	3341792	13798195
27	1036377	5185056	72194746	13405438	4139984	3426734	7595100	668891	34131	452255	298745	107265	66271	1432783	402783	921582	1590473	9185573
28	......	......	......	......	......	......	......	......	......	......	......	......	......	......	......	......	......	......
29	2932175	7585846	148701861	19416910	10761252	7261869	18051503	2109023	28470	794562	270776	247455	132640	1673710	482380	2823242	4932265	22983768
30	2065974	......	70142813	5581845	5630943	2968750	8599693	1206115	......	612129	......	......	36017	233909	983743	1865798	3071913	11671606
31	866201	......	78559048	13835065	5130309	4293119	9451810	902908	......	341353	......	......	96623	1439801	957444	957444	1860352	11312162
32	......	......	......	......	......	......	......	......	......	......	......	......	......	......	501363	......	......	......
33	2932175	7585846	148701861	19416910	10761252	7261869	18051503	2109023	28470	794562	270776	247455	132640	1673710	482380	2823242	4932265	22983768
34	1032292	......	42383332	4527913	4984795	1916749	6911544	1344202	......	......	76	......	5459	70	902981	908386	2252788	9154332
35	1899883	......	106318529	14888997	5776457	5345120	11139959	764821	......	......	270700	127181	127181	1673640	......	1914656	2694417	13829436
36	......	......	......	......	......	......	......	......	......	......	......	......	......	......	......	......	......	......

PAROCHIAL REPORT OF THE UNITED LUTHERAN CHURCH IN AMERICA—1928
1928 and 1927 Gains Compared

PAROCHIAL

Index Number		PASTORS	Parishes (4)	Membership — Congregations (5)	Baptized (6)	Confirmed (7)	Communing (8)	Accessions — Children: Baptism (9)	Otherwise (10)	Adult: Baptized (11)	Confirmation (12)	Certificate (13)	Otherwise (14)	Losses — Children: Death (15)	Otherwise (16)	Adult: Death (17)	Certificate (18)	Otherwise (19)	Church Papers — No.Sub.to Official Papers (20)	No.S.S.Papers Distributed (21)	No.Sub.to Oth'r Ch.P'rs (22)
1	1928 Gain	88	101	25	48403	15538	343	2138	670	501	1615	1979	2506	13	1641	507	876	1512	2108	781	7298
2	1928 Decrease																				
3	1927 Gain	57		5	6160	16792									1983	919		1633	6767		11252
4	1927 Decrease		17				791	2106	691	219	8420	1838	231	40			650			5172	
5	1928 Net Gain	31	118	20	42243		1134	4244	1361	720	10035	3817	2737	53			1526			5953	
6	1928 Net Decrease					1254									342	412		121	4659		3954

FINANCIAL · PAROCHIAL

Index Number		Church Schools — Sunday: Number (23)	Officers & Teacher (24)	Scholars (25)	Home Dept. (26)	Cradle Roll (27)	Weekday: Number (28)	Teachers (29)	Scholars (30)	Catechetical: Catechumens (31)	Students: Ministry (32)	Deaconess (33)	In Lutheran Institutions (34)	In Non-Luth. Institutions (35)	Church Societies — Men's: Number (36)	Members (37)	Women's: Number (38)	Members (39)	Young P.: Number (40)	Members (41)	Valuation Church Property — Church Edifices (42)	Parsonages (43)	School & Parish Houses (44)
1	1928 Gain	20	1253	11045	220	243	105	330	6632	2389	52	8	52	629	53	500	141	1315	399	577	5490201	166248	655864
2	1928 Decrease																						
3	1927 Gain	127	1603	5602	1483	394	281	1026	13125	551	90	27	6	783	89	3956	351	8148	161	3130	9062160	716573	1631981
4	1927 Decrease																						
5	1928 Net Gain			5443	1703	637				1838			46						238				
6	1928 Net Decrease	107	350				107	696	6493		38	19		154	33	3456	210	6833		3307	3571959	550325	976117

PAROCHIAL REPORT OF THE UNITED LUTHERAN CHURCH IN AMERICA—1928
1928 and 1927 Gains Compared—Concluded

FINANCIAL

INDEX NUMBER	VALUATION OF CHURCH PROPERTY				CONGREGATIONAL EXPENSES			CONGREGATIONAL BENEVOLENCE										SUMMARY	
	Endowment	Other Property	Total Valuation	Indebtedness	Current	Unusual	Total	APPORTIONED			UNAPPORTIONED					Total Un-apportioned Benevolence	Total Benevolence	Total Expenditures		
								Paid	Excess	Deficit	Education	Foreign Missions	Home Missions	Inner Missions	Other Benevolence			
	45	46	47	48	49	50	51	52	53	54	55	56	57	58	59	60	61	62
1	174309	62286	8091991	1532980	274251	772355	469723	47368	3455	171079	164141	73192	3281	1193179	33437	941971	894603	424880
2	210803	81815	11645606	2583821	1043823	616789	427125	303166	1787	163149	134097	51772	29296	165834	74211	455216	758336	1185411
3										7930								
4	36494	19529	3553615	1050841	769572	1389144	896848	350534	5242		298238	124961	26015	1359013	107648	486755	136267	760531

PAROCHIAL REPORT OF THE UNITED LUTHERAN CHURCH IN AMERICA—1928
Including Statistics Outside Continental United States and Canada

PAROCHIAL

Index No.	Country (1)	Province (2)	When Organized (3)	Pastors (4)	Congregations (5)	Baptized (6)	Confirmed (7)	Communing (8)	Children Baptism (9)	Children Otherwise (10)	Adult Baptism (11)	Confirmation (12)	Certificate (13)	Otherwise (14)	Children Death (15)	Children Otherwise (16)	Adult Death (17)	Adult Certificate (18)	Adult Otherwise (19)
1	India	Madras	1843	For. 19 Native	1471	140462	58382	45458			8603	2879		1421			2742		5464
2	Africa	Liberia	1860	For. 11 Native	45	300	215	150											
3	Japan	Kyushu-Hondo	1893	For. 14 Native	25	2500	1000	1047					3						
4	China	Shantung	1897	For. 6 Native	35	2390	1237	620	55						15	6	40	10	
5	Virgin Islands		1666	U.L.C.	9	2032	805	760											
6	British Guiana	New Amsterdam	1898	For. 2 Native	11	300	200	200			2								
7	Porto Rico		1898	U.L.C. 7 Other	3	1631	780	555	68	13			8	3	13	10	10	12	22
8	Argentina	Buenos Aires	1908	For. 2 Native	10	664	500	68											
9	Total outside U.S. and Canada			141	1609	150279	63119	48858	123	13	8605	4414	11	1424	28	16	2792	22	5486
10	Total U.S. and Canada			3272	3906	1370183	949188	676839	34530	17594	4896	32256	16725	17506	2010	16413	13184	11241	25976
11	World Total U.L.C. in A.			3413	5515	1520462	1012307	725697	34653	17607	13501	36670	16736	18930	2038	16429	15976	11263	31462

PAROCHIAL / FINANCIAL

Index No.	No. Sub. to Official Papers (20)	No. S.S. Papers Distributed (21)	N. Sub. to Other Ch. Paprs (22)	Sunday Number (23)	Sunday Officers & Teachers (24)	Sunday Scholars (25)	Home Dept (26)	Cradle Roll (27)	Weekday Number (28)	Weekday Teachers (29)	Weekday Scholars (30)	Catechumens Catechetical (31)	Ministry (32)	Deaconess (33)	In Lutheran Institutions (34)	In Non-Luth Institutions (35)	Men's Number (36)	Men's Members (37)	Women's Number (38)	Women's Members (39)	Young P. Number (40)	Young P. Members (41)	Church Edifices (42)	Parsonages (43)	School and Parish Houses (44)
1			1032		1836	44632			1032	1606	34712		172										1116600		
2					25	500			8	25	500												75000		
3					30	800			9	30	700	65											600000		
4					52	300			41	52	1669												185000		
5					60	760			5		130												113000	6000	4800
6					10	250			6		250												13700		
7				17	88	1765				10	195	45											71000	30000	7000
8					46	536				46	1560												208000		
9	36		1032	1054	2147	49543			1114	1783	39716	110	188		3	18			5	78	8	177	2382300	36000	11800
10	41800	163027	56091	3671	65465	624908	26046	65787	1033	4513	65123	51212	709	44	2678	8967	1436	63646	5322	209318	4385	133105	114446734	14764569	7486380
11	41836	163027	57123	4725	67612	674451	26046	65787	2147	6296	104839	51322	897	44	2681	8985	1436	63646	5327	209396	4393	133282	116829034	14800569	7498180

PAROCHIAL REPORT OF THE UNITED LUTHERAN CHURCH IN AMERICA—1928
Including Statistics Outside Continental United States and Canada—Continued

FINANCIAL

Index Number	Valuation of Church Property				Congregational Expenses			Congregational Benevolences									Summary	
								Apportioned			Unapportioned							
	45 Endowment	46 Other Property	47 Total Valuation	48 Indebtedness	49 Current	50 Unusual	51 Total	52 Paid	53 Excess	54 Deficit	55 Education	56 Foreign Missions	57 Home Missions	58 Inner Missions	59 Other Benevolence	60 Total Un-apportioned Benevolence	61 Total Benevolence	62 Total Expenditures
4			1116600		151340		151340								29734	29734	29734	181074
5			75000		8000		8000											8000
6		30000	600000		2000		2000											2000
7	25000	2500	185000		3900		3900								927	927	927	4827
8		16000	143000		2951		2951								781	781	781	3732
9			52000		3000		3000											3000
10			124000															
11			208000															
	25000	48500	2503600		171191		171191								31442	31442	31442	202633
	2932175	7585846	148701861	19416910	10761252	7261869	18051503	2109023	28470	794562	270776	247455	132640	167310	482380	2823242	4932265	22983768
	2957175	7634346	151205461	19416910	10932443	7261869	18222694	2109023	28470	794562	270776	247455	132640	167310	513822	2854684	4963707	23186401

UNITED LUTHERAN CHURCH IN THE UNITED STATES AND CANADA

COMPARISON OF TOTALS OF ACCESSIONS AND LOSSES, NET VALUATION AND PER CAPITAS

COMPARISON OF TOTALS OF ACCESSIONS AND LOSSES

1928 Total Accessions	123,507	1928 Total Losses	68,824
1927 Total Accessions	132,916	1927 Total Losses	66,053
1928 Decrease in Accessions	9,409	1928 Increase in Losses	2,771
1927 Increase in Accessions.	13,505	1927 Increase in Losses	5,225
1928 Net Decrease in Accessions	22,914	1928 Net Decrease in Losses	2,454

1928 Accessions gain over Losses 54,683
1927 Accessions gain over Losses 66,863
1928 Loss in Accessions gain over Losses 12,180
1927 Gain in Accessions gain over Losses 8,280
1928 Net Loss 20,460

NET VALUATION

1928 Total Valuation .	$148,701,861	1925 Net Valuation ..	$100,398,878
1928 Total Indebtedness	19,416,910	1924 Net Valuation ..	92,103,946
1928 Net Valuation ..	129,284,951	1923 Net Valuation ..	83,389,965
1927 Net Valuation ..	122,725,940	1922 Net Valuation ..	74,926,113
1928 Gain Net Valuation	6,559,011	1921 Net Valuation ..	70,495,643
1926 Net Valuation ..	113,664,155	1920 Net Valuation ..	64,560,968
		1919 Net Valuation ..	37,855,419

PER CAPITAS

	Current Expenses	Unusual Expenses	Total Congregational	Apportiomment Benevolence Paid	Total Benevolence	Total Expenditures
1928 Per Capita .... (949,188 cf.m.)	$11.33	$7.65	$19.01	$2.22	$5.11	$24.21
1927 Per Capita .... (933,650 cf.m.)	11.23	8.59	19.84	2.31	4.32	24.16
1928 Gain Per Capita	.10				.79	.05
1928 Loss Per Capita		.94	.83	.09		
1926 Per Capita .... (916,858 cf.m)	10.30	9.44	19.73	2.02	3.58	23.31
1927 Gain Per Capita	.93		.11	.29	.74	.85
1927 Loss Per Capita		.85				
1925 Per Capita .... (886,840 cf.m.)	9.78	7.91	17.69	2.06	4.19	21.88
1924 Per Capita .... (856,180 cf.m.)	9.39	7.96	17.36	2.04	4.10	21.46
1923 Per Capita .... (839,279 cf.m.)	8.80	5.52	14.33	1.91	3.52	18.00
1922 Per Capita .... (819,063 cf.m.)	8.32	4.89	13.21	1.84	3.71	16.93
1921 Per Capita .... (801,250 cf.m)	8.26	4.79	13.05	1.79	4.17	17.22
1920 Per Capita .... (791,400 cf.m)	7.15	3.75	10.90	1.52	3.88	14.78
1919 Per Capita .... (776,582 cf.m)	6.42	2.46	8.88	1.73	2.90	11.78

STATISTICAL REPORT OF THE UNITED LUTHERAN CHURCH IN AMERICA FOR THE YEAR 1929

Index	Synod	When Organized	Pastors	Parishes	Congregations	Membership: Baptized	Membership: Confirmed	Membership: Communing	Accessions Children: Baptism	Accessions Children: Otherwise	Accessions Adult: Baptism	Accessions Adult: Confirmation	Accessions Adult: Certificate	Accessions Adult: Otherwise	Losses Children: Death	Losses Children: Otherwise	Losses Adult: Death	Losses Adult: Certificate	Losses Adult: Otherwise	No. Sub. to Official Papers	No. S.S. Papers Distributed	No. Sub. to Other Ch. Prs.
1	Ministerium of Penna.	Aug. 15, 1748	469	372	593	288364	197023	141335	7023	4058	598	7952	3056	2498	521	2970	3327	2144	4599	7647	17558	6286
2	United Synod of N.Y.	Oct. 23, 1786	447	403	415	219973	148481	98490	5326	4285	489	5013	2314	3959	342	4037	2176	1139	5050	5547	15088	3159
3	United Synod of N.C.	May 2, 1803	107	90	161	35022	24749	18758	819	275	161	886	595		24	381	255	406	137	1114	2203	2728
4	Synod of Maryland.	Oct. 11, 1820	133	101	139	65892	47660	30761	1507	452	176	1483	701	558	42	381	656	585	826	1758	5027	2089
5	Synod of S. Carolina.	Jan. 14, 1824	67	67	160	27203	19912	13250	531	143	63	522	527	41	24		219	379	223	1113	1801	1836
6	Synod of West Penna.	Sept. 5, 1825	113	93	100	59432	44455	34128	1290	323	229	1162	720	419	26	262	642	549	616	1643	3551	1145
7	Synod of Virginia.	Aug. 10, 1829	89	77	171	24206	19219	12092	365	138	205	430	388	122	83	110	234	223	310	1292	2967	2915
8	Synod of Ohio.	Nov. 7, 1836	240	206	283	82698	57204	48133	1860	1055	609	2040	1343	1081	18	737	920	1129	2751	2838	22493	1843
9	East Penna. Synod.	May 2, 1842	174	127	176	70630	50982	33984	1138	659	358	1438	1177	852	98	431	665	693	1328	2192	7527	1742
10	Alleghany Synod.	Sept. 9, 1842	273	67	146	40092	30472	20563	659	155	273	719	335	184	112	482	409	335	595	1044	6963	2488
11	Pittsburgh Synod.	Jan. 15, 1845	226	226	318	119572	82146	52690	2930	1304	340	2787	1693	1857	224	1843	1007	1354	2381	3431	23724	21432
12	Indiana Synod.	Oct. 28, 1848	59	59	140	16376	12412	8660	332	235	127	377	234	222	5	107	176	150	118	569	3958	680
13	Illinois Synod.	Sept. 18, 1851	149	122	164	52582	35128	25959	1503	1417	332	1787	674	1197	73	977	422	496	1485	1201	12791	1019
14	Texas Synod.	Nov. 10, 1851	18	19	12	6222	4131	3231	123	87	12	206	83		2	55	46	29	62	190	300	733
15	Susq. Syn. of Cen. Pa.	Nov. 21, 1855	112	82	132	51217	38883	26699	913	249	257	987	640	396	49	975	536	410	955	1066	5153	772
16	Mississippi Synod.	July 25, 1855	8	5	12	777	621	289	23	23	10	23	15				46	29	21	28	61	36
17	Synod of Iowa.	Sept. 3, 1855	29	32	88	14974	9494	6248	431	213	128	488	284	213	13	86	86	154	189	452	3722	401
18	Michigan Synod.	Oct. 27, 1855	88	64	29	21344	15592	9461	521	518	147	465	471	425	19	588	182	142	615	612	5398	1074
19	Synod of Georgia-Ala.	July 20, 1860	18	15	87	6280	4025	2712	91	61	34	106	164	30	3	26	49	56	73	340	773	475
20	Synod of Canada.	July 5, 1861	57	57	51	26001	17193	13263	723	240	19	653	212	315	39	163	246	187	249	1426	2115	581
21	Synod of Kansas.	Nov. 5, 1868	51	36	44	10099	7287	5081	150	150	94	202	166	195	6	137	115	119	209	394	2577	618
22	Synod of Nebraska.	Sept. 1, 1871	48	44	50	19254	13014	8698	658	191	128	583	196	332	15	402	104	215	331	478	4006	740
23	Wartburg Synod.	1875	85	82	86	19034	13910	9110	398	189	34	281	23	137	21	74	146	50	101	758	1585	557
24	German Neb. Synod.	July 24, 1890	60	36	60	17623	11689	8725	423	164	80	428	226	137	23	45	118	55	61	570	1003	239
25	Synod of California.	Apr. 6, 1891	29	36	61	9121	6024	4254	251	269	26	248	120	386	4	203	80	87	314	278	1633	61
26	Rocky Mount. Synod	May 22, 1891	16	16	55	3472	2442	1638	77	77	24	117	465	124	3	95	26	61	190	218	1080	1352
27	Synod of the N. W.	Sept. 22, 1897	83	83	94	47080	29739	22464	1462	1163	198	1673		1635	62	1251	256	279	2725	1213	6781	
28	Manitoba Synod.	July 26, 1897	45	36	94	12860	7239	5310	525	234	35	418	161	225		121	140	109	181	199	1601	338
29	Pacific Synod.	Sept. 26, 1901	24	26	31	5671	3381	2169	202		1	188	20	7	3	4	39	11	2	236	1860	67
30	Nova Scotia Synod.	July 10, 1903	7	8	31	5351	3004	1628	111			96		73	11	26	38	84	144	379	156	1087
31	Synod of W. Virginia.	Apr. 17, 1912	22	24	37	6486	4241	3111	151	31	39	161	88		11		50					
32	Slovak "Zion" Synod.	June 10, 1919	22	18	31	12606	8001	6943	403	31		299		52		37	176	43	89	103	325	12
33	Florida Synod.	Jan. 15, 1929	13	13	13	1894	1434	999	44	75	9	43	68				13	43				
34	Totals for U. S. and Canada.		3274	2750	3925	1399408	971187	680836	33195	18412	5235	34247	17181	17889	1913	16855	13561	11678	27406	40329	165940	58505
35	Total Outside U. S. and Canada.		142	....	1633	156268	63975	49125	141	16	8607	3706	16	2876	41	16	2788	28	5478	27	....	....
36	U. L. C. World Total.		3416	2750	5558	1555676	1035162	729961	33336	18428	13842	37953	17197	20765	1954	16871	16349	11706	32884	40356	165940	58505

STATISTICAL REPORT OF THE UNITED LUTHERAN CHURCH IN AMERICA FOR THE YEAR 1929—Continued

Column key:

CHURCH SCHOOLS — SUNDAY: 23 Number, 24 Officers and Teachers, 25 Scholars, 26 Home Dep't., 27 Cradle Roll. WEEKDAY: 28 Number, 29 Teachers, 30 Scholars. 31 Catechetical Catechumens.

PAROCHIAL — STUDENTS: 32 Ministry, 33 Deaconess, 34 In Lutheran Institutions, 35 In Non-Luth. Institutions.

CHURCH SOCIETIES — MEN'S: 36 Number, 37 Members. WOMEN'S: 38 Number, 39 Members. YOUNG P.: 40 Number, 41 Members.

FINANCIAL — Valuation of Church Property: 42 Church Edifices, 43 Parsonages, 44 School and Parish Houses.

Index No.	23	24	25	26	27	28	29	30	31	32	33	34	35	36	37	38	39	40	41	42	43	44
1	592	12327	120355	5622	12395	126	836	12134	7992	93	9	361	1583	226	11405	788	36841	660	24119	22173002	2303432	1984300
2	413	7685	64710	1510	9905	104	440	5114	6830	87	4	192	213	278	13883	699	33342	742	21147	22073066	2980200	3185552
3	151	2165	24518	138	715	78	348	6156	2495		1	162	509	52	1198	160	4309	203	5733	2843316	412386	110040
4	142	3510	35054	2020	4098	23	166	1909	2106	40	8	206	247	58	954	217	10340	201	7239	6691120	721350	335600
5	105	1305	13918	196	566	56	361	5157	1538	17	3	137	430	28	2172	143	4568	166	4598	1257500	258199	127500
6	159	3937	44649	1293	3360	26	164	2607	3126	33	1		166	38	832	227	9196	170	6942	4950700	587550	292200
7	143	1674	15001	1317	1198	49	255	2730	857	11		65	74	26	5316	157	4175	127	3917	1883470	382065	122600
8	275	5124	50861	1452	3760	29	120	1980	2813	15		329	585	127	4924	489	18739	285	6897	9102200	979050	564500
9	158	3927	39765	3700	3516	50	309	3899	2965	42		133	380	97	5706	287	12681	363	8021	7663567	1036182	646451
10	656	2491	22800	1159	2269	49	329	4401	1499	29		94	808	24	805	160	5190	124	3993	3152500	456429	169616
11	302	5596	51467	2861	6858	71	376	5245	4549	9	1	216	142	150	3676	530	18174	398	11329	10315379	1437982	416900
12	68	1092	9034	403	953	13	81	926	584			28	23	26	121	120	4015	215	1450	1605000	216300	116500
13	141	3082	27466	371	2736	29	203	1898	1798	32	2	143	405	77	2334	268	9302	32	6591	5014535	658263	232750
14	28	243	1963		195	30	18	214	170			1	5	6	10	33	1028	129	856	144706	49300	29900
15	165	3169	34386	1584	2543	205	205	2531	1995	25	4	133	432	42	457	210	5727		4124	4312100	503800	55500
16	36	36	177			1		40	19					1	803	8	78	66	94	29550	3500	3000
17	31	647	5715	45	813	9	48	403	940	8	1	1	142	13	243	60	2310	83	1994	993993	156500	98500
18	82	1350	10943	259	1100	12	41	512	701	8	1	43	192	21	223	123	4403	40	1922	2815775	230700	109000
19	23	349	2593		201	5	37	443	218	5		16	66	10	490	40	1233	64	866	632900	53700	71650
20	81	850	6485	8	904	23	28	537	549	12	1	19	51	8	301	68	2788	57	2065	1084080	192325	49000
21	42	688	5453	53	379	6	30	514	294	28	1	94	134	17	738	86	2732	67	1223	1375740	205900	15000
22	51	969	8099	150	1060	13	62	603	1234	6			242	12		65	2695	42	1792	1220050	164475	
23	39	545	5543			17	28	514	449	6					555	55	2822	35	1233			15150
24	57	382	3896	54	171	28	35	582	520	7		19	37	15	133	73	1532	45	1078	791700	225600	5000
25	36	459	3711	49	383	5		110	375	3	2	20	104	15	2140	30	763	20	985	1540800	72000	3000
26	15	241	1772	137	290	3	9	197	176	24		3	57	30		159	5723	170	428	490100	36700	174600
27	86	1747	14654	36	2198	24	15	1126	2522	23	1	57	408	58	294	17	324	26	4281	4079769	342100	
28	60	141	2054			26	72	1887								45	1051	43	598			3800
29	26	274	2421	41	313	69	54	92	177	3		6	75	15	349	14	485	3	972	424500	61300	40
30	15	128	878			3	14		151	3		3	13			45	1114	33	77	190875	30400	2000
31	31	466	3594	84	306		25	496	317	2		7	76	13					809	711200	126801	23500
32	22	66	1112			84	149	3044							349	21	499	17		530000	129000	3200
33	13	135	1074		20	2	7	81	50			5	8	3	44				251	387375	67500	
34	4215	66800	636121	24564	63218	1056	4870	68082	50009	661	33	2635	9034	1471	63799	5488	210328	4698	137624	120574104	15170989	8966309
35	1055	2197	56198			1115	1794	39678	145	191		3	18			6	91	8	273	2413300	61000	16163
36	5270	68997	692319	24564	63218	2171	6664	107760	50154	852	33	2638	9052	1471	63799	5494	210419	4706	137897	122987404	15231989	8982472

STATISTICAL REPORT OF THE UNITED LUTHERAN CHURCH IN AMERICA FOR THE YEAR 1929—Concluded

FINANCIAL

Index Number	Valuation of Church Property				Congregational Expenses			Financial — Congregational Benevolence									Summary	
								Apportioned			Unapportioned							
	Endowment 45	Other Property 46	Total Valuation 47	Indebtedness 48	Current 49	Unusual 50	Total 51	Paid 52	Excess 53	Deficit 54	Education 55	Foreign Missions 56	Home Missions 57	Inner Missions 58	Other Benevolence 59	Total Un-apportioned Benevolence 60	Total Benevolence 61	Total Expenditures 62
1	1119408	1019014	28689156	3907161	1700538	1437014	3137552	402814	4197	194143	13438	45761	14572	217093	56625	347489	750303	3887855
2	715002	1870405	30824225	4841164	2018063	1427813	3445876	333028			79182	29655	14535	210234	37921	371527	704555	4150431
3	14650	305005	3509190	303256	194093	147159	341252	45613	284	24132	4103	9558	10588	20014	10929	55192	100805	442057
4	99695	171525	8152770	1187140	522832	322772	845604	114802	2143	21227	8719	24570	9711	79330	15307	137637	252439	1098043
5	274748	315367	6420565	196610	147372	66181	213553	38047	815	24069	9195	4555	4283	12919	9831	40783	78830	292383
6	66247	120150	2574532	326299	434943	405440	840383	126819	6516	24936	4526	19319	5731	50380	20290	100246	227065	1067448
7	124103	532008	11301861	149198	179631	124790	304421	37142	46	21600	3219	6283	4260	26558	8801	49131	86273	390694
8	175532	338461	9860193	1234396	863470	331459	1194929	220877	2406	42101	7120	34113	17481	103175	39493	201382	422259	1617188
9	42952	104445	3925942	1606228	723343	301586	1024929	133422	548	23024	9359	42698	9813	80384	37763	180017	313439	1338368
10	152217	943989	13266467	345477	296959	164660	461619	87582	5867	8252	4901	7822	2479	34575	20712	70489	158071	619690
11	99400	154989	2191879	2193081	1021750	593180	1614930	199167		43183	9716	25677	15604	121691	41210	213898	413515	2028445
12	60089	241944	6207581	377975	195017	65801	260818	40449	197	9760	1348	4112	3989	19236	4183	32868	73317	334135
13	150	13729	237785	1443698	563821	208331	772152	111311	65	17877	7341	16116	8044	48762	15379	95642	206953	979105
14	63348	175630	5110378	463129	33157	10435	43592	4132	2879	8035	276	749	378	5174	648	7225	11357	54949
15			33050		378285	143539	521824	96490		19895	4193	11748	2249	30260	9002	57452	153942	675766
16	200	48650	1202343	303084	4334	1315	5649	889	6	135	99	41	47	768	218	1173	2062	7711
17	9725	39833	3194533	808787	152101	29871	181972	15073		14289	85	1877	450	6544	3616	12572	27645	209617
18	20000	28466	844066	155400	215469	116266	331735	34506	344	14096	624	2655	1655	9756	3112	21049	55555	387290
19	27800	37100	1432955	119098	59201	41152	100353	12099		1901	875	640	757	6475	6814	12265	24364	124717
20	6850	2672	1640162	231165	158399	63927	222326	31482	66	45777	4303	2034	436	6615	4030	20202	51684	274010
21	6780	145393	1551698	116120	130621	67184	197805	23385	105	5101	291	1814	860	7312	5399	14307	37692	235497
22		1166971	1169971	108860	110975	40622	184885	36577		14713	1217	4630	1015	16649	29410	29410	65987	253872
23		10530	1042980	27153	75062	13185	124160	7294							2418	2418	9712	133872
24	4337	61200	1681337	275544	119949	16159	91221	8060	122	2565	2461	842	900	5548		12863	20923	112144
25	364	10233	542397	236590	42913	37418	157367	14606	87	895	393	878	541	7291	4057	13160	27766	185133
26	32900	79647	4709016	1776151	406834	39007	79920	6583			194	344	430	3464	1626	6058	12641	92561
27		327859	327859		49052	219389	626223	77628			3900	8565	3807	31940	21120	69332	146960	773183
28		18500	508100	196753	59162		76678	8541	3	688					2944	2944	11485	60537
29	200	229474	229474	20905	14171	17156	21327	8935		3372	806	428	461	3508	1508	6711	15646	92324
30	7999	76100	917151	176161	73878	7156	103557	1959		4107	147	237	75	1765	1190	3414	5373	26700
31	1050	6000	688500	91858	75120	29679	75320	10867	45		159	2021	521	5536	2068	10305	21172	124729
32		2400	461725	176840	29791	18993	48784	1191							1968	1968	3159	78479
33	1250							3792		621	100	424	186	884	1162	2756	6548	55332
34	3133547	8525702	156370651	23432357	11197569	6507199	17704768	2295612	26748	590494	182290	310166	135858	1173850	401721	2203885	4499497	22204265
35	25000	60500	2575963		170917		170917								31501	31501	31501	202418
36	3158547	8586202	158946614	23432357	11368486	6507199	17875685	2295612	26748	590494	182290	310166	135858	1173850	433222	2235386	4530998	22406683

COMPARATIVE STATISTICAL REPORT OF THE UNITED LUTHERAN CHURCH IN AMERICA FOR THE YEARS 1919, 1920, 1921, 1922, 1923, 1924, 1925, 1926, 1927, 1928, 1929

PAROCHIAL

Index No.	Year	Pastor (2)	When Organized (3)	Parishes (4)	Congregations (5)	Membership – Baptized (6)	Membership – Confirmed (7)	Membership – Communing (8)	Access. Children Baptism (9)	Access. Children Otherwise (10)	Access. Adult Baptism (11)	Access. Adult Confirmation (12)	Access. Adult Certificate (13)	Access. Adult Otherwise (14)	Loss Children Death (15)	Loss Children Otherwise (16)	Loss Adult Death (17)	Loss Adult Certificate (18)	Loss Adult Otherwise (19)	No. Sub. to Official Papers (20)	No. S.S. Papers Distributed (21)	No. Sub. to Other Ch. P'rs. (22)
1	1929	3274		2750	3925	1399408	971187	680836	33195	18412	5235	34247	17181	17889	1913	16855	13561	11678	27406	40329	165940	58505
2	1928	3272		2790	3906	1370183	949188	676839	34530	17594	4896	32256	16725	17506	2010	16413	13184	11241	25976	41809	163027	57123
3	1 Years' Gain	2			19	29225	21999	3997		818	339	1991	456	383		442	377	437	1430		2913	1382
4	1 Years' Decrease			40					1335						97					1480		
5	1929	3274		2750	3925	1399408	971187	680836	33195	18412	5235	34247	17181	17889	1913	16855	13561	11678	27406	40329	165940	58505
6	1927	3184		2689	3881	1321780	933650	676496	36668	18264	5397	33871	15658	20012	2023	14772	12677	12117	24464	43917	162246	49825
7	2 Years' Gain	90		61	44	77628	37537	4340		148		376	1523			2083	884		2942		3694	8680
8	2 Years' Decrease								3473		162			2123	110			439		3588		
9	1929	3274		2750	3925	1399408	971187	680836	33195	18412	5235	34247	17181	17889	1913	16855	13561	11678	27406	40329	165940	58505
10	1926	3127		2706	3876	1315620	916858	677287	34562	17573	5178	25451	16866	19781	1983	12789	11758	11467	22831	50684	167418	38573
11	3 Years' Gain	147		44	49	83788	54329	3549		839	57	8796	315			4066	1803	211	4575			19932
12	3 Years' Decrease								1367					1892	70					10355	1478	
13	1929	3274		2750	3925	1399408	971187	680836	33195	18412	5235	34247	17181	17889	1913	16855	13561	11678	27406	40329	165940	58505
14	1925	3011		2649	3875	1276176	886840	669695	35307	16658	5536	31071	17366	18504	2004	12335	11454	12111	23935	50735	174407	36101
15	4 Years' Gain	263		101	50	123232	84347	11141		1754		3176				4520	2107		3471			22404
16	4 Years' Decrease								2112		301		185	615	91			433		10406	8467	
17	1929	3274		2750	3925	1399408	971187	680836	33195	18412	5235	34247	17181	17889	1913	16855	13561	11678	27406	40329	165940	58505
18	1924	2983		2643	3829	1238009	856180	645836	35138	14029	5746	31020	17314	18090	1982	9918	11250	11887	23356	50224	162037	39471
19	5 Years' Gain	291		107	96	161399	115007	35000		4383		3227				6937	2311		4050		3903	19034
20	5 Years' Decrease								1943		511		133	201	69			209		9895		
21	1929	3274		2750	3925	1399408	971187	680836	33195	18412	5235	34247	17181	17889	1913	16855	13561	11678	27406	40329	165940	58505
22	1923	2924		2566	3812	1201401	839279	633184	33837	12419	4472	28188	15600	16125	2244	9788	11518	11016	25436	47618	152731	34708
23	6 Years' Gain	350		184	113	198007	131908	47652		5993	763	6059	1581	1764		7067	2043	662	1970		13209	23797
24	6 Years' Decrease								642						331					7289		
25	1929	3274		2750	3925	1399408	971187	680836	33195	18412	5235	34247	17181	17889	1913	16855	13561	11678	27406	40329	165940	58505
26	1922	2900		2501	3732	1164550	819063	621123	36016	12704	5599	30954	16345	16445	2334	9370	11741	10934	25650	49267	144631	33867
27	7 Years' Gain	374		249	193	234858	152124	59713		5708		3293	836	1444		7485	1820	744	1756		21309	24638
28	7 Years' Decrease								2821		364				421					8938		
29	1929	3274		2750	3925	1399408	971187	680836	33195	18412	5235	34247	17181	17889	1913	16855	13561	11678	27406	40329	165940	58505
30	1921	2887		2492	3803	1147007	801250	597768	37403	11773	5302	30467	16456	16500	2392	8921	11051	11475	25485	36969	118139	21454
31	8 Years' Gain	387		258	122	252401	169937	83068		6639		3780	725	1389		7934	2510	203	1921	3360	47801	37051
32	8 Years' Decrease								4208		67				479							
33	1929	3274		2750	3925	1399408	971187	680836	33195	18412	5235	34247	17181	17889	1913	16855	13561	11678	27406	40329	165940	58505
34	1920	2812			3775	1117938	791400	580018	36438		4834	29380	15214	14571			11554	11610	26550			
35	9 Years' Gain	462			150	281470	179787	100818			401	4867	1967	3318			2007	68	856			
36	9 Years' Decrease								3243														
37	1929	3274		2750	3925	1399408	971187	680836	33195	18412	5235	34247	17181	17889	1913	16855	13561	11678	27406	40329	165940	58505
38	1919	2843			3473	1094153	776582	474553	34785		4400	27645	13915	8654			14073	10664	23467			
39	10 Years' Gain	431			452	305255	194605	206283			835	6602	3266	9235				1014	3939			
40	10 Years' Decrease								1590								512					

COMPARATIVE STATISTICAL REPORT OF THE UNITED LUTHERAN CHURCH IN AMERICA FOR THE YEARS 1919, 1920, 1921, 1922, 1923, 1924, 1925, 1926, 1927, 1928, 1929—Continued

PAROCHIAL

Index Number	CHURCH SCHOOLS							Cate-chetical	STUDENTS				CHURCH SOCIETIES						FINANCIAL		
	SUNDAY				WEEKDAY								MEN'S		WOMEN'S		YOUNG P.		Valuation Church Property		
	Number	Officers and Teachers	Scholars	Home Dept.	Cradle Roll	Number	Teachers	Scholars	Catechumens	Ministry	Deaconess	In Lutheran Institutions	In Non-Luth. Institutions	Number	Members	Number	Members	Number	Members	Church Edifices	Parsonages	School and Parish Houses
	23	24	25	26	27	28	29	30	31	32	33	34	35	36	37	38	39	40	41	42	43	44
1	4215	66800	636121	24564	63218	1056	4870	68082	50009	661	33	2635	9034	1471	63799	5488	210328	4698	137624	120574104	15170989	8966309
2	3671	65465	624908	24046	65787	1033	4513	65123	51212	709	11	44	8967	1436	63646	5322	209318	4385	133105	114446734	14764569	7486380
3	544	1335	11213	1432	2569	23	357	2959	1203	48		2678	67	35	153	166	1010	313	4519	6127370	406420	1479929
4	4215	66800	636121	24564	63218	1056	4870	68082	50009	661	33	2635	9034	1471	63799	5488	210328	4698	137624	120574104	15170989	8966309
5	3651	64212	613863	25826	65544	928	4183	58491	48823	261	33	2626	8338	1383	63146	5181	208003	3986	133682	108956533	14598321	6830516
6	564	2588	22258	1262	2326	128	687	9591	1186	400	52	696		88	653	307	2325	712	3942	11617571	572668	2135793
7	4215	66800	636121	24564	63218	1056	4870	68082	50009	661	33	2635	9034	1471	63799	5488	210328	4698	137624	120170984	15170989	8966309
8	3524	62609	608261	27309	65938	647	3157	45366	48272	851	79	2632	7555	1294	59190	4830	199855	3835	130052	99894373	13381748	5198535
9	691	4191	27860	2745	2720	409	1713	22716	1737	190	19	1479		177	4609	658	10473	873	7072	20679731	1289241	3767774
10	4215	66800	636121	24564	63218	1056	4870	68082	50009	661	33	2635	9034	1471	63799	5488	210328	4698	137634	120574104	15170989	8966309
11	3531	59940	590169	28187	65706	651	2704	42372	49216	826	46	2551	6753	1211	56892	4515	184475	3547	122380	86288340	12532190	3919080
12	684	6860	5952	2745	635	405	2166	25710	793	826	90	84	2281	260	6907	973	25853	1151	15244	34285764	2638799	5047220
13	4215	66800	636121	24564	63218	1056	4870	68082	50009	661	33	2635	9034	1471	63799	5488	210328	4698	137624	120574104	15170989	8966309
14	3515	59205	571737	28028	63853	557	2051	38824	49310	828	68	2530	5841	1213	56605	4307	181449	3400	120277	78525563	11169150	3136620
15	700	7595	64384	3623	2488	499	2819	29258	699	167	57	254	3632	258	7194	973	35793	1298	17347	42048541	2638799	5829689
16	4215	66800	636121	24564	63218	1056	4870	68082	50009	661	33	2635	9034	1471	63799	5488	210328	4698	137624	120574104	15170989	8966309
17	3440	56863	552872	28164	61995	523	1638	28438	45238	717	67	2381	5402	1137	53706	4151	174535	3200	115726	70971368	10415614	2463970
18	775	9937	83249	3464	1223	533	3232	39644	4771	746	35	105	3193	334	10093	1337	37058	1498	21898	49602736	4001839	6502339
19	4215	66800	636121	24564	63218	1056	4870	68082	50009	661	34	2635	9034	1471	63799	5488	210328	4698	137624	120574104	15170989	8966309
20	3465	55330	555510	28446	59264	490	1453	25149	35311	661	59	2015	4520	1102	52525	4013	173270	3132	115234	65598841	9237584	1584150
21	750	11470	80611	2400	3954	566	3417	42933	14698	717	26	4514		369	11274	1475	37058	1566	22390	54975263	5933405	7382159
22	4215	66800	636121	24564	63218	1056	4870	68082	50009	661	33	2635	9034	1471	63799	5488	210328	4698	137624	120574104	15170989	8966309
23	3682	54268	522691	26142	52148	375	954	17534	34034	582	85	1712	4292	967	47052	3618	154089	3694	106842	63193694	8138433	878400
24	533	12532	113430	2400	11070	681	3916	50548	15975	79		923	4742	504	16747	1870	56239	2004	30782	57380410	7032556	8087909
25	4215	66800	636121	24564	63218	1056	4870	68082	50009	661	33	2635	9034	1471	63799	5488	210328	4698	137624	120574104	15170989	8966309
26	3399	52939	515815	23506	46300	190	326	7070	44334	577	46	1838	4316	892	42373	3547	139205	2367	92822	63193694	8242533	
27	816	13861	120306	1058	16918	866	4544	61012	5675	84	13	797	4718	579	24373	1941	71123	2331	44802	57380410		8966309
28	4215	66800	636121	24564	63218	1056	4870	68082	50009	661	33	2635	9034	1471	63799	5488	210328	4698	137624	120574104	15170989	8966309
29	3412	53524	514924	19019	32228	109	130	4779	36689	526	14	223	611	708	32350	2811	104760	2114	81746		2071193	
30	803	13276	121197	5545	30990	947	4740	63303	13320	135	19	2412	8423	763	31249	2677	105568	2584	55878	120574104	13099796	8966309

COMPARATIVE STATISTICAL REPORT OF THE UNITED LUTHERAN CHURCH IN AMERICA FOR THE YEARS 1919, 1920, 1921, 1922, 1923, 1924, 1925, 1926, 1927, 1928, 1929—Concluded

FINANCIAL

Index	VALUATION OF CHURCH PROPERTY				CONGREGATIONAL EXPENSES			CONGREGATIONAL BENEVOLENCE — APPORTIONED				UNAPPORTIONED					SUMMARY	
	45 Endowment	46 Other Property	47 Total Valuation	48 Indebtedness	49 Current	50 Unusual	51 Total	52 Paid	53 Excess	54 Deficit	55 Education	56 Foreign Missions	57 Home Missions	58 Inner Missions	59 Other Bene.	60 Total Unapportioned Bene.	61 Total Benevolence	62 Total Expenditures
1	3133547	8525702	156370651	23432357	11197569	6507199	17704768	2295612	26748	590494	182290	310166	135858	1173850	401721	2203885	4499497	22204265
2	2932172	7585846	148701861	19416910	10761252	7290251	18051503	2100023	28470	794562	270776	247455	132640	1673710	482380	2823342	4932265	22983768
3	201372	939856	7668790	4015447		186589	346735	186589	1722	204068	88486	62711	3218	499860	80659	619357	432768	779503
4																		
5	3133547	8525702	156370651	23432357	11197569	6507199	17704768	2295612	26748	590494	182290	310166	135858	1173850	401721	2203885	4499497	22204265
6	2757866	7523560	140609870	17883930	11487001	7034225	18521226	2156391	26748	590494	252627	320647	129359	480531	515817	1881271	4037662	22558888
7	375681	1002142	15760781	5548427				139221	5177	623483	434917	10481	6499	693319	114096	322614	461835	354623
8																		
9	3133547	8525702	156370651	23432357	11197569	6507199	17704768	2295612	26748	590494	182290	310166	135858	1173850	401721	2203885	4499497	22204265
10	7441745	2547063	128964264	15300109	9443178	8650813	18093991	1853225	26748	460334	300820	268875	100063	314697	441606	1426061	3279286	21373277
11	586484	1083957	27406387	8132248				442387	30138	130160	118530	41291	35795	859153	39885	777824		830788
12																		
13	3133547	8525702	156370651	23432357	11197569	6507199	17704768	2295612	26748	590494	182290	310166	135858	1173850	401721	2203885	4499497	22204265
14	2383469	6733780	111856868	11457989	8676760	7014663	15691423	1828761	3390	458335	623116	218881	110766	403638	526722	188323	3711884	19403307
15	750078	1791922	44513783	11974368			2013345	466851		132159	440826	91285	25092	770212	125001	2015562	787613	2800958
16																		
17	3133547	8525702	156370651	23432357	11197569	6507199	17704768	2295612	26748	590494	182290	310166	135858	1173850	401721	2203885	4499497	22204265
18	2281248	5806395	101366975	9265083	8041334	6818426	14859760	1748347	14647	390112	320448	256587	160597	354336	672022	1763990	3512337	18372097
19	852299	2719307	55001675	14167274			2845008	547265	44595	200382	138158	53579	24739	819514	270301	439895	987160	3832168
20																		
21	3133547	8525702	156370651	23432357	11197569	6507199	17704768	2295612	26748	590494	182290	310166	135858	1173850	401721	2203885	4499497	22204265
22	2007027	4973232	90831211	7441246	7387593	4635721	12023314	1605290	26748	378486	318056	227718	86762	261050	596888	1488474	3093764	15117078
23	1126520	3552470	65539440	15991111			5681454		48060	212008	133766	82448	49096	912800	195167	715411	1405733	7087187
24																		
25	3133547	8525702	156370651	23432357	11197569	6507199	17704768	2295612	26748	590494	182290	310166	135858	1173850	401721	2203885	4499497	22204265
26	1851134	3701544	81973053	7047140	6816399	4009146	10825545	1513077	21312	368687	292682	155599	72287	233324	777002	1530894	3043971	13869516
27	1282413	4824158	74397398	16385217			6879223	782535	45328	221807	110392	154567	63571	940526	375281	672991	1455526	8334749
28																		
29	3133547	8525702	156370651	23432357	11197569	6507199	17704768	2295612	26748	590494	182290	310166	135858	1173850	401721	2203885	4499497	22204265
30	1895798	2400790	76507115	6011472	6621268	3835135	10456403	1449132	18580	342307	569521	140190	66369	240927	884653	1901660	3341792	13798195
31	1237749	6124912	79863536	17420885			7248365	855480	62601	248187	387231	169976	69489	932923	482932	302225	1157705	8406070
32																		
33	3133547	8525702	156370651	23432357	11197569	6507199	17704768	2295612	26748	590494	182290	310166	135858	1173850	401721	2203885	4499497	22204265
34	2065974		70142813	5581845	5630943	2968750	8599693	1206115		342307	612129		36017	233909	743909	1865798	3071913	11671606
35	1067573		86227838	17850512			9105075	1089497	35853	248187	429839		99841	939941	582022	338087	1427584	10532659
36																		
37	3133547	8525702	156370651	23432357	11197569	6507199	17704768	2295612	26748	590494	182290	310166	135858	1173850	401721	2203885	4499497	22204265
38	1032292		42383332	4527913	4984795	1926749	6911544	1344202	26748				5459	1173780	501260	908586	2257788	9154332
39	2101255		113987319	18904444			10793224	951410			182214		130399			1295299	2246709	13049933
40																		

PAROCHIAL REPORT OF THE UNITED LUTHERAN CHURCH IN AMERICA—1929
1929 and 1928 Gains Compared

Index Number		Pastors	When Organized	Parishes	Congregations	Membership Baptized	Membership Confirmed	Membership Communing	Accessions Children Baptism	Accessions Children Otherwise	Accessions Adult Baptism	Accessions Adult Con-firmation	Accessions Adult Certificate	Accessions Adult Otherwise	Losses Children Death	Losses Children Otherwise	Losses Adult Death	Losses Adult Certificate	Losses Adult Otherwise
		2	3	4	5	6	7	8	9	10	11	12	13	14	15	16	17	18	19
1	1929 Gain	2		40	19	29225	21999	3997	1335	818	339	1991	456	383	97	442	377	437	1430
2	1929 Decrease																		
3	1928 Gain	88		101	25	48403	15538	343	2138	670	501	1615	1979	2506	13	1641	507	876	1512
4	1928 Decrease																		
5	1929 Net Gain																		
6	1929 Net Decrease	86		141	6	19178	6461	3654	803	1488	840	3606	2435	2889	84	1199	130	1313	82

STATISTICAL REPORT OF THE UNITED LUTHERAN CHURCH IN AMERICA—1929
Including Statistics Outside Continental United States and Canada

Index Number	Country	Province	When Organized	Pastors	Congregations	Membership Baptized	Membership Confirmed	Membership Communing	Accessions Children Baptism	Accessions Children Otherwise	Accessions Adult Baptism	Accessions Adult Con-firmation	Accessions Adult Certificate	Accessions Adult Otherwise	Losses Children Death	Losses Children Otherwise	Losses Adult Death	Losses Adult Certificate	Losses Adult Otherwise
			3	4	5	6	7	8	9	10	11	12	13	14	15	16	17	18	19
1	India	Madras	1843	For. 19, Nat. 53	1496	146122	58995	45458			8603	2879		2872			2742		5464
2	Africa	Liberia	1860	For. 11, Nat. 0	5	350	215	150				51							
3	Japan	Kyushu-Hondo	1893	For. 14, Nat. 20	25	3167	1160	1047				285							
4	China	Shantung	1897	For. 6, Nat. 20	71	1613	1298	620	63			190							
5	Virgin Islands		1666	U. L. C. 3	3	2137	1012	905				78	5		21	5	32	12	
6	British Guiana	N. Amsterdam	1898	For. 2, Nat. 0	5	400	200	200	78			44							
7	Porto Rico			U. L. C. 8, O. 1	18	1771	1061	677			4	145	11		20	11	14	16	14
8	Argentina	Buenos Aires	1908	For. 2, Nat. 3	8	708		68				34				16	14	16	14
9	Total Outside U.S. and Can.			142	1633	156268	63975	49125	141	16	8607	3706	16	2876	1913	41	2788	28	5478
10	Total U.S. and Canada			3,274	3925	1399408	971187	680836	33195	18412	5235	34247	17181	17181	13561	16855	13561	1678	27406
11	World Total U. L. C. in A.			3,416	5558	1555676	1035162	729961	33336	18428	13842	37953	17197	20765	1954	16871	16349	1706	32884

PAROCHIAL REPORT OF THE UNITED LUTHERAN CHURCH IN AMERICA—1929
1929 and 1928 Gains Compared

Index Number	Church Papers			Church Schools									Students				Church Societies						Valuation Church Property		
				Sunday					Weekday			Catechumens					Men's		Women's		Young P.				
	No. Sub. to Official Papers	No. S. S. Papers Distributed	No. Sub. to Other Ch. P'rs	Number	Officers and Teachers	Scholars	Home Dep't	Cradle Roll	Number	Teachers	Scholars	Catechical	Ministry	Deaconess	In Lutheran Institutions	In Non-Luth. Institutions	Number	Members	Number	Members	Number	Members	Church Edifices	Parsonages	School and Parish Houses
	20	21	22	23	24	25	26	27	28	29	30	31	32	33	34	35	36	37	38	39	40	41	42	43	44
1		2913	1382	544	1335	11213	1482	2569	23	357	2959	1203	48	11	43	67	35	153	166	1010	313	4519	6127370	406420	1479927
2	1480	781	7298	20	1253	11045	220	243	105	330	6632	2389			52	629	53	500	141	1315	399	577	5490201	166248	653864
3														8					25						
4	2108	2132	524	524	82	168	1702	2812	82	27	3673	3592	52	3	95	562	18	347	25	305	86	5096	637169	240170	824065
5	628	2132																							
6			5916																						

STATISTICAL REPORT OF THE UNITED LUTHERAN CHURCH IN AMERICA—1929
Including Statistics Outside Continental United States and Canada

Index Number	Church Papers			Church Schools									Students				Church Societies						Valuation Church Property		
				Sunday					Weekday			Catechumens					Men's		Women's		Young P.				
	No. Sub. to Official Papers	No. S. S. Papers Distributed	No. Sub. to Other Ch. P'rs	Number	Officers and Teachers	Scholars	Home Dep't	Cradle Roll	Number	Teachers	Scholars	Catechical	Ministry	Deaconess	In Lutheran Institutions	In Non-Luth. Institutions	Number	Members	Number	Members	Number	Members	Church Edifices	Parsonages	School and Parish Houses
	20	21	22	23	24	25	26	27	28	29	30	31	32	33	34	35	36	37	38	39	40	41	42	43	44
1				1032	1836	48375			1032	1606	35174		172										1116600		
2					25	377			8	25	336												75000		
3					30	2073			9	30	1273		8										600000		
4				5	52	854			41	52	1536	78	4		1	8			3	55	2	67	185000	15000	4800
5	12				86	1095			2	11	146		1										113000	6000	11363
6					10	470			10	10	259		4										13700		
7	15				112	2438			6	14	220	67	2		2	10			3	36	6	206	102000	40000	
8				18	46	516			11	46	734												208000		
9	27			1055	2197	56198	24564	63218	1115	1794	39678	145	191	18	3	18	6	91	6		8	273	2413300	61000	16163
10	40329	165940	58505	4215	66800	636121	24564	63218	1056	4870	68082	50009	661	33	2635	9034	1471	63799	5488	210328	4698	137624	120574104	15170989	8966309
11	40356	165940	58505	5270	68997	692319	24564	63218	2171	6664	107760	50154	852	33	2638	9052	1471	63799	5494	210419	4706	137897	122987404	15231989	8982472

PAROCHIAL REPORT OF THE UNITED LUTHERAN CHURCH IN AMERICA—1929
1929 and 1928 Gains Compared—Concluded

FINANCIAL

Index No.	Valuation of Church Property — Endowment (45)	Other Property (46)	Total Valuation (47)	Indebtedness (48)	Congregational Expenses — Current (49)	Unusual (50)	Total (51)	Apportioned — Paid (52)	Excess (53)	Deficit (54)	Congregational Benevolence — Education (55)	Unapportioned — Foreign Missions (56)	Home Missions (57)	Inner Missions (58)	Other Benevolence (59)	Summary — Total Unapportioned Benevolence (60)	Total Benevolence (61)	Total Expenditures (62)
1	201372	939856	7668790	4015447	436317	754670	346735	186589	1722	204068	88486	62711	3218	499860	80659	619357	432768	779503
2	174309	62286	8091991	1532080	274251	772355	469723	47368	3455	171079	164141	73192	3281	1193179	33437	941971	894603	424880
3	27063	877570	423201	2482467	162066	17685	122988	233957	1733	375147	75655	135903	63	693319	47222	1161328	1327371	1204383

STATISTICAL REPORT OF THE UNITED LUTHERAN CHURCH IN AMERICA—1929
Including Statistics Outside Continental United States and Canada—Concluded

FINANCIAL

Index No.	Valuation of Church Property — Endowment (45)	Other Property (46)	Total Valuation (47)	Indebtedness (48)	Congregational Expenses — Current (49)	Unusual (50)	Total (51)	Apportioned — Paid (52)	Excess (53)	Deficit (54)	Congregational Benevolence — Education (55)	Unapportioned — Foreign Missions (56)	Home Missions (57)	Inner Missions (58)	Other Benevolence (59)	Summary — Total Unapportioned Benevolence (60)	Total Benevolence (61)	Total Expenditures (62)
1			1116600		151340		151340								29734	29734	29734	181074
2			75000		8000		8000											8000
3			600000		2000		2000											2000
4		30000	185000		3500		3500								962	962	962	4462
5	25000	2500	158000		3077		3077								805	805	805	3882
6			52000		3000		3000											3000
7	25000	28000	181363															
8			208000		170917		170917											
9		60500	2575963		170917		170917								31501	31501	31501	202418
10	3133547	8525702	156370651	24332357	11197569	6507199	17704768	2295612	26748	590494	182290	310166	135858	1173850	401721	2203885	4499497	22204268
11	3158547	8586202	158946614	24332357	11368486	6507199	17875685	2295612	26748	590494	182290	310166	135855	1173850	433222	2235386	4530998	22406683

UNITED LUTHERAN CHURCH IN THE UNITED STATES AND CANADA
COMPARISON OF TOTALS OF ACCESSIONS AND LOSSES, NET VALUATION AND PER CAPITA

COMPARISON OF TOTALS OF ACCESSIONS AND LOSSES

1929 Total Accessions............	126,159	1929 Total Losses.................	71,413
1928 Total Accessions............	123,507	1928 Total Losses.................	68,824
1929 Increase in Accessions........	2,652	1929 Increase in Losses............	2,589
1928 Decrease in Accessions........	9,409	1928 Increase in Losses............	2,771
1929 Net Increase in Accessions....	12,061	1929 Net Decrease in Losses.......	182

1929 Accessions Gain Over Losses............................ 54,746
1928 Accessions Gain Over Losses............................ 54,683
1929 Gain in Accessions Gain Over Losses..................... 63
1928 Loss in Accessions Gain Over Losses..................... 12,180
1929 Net Gain.. 12,243

NET VALUATION

1929 Total Valuation.........	$156,370,651	1925 Net Valuation...........	$100,398,878
1929 Total Indebtedness......	23,432,357	1924 Net Valuation...........	92,103,946
1929 Net Valuation...........	132,938,294	1923 Net Valuation...........	83,389,965
1928 Net Valuation...........	129,284,951	1922 Net Valuation...........	74,926,113
1929 Gain Net Valuation......	3,653,343	1921 Net Valuation...........	70,495,643
1927 Net Valuation...........	122,725,940	1920 Net Valuation...........	64,560,968
1926 Net Valuation...........	113,664,155	1919 Net Valuation...........	37,855,419

PER CAPITAS

	Current Expenses	Unusual Expenses	Total Congregational	Apportionment Benevolence Paid	Total Benevolence	Total Expenditures
1929 Per Capita........(971,187 cf.m.)	$11.42	$6.70	$18.23	$2.36	$4.63	$22.86
1928 Per Capita........(949,188 cf.m.)	11.33	7.65	19.01	2.22	5.11	24.21
1929 Gain Per Capita................	.09	.....	......	.14	.....	......
1929 Loss Per Capita................	......	.95	.78	.....	.48	1.35
1927 Per Capita........(933,650 cf.m.)	11.23	8.59	19.84	2.31	4.32	24.16
1928 Gain Per Capita................	.10	.....	......	.....	.79	.05
1928 Loss Per Capita................	......	.94	.83	.09	.....	......
1926 Per Capita........(916,858 cf.m.)	10.30	9.44	19.73	2.02	3.58	23.31
1925 Per Capita........(886,840 cf.m.)	9.78	7.91	17.69	2.06	4.19	21.88
1924 Per Capita........(856,180 cf.m.)	9.39	7.96	17.36	2.04	4.10	21.46
1923 Per Capita........(839,279 cf.m.)	8.80	5.52	14.33	1.91	3.52	18.00
1922 Per Capita........(819,063 cf.m.)	8.32	4.89	13.21	1.84	3.71	16.93
1921 Per Capita........(801,250 cf.m.)	8.26	4.79	13.05	1.79	4.17	17.22
1920 Per Capita........(791,400 cf.m.)	7.15	3.75	10.90	1.52	3.88	14.78
1919 Per Capita........(776,582 cf.m.)	6.42	2.46	8.88	1.73	2.90	11.78

PAROCHIAL REPORT OF THE UNITED LUTHERAN CHURCH IN AMERICA—UNITED STATES AND CANADA
Comparisons, Percentages and Averages—1919 to 1929 Inclusive

Index No. (1)		Pastors (2)	Parishes (3)	Congregations (4)	MEMBERSHIP Baptized (5)	MEMBERSHIP Confirmed (6)	MEMBERSHIP Communing (7)	ACCESSIONS Children Baptism (8)	ACCESSIONS Children Otherwise (9)	ACCESSIONS Adult Baptism (10)	ACCESSIONS Adult Confirmation (11)	ACCESSIONS Adult Certificate (12)	ACCESSIONS Adult Otherwise (13)	LOSSES Children Death (14)	LOSSES Children Otherwise (15)	LOSSES Adult Death (16)	LOSSES Adult Certificate (17)	LOSSES Adult Otherwise (18)
1	1929	3274	2750	3925	1399408	971187	680836	33195	18412	5235	34247	17181	17889	1913	16855	13561	11678	27406
2	1928	3272	2790	3906	1370183	949188	676833	34530	17594	4896	32256	16725	17706	2010	16413	13184	11241	25976
3	1 Year's Gain	2		19	29225	21999	3997		818	339	1991	456	383		442	377	437	1430
4	1 Year's Decrease		40					1335						97				
5	1 Year's Percentage Gain	.06		.48	2.13	2.31	.59		4.64	6.92	6.17	2.72	2.18		2.69	2.85	3.88	5.50
6	1 Year's Percentage Decrease		1.43					3.86						4.82				
7	1927	3184	2689	3881	1321780	933650	676496	36668	18264	5397	33871	18704	20012	2023	14772	12677	12117	24464
8	2 Years' Gain	90	61	44	77628	37537	4340		148		376				2083	884		2942
9	2 Years' Decrease							3473		162		1523	2123	110			439	
10	2 Years' Percentage Gain	2.82	2.27	1.13	5.87	4.02	.64		.81		1.11				14.10	6.09		12.02
11	2 Years' Percentage Decrease							9.47		3.00		8.14	10.60	5.43			3.62	
12	2 Years' Average Percentage Gain	1.41	1.14	.57	2.94	2.01	.32		.40		.56				7.05	3.05		6.01
13	2 Years' Average Percentage Decrease							4.74		1.50		4.07	5.30	2.72			1.81	
14	1926	3127	2706	3876	1315620	916858	677287	34562	17573	5178	25451	16866	19781	1983	12789	11758	11447	22831
15	3 Years' Gain	147	44	49	83788	54329	3549		839	57	8796	315			4066	1803	211	4575
16	3 Years' Decrease							1367					1892	70				
17	3 Years' Percentage Gain	4.70	1.62	1.26	6.36	5.92	.52		4.77	1.11	34.56	1.86			31.79	15.33	1.84	20.03
18	3 Years' Percentage Decrease							3.95					9.56	3.53				
19	3 Years' Average Percentage Gain	1.83	.54	.42	2.12	1.97	.17		1.59	.37	11.52	.62			10.60	5.11	.61	6.68
20	3 Years' Average Percentage Decrease							1.32					3.19	1.18				
21	1925	3011	2649	3875	1276176	886840	669695	35307	16658	5536	31071	17366	18504	2004	12335	11454	12111	23935
22	4 Years' Gain	263	101	50	123232	84347	11141		1754		3176				4520	2107		3471
23	4 Years' Decrease							2112		301		185	615	91			433	
24	4 Years' Percentage Gain	8.73	3.81	1.29	9.65	9.51	1.66		10.52		10.22				36.64	18.30		14.50
25	4 Years' Percentage Decrease							5.98		5.43		1.06	3.32	4.54			3.57	
26	4 Years' Average Percentage Gain	2.18	.95	.32	2.41	2.38	.41		2.63		2.55				9.16	4.57		3.62
27	4 Years' Average Percentage Decrease							1.49		1.36		.26	.83	1.13			.89	
28	1924	2983	2643	3829	1238009	856180	645836	35138	14029	5746	31020	17314	18090	1982	9918	11250	11887	23356
29	5 Years' Gain	291	107	96	161399	115007	35000		4382		3227				6937	2311		4050
30	5 Years' Decrease							1943		511		133	201	69			209	
31	5 Years' Percentage Gain	9.7	4.04	2.5	13.03	13.43	5.41		31.24		10.40				69.94	20.54		17.34
32	5 Years' Percentage Decrease							5.52		8.89		.76	1.11	3.48			1.75	
33	5 Years' Average Percentage Gain	1.94	.8	.50	2.60	2.68	1.08		6.25		2.08				13.99	4.10		3.47
34	5 Years' Average Percentage Decrease							1.10		1.78		.15	.22	.69			.35	
35	1919	2843		3473	1094153	776582	474553	34785		4400	27645	13915	9235			14073	10664	23467
36	10 Years' Gain	431		452	305235	194605	206283			835	6602	3266	8654				1014	3939
37	10 Years' Decrease							1590								512		
38	10 Years' Percentage Gain	15.16		13.01	27.89	25.05	43.46			18.97	23.88	23.47	93.70				9.50	16.77
39	10 Years' Percentage Decrease							4.57								3.63		
40	10 Years' Average Percentage Gain	1.52		1.30	2.79	2.50	4.35			1.89	2.39	2.35	9.37				.95	1.68
41	10 Years' Average Percentage Decrease							.46								.36		

PAROCHIAL REPORT OF THE UNITED LUTHERAN CHURCH IN AMERICA—UNITED STATES AND CANADA
Comparisons, Percentages and Averages—1919 to 1929 Inclusive—Continued

Idx	19 Off. Papers	20 S.S. Papers	21 Oth'r Ch. Prs.	22 No. (Sun.)	23 Off. & Teach.	24 Scholars	25 Home Dept.	26 Cradle Roll	27 No. (Wk.)	28 Teachers	29 Scholars	30 Catechu.	31 Ministry	32 Deaconess	33 Luth. Inst.	34 Non-Luth.	35 Men's No.	36 Men's Mem.	37 Wom. No.	38 Wom. Mem.	39 Y.P. No.	40 Y.P. Mem.	41 Ch. Edifices	42 Parsonages
1	40329	165940	58505	4215	66800	636121	24564	63218	1056	4870	68082	50009	661	33	2635	9034	1471	63799	5488	210328	4698	137624	120574104	15170989
2	41809	163027	57123	3671	65465	624908	26046	65787	1033	4513	65123	51212	709	44	2678	8967	1436	63646	5322	209318	4385	133105	114446734	14764569
3	1480	2913	1382	544	1335	11213	1482	2569	23	357	2959	1203	48	11	43	67	35	153	166	1010	313	4519	6127370	406420
4	3.53	1.78	2.41	14.81	2.03	1.79	5.68	3.90	2.22	7.91	4.53	2.34	6.77	25.0	1.60	.74	2.43	.24	3.11	.48	7.13	3.39	5.17	2.75
5	43917	162246	49825	3651	64212	613863	25826	65544	928	4183	59491	48833	261	52	2626	8338	1383	63146	5181	208003	3986	133682	108956533	14598321
6	3588	3694	8680	564	2588	22258	1262	2326	128	687	9591	1186	400	19	9	696	88	653	307	2325	712	3942	11617571	572668
7	8.16	2.27	11.30	15.43	4.03	3.62	4.88	3.54	13.78	16.42	16.39	2.43	153.25	36.53	.34	8.34	6.36	1.03	5.92	1.11	17.86	2.94	10.66	3.89
8	4.08	1.14	5.65	7.72	2.02	1.81	2.44	1.77	6.89	8.21	8.15	1.22	76.63	18.27	.17	4.17	3.18	.52	2.96	.56	8.93	1.47	5.33	1.95
9	50684	167418	38573	3524	62609	608261	27309	65938	647	3157	45366	48272	851	79	2632	7555	1294	59190	4830	199855	3825	130552	99894373	13381748
10	10355	1478	19932	691	4191	27860	2745	2720	409	1713	22716	1737	190	46	3	1479	177	4609	658	10473	873	7072	20679731	1289241
11	20.43	.88	51.67	19.60	6.69	4.58	10.05	4.12	63.21	54.26	50.07	3.59	22.32	58.22	.11	19.57	13.67	7.78	13.56	5.24	22.82	5.41	20.70	9.28
12	6.81	.29	17.22	6.65	2.23	1.53	3.35	1.37	21.07	18.09	16.69	1.20	7.44	19.40	.04	6.52	4.56	2.59	4.52	1.75	7.61	1.80	6.90	3.09
13	50735	174407	36101	3531	59940	590169	28197	65706	651	2704	42372	49216	826	90	2551	6753	1211	56892	4515	184475	3547	122380	86288340	12532190
14	10406	8467	22404	684	6860	5952	3623	2488	405	2166	25710	793	165	57	84	2281	260	6907	973	25853	1151	15244	34285764	2638799
15	20.51	4.85	62.05	19.37	11.44	1.00	12.85	3.78	62.21	80.10	60.67	1.69	19.97	63.33	3.29	33.77	21.46	12.14	21.55	14.06	32.44	12.45	39.74	21.04
16	5.13	1.21	15.51	4.84	2.86	.25	3.21	.94	15.55	20.02	15.17	.42	4.99	15.83	.82	8.44	5.37	3.04	5.39	3.52	8.11	3.11	9.94	5.26
17	50224	160203	39471	3515	55205	571737	28028	63853	557	2051	38824	49310	828	68	2530	5841	1213	56605	4307	181449	3400	120277	78525563	11169150
18	9895	3903	19034	700	7595	64384	3464	635	499	2819	29258	699	167	35	105	3193	258	7194	1181	28879	1298	17347	42048541	4001839
19	19.70	2.40	48.22	19.91	12.82	11.26	12.35	.99	89.58	137.44	75.36	1.41	20.16	51.47	4.15	54.66	21.26	12.79	27.42	15.97	35.23	14.42	53.54	35.82
20	3.94	.48	9.64	3.98	2.56	2.25	2.47	.20	19.72	27.49	15.07	.28		10.29	.83	10.93	4.25	2.56	5.48	3.19	7.05	2.88	10.71	7.16
21				3412	53554	514924	19019	32228	109	130	4779	36689	526	14	223	611	708	32550	2811	104760	2114	81746		2071193
22				803	13276	121197	5545	30990	947	4740	63303	13330	135	19	2412	8423	763	31249	2677	105568	2584	55878		13099796
23				23.53	24.80	23.53	29.15	96.15	868.80	3646.19	1324.60	36.30	25.66	135.71	1081.61	1378.55	107.76	96.03	95.23	100.77	122.23	68.35		632.47
24				2.35	2.48	2.35	2.91	9.61	86.88	364.60	132.46	3.63	2.57	13.57	108.16	137.85	10.78	9.60	9.52	10.07	12.22	6.84		63.25

Column groups: CHURCH PAPERS (19 No. Sub. to Official Papers; 20 No. S.S. Papers Distributed; 21 No. Sub. to Oth'r Ch. Prs.). CHURCH SCHOOLS — SUNDAY (22 Number; 23 Officers and Teachers; 24 Scholars; 25 Home Dept.; 26 Cradle Roll); WEEKDAY (27 Number; 28 Teachers; 29 Scholars); 30 Catechical Catechumens. STUDENTS (31 Ministry; 32 Deaconess; 33 In Lutheran Institutions; 34 In Non-Luth. Institutions). CHURCH SOCIETIES — MEN'S (35 Number; 36 Members); WOMEN'S (37 Number; 38 Members); YOUNG P. (39 Number; 40 Members). FINANCIAL (41 Church Edifices; 42 Parsonages).

PAROCHIAL REPORT OF THE UNITED LUTHERAN CHURCH IN AMERICA—UNITED STATES AND CANADA

Comparisons, Percentages and Averages—1919 to 1929 Inclusive—Concluded

Index No.	VALUATION OF CHURCH PROPERTY					CONGREGATIONAL EXPENSES			FINANCIAL — APPORTIONED			CONGREGATIONAL BENEVOLENCE — UNAPPORTIONED						SUMMARY	
	School and Parish Houses (43)	Endowment (44)	Other Property (45)	Total Valuation (46)	Indebtedness (47)	Current (48)	Unusual (49)	Total (50)	Paid (51)	Excess (52)	Deficit (53)	Education (54)	Foreign Missions (55)	Home Missions (56)	Inner Missions (57)	Other Benev. (58)	Total Unapportioned Benev. (59)	Total Benevolence (60)	Total Expenditures (61)
1	8966309	3133547	8525702	156370651	23432357	11197569	6507199	17704768	2295612	26748	590494	82290	310166	135858	1173850	401721	2203885	4499497	22204265
2	7486380	2932175	7585846	148701861	19416910	10761252	7261869	18051503	2109023	28470	794562	270776	247455	132640	1673710	483380	2823342	4932265	22983768
3	1479929	201372	939856	7668790	4015447	436317	754670	346735	186589	1722	204068	88486	62711	3218	499860	80659	619357	432768	779503
4	19.76	6.86	12.38	5.15	20.68	4.05	10.39	1.92	8.84	6.04	25.68	32.67	25.34	2.42	29.86	16.72	21.93	8.77	3.39
5																			
6	6830516	2757866	7523560	140609870	17883930	10487001	8034224	18521226	2156391	31925	623483	434917	320647	129359	480531	515817	1881271	4037662	22558888
7	2135793	375681	1002142	15760781	5548427	710568	1527025	816458	139221	5177	32989	252627	10481	6499	693319	114096	322614	461835	354623
8	31.26	13.62	13.32	11.20	31.02	6.77	19.0	4.40	6.45	16.21	5.29	58.08	31.33	5.02	144.28	22.11	17.14	11.43	1.57
9	15.63	6.81	6.66	5.60	15.51	3.39	9.50	2.20	3.23	8.10	2.65	29.04	15.66	2.51	72.14	11.06	8.57	5.72	.79
10																			
11	5198535	2547063	7441745	128964264	15300109	9443178	8651013	18094191	1853225	30138	460334	300820	268875	100063	314697	411606	1426061	3779286	21373477
12	3767774	586484	1083957	27406387	8132248	1754391	2143814	389423	442387	3390	130160	118530	41291	35795	859153	777824	777824	1220211	830788
13	72.47	23.02	14.56	21.25	53.15	18.50	24.78	2.15	23.87	11.24	28.27	39.40	15.35	35.77	273.01	39885	54.55	37.20	3.88
14	24.16	7.67	4.85	7.08	17.72	6.17	8.26	.72	7.96	3.75	9.42	13.13	5.12	11.92	91.0	8.94	18.18	12.40	1.29
15																.98			
16	3919089	2383469	6733780	111856868	11457989	8676760	7014663	15691423	1828761	41395	132159	623116	218881	110766	403638	526722	188323	3711884	19403307
17	5047220	750078	1791922	44513783	11974368	2420809	507464	2013345	466851	14647	458335	440826	91285	25092	770212	125001	2015562	787613	2800958
18	128.78	31.47	26.61	39.79	104.49	27.32	7.14	12.83	25.52	35.38	28.83	70.74	41.70	22.65	190.81	23.73	1070.26	21.21	14.43
19	32.20	7.87	6.65	9.95	26.12	6.83	1.79	3.21	6.38	8.85	7.21	17.69	10.43	5.66	47.70	5.93	267.57	5.30	3.61
20																			
21	3136620	2281248	5806395	101368976	9265083	8041334	6818421	14859760	1748347	44595	390112	320448	256887	160597	354336	672022	1763990	3512337	18372097
22	5829689	832299	2719307	55001675	14167274	3156235	311222	2845008	547265	17847	390382	138158	53579	24739	819514	270301	439895	987160	3832168
23	185.85	37.36	46.83	54.25	152.91	39.24	4.56	19.21	31.30	40.02	50.33	43.11	20.88	15.40	231.30	40.22	24.93	28.10	20.85
24	37.17	7.67	9.37	10.85	30.58	7.85	.91	3.84	6.26	8.00	10.07	8.63	4.18	3.08	46.26	8.04	4.99	5.62	4.17
25																			
26																			
27																			
28																			
29																			
30																			
31																			
32																			
33																			
34																			
35																			
36		1032292	4238332	42383332	4527913	4984795	1916749	6911544	1344202			182214		130399	1173780	902981	908586	2257788	914432
37		2101255		113987319	18904444	6212774	4590450	10793224	951410							501260	1295299	2246709	13049933
38												239755.26		2388.69	1676828.57				
39												23975.53		238.87	167682.86				
40	203.55	203.55	417.50	268.94	417.50	124.63	239.49	156.16	70.77							55.51	142.56	99.73	142.55
41	20.36	20.36	41.75	26.89	41.75	12.46	23.95	15.62	7.08							5.55	14.26	9.97	14.25

PAROCHIAL REPORT OF THE UNITED LUTHERAN CHURCH IN AMERICA—UNITED STATES AND CANADA
1927 Gains and Decreases and 1929 Gains and Decreases Compared

Index Number					MEMBERSHIP			PAROCHIAL										
								ACCESSIONS						LOSSES				
								CHILDREN		ADULT				CHILDREN		ADULT		
		PASTORS	PARISHES	Congregations	Baptized	Confirmed	Communing	Baptism	Otherwise	Baptism	Confirmation	Certificate	Otherwise	Death	Otherwise	Death	Certificate	Otherwise
	1	2	3	4	5	6	7	8	9	10	11	12	13	14	15	16	17	18
42	10 Year Gain from 1919 to 1929	431		452	305255	194605	206283	1590		835	6602	3266	8654					
43	10 Year Decrease from 1919 to 1929															512	1014	3939
44	10 Year % Gain from 1919 to 1929	15.16		13.01	27.89	25.05	43.46	4.57		18.97	23.88	23.47	93.70					
45	10 Year % Decrease from 1919 to 1929															3.63	9.50	16.77
46	10 Year Average % Gain from 1919 to 1929	1.52		1.30	2.79	2.50	4.35	.46		1.89	2.39	2.35	9.37					
47	10 Year Average % Dec. from 1919 to 1929															.36	.95	1.68
48	8 Year Gain from 1919 to 1927	341		408	227627	157068	201943	1883		997	6226	4789	10777					
49	8 Year Decrease from 1919 to 1927															1404	1453	997
50	8 Year % Gain from 1919 to 1927	11.99		11.74	20.79	20.22	42.55	5.41		22.65	22.52	34.41	116.69					
51	8 Year % Decrease from 1919 to 1927															9.97	13.62	4.24
52	8 Year Average % Gain from 1919 to 1927	1.50		1.47	2.59	2.53	5.32	.68		2.83	2.82	4.30	14.59					
53	8 Year Average % Decrease from 1919 to 1927															1.25	1.58	.53
54	Net 2 Year Gain	90		44	77628	37537	4340	293		162	376	1523	2123					
55	Net 2 Year Decrease															892	439	2942
56	Net 2 Year Percentage Gain	3.17		1.27	7.1	4.83	.91	.84		3.68	1.36	.94	22.99					
57	Net 2 Year Percentage Decrease															6.34	4.12	12.53
58	Net 2 Year Average Percentage Gain	1.59		.64	3.5	2.42	.45	.42		1.84	.68	.47	11.49					
59	Net 2 Year Average Percentage Decrease															3.17	2.06	6.26

PAROCHIAL REPORT OF THE UNITED LUTHERAN CHURCH IN AMERICA—UNITED STATES AND CANADA
1927 Gains and Decreases and 1929 Gains and Decreases Compared—Continued

Index No.	19 No. Sub. to Official Papers	20 No. S.S. Papers Distributed	21 No. Sub. to Oth'r Ch. P'rs.	22 Number (Sunday)	23 Officers and Teachers	24 Scholars	25 Home Dept.	26 Cradle Roll	27 Number (Weekday)	28 Teachers	29 Scholars	30 Catechumens	31 Ministry	32 Deaconess	33 In Lutheran Institutions	34 In Non-Luth. Institutions	35 Number (Men's)	36 Members (Men's)	37 Number (Women's)	38 Members (Women's)	39 Number (Young P.)	40 Members (Young P.)	41 Church Edifices	42 Parsonages
42	…	…	…	803	13276	121197	5545	30990	947	4740	63303	13320	135	19	2412	8423	763	31249	2677	105568	2584	55878	…	13099796
43	…	…	…	23.53	24.80	23.53	29.15	96.15	868.80	3646.19	1324.60	36.30	25.66	135.71	1081.61	1378.55	107.76	96.03	95.23	100.77	122.23	68.35	…	632.47
44	…	…	…	2.35	2.48	2.35	2.91	9.61	86.88	364.60	132.46	3.63	2.57	13.57	108.16	137.85	10.78	9.60	9.52	10.07	12.22	6.84	…	63.25
45	…	…	…	…	…	…	…	…	…	…	…	…	…	…	…	…	…	…	…	…	…	…	…	…
46	…	…	…	…	…	…	…	…	…	…	…	…	…	…	…	…	…	…	…	…	…	…	…	…
47	…	…	…	…	…	…	…	…	…	…	…	…	…	…	…	…	…	…	…	…	…	…	…	…
48	…	…	…	239	10688	98939	6807	33316	819	4053	53712	12134	235	38	2403	7727	675	30596	2370	103243	1872	51936	…	12527128
49	…	…	…	7.00	19.96	19.21	35.79	103.37	751.37	3117.69	1123.91	33.07	44.67	271.42	1077.57	1264.64	95.33	93.99	84.31	98.55	88.55	63.53	…	604.82
50	…	…	…	.88	2.50	2.40	4.47	12.92	93.92	387.21	140.49	4.13	5.58	33.93	134.70	158.18	11.92	11.75	10.54	12.32	11.07	7.94	…	75.60
51	…	…	…	…	…	…	…	…	…	…	…	…	…	…	…	…	…	…	…	…	…	…	…	…
52	…	…	…	…	…	…	…	…	…	…	…	…	…	…	…	…	…	…	…	…	…	…	…	…
53	…	…	…	…	…	…	…	…	…	…	…	…	…	…	…	…	…	…	…	…	…	…	…	…
54	…	…	…	564	2588	22258	1262	2326	128	687	9591	1186	100	19	9	696	88	653	307	2325	712	3942	…	572668
55	…	…	…	16.53	4.84	4.32	6.64	7.22	117.43	528.5	200.69	3.23	19.01	135.71	4.04	113.91	12.43	2.04	10.92	2.22	33.68	4.82	…	27.65
56	…	…	…	8.26	2.42	2.16	3.32	3.61	58.72	264.3	100.35	1.62	9.5	67.85	2.02	56.95	6.22	1.02	5.46	1.11	16.84	2.41	…	13.82
57	…	…	…	…	…	…	…	…	…	…	…	…	…	…	…	…	…	…	…	…	…	…	…	…
58	…	…	…	…	…	…	…	…	…	…	…	…	…	…	…	…	…	…	…	…	…	…	…	…
59	…	…	…	…	…	…	…	…	…	…	…	…	…	…	…	…	…	…	…	…	…	…	…	…

Column group headings: Church Papers (19–21); Church Schools — Sunday (22–26), Weekday (27–29), Catechetical (30); Students (31–34); Church Societies — Men's (35–36), Women's (37–38), Young P. (39–40); Financial (41–42).

PAROCHIAL REPORT OF THE UNITED LUTHERAN CHURCH IN AMERICA—UNITED STATES AND CANADA
1927 Gains and Decreases and 1929 Gains and Decreases Compared—Concluded

FINANCIAL

Index Number	43 School and Parish Houses	44 Endowment	45 Other Property	46 Total Valuation	47 Indebtedness	48 Current	49 Unusual	50 Total	51 Paid	52 Excess	53 Deficit	54 Education	55 Foreign Missions	56 Home Missions	57 Inner Missions	58 Other Benevolenc	59 Total Un-apportioned Benev.	60 Total Benevolence	61 Total Expenditures
42		2101255		113987319	18904444	6212774	4590450	10793224	951410			182214		130399	1173780	501260	1295299	2246709	13049933
43		203.55		268.94	417.50	124.63	239.49	156.16	70.77			239755.26		2388.69	1676828.57	55.51	142.56	99.73	142.55
44																			
45		20.36		26.89	41.75	12.46	23.95	15.62	7.08			23975.53		238.87	167682.86	5.55	14.26	9.97	14.25
46																			
47		1725574		98226538	13356017	5496206	6117475	11609682	812189			434841		123900	480461	387164	972685	1784874	13404556
48																			
49		167.15		231.75	294.08	110.25	319.15	167.97	60.42			572157.89		2086.46	686372.85	42.87	107.05	83.66	146.42
50																			
51		20.89		28.97	36.76	13.78	39.89	20.99	7.55			71519.74		260.81	85796.37	5.36	13.38	10.46	18.30
52																			
53		375681		15760781	5548427	716568	527025	816458	139221			252627		6499	693319	114096	322614	461835	354623
54																			
55		36.40		37.19	123.42	14.33	79.66	11.81	10.35			332402.63		302.23	990455.72	12.64	35.51	16.07	3.87
56																			
57		18.20		18.59	61.71	7.19	39.83	5.90	5.17			166201.31		151.11	495227.86	6.32	17.75	8.03	1.93
58																			
59																			

UNITED LUTHERAN CHURCH IN THE UNITED STATES AND CANADA

COMPARISONS, PERCENTAGES AND AVERAGES 1927, 1928 AND 1929 ON ACCESSIONS, LOSSES AND NET ACCESSIONS

1929 Total Accessions................	126,159		1929 Total Losses....................	71,413
1928 Total Accessions................	123,507		1928 Total Losses....................	68,824
1929 Increase in Accessions............	2,652		1929 Increase in Losses...............	2,589
1 Year Percentage Increase............	2.14%		1 Year Percentage Increase............	3.76%
1928 Decrease in Accessions...........	9,409		1928 Increase in Losses...............	2,771
2 Year Net Increase in Accessions.......	12,061		2 Year Net Decrease in Losses.........	182
2 Year Percentage Increase in Accessions.	9.07%		2 Year Percentage Decrease............	.27%
2 Year Average Percentage Increase.....	4.53%		2 Year Average Percentage Decrease.....	.14%

1929 Accessions Gain over Losses.........................	54,746
1928 Accessions Gain over Losses.........................	54,683
1929 Gain in Accessions Gain over Losses...................	63
1 Year Percentage Gain......................................	.11%
1928 Loss in Accessions Gain over Losses...................	12,180
2 Year Net Gain...	12,243
2 Year Percentage Gain....................................	18.31%
2 Year Average Percentage Gain.............................	9.15%

NET VALUATION

1929 Total Valuation..............	$156,370,651		1919 Net Valuation................	$37,855,419
1929 Total Indebtedness............	23,432,357		10 Year Net Gain....................	95,082,875
1929 Net Valuation................	132,938,294		10 Year Percentage Gain..............	251.17%
1928 Net Valuation................	129,284,951		10 Year Average Percentage Gain......	25.12%
1 Year Net Gain....................	3,653,343		8 Year Net Gain....................	84,870,521
1 Year Percentage Gain..............	2.82%		8 Year Percentage Gain..............	224.19%
1927 Net Valuation................	122,725,940		8 Year Average Percentage Gain......	28.02%
2 Year Net Gain....................	10,212,354		Net 2 Year Gain....................	10,212,354
2 Year Percentage Gain..............	8.32%		Net 2 Year Percentage Gain........	26.98%
2 Year Average Percentage Gain......	4.16%		Net 2 Year Average Percentage Gain..	13.49%

COMPARISONS, PERCENTAGES AND AVERAGES 1919 TO 1929 INCLUSIVE
PER CAPITAS

	Current Expenses	Unusual Expenses	Total Congregational	Apportionment Benevolence paid	Total Benevolence	Total Expenditures
1929..	$11.42	$6.70	$18.23	$2.36	$4.63	$22.86
1928..	11.33	7.65	19.01	2.22	5.11	24.21
1 Year Gain....................................	.09	......	......	.14	......	......
1 Year Loss....................................	......	.95	.78	......	.48	1.35
1 Year Percentage Gain...........................	.8%	......	......	6.30%	......	......
1 Year Percentage Loss...........................	......	12.41%	4.10%	......	9.39%	5.57%
1927..	$11.23	$8.59	$19.84	$2.31	$4.32	$24.16
2 Year Gain....................................	.19	......	......	.05	.31	......
2 Year Loss....................................	......	1.89	1.61	......	......	1.30%
2 Year Percentage Gain...........................	1.69%	......	......	2.16%	7.17%	......
2 Year Percentage Loss...........................	......	22.0%	8.11%	......	......	5.36%
2 Year Average Percentage Gain....................	.84	11.0	4.05	1.08	3.58%	......
2 Year Average Percentage Loss....................	......	......	......	......	......	2.68
1919..	$6.42	$2.46	$8.88	$1.73	$2.90	$11.78
10 Year Gain...................................	5.00	4.24	9.35	.63	1.73	11.08
10 Year Loss...................................	......	......	......	......	......	......
10 Year Percentage Gain..........................	77.88%	172.35%	105.29%	36.41%	59.65	94.05
10 Year Percentage Loss..........................	......	......	......	......	......	......
10 Year Average Percentage Gain...................	7.78	17.23	10.53	3.64	5.96	9.40
10 Year Average Percentage Loss...................						

U.L.C. in A.
TOTAL ADULT ACCESSIONS
Confirmations—Catechumens
Membership Weekday Schools
and Societies
1919—1929

THOUSAND

	Increase 8 Years %	Increase 10 Years %
	98.55	100.77
	63.53	68.35
	41.28	35.07
	116+.51	138.08
	93.99	36.03
	33.07	36.30
	23.52	28.88

WOMEN'S SOCIETIES

YOUNG PEOPLE'S SOCIETIES

ADULT ACCESSIONS

MEN'S SOCIETIES

CATECHUMENS

CONFIRMATIONS

WEEKDAY SCHOOLS

220 200 180 160 140 120 100 80 60 40 20 0

1919 1920 1921 1922 1923 1924 1925 1926 1927 1928 1929

U.L.C. in A.
MEMBERSHIPS
U.S. and Canada
1919—1929

MEMBERS

	Increase 8 Years %	Increase 10 Years %
	20.79	27.89
	20.22	25.05
	24.16	29.02
	42.55	43.46

BAPTIZED

CONFIRMED

SUNDAY SCHOOLS

COMMUNING

1,500,000 1,400,000 1,300,000 1,200,000 1,100,000 1,000,000 900,000 800,000 700,000 600,000 500,000 0

1919 1920 1921 1922 1923 1924 1925 1926 1927 1928 1929

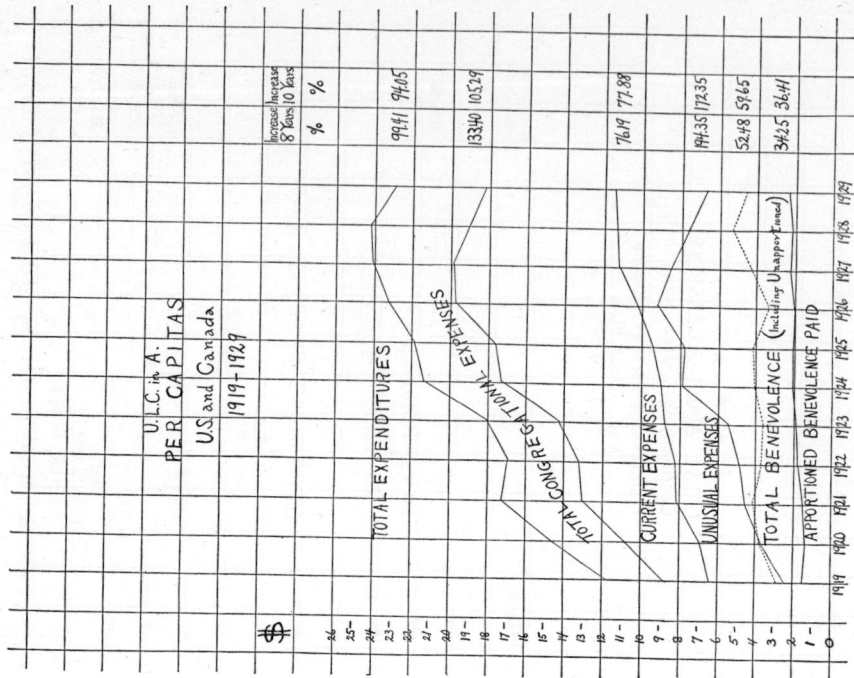

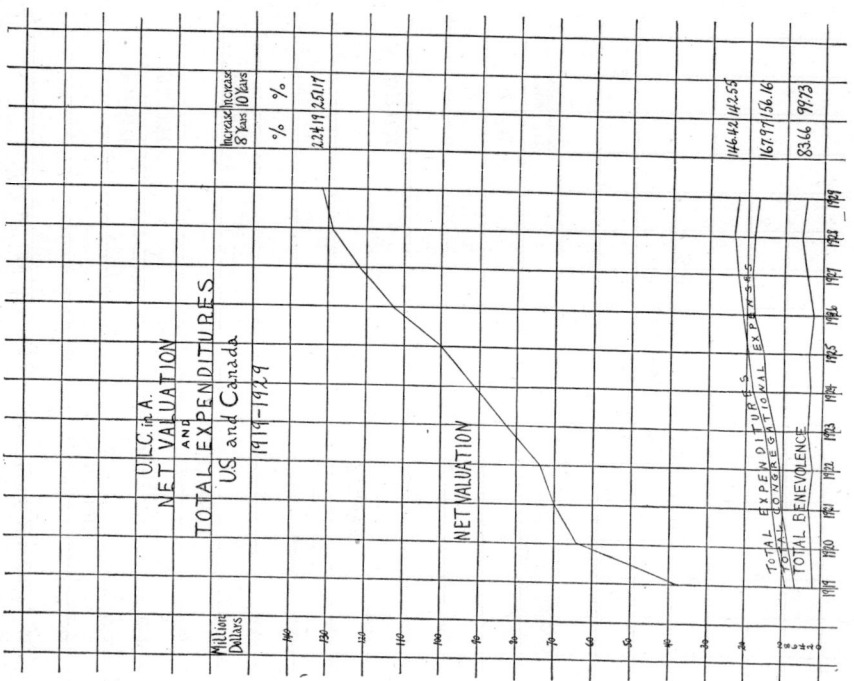

U.L.C. in A.
PER CAPITAS
US and Canada
1919-1929

Increase Increase
8 Years 10 Years
%   %

99.41 94.05
133.40 105.9
76.19 77.88
199.35 172.35
52.48 57.65
34.25 36.41

TOTAL EXPENDITURES
TOTAL CONGREGATIONAL EXPENSES
CURRENT EXPENSES
UNUSUAL EXPENSES
TOTAL BENEVOLENCE (including Unapportioned)
APPORTIONED BENEVOLENCE PAID

1919 1920 1921 1922 1923 1924 1925 1926 1927 1928 1929

U.L.C. in A.
NET VALUATION
AND
TOTAL EXPENDITURES
US and Canada
1919-1929

Increase Increase
8 Years 10 Years
%   %

224.19 250.19
146.42 142.55
167.97 156.16
83.66 99.73

Million Dollars

NET VALUATION

TOTAL EXPENDITURES
TOTAL CONGREGATIONAL EXPENSES
TOTAL BENEVOLENCE

1919 1920 1921 1922 1923 1924 1925 1926 1927 1928 1929

The Rev. Frank Wolford was called upon by the President and addressed the Convention in recognition of the centennial of the New York Synod, recently merged into the United Lutheran Synod of New York.

At twelve o'clock the Convention adjourned with prayer by the Rev. C. N. Swihart.

———————•—•———————

Afternoon Session

Monday, October 13, 1930, 2:00 o'clock.

Devotions were conducted by the Rev. M. L. Stirewalt.

The President called the Convention to order.

The Rev. J. A. Leas presented the report of the Committee of Reference and Counsel as follows:

1. We recommend that a message of Christian sympathy be sent to the Rev. Chas. E. Hay, D.D., for twenty-five years pastor of the Baltimore Motherhouse, and who has been seriously ill for some months; and we further recommend that prayer be made for his recovery and for our heavenly Father's sustaining care.

2. We recommend that the Secretary of the Convention be authorized to send greetings to one of the Lord's faithful and efficient servants, the Rev. L. A. Bikle, D.D., of Concord, N. C., who will be ninety-six years of age on November 6th.

3. We recommend that the Convention, feeling deeply the untimely death of Missionary J. D. Curran, of Africa, authorize the Secretary to extend to the bereaved family the sympathy of this body.

4. Your committee recommends the adoption of the following resolution:

Resolved, that the Convention hereby places on record the Church's especial and grateful recognition and appreciation of the many years of efficient and valuable service rendered by the Hon. E. F. Eilert, C.S.D., retiring President of the Board of Publication; by the Rev. C. Theodore Benze, D.D., retiring President of the Board of Foreign Missions; by the Rev. August Steimle, D.D., retiring President of the Board of Education; by the Rev. E. F. Bachman, D.D., retiring President of the Inner Mission Board; by the Rev. Henry Eyster Jacobs, D.D., LL.D., S.T.D., retiring President of the Commission of Adjudication; and by the Rev. F. P. Manhart, D.D., as a member of the Board of Publication and earlier as secretary of the Publication Society of the former General Synod.

5. We recommend that the Rev. Wm. M. Horn be permitted, at this time, to read certain resolutions as touching our missionaries in Japan.

Recommendation 1 was adopted by a rising vote.

The Rev. H. C. Alleman led the Convention in prayer.

Recommendations 2, 3, 4 and 5 were adopted.

In connection with recommendation 5, the Rev. Wm. M. Horn read the following resolution which was adopted:

The United Lutheran Church in America, in convention assembled at Milwaukee, Wis., has received and heard with interest and concern the communication signed by all of you and amplified and brought home to its delegates in the earnest addresses of your two co-workers, Revs. J. K. Linn and S. O. Thorlaksson. It appreciates and sympathizes with the situation confronting you and thanks God that in the present crisis in Japan He has given us such faithful and devoted men and women to proclaim the Gospel of our Blessed Savior. The story which your two representatives, fresh from the field, have told, has stirred our hearts and has made us see more clearly the obstacles you face and the sacrifices you are making to carry on.

The United Lutheran Church sends to each of you its loving appreciation, its prayers, and its pledge to stand by. We commit to our agency for work in Japan, the Board of Foreign Missions, the working out of plans for your relief, and we commend to our congregations the raising of their whole apportionment as the best means of showing our affection.

In sending this to you we are conscious that the same conditions as you meet obtain in every section of our mission field, and that men and women, as faithful and devoted as those in Japan, are laboring in India, Africa, China and South America, and we cannot but send to them the same affection, prayers and pledges.

The Rev. H. C. Alleman presented his report as representative in the Advisory Board of the American Bible Society and introduced Dr. George William Brown, Secretary of the American Bible Society. Dr. Brown addressed the Convention. The report follows:

REPORT OF REPRESENTATIVE IN THE ADVISORY BOARD OF THE AMERICAN BIBLE SOCIETY

Your representative in the Advisory Board of the American Bible Society begs leave to submit his sixth biennial report.

The Advisory Board is composed of delegated representatives from the supporting denominations, three of them being Lutheran, namely, the Augustana Synod, the Norwegian Church in America, and the United Lutheran Church in America. The Board meets annually at the Bible House, Astor Place, New York City, to consider the recommendations of the secretaries and the treasurer of the Society, and to submit its findings to the Board of Managers, with whom it is invited to sit throughout their consideration. Your representative was present at the meetings of the Advisory Board in 1928 and 1929.

The American Bible Society, which is rounding out the one hundred and fifteenth year of its service, is one of the pillars of our American Christianity, and one of the great missionary organizations of the world. Its sole object is "to encourage a wider circulation of the Holy Scriptures without note or comment." The latest statistics show that the Bible, in whole or in part, has been translated into 886 languages. It is estimated that, due to the combined interested agencies, some portion of the Bible appears in a new language or dialect as often as once every five weeks. During 1929 the four Gospels were published for the first time in the language spoken by the Kuskokwim Eskimos in southwestern Alaska; an edition of the four Gospels and the Acts of the Apostles in Benga for use in West Africa; the four Gospels in Hopi, the first of the Scriptures to be published for the Indians of that name living near the Grand Canyon; a "diglot" edition of the Gospel of St. John, with Portuguese and Japanese in parallel columns for use among the Japanese immigrants now pouring into Brazil; and the Psalms in Bolivian Quechua for use among a large Indian population in the Andes.

In the years of its history the American Bible Society has distributed over 216 million copies of Bibles, Testaments and Portions. During 1929, for the second time, it passed the eleven million mark in its distribution. Particularly interesting is the report of the Society's agency Secretary for China that the circulation there in 1929 exceeded that of 1928 by 651,170 copies.

The year 1929 saw a new record established in the number of volumes of embossed Scriptures distributed to the blind, namely, 3,725, or an increase of fifty per cent. The Society is now able to furnish the embossed Scriptures in any system at fifty cents a volume. An entire Bible in revised Braille may be secured for $10.50.

The annual budget of the Society is over a million dollars. The Society enjoys an income of a quarter of that amount from invested funds and rentals, about $200,000 from individual gifts and annuities, and upwards of $375,000 from sales. For the balance, or $225,000, it must look to the churches. Last year the churches contributed $208,405.59.

After an all-day meeting, December 4th last, the Advisory Council unanimously adopted the following resolutions and requested their reference to the several churches:

"The Advisory Council of the American Bible Society in its eleventh annual session desires to put itself on record as follows:

"1. We are impressed anew with the magnitude of the trust administered by the American Bible Society. Its task, with similar organizations in other lands, is to distribute the Word of God in the languages of the people to the ends of the earth. Over 11,000,000 volumes of the Scriptures in over 182 tongues were issued last year by the American Bible Society alone. This work is done within a budget of a little more than $1,000,000. It is a great work.

"2. We are impressed anew with the needs of the work. Doors of opportunity are opened of which we cannot avail ourselves. The budget must be cut to the income of the society.

"3. We are impressed again with the tardiness of the churches to support this work as it deserves. One-fourth of the income of the society must come from the churches in order to sustain the budget, yet many denominations recognize the society financially in an inadequate way. We call on our several denominations to give this cause its rightful place.

"4. We are impressed with the fitness of the several officers of the society for their tasks. Their co-operation and efficiency not only make the task of the Advisory Council a pleasure, but we are convinced that the administration of the society's work is in competent hands.

"5. We commend to our churches the observance of the second Sunday in Advent as Universal Bible Sunday.

"6. As the Word of God is the organ of the divine Spirit's operation, we call upon all Christian people to observe the nineteen hundredth anniversary of the advent of the Holy Spirit by a new and larger use of this Word in the home, the school and the church."

Your representative recommends:

That the United Lutheran Church in America continue its representation in the Advisory Council.

Respectfully submitted,
HERBERT C. ALLEMAN,
Representative of the U. L. C.

The recommendation was adopted.

The Rev. E. F. Bachmann presented the report of the Inner Mission Board as follows:

REPORT OF THE INNER MISSION BOARD

Your Inner Mission Board rejoices to report a steady growth of Inner Mission interest and activities throughout the Church. The fact that only $1.50 out of every $100 contributed by the Church for all her causes is available for the purposes of your Board, has led many to believe its work of minor importance, yet the Inner Mission activities throughout our Church present an array of figures which place her well in the front rank among the Protestant bodies in this country for what is often termed welfare work. 1,281 orphaned boys and girls have found an opportunity for education and training in fifteen homes of the Church, while seventeen provide a carefree evening of life to 308 of her aged men and women. She has eight hospitals which every year admit about 30,000 patients, four homes for 120 defective children and adults, fifteen other institutions for children and adults in need of various forms of care, fifteen Inner Mission societies in as many cities reaching out the helping hand in Christ's Name to thousands of persons, young and old, who by this service feel the touch of God's seeking and saving love. Nor are the strangers within our gates ignored. In eleven cities are hospices for young men and young women who have ventured away from home in search of better opportunities and who find in these hospices not a mere boarding house, but a home under sympathetic leadership and with a Christian atmosphere. The immigrant reaching the shores of this land of promise is welcomed by six pastors and three helpers devoting their entire time to this service in New York and Philadelphia, in Montreal and in Winnipeg, that great distributing point for Canada's vast Northwest. And the seamen, rendering mankind their indispensable service at the sacrifice of their own personal comforts, find a home with congenial comradeship provided in the harbors of New York and Philadelphia. All this work is carried on by a force of consecrated men and women, and at a total annual expense of $3,000,000.00. About half of these institutions and agencies are directly controlled by the United Lutheran Church or its constituent synods. The others draw their support partly from our membership and closely co-operate with our congregations.

This organized expression of the Inner Mission spirit within our church, goes back for more than eighty years to that great pioneer, the Rev. W. A. Passavant, who besides other Inner Mission institutions, founded also the Milwaukee hospital, and, gaining momentum especially during the past two decades, gives reasonable assurance of a still more rapid development in the near future. The Macedonian cry, "Come and help us," reaches your Board's executive office from many important groups which we dare not ignore. Our Church in America, the most favored land in the world today, cannot with Cain ask: "Am I my brother's keeper?" When for instance, tens of thousands of Lutheran seamen from abroad find not even a reading room provided by our Church in any of the ports on our eastern or western shores, except in New York and Philadelphia. In a few other ports provision has been made for Scandinavians. During the past biennium an open door for beginning effective work among seamen in one of the most important gulf ports could not be entered, because your Board did not have the funds necessary to rent, equip and maintain a reading room for at least a year, after which time support from local business interests could be enlisted. This is but one of several Christian obligations not yet adequately met by the Church.

Today, however, there is one group above all others which puts to the test the Church's faith in God and her love to the brethren—the *unemployed*. While we must always expect to have with us some persons temporarily out of work, their number has within the past twelve months increased to proportions which affect the entire nation. The united efforts of Federal, State and Municipal governments in co-operation with great corporations and private enterprises will not be able to cope successfully with the situation without the moral and material support of the religious forces. Our Church must take its place in the ranks of the agencies seeking to relieve distress. At the same time, she must clearly and fearlessly proclaim those fundamental truths of the gospel which, if honestly applied to the causes underlying the strained economic conditions of today, would prevent their recurrence and a possible disaster.

The present unemployment with its long train of soul-harrowing hardships and with a bitterness which may lead to lawlessness, is the more serious because it is world-wide, and threatens a world crisis under radical leadership. It requires more than mere welfare work, for this leaves the souls of men untouched; and more than mere preaching, for this leaves unsatisfied the pangs of hunger. The world today needs the combination of both, the preaching of the gospel as the message of God's love to men and the works of mercy as the proof of the truth of the gospel. This combination of both, found in Christ and the apostles, must be made more real, so that the Church may honestly confess: "Love is mine even as faith."

Following the example of her Lord, the Church will avoid the pitfalls of partisanship in the struggle between capital and labor, will retain clear vision and sound judgment, will be sincerely concerned about the welfare of *all,* and will not stoop to make a bid for the favor of one party by condemning the other. She will fearlessly proclaim to all men alike, "Thou shalt love thy neighbor as thyself" and will call upon employers to pay fair wages, and on employees really to earn their wages by conscientious work. She will also like her Lord, feed the hungry, and like the Mother Church in Jerusalem she will see to it that no needy person be neglected (Acts 6).

Your Inner Mission Board would therefore urge upon our Church assembled in convention, not vague pronouncements of sentiments and opinions, nor resolutions recommending to our government or to industrial leaders specific actions the effects of which the Church is not qualified to estimate, but would rather submit two resolutions of practical value. The one should commend President Hoover for his statesmanship exhibited last fall in calling conferences of representatives of state governments and leading industries to provide additional employment. The other should call on every congregation of the United Lutheran Church in America to appoint a "Committee on Employment" for the purpose of assisting members to secure work or support, and also to co-operate with similar religious and secular agencies of their community for general relief. **(See Resolutions 1 and 2.)**

This unemployment situation presents the greatest opportunity and the most urgent call of this generation for the exercise of a true Inner Mission spirit throughout our entire Church.

I. ORGANIZATION

The Board was organized for the biennium at a meeting held on December 5, 1928. The members of the Board elected at the last convention are: Rev. F. B. Clausen, Rev. J. F. Fedders, D.D., Rev. J. S. Schantz, Mr. A. H. Durboraw and Mr. W. J. Showalter, Sc.D. Mr. Showalter found it necessary to resign from membership in the Board as he was already a member of one Board and a major committee of the Church. In place of Mr. Showalter, Mr. T. P. Hickman, of Washington, D.C., was nominated to the Executive Board and elected by that body.

The following officers were elected for the biennium: President, Rev. E. F. Bachmann, D.D.; vice-president, Rev. F. B. Clausen; secretary and treasurer, Rev. William Freas, D.D.

Having completed a faithful service of ten years as a member of the Board it was a delight to acknowledge and give testimony to the service of Rev. J. F. Ohl, D.D., Mus.D. Dr. Ohl has been one of the Inner Mission pioneers in this country. He was the first Lutheran City Missionary in this country, having been called to Philadelphia to such position by the Ministerium of Pennsylvania in 1898. He was the first superintendent of Lutheran City Missions, serving in that capacity since 1903. He was also largely instrumental in organizing a Deaconess Motherhouse in Milwaukee, of which he was the pastor before coming to Philadelphia. Dr. Ohl has been an outstanding defender of the principles of the Inner Mission and out of a ripe experience of its practice has rendered an invaluable and stimulating service to the Church in the development of its Inner Mission work.

The Board was glad to welcome as representatives of the Women's Missionary Society, Mrs. W. A. Snyder and Mrs. M. J. Bieber. These representatives have been of real service in our counsels. We hereby acknowledge our gratitude to them for their helpfulness.

The matter of finances has long been a perplexing matter to the Board. An effort is now being made to solve this difficulty. One step in this direction is the Board's pledging itself to a balanced budget, upon the basis of actual receipts. In doing so it has been necessary to refrain from certain important activities except for small contributions. This is true of such an important work as the caring for seamen at the Port of Houston, Texas.

II. CONGREGATIONAL INNER MISSION WORK

The chief function of the Board as laid upon it by the Church is the development of that spirit in our congregations which shall lead to works of mercy on the part of all our people. This spirit will show itself in service in the congregation and in the community in which the Church is located.

Much yet remains to be done towards realizing the ideal of a fully active membership in our congregations. It is gratifying to note in the Church the growth of this spirit and activity. This is best evidenced by the fact that more and more men and women are becoming interested in some form of personal service in connection with the work of the congregation. Out of this interest, new activities, agencies and institutions have come.

Our congregations have been seeking for some time a congregational program. Upon this the Board has been working. While not yet ready to submit such a program, we can report that progress is being made upon it and that such program will soon be available.

As a step in the utilizing of the spirit of love in our churches there have been submitted to our Synodical Inner Mission Committees suggestions for seeking out our Lutheran people or others in need of spiritual care in the many institutions (other than those of the Church) operated by the state, county, philanthropic agencies, and so forth. Local pastors and congregations in certain places have been doing this sort of work. They have given a regular ministry and have come with gifts of love to bring something more of peace and joy into the lives of these often neglected folks.

That there are many people in such institutions for which no spiritual and social provision is made has been clearly shown. Numerous letters have come to the Board asking that they might have some Lutheran pastor come to them. In a number of instances some of these people have had no spiritual ministry for five or more years, though a number of Lutheran congregations are found near the institutions. Synodical Inner Mission committees are urging the seeking out of these people and arranging for them a regular service. Such committees are keeping in touch with the congregations so that this service may not only be begun but regularly continued.

A constant check-up is made difficult by the changing personnel of committees. The Inner Mission Board is urging upon all of its synods (where it seems to be at all wise) to plan for the establishment of an Inner Mission Board rather than a committee. This Board should retain at least two-thirds of its membership constantly. If possible all the conferences of the synod should be represented upon the Board. An appropriation for the work of this Board according to the needs of the territory should be made. **(See Resolution 4.)**

III. FOREIGN CONTACTS

One of the most important developments of the biennium has been the establishment of new foreign contacts with Inner Mission workers and organizations. Rev. Dr. Johannes Steinweg, executive secretary of the

Welfare Division of the Central Commission for the Inner Mission of the Evangelical Church in Germany was a visitor to this country and met many groups of people interested in Inner Mission work. It was very interesting to observe that the problems in Inner Mission work both here and abroad are the same. At a luncheon given in his honor by Dr. Knubel, Dr. Steinweg spoke of the harmony of principles of our work here and abroad. The much larger development in Germany is indicated by the fact that a force of 40,000 deaconesses and of 4,100 deacons is engaged in Protestant charitable work. In addition, there are 1,600 pastors, physicians and lawyers who devote their full time to Inner Mission work, together with 3,500 welfare workers and 10,000 employees and assistants. The volunteer workers on part time number several hundred thousand. The great difficulty faced is the increasing undenominational and purely secular form of welfare work by social agencies, but supported largely by the members of the Christian Church.

Growing out of this visit of Dr. Steinweg was the decision of the Board to send a representative to the meeting of the International Federation for Inner Mission and the Diaconate. Without much expense to the Board, Dr. Brueckner as representative of the Inner Mission Board, attended the meetings of the federation in the summer of 1929 in Bonn and Kaiserswerth. Dr. Brueckner submitted a report of the deepest interest. The following recommendations were made by Dr. Brueckner:

1. That, the United Lutheran Church in America, in consideration of the common battlefront forced upon the Inner Mission work of the churches by secular attempts to exclude it, join the International Federation for Inner Mission and the Diaconate.

2. That, the Inner Mission Board of the United Lutheran Church in America be authorized to acquire membership and cast the votes for the United Lutheran Church.

3. That, since under the conditions prevailing in the United States of America we cannot claim votes in proportion to the Protestant population of our country, the Federation for Inner Mission and the Diaconate be asked to allot to the United Lutheran Church in America a number of votes according to its baptized membership.

4. That, the desideria submitted by the federation be received and presented to the Church.

5. That, the outline of general statistics prepared by the federation be handed over through this Board to the statistician of the United Lutheran Church with the request to co-operate through this Board with the International Federation toward the procuring of world-wide statistics of the service of love of the Protestant Churches.

The Board adopted these resolutions and sought membership in the International Federation. This action was approved by the Executive Board. It was also decided to make a yearly contribution to the work of this organization.

Another contact of interest was that formed by Rev. J. J. Scherer, Jr.,

D.D., in connection with the Lutheran World Convention. Dr. Scherer was named by the Board to represent it at the conferences on Immigrant Work. We wish to express our gratitude to Rev. E. C. J. Kraeling, D.D., for his helpfulness to Dr. Scherer in this connection. The contacts thus formed are proving of value.

Pastor Heine, the Immigrant Pastor at the port of Bremen, and Dr. Wagner, the Immigrant Pastor at the port of Hamburg, were visitors to this country and conferred with those doing immigrant work both here and in Canada. These visits helped to give to us a better understanding of the problems which are faced by the immigrant pastor abroad, and at the same time to have them understand something of the difficulties involved in our work in America.

IV. INSTITUTIONS OF MERCY

The biennium has marked the establishment or taking over of three Inner Mission institutions. Of these two are in Milwaukee. Bethany Home for Girls is a most admirable home which is seeking to be of service to girls who need safeguards against trouble. The results already growing out of the work have been most enviable. This home is conducted by the Milwaukee Inner Mission Society. St. Luke's Hospital in Milwaukee has been taken over by a group of Lutherans representing the various General Bodies. It is situated in a section of Milwaukee where there is ample opportunity for service to those who need this help which the Church can give to them.

The Lutheran Brotherhood has undertaken a work for old people by securing the old Weidner Institute. With certain alterations to the property this makes an admirable place for the care of some of the old people of our church. It is of ready access from much of the surrounding territory and can serve it well. It is expected that the home will be open on August 1st.

In this biennium two offers of property, each with an institution, has been made to our Board—one a hospital and the other an old folks' home. After numerous conferences and investigations it was thought unwise to proceed with either of these propositions. The president and certain brethren of the Iowa Synod were exceedingly helpful in connection with one of these offers.

A study of the subject of sub-normal children in our orphanages is under way. It is impossible however, to make a final report upon the matter at this time. It is, however, rather surprising to learn how small a percentage of problem children are residents in our orphanages today. This is a cause for real gratitude.

The classification of our Institutions of Mercy has been unsatisfactory. After a long study of the problems involved the Board has decided to suggest a single classification of these institutions. This new listing does not claim perfection. Relationships with other Lutheran General Bodies are often involved which make a proper listing difficult. It is prepared upon the basis of the best information which we have been able to secure. It is now presented to this convention for approval. We believe that it will present more adequately the institutional work which is now being done by the Church. (See Resolution 5.)

V. LITERATURE

One of the best services which our Board has rendered to the Church is in the supply of helpful literature. Among this literature the outstanding publication is "A Message for the Day." There is now a subscription list of 7,800, an increase during the biennium of 1,170. This little leaflet, going out to our "shut-ins" and "shut-outs," has been the means of rich blessing. We have received many letters telling us how deeply the "Message" is appreciated by those into whose hands it comes. A quantity of other literature has been distributed during the year, some having been sent to all synodical conventions, and to the conventions of church organizations.

June has been set aside by the Church as the time for the particular presentation of the Inner Mission Work of the Church. Plans for the larger use of this month as the particular time to urge the Inner Mission upon our people are being made. Inner Mission sermon outlines and material were sent to all the pastors of the Church with the request to preach a sermon on the Inner Mission. Many did so. Articles also appeared in *The Lutheran*.

A yet unsolved problem before the Church is the training of workers for special forms of activity. Except in certain places where Inner Mission work has become well established there has been great difficulty in securing properly trained workers. There are a growing number of our young people who are interested in social work. Many of them specialize in some form of it in college and university. There is, however, a real need of workers trained in our Lutheran colleges and schools for such service. Our big opportunity at this time is so to train our young people that they may carry the spirit of Christ with them into social work of a purely secular character. The possibility of leadership is open to them if they have technical training in a recognized school. Some progress is being made in one of our Lutheran colleges towards the development of such technical courses. A great difficulty is to do the field work that is required. Those who do not have such technical training have but little opportunity for a part in the rapidly growing field of social work. The influence of the Church could be spread abroad by such leaders and workers. The Church itself needs to train its young people so that they may be of service in the development of new forms of Inner Mission activities. Those who come to us from other training schools with but few exceptions do not seem to fit into our work. (See Resolution 6.)

VI. Work for the Deaf-Mutes

Following the last convention the development of Work for the Deaf was committed to the Board. The Board is directly concerned at this time with this work in Eastern Pennsylvania through the Ministerium of Pennsylvania, and in Kansas and adjacent states. This is only the beginning of this important work. Plans for its expansion are being urged. The results already accomplished indicate the possibilities for the future for a most blessed service to some of Christ's unfortunate children. A brief statement of what has been accomplished follows. The work of the Board of Inner Missions of the Ministerium of Pennsylvania is summarized below:

Forty-two services were held in the following places: Philadelphia, Allentown, Reading, Lancaster, Wilkes-Barre, Scranton, Norristown, Hazleton, Trenton, N. J.; Washington, D.C., and New York City. The total attendance was 1,133. Two new points were entered. On invitation of the Inner Mission Committee of the New York Synod, services are held every six weeks at the Church of the Transfiguration, New York City, for the negro deaf. The largest number present was fifty-one. In order to conserve the interest of the Lutheran students at Gallaudet College, Washington, arrangements have been made for periodic services together with the celebration of the Holy Communion in the Church of Pastor Snyder. In addition to personal work among the students, Pastor Kaercher has also conducted services in the college chapel at the invitation of the faculty.

Regular visits are made to the Home for the Aged and Infirm, Deaf and Blind, in Philadelphia.

At St. Phillips in Philadelphia an adult catechetical class of five has been organized and two persons have been added by letter. One deaf blind man was confirmed. Two members were received by confirmation at Allentown and one at Reading. Two children of deaf parents have been baptized.

Pastor Kaercher has been engaged in systematic visitation and just concluded a two weeks' trip which covered 1,650 miles, during which time he visited about two hundred deaf families. It extended as far south as Chambersburg and north to Scranton and covered altogether thirty communities.

In September the secretary of the Board will visit all the church councils as well as the congregations in company of the pastor.

The salary of the pastor to the deaf is paid in part by the Inner Mission Board of the United Lutheran Church in America.

Following many negotiations and with the full approval of the Kansas Synod, work for deaf-mutes was initiated on the territory of that synod on October 15, 1929. Previous to this date Rev. E. C. Sibberson, who had learned the sign language had been doing some work while still serving a congregation. Under the direction of the Inner Mission Commit-

THE UNITED LUTHERAN CHURCH IN AMERICA   501

tee of the Kansas Synod the work has been going on steadily and with
most happy results. There follows a brief statement of the activities for
deaf-mutes in Kansas and adjacent states:

Regular monthly services for the deaf-mutes are held at Topeka, Em-
poria, and Chanute. Irregular services are held at six other points. We
are happy to report that the Nebraska, German Nebraska, and Rocky
Mountain Synods have officially endorsed our work and have promised
hearty co-operation in our pastor's visitations. The following cities and
towns have been visited in the interest of the work, in many of which
deaf-mutes have been found and ministered to: In Kansas: Vilas, Valley
Falls, Atchison, Nortonville, Eureka, Florence, Dorrance, Russell, Hays,
Bunker Hill, Excelsior, Iola, Wichita, Wellington, Greenleaf, Linn, Glasco,
Hoisington, Fort Scott and Chaney. In Nebraska: Wolbach, Dunbar,
Nebraska City Lincoln, Fontanelle, Auburn, Johnson, Omaha, Walton,
and Eagle. In Missouri: St. Joseph, Langdon and Rockport.

State institutions for the deaf and blind in both Kansas and Nebraska
have been visited. Semi-monthly instruction in the sign language is
being given to a class of seventeen students in the Martin Luther Seminary
at Lincoln, Nebraska, and also at Tabitha Home, and contacts have been
made with civic clubs and secular organizations. Presbyterian, Episcopal,
and Methodist churches have been open to him. A number of Missouri
Synod churches have asked for the presentation of this work to them.
The missionary has ministered to white and colored people and so far
as the committee knows, maybe some orientals. He has performed many
ministerial acts, administered the Sacrament of the Lord's Supper at stated
intervals, has had three weddings, two funerals and seven baptisms of
adults.

Special mention should be made of a glove by which it is possible to
communicate with the blind deaf-mutes. Pastor Sibberson is responsible
for this glove and its distribution. It has already been sent to many
of the states of the union and as far away as China. The letters which
have come following the use of this glove have been most grateful. It
has served to open a new world to many of these afflicted folks. An effort
was made by the Board to copyright the glove, but this was found to be
impossible.

No doubt there are certain individuals who have met this problem of
deaf-mutes and have learned the sign language so that they might serve.
We know of at least one instance where this is true and are hopeful that
it will grow into a synodical service to the deaf-mutes upon that territory.
The Board is working towards the development of other centers of service.
We look forward to the securing of a promising young deaf-mute to be
educated and enter this work. (See Resolution 7.)

VII. IMMIGRANT WORK

Work for Immigrants and Seamen.

The change in the name of this department of your Board's work from "Work for Immigrants" to "Work for Immigrants and Seamen" was made necessary through the extension of the work to include seamen also.

Work for Seamen.

In the mind of the average person the seamen are not thought of as immigrants. The immigration laws of our country, however, list the seamen among immigrants, though in a class by themselves—with special ruling, governing the sojourn on our shores of all such whose status is that of the seamen.

It is this branch of port work which has caused your Board much concern. Here is a wonderful opportunity to serve those of our brethren whose mode of living deprives them of many comforts their fellowmen enjoy, including the regular ministry of the Church. It is obvious that the Church should interest herself in these men much more than she has, when her own sons constitute the bulk of this vast army of seafaring men.

Our secretary for Immigrant and Seamen's Work has investigated the ports of Seattle, San Francisco, Los Angeles, Vancouver, B. C., on the west coast, and Houston, Galveston, New Orleans and Mobile on the Gulf of Mexico, and in all of them opportunity to do port work for seamen is present.

Such work by the Lutheran Church is done in but few of these ports. Even the harbor of New York, this great field, where various organizations are engaged in port work for seamen, is not covered. We have a splendid and extensive work in Hoboken, but the Manhattan and Brooklyn side should also be cared for by the Lutheran Church. Then there are the ports of the Great Lakes to which repeatedly the attention of your Board has been called and which will be investigated. To these may be added the great Canadian ports in the east—St. Johns, Halifax and Quebec.

Men by the hundred thousand are utterly neglected by the Church while in the ports of the territory covered by the United Lutheran Church in America. Is it because they are not prospects for membership in our congregations; or because they have their peculiarities as a class that the Church neglects them? Are they not our brethren? Are they not commended to our care as strangers in our gates and fellows of our faith? From various of the above-mentioned ports the Macedonian cry has come to your Board. These communities are too weak to support a work of this kind themselves, nor are they alone indebted to the seamen. Circles far beyond the local port communities are benefitted by the labors of the seamen. The Church should therefore be concerned about their welfare. Your Board is willing to undertake such work where needed most, but with no financial provisions made for it, the hands of your Board are tied. The Church entrusted this work to the Inner Mission Board, but has not willed that it be the domain of this Board to initiate or do such work, nor has it granted the necessary funds for it. *The Inner Mission Board therefore pleads with the United Lutheran Church to provide for this most necessary work of Christian love.* (See Resolution 9.)

Work for Immigrants.

To state briefly the scope of this work is accomplished best by summarizing it under the five points of the program laid down by the Church for its execution.

1. Port Work at New York.
2. Port Work in other ports of the United States.
3. Port Work in the ports of Canada.
4. Follow-up Work.
5. Contracts with Foreign Ports.

1. Port work for immigrants in the harbor of New York has been • actively and successfully carried on in co-operation with the Lutheran Emigrant House Association. A word of appreciation to this organization for its co-operation would not be amiss. The Lutheran Emigrant House Association has not only entered into close co-operation with your Board, whereby the secretary for Immigrant Work is entrusted with the supervision of the port work, but also provides office room, a working force of two, and a home for the secretary for Immigrant Work. This constitutes a large saving financially to your Board, though the Lutheran Emigrant House Association must meet a deficit every year.

Through this co-operation it is possible that incoming steamers are regularly met and the immigrants assisted in every way possible at the docks and railroad stations. Frequently lodging, or work, or both are secured for the strangers who appeal for such help. .

During the past biennium, April 1, 1928, to March 31, 1930, 3,614 strangers were ministered unto.

2. Other ports in the United States have been investigated by our secretary for Immigrant Work with the view of inaugurating port work for immigrants. Of these ports, Boston, Mass., and Houston, Texas, in the east, and Seattle and San Francisco in the west, should have the first consideration. The work in these ports will of necessity h a v e to be financed entirely by your Board as the United Lutheran Church in America does not possess a constituency at these ports strong enough to warrant much local support. The one exception under this point is the port of Philadelphia. In this port the work is most admirably and adequately carried on by the Board of Inner Missions of the Ministerium of Pennsylvania.

3. A splendid work has developed in the Canadian ports of Montreal and Winnipeg. It has flourished from its very inception, and grows in its demands upon the immigrant pastors in these centers as the influx of immigrants increases year after year. The pastors in charge of the work

perform their duties under the direction of their respective synodical Inner Mission committees. These committees report monthly to our secretary for Immigrant Work on the progress of work carried on in their respective immigration centers. According to t h e s e reports, during the biennium from May 1, 1928, to April 30, 1930, there arrived and were admitted into Canada the total of 38,039 Lutheran immigrants.

4. Contacts with foreign ports have been established. The main ones are through the pastors in charge of the Emigrant Missions in the ports of Hamburg and Bremen. These mission pastors gather and forward to our secretary for Immigrant Work the names and addresses of emigrants whose destination is the United States. They also gather such other information as may be desired by us in connection with the work. For their services these men receive a monthly remuneration from our Board.

Some other outstanding contacts w h i c h we have abroad are, "Das deutsche Auslands Institut" in Stuttgart, "The City Missionary Bock in Nuernberg," "Der Evangelische Hauptverein fur deutsche Ansiedler und Auswanderer" in Berlin, and a number of smaller agencies from whom we hear occasionally.

5. The most important branch in the Immigrant Work is the Follow-up Work. Much time and money is spent in gathering the names and addresses of immigrants before and at the time of their arrival in this country and in Canada. The names are sent to the pastors and congregations of the communities which have been given us as the destination of the immigrant. This information is gained either from the immigrant himself upon landing, our contacts abroad, or such other sources as may be available for the information needed.

The object of this work is that these immigrants be looked up, welcomed into the community, invited to church or referred to a church where they can worship in their language, if the visiting pastor or layman represents a church that is not in position to minister unto their spiritual needs.

This work is done for the United States through the office of our secretary for Immigrant Work at 218 Seventh Avenue, New York City, and has grown to such an extent that another worker had to be engaged. For Canada this work is done through the Inner Mission Committee of the Canada Synod for the east and through the Inner Mission Committee of the Manitoba Synod for the west. We know that pastors frequently meet with difficulties and disappointment when looking up such immigrants. They may not be Lutheran or they may be no longer at the given address. Sometimes even the address given does not exist at all. Then also the language presents difficulties to those of our pastors who cannot converse with the foreigner in his tongue. We appreciate these experiences on the part of pastors, but we m u s t ask them to bear with us. Our secretary can only send out the addresses as he receives them and has no way of finding out if they are right or wrong. Sometimes it is possible to intercept immigrants who are not going to the destination given and obtain the right address from them. The United States does not require the registration of the religious persuasion of the immigrant, consequently the only ones who can find out what they are are those who visit them when they arrive at their destination. In Canada where the registration of religious persuasion of the immigrants is required, our immigrant pastors are put in position to know "who's who" religiously. Therefore we can report with confidence the number of Lutherans entered and accordingly follow them up. During the biennium from April 1, 1928, to March 31, 1930, we have sent out from our New York office 5,432 addresses and received report on only one out of every three. This does not mean that only one-third of the addresses sent out are looked up. We are rather under the impression that more than 50 per cent are visited, but not reported to us. To substantiate our viewpoint our secretary reports that recently he received about fifty addresses from one pastor who had them in possession over one year but finally sent them in with the remark that all of them had been looked up. Sometimes pastors are too busy to look up the addresses sent them. If such pastors would delegate some organization or laymen of their congregation to look up the new arrivals it would not only suffice to make the first contact between the new arrival and the Church in this way, but it would be a means to enlist the interest of their church members also.

A much desired co-operation in our Follow-up Work would be if pastors or visiting parties would secure the new address of the person whom they find has moved from the address sent them and inform our secretary. This would enable him to continue following up the immigrants and establish a contact between them and the Church.

Some pastors find it difficult to interest immigrants or to hold them in the Church. It might prove beneficial for stimulation of interest if immigrants would be gathered in groups by themselves. This would make them feel at home among themselves and keep them in touch with the Church. Perhaps some room in the parish house or basement of the church could be opened to them where they could meet for social gathering. English congregations could participate in extending this help and courtesy to immigrants. In this case we would suggest that some provision be made at some suitable hour for devotion or divine service in the language of the immigrant. Even in small communities this practice should prove beneficial both to the immigrant and to the Church. If it is impossible to provide for such services it would be well to arrange that someone out of the group itself lead in devotion.

We acknowledge gratefully the spirit of co-operation expressed by the Board of American Missions in permitting one of the Home Mission pastors under its direction to give to seamen's work at Houston, Texas, such time as would not interfere with the regular activities of his parish. (See Resolution 8.)

VIII. MOUNTAIN WORK

The Women's Missionary Society carries on the work for girls through this Board. On the average of thirty-five girls from the mountains around Konnarock, Va., are at the Konnarock Training School. In addition, from fifty to sixty girls and boys come to the school during the day for regular school instruction. This is done by arrangements with the Public School authorities of Smyth County, in which Konnarock lies.

In addition to regular school work in the grammar grades (some of the older girls attend the high school at Konnarock) great emphasis is laid upon instruction in home economics. Two to four hours a week is required for each girl. This training is arranged to fit them to meet better the conditions in their homes in the mountains.

Religious education naturally has a large place in the School. During the average of three years that the girls remain much time is given to teaching them to know Christ, and take Him back with them to their mountain homes.

It will be the cause of real gratification to the Church to know that Konnarock was selected as a typical Southern Mountain School in the survey made by the Southern Women's Educational Alliance. This survey report, now in permanent form, gives to Konnarock a high rating, and indicates that fewer mistakes have been made there than in many other similar Schools. We can be proud of this work of the women of our Church.

A dispensary under a registered nurse is now in operation. The nurse also goes through the whole community. She has carried on this work particularly in connection with the five Daily Vacation Bible Schools conducted at as many different locations in the mountains.

The work is supported entirely by the Women's Missionary Society, to which Auxiliary of the Church we express our grateful thanks for the fullest sort of co-operation.

For some time there has been a growing conviction that something should be done for mountain boys as well as for the girls. With this end in view the Board approached the Lutheran Brotherhood and the Luther League to help realize this service. It was found that the Luther League could do nothing in the matter because of its previous commitments and the limitations upon its work approved by the Church.

However, the Lutheran Brotherhood has interested itself deeply in this matter. Preliminary negotiations for the purchase of property and plans for the operation of a school for boys at Konnarock have now been matured. Before the final step is taken it is necessary only that the Brotherhood at its convention shall approve the work. Much enthusiasm has already been aroused among the men by the plans for this new work. The Board sincerely hopes that this matter will be endorsed fully at the convention of that organization.

IX. TREASURER'S REPORT
STATEMENT OF RECEIPTS AND DISBURSEMENTS
For the Year Ended June 30, 1929

RECEIPTS

	General Fund	Mountain Work	Immigrant Work	Deaf Work
United Lutheran Church	$15,855.00		$6,795.00	
Women's Missionary Society ...		$11,666.62		
Konnarock School Scholarship..		200.00		
Konnarock School, Boys' Work.		179.50		
Donations From Individuals....	72.87			$85.00
Sales of Literature	942.54			
Loans	7,800.00			
	$24,670.41	$12,046.12	$6,795.00	$85.00

DISBURSEMENTS

	General Fund	Mountain Work	Immigrant Work	Deaf Work
Salaries of Secretaries	$3,999.96		$3,125.00	
Salaries of Clerks, Stenographers, etc.	1,385.25			
Salary of School Superintendent.		$1,400.00		
Other School Expenses		10,266.62		
Salaries of Pastors			3,599.91	$125.00
Expenses of Secretaries	4,803.27		246.92	
Expenses of Board Members, etc.	903.11			
Literature Purchased	769.52			
Maintenance contributions, Lutheran Church House	725.00			
Advertising	201.00			
Printing and Stationery	154.00			
Postage and Express	553.12			
Auditing	150.00			
Office Supplies and Expenses ..	437.62		35.58	
Loans Repaid	8,900.00			
Interest on Bank Loans	40.15			
Lutheran Emigrant House Association of New York			700.00	
Home Missions Council			100.00	
Office Furniture and Fixtures..	92.50			
Konnarock School Scholarship..		200.00		
	$23,114.50	$11,866.62	$7,807.41	$125.00
Excess or Deficiency of Receipts	$1,555.91	$179.50	$1,012.41	$40.00

RECONCILEMENT OF CASH, JUNE 30, 1929

	General Fund	Mountain Work	Immigrant Work	Deaf Work
Balances, July 1, 1928	$7,520.00		$7,416.51	
Transfer of Immigrant Work Deficit to General Fund	7,416.51		7,416.51	

Adjusted Balances, July 1, 1928.	103.49			
Add Receipts	24,670.41	$12,046.12	6,795.00	$85.00
	24,773.90	12,046.12	6,795.00	85.00
Deduct Disbursements	23,114.50	11,866.62	7,807.41	125.00
Balances, June 30, 1929	$1,659.40	$179.50	$1,012.41	$40.00

$786.49

RECEIPTS AND DISBURSEMENTS
For the Year Ended June 30, 1930

RECEIPTS

	General Fund	Mountain Work	Immigrant Work	Deaf Work
United Lutheran Church, apportionments	$12,525.30	$58.69	$8,004.50	$1,011.51
Women's Missionary Society ..		9,999.96		
Sales of Literature	963.80			
Donations From Individuals ...	173.09		4.00	230.92
Special, for Konnarock School, Boys' Work		69.30		
Loans	9,675.00			
	$23,337.19	$10,127.95	$8,008.50	$1,242.43

DISBURSEMENTS

	General Fund	Mountain Work	Immigrant Work	Deaf Work
Salaries of Secretaries	$3,999.96	$1,200.00	$3,000.00	
Salaries of Clerks, Stenographers, etc.	1,421.00		66.00	
Other School Expenses		8,799.96		
Salaries of Pastors			4,329.96	$2,499.98
Expenses of Secretaries, traveling	3,204.88	22.25	442.95	
Expenses of Board Members....	960.33			
Maintenance Contributions, Lutheran Church House	870.00			
Advertising	85.68			
Printing and Stationery	615.22			
Postage	353.76		225.00	
Office Supplies and Expenses..	618.80		83.17	5.00
Loans Repaid	9,675.00			
Interest on Bank Loans	47.80			
Contribution to Lutheran Emigrant House Assn. of New York			200.00	
Purchase of Office Furniture and Fixtures			79.00	
Special, for Konnarock School, Boys' Work		49.30		
	$21,852.43	$10,071.51	$8,426.08	$2,504.98
Excess or Deficiency of Receipts	$1,484.76	$56.44	$417.58	$1,262.55

SUMMARY OF CASH ACCOUNTS
For the Year Ended June 30, 1930

	General Fund	Mountain Work	Immigrant Work	Deaf Work
Balances, July 1, 1929	$1,659.40	$179.50	$1,012.41	$40.00
Transfers From General Fund.	3,549.30		2,460.22	1,089.08
	1,889.90	179.50	1,447.81	1,049.08
Add Receipts, as Annexed ..	23,337.19	10,127.95	8,008.50	1,242.43
	21,447.29	10,307.45	9,456.31	2,291.51
Deduct Disbursements, as Annexed	21,852.43	10,071.51	8,426.08	2,504.98
	405.14	235.94	1,030.23	213.47
Add Stamp Funds Not Previously Reported as Assets.	3.10		32.60	
Balances, June 30, 1930....	$402.04	$235.94	$1,062.83	$213.47

$683.26

THE INNER MISSION BOARD OF HE UNITED LUTHERAN CHURCH IN AMERICA
BALANCE SHEET AT JUNE 30, 1930

ASSETS

Cash in Bank and on Hand	$683.26
Inventory of Salable Literature, at Estimated Value	1,322.30
Advance to Secretary of Immigrant Work for Traveling Expenses	100.00
	$2,105.56
Land, 335.7 Acres, Konnarock, Va.	$7,140.00
School Buildings and Equipment, Konnarock, Va.	43,751.08
Office Furniture and Fixtures, at Estimated Value	379.00
	$53,375.64

LIABILITIES

Vouchers Payable:		
General Fund, For Printing	2,800.00	
General Fund, For Other Expenses	195.00	
Mountain Work, For Boys' Work	199.50	
Immigrant Work, For Expenses	400.00	$3,594.50

FUNDS

General Fund	$1,774.74	
Mountain Work	50,927.52	
Immigrant Work	841.83	
Deaf Work	213.47	49,781.14
		$53,375.64

Respectfully submitted,
WM. FREAS, *Treasurer.*

Philadelphia, August 1, 1930.
We have audited the accounts of the Treasurer of The Inner Mission Board of the United Lutheran Church in America for the two years ended June 30, 1930, and we certify that, in our opinion, the foregoing balance sheet at June 30, 1930, and the statements of receipts and disbursements for the years ended June 30, 1929 and 1930, are in accordance with the books of account and are correct.

LYBRAND, ROSS BROS. & MONTGOMERY,
Accountants and Auditors.

X. CLASSIFICATION OF INNER MISSION INSTITUTES AND ORGANIZATIONS

Unless otherwise noted the institutions and organizations on the following list are owned, controlled and supported entirely by the United Lutheran Church in America, one or more of its constituent synods, one or more of its congregations, or by associations within constituent synods.

(Intersynodical—with one or more other Lutheran General Bodies.)

(Non-synodical self-perpetuating Board of Managers, majority Lutheran with full control.)

Date of Founding

I. *General Inner Mission Board*

1918 1. Inner Mission Board of the United Lutheran Church in America.
    (a) Work for the Deaf (with Ministerium of Pennsylvania and Kansas Synod).
    (b) Seamen's and Immigrant Work (with Lutheran Emigrant House Association).
    (c) Work for Southern Mountain Girls (with Women's Missionary Society).

II. *Synodical Inner Mission Boards*

1923 1. Board of Inner Missions of the Ministerium of Pennsylvania.
    A. Activities of Board
1899   (a) City Mission, Philadelphia, Pa.
1908   (b) Lutheran Seamen's and Immigrant Mission, Philadelphia, Pa.
1922   (c) Lutheran Children's Bureau, Philadelphia, Pa.
1922   (d) Lutheran Bureau, Philadelphia, Pa.
1925   (e) Mission to the Deaf.
1929   (f) Mission to the Blind.

    B. Other Inner Mission Institutions and Organizations on the territory of the Ministerium of Pennsylvania.
1859   (a) Orphans' Home and Asylum for the Aged and Infirm of the Evangelical Lutheran Church at Germantown, Philadelphia, Pa.
1884   (b) Mary J. Drexel Home and Philadelphia Motherhouse of Deaconesses, Philadelphia, Pa.
1897   (c) The Lutheran Orphans' Home, Topton, Pa.
1902   (d) The Inner Mission Society of the Evangelical Lutheran Church of Philadelphia, Pa.
1905   (e) The Luther Hospice for Young Men, Philadelphia, Pa.
1905   (f) The Lutheran Settlement, Philadelphia, Pa.

1906   (g) Kensington Dispensary for the Treatment of Tuberculosis, Philadelphia, Pa. (Non-synodical).
1908   (h) Tabor Home for Children, Doylestown, Pa.
1908   (i) Good Shepherd Home, Allentown, Pa.
1913   (j) River Crest Preventorium of Kensington Dispensary, Mont Clare, Pa. (Non-synodical).
1915   (k) Artman Home for Lutherans, Ambler, Pa.
1920   (l) Tryon Hall, Philadelphia, Pa.
1923   (m) The Lutheran Inner Mission Society of Trenton, N. J., and vicinity.
        (n) The Lutheran Inner Mission Society of Reading and vicinity.

C. "The Institution of Protestant Deaconesses," Pittsburgh Synod
    (a) Passavant Hospital, Pittsburgh, Pa. (Intersynodical).
    (b) Memorial Homes for Epileptics, Rochester, Pa. (Intersynodical).
    (c) Orphans' Home and Farm School, Zelienople, Pa.

III. *Children's Homes*
1806   1. Emaus Orphans' Home, Middletown, Pa. (Non-synodical).
1852   2. Orphans' Home and Farm School, Zelienople, Pa.
1859   3. Orphans' Home (and Asylum for the Aged) at Germantown, Philadelphia, Pa.
1864   4. St. John's Orphans' Home, Buffalo, N. Y.
1866   5. Wartburg Orphans' Farm School of the Evangelical Lutheran Church (Intersynodical).
1868   6. Tressler Orphans' Home, Loysville, Pa.
1888   7. Tabitha Home (also Old People's Home), Lincoln, Nebr.
1888   8. The Lutheran Orphan Home of the South, Salem, Va.
1897   9. The Lutheran Orphans' Home in Berks County, Pa., Topton, Pa.
1903 10. Oesterlen Orphans' Home, Springfield, Ohio.
1904 11. Nachusa Lutheran Orphanage, Nachusa, Ill.
1904 12. Kinderfreund, Jersey City, N. J. (also Old Peoples' Home).
1908 13. Ebenezer (Orphanage for Girls), Frederiksted, Virgin Islands (Board of American Missions).
1908 14. Good Shepherd Home, Allentown, Pa. (Non-synodical).
1908 15. Tabor Home for Children, Doylestown, Pa. (Non-synodical).
1919 16. Children's Receiving Home, Maywood, Ill. (Intersynodical).
1919 17. Children's Receiving Home, St. Paul, Minn. (Intersynodical).
1920 18. Bethesda Home, Meadville, Pa.
1924 19. Inner Mission Center, Brooklyn, N. Y. (Intersynodical).

IV. *Fresh Air Camps and Homes*
1922   1. Wilbur J. Herrlich Memorial Home, Towners, N. Y. (New York Inner Mission Society).
        2. Jolly Acres (Baltimore Inner Mission Society).
        3. Fresh Air Home (Lutheran Welfare Society, Minneapolis, Minn.).
        4. Summer Camp (Pittsburgh Inner Mission Society).

V. *Homes for Problem Children*
1920   1. Bethesda Home, Meadville, Pa.
1927   2. Williams-Henson Home for Boys, Knoxville, Tenn.
1928   3. Bethany Home, Milwaukee, Wisc. (Intersynodical).

VI. *Old People's Homes*

1859 1. Asylum for the Aged and Infirm of the Evangelical Lutheran Church at Germantown, Philadelphia, Pa. (also Orphans' Home).

1888 2. Tabitha Home, Lincoln, Nebr. (also Orphans' Home).

1888 3. Mary J. Drexel Home, Philadelphia, Pa. (also Deaconess Motherhouse).

1890 4. National Lutheran Home for the Aged, Washington, D. C.

1896 5. Lutheran Church Home for the Aged and Infirm of Buffalo and Erie Co., N. Y.

1896 6. The Franke Home, Charleston, S. C.

1897 7. Mary Louise Heins' Home for the Aged and Infirm, Mt. Vernon, N. Y. (Intersynodical).

1904 8. Kinderfreund, Jersey City, N. J.

1905 9. Old Peoples' Home of the Pittsburgh Synod, Zelienople, Pa.

1906 10. Lutheran Home for the Aged, Erie, Pa.

1906 11. Feghtly Lutheran Home, Tippecanoe City, Ohio.

1908 12. Good Shepherd Home, Allentown, Pa. (Non-synodical).

1911 13. Lowman Home for the Aged and Helpless, White Rock, S. C.

1918 14. Lutheran Home for the Aged, Southbury, Conn.

1919 15. The Lutheran Church Home for the Aged and Infirm of Central, N. Y., Clinton, N. Y.

1927 16. The Louisville Lutheran Home, Jeffersonville, Ky.

1930 17. The Mulberry Lutheran Home for the Aged, Mulberry, Ind.

VII. *Homes for Dependents, Destitute and Helpless*

1908 1. Good Shepherd Home, Allentown, Pa. (Non-synodical).

1911 2. Lowman Home for the Aged and Helpless, White Rock, S. C.

VIII. *Homes for Epileptics*

1895 1. Passavant Memorial Homes for the Care of Epileptics, Rochester, Pa. (Intersynodical).

1911 2. Lowman Home for the Aged and Helpless, White Rock, S. C.

IX. *Hospitals*

1849 1. Passavant Hospital, Pittsburgh, Pa. (Intersynodical).

1890 2. Children's Hospital of Mary J. Drexel Home, Philadelphia, Pa.

1895 3. Women's and Children's Hospital, Guntur, India (Board of Foreign Missions).

1898 4. The California Hospital (Lutheran), Los Angeles, Calif. (Intersynodical).

1898 5. Robinwood Hospital, Toledo, Ohio (Intersynodical).

1898 6. Lutheran Hospital of Manhattan, New York City (Non-synodical).

1910 7. Women's and Children's Hospital, Chirala, India (Board of Foreign Missions).

1911 8. Women's and Children's Hospital, Rajahmundry, India (Board of Foreign Missions).

1916 9. General, Rentichintala, India (Board of Foreign Missions).

1922 10. General Hospital, Tarlupad, India (Board of Foreign Missions).

1925 11. General Nidadavole, India (Board of Foreign Missions).

1926 12. General Hospital, Zorzor, Africa (Board of Foreign Missions).

1927 13. National Lutheran Sanitarium, Albuquerque, New Mexico.

1928 14. Lutheran Hospital Reuss Memorial, Cuero, Texas.

1928 15. St. Luke's Lutheran Hospital, Milwaukee, Wisc. (Intersynodical).
      16. Muhlenberg, Monrovia, Liberia, Africa (Board of Foreign Missions).
      17. General, Tsingtao, China (Board of Foreign Missions).

X. Seamen's and Immigrants' Missions
1869 1. Lutheran Emigrant House Association of New York (Nonsynodical).
1907 2. Seamen's Mission, Hoboken, N. J. (Non-synodical).
1908 3. Seamen's and Immigrant Mission of the Ministerium of Pennsylvania for Philadelphia, Pa.

XI. Hospices
1905 1. The Luther Hospice for Young Men, Philadelphia, Pa.
1917 2. Lutheran Hospice for Girls, Baltimore, Md. (Intersynodical).
1918 3. Lutheran Hospice for Young Women, Pittsburgh, Pa. (Intersynodical).
1919 4. Trabert Hall (for Young Women), Minneapolis, Minn. (Intersynodical).
1920 5. Tryon Hall (for Young Women), Philadelphia, Pa.
1921 6. The Lutheran Hospice for Girls, Akron, Ohio.
1921 7. Lutheran Hospice for Girls, Milwaukee, Wisc. (Intersynodical).
1924 8. United Lutheran Church Girls' Home, Chicago, Ill.
1925 9. State Luther League Hospice, Omaha, Nebr.
1928 10. Lutheran Hospice for Girls, Reading, Pa.

XII. Settlements
1890 1. St. John's Lutheran Settlement House, Knoxville, Tenn.
1905 2. The Lutheran Settlement, Philadelphia, Pa.
1914 3. The Luther House ,Minneapolis ,Minn. (Intersynodical).   ➤

XIII. Miscellaneous Institutions and Agencies
1899 1. City Mission, Philadelphia, Pa.
1904 2. Queen Louise Home (for sick and neglected babies), Frederiksted, St. Croix, Virgin Islands (Board of American Missions).
1906 3. Kensington Dispensary for the Treatment of Tuberculosis, Philadelphia, Pa. (Non-synodical).
1907 4. Queen Louise Home (for sick and neglected babies), Christensted, St. Croix, Virgin Islands (Board of American Missions).
1913 5. River Crest Preventorium of Kensington Dispensary, Mont Clare, Pa. (Non-synodical).
1915 6. Artman Home for Lutherans, Ambler, Pa. (Non-synodical).
1922 7. Lutheran Children's Bureau, Philadelphia, Pa.
1922 8. Lutheran Bureau, Philadelphia, Pa.
1922 9. Wilbur J. Herrlich Memorial Farm, Towners, N. Y.
1924 10. Inner Mission Center, Brooklyn, N. Y. (Intersynodical).
1930 11. Inner Mission—Social Service Branch, Pittsburgh, Pa. (Intersynodical).

XIV. Inner Mission Societies
1902 1. The Inner Mission Society of the Evangelical Lutheran Church, Philadelphia, Pa.
1905 2. The Lutheran Welfare Society in the Twin Cities, Minn. (Intersynodical).

1907 3. The Lutheran Inner Mission Society of Pittsburgh, Pa. (Intersynodical).
1907 4. The Inner Mission Society of the Evangelical Lutheran Church
in New York City (Intersynodical).
1909 5. The Inner Mission and Rescue Society, Brooklyn, N. Y. (Non-
synodical).
1910 6. The Inner Mission Society of the Evangelical Lutheran Church
in Brooklyn, New York and vicinity (Intersynodical).
1914 7. The Inner Mission Society of the Evangelical Lutheran Church
of Baltimore, Md., and vicinity (Intersynodical).
1917 8. The Inner Mission Society of the State of Connecticut.
1917 9. The Inner Mission Society of the Chicago Area, Chicago, Ill.
1917 10. The Inner Mission Society of Washington, D. C.
1921 11. The Milwaukee Inner Mission Society of the Evangelical Lutheran Church, Milwaukee, Wisc. (Intersynodical).
1923 12. The Inner Mission Society, Trenton, N. J.
     13. The Inner Mission Society, Charleston, S. C.
     14. The Inner Mission Society of the Evangelical Lutheran Church,
of Reading, Pa.

XV. Deaconess Motherhouses

1884 1. Philadelphia Motherhouse for Deaconesses, Philadelphia, Pa.
1895 2. The Lutheran Deaconess Motherhouse and Training School,
Baltimore, Md.
Total, Inner Mission institutions and agencies............................... 104
    Less, duplications in listing under different general head-
    ings 13

Number of institutions and agencies supported in whole or in
    part by the members of the United Lutheran Church in
    America. (See Resolution 5) 91

XI. RECOMMENDATIONS

1. *Resolved,* that the United Lutheran Church in convention assembled,
record its appreciation of the statesmanship shown by President Hoover
last Fall in calling conferences of governors of states and of leaders of
industry and commerce for a nation-wide concerted effort to reduce the
rising menace of unemployment; and that, we pledge to him the support
of our Church in helping to make effective whatever measures proposed
may come within the scope of her ability.

2. *Resolved,* furthermore, that the United Lutheran Church urge every
congregation directly affected by unemployment to appoint a special committee to assist its members in finding work and to co-operate with other
religious and secular agencies of their community for relief of the situation
in general.

3. *Resolved,* that the constitution of the Inner Mission Board be interpreted to permit said Board to inaugurate and if necessary to continue and
conduct such forms of Inner Mission work as are plainly the duty of the
entire Church, provided that the Executive Board previously give its approval.

4. *Resolved,* that the United Lutheran Church call upon every constituent synod for the most effective organizing of its Inner Mission Work
and for the closest possible co-operation with the Inner Mission Board.

5. *Resolved,* that this Convention approve the new classification of Inner Mission Institutions and Agencies found in this Report.

6. *Resolved,* that the Inner Mission Board be instructed to confer with one or more Educational Institutions of the Church for the purpose of providing courses of instruction and training for Inner Mission workers up to the standards required by Social Service agencies.

7. *Resolved,* that we recommend to our synods and congregations the development of a helpful Christian service to deaf-mutes, following generally the suggestion for the beginning and prosecution of such work as made to Synodical Committees by the Board.

8. *Resolved,* that the pastors of the United Lutheran Church in America be urged to co-operate in the Follow-up Work for Immigrants by visiting at once the people whose addresses are sent to them; by reporting regularly their findings to the secretary for Immigrant Work; by gathering people visited regularly into special groups and providing for their spiritual and social needs.

9. *Resolved,* that, realizing the need for a Christian service to seamen entering the ports of our country in such large numbers, that we urge upon our people interest and personal service in the initiation and carrying on of such activity.

Respectfully submitted,
WILLIAM FREAS, *Secretary.*

XII. REPORTS FROM INSTITUTIONS

II-1. *Report of the Board of Inner Missions for the Year* 1929

In carrying out the work of its various departments, the Board has the services of five pastors, three women missionaries, a part-time worker for the blind, and two office secretaries. The Board operates through its executive secretary who is also in charge of the Lutheran Children's Bureau and the Lutheran Bureau.

During the biennium a study has been made on the subject of the care of the aged and the Board also has under way a study of the rural churches on its territory.

A program of congregational inner missions for both urban and rural churches has been prepared and was adopted at the recent meeting of the Ministerium.

The Board operates through the conferences, having Inner Mission committees in each of the ten. Through them services are held in the various public institutions on their territory and special service rendered to our people.

The Board through its secretary maintains contacts with the Inner Mission activities in the principal centers of America and also has working agreements with the Inner Mission agencies on the continent.

The total expenses for the biennium were $154,555, of which the Ministerium appropriated $47,250.

The four departments of the Board carry on the following work:

Philadelphia City Mission:

In its thirty-one years the City Mission has extended its work through its two missionaries, Dr. Ohl and Pastor Weaver, to reaching practically every institution in the city. The missionaries are aided in their work by the volunteer services of eight pastors and one layman, together with the young people of our Luther Leagues. An effective service is rendered discharged and paroled prisoners. It also has an extensive relief work among the transients.

During the past biennium over one thousand services were held and 30,000 individual visits were made in hospitals, homes, and prisons. Holy baptism was administered to one adult and ten children and the Holy Communion was administered to ninety persons. Twenty-eight funerals were conducted. The junior missionary represents the Children's Bureau in the Juvenile Court.

The Seamen and Immigrant Mission:

A shore line of more than thirty miles on the Delaware and Schuylkill Rivers, is the extent of the parish of the seamen's pastor. Since the last report he has visited more than four hundred vessels and met 2,900 sailors in the course of these visits. A large quantity of religious literature was distributed. A regular service is held at the Seamen's Home every Sunday with a goodly attendance of seamen. The seamen's pastor in addition to taking splendid care of the spiritual welfare of the sailors, also looks after their finances and provides social entertainment for them. An important part of his work is securing employment and in spite of the depression 355 men were helped in that way.

In connection with the executive office hundreds of newly arrived immigrants were assisted in finding a church home and in solving some of the problems that come to newcomers in a strange land.

Lutheran Children's Bureau:

On January 1st the Children's Bureau had 425 children in care. During the biennium 125 children were received and 53 were discharged; 250 of these children were placed in private families. Statistics cannot show everything that was done in the way of studying the conditions that made the removal of the children necessary. The outstanding cause was not death, as is commonly supposed, but the separation of parents. Especial attention is paid to the health of the children. Through this service we have been able to care for a number of crippled children who have been kept in private families during the time that their handicaps were being removed. In addition to caring for children out of their homes, it is necessary to carry on family relief work in order to prevent the breaking-up of homes. The care of unmarried mothers also demanded our attention in twenty-nine cases. The placement of a number of feebleminded children, epileptic and incurable persons also was effected.

Lutheran Bureau:

Sleighton Farm:

Sleighton Farm has continued as a field of great usefulness in helping to rehabilitate delinquent Lutheran girls. During the biennium thirty-six girls were admitted to the Church by baptism and confirmation. Contacts are maintained after discharge by personal visitation and correspondence.

Hamburg and White Haven:

At these two colonies for the tubercular services are conducted by the local pastors, the Rev. R. E. Kern and W. M. Geiger, assisted by one of our missionaries.

Mission to the Deaf. (See Report of the Board).

Mission for the Blind:

By direction of the Ministerium our Board undertook a service to these handicapped brethren. Its first work was the embossing of Luther's Small Catechism. This was followed by Habermann's Prayer Book. The Common Service is in course of preparation. These publications have been distributed free and many words of praise have been spoken by the blind concerning them.

Through our part-time worker, Miss Anna Drissel, we are gathering the names of all the Lutheran blind on our territory, for the purpose of establishing them in our churches and providing them with Lutheran literature. Through the cordial co-operation of the Committee for the Blind of the Synodical Conference, we have been able to place the *Lutheran Messenger,* a monthly, in the homes of a number of our people.

The library of the Information Bureau has had added to it a large number of foreign and American publications, together with many pamphlets. After it is catalogued it will be of great service to all interested in this phase of work.

This report cannot include all the activities of the Board.

III-5. *Wartburg Orphans' Farm School, Mount Vernon, N. Y.*

During the past two years the Wartburg Home, founded in 1866 by Dr. W. Passavant, has made the usual strides. Two new buildings have been reared at a cost of $87,000. One of these, the Bultmann Memorial, was in the nature of an experiment. It was intended to house twelve children, sisters and brothers remaining under the same roof. The experiment has proved successful. A second cottage, the Stubenrauch-Treckman Memorial, was opened on July 1st of this year and is intended for undernourished and convalescent children of the Home. It is caring for fifteen children at the present time. Beside these major buildings the Home has built three smaller cottages for its agricultural work at a total cost of $15,000. The number of buildings belonging to the Home now totals 29.

In the matter of methods the Home has kept pace with modern demands. Every case is considered on its own merits and children have been received from ten states of this country, where no provision was made in Lutheran homes to meet their respective needs. Another Old People's Home has been planned and is expected to be finished within the year. During the past two years the home has cared for more than six hundred different children. Voluntary contributions still remain the chief source of income. Only three directors have served the home since its beginning, Pastors G. C. Holls, Dr. G. C. Berkemeier and S. G. von Bosse. The president of the Board of Trustees is the Hon. William H. Steinkamp.

III-6. *Tressler Orphans' Home*

Tressler Orphans' Home, Loysville, Pa., continues to make advancement particularly in the line of the education of its children. Besides graded schooling from the kindergarten to the completion of a four-year high school course which admits its graduates to leading colleges, special courses and electives provide for trades, drafting, domestic science and commercial education. Six former pupils of Tressler are now taking hospital training in nursing, seven are students in colleges and one in theological seminary. Several have recently secured good positions following their advanced education, and others jobs in trades that they learned while pupils at Loysville.

All building and repair work at the home is done by the Trade School force. Some projects are: remodeling a building from a combined school building and dormitory into a modern school building, changing an open dormitory into groups of rooms that four large girls may occupy each room, building a brick fire tower, a paint shop, brooder houses, garage, etc.

Endowment is now $332,680.

Appraised value of property, $688,600.

Yearly cost of operation, $95,000.

III-7. *Tabitha Home*

Our heavenly Father's loving kindness helped Tabitha Home to another biennium. We felt the great need of the Ministry of serving love more than ever before. Many applications from needy aged, especially from invalids and helpless ones, as well as for homeless children could not be given any consideration for lack of room. The contemplated Bethesda building for the invalid and helpless aged is our greatest need. $11,500 is in this building fund. $30,000 more is needed.

One hundred and seventy-three persons were given care during the biennium. Seventeen of the eighty-four aged died and six were given only temporary care. Sixty-one in the home, July 1, 1930. Of the eighty-nine children, nineteen were dismissed. Seventy in the home July 1, 1930.

III-9. *The Lutheran Orphans' Home, Topton, Pa.*

The Lutheran Orphans' Home in Berks County, Pa., at Topton, was founded in 1896. It has been blessed with a remarkable growth in these thirty-four years. Beginning with a single dollar it now has a property valued at over half a million, free of debt. There are two large farms, upon which are located the main (administration) building, the Holton Memorial for Infants, the Lowry Memorial Infirmary, School Building, Allentown Conference Cottage for Boys, and the two farmhouses, and barns. Another small tract with building was purchased for the water supply, which furnishes an abundant supply of pure water from mountain springs, with sufficient fall to throw a stream over the highest point of the buildings. A Girls' Cottage, to cost approximately $30,000, as a complement to the Boys' Cottage, is in course of erection.

Our schools, eight grades, employing four teachers, besides a music teacher, and kindergarten teacher, are under state supervision. 159 children— 91 boys and 68 girls—are under our care at present. The average cash cost of maintenance at present is $36,000 per year. This is supplied by voluntary contributions. Our endowment fund amounts to $64,000. Through the generosity of friends, capable children pursue courses of higher education. Two boys are at present at Muhlenberg College, Allentown.

Two members of the original Board of Trustees still serve actively.

III-10. *The Oesterlen Orphans' Home, Springfield, Ohio*

The home was founded in 1903 by the funds provided by Mrs. Amelia Oesterlen, of Findlay, Ohio.

The object of the home is to care for unfortunate Lutheran children and other worthy children who are homeless. It is the aim of the home to give to all at least an elementary education and to encourage those who show the ability to pursue a high school and college training.

During the twenty-six years of Oesterlen's being more than two hundred and fifty children have enjoyed the training and care such as is offered by the home.

Oesterlen Home is at the present time caring for ninety-four children from the ages of three years to the twenties. During the past two years many improvements have been made. The band has been organized and the children are receiving music instructions regularly. A frigidaire system has been installed on both floors of the administration building. Playground equipment for boys and girls has been secured. Walks and a new driveway have been built around the administration building. The planting of trees and shrubbery was done on an extensive scale. New beds and new lockers are now being bought for the senior boys' cottage.

Improvements suggested are the re-opening and the re-modeling of the older girls' dormitory for the future use of boys. New walks are badly needed from the building to the road.

The endowment fund at the present is the sum of $80,000. The cost of operation for our institution is approximately $24,000 a year. The value of the farm and all the buildings is $300,000.

III-11. *The Nachusa Lutheran Orphanage*

The Nachusa Lutheran Orphanage, Nachusa, Ill., showed a marked development and improvement during the biennium.

The chief improvement was the erection and dedication °of a new Administration Building, the building providing a home for the smaller children also.

Seventy children can be cared for in three well furnished and equipped cottages, with almost private home conditions prevailing. Considerable progress has been made toward the development of the private home life among the children under the cottage system. It was largely due to the fact that every child has the opportunity of self-development that a boy from the Nachusa Home represented the State of Illinois in the 1929 Edison Contests.

An advance step was also taken in the grade school, which is maintained by the Orphanage. All the grade school children received instruction under one teacher, but for the first time they were placed under two teachers, thus permitting more time for individual attention.

An average of fifty-five children were cared for.

Endowment funds, $10,500.

Value of land, buildings and equipment, $135,000.

Cost of operation, $17,000.

III-14. *The Good Shepherd Home, Inc., Allentown, Pa.*

The Good Shepherd Home, Allentown, Pa., was founded by Rev. John H. Raker, D.D., when on the 21st day of February, 1908, he received into his private home a crippled girl. Its policy is to provide a Christian home for crippled, blind and infant orphans, destitute children, old people (many of whom cannot be admitted into other homes because of their physical deformities or disabilities) and aged or disabled ministers, regardless of money, creed, color, or nationality.

The work has expanded until now five buildings house this present family of seventy children and thirty old people.

Recently the Board of Trustees adopted new by-laws, defining the duties of those in charge of the various departments and increasing the number of Board members from five to eleven, two of whom are elected by the Ministerium of Pennsylvania and two are women.

Our children attend the public schools and a teacher is employed in the home for those unable to go to the public schools. We endeavor to train and educate these crippled children so that they may go out into the world self-supporting.

Our present urgent need is an administration building, so that certain space in the boys' dormitory may be released for training, and other rooms may be provided for our help, away from their work.

The value of our property is said by competent judges to be about $600,000. Our endowment fund is $23,100. It requires between fifty-five and sixty thousand dollars per year to carry on the work.

VI-4. *The National Lutheran Home for the Aged, Washington, D. C.*

The National Lutheran Home for the Aged, Washington, D. C., has never had a better biennium than the one now closing. The trials have been many; the triumphs fair. Appeal for admission seem to be on the increase from month to month.

The Board of Lady Managers, composed of two or more representatives, from every Lutheran congregation in our city, has been very diligent in attending to the personal needs of the aged, and assisting the worthy matron, Sister Mabel Stanley. The task is by no means a small one.

Apeals for admission are coming from all sections of our country.

There are fifty names on the waiting list. Everyone of them seems to be worthy but we cannot admit them because of lack of room.

The approximate cost per member per day, including all expenses, is one dollar.

VI-6. *The Franke Home ,Charleston, S. C.*

The Franke Home, Charleston, S. C., was founded thirty years ago by a bequest of Jacob Washington Franke and incorporated under the terms of his will with the four Lutheran pastors and two laymen from each of the four parishes constituting the Lutheran Charities Society—the administrator of the fund and the director of the Home.

The Home is caring for twelve persons (men and women) and is in charge of Sister Dorothea Hesse of the Baltimore Motherhouse of Deaconesses.

There is a choice property and quite ample invested funds in the possession of the society and additional revenue is secured through the agency of an efficient Ladies' Auxiliary Society.

VI-7. *Marie Louise Heins Memorial Home for the Aged,*
Mt. Vernon, N. Y.

There is little to report for the past two years in the life of this Home, which is controlled and managed by the Wartburg Orphans Farm School. Begun in 1897, the Home has ministered to 200 aged men and women of Lutheran faith. It was built by John D. Heins as a memorial to his daughter, Marie. Every inmate has a room of its own. The requirements include a minimum age limit of sixty-five years; membership in a Lutheran Church in New York City or vicinity; an entrance fee of

$1,000.00. The capacity of the Home is 36. From the beginning it has been presided over by Lutheran deaconesses, trained mostly at the Elisabeth-Stift in Hanover, Germany. A waiting list is maintained for eight persons. The Home has its own burial plot in New Rochelle, N. Y. The Director is Pastor S. G. von Bosse.

Endowment Funds $17,500
Value of Property 100,000
Cost of Operation for 1929 12,655

VI-10. *Lutheran Home for the Aged, Erie, Pa.*

This Home is maintained by the Lutheran Churches of Erie and vicinity, in connection with the Pittsburgh Synod of the Evangelical Lutheran Church. Sister Frieda, of the Philadelphia Motherhouse is the Directing Sister, assisted by two additional Sisters. During the past year it cared for 60 inmates; with the Sisters and the required help, a total of 71 persons. There were 9 deaths and 14 admissions.

Its property is valued at $190,000, and it has invested funds amounting to $27.600. $15,000 were paid off on the indebtedness during the past two years.

The receipts during the past year were $39,672.64, and the expenditures $37,293.85.

The Home receives $4,500 per year from the Erie Community Chest.

VI-11. *Feghtly Lutheran Home, Tippecanoe City, O.*

The Feghtly Lutheran Home has continued through another biennium its helpful service of caring for indigent women, who find here the efficient management and the home-like atmosphere so much desired and unsurpassed elsewhere.

The institution (formerly controlled by the Miami Synod of the General Synod) several years ago came under the supervision of the Synod of Ohio. The Home constitution has been amended to provide for this change of management.

An "expansion program," with the building to the Home of eight to twelve additional rooms, awaits the action of Synod.

Recently an automatic sprinkler system was installed in the Home at a cost of $2,500.00. Better fire protection, long desired, is hereby secured.

Within the past two years a suitable marker has been placed on the Home burial plot in "Maple Hill" cemetery—a monolith, white Barre granite, eight feet in height, with the inscription:

SARAH FEGHTLY MEMORIAL

FEGHTLY LUTHERAN HOME

Feghtly's resources are $94,103.37, the interest therefrom caring for the annual expense of $5,600.00. This means $400.00 each year per member

for the fourteen guests.   The estimated property value is $35,000.00.
Feghtly Home is self-supporting.

VI-15. *The Lutheran Church Home for the Aged and Infirm*
of Central New York, Inc., Utica-Clinton, N. Y.

This Lutheran Home for the Aged is finishing the first decade of service. The blessings of God are manifest. The hope of faith has met its
fulfillment. Not only has the treasury been supplied to meet all obligations,
but the various requirements and problems that arise in the care of
the aged have been met courageously by the combined wisdom and
charity of a loyal group of Christians. The Home accommodates a
family of twelve. There is need for a larger Home. A small endowment fund and a good beginning of a building fund are on hand,
beckoning for renewed vision and sacrifice to make possible increased
accommodations. Old age reflects the complexities of life which are not
lessening. Old age pensions are a great help, but they do not substitute.
Our Home admits men and women, single and couples, giving first opportunity to those of the Lutheran faith. In the providence of a gracious
Heavenly Father, and by the inspiration of the Shepherd of souls, we
discover and meet some of the perplexities of life and the mystery of
the true spirit of charity, praying for His guidance and for the good
will of the people.

Value of Property $23,000.00
Endowment Fund 6,000.00

Yearly Cost of Operation, $5,500.00, or about $500.00 per resident.

VI-16. *The Louisville Lutheran Home at Jeffersontown, Ky.*

The Louisville Lutheran Home, situated in Jeffersontown, Ky., a suburb
of Louisville, Ky., became an institution under the control of the Indiana
Synod at its last convention, at Columbus, Indiana in May of this year.
The Home is controlled by a board of directors two from each Church
in Jefferson County, Ky., and each pastor, and two delegates from without
the county elected by the Indiana Synod. These latter are: Mr. H. H.
Coombs, of Shepherdsville, Ky., and Rev. I. W. Gernert, of Nashville,
Tenn. The Board meets annually in January. The Home owns property
valued at $60,000, with 30 acres of land, with modern limestone building
of 27 rooms, steam heat, running water in every room, and beautiful
landscaping around the main building and outlying buildings. Mr. and
Mrs. Charles Graff are Superintendent and Matron, and maid and physician
are employed, and such other help as is necessary. The President of the
Board is Rev. Courtland Miller, and its treasurer Mr. George Deckman,
of Jeffersontown, Ky. Entrance fee of $500 is required of members of
United Lutheran Church Indiana Synod members, and of other denominations of Louisville and vicinity, $1500. This latter sum is to be laid

aside until a sufficient amount is accrued to build a men's wing to the building. There is a $1500 debt, and a $1700 endowment fund. Cost of operation per member of Home now is $350 annually, exclusive of depreciation of property. There are eight members. The most active agency, financially speaking, is an aid society in Louisville.

VI-17. *The Mulberry Lutheran Home for the Aged, Mulberry, Ind.*
The Brotherhood of the Central States has opened a Home for Aged at Mulberry, Ind., on the property formerly known as the Weidner Institute. The Brotherhood has assumed the outstanding indebtedness against the property, and this, with the repairs and alterations necessary, will require an outlay of approximately twenty-five thousand dollars. When these changes are made we will then have a property of twenty acres of land and three buildings, capable of housing a family of forty-five people, and worth to us, for this purpose, at least one hundred thousand dollars.

IX-1. *The Passavant Hospital, Pittsburgh, Pa.*

Patients remaining	109	Surgical	832
Patients admitted	3,004	Genito-Urinary	148
Staff Doctors' cases	2,190	Gynecology	129
Non-Staff Doctors' cases	814	Ear, nose and throat	401
Private and semi-private room patients	1,901	Eye	122
		Orthopedic surgery	16
Ward patients	1,103	Neurology	12
Operations	1,375	Obstetrical	348
Emergencies	2,786	Births	282
Physiotherapy treatments	3,718	Still births	18
Discharged patients	2,852	Cardiac	148
Deaths	162	Dental	12
Patients remaining	99	Dermatology	4
Dispensary visits	12,345	Pediatric	107
Medical	333	Chest	92

White race 2,130
Colored (Chinese) 874

Total receipts $160,655.49
Total expenditures 160,495.22

Cost per day $4.53
Average length of stay ....11 days

Nursing days:
Ward—Pay 3,285

Ward—Part pay 4,249
Ward—Free 11,175

Ward—Total 18,709
Private room 15,509

Grand Total 34,218

IX-5. *Robinwood Hospital, Toledo, Ohio*

Robinwood Hospital is an intersynodical institution. It was founded in 1898 as a private hospital.

In 1920 "The Federated Lutheran Benevolent Society of Toledo and Vicinity," on behalf of the Lutheran Church, entered into a contract of purchase extending over a period of years. On January 1, 1925, it came under Lutheran control and management.

In the five years, 1925-1929, 8800 patients were admitted, with 111,000 days of care, and current expenditures of $612,000. During the same period the Lutheran equity in the property, now valued at $400,000, increased from $75,000 to $210,000.

Robinwood has a medical staff of twenty-five, a nursing staff of sixty-five, a school of nursing with fifty-six students and a bed capacity of one hundred and two, housed in three buildings, the Hospital proper, the Nurses' Home, and Faculty House.

It is rated as a Class A Hopsital by the American College of Surgeons. Its classification is that of a General Hospital, maintaining, in addition to beds for general cases, a maternity department, children's ward and nursery, and X-Ray and Pathalogical departments equipped with the latest scientific apparatus, in charge of skilled specialists.

The Hospital is managed by a Board of Trustees, with eleven laymen and four clerical members.

IX-6. *Lutheran Hospital of Manhattan*

During the year 1928 the hospital took care of 2395 patients, who received 28,041 days of treatment. The cost of caring for free and part free patients amounted to $24,131.62.

The personnel of the hospital totaled 90.

In connection with the hospital a clinic for out patients is maintained. During 1928, 3,886 patients were treated in the various departments of the clinic.

During 1929 the hospital took care of 2,639 patients, receiving 30,653 days of treatment. The cost of caring for free and part free patients amounted to $24,422.43.

The personnel of the hospital totaled 91.

In the clinic 2,776 patients were treated.

Comparing figures of the two years you will note that 244 more patients were admitted to the hospital in 1929. There were 2,612 hospital days more as compared with 1928, and the daily census increased from 76 to 84. The attendance in our clinic decreased by 1,110 treatments.

We want to state that the work in the clinic was greatly aided through the co-operation of the representatives of the Inner Mission Society.

We are sorry to state that the hospital at present has no endowment funds. The property of the hospital is valued at $300,000. The approximate yearly cost of operation is $220,000.

X-1. *The Lutheran Emigrants House Association*

The Lutheran Emigrants House Association was incorporated in 1871, and has been for many years the port mission for the Lutheran Church in the Harbor of New York.

Founded by a group of Pastors and Laymen as an independent organization, its object was from the beginning to serve the entire Lutheran Church. Its present relation to the Inner Mission Board of the United Lutheran Church in America makes it the recognized "Port Mission for Immigrants" in the Harbor of New York of that body.

An office, with the necessary staff of workers, is maintained at 218 Seventh avenue, New York City. Its activities are varied and numerous:

a. Steamships are regularly met upon landing.
b. Immigrants are assisted on their way to their destination as circumstances may require, at the piers and railroad stations.
c. Lodgings are secured if desired or needed by immigrants or tourists.
d. Tourists, if requested, are met at railroad stations and conducted to ships, etc.
e. Reservations for sailings are secured upon application.
f. Monies are transmitted by ship money orders.
g. Assistance is rendered in securing employment.
h. Requests to seek lost relatives and friends are honored to the best ability.
i. Information pertaining to immigration, sailings, etc., is gladly given upon request.

The one thing lacking and missed much in this work is a Home wherein to house the newcomers. The hope some day to come into possession of one is still alive, and is the cherished outlook for the future!

X-3. *Lutheran Seamen's and Immigrant Mission of the Ministerium of Pennsylvania.*

The Seamen's Home in Philadelphia is maintained by the Philadelphia Association for the care of German seamen. It is located at 1402 East Moyamensing avenue, and can accommodate 26 men. It is open to sailors of all nationalities, but is especially patronized by Germans, Scandinavians, Finns, Austrians and Americans. The Seamen's pastor is supported by the Ministerium of Pennsylvania, who pays his salary. The housefather is supported by the Association. The cost of operation is $5,000 per annum. A debt of $12,000 remains on the Home. Its value is about $30,000. During the last two years 1132 persons lived temporarily at the Home in 10,943 sleeping nights. 1840 were given free sleeping quarters. At 89 services held at the Home 1159 men were present. 410 vessels were visited by the Pastor, 2,889 sailors met, about 6,000 periodicals and 700 Testaments distributed. At hospitals 745 sick seamen were spiritually cared for. 354 needy persons were assisted with $3,322.93. The greater part of this amount is paid back.

XI-1. *The Luther Hospice for Young Men, Philadelphia, Pa.*

The work at The Luther Hospice for Young Men, located at 157 N. 20th street, progressed satisfactorily during the last biennium. The work presented some difficulties from time to time. Difficulties which had their origin in the freedom young people, and old as well, claim is theirs today. However, by counselling as well as we knew how, and by the process of elimination, for a Hospice is no reformatory, we kept together a body of young men whose fellowship was helpful and appreciated by incoming guests. The average number of men entertained was 65. This was somewhat below the previous biennium. The removal of medical and dental colleges from the centre of the city, and the tendency of students to join fraternities and live in fraternity houses, accounts in part for the smaller number of guests. However, as our house only accommodates 64 guests, we are still running capacity houses. Formerly accommodations were secured for men in the neighborhood. An average of seven young men paid less than the average rate of $10.50. Young men, who had not the means of paying the regular rate when starting to work, were given a special rate. With the daily evening prayers and especial Lenten services, a good Christian atmosphere was maintained. The Hospice offers accommodations to the traveling public, and many of our people continually avail themselves of this privilege.

Average annual receipts for room and board, $31,000. Value of property, $225,000. No endowment.

XI-7. *Lutheran Hospice for Girls, Akron, Ohio*

Our Hospice is operated primarily for young ladies, and is the property of the Trinity Lutheran Church of Akron and adjoins the church property. The Home accommodates twenty-five young women.

It is operated by the congregation for no profit. With moderate charges made to the occupants, together with donations from members of the congregation and their friends we are able to operate without a loss. During the year 1929-1930 our income from the young ladies for room and board amounted to $5,544. Disbursements for all purposes over the same period of time amounted to $5,385.

The Deaconess of our congregation makes her home at the Hospice and several members of the church whose parents have died and who are not physically able to earn a livelihood make their home here. At the present time it is the home of a lady who is totally blind and teaching in a local school for the blind. In addition to the above mentioned, our Hospice makes a home for young ladies who come to Akron without their parents, to work in the factories. It is open to young ladies of all denominations, but Lutheran girls are given the preference.

We have no endownment fund. With the proper management we are able to keep free from debt. The value of the Hospice property is $50,000. The Trinity Lutheran congregation hold the deed for same.

XI-8. *United Lutheran Church Girls' Club*

The United Lutheran Church Girls' Club, of 5402 Magnolia avenue, Chicago, Ill., has continued its program of being helpful to girls as opportunity has afforded. Room and two meals are provided for $7.50—$9.00 per week according to the room.

Several of the girls are Lutheran, but there are no demoninational restrictions. Owing to present economic and working conditions changes have been more frequent.

The girls have such diversified interests and activities that lectures and classes are not attempted. Professional schools and colleges and evening classes, which give credits, afford splendid educational and cultural privilege.

After dinner talks by visitors at the club have been much appreciated.

The aim of the club is to provide a homelike environment where loyalty, friendship and the Christian life are the predominating factors.

The indebtedness has been reduced to $11,000, with an equity of $21,000.

XI-10. *Lutheran Hospice for Girls, Reading, Pa.*

The Hospice has been very active during the year. By the grace of God we have been privileged to serve a number of girls. Not only administering to their physical needs, but endeavoring to strengthen their spiritual life.

Residents—Thirty girls have made it their permanent home, at times overtaxing the capacity. At present the family numbers 14 residents, besides two others who are taking their meals with us and enjoying the advantages of the Hospice. Most of these girls are employed in industry, and come from Reading homes that are broken up because of the death of a parent or parents.

You will be interested to know that 50 per cent of the girls thus far are of the Lutheran faith, 33 per cent belong to other Protestant denominations, while 17 per cent are Catholic.

Seventeen transients have been cared for. Some only for a day. Others for a period of a week and longer. 115 people have been served with meals.

Through our Room's Registry we have found homes for several people not eligible to the Hospice. One of our problems is finding homes that are willing to supply meals.

Total receipts $6,475.82

Total expenditures 6,308.82

XII-2. *Lutheran Settlement House, Philadelphia, Pa.*

Our activities for the past two years were as follows: Church Services, Sunday School, Childrens' Vespers, Luther Leagues, Light Brigade, Weekday Church School, Daily Vacation Bible School, Daily Kindergarten. Classes for Boys and Girls as well as clubs, also Clubs for Men and Women; Baby Clinic, Free Library, Savings Fund, Educational Lectures and Pictures, Music, Art, Family Welfare Work, Neighborhood Visitation, Outings for Mothers and Children in the summer.

The activities were conducted by a Resident Staff of five women workers, the Pastor, Rev. Schantz, and about 60 volunteers.

The property is worth $100,000.

Approximate yearly cost $11,000.

XIV-1. *The Inner Mission Society of the Evangelical Lutheran Church, Philadelphia, Pa.*

This first Inner Mission Society of the Lutheran Church in America, organized in 1902, incorporated 1911, established and maintains *The Luther Hospice for Young Men and The Lutheran Settlement,* both pioneers in their respective fields. At the former an average of seventy men enjoy all the comforts and quiet influences of a Christian home, and the latter has more than ever become a powerful agency for good in the neighborhood in which it is located. The Society owns property to the value of at least $250,000, with an annual budget of over $50,000. For details see the separate statement of each activity.

XIV-2. *Lutheran Welfare Society in the Twin Cities, Minnesota*

The Society maintains a general office in Minneapolis, and City Mission offices in Minneapolis and St. Paul. The Society membership is over 5,500, and the bi-monthly paper, "Lutheran-Welfare," has about 6,000 subscribers. A staff of 18 workers, 3 of whom are pastors, assisted by over 100 volunteers, have charge of the activities of the Society. The General Board functions through ten department committees, most of which meet monthly.

The 1930 budget of the Society requires $90,301.83, of which amount $36,878 is estimated as fees and earnings. The property valuation is about $110,000. The Minneapolis Community Fund appropriates $14,500, the

Norwegian Lutheran Church $5,000, Northwest Synod $425, and the two women's auxiliaries of the Society $3,200. The balance must be provided by memberships and voluntary offerings gathered chiefly during the annual "Lutheran Welfare Week," third week after Easter. Mr. S. H. Holstad has been the general campaign chairman.

The transfer of the Twin City charity work and state-wide children's case work of the Norwegian Lutheran Church, Board of Charities, two years ago, is working out successfully, and was endorsed at the recent general convention of that body. An extensive survey of the Society's work by the Minneapolis Council of Social Agencies called attention to the high quality of the service, and recommended the consolidation of the settlement work at The Luther House and the Washington Neighborhood House. The Society has recently been petitioned to take over the management of the Lutheran Girls' Home, a shelter for unmarried mothers, located in Minneapolis.

DEPARTMENTS: (1) *Twin City Institutional Visitations.* (Figures are for 1929) 10,361 visits in 26 institutions, and 224 mission services conducted; (2) *Personal Service:* 1,029 distressed families served; 3,714 interviews and 2,474 visits by staff workers. (3) *The Luther House,* settlement nursery school, boys and girls clubs, mothers' meetings and employment bureau and hospice department, served 1,214 different individuals; (4) *Unmarried Mothers:* 51 mothers and their babies; (5) *Child Welfare,* 188 children served in placement work, 190 juvenile court children accepted for visitation, 32 older orphanage boys and girls enrolled in group work; (6) *Trabert Hall,* for young women, Minneapolis, sheltered 481 women; (7) *Children's Receiving Home,* 875 Aldine avenue, St. Paul, cared for 55 dependent children, and (8) the Children's Summer Camp, Pepin, Wisconsin, provided health service to 109 children. A total of 231 were connected with Sunday school, 189 with Church, 46 children and adults were baptized, 12 funerals conducted, and 86 individuals were referred to pastors for ministerial acts. During the summer weekly Street Preaching Services were conducted in both cities, and weekly radio broadcasting, "Fireside Vespers," during the rest of the year. Appropriate observance of the Twenty-fifth Anniversary of the organization of the Society is planned for the fall of 1930.

XIV-4. *The Inner Mission Society of the Lutheran Church in New York City*

This Society is an individual membership corporation, with no Synodical lines. There is a Board of fifteen members responsible to an annual meeting of all members.

The staff of Superintendent, a City Missionary (ordained), a woman lay worker, office force and two part time salaried workers operates four departments of work: Institutional Visitation, Family and Child Welfare,

Hospital Social Service Department, and a Fresh Air Vacation Home for Children.

During the past biennium the Society has made progress along all four lines. Hospital visitation includes regular bedside visit in city and private institutions, preaching services in two languages, and the supply of material comforts and necessities. An average of 1,000 visits per month is maintained through the year.

The Society has developed an ever increasing family and child welfare service, which it offers all Lutheran pastors in the city. Homeless men and women are provided with clothing, shelter, and when possible, employment. Social case work with religious contact is substantially carried on.

The Lutheran Hospital Social Service Department is under the care of the Society. Our lay worker spends the larger part of each week-day in the dispensary, wards, and private homes of patients. Many avenues of fruitful service are opening up in this work.

The Society maintains and operates each summer a vacation home poor children, known as the Wilbur A. Herrlich Memorial Farm. Here more than 425 children each summer are given free vacations for two weeks each. A program of Christian culture is combined with recreation, hand work, nature study and song. Christian men and women are employed as Counsellors and Guardians. The farm comprises forty acres of land in beauitful rolling country in New York State.

The Society has a permanent endowment fund of $16,000, and property valued at $30,000. The income from all sources in 1929 was $28,054.72, and expenses of operation $25,534.19.

XIV-5. *The Lutheran Inner Mission Society of Brooklyn and Vicinity*
The Society was organized in 1915 as a non-Synodical organization. Its Board members and contributions come entirely from members of the United Synod of New York and several independent congregations.

The work of the Society is carried on by these departments:

The Institutional Visitation Department sends a city missionary into various city hospitals to minister to all patients, and particularly to find non-churched Lutherans and bring them into communion with a congregation. Religious services are conducted at a Poor House for Men, a Home for Friendless Women, a Home for Incurables, and a Home for the Aged. Groups of women are organized to bring treats of various kinds to these friendless, sick and suffering. Approximately 15,000 bedside visits are made annually, and 200 religious services conducted in institutions.

The Family Welfare Department gives temporary relief to families suffering in a financial way. Cases requiring enormous sums of money cannot be cared for, save for spiritual ministration. These are referred to other agencies. Of the 300 cases dealt with annually, few needed more than temporary relief. Most family difficulties are due to sin, and then application of the law and the Gospel are quickly helpful.

The Child Welfare Department is maintained under the name of "The Lutheran Children's Bureau," and is under the supervision of the State Department of Social Welfare. During the past two years a Tiding Over Home for Children was opened. Here 22 children are given temporary care for any number of reasons. More than 250 children have passed through the institution. Children are returned either to their re-established homes, placed out, or sent to other institutions.

100 children are sent every summer to various camps, for two weeks vacation. The Society does not own its own camp, but pays board at the camp it selects.

A staff of seven paid employees and many volunteers do an enormous work at an expenditure of $18,000 annually. Except for about $1,800, payments of board for children, the budget is met by voluntary contributions from churches and individuals.

XIV-9. *Inner Mission Society of the Chicago Area, Chicago, Illinois*
Supplemental to their local programs and general activities United Lutheran Ministers and members and friends of Chicagoland, through the Inner Mission, have been "giving the helping hand":

To children—deserted, destitute, deprived, physically under-nourished, spiritually under-privileged.
To young people—young men and young women caught in the whirlpool of pleasure and passion and pelf.
To men and women—buffeted, baffled, discouraged, desperate and some of them depraved.
To the aged—who seek a quiet haven in which to complete this earthly voyage.
To the lowly—the lonely, the homeless, the hopeless, the unemployed.
To the sinning—suffering, sorrowing, sinking souls on life's turbid sea.

In addition to family and individual welfare work, there has been institutional visitation at Passavant Memorial Hospital, at Research and Educational Hospitals of the University of Illinois, at Cook County Hospital, in the prisons and other public institutions.

Bibles, tracts, "The Message for the Day," and other literature have been distributed. Appropriate gifts are given at Christmas, Easter and Thanksgiving. Thousands thus are inspired through the co-operation of our pastors, church choirs and theological students as volunteer workers.

Lutheran children at the Mooseheart Home have been afforded spiritual care through Pastor John J. Clemens and our Aurora Church. There two splendid classes of young people were confirmed during the biennium.

"Inner Mission Message" is published, and there is the manifold Ministry of Mercy "In Jesus' Name."

The Society celebrates its fifth anniversary this Fall.

XIV-14. *Lutheran Inner Mission Society of Reading and Vicinity*
The activities in the Reading Inner Mission Society are: The Girls'

Hospice, 1520 Mineral Spring road; institutional visitation; family and child welfare; preaching services; general information bureau.

XV-2. *The Baltimore Motherhouse*

The total number of deaconesses at present connected with the Baltimore Motherhouse is sixty-three. Of this number thirty-two are serving as parish deaconesses and twelve are engaged in institutional activities.

Seventeen of the young women, who, during the past two years, completed the special courses for Christian workers, are now rendering full time service in congregations and institutions of the Church.

The total number of young women enrolled in the Training School during this two-year period is fifty-two—from twelve states, the District of Columbia and Nova Scotia.

One of the interesting events was the Triennial Homecoming, a custom inaugurated a few years ago of having all the consecrated sisters return to the Motherhouse once in three years, in the month of June, for a period of two weeks, for study and fellowship.

During the biennium the training courses have been revised and readjustments have been made whereby the efficiency of the Training School has been considerably increased. Leadership Training in Young People's Work and Missionary Organizations, Department Methods, Recreational Leadership and Public Speaking are among the subjects that have been added recently. Typewriting and stenography have been made elective studies for seniors of the two-year special course. These special courses for Christian workers seem to be constantly growing in popularity.

Among the outstanding events of the biennium have been the commemoration of Dr. Hay's twenty-fifth anniversary as Pastor of the Motherhouse, and the installation of Dr. Gift as Pastor and Superintendent of Instruction. Dr. Hay became Pastor Emeritus on June 1, 1929. By action of the Board, the two offices of Pastor and Superintendent of Instruction were combined, with the understanding that later on a pastor's assistant be called.

The Rev. Wm. Freas, Secretary of the Board, introduced the Rev. W. H. Greever, who spoke in regard to the Lowman Home; the Rev. E. A. Sievert, Secretary for Immigrant and Seamen's Work; the Rev. G. H. Bechtold, Executive Secretary of the Inner Mission Bureau of the Ministerium of Pennsylvania; the Rev. E. C. Sibberson, missionary to the deaf mutes; Miss Amelia Kemp, Executive Secretary of the Women's Missionary Society; and the Rev. Ernst Walter, Superintendent of the Tabitha Home, each of whom briefly addressed the Convention.

Recommendations 1, 2, 3, 4, 5, 6, 7, 8 and 9 were adopted. (See Division XI of the Report.—Secretary.)

The auditor's report was accepted.

The Rev. John Weidley presented the report of the National Lutheran Home for the Aged.

REPORT OF THE NATIONAL LUTHERAN HOME FOR THE AGED

"When Jesus therefore saw his mother, and the disciple whom he loved, he saith unto his mother, Woman, behold thy son! Then saith he to the disciple, Behold thy mother! And from that hour the disciple took her unto his own home."

Tragic as was the treatment of Jesus, filled with thoughts of his supreme mission, in pain of body, in anguish of soul, yet Jesus had filial regard for his dear mother. As she was standing nearby, helpless before the mob, with tearful eyes beholding the infamous treatment of her beloved son, He looked down from the uplifted cross; He thought of not only her present grief but future care. He had been her support from the time He was old enough to minister to her comfort. Now that He is gone, what can she do? He left her no money, no property. Even the clothing He wore was taken by the Roman soldiers. Was she to be thrust upon the world as a dependent? The apostle Paul said, "If any provideth not for his own, and especially his own household, he hath denied the faith, and is worse than an unbeliever."

To his closest friend Jesus said, "Behold thy mother! And from that hour the disciple (John) took her unto his own home." With what tender solicitude must he have cared for her until the day of her death!

Jesus committed His mother to the care of His Church. From that day to this the Church has provided for the aged, the orphan, and the helpless. There is no finer bit of work she has done or is doing.

When the Saviour was in the house of Simon, a woman poured alabaster, an exceeding precious ointment, upon His head. When the disciples saw it they had indignation, saying, "To what purpose is this waste? For this ointment might have been sold for much, and given to the poor." Perceiving their thoughts, Jesus said, "The poor ye always have with you." Did He say this ironically, or was it a prophecy of the future? That is, were there always to be poor people to be supported by the Church It is true, there always have been persons dependent upon the gifts of their fellows. Even in our beloved America, richer than was Eden, there are many who would be without creature comfort were it not for the ministry of the Church. So insistent is the problem that the states and the Federal

Government are giving it careful consideration. The subject of pensions is vital to the welfare of our nation.

In the District of Columbia, the seat of our national government, the richest nation in the world, there are many homes for the aged, supported by the government, by churches, by individuals. Nearly every denomination is represented. In addition to these there are independent homes. There are two heavily endowed homes located in the fairest portions of our city. One is for aged men. One is for aged women. Everyone is filled to capacity and has a long waiting list. This is also true of every similar institution throughout the land.

We are truly thankful for the homes maintained by our great denomination. It is a ministry the Church must not neglect. The Saviour said, "I was hungry, and ye gave me to eat; I was thirsty, and ye gave me to drink; I was a stranger, and ye took me in; naked, and ye clothed me; I was sick, and ye visited me; I was in prison, and ye came unto me."

The work for the National Lutheran Home for the Aged, Washington, D. C., has been well sustained since the last report rendered to this body. The receipts from the appropriation on its behalf by the United Lutheran Church in America have been far below the amount promised. It was necessary to secure funds from other sources.

The capacity of the home is fifty-seven members. The rooms are always filled. The family at present consists of forty-eight women, nine men. There are fifty applicants on the waiting list.

The home is well located in the center of a thirty acre plot within the District of Columbia.

Sister Mabel Stanley, a deaconess from the Baltimore Motherhouse, is the efficient matron. She has held this position for twelve years. She is assisted by Deaconess Marie Stork from the Baltimore Motherhouse, and by a graduate nurse.

For forty years this home has been supported by the Church and ministering as best it can to the aged men and women from all sections of our country. There are now in the family men and women who in former years were prominent in the affairs of our denomination, in the home and foreign fields. Now that their physical strength is gone it is no more than just that the Church should tenderly care for them.

We appeal to the Church for its continued support, for annuities, for legacies, for personal contributions. A fund has been started with the hope that soon there will be sufficient money on hand to endow the home perpetually. We are thankful to all for gifts and prayers. When you come to see your beautiful National Capital do not fail to visit the home. The door is always open. A glad welcome awaits you.

Respectfully, for the Board,

JOHN WEIDLEY, *President.*

REPORT OF THE TREASURER OF THE NATIONAL LUTHERAN HOME FOR THE AGED

For the two years ended June 30, 1930 *and* 1929

BALANCE SHEET

June 30, 1930

ASSETS:

Cash:

American Security and Trust Co.	$ 6,769.88	
Columbia National Bank	2,006.29	
The National Savings and Trust Co.	2,127.19	
Washington Loan and Trust Co.	318.23	
In transit from General Treasurer	814.00	
		$ 12,035.59
Certificate of deposit, People's Bank of Hanover, Pa.		550.87
Securities, at book values, as annexed		109,375.00
Real estate, etc., at book values:		
National Lutheran Home Property, Washington, D. C.	$39,469.48	
New building	91,555.64	
Farmer's cottage	3,000.00	
New barn	2,000.00	
Grundy County Tract, Tennessee	200.00	
		136,225.12
		$258,186.58

FUNDS:

Trust funds	$41,892.46	
Annuity funds	19,833.34	
New building fund	91,955.64	
Maryland Synod building fund	39,674.05	
Endowment fund	1,000.00	
General fund	63,831.09	
		$258,186.58

BALANCE SHEET, June 30, 1929

ASSETS:

Cash:

American Security and Trust Co.	$15,376.33	
Columbia National Bank	1,435.07	
The National Savings and Trust Co.	488.92	
Washington Loan and Trust Co.	318.23	
		$ 17,618.55
Certificate of deposit, Peoples' Bank of Hanover, Pa.		550.87
Securities, at book values		82,975.00
Real estate, etc., at book values:		

National Lutheran Home Property, Washington,
D. C. $39,469.48
New building 91,555.64
Farmer's cottage 3,000.00
New barn 2,000.00
Grundy County Tract, Tennessee............................... 200.00
                                                       136,225.12

                                                       $237,369.54

FUNDS:

Trust funds $34,603.53
Annuity funds 19,333.34
New building fund 91,955.64
Maryland Synod building fund.. 34,303.05
Endowment fund 1,000.00
General fund 56,173.98
                                                       $237,369.54

CASH RECEIPTS AND DISBURSEMENTS

For the year ended June 30, 1930

RECEIPTS

	General Fund	Trust Funds	Maryland Synod Building Fund	Annuity Funds
United Lutheran Church, apportionment	$11,004.00*			
Inmates of Home		$ 8,743.93		
Legacies	6,077.29			
Donations, general	615.48			
Donations for specific purposes			$ 6,211.00	$ 500.00
Admission fees	1,650.00			
Sale of farm products	30.00			
Income from securities, etc.	4,729.42			
Interest on bank balances	679.43			
"The Home News"	79.90			
Miscellaneous receipts	1,032.81			
Proceeds of sales or redemption of investments		100.00		
	$25,898.33	$ 8,843.93	$ 6,211.00	$ 500.00

* Includes $814 for June, 1930, apportionment not entered on books nor deposited in bank until July, 1930.

DISBURSEMENTS

Board of Lady Managers for domestic expenses ....$ 7,150.00			
Farm labor and expenses............ 2,889.84			
Gas, electricity and fuel............ 573.03			
Engineers' wages 985.00			
Medical and nursing expense.... 2,525.69			
Religious services 230.00			
Funeral expenses 695.90			
Repairs to building, plumbing, etc. 749.31			
Salary of president 310.00			
Salary of treasurer 500.00			
Expenses of board meetings........ 58.31			
Auditing expenses 141.11			
Printing, stationery and postage 83.04			
Telephone 182.40			
Taxes and water rent 262.61			
Insurance 785.68			
Architect's fees		840.00	
"The Home News" 255.68			
General expenses 196.87			
Interest and annuities paid........ 3,546.75			
Investments purchased	19,400.00	4,675.00	
$22,121.22	$19,400.00	$ 5,515.00	

Excess or deficiency of cash
receipts ....$ 3,777.11 $10,556.07 $ 696.00 $ 500.00

$ 5,582.96
Cash Balance, July 1, 1929 .... 17,618.55

Cash balance, June 30, 1930 ....$12,035.59

CASH RECEIPTS AND DISBURSEMENTS

For the year ended June 30, 1929

	General Fund	Trust Funds	Maryland Synod Building Fund	Annuity Funds	Endowment Fund
Receipts					
United Lutheran Church apportionment	$10,880.00				
Inmates of Home		$ 4,915.70			
Legacies	1,593.96				
Donations, general	584.21				
Donations for specific purposes			$ 2,412.79	$ 2,000.00	$ 1,000.00
Admission fees	2,200.00				
Sale of farm products	128.45				
Income from securities, etc....	3,613.63				
Interest on bank balances	1,152.89				
"The Home News"	103.00				
Miscellaneous receipts	1,163.58				
Proceeds of sales or redemption of investments	8,000.00	5,300.00	7,100.00	8,500.0	
	$29,419.72	$10,215.70	$ 9,512.79	$10,500.00	$ 1,000.00
Disbursements					
Board of Lady Managers for domestic expenses	$ 7,150.00				
Farm labor and expenses	2,630.51				
Gas, electricity and fuel	2,402.06				
Engineer's wages	960.00				
Medical and nursing expense	2,790.63				
Religious services	195.00				
Funeral expenses	1,397.38				
Repairs to building, plumbing, etc.	1,240.26				
Salary of president	310.00				
Salary of treasurer	500.00				
Expenses of board meetings	47.76				
Auditing expenses	145.66				
Printing, stationery and postage	65.22				
Telephone	182.04				
Taxes and water rent	261.87				
Insurance	213.34				
"The Home News"	225.30				
General expenses	236.15				
Interest and annuities paid....	4,196.28				
Investments purchased	6,000.00	5,412.30	37,500.00	8,810.20	1,000.00
	$31,149.46	$ 5,412.30	$37,500.00	$ 8,810.20	$ 1,000.00
Excess or deficiency of cash receipts	$ 1,729.74	$ 4,803.40	$27,987.21	$ 1,689.80	
Cash balance, July 1, 1928		23,223.75 40,842.30			
Cash balance, June 30, 1929		$17,618.55			

RECONCILEMENT OF FUNDS
For the year ended June 30, 1930

	General Fund	Trust Funds	New Building Fund	Annuity Fund	Maryland Synod Building Fund	Endowment Fund
Balances, July 1, 1929	56,173.98	$34,603.53	$91,955.64	$19,333.34	$34,303.05	$ 1,000.00
Add, Cash receipts	25,898.33	8,843.93		500.00	6,211.00	
	82,072.31	43,447.46	91,955.64	19,833.34	40,514.05	1,000.00
Deduct, Cash disbursements	22,121.22	19,400.00			5,515.00	
	59,951.09	24,047.46	91,955.64	19,833.34	34,999.05	1,000.00
Add: Investments purchased, at cost	250.00	19,400.00				
U. S. Fourth Liberty Loan bonds received from inmate, at par value		250.00				
Write-up from cost to par value, of securities purchased during the year	1,925.00				4,675.00	
	62,126.09	43,697.46	91,955.64	19,833.34	39,674.05	1,000.00
Deduct, proceeds of bond redeemed		100.00				
	62,126.09	43,597.46	91,955.64	19,833.34	39,674.05	1,000.00
Transfer of funds, due to deaths of inmates	1,705.00	1,705.00				
Balances, June 30, 1930	$63,831.09	$41,892.46	$91,955.64	$19,833.34	$39,674.05	$ 1,000.00

RECONCILEMENT OF FUNDS
For the year ended June 30, 1929

	General Fund	Trust Funds	New Building Fund	Annuity Fund	Maryland Synod Building Fund	Endowment Fund
Balances, July 1, 1928	$56,638.87	$32,691.14	$91,955.64	$17,333.34	$31,890.26	$ 1,000.00
Add, Cash receipts	29,419.72	10,215.70		10,500.00	9,512.79	
	86,058.59	42,906.84	91,955.64	27,833.34	41,403.05	1,000.00
Deduct, Cash disbursements	31,149.46	5,412.30		8,810.20	37,500.00	1,000.00
	54,909.13	37,494.54	91,955.64	19,023.14	3,903.05	
Add: Investments purchased, at cost	6,000.00	5,412.30		8,810.20	37,500.00	1,000.00
Stock and certificate of deposit received from inmates, at par value		1,050.87				
	$60,909.13	$43,957.71	$91,955.64	$27,833.34	$41,403.05	$ 1,000.00
Deduct: Proceeds of investments sold or redeemed	8,000.00	5,300.00		8,500.00	7,100.00	
Loss on Fetterly bequest	256.83					
Investment in Garford Motor Truck Co., written off	10.00					
Reduction of investments purchased to par value	522.50					
	$ 8,789.33	$ 5,300.00		$ 8,500.00	$ 7,100.00	
	52,119.80	38,657.71	91,955.64	19,333.34	34,303.05	1,000.00
Transfer of funds, due to deaths of inmates	4,054.18	4,054.18				
Balances, June 30, 1929	$56,173.98	$34,603.53	$91,955.64	$19,333.34	$34,303.05	$ 1,000.00

SECURITIES OWNED
June 30, 1930
BONDS

Par Values	Descriptions	Book Values
$ 200	Boro of North York, Pa., School District 4½'s, 1944	$ 200.00
15,000	Capital Traction Co., 1-5s, 1947	15,000.00
500	Fort Spring Magisterial District, County of Greenbrier, W. Va., Road 5s, 1934	500.00
500	Island Oil and Transport Co. 8 Pct. Participating Gold Note Certificate of Deposit	500.00
500	Milford Improvement Co., N. J., 5s, April 1, 1930	500.00
1,000	Potomac Electric Power Co., Cons. 5s, 1936	1,000.00
1,000	United Rys. and Electric Co. of Baltimore Income 4s, 1949	1,000.00
50	U. S. First Liberty Loan 3½s	50.00
550	U. S. Fourth Liberty Loan 4¼s	550.00
16,000	Washington Gas Light Co. 10-year 6s, 1933, Series "A"	16,000.00
5,000	Washington Ry. and Electric Co. 6s, 1933	5,000.00
10,000	Washington Ry. and Electric Co. Cons. 4s, 1951	10,000.00
500	York and Peach Bottom Ry. Co. 5s, 1932	500.00
		$50,800.00

STOCKS

Shares		
25	American Telephone and Telegraph Co.	$ 2,500.00
4	Baltimore and Ohio R. R. com	400.00
5	Capital Traction Company	500.00
1	Codorus Canning Co. (In name of Susanna Rebert)	100.00
4	Codorus National Bank of Jefferson, Codorus, Pa.	400.00
4	Drovers and Mechanics National Bank, York, Pa.	400.00
30	Potomac Electric Power Co. 5½ Pct. Preferred	3,000.00
11	Union National Bank, Westminster, Md	275.00
		7,575.00

REAL ESTATE NOTES

Secured by First Deeds of Trust:

The Broadmoor Corp., 6 Pct., due November 15, 1933	5,000.00
Rogers M. Fred, 6 Pct., due November 20, 1931	5,000.00
Ethel Evans Holland, 6 Pct., due February 12, 1932	5,000.00
A. Joseph Howar, 6 Pct., due October 6, 1931	1,500.00
Bryce G. Payne, 6½ Pct., due June 30, 1930 (Guaranteed by Howard M. Etchison)	2,500.00
Howard A. Schladt, 6 Pct., due July 30, 1930 (Guaranteed by Harry Wardman and Thomas P. Bones)	5,000.00
Archie L. Straub, 6 Pct., due September 24, 1931 (Guaranteed by David L. Stein)	5,000.00
Rose J. Waggaman, 6 Pct., due May 1, 1931	2,000.00

Harry Wardman and Thomas P. Bones, 6 Pct., due
   August 1, 1933 .... 5,000.00
Lena Weitzman, 6 Pct., due March 28, 1932............... 15,000.00
                                                            ——————— 51,000.00

                                                                    $109,375.00
                              Respectfully submitted,
                              HARRY T. DOMER, *Treasurer.*

                                       Baltimore, Md., July 16, 1930.
   We have audited the accounts of the National Lutheran Home for the
Aged for the two years ended June 30, 1930, and we certify that, in our
opinion, the foregoing statements submitted by its treasurer are correct.
                              LYBRAND, ROSS BROS. & MONTGOMERY,
                                       Accountants and Auditors.

   The report of the auditors was accepted.

   The Rev. William A. Wade presented the report of the Board
of Deaconess Work and introduced the Rev. Foster U. Gift,
pastor of the Baltimore Motherhouse, who addressed the Convention.

REPORT OF THE BOARD OF DEACONESS WORK

   The Board of Deaconess Work respectfully presents the following report
for the biennium, closing July 31, 1930:
   The Board met on October 23, 1928, in the Mary J. Drexel Home and
Motherhouse of Deaconesses, Philadelphia, for the annual meeting. The
following officers were elected: Rev. William A. Wade, D.D., president;
Rev. J. F. Ohl, D.D., vice-president; Rev. Charles E. Hay, D.D., secretary; Mr. Pearre E. Crowl, treasurer.

I. GENERAL INTEREST AND FUTURE OUTLOOK

   The Deaconess cause is making substantial progress within the United
Lutheran Church. General interest in the diaconate is continually increasing, and the intelligent interest and sympathetic attitude toward the diaconate
is most gratifying to your Board and those who have dedicated their lives
to this calling. The work has been presented by the pastors of our two
motherhouses, members of the Board, deaconesses, and others at the various
synodical conventions, women's missionary conventions and educational
institutions. The Board is endeavoring to spread constructive information
throughout the Church by means of articles in the Church papers, leaflets
and booklets and personal presentations generally. The Women's Missionary Society of the United Lutheran Church, through its officers and
Department of Deaconess Work, is furnishing a most effective publicity
for which we are very grateful. Thus the appeal is reaching every local
society and the young women of the Church, who will determine the future
growth and development of the deaconess cause in the future.

The Luther League is also an agency of great value in our effort to enlist young women in this ministry of mercy. The Department of Life Service brings the work to the serious attention of young women who may be led to consecrate their talents to the splendid cause of the diaconate.

A special committee, appointed by the Board, has been studying the entire question of the future of the Deaconess Movement. The president of the Board and the pastors of our two motherhouses were appointed a committee to undertake an active campaign for candidates for the deaconess calling, including in this effort a definite appeal to women of advanced education, in order to meet more quickly and more effectively the present demands of the Church.

We are greatly encouraged with the growing interest in the deaconess cause throughout the Church. However, the response to the call for candidates is not as hearty as it should be, and consequently the Board urges that the cause be stressed by our pastors of all the congregations, especially on Septuagesima Sunday, the day designated for that cause by the United Lutheran Church. (See **Resolution No. 5**)

II. Board Represented

Dr. Brueckner represented the Board of Deaconess Work at the General Conference of the Kaisersworth Union, which was held in September, 1929.

Rev. U. S. G. Rupp, D.D., was the Board's official representative at the annual convention of Lutheran Deaconess Motherhouses in America, which was held at Columbus, Ohio, May 12, 13, 1930.

III. Passing of Valuable Member

On December 12, 1929, the Hon. John D. Cappelmann, of Charleston, S. C., for a number of years a most faithful member of the Board of Deaconess Work, was called to his eternal reward. Distinguished in his legal profession and zealously active in the service of the Master to the last moment of his life, his wise counsel and his influence in the Church at large fitted him in a large way for most valuable service as a member of the Board of Deaconess Work. An appropriate memorial service was held for him in the chapel of the Baltimore Motherhouse, on January 23, 1930, in connection with the regular board meeting.

IV. Change in Administration of Baltimore Motherhouse

Rev. Charles E. Hay, D.D., who for twenty-five years has been pastor of the Baltimore Motherhouse, on June 1, 1929, retired as pastor, and by action of the Board, became pastor *emeritus*. He retained the office of general secretary of the Board together with other publicity work. In appreciation of the splendid service rendered by Dr. Hay, the twenty-fifth anniversary of his pastorate was celebrated in a special service in the chapel on Wednesday evening, June 19, 1929. Addresses were made by a number of those active in the work during Dr. Hay's time of service, all of them paying beautiful tributes to his fine contribution of life service, covering a period of a quarter of a century.

On the following evening Rev. Foster U. Gift, D.D., who for a number of years had been superintendent of instruction at the Baltimore Motherhouse, was installed pastor by the president of the Maryland Synod. In electing Dr. Gift to succeed Dr. Hay as pastor, the office of superintendent of instruction was eliminated and the work of the two combined with that of pastor with the understanding that later an assistant will be called. Dr. Gift is well qualified for his new office.

V. Appreciation of Service of Retiring Members

At the June meeting the Board adopted resolutions of appreciation of the service rendered by the members whose terms expire at this time. The following members have rendered faithful and fruitful service to the cause of the diaconate: Rev. J. F. Ohl, D.D., Rev. E. F. Bachmann, D.D., Rev. J. F. Crigler, D.D., Mr. F. G. Hassold and Mrs. James P. Reese, Advisory Member. The Board records its highest appreciation of their devotion and service to the cause.

VI. Baltimore and Philadelphia Motherhouses

The following reports of the Baltimore and Philadelphia Motherhouses have been prepared by Dr. F. U. Gift and Dr. E. F. Bachmann, pastors, respectively:

(a) Baltimore Motherhouse Training School

With the hope of increasing the efficiency of the training school, the courses of instruction have, from time to time, been revised to meet the growing needs of the Church. It may be in place here to list the chief subjects which are now included in these courses: English Bible, Old Testament History, New Testament History, Bible Geography, Life of Christ, Bible Story Telling, Christian Evidences, Christian Doctrine, Church History, Catechetics, Religions of the World, Educational Psychology, Personal Work, Diaconics, Departmental Methods (Beginners, Primary, Junior and Intermediate), Medical Lectures, Nursing, Church Music, Book Reviews, English, Weekday Religious Education, Recreational Leadership, Leadership Training, Public Speaking and Church Administration.

In addition to the regular classroom instruction given by the pastor, the Head Sister and the Training Sister, Rev. Charles J. Hines, Rev. J. William McCauley, Mrs. Charles E. Hay, Miss Lillian E. McCormick, Rev. J. E. Cudlipp, Dr. George A. Bawden and Dr. C. Wilbur Stewart have rendered faithful service as members of the teaching staff.

Special addresses and lectures have been given during the biennium by the following: Rev. E. H. Delk, D.D., Rev. C. H. B. Lewis, D.D., Rev. Charles F. Steck, D.D., Rev. L. M. Zimmerman, D.D., Rev. L. B. Wolf, D.D., Rev. A. Pohlman, D.D., Rev. F. P. Manhart, D.D., Rev. J. C. Bowers, D.D., Rev. F. H. Knubel, D.D., Rev. William Freas, D.D., Rev. Paul Koller, D.D., Rev. N. R. Melhorn, D.D., Rev. Amos Traver and Rev. James Oosterling.

The Weekday Church School, with an enrolment of about two hundred children, continues to furnish fine opportunities for practical experience in teaching. It is conducted by the Motherhouse under the direct supervision of the Pastor and Training Sister, and, since its organization eight years ago, has had a splendid history.

The work of the Kindergarten began last fall with bright prospects for a very successful year. However, on account of the illness of Sister Carolyn it became necessary, in February of this year, to discontinue it temporarily.

Under the direction of the Training Sister, the students spend much time each week in what may be called practical training. This practical work of the training school includes a variety of activities such as: the conducting of teacher training classes; teaching in Sunday schools; conducting a Sunday school at Camp Holabird; assisting Sister Christine at the Montrose School; conducting Sunday afternoon services at the Orphans' Home in Catonsville; visiting the children of the weekday church school and spending almost every Tuesday afternoon in field work under the direction of the Baltimore Inner Mission Society.

NUMBER OF SISTERS

At the present time there are forty-eight consecrated sisters and fourteen probationers connected with the Motherhouse. On April 1, 1930, the Sisterhood suffered a severe loss in the death of Sister Eleanor Frank, one of the younger deaconesses, who was greatly beloved by all who knew her, and as a parish deaconess, left a very fine record of real Christian service. She was consecrated on April 22, 1926. The funeral service was held on Friday, April 4th, in the Motherhouse chapel, after which the body was laid to rest in the beautiful Motherhouse burial plot in Lorraine Cemetery.

CONSECRATION SERVICES

On June 20, 1929, in the Motherhouse Chapel, Sisters Meta Fellerman, Mary Junas, Margaret Lang and Ida Steuerwald were solemnly consecrated as deaconesses. Rev. L. M. Zimmerman, D.D., preached the sermon. On June 26, 1930, Sisters Delphine Dasher and Madaline Schaefer were admitted to full membership in the Sisterhood by consecration. The sermon was preached by Rev. A. Steimle, D.D.

THE WORK OF THE SISTERS

Our Sisters are engaged in many different kinds of work as may be seen by the following list of stations in which they are at present rendering very effective service: First Church, Second Church, Reformation and St. Paul's, Baltimore, Md.; Trinity, Canton, Ohio; Church of the Reformation, Rochester, N. Y.; St. John's (Christopher St.), St. John's (Bronx), Advent, Our Saviour's Atonement, Christ Church (Washington Heights), New York City; St. Matthew's and Gethsemane, Philadelphia, Pa.; Memorial Church, Harrisburg, Pa.; Zion, Syracuse, N. Y.; First Church, Richmond, Va.; Trinity, Akron, Ohio; Trinity, Germantown, Philadelphia,

Pa.; Glenwood Avenue Church, Toledo, Ohio; St. Luke's and St. John's, Brooklyn, N. Y.; Seventh Street Church, Lebanon, Pa.; St. Paul's, Allentown, Pa.; First Church, Albany, N. Y.; Trinity, Hagerstown, Md.; Keller Memorial, Washington, D. C.; St. John's German, Reading, Pa.; First Church, Mansfield, Ohio; English Lutheran Church, Pottsville, Pa.; St. Matthew's, Hanover, Pa.; St. Peter's, Middletown, Pa.; Evangelical Lutheran Church, Frederick, Md.; St. Mark's, Williamsport, Pa.; St. Stephen's, Wilmington, Del.; Tabitha Home, Lincoln, Nebraska; Good Shepherd Home, Allentown, Pa.; National Home for the Aged, Washington, D. C.; Muhlenberg Mission, Africa; Lowman Home, White Rock, S. C.; Franke Home, Charleston, S. C.; Inner Mission Society, Brooklyn, N. Y.; Lutheran Girls' Hospice, Baltimore, Md.; Lutheran Settlement, Philadelphia, Pa.; Children's Mission Home, Knoxville, Tenn.; and Tressler Orphans' Home, Loysville, Pa.

THE TRIENNIAL HOMECOMING

The custom inaugurated some years ago of having all the consecrated Sisters return to the Motherhouse once in three years for a period of two weeks for study and fellowship has proved to be very satisfactory. In June, 1929, the second such Triennial Homecoming was held and it was a very pleasant event from every standpoint.

SPECIAL STUDENTS

The special courses for Christian workers continue to attract a large number of students, and evidently are offering the kind of preparation which our churches and institutions want. During the biennium forty-six young women, representing fourteen states, the District of Columbia and Nova Scotia, embraced this opportunity for Christian leadership training. Quite a number of those, who during the past two years completed these courses, are now filling full time positions in parishes and institutions of the church.

(b) PHILADELPHIA MOTHERHOUSE

During the past biennium the Philadelphia Motherhouse has experienced in many ways that the Lord is fulfilling His promise, "Lo, I am with you always." In our work we can point to His sustaining power and blessing, in our perplexing problems to His remarkable guidance, and in our tribulations to His consolation.

MINISTRY OF MERCY

Our work is an important part of the Ministry of Mercy in the United Lutheran Church. In the care of our Sisters are almost one hundred aged men and women in the Mary J. Drexel Home in Philadelphia and in the Lutheran Home in Erie; seventy-seven boys and girls taken from broken-up families by the Tabor Home, near Doylestown, Pa.; about sixty children, increased to one hundred during the summer, coming from families afflicted with tuberculosis, and during a stay of several weeks or months, seeking new strength at the Preventorium River Crest, near Phoenixville, Pa.; and about fifteen native girls at the Eben-Ezer Orphans' Home in Fredericksted, St. Croix. One of our deaconesses has been at the head of the Kensington Dispensary since its organization twenty-four years ago, during which time almost 6,500 tuberculosis patients, mostly mill workers, have been aided in their fight for health, and about four hundred are under treatment at present.

CHILDREN'S HOSPITAL

The Children's Hospital of the Motherhouse admitted 2,313 little patients in 1928 and 1929, and gave 5,029 children 38,889 treatments in the dispensary, while the Lankenau Hospital, our largest field of labor, had during the same time 8,027 house patients and 14,372 dispensary patients with 65,594 treatments.

INNER MISSION WORK

An important work is done by two of our Sisters under the direction of the Berks County Inner Mission Society in Reading, Pa., where the one is executive secretary and field worker and the other in charge of a hospice with rooms for sixteen working girls. The former Sister reports for the past two years.

A new activity was added to our list on March 7, 1930, when upon request of the Inner Mission Bureau of the Ministerium of Pennsylvania, two of our deaconesses made their first visit to Moyamensing Prison. They have been elected members of the Pennsylvania Prison Society, which authorizes them to visit female prisoners in any penal institution of the state. For the present they conduct, twice a month, a simple service for the few Lutheran women, and for others, and follow that with personal work as circumstances require.

PARISH WORK

Nine congregations have parish deaconesses from our Motherhouse, Zion's, Trinity and Tabor, in Philadelphia; St. John's, Easton; Trinity, Pottsville; Christ, Hazleton; St. Paul's, New York; Trinity, New Haven; and St. John's, Erie. Each of these congregations differs widely from every other in its local conditions and peculiar problems, except the two in the mining region with a communicant membership of over 2,000 each. We sincerely deplore the fact that the shortage of Sisters alone prevents us from expanding this important branch of the diaconate.

LANKENAU SCHOOL FOR GIRLS

A unique and richly blessed department of our Motherhouse work observes its fortieth anniversary this fall—the Lankenau School for Girls. Beginning in a very modest way, in September, 1890, with three classes accommodated on the fourth floor of the Motherhouse building, it outgrew those quarters, and in 1910 moved into its own home, on a spacious property, directly west of the Motherhouse. It is the only school conducted by Lutheran deaconesses in this country, and under their leadership has developed into a school for resident and day pupils with kindergarten and a full twelve-year course, parallel to that of the public school system. The High School Department has been accredited by the Department of Education of Pennsylvania for many years, and in November, 1929, it also became a fully accredited member of the Association of Colleges and Secondary Schools of the Middle Atlantic States and Maryland. While most of the one hundred girls enrolled are from Pennsylvania and New York, the rest represent five other states and Mexico. This year's roll of one hundred and seven fairly shows the usual denominational proportions: 47 Lutheran, 14 Presbyterian, 11 Episcopalian, 8 Methodist, 8 Protestant, 8 Roman Catholic, and the remainder scattered among eight different religious bodies. Though every pupil shares the same religious instructions for three or four periods a week, the thorough teaching and the character building influences of the school have won for it the unqualified confidence of many outside of our own church.

THE LORD'S GUIDANCE IN OUR PROBLEMS

In all our perplexing problems as they arise in the daily routine and through unexpected circumstances, we have experienced the Lord's guidance, often in a remarkable manner. Many problems of our work we discuss at the monthly meetings of the Sisters' Council, which brings the most important before the Sisters' Conference. The parish deaconesses meet at the Motherhouse for a two-day conference at the close of the year, and the Sisters in charge of institutions shortly before Easter for the consideration of their special tasks and difficulties. Nevertheless, frequently, not we, but circumstances uncontrollable by us, have so solved our difficulties and shaped our course, that our faith has been strengthened in the Lord's special providence.

One of the vexing problems is financial. The regular income from all sources was, in 1928, $84,587.69, over against an expense of $112,227.22. This shortage of $27,689.53 was reduced by $4,731 received on the $5,000 appropriation by the United Lutheran Church and by $6,556 received from the Donation Day in November. In 1929 the regular receipts were $85,432.91, the expenses $101,227.39. The deficit of $15,794.48 was lower than that of the previous year, chiefly because of the lower item for repairs and improvements. This year we received $3,000 from the United Lutheran Church and $8,954.49 from Donation Day. For the inauguration and management of Donation Day, first held in 1923, we are indebted to a number of ladies, personal friends of Sister Else, for many years at the head of our Children's

Hospital. It was certainly providential that these ladies organized themselves as an Auxiliary on December 13, 1929, to make these Children's hospital days a permanent feature. This was less than one month before the unexpected death of Sister Else.

THE HAND OF DEATH

Unusual tribulations came upon our Motherhouse during the biennium, but in them all we experienced the Lord's presence and consolation. During the year 1928 the Sisterhood did not sustain any loss, by death or by resignation, but in 1929 one deaconess and three probationers left us, and on July 13th our Directing Sister, Julia Mergner, was called to her heavenly home after an illness of less than a week; and within less than six months, on January 7, 1930, her successor, Sister Else Dodenhoff, installed in her office on October 13th, followed her. We were plunged into deepest sorrow, and have hardly recovered from the shock. Largely to Sister Julia was due the development of the Lankenau School, and to Sister Else that of our Children's Hospital. Sister Else was in the diaconate forty-three years, Sister Julia thirty-four. By their death we lost not merely their valuable services, but above all, the influence of their unusual personality.

NUMBER OF SISTERS

We began the biennium with 106 Sisters. We lost six, but we added four probationers in 1929 and five in 1930, and one deaconess, who had honorably left twelve years ago to assist her family, re-entered the work. On May 1, 1930, we therefore have 80 deaconesses and 30 probationers, or 110 Sisters. Of this number fifty-one came to us from congregations of the Ministerium of Pennsylvania, and of these, twenty are from Philadelphia. Evidently the Motherhouse attracts most where it is known best. If the entire United Lutheran Church, with about thirty times as many communicant members as the two Philadelphia Conferences of the Ministerium, from which we have twenty-six Sisters, had furnished the same proportion of young women, we should have today about 750 Sisters in both Motherhouses of the United Lutheran Church. This comparison justifies our confidence in the greater future of the deaconess work within our church.

NEW DIRECTING SISTER

Our Sisterhood and Board of Trustees looked forward to a larger development of the deaconess work when they approached the election of a new Directing Sister. Realizing the grave situation into which our Motherhouse has been led by the Lord, when He took away Sister Else, within less than three months after her installation, everyone prayed the more earnestly for His special guidance. Thanks also to the vision of our older Sisters. The choice fell on one of our younger deaconesses, Sister Anna Ebert, the daughter of the Rev. A. O. Ebert, of New Tripoli. She is a graduate of the Kutztown State Normal School, of the Lankenau Training School for Nurses and of Temple College. Together with Sister Grace Lauer, our Training Sister, she was sent to some of the leading Motherhouses in this country and on June 26th left for abroad to study the present situation of the diaconate to learn the most advanced ideas in the training of deaconesses and the conduct of the work, and to form those personal contacts with leaders so important to anyone bearing the grave responsibility of leadership. Sister Anna is to be installed in her new office on Reformation Day. We bespeak for her and for our Motherhouse the special prayers of the Church.

MORE YOUNG WOMEN NEEDED

We cannot overstate the plea for capable and consecrated young women for the diaconate. Requests for deaconesses have so uniformly received a negative answer, that pastors have been discouraged and some even embittered. This situation will change as soon as capable young women in larger numbers will respond to the call for laborers. How sorely they are needed is evident from the fact that our Motherhouse has had to refuse new work during the past five years for which fifty-eight trained deaconesses would have been needed. We should also have in the near future at least twenty-five additional trained Sisters for our present fields to continue the work effectively.

The Lord is with us always, and among the aged and the little ones, among the sick and the sorrowing, among the strangers and the destitute. May our Church in its entirety arise to serve Him! Our Motherhouse is prepared to do its share.

VII. RESOLUTIONS SUBMITTED BY THE BOARD

1. That the United Lutheran Church records its gratitude to God for the permanent establishment of the Deaconess Work in this country by the Rev. William A. Passavant and Mr. John D. Lankenau, and for the development of the work by those whom God has called as leaders since that time.

2. That the Church records its deep appreciation of the splendid service rendered by the deaconesses of the different Motherhouses; and rejoices in the fact that in the female diaconate there is offered to the consecrated young womanhood of the Church an opportunity for life service so varied in its demands as to utilize every talent so Christ-like in spirit, challenging the devotion of all who love the Lord.

3. That we bespeak for our Deaconess Work the hearty support of our pastors and of the official representatives of the various agencies of the Church, in view of the fact that our sisters are serving in parishes and institutions under the auspices of the various boards of the Church.

4. That we urge upon parents, pastors, superintendents of Church schools, teachers of young women's Bible classes and leaders of young

people's organizations that they make frequent reference to the helpful ministry of deaconesses in the Church, and bring to the attention of suitable young women the large opportunities thus afforded for fruitful Christian service.

5. That we urge all our pastors to present the Deaconess Cause to their congregations, especially on Septuagesima Sunday, appealing to the young women of the Church to consider the high calling of the diaconate.

6. That we commend the Annuity Bond Plan of the Board of Deaconess Work, which affords an attractive investment for those desiring perfect security and liberal interest with prompt payments, the proceeds of which are to be used eventually through our Endowment Fund for the support of aged Sisters.

Respectfully submitted,

WILLIAM A. WADE, *President.*
CHARLES E. HAY, *Secretary.*

TREASURER'S REPORT

For the Two Years Ended June 30, 1930, and 1929

BALANCE SHEET, June 30, 1930

ASSETS:

Cash: The Baltimore Trust Company, Exchange Bank Office	$ 8,623.03	
Hopkins Place Savings Bank	12,919.92	
Maryland Trust Company	330.83	
Imprest Funds at Motherhouse	900.00	
		$ 22,773.78
Real estate, buildings, etc., at book values: Motherhouse, North and Thomas Avenues, Baltimore, Md.	$200,000.00	
Properties at 1901 and 1905 Thomas Avenue, Baltimore, Md.	18,944.18	
Ground rents	27,358.33	
Lorraine Park Cemetery burial lot	600.00	
		246,902.51
		$269,676.29

FUNDS:

New building fund	$ 20,387.63	
Endowment funds	9,562.14	
Annuity funds	21,400.00	
General fund	218,326.52	
		$269,676.29

Note: Commitments at June 30, 1930, for practically completed alterations and repairs to Motherhouse are estimated by Board Treasurer to aggregate $10,400.

BALANCE SHEET, June 30, 1929

ASSETS:

Cash: The Baltimore Trust Company, Exchange Bank Office	$ 6,435.92	
Hopkins Place Savings Bank	11,120.88	
Maryland Trust Company	326.38	
Imprest funds at Motherhouse	800.00	
		$ 18,683.18

Real estate, buildings, etc., at book values:

Motherhouse, North and Thomas Avenues, Baltimore, Md.	$200,000.00	
Properties at 1901 and 1905 Thomas Avenue, Baltimore, Md.	18,944.18	
Ground rents	25,758.33	
Lorraine Park Cemetery burial lot	600.00	
		245,302.51
		$263,985.69

FUNDS:

New building fund	$ 19,976.61	
Endowment fund	8,174.12	
Annuity funds	20,400.00	
General fund	215,434.96	
		$263,985.69

CASH RECEIPTS AND DISBURSEMENTS

For the Year Ended June 30, 1930

RECEIPTS:

	General Fund	Endowment Fund	New Building Fund	Annuity Fund
United Lutheran Church, apportionment	$30,254.84			
United, general and branch synods	58.43			
Donations	271.34	$1,243.90	$26.70	
Tuition	3,464.22			
Kindergarten	239.50			
Nursing	303.95			
Stations	8,445.54			
Annuity				$1,000.00
Bank Interest	159.37	144.12	384.32	
Income from investments	1,545.50			
	$44,742.69	$1,388.02	$411.02	$1,000.00
Total cash receipts		$47,541.73		

DISBURSEMENTS:

Salaries of superintendent and assistant	$ 4,000.00	
Superintendent's traveling expenses	200.06	
Wages of general and domestic help	4,153.00	

Maintenance and miscellaneous expenses of Motherhouse and cottages	2,870.87	
Furniture and fixtures purchased....	1,024.17	
Insurance	645.22	
Expenses of other officers and board representatives	708.05	
Expenses of grounds	129.10	
Household expenses	5,500.00	
Personal expenses of sisters	2,085.97	
Vacation allowance, Dr. Gift	300.00	
Professional services for sisters	957.72	
Sisters' allowances	5,866.25	
Wearing apparel	1,207.71	
Lectures and class instructions	856.49	
Class and library books	441.84	
Printing and stationery	1,021.66	
Advertising	200.86	
Office salary and expenses	1,045.82	
Fuel and light	2,120.74	
Contribution to Mary J. Drexel Home and Philadelphia Motherhouse of Deaconesses	3,000.00	
Sewing room expenses	75.00	
Grain, feed and garden supplies....	620.71	
Auditing	110.00	
Annuities paid	1,401.00	
Ground rent purchased	600.00	$1,000.00
*Partial payment for alterations to Motherhouse heating system	1,200.00	
Discounts earned	141.11	
Reimbursement to Dr. Gift against expenses not detailed	250.00	
	$42,451.13	$1,000.00

Total cash disbursements	$43,451.13	
Cash balance, July 1, 1929	18,683.18	
Total cash receipts	47,541.73	
	66,224.91	
Less, total cash disbursements	43,451.13	
Cash balance, June 30, 1930	$22,773.78	

* Additional cost of alterations and repairs estimated by Board Treasurer at approximately $10,400.

CASH RECEIPTS AND DISBURSEMENTS
For the Year Ended June 30, 1929
RECEIPTS:

	General Fund	Endowment Fund	New Building Fund	Annuity Fund
United Lutheran Church apportionment	$28,560.00			
United, general and branch synods	57.42			

Donations	75.77	$445.00	$561.00	
Tuition	3,988.50			
Kindergarten	421.21			
Nursing	787.57			
Stations	8,779.06			
Annuity				$1,600.00
Bank interest	18.86	100.93	357.88	
Income from investments	1,479.58			
	$44,167.97	$545.93	$918.88	$1,600.00
Total cash receipts		$47,232.78		

DISBURSEMENTS:

Salaries of superintendent and assistant	$ 4,916.67
Superintendent's traveling expenses	204.87
Wages of general and domestic help	4,678.00
Maintenance and miscellaneous expenses of Motherhouse and cottages	1,861.15
Furniture and fixtures purchased	216.71
Advertising	170.50
Expenses of other officers and Board representatives	710.21
Expenses of grounds	62.50
Household expenses	6,300.00
Personal expenses of sisters	2,215.98
Tuition fees refunded	130.00
Sisters' training fund	75.00
Professional services for sisters	449.72
Sisters' allowances	6,000.63
Sisters' traveling expenses	711.70
Wearing apparel	2,124.98
Lectures and class instruction	507.00
Class and library books	425.34
Printing and stationery	1,062.46
Office salary and expenses	456.04
Fuel and light	2,156.26
Contribution to Mary J. Drexel Home and Philadelphia Motherhouse of Deaconesses	3,000.00
Sewing room expenses	250.00
Grain, feed and garden supplies	683.68
Auditing	135.00
Annuities paid	1,428.50
Ground rent purchased	$1,166.67
New heating system, 1905 Thomas Avenue	1,447.18
Discounts earned	121.69
	$42,258.39 $1,166.67

Total cash disbursements	$43,425.06
Cash balance, July 1, 1928..................................	14,875.46
Total cash receipts	47,232.78
	62,108.24
Less, total cash disbursements..........................	43,425.06
Cash balance, June 30, 1929................................	$18,683.18

RECONCILEMENT OF FUNDS

For the Year Ended June 30, 1930

	General Fund	Endowment Fund	New Building Fund	Annuity Fund
Balances, July 1, 1929..............	$215,434.96	$8,174.12	$19,976.61	$20,400.00
Add, Cash receipts	44,742.69	1,388.02	411.02	1,000.00
	260,177.65	9,562.14	20,387.63	21,400.00
Deduct, Cash disbursements..	42,451.13			1,000.00
	217,726.52	9,562.14	20,387.63	20,400.00
Add, Purchase of ground rent	600.00			1,000.00
Balances, June 30, 1930............	$218,326.52	$9,562.14	$20,387.63	$21,400.00

RECONCILEMENT OF FUNDS

For the Year Ended June 30, 1929

	General Fund	Endowment Fund	New Building Fund	Annuity Fund
Balances, July 1, 1928..............	$212,078.20	$6,128.19	$19,057.73	$20,300.00
Add, Cash receipts	44,167.97	545.93	918.88	1,600.00
	256,246.17	6,674.12	19,976.61	21,900.00
Deduct, Cash disbursements	42,258.39			1,166.67
	213,987.78	6,674.12	19,976.61	20,733.33
Add, Purchase of ground rent and cost of addition to building	1,447.18			1,166.67
	215,434.96	6,674.12	19,976.61	21,900.00
Transfer of funds (annuitant deceased)		1,500.00		1,500.00
Balances, June 30, 1929............	$215,434.96	$8,174.12	$19,976.61	$20,400.00

Respectfully submitted,

PEARRE E. CROWL, *Treasurer.*

Baltimore, Md., July 16, 1930.

We have audited the accounts of the Board of Deaconess Work of the United Lutheran Church in America for the two years ended June 30, 1930, and we certify that, in our opinion, the foregoing statements submitted by its treasurer are correct.

LYBRAND, ROSS BROS. & MONTGOMERY,
Accountants and Auditors.

Recommendations 1, 2, 3, 4, 5, and 6 were adopted.

The report of the auditors was accepted.

Mr. Harry Hodges, Secretary of the Board of Ministerial Pensions and Relief, presented the report of the Board.

THE REPORT OF THE BOARD OF MINISTERIAL PENSIONS AND RELIEF

The past biennium has been largely a collection period of the subscriptions to the Endowment Fund.

The total amount subscribed was $4,178,065, to be paid over a period of two and one half years, the last installment due April 1st, 1930.

At this date (July 1st, 1930) there has been paid $2,820,076, but 67 per cent. The status by synods follows:

Synod	Quota	Subscription	Paid	Per Cent
Pennsylvania Ministerium	$844,446	$849,220	$620,331.04	73
United Synod of New York	644,916	660,177	460,055.85	69
Pittsburgh	301,038	341,509	229,275.35	67
Ohio	273,306	345,000	229,918.79	67
West Pennsylvania	209,388	191,023	134,690.23	70
East Pennsylvania	202,992	285,364	180,808.30	63
Maryland	184,302	222,487	154,536.01	69
Susquehanna	160,416	128,626	78,397.62	61
Illinois	136,866	172,903	97,688.44	56
Alleghany	128,706	140,563	82,428.00	59
Northwest	102,540	114,200	62,967.02	55
North Carolina	99,858	84,214	45,553.33	54
Canada	84,726	45,604	34,915.60	76
South Carolina	82,212	55,028	32,506.66	59
Virginia	65,868	67,939	43,542.96	64
German Nebraska	53,220	26,953	22,906.72	85
Michigan	52,770	54,169	32,067.43	59
Indiana	51,156	48,492	34,335.05	71
Nebraska	49,410	54,842	36,772.40	67
Wartburg	46,590	27,600	23,378.85	84
Slovak Zion	32,478	1,710	1,999.45	117
Kansas	31,368	35,160	20,682.31	59
Iowa	30,012	26,500	14,998.87	57
Manitoba	29,748	3,000	3,160.65	105
California	28,938	31,924	19,325.62	60
West Virginia	21,480	28,273	18,796.76	66
Georgia	21,660	22,975	15,483.20	67

Texas	18,096	11,810	8,150.00	69
Pacific	12,372	19,116	9,995.18	52
Rocky Mountain	8,880	12,968	6,760.26	52
Nova Scotia	7,458	7,902	5,304.25	67
Florida	5,000	4,988	2,219.00	45
United Lutheran Pub. House	....	50,000	50,000.00	100
Mississippi	2,214	3,225	1,662.97	61
Porto Rico	....	2,601	....	......
Miscellaneous	....	....	4,462.25	......
Total		$4,178,065	$2,820,076.42	

The synodical presidents received the status of their respective synods prior to the conventions and were urged to inaugurate follow-up proceedings. Several of the synods have inaugurated such proceedings.

The campaign goal was to double the pensions. On the first of May of the current year, the Board advanced the pensions to ministers, missionaries, and widows, $100 per year. It cannot complete its program until the entire subscription is paid. This fact should be an urge to both clergymen and laymen to complete the task.

STATISTICS

Since our last report the following deductions and additions have been made in our roll:

Additions: Ministers 94, widows 72, children 38, missionaries 2; total, 206.

Deductions: Ministers 50, widows 44, children 30, missionaries 0; total, 124.

The Roll by Synods is appended hereto.

During the biennium thirty special grants were made amounting to $1,925.00.

ANNUITY BONDS AND BEQUESTS

During the past biennium five annuity bonds to the amount of $6,350.00 have been sold, and twelve bequests received to the amount of $20,095.35.

The attention of the Church is called to the fact that the Board issues annuity bonds at a liberal rate of interest and pastors and attorneys are asked to call the attention of their parishioners to these bonds and to suggest the Board of Ministerial Pensions and Relief as an institution worthy of remembrance in their wills.

WOMEN'S MISSIONARY SOCIETY

The Board herewith records its high appreciation of the $5,000 annual appropriation from the Women's Missionary Society and of the faithful attendance of its two members who attend its meetings in an advisory capacity.

SPECIAL REPRESENTATIVES

The Board has sent its president, Paul F. Myers, Esq., and its vice-president, the Rev. M. H. Valentine, D.D., to represent it at this convention and requests that they be given a hearing in connection with the presentation of this report.

NOMINATIONS

At this convention the terms of the following members expire:

The Rev. Ross H. Stover, D.D.
The Rev. M. H. Valentine, D.D.
The Rev. C. L. Miller, D.D.
Mr. George P. Tustin.
Mr. J. Harvey Wattles.

The Board places in nomination the following:

The Rev. Ross H. Stover, D.D., Philadelphia, Pa. (East Pennsylvania Synod).
The Rev. J. H. Reble, Hamilton, Ont., Canada (Canada Synod).
W. T. Stauffer, Esq., Newport News, Va. (Virginia Synod).
H. J. Herbst, Fort Wayne, Ind. (Michigan Synod).
William A. Granville, Ph.D., LL.D., Chicago, Ill. (Illinois Synod).

RECOMMENDATION

That the synods be requested to continue their Pension Campaign Committees to clean up the subscriptions and urge the fullest co-operation on the part of congregations and conference officials with the Board in any plans that it may inaugurate.

Respectfully submitted,
HARRY HODGES, *Executive Secretary.*

The Pension Roll by Synods—June 30, 1930

Synod	Retired	Dis-abled	Widows	Children	Daugh-ters	Pension	Relief
Alleghany	7	0	11	0	0	$ 6,100	$ 480
California	8	3	7	1	0	6,550	450
Canada	11	1	12	2	0	8,500	600
East Pennsylvania	9	1	36	5	1	15,350	840
Florida	1	1	1*	2	0	1,200	100
Georgia	1	2	7	3	1	3,750	290
German Nebraska	7	3	14	10	0	8,700	480
Illinois	11	0	22	13	2	12,250	500
Indiana	4	1	8	2	1	4,800	350
Iowa	2	0	2	0	0	1,400	......
Kansas	4	1	9	3	0	4,850	350
Manitoba	2	3	4	2	0	3,300	480
Maryland	5	0	32	2	1	12,000	820
Michigan	5	0	12	2	0	5,700	......
Mississippi	1	0	0	0	0	400	
Nebraska	4	0	8	2	0	4,100	100
United New York	20	4	68	13	2	31,250	2,770
North Carolina	9	0	22	4	0	10,400	810
Northwest	3	0	4	1	0	2,450	80
Nova Scotia	0	0	0	0	0	....	......
Ohio	18	4*	39	17	0	21,350	1,210
Pacific	2	0	4	1	0	2,050	......
Min. of Pennsylvania	18	10*	56	13	0	28,650	2,390
Pittsburgh	16	4**	31	7	1	18,250	520

Note: *Includes a missionary.

Rocky Mountain	6	0	1	1	0	2,750	350
Slovak Zion	0	1	0	0	0	400	......
South Carolina	2	1	17	3	0	6,450	640
Susquehanna	11	1	13	0	0	8,700	760
Texas	0	1	5	4	0	2,100	430
Virginia	6	2	18	5	0	8,850	400
Wartburg	5	1	5	0	0	3,900	550
West Pennsylvania	10	1	31	13	0	14,350	970
West Virginia	0	0	3	0	0	900	100
Total (1930)	208	46	502	131	9	$261,750	$17,820
Total (1928)	180	28	470	119	6	$163,750	$13,472

REPORT OF THE TREASURER OF THE BOARD OF MINISTERIAL PENSIONS AND RELIEF

Statement of Assets and Liabilities 6-30-30.
Statement of Receipts and Disbursements for year ending June 30, 1930.
Bonds owned June 30, 1930.

PETER P. HAGAN,
Treasurer.

BOARD OF MINISTERIAL PENSIONS AND RELIEF OF THE UNITED LUTHERAN CHURCH IN AMERICA
BALANCE SHEET, JUNE 30, 1930

ASSETS

Cash in banks and on hand		$201,489.27
Investments, at ledger values:		
U. S. Liberty loan bonds, as annexed	$10,504.12	
Other bonds, as annexed	674,288.29	
Mortgages	2,233,200.00	
Miscellaneous		
(Adjusted War Service Certificate)	1.00	
		2,917,993.41
Real estate, at ledger value:		
Sime's Farm, Wheatland County, Montana		1.00
Office furniture and fixtures		1,696.49
		$3,121,180.17

LIABILITIES

Annuities		84,350.00
Funds:		
Endowment	3,010,608.35	
General	26,221.82	
		3,036,830.17
		$3,121,180.17

STATEMENTS OF RECEIPTS AND DISBURSEMENTS
For the Year Ended June 30, 1929

RECEIPTS:

	Pension Endowment	Pension General	Relief Endowment	Relief General
Campaign Fund	$1,246,392.12			
Proportion of apportionment		$159,800.00		
Women's Miss. Society		5,000.00		
Bequests	10,197.31	1,998.82	$1,796.42	$5,200.00
Donations	91.96	1,010.73		4,337.04
Interest:				
On Bank Balances	21,149.61	1,467.14	968.90	
On Investments	23,110.31		3,450.00	
Annuity contracts sold	6,850.00			
Investments matured	7,350.00		6,507.50	
Refund Montana property	32.00			
	$1,315,173.31	$169,276.69	$12,722.82	$ 9,537.04

DISBURSEMENTS:

	Pension Endowment	Pension General	Relief Endowment	Relief General
Pensions and relief:				
Retired Ministers		57,179.17		7,198.50
Disabled Ministers		10,775.40		
Widows & Mothers of Ministers		96,304.96		8,512.50
Children of Ministers		5,505.25		
Annuity interest		3,943.30		1,596.00
Salary of Executive Secretary		3,600.00		
Salary of Office Secretary		1,820.00		
Travel. Exp. Executive Sec.		678.77		
Exp. Treas. & Bd. Members		1,326.99		
Printing & Stationery		96.75		
Office supplies & expenses		625.63		
Rental of office		765.00		
Auditing		350.00		
Advertising		250.00		
General expenses		916.17		
Campaign expenses	6,578.66			
Equipment purchased		27.60		
Investments purchased	1,867,800.00			
	$1,874,378.66	$184,164.99		$17,307.00

RECONCILEMENT OF CASH:

	Pension Endowment	Pension General	Relief Endowment	Relief General
Balances, July 1, 1928	758,336.29	59,597.72	31,800.37	492.88
Cash receipts for the period	1,315,173.31	169,276.69	12,722.82	9,537.04
	2,073,509.60	228,874.41	44,523.19	9,044.16
Disbursements	1,874,378.66	184,164.99		17,307.00
	199,130.94	44,709.42	44,523.19	8,262.84
Transfers between funds as of June 30, 1929	25,332.23	25,332.23	5,081.40	5,081.40
	$173,798.71	$70,041.65	$39,441.79	$3,181.44

Balance, June 30, 1929 $280,100.71

STATEMENTS OF RECEIPTS AND DISBURSEMENTS
For the Year Ended June 30, 1930
RECEIPTS:

	Endowment Fund	General Fund
Campaign for Endowment Fund	$739,793.31	
United Lutheran Church, Apportionment		$169,200.00
Board of Publication of the United Lutheran Church	20,000.00	
Women's Missionary Society		5,000.00
Bequests	1,298.66	
Donations	68.00	5,258.36
Interest:		
On bank balances	2,991.80	180.93
On investments	135,039.47	
Annuity contract sold	500.00	
Investments:		
Bonds matured or sold	20,286.94	
Mortgages paid in full or on account	164,500.00	
Satisfaction fees received on mortgages		5.00
	$1,084,478.18	$179,644.29

DISBURSEMENTS:

Pensions and relief:		
Retired ministers		72,340.35
Disabled ministers		13,516.95
Widows and mothers of ministers		118,119.73
Children of ministers		5,159.19
Missionaries		1,833.30
Annuity interest		5,793.40
Salary of Executive Secretary		3,600.00
Salary of Office Secretary		1,820.00
Traveling expenses of Executive Secretary		1,480.00
Expenses of Treasurer and other Board members		2,450.53
Printing and stationery		247.50
Office supplies and expenses		1,389.42
Rental of office		765.00
Auditing		650.00
Advertising		183.73
Campaign expenses	1,605.55	
Equipment purchased		232.50
Investments purchased:		
Bonds	580,646.76	
Mortgages	530,900.00	
	$1,113,152.31	$229,581.60

RECONCILEMENT OF CASH:

Balances, July 1, 1929	213,240.50	66,860.21
Cash receipts for the period	1,084,478.18	179,644.29
	1,297,718.68	246,504.50

Disbursements 1,113,152.31   229,581.60

184,566.37	16,922.90
Transfers between funds 7,602.43	7,602.43

$176,963.94 $24,525.33

Balance, June 30, 1930 $201,489.27

BONDS OWNED, ENDOWMENT FUND, June 30, 1930

Ledger Values

U. S. GOVERNMENT OBLIGATIONS:

$10,950 U. S. Fourth Liberty Loan 4¼s $10,504.12

OTHER BONDS:

$25,000	American Telephone & Telegraph Co., 5s, 1965......	25,175.00
25,000	Appalachian Electric Power 5s, 1956	24,425.00
25,000	Atchison, Topeka & Santa Fe 4s, 1995	23,570.00
25,000	Baltimore & Ohio R. R. 5s, 1995	25,515.00
5,000	Bell Telephone Co. of Penna. 5s, 1960	5,041.25
25,000	Buffalo, Rochester & Pittsburgh Cons. 4½s, 1957....	23,187.50
25,000	Canadian Pacific R. R. Equipment Trust 5s, 1944..	25,375.00
25,000	Carolina Power & Light Co. 5s, 1956..............	25,175.00
5,000	Central District Telephone Co. 5s, 1943...........	4,875.00
25,000	Chesapeake & Ohio R. R. Equipment 4½s, 1940....	24,900.33
6,000	Chicago, Indianapolis & Louisville 5s, 1966.........	6,000.00
25,000	Chicago & Northwestern 4¾s, 1949................	24,925.00
10,000	City of Ottawa 4½s, 1954........................	9,309.96
1,000	Des Moines City Ry. Co. 5s, 1936................	950.00
25,000	Georgia Power Co. 5s, 1967	24,425.00
25,000	The Harbour Commission of Montreal 5s, 1969......	25,412.50
1,000	Howard Gas & Coal 6s, 1937	1,000.00
5,000	Lehigh Valley R. R. Co. 5s, 2003	5,110.00
10,000	The Montreal Metropolitan Commission 4½s, 1953	9,262.50
1,000	Pacific Telephone & Telegraph Co. 5s, 1937........	1,000.00
25,000	Pennsylvania Co. Secured 4¾s, 1963	24,675.00
25,000	Pennsylvania R.R. Debenture 4½s, 1970............	23,812.50
5,000	Pennsylvania R. R. General 4½s, 1965	5,000.00
25,000	Pere Marquette Equipment 4½s, 1942..............	24,885.22
25,000	Philadelphia Co. 5s, 1967	24,675.00
5,000	Philadelphia Electric Co. 5s, 1960................	4,990.28
50,000	Philadelphia Electric Power Co. 5½s, 1972.........	51,487.50
24,500	Philadelphia Rapid Transit Co. 6s, 1944............	24,500.00
5,000	Pittsburgh, Cincinnati & St. Louis 5s, 1975........	4,985.00
20,000	Province of Alberta, Canada, 5s, 1959............	19,775.00
10,000	Province of Manitoba, Canada, 5s, 1959	9,937.50
25,000	Province of Ontario, Canada, 5s, 1960............	25,750.00
25,000	Province of Saskatchewan, Canada, 5s, 1959......	25,112.50
25,000	Southern Pacific R. R. 4½s, 1969, w. w.	24,281.25
25,000	Southern Pacific Oregon Lines, 4½s, 1977........	24,375.00
2,000	Tennessee Power Co. 5s, 1962.....................	1,600.00
25,000	Texas Corporation Conv. 5s, 1944	25,312.50

5,000	Virginia Power Co. 5s, 1942	4,500.00
10,000	Walnut St. Trust Building 6s, 1932...............	10,000.00

$674,288.29

PETER P. HAGAN,
Treasurer.

Philadelphia, July 21, 1930.

We have audited the accounts of the Treasurer of the Board of Ministerial Pensions and Relief of the United Lutheran Church in America for the two years ended June 30, 1930, and we certify that, in our opinion, the annexed statements:

Balance Sheet, June 30, 1930

Statement of Receipts and Disbursements for the year ended June 30, 1929

Statement of Receipts and Disbursements for the year ended June 30, 1930

Bonds Owned, Endowment Fund, June 30, 1930

are in accordance with the books of account and are correct.

LYBRAND, ROSS BROS., & MONTGOMERY,
Accountants and Auditors.

BOARD OF MINISTERIAL PENSIONS AND RELIEF
ENDOWMENT FUND

Mortgages Owned, June 30, 1930, In Safe Deposit Box

Bank of Philadelphia & Trust Company

Nos.	1 to 25	$81,000.00
Nos.	26 to 50	134,000.00
Nos.	51 to 75	135,000.00
Nos.	76 to 100	135,200.00
Nos.	101 to 125	138,300.00
Nos.	126 to 150	94,500.00
Nos.	151 to 175	176,400.00
Nos.	176 to 200	157,300.00
Nos.	201 to 225	85,600.00
Nos.	226 to 250	563,700.00
Nos.	251 to 275	102,000.00
Nos.	276 to 300	156,900.00
Nos.	301 to 325	168,500.00
Nos.	326 to 341	100,500.00

Total $2,228,900.00

Participating Trust Certificate, Property in Park
County, Mont., 6 per cent $800.00

Mortgage, Wm. Hoppe, 17 W. 106th St., New York
City 3,500.00

4,300.00

$2,233,200.00

Mtg. Nos.	Title Nos.	Amounts	Premises	Due Dates
1	6100	3,000	522 Godfrey Ave.	12-28-29
2	6098	3,500	528 Godfrey Ave.	12-31-29
3	6088	3,500	532 Godfrey Ave.	12-28-29
4	6096	3,000	538 Godfrey Ave.	12-24-29
5	6106	3,500	542 Godfrey Ave.	12-30-29
6	6099	3,000	544 Godfrey Ave.	12-30-29
7	6090	1,800	2762 N. Ringgold St.	4-12-31
8	6092	2,500	2531 W. Seltzer St.	6-7-31
9	6094	4,000	1717 W. Norris St.	4-18-31
10	6091	2,500	3102 N. 27th St.	5-23-31
11	6095	2,200	2356 N. 15th St.	1-24-31
12	6097	4,000	599 E. Cheltenham Ave.	6-22-31
13	6102	3,500	5916 Palmetto St.	4-9-31
14	6103	3,500	5922 Palmetto St.	5-24-31
15	6104	3,500	5962 Palmetto St.	4-9-31
16	6105	6,500	1329-65th Ave., North	5-10-33
17	6107	2,200	3022 "B" St.	3-19-31
18	6108	2,500	7308 Palmetto St.	4-9-31
19	6109	3,000	723 Rhawn St.	1-6-29
20	6110	3,300	NEs Afton St., N W Bustleton Ave.	5-8-31
21	6111	3,300	NEs Afton St., N W Bustleton Ave.	5-8-31
22	6112	3,500	NWs Claridge St. SW Faunce St.	6-11-31
23	6114	2,000	SEs Elm Ave., N E Montgomery Ave.	1-23-29
24	6115	4,200	6547 North 18th St.	7-25-31
25	6116	3,500	NEs Chandler St. SE Verree Ave.	7-14-31
26	6117	3,500	NEs Chandler St. SE Verree Ave.	7-14-31
27	6388	15,000	Ws Limekiln Tpke N Central Ave., Edge Hill SEs Tennis Ave., NE Elm Ave.	8-14-31
28	6389	6,000	5708 Virginian Road	4-1-31
29	6390	9,000	8514 Cypress Ave., Abington Twp., Pa.	8-9-31
31	6392	3,500	1939 Independence Ave.	7-26-31
32	6394	2,500	1133 Faunce St.	8-13-31
33	6395	15,000	300 S. Easton Road, Willow Grove.	8-23-31
34	6396	9,000	SEs High School Rd., NE Marvin Rd., Elkins Park	8-9-31
35	6397	4,000	3357 St. Vincent St.	7-26-31
36	6398	2,000	2124 Spencer St.	7-2-31
37	6399	5,000	Ns Chelten Ave. E Old York Rd.	8-27-31
40	6402	2,000	3031 N. Bonsall St.	7-17-31
41	6463	20,000	Lot 33 & NW ½ Lot No. 32, Noble Hills, Pa.	9-15-31
42	6495	7,000	Lot No. 74, Penrose Homestead, Elkins Park, Pa.	1-13-28
43	6526	2,500	1221 W. Atlantic St.	9-21-31
44	6464	8,000	6506 E. Rising Sun Ave.	9-17-31

Mtg. Nos.	Title Nos.	Amounts	Premises	Due Dates
45	6527	4,500	78 E. Bringhurst St. 9-10-31	
46	6528	3,500	5928 Webster St. 9-1-31	
47	6547	3,000	423 Passmore St. 9-28-31	
48	6548	3,000	425 Passmore St. 9-28-31	
49	6549	3,000	427 Passmore St. 9-28-31	
50	6711	3,000	2836 N. 27th St. 11-28-32	
51	6722	1,500	931 Edgeley St. 10-19-31	
52	6723	20,000	32 East Armat St. 9-12-31	
53	6724	4,000	312 Chandler St. 11-26-31	
54	6726	3,000	8431 High School Road, Elkins Park, Pa. 9-17-32	
55	6727	3,000	8435 High School Road, Elkins Park, Pa. 12-16-29	
59	6733	3,800	3310 St. Vincent St. 10-10-31	
61	6732	3,500	4519 McKinley St. 10-4-31	
62	6729	3,000	SWs St. Vincent St. SE Summerdale Ave 12-16-29	
63	6776	15,000	514 Chelten Ave., Jenkintown....11-1-31	
64	6777	2,000	2355 N. Garnet St. 10-24-31	
65	6778	9,000	1421 W. Westmoreland St.......10-22-31	
66	6779	2,200	2311 N. Garnet St. 10-22-31	
67	6780	3,500	7212 Lawndale Ave. 10-24-31	
68	6781	12,000	1411 Hunting Park Ave.........10-26-31	
69	6782	3,500	7248 Tabor St. 9-3-31	
70	6783	3,500	2231 N. Uber St. 10-23-31	
71	6651	6,000	York & Keith Rds., Highland Farms Tract, Abington Twp., Montg. Co. 9-25-28	
72	6806	15,000	NWs Cadwalader Ave., NE Waring Road 10-27-31	
73	6882	5,500	6407 Rising Sun Ave. 9-23-31	
74	6903	8,000	117 York Road, Hatboro, Pa.....11-16-31	
75	6904	8,000	115 York Road, Hatboro, Pa.....11-16-31	
76	6905	1,500	467 Devereaux St. 11-9-31	
77	6906	3,000	4277 Leidy Ave. 11-14-31	
79	6908	6,000	Weisel Road lead. from Limekiln Pike to Bristol R., Warrington Twp. 11-1-31	
80	6909	3,800	3320 St. Vincent St. 11-14-31	
81	6910	3,500	6221 Hasbrook St. 11-15-31	
82	6911	3,500	473 Devereaux St. 11-15-31	
83	6912	6,000	SEs Evergreen Rd., SW of Jenkintown Road 11-13-31	
84	6913	3,000	5949 Elsinore St. 11-19-31	
85	6914	3,000	5957 Elsinore St. 11-19-31	
86	6915	3,000	5961 Elsinore St. 11-19-31	
89	7150	25,000	NWs Sumac St. NE Cor. Righter & Sumac 11-24-31	
90	7151	20,000	3401 N. 16th St. 11-23-31	
91	7152	3,500	7531 Lawndale Ave. 12-4-31	
92	7153	15,000	Es 5th St. & Ss Spencer Sts.....3-30-31	
93	7154	1,600	1919 Airdrie St. 10-14-31	

Mtg. Nos.	Title Nos.	Amounts	Premises	Due Dates
94	7155	6,000	6888 N. 20th St. 11-21-31	
95	7156	3,800	3337 St. Vincent St. 9-10-31	
96	7157	3,000	305 Corinthian Ave., Overlook Hill, Willow Grove, Pa. 12-8-31	
97	7158	12,000	SW Cor. Jenkintown & Evergreen Rds., Jenkintown, Pa...12-7-31	
100	7161	9,000	8237 Manor Road, Elkins Park..12-7-31	
101	7331	4,000	3459 Princeton Ave. 1-4-32	
102	7332	8,000	7214 Frankford Ave. 1-3-32	
103	7333	4,000	337 Hellerman St. 11-11-31	
104	7336	12,000	148-150 W. Girard Ave. 12-27-31	
105	7337	15,000	NE Cor. 5th & Fern Sts. 3-30-31	
106	7347	30,000	SEs Haines St. SW of Rodney St. 1-4-34	
107	7356	3,000	7215 Oak Ave. 10-13-31	
108	7355	6,500	143 W. Wyoming Ave. 1-11-32	
109	7357	3,000	5345 Bellfield Ave. 1-3-32	
110	7358	5,000	435 Sanger St. (now Sentner St.)1-11-32	
111	7029	3,000	206 W. Widener St. 2-15-32	
112	5030	3,200	4015 Teesdale St. 1-26-32	
113	5031	3,200	4017 Teesdale St. 1-26-32	
114	5039	3,200	4033 Teesdale St. 1-26-32	
115	5040	3,200	4035 Teesdale St. 1-26-32	
116	5041	3,200	4037 Teesdale St. 1-26-32	
117	5042	3,200	4039 Teesdale St. 1-26-32	
118	5043	3,200	4041 Teesdale St. '..............1-26-32	
119	5044	3,200	4043 Teesdale St. 1-26-32	
120	5053	3,200	4061 Teesdale St. 1-26-32	
121	5045	3,200	4045 Teesdale St. 1-26-32	
122	5046	3,200	4047 Teesdale St. 1-26-32	
123	5047	3.200	4049 Teesdale St. 1-26-32	
124	5048	3,200	4051 Teesdale St. 1-26-32	
125	5049	3,200	4053 Teesdale St. 1-26-32	
126	5050	3,200	4055 Teesdale St. 1-26-32	
127	5051	3,200	4057 Teesdale St. 1-26-32	
128	5054	3,600	4063 Teesdale St. 1-26-32	
129	7015	12.000	1622 W. Erie Ave. 1-19-32	
130	7017	3,000	184 W. Fern St. 8-23-32	
131	7023	3,000	258 W. Linton St. 3-10-32	
132	7024	3,000	223 W. Widener St. 2-14-32	
133	5170	4,000	601 Godfrey Ave. 3-16-32	
134	5174	3,500	609 Godfrey Ave. 3-16-32	
135	5175	3,500	611 Godfrey Ave. 3-16-32	
136	5176	3.500	613 Godfrey Ave. 3-16-32	
137	5177	3,500	615 Godfrey Ave. 3-16-32	
138	5178	3,500	617 Godfrey Ave. 3-16-32	
139	5179	3,500	619 Godfrey Ave. 3-16-32	
140	5180	3,500	621 Godfrey Ave. 3-16-32	
141	5181	3,500	623 Godfrey Ave. 3-16-32	
142	5182	3.500	625 Godfrey Ave. 3-16-32	
143	5183	3,500	627 Godfrey Ave. ....:3-16-32	
144	5184	3,500	629 Godfrey Ave. 3-16-32	
145	5185	3,500	631 Godfrey Ave. 3-16-32	

Mtg. Nos.	Title Nos.	Amounts	Premises	Due Dates
146	5186	3,500	633 Godfrey Ave.	3-16-32
147	5187	3,500	635 Godfrey Ave.	3-16-32
148	5188	3,500	637 Godfrey Ave.	3-16-32
149	5189	3,500	639 Godfrey Ave.	3-16-32
150	5190	3,500	641 Godfrey Ave.	3-16-32
151	5191	3,500	643 Godfrey Ave.	3-16-32
152	5192	3,500	645 Godfrey Ave.	3-16-32
153	5193	3,500	647 Godfrey Ave.	3-16-32
154	5194	3,500	649 Godfrey Ave.	3-16-32
155	5195	3,500	651 Godfrey Ave.	3-16-32
156	5196	3,500	653 Godfrey Ave.	3-16-32
157	5197	3,500	655 Godfrey Ave.	3-16-32
158	5198	3,500	657 Godfrey Ave.	3-16-32
159	5199	4,000	659 Godfrey Ave.	3-16-32
160	7031	25,000	Waverly Rd., NW Mill Road	5-15-30
161	7301	40,000	5809-11 Torresdale Ave.	12-19-31
162	7327	3,000	531 E. Godfrey Ave.	12-26-31
163	7328	12,000	1111 Stratford Ave.	12-27-31
164	7329	5,000	2445 W. Columbia Ave.	12-19-31
165	7330	9,000	6529 Rising Sun Ave.	1-5-32
166	7014	3,000	417 W. Cumberland St.	11-8-31
167	7020	3,000	218 W. Linton St.	3-26-32
168	7021	3,000	230 Linton St.	3-19-32
169	7030	3,000	243 W. Widener St.	2-14-32
170	7028	2,900	227 W. Widener St.	3-6-32
171	7338	15,000	1004-66th Ave., North	12-26-31
172	7396	3,500	517 Ryers Ave.	1-25-32
173	7431	3,000	2514 W. Somerset St.	12-21-31
174	7432	4,000	5415 Tacoma St.	1-26-32
175	7433	10,000	2915 N. 22d St.	2-17-32
178	7436	3,600	7611 Verree Ave.	1-15-32
179	7437	20,000	22-24 Park Ave., Upper Darby Twp.	1-13-32
180	7016	3,000	4704 N. Lawrence St.	5-9-32
181	7018	3,000	6032 N. Phillip St.	3-18-32
182	7022	3,000	232 Linton St.	3-19-32
183	7025	3,000	240 W. Widener St.	3-26-32
184	7027	2,900	229 W. Widener St.	3-6-30
185	7045	3,000	208 Linton St.	4-1-32
186	7564	5,000	620 Levick St.	12-11-31
187	7565	3,500	3429 Englewood St.	2-20-32
188	7566	3,800	3353 St. Vincent St.	1-29-32
189	7567	10,000	5901 Belden St.	2-6-32
190	7568	7,500	Lots Nos. 215, 16, 17 Somerton Gardens	2-14-32
191	7569	12,000	7116 Old York Road	2-17-32
192	7570	3,000	2505 N. 18th St.	3-25-31
193	7667	45,000	5528 Wayne Ave.	2-16-32
194	7398	10,000	2612 W. Lehigh Ave.	3-6-32
195	5079	3,200	4058 Teesdale St.	1-26-32
197	5055	3,200	4010 Teesdale St.	1-26-32
198	5056	3,200	4012 Teesdale St.	1-26-32
199	5057	3,200	4014 Teesdale St.	1-26-32
200	5066	3,200	4032 Teesdale St.	1-26-32

Mtg. Nos.	Title Nos.	Amounts	Premises	Due Dates
201	5067	3,200	4034 Teesdale St.	1-26-32
202	5069	3,200	4038 Teesdale St.	1-26-32
203	5070	3,200	4040 Teesdale St.	1-26-32
204	5071	3,200	4042 Teesdale St.	1-26-32
205	5072	3,200	4044 Teesdale St.	1-26-32
206	5073	3,200	4046 Teesdale St.	1-26-32
207	5074	3,200	4048 Teesdale St.	1-26-32
208	5075	3,200	4050 Teesdale St.	1-26-32
209	5076	3,200	4052 Teesdale St.	1-26-32
210	5078	3,200	4056 Teesdale St.	1-26-32
211	5077	3,200	4054 Teesdale St.	1-26-32
212	7668	3,300	2919 Hale St.	12-12-31
213	7669	3,300	2921 Hale St.	12-12-31
214	7670	3,300	2917 Hale St.	12-12-31
215	7671	3,300	2925 Hale St.	12-12-31
216	7672	3,300	2923 Hale St.	12-12-31
217	8064	13,000	6801 Marshall Road	3-14-32
218	8065	3,000	5952 Elsinore St.	2-5-32
219	8066	2,500	2552 N. Corlies St.	3-22-32
220	8067	3,000	2009 Norris St.	1-28-32
221	8068	3,000	5959 Elsinore St.	3-30-32
222	8069	3,000	618 E. Brill St.	3-27-32
223	8070	2,000	2269 N. Colorado St.	2-21-32
224	8071	1,400	2862 N. Stillman St.	2-23-32
225	8072	3,000	658 E. Brill St.	3-27-32
226	8073	2,200	2605 N. Douglass St.	2-17-32
227	8074	3,000	622 E. Brill St.	3-27-32
228	8075	3,000	5945 Elsinore St.	3-30-32
229	8076	3,500	6429 Lawndale Ave.	2-15-32
230	8077	3,500	3436 Englewood St.	3-5-32
231	8078	3,500	2204 N. 18th St.	3-20-32
232	8079	3,000	602 E. Brill St.	2-25-32
233	8080	4,000	924 W. Rockland St.	3-18-32
234	8081	18,000	5300 Wayne Ave.	4-11-32
235	7013	15 000	2642 Germantown Ave.	4-24-32
236	7019	2,000	263 Linton St.	4-18-32
249	8117	500,000	1327-29-31-33 Airdrie St. (3701-3 N. Broad)	5-10-30
250	8280	3,000	610 E. Brill St.	5-18-32
251	8286	5,000	SW Cor. Rhawn & Ridgway Sts.	5-9-32
252	8287	2 500	2759 N. Croskey St.	5-21-32
253	8288	3,000	616 E. Brill St.	5-10-32
254	8289	2,500	7907 Queen St.	5-20-32
255	8290	2,500	1029 Pleasant St.	5-20-32
256	8291	2,500	1031 Pleasant St.	5-20-32
257	8292	4,000	3427 Princeton Ave.	5-28-32
258	8293	2 200	2843 N. Ringgold St.	5-25-32
259	8294	3,800	3425 Princeton Ave.	5-17-32
260	8295	3,500	36 Robbins Ave.	5-6-32
261	8296	3,000	3228 N. Carlisle St.	5-28-32
262	8297	10,000	20 W. Queen Lane	5-24-32
263	8298	3 000	626 E. Brill St.	5-25-32
264	8309	3,000	6058 Beechwood St.	4-25-32
265	8310	3,000	6056 Beechwood St.	4-25-32

Mtg. Nos.	Title Nos.	Amounts	Premises	Due Dates
266	8311	3,000	6054 Beechwood St.	4-25-32
267	8312	2,500	6128 Palmetto St.	5-27-32
268	8313	4 000	3405 Princeton Ave.	5-25-32
269	8194	5,000	224 Forest Ave., Narberth	1-24-32
270	8195	8,000	6631 Chew St.	5-29-32
271	8196	8,000	6633 Chew St.	5-29-32
272	8197	2,000	2404 N. 26th St.	5-15-32
273	8198	10,000	2040-42-44-46 Germantown Ave.	5-13-32
274	8217	2,000	5127 Shelton St.	5-6-32
275	8218	4,000	7526 Tabor Ave.	5-14-32
276	8681	4,000	3451 Princeton Ave.	6-4-32
277	8682	2,000	2764 N. 22d St.	6-4-32
278	8683	15,000	3300-02 Kensington Ave.	6-12-32
279	8684	3,000	461-63 E. Girard Ave.	6-11-32
280	8685	2,000	2248 W. Huntingdon St.	6-8-32
281	8686	5,500	6064 N. 21st St.	6-7-32
282	8687	3,800	3435 Princeton Ave.	7-1-32
283	8688	3,800	3445 Princeton Ave.	5-14-32
284	8689	14,000	SEs Easton Rd. & SWc Toxony Ave.	2-25-33
285	8690	3,000	656 E. Brill St.	6-7-32
286	8691	20,000	2943-45 Kensington Ave.	6-1-32
288	8693	3,500	1942 Spencer St.	4-23-32
289	8694	10,000	535 E. Church Rd., Elkins Park	10-29-31
290	8695	10,000	537 E. Church Rd., Elkins Park	10-29-31
291	8696	12,000	Lot No. 25, Penrose Homestead	6-11-32
292	9606	5,500	6520 N. 16th St.	5-20-32
293	9607	5,500	6167 Oakley St.	4-7-32
294	9608	5.500	3470 Bowman St.	4-15-32
295	8176	5,200	3430 Midvale Ave.	5-20-34
296	9610	5,000	2002 Haines St.	5-23-32
297	9611	5,000	614 Boyer Road, Rowland Park	8-14-32
298	9612	4,600	401 Sanger St.	1-3-32
299	9613	4.500	120 W. Tabor Road	8-8-32
300	9614	4,500	600 E. Brill St.	10-11-32
302	9616	4,000	4239 Cottman St.	9-24-32
303	9617	4,000	4237 Cottman St.	10-16-32
304	9618	4,000	4235 Cottman St.	9-13-32
305	5762	3,500	5949 Bingham St.	8-30-32
306	5749	3 500	5923 Bingham St.	8-30-32
307	5746	3,500	5917 Bingham St.	8-30-32
308	9622	3,500	555½ Cheltenham Ave.	5-28-31
309	9623	18,000	5340 Germantown Ave.	8-12-32
310	9624	11,000	213 Evergreen Rd., Jenkintown Manor	9-25-32
311	9625	9,000	NWs Ogontz Ave., SW Manor Road	10-5-32
312	9626	9,000	5900-02-04 Kemble Ave.	9-20-32
313	9627	8,000	6236 Hasbrook Ave.	8-7-32
314	9628	7,200	2853-55 Oakdale St.	5-17-32
315	9629	6,000	600 E. Woodlawn Ave.	9-3-32
316	9630	6,000	NW cor. Buxmont St. & Over-hill Road	10-10-32

Mtg. Nos.	Title Nos.	Amounts	Premises	Due Dates
317	9841	35,000	SW Cor. Wellington Road & Sunset Ave., Jenkintown, Pa.	2-21-30
318	10081	7,000	4149 N. Broad St.	10-11-29
319	10082	5,000	2004 Haines St.	5-23-32
320	10083	3,800	3443 Princeton Ave.	4-29-32
321	10084	3,000	612 Brill St.	12-21-31
322	10085	3,000	614 E. Brill St.	7-31-32
323	10086	4,200	525 E. Vankirk St.	8-17-32
324	10087	3,300	532 Fanshawe St.	9-23-29
325	10088	4,000	4215 Cottman St.	10-19-32
326	10089	4,000	4225 Cottman St.	10-16-32
327	10090	18,000	711 Chelten Ave.	4-16-32
328	10091	4 000	1310 Butler St.	11-20-32
329	10092	12,000	231-33 Coulter St.	11-8-32
330	10093	4,500	2226 N. 13th St.	7-6-31
331	10094	4,000	4221 Cottman St.	9-24-32
332	10095	9,000	4630 N. 5th St.	7-12-32
333	10096	8,000	2208-10 Hunting Park Ave.	10-2-32
334	10097	3 000	5961 Bingham St.	8-30-32
335	10098	7,500	5900 N. 21st St.	8-25-32
336	10099	6,000	213 Church Road, Elkins Park	10-14-32
337	10100	4,000	755 E. Herkness St.	9-4-32
338	10101	7,500	NE Cor. 16th & McKean Sts.	8-5-32
339	10106	3.000	4217 Stirling St.	9-3-32
340	10104	3,000	4215 Stirling St.	7-26-32
341	10103	3,000	4209 Stirling St.	8-30-32

2,228,900

In Safe Deposit Box Fidelity-Philadelphia Trust Co.

800   Participating Trust Certificates, property in Park Co., Montana, 6%.

3,500   Wm. Hoppe, 17 W. 106th St., New York City.

$2,233,200   Total Mortgages Owned.

Philadelphia, October 14, 1930.

We have examined the mortgages owned by the Board of Ministerial Pensions & Relief of the United Lutheran Church in America at June 30, 1930, and we certify that the foregoing schedule of mortgages, aggregating $2,233,200, is in accordance with the books of account and is correct.

LYBRAND, ROSS BROS. & MONTGOMERY,
Accountants and Auditors.

In connection with the presentation of the report, Mr. Peter P. Hagan, Treasurer; Paul F. Meyers, Esq., President, and the Hon. Henry W. Harter, addressed the Convention.

The recommendation was adopted.

The report of the auditors was accepted.

The Convention voted an expression of its appreciation to Mr. Peter P. Hagan for his services as Treasurer.

The Rev. James F. Lambert presented the report of the Necrologist as follows:

NECROLOGY REPORT

Material for biographies of eighty-eight ministers, who died during the biennium closed July the first, has been compiled and shall be deposited in the library at Gettysburg Seminary, Gettysburg, Pa., and the Krauth Memorial Library in Mt. Airy, Philadelphia, Pa.

Of laymen, reported outstanding by virtue of services rendered to the Church at large, there are fifteen, and of lay-women six.

Necrologists of synods are importuned annually for data on the lives of their deceased brethren, and a final check-up is asked for before the list for the biennium is submitted for the bulletin.

Name	Born Where	Born When	Ordained When	Synod at Death	Died Where	Died When	Where Buried	Age Y	Age M	Age D	Years of Service
Adams, Samuel S.	Somerset, Pa.	May 4, 1857	1886	Al.	Springfield, O.	Nov. 11, 1929	Springfield, O.	72	6	7	40
Aue, Carl G., D.D.	Richmond, Ind.	Apr. 23, 1871	1895	Id.	Louisville, Ky.	Aug. 27, 1929	Yellow Springs, O.	58	4	4	34
Bearden, George S.	Columbia, S.C.	June 29, 1868	1895	SC.	Columbia, S.C.	Dec. 5, 1928	Columbia, S.C.	60	7	6	32
Beck, William McC.	Near Lancaster, O.	July 28, 1855	1881	Il.	Sedgewickville, Mo.	Mar. 24, 1929	Springfield, O.	69	7	26	33
Bell, Albert, D.D.	Leitersburg, Md.	Sept. 28, 1855	1881	WP.	Washington, D.C.	Feb. 27, 1930	Gettysburg, Pa.	74	4	29	46
Boethel, Richard R. F.	Kreibau, Silesia	Oct. 7, 1849	1875	Pg.	Cleveland, O.	Feb. 7, 1930	Mansfield, O.	80	4	0	53
Bowers, Andrew J., D.D.	Helena, S.C.	Oct. 1, 1860	1883	Ga.	Newberry, S.C.	June 14, 1930	Newberry, S.C.	69	8	13	44
Brackebusch, Carl E. J. F.	Berkum, Germany	Sept. 26, 1860	1888	Cn.	Waterloo, Cn.	Nov. 15, 1929	Waterloo, O.	69	1	19	40
Conder, Irenaeus	Union County, Va.	Oct. 17, 1832	1861	Va.	McGaheysville, Va.	Aug. 31, 1928	McGaheysville, Va.	95	11	14	66
Corleis, Harry G.	Brooklyn, N.Y.	Jan. 18, 1893	1916	NY.	Brooklyn, N.Y.	Sept. 17, 1928	Brooklyn, N.Y.	35	7	29	12
Cox, George H., D.D.	Boston, Mass.	Aug. 9, 1838	1872	NC.	Salisbury, N.C.	Dec. —, 1928	Mt. Pleasant, N.C.	90	3	28	56
Crickenberger, David P. T.	Port Republic, Va.	About 1859	1884	WV.	Grafton, W. Va.	July 22, 1929	Grafton, W. Va.	About 70 yrs.			45
Cronk, Eli C., D.D.	Floyd, Va.	Sept. 15, 1864	1895	Va.	New York, N.Y.	Feb. 25, 1929	Richmond, Va.	64	4	29	34
Cross, William Morgan	Emmitsburg, Md.	Sept. 25, 1871	1897	WP.	Greencastle, Pa.	July 14, 1928	Greencastle, Pa.	56	9	19	8
Dattan, Hermann G., D.D.	Rudensdorf, Germany	Jan. 25, 1853	1875	NY.	Syracuse, N.Y.	Sept. 14, 1928	Syracuse, N.Y.	75	7	28	50
Deck, Luther B.	Chester Springs, Pa.	Sept. 12, 1883	1908	Il.	Vancouver, Wash.	Apr. 10, 1930	Vancouver, Wash.	46	6	22	22
Doering, Emil W.	Niedeck, Germany	Sept. 2, 1886	1915	Pt.	Vandalia, Ill.	Dec. 24, 1929	Vandalia, Ill.	43	3	15	14
Earnheart, Turner	Salisbury, N.C.	Nov. 21, 1894	1918	Tx.	Oklahoma City, Okla.	Apr. 17, 1930	Oklahoma City, Okla.	35	4	26	12
Eberhardt, Frank D., B.D.	Jersey City, N.J.	May 21, 1866	1893	PM.	Cuero, Tx.	Jan. 17, 1930	Cuero, Tx.	62	7	26	35
Ettwein, Oliver F.	Northampton Co., Pa.	Jan. 1, 1858	1880	Cf.	Gilbert, Pa.	Nov. 29, 1928	Moorestown, Pa.	72	8	16	49
Feix, Henry S.	Cannelton, Ind.	May 8, 1850	1873	Id.	San Francisco, Cal.	Jan. 17, 1930	San Francisco, Cal.	68	8	10	56
Fenner, Harlan K., D.D.	Mansfield, O.	Apr. 8, 1862	1891	Sq.	Louisville, Ky.	Jan. —, 1929	Selinsgrove, Pa.	66	4	25	36
Fetterolf, Robert F.	Spring Mills, Pa.	Sept. 16, 1852	1880	PM.	Selinsgrove, Pa.	Sept. 3, 1928	Philadelphia, Pa.	71	9	18	37
Fluck, John F. C.	Telford, Pa.	Dec. 4, 1852	1883	Va.	Telford, Pa.	July 4, 1928	Morristown, Tenn.	76	4	29	46
Graichen, William G.	Baltimore, Md.	Mar. 17, 1856	1895	O.	Morristown, Tenn.	May 3, 1929	Darrtown, O.	74	1	20	35
Guiney, James B.	Franklin, Pa.	Nov. 18, 1857	1895	Va.	Darrtown, O.	Apr. 27, 1930	Brooklyn, N.Y.	72			39
Hasskarl, Gottlieb C. H., Ph.D., C.D.L.	East Eden, N.Y.	Aug. 31, 1851	1889	Il.	Brooklyn, N.Y.	Aug. 2, 1929	Joliet, Ill.	78	11	8	39
Heilman, Howard M., D.D.	Abbottstown, Pa.	Nov. 18, 1856	1889	Il.	Joliet, Ill.	Oct. 26, 1928	Baltimore, Md.	78	4	4	51
Heilman, Philip A., D.D.	Muncy Station, Pa.	Aug. 31, 1852	1878	PM.	Baltimore, Md.	Dec. 28, 1929	Bethlehem, Pa.	76	6	7	41
Hemsath, Charles H.	Near White Haven, Pa.	Mar. 31, 1858	1878	NY.	Bethlehem, Pa.	Aug. 1, 1929	Brooklyn, N.Y.	70	6	24	50
Heischman, John J. P., D.D.	Lyons, N.Y.	Jan. 7, 1858	1879	NY.	Brooklyn, N.Y.	Mar. 1, 1929	Carthage, Ill.	65	9	11	
Holtgreve, Paul B., D.D.	Beaufort, Mo.	Aug. 26, 1864	1888	Pm.	Peoria, Ill.	Nov. 29, 1930	Wilmington, Del.	85	10	29	55
Isenschmid, Paul, M.D.	Zweisimmen, Switz.	July 31, 1844	1869	PM.	Wilmington, Del.	June 13, 1930	Petawawa, Cn.	About 62 yrs.			
Jannau, Ivan C.	Russia	July 16, 1870	1925	Cn.	Petawawa, Cn.	Apr. 13, 1930	Chicago, Ill.	59	2	28	34
Kaltschuk, Albert A.	Chicago, Ill.	July 1, 1838	1895	Wg.	Chicago, Ill.	Oct. 13, 1929	Chicago, Ill.	91	9	15	64
Kemerer, Duncan McV., D.D.	Schellsburg, Pa.	Aug. 7, 1838	1865	Pg.	Pittsburgh, Pa.	May 22, 1930	New Rumley, O.	79	8	17	49
Kiefer, Cornelius J., D.D.	Smithville, O.	Apr. 12, 1849	1879	O.	Annapolis, Md.	Dec. 29, 1928	Springfield, O.	80	3	17	43
Kistler, John L., D.D.	Icksburg, Pa.	Sept. 25, 1849	1877	NY.	Gettysburg, Pa.	Jan. 2, 1930	Hartwick Sem., N.Y.	85	3	0	50
Koser, David T., D.D.	Shippensburg, Pa.	Mar. 7, 1845	1874	WP.	Gettysburg, Pa.	Apr. —, 1930	Gettysburg, Pa.	85	1	1	50
Kreps, Muller O. J., D.D.	Lexington Co., S.C.	Dec. 29, 1857	1883	SC.	Columbia, S.C.	Feb. 18, 1929	Columbia, S.C.	71	1	19	45
Kronsbein, William R.	Klekevitz, Germany	Jan. 7, 1858	1895	Wg.	Campbell Hill, Ill.	July —, 1928					
Krueger, Carl, D.D.		Jan. 7, 1858	1886	NY.	New York, N.Y.	Nov. 23, 1929	Stratford, Conn.	71	10	16	40

Name	Born Where	Born When	Or-dained	Synod at Death	Died Where	Died When	Where Buried	Age Y	Age M	Age D	Years of Service
Lenker, John N., D.D.	Sunbury, Pa.	Nov. 28, 1858	1880	NW	Minneapolis, Minn.	May 16, 1929	Minneapolis, Minn.	70	5	18	49
Lindenstruth, Louis, D.D.	Philadelphia, Pa.	June , 1853	1877	PM	Wilkes-Barre, Pa.	Jan. , 1930	Wilkes-Barre, Pa.	76	6	17	53
Long, Simon P., D.D., L.L.D.	McZena, O.	Oct. 7, 1860	1886	Il.	Chicago, Ill.	Jan. 3, 1929	Chicago, Ill.	68	2	26	43
Lundh, Hans, B.S., B.D.	Osterkorsberga, Swd.	Oct. 16, 1901	1929	Ga.	Chicago, Ill.	June 15, 1930	Osterkorsberga, Swd.	28	7	29	1
Maclaughlin, Charles P., D.D.	Pittsburgh, Pa.	Mar. 28, 1870	1900	Ga.	Atlanta, Ga.	Nov. 13, 1928	Atlanta, Ga.	58	7	15	28
Mattern, John W.	Allentown, Pa.	Dec. 30, 1847	1878	PM	Allentown, Pa.	Apr. 24, 1930	Allentown, Pa.	82	3	24	40
McLinn, Milton E., D.D.	Thompsontown, Pa.	Sept. 20, 1848	1886	EP	Princeton, N.J.	Jan. 15, 1929	Near Narberth, Pa.	80	3	25	42
Mehrkam, A. Milles, Ph.D.	Little Gap, Pa.	Mar. 23, 1862	1888	PM	Columbia, Pa.	Dec. 27, 1928	Columbia, Pa.	66	9	19	40
Melchior, Oliver H.	Bucks County, Pa.	Dec. 23, 1848	1879	EP	Springtown, Pa.	Sept. 7, 1928	Durham, Pa.	79	8	4	49
Melville, Frederick J.	Newark, N.J.	Sept. 13, 1896	1921	NY	White Plains, N.Y.	Mar. 12, 1930	Middle Village, N.Y.	33	5	29	9
Meyer, John H., D.D.	Germany	Aug. 30, 1874	1902	NY	Jersey City, N.J.	July 6, 1929	Gettysburg, Pa.	54	10	6	27
Minkus, Oscar F.	Bethen, Germany	Mar. 5, 1863		NY	Allentown, Pa.	Mar. 29, 1929	Allentown, Pa.	66	0	24	
Miller, Charles D., Ph.D.	Germano, O.	Oct. 26, 1879	1907	O.	Cleveland, O.	Aug. 20, 1929	Germano, O.	49	9	24	22
Miller, J. C.	Millertown, Tenn.	Sept. 28, 1851	1874	Fl.	Asheville, N.C.	July 26, 1929	Near Knoxville, Tenn.	77	10	18	
Mullaney, James I., B.D.	Utica, N.Y.	Aug. 20, 1865	1892	Id.	Near Corydon, Ind.	Mar. 2, 1929	Near Urbana, O.	63	4	12	31
Patterson, Richard S., D.D.	Concord, N.C.	Aug. , 1866	1892	Md.	Westminster, Md.	Feb. 26, 1930	Gettysburg, Pa.	63			38
Paules, Howard S.	Slatedale, Pa.	Feb. 16, 1884	1911	PM	Lansdale, Pa.	Sept. 11, 1928	Lansdale, Pa.	44	6	25	17
Peterson, Daniel W.	Otterndorf, Germany	Dec. 31, 1842	1875	NY	Hollis, L.I.	Apr. 7, 1929	Middle Village, N.Y.	86	3	6	54
Puhl, Max O., D.D.	Berlin, Germany	June 5, 1857	1887	Md.	Silver Springs, Md.	May 16, 1929	Lancaster, Pa.	71	11	1	42
Rabbow, C. B.	Nuernberg, Bavaria	Oct. 6, 1868	1895	NY	Port Chester, N.Y.	July 16, 1930	Brooklyn, N.Y.	60	9	10	34
Ramer, Adam L., Ph.D.	Near Kutztown, Pa.	Jan. 5, 1867	1893	PM	Camden, N.J.	Mar. 8, 1929	Allentown, Pa.	62	2	3	34
Reed, John K.	Lehighton, Pa.	Mar. 16, 1856	1893	Ms.	Algona, Ia.	May 11, 1930	Sterling, Ill.	74	2	10	37
Rehrig, Wilson M., Ph.D.	Lehighton, Pa.	Nov. 16, 1853	1882	PM	Mauch Chunk, Pa.	Dec. 23, 1929	Mauch Chunk, Pa.	75	0	22	46
Reissig, F. Ernst.	Saxony, Germany	Nov. 14, 1847	1883	NY	East Potter, N.Y.	May 9, 1929	East Potter, N.Y.	81	6	9	46
Richard, Asa.	Frederick Co., Va.	Oct. 10, 1844	1887	Va.	Chambersburg, Pa.	May 8, 1930	Winchester, Va.	85	6	28	28
Rinker, Michael F.	Near Gettysburg, Pa.	Jan. 10, 1841	1860	Cf.	Los Angeles, Cal.	Apr. 22, 1930	Glendale, Cal.	89	2	4	
Rudisill, Martin L.	Clarion Co., Pa.	June 18, 1846	1875	WP	Two Taverns, Pa.	Aug. 12, 1928	Two Taverns, Pa.	82	1	25	11
Scheffer, John A.	Ettensdadt, Germany	Oct. 17, 1858	1879	PM	Knox, Pa.	Oct. 20, 1928	Allentown, Pa.	70	0	10	21
Schmidtkonz, Adam	Nr. Connersville, Ind.	Apr. 22, 1841	1869	WP	Kingston, N.Y.	Aug. 30, 1928	Kingston, N.Y.	88	4	8	49
Scholl, George, D.D.	Near Waterville, Kan.	Dec. 10, 1859	1906	Md.	Baltimore, Md.	Dec. 25, 1928	Baltimore, Md.	69	0	15	60
Shirck, Frederick R.	Haley, Tenn.	Aug. 10, 1859	1888	Mh.	Near Bippus, Ind.	Apr. 6, 1930	Fort Wayne, Ind.	70	7	26	22
Slater, Samuel E., D.D.	Near Gettysburg, Pa.	Jan. 29, 1846	1875	Md.	Washington, D.C.	Feb. 16, 1929	Washington, D.C.	83	0	17	42
Slaybaugh, George H.	Boliver, O.	Dec. 21, 1862	1893	O.	Boliver, O.	Apr. 6, 1930	Boliver, O.	67	3	15	54
Smith, Gideon C., D.D.	Salem, Pa.	Apr. 4, 1859	1872	EP	Columbus, O.	Apr. 27, 1930	Columbus, O.	67	0	23	36
Snyder, John.			1900	EP	Selinsgrove, Pa.	Mar. 19, 1927	Selinsgrove, Pa.				27
Snyder, M. Luther.	Seward, N.Y.	Nov. 23, 1847	1874	NV	Liverpool, Pa.	Apr. 4, 1930	Fort Plains, N.Y.	82	11	16	54
Strail, Hammie A.	Rhinebeck, N.Y.	June 24, 1848	1876	NV	New York, N.Y.	Apr. , 1930	New York, N.Y.	81	7	0	41
Traver, Chester H., D.D.	Clinton, N.Y.	Jan. 24, 1847	1873	NV	Clinton, N.Y.	June 29, 1929	Germantown, N.Y.	83	0	6	57
Traver, William E.	Maxatawney, Pa.	May 30, 1862	1889	NV	Bechtelsville, Pa.	Jan. 31, 1930	Lobach's, Pa.	67	0	5	41
Warmkessel, Henry W.	Venango Co., Pa.	Apr. 30, 1853	1876	Pg.	Renovo, Pa.	Mar. 27, 1930	Renovo, Pa.	76	10	7	53
Weicksel, Luther M. C.	Wildberg, Germany	Apr. 13, 1857	1882	PM	Trenton, N.J.	Sept. 3, 1929	Trenton, N.J.	71	8	24	47
Wendel, J. H. A., D.O.						Jan. 6, 1929					

Name	Born — Where	Born — When	Ordained	Synod at Death	Died — Where	Died — When	Where Buried	Age Y	M	D	Years of Service
Whitman, N. A.	Asterode, Germany	Sept. 9, 1880	1878	Id.	Pine Bluff, Ark.	July 2, 1926	Syracuse, N. Y.	49	7	11	23
Wittekind, John	Belleville, Pa.	July 12, 1872	1907	NY	Syracuse, N. Y.	Apr. 20, 1930		56	6	19	25
Young, Levi P., D.D.			1904	Al.	Elk Lick, Pa.	Feb. 1, 1929	Elk Lick, Pa.				
Zerger, James E., D.D.	Columbia, Pa.	Nov. 3, 1858	1885	Id.	Louisville, Ky.	June 23, 1929	Louisville, Ky.	70	6	22	38
Laymen											
Allen, Charles S., Prof.	Bloomsburg, N. J.	June 1, 1898		PM	Saranac Lake, N. Y.	Dec. 23, 1929	Easton, Pa.	31	6	22	
Boschen, George D.	New York, N. Y.	Dec. 24, 1869		NY	Englewood, N. J.	June 30, 1929	Woodlawn, N. Y.	59	6	6	
Capplemann, John D., Esq.	Walhalla, S. C.	July 24, 1847		SC	Charleston, S. C.	Dec. 13, 1929	Walhalla, S. C.	82	10	19	
Daub, William J.	Germany.	Jan. 19, 1848		PM	Easton, Pa.	Dec. 16, 1928	Easton, Pa.	80	10	27	
Dinkey, John.	Easton, Pa.	Oct. 16, 1854		NY	Rochester, N. Y.	Jan. 23, 1930	Rochester, N. Y.	75	3	7	
Glatfelter, William L.	Spring Grove, Pa.	Apr. 27, 1865		WP	Pinehurst, N. C.	Apr. 20, 1930	Spring Grove, Pa.	64	11	23	
Heilig, James D.	Rowan Co., N. C.	Nov. 6, 1857		NC	Salisbury, N. C.	Sept. 2, 1929	Salisbury, N. C.	71	9	26	
Larson, Adolph, Sr.	Fredrikshald, Norway.	Sept. 15, 1856		Cf.	Los Angeles, Cal.	Feb. 25, 1930	Los Angeles, Cal.	73	5	10	
Lemhuis, Peter L.	Lafayette, Ind.	Apr. 18, 1851		Pg.	Erie, Pa.	Dec. 23, 1928	Erie, Pa.	77	8	5	
Moser, Franklin W., Prof.	Shepherdstown, W. Va.	May 12, 1886		EP	York, Pa.	Jan. 30, 1930	Gettysburg, Pa.	43	8	18	
Potteiger, Samuel N., Esq.	Reading, Pa.	Aug. 31, 1864		PM	Reading, Pa.	Oct. 11, 1928	Reading, Pa.	64	1	10	
Schofer, James A.	Berks Co., Pa.	Dec. 30, 1858		PM	Reading, Pa.	Nov. 28, 1929	Reading, Pa.	70	10	28	
Wichmann, Charles J.	Germany.	Dec. 1855		NY	Bronx, N. Y.	Oct. 31, 1929	Rochester, N. Y.	74			
Wolfe, James H. Esq.	Hilltown, Bucks Co., Pa.	Dec. 2, 1848		PM	Philadelphia, Pa.	Feb. 28, 1929	Sellersville, Pa.	80	2	26	
Wurtz, John C.	Norristown, Pa.	Feb. 15, 1902		PM	Norristown, Pa.	May 15, 1930	Norristown, Pa.	28	3	1	
Laywomen											
Belmer, Lydia L.	Near Sunbury, Pa.	Mar. 17, 1844		EP	Philadelphia, Pa.	Aug. 26, 1929	Macungie, Pa.	85	4	9	
Dodenhoff, Sister Else.	Baden, Germany.	Sept. 30, 1867		PM	Philadelphia, Pa.	Jan. 7, 1930	Philadelphia, Pa.	62	3	7	
Frank, Sister Eleanor.	Allentown, Pa.	June 17, 1902		Md.	Baltimore, Md.	Apr. 1, 1930	Baltimore, Md.	27	9	14	
Keck, Laura V.	Philadelphia, Pa.	Feb. 4, 1853		PM	Allentown, Pa.	Dec. 2, 1928	Allentown, Pa.	75	9	28	
Mergner, Sister Julia.	Ditterswind, Bavaria.	Dec. 25, 1857		PM	Philadelphia, Pa.	July 9, 1929	Philadelphia, Pa.	72	6	14	
Sadtler, Katherine S.	Shippensburg, Pa.	Aug. 7, 1849		Md.	Baltimore, Md.	May 14, 1929	Baltimore, Md.	79	10	7	

Humbly submitted,
JAMES F. LAMBERT, *Necrologist.*

The Rev. F. A. Kahler read portions of Scripture and led in prayer while the Convention stood.

At five o'clock the Convention adjourned with prayer by the Rev. C. H. Stein.

———————•———————

Evening Service

The Inner Mission Board was in charge of the program for Monday evening. It presented six Inner Mission illustrations so that not only the ideal of the Inner Mission might be known, but that its practice also might be seen.

The service was in charge of the President of the Board, the Rev. E. F. Bachmann. Dr. Bachmann read a Scripture Lesson and offered a prayer. The music for the evening was furnished by the choir of Lake Park Lutheran Church and a solo sung by Mrs. Harris G. Nelson.

The illustrations presented were the use of "A Message for the Day," a day at the Girls' Hospice, work for deaf-mutes and blind deaf-mutes, work for immigrants, Southern Mountain work for boys and girls and the activity of Inner Mission societies.

Some of those who took part in the evening program were: the Rev. Wm. Freas, Executive Secretary of the Board; the Rev. and Mrs. E. C. Sibberson, Topeka, Kansas; a Milwaukee blind deaf-mute lady; the Rev. E. A. Sievert, Secretary for Immigrant and Seamen's Work; the Rev. Kenneth Killinger, Virginia Synod's Southern Mountain pastor; Miss Wolf and about forty-five local Milwaukee people. Three Inner Mission Superintendents presented the last illustration, the Rev. G. H. Bechtold, Secretary of the Board of Inner Missions of the Ministerium of Pennsylvania; the Rev. C. E. Krumbholz, Superintendent of the New York Inner Mission Society; and the Rev. James Oosterling, Superintendent of the Baltimore Inner Mission Society.

The evening was closed with the praying of the Lord's Prayer and the Benediction.

SIXTH MEETING

HOTEL SCHROEDER

Milwaukee, Wisconsin

Tuesday, October 14, 1930, 8:45 o'clock.

Matins were conducted by the Rev. P. H. Roth.

The Convention was called to order by the President.

The Minutes of the Monday morning and afternoon sessions were read by the Secretary and approved.

The Rev. J. A. Leas presented the report of the Committee of Reference and Counsel as follows:

We recommend that we note with sorrow the death, on last Sunday, of the Rev. E. F. Aksim, S.T.M., of the Waterloo Seminary and that the Secretary of the Convention be authorized to convey to the bereaved family the sympathy of this body.

Recommendation adopted.

The Rev. A. Steimle, Chairman of the Commission on Theological Education, addressed the Convention.

Dr. Steimle introduced the Rev. G. Morris Smith, Secretary, who presented the report of the Commission and moved the adoption of Principles 1 and 2.

REPORT OF THE COMMISSION ON THEOLOGICAL EDUCATION

The Commission on Theological Education in the United Lutheran Church, authorized at the Chicago Convention, continued by the Richmond convention, and enlarged by the Erie convention (see page 409, minutes of the Erie convention) has held two meetings in the past biennium, one on April 3, 1929, Muhlenberg Building, Philadelphia, the other on June 20, 1930, at Springfield, Ohio.

At the Philadelphia meeting, the Commission organized by electing Dr. A. Steimle as chairman, and Dr. G. Morris Smith as secretary. The members of the Commission are:

Rev. John Aberly, Gettysburg, Pennsylvania.
Rev. R. D. Clare, Baltimore, Maryland.
Rev. F. O. Evers, Baltimore, Maryland.
Rev. L. F. Gruber, Maywood, Illinois.
Rev. J. A. W. Haas, Allentown, Pennsylvania.
Rev. A. S. Hardy, Long Island, New York.
Hon. H. W. Harter, Canton, Ohio.
Rev. C. M. Jacobs, Mt. Airy, Philadelphia.
Rev. L. H. Larimer, Springfield, Ohio.

Rev. J. Sittler, Lancaster, Ohio.
Rev. G. Morris Smith, Selinsgrove, Pennsylvania.
Rev. A. Ste.mle, New York City.
Rev. A. G. Voigt, Columbia, South Carolina.
Rev. A. A. Zinck, Milwaukee, Wisconsin.
Judge J. W. King, Kittanning, Pennsylvania.

During the past biennium the Commission has posited its work upon the proposit.ons previously adopted by the United Lutheran Church at the Richmond and Erie conventions.

COMMUNICATES RICHMOND AND ERIE PROPOSITIONS TO SYNODICAL PRESIDENTS

In order that Synodical Presidents might definitely know the action so far approved by the United Lutheran Church with reference to Theological Education, the Commission addressed the following letter to each Synodical President:

"My dear President:
"At a meeting of the Theological Commission of the United Lutheran Church, held on April 3, the Commission voted to bring to the attention of Synodical Presidents a statement of principles heretofore approved by the Richmond and Erie conventions. They are as follows:
"Richmond recommendations, page 541.
"1. That it be the sense of the convention that no Syno, or group of Synods should hereafter organize or locate a theological sem.nary w:thout first securing the consent of the United Lutheran Church.
"2. That seminaries located in contiguous territory be urged to consider whether the needs of the Church may not be best served by consolidation or by such affiliation as may unify and correlate their work.
"3. That we commend the holding of informal conferences among our seminary faculties and executives looking to a hearty co-operation in the whole work of theological education and the joint study of the various problems involved in furthering the interests and efficiency of all our seminaries.
"Erie propositions, page 409.
"1. We believe that for the best interest of the Church the theological seminaries should be more definitely bound to the United Lutheran Church.
"2. We believe from our survey and data in hand, that only one seminary should serve a definite territory, and where there is more than one seminary on that territory that they should take steps to consolidate.
"3. We believe that the number and boundaries of such territory should be fixed by the United Lutheran Church in such manner as it shall determine.
"Respecting the proposed merger of the three theological seminaries in Pennsylvania, the Commission passed the following resolution: 'It was moved and carried that we express our approval of efforts now being made to effect a merger of the three Pennsylvania seminaries.' "

A. STEIMLE, *President.*
G. MORRIS SMITH, *Secretary.*

CONSOLIDATION OF SEMINARIES

For the information of the Church we report that resolutions of merger drawn up and prepared by a joint commission of representatives of the Boards of Directors of the three seminaries in Pennsylvania, were submitted to their supporting Synods at their meetings in 1929, and these resolutions to merge the Gettysburg, Philadelphia and Susquehana Seminaries were approved by the Pittsburgh Synod, the Ministerium of Pennsylvania and the Maryland Synod. Other Synods not yet ready to approve the merger were: Susquehanna Synod of Central Pennsylvania, the Alleghany Synod, the East Pennsylvania Synod, and the West Pennsylvania Synod.

The United Lutheran Synod of New York, at its convention held in Rochester, June 16-19, 1930, voted to approve the action of the Board of Trustees of the Hartwick Theological Seminary to remove said institution from its present location to St. Luke's Parish House, Brooklyn, in September, 1930, and provisions were made for approaches to the Ministerium of Pennsylvania looking toward the merger of the Philadelphia and the Hartwick Seminaries.

CONFERENCES OF MID-WESTERN SEMINARIES IN CHICAGO

Under the auspices of the Theological Commission, a meeting of the representatives of the Mid-Western Seminaries and representatives of the Theological Commission was held in Chicago, at the Edgewater Beach Hotel, on April 19, 1929, which resulted in a helpful interchange of thought concerning the problems which confront these institutions.

CONFERENCES OF SEMINARY FACULTIES

Your Commission is gratified to report that annual faculty conferences are being held, to which representatives of the faculties of the several seminaries of the United Lutheran Church are invited. In the past biennium these conferences have been held (1929) at Susquehana University, Selinsgrove, Pennsylvania, and (1930) in Springfield, Ohio, with Hamma Divinity School as host. It is felt that these faculty conferences are productive of great good in bringing out papers on theological subjects of genuine merit and also in promoting a better understanding of our common theological problems.

The Commission on Theological Education would submit for the approval of this convention the following principles and recommendations:

Principles:
1. Our Theological Seminaries are engaged in the preparation of ministers for the whole church and not for any section of it only.
2. In order that the best interests of the whole church shall be served and an adequate ministry be provided, it is needful that a more definite relationship between the seminaries and the United Lutheran Church be established.

Recommendations:
We therefore recommend:
1. That the Seminaries be requested to send annual reports similar to those submitted to their supporting Synods to the United Lutheran Church through the proper channels.
2. That the charters and constitutions of the several seminaries be submitted for examination in order that any necessary adjustments for the closer identification of the seminaries with the United Lutheran Church may be recommended to the seminaries, Synods and the United Lutheran Church.
3. That to promote a closer relationship of the seminaries to the United Lutheran Church, conferences be held to consist of the Presidents and Deans of the several seminaries, the Presidents of their Board of Trustees, and the Presidents of their supporting Synods, together with the Commission on Theological Education, the call to be issued by the Chairman of the Theological Commission.

The subjects for discussion shall be concerning:
a. Curricula, how they may be improved, enlarged and standardized in conformity with the ideals and cultus of the whole Church.
b. Standards for faculty requirements.
c. The matter of mergings where territories overlap, and a better distribution of locations to cover the entire field.
d. A consideration of the desirability of the establishing of a general post-graduate seminary under the direct supervision of the United Lutheran Church.
The proceedings and recommendations of such conferences shall be reported to the Convention of the United Lutheran Church by the Commission on Theological Education.
4. We believe that the United Lutheran Church as now constituted can be adequately served by five or six theological seminaries.
We therefore recommend that the conferences of seminaries herein provided for be requested to recommend locations.
5. It is further recommended that a Theological Commission be appointed by the Executive Board of the United Lutheran Church in consultation with the Board of Education, the same to function as its department on Theological Education.

A. STEIMLE, *President.*
G. MORRIS SMITH, *Secretary.*

Upon motion of the Rev. P. H. Roth, duly seconded and carried, Principles 1 and 2 were laid on the table.

Moved and carried, that the Convention consider recommendation No. 5.

The Rev. Henry H. Bagger moved the following substitute taken from the President's Report:

"Recommended that the Executive Board, in consultation with the Conference of Synodical Presidents and with the Board of Education, study the Church's arrangements for the training of ministers and teachers and bring recommendations for changes therein to the next convention."

In connection with the proposed substitute recommendation the Rev. C. P. Swank read the report of the Committee on President's Report for information.

The Rev. R. E. Tulloss was called to the Chair and the President addressed the Convention. After discussion the proposed substitute offered by the Rev. Henry H. Bagger was adopted.

Recommendations 1, 2, 3 and 4 were referred to the agency created by the substitute recommendation of the Rev. Mr. Bagger.

On motion of the Rev. A. Steimle, Principles 1 and 2 were taken from the table and, on further motion, the Principles were referred to the same agency.

The Rev. F. M. Urich presented the report of the Parish and Church School Board and introduced the Rev. Paul J. Hoh who addressed the Convention.

THE REPORT OF THE PARISH AND CHURCH SCHOOL BOARD

Religious Education Texts

The outstanding purpose of the Parish and Church School Board is to provide our own literature for all departments and phases of religious education in our congregations. In the biennium, the Vacation Church School texts have been completed, so that now there are available three texts for the Primary group and three texts for the Junior group. These cover the ages from six to eleven inclusive. These texts have been found satisfactory and helpful.

Hymns and Services

The Children's Hymnal and Service Book has been completed and is now in use in many of our schools. This hymnal has met a great need and is receiving high praise.

Special services have been prepared for the festival days. These services have been in harmony with the principles and practices of the Lutheran Church. Christmas, Easter, Children's Day and Rally Day Services have been issued and have met with general favor.

After careful consideration, the Board decided to encourage the preparation of suitable dramas and pageants for special days in our church schools.

At the request of the Board the Order of Service for the Dedication of a Church House was prepared by Paul Z. Strodach, D.D., of the Sub-committee of the Common Service Book Committee. This service is now available.

CONTINUED COURSES

The preparation of the various units of the Lutheran Graded Series and of the International (Augsburg) Uniform Series has continued during the biennium. The tenth annual volume of the Lesson Commentary on the Uniform Lessons for 1931 has been published. The *Parish School* appeared under a new form early in the biennium. It is published ten months each year. It carries general articles and special articles arranged under departments. The purpose of this magazine is to make available for our leaders and teachers the best materials for their guidance in carrying on their work. It is the desire of the Board that the magazine be more generally circulated among our Church School Leaders.

THE CHRISTIAN LIFE COURSE

Considerable progress has been made since our last report to the United Lutheran Church, on the new graded course, known as The Christian Life Course. Although it will not be available for use in our schools before the fall of 1931, we believe the Church will be amply rewarded for its patience by the improvements which are being made. Sunday schools have been advised by letter of the progress of the work and have been informed that the literature now in use will be continued until the appearance of the new course. There will, therefore, be no interruption and no need of change in the work of our schools until the new materials are ready for use.

In the Christian Life Course five principles will find expression. The course will be:

1. Christo-centric.
2. Biblical.
3. Lutheran.
4. Vital (dealing with the actual life of the persons taught).
5. Practicable.

The writers of the literature are being governed by these principles.

The curriculum, which will make provision for those between the ages of four and seventeen, is being constructed upon the basis of five comprehensive aims:

1. Understanding of and response to the grace of God;
2. Growth in Christian faith;
3. Training in personal and social Christian living;
4. Understanding and use of the Bible as the revealed Word of God;
5. Personal and wholehearted participation in the life and work of the Church.

In outline, the course will be divided as follows:

1. Beginners' Department—two years; ages 4 and 5;
2. Primary Department—three years; ages 6 to 8;

3. Junior Department—three years; ages 9 to 11;
4. Intermediate Department—three years; ages 12 to 14.
5. Senior Department—three years; ages 15 to 17.

For the Beginners' and the Primary Departments, weekly lesson leaflets with colored pictures will be provided for the pupil. The teachers will be supplied with substantial quarterlies. In the other departments there will be two sets of quarterlies, one for the pupil, another for the teacher.

The titles of the various years, beginning with the first year of the Primary Department, are as follows: "The Christian's Home," "The Christian's World," "The Christian's Friends," "God's Heroes," "God's Workers," "God's Instruments," "Christian Boys and Girls," "Men and Women of God," "The Story of God's People," "The Christian Church," "The Christian Life," "Life Problems."

The substantial gains of modern pedagogy are being utilized in the development of the course, while at the same time the convictions and the spirit of our Church are being carefully maintained.

The Rev. Paul J. Hoh, Pastor of the Ascension Lutheran Church at Mt. Airy Seminary, Philadelphia, has been called as the editor who shall have special responsibility for the preparation of the Christian Life Course. Pastor Hoh assumed his duties March 1, 1930. He is eminently qualified for this important task and under his supervision and guidance we have every reason to believe that the preparation of our new graded course of Sunday school texts will proceed without delay to a successful issue.

RETIREMENT OF DR. W. L. HUNTON

Due to declining health and acting upon the advice of his physicians, the Rev. W. L. Hunton, Ph.D., D.D., one of our editors and the secretary of the Parish and Church School Board, was compelled to relinquish his work in connection with our publications.

His resignation was accepted with deep regret and became effective May 1, 1930.

Dr. Hunton's long years of faithful and efficient service, his valuable work in the field of our Sunday school literature and his conscientious application to duty in many other spheres of activity have enriched the Church and entitle him to lasting recognition.

FIELD SECRETARIES

The Church schools of the United Lutheran Church are scattered over a large area. The two field secretaries, Dr. Charles H. B. Lewis and Rev. S. White Rhyne have been doing a remarkable piece of constructive work in spite of the great extent of their fields. They have encouraged schools, set up and conducted institutes, promoted and directed leadership training and above all, have unified the schools on their territories with the plans of the Parish and Church School Board.

On June 1, 1930, Rev. Paul E. Keyser became the third field secretary for the Parish and Church School Board. The territory he is to cover is that occupied by six synods: Alleghany, Indiana, Michigan, Ohio, Pittsburgh and West Virginia.

LEADERSHIP TRAINING

No phase of the religious education work is demanding more careful attention than leadership training. Those who are responsible for education in the congregations are convinced that those who lead and teach must be more thoroughly trained for their vital task. It is encouraging to know that there is a constant increase of pupils in training classes. Young people are impressed with the challenge that is given them to become efficient workmen in the church schools. The Board has been planning and working toward the end of providing adequate leadership training literature. The courses which are in use have proved effective in the training of teachers and leaders, but there is a constant advance being made in the type of literature demanded for this work. Your Board realizes the necessity of providing for our workmen the best possible literature. A significant action has been taken which points to the development of a literature for our teachers and leaders which shall conform in every respect with the educational demand of the day and at the same time be prepared by our Church.

The Board has decided to call an editor whose whole time shall be given to planning and supervising an adequate course of leadership training for the United Lutheran Church .

The Board is convinced that it has done no better service to leadership training than in providing the Leadership Training Camp in Adams County, Pa. The name of the camp is " Nawakwa, " or " The Camp in the Woods. " The name is very appropriate for the setting in which the camp is placed. The results of the first year of the camp's operation justify this conviction. The different groups of boys and girls, young people and leaders who availed themselves of the privileges of the camp in 1929, more than balance the effort and expenditure put on the camp. There is no mathematical method for measuring growth in character. It is gratifying to know that in the first boys' camp two boys decided to study for the ministry, two to enter the mission field and others to prepare for various lines of Christian service. The camp is under the immediate direction of Dr. M. Hadwin Fischer, Gettysburg, Pa., and his assistant, Miss LaVene Grove, Harrisburg, Pa. The enrolment for the camp in 1930 is larger than for 1929.

The faculty for 1930 has been selected with the greatest care. The faculty and group counselors for the Junior High boys represent fifteen colleges and universities in America, and Berlin, and Leipsic. This high standard will be maintained throughout the summer. The plans are already made for the selection of curriculum, faculty and counselors for 1931. The Board shares in the preparation and distribution of promotion literature for the camp.

CHURCH SCHOOL PLANS AND EQUIPMENT

It was found advisable to change the name of the Committee on Architecture to the Committee on Church School Plans and Equipment. This committee is gathering data concerning buildings and equipment throughout the Church. Its purpose is to make available for our schools helpful suggestions for the remodeling of present buildings, for the erection of new buildings and for equipping them.

The committee acts in the capacity of consultants and is willing to give such advice and help as may be needed. Church school committees desiring to meet the needs of a modern educational program for the church school will find it helpful to consult with this committee.

APPOINTMENTS

The Intersynodical Conference on Elementary Christian Education held two meetings in the biennium attended by the representatives appointed by the Board, Charles P. Wiles, D.D., and D. Burt Smith, D.D. At these conferences, principles and methods were discussed, looking toward a better understanding of the conceptions held by the different Lutheran bodies of the conferences in the matter of elementary Christian education. Well prepared papers were presented and thoroughly discussed. While there is no tangible outcome from this conference to be expected in the near future, yet it seems advisable to continue them. The Board is glad to have its representatives take part in the conferences and will continue their appointment.

NOMINATIONS

The terms of four members of the Board expire at this meeting:

T. Bruce Birch, Ph.D., D.D.
Charles F. Dapp, Ph.D., D.D.
William L. Hunton, Ph.D., D.D.
Gilbert P. Voigt, Ph.D.

The Board desires to express its appreciation of the faithful service rendered by these four retiring members and to express its regret that their presence and influence in the Board will be lost.

None of these being eligible for re-election the following were nominated for the six-year period, 1930-1936:

Geo. H. Rhodes, D.D., Albemarle, N. C.
Wm. C. Schaeffer, Jr., D.D., Allentown, Pa.
Rev. Paul H. Heisey, Ph.D., Springfield, Ohio.
Mr. Dan Smith, Williamsport, Pa.

CORRELATION

In accordance with the action taken by the United Lutheran Church at its Convention in 1928 (Page 65, Section V, Co-ordination), the Parish and Church School Board authorized a call to the boards and agencies of the Church to send representatives to a meeting to be held in the Muhlenberg Building, Philadelphia, Pa., October 4, 1929. This call was issued by the Executive Committee of the Parish and Church School Board and the meeting was held.

President Knubel and appointed representatives of the following boards and agencies were present:

Foreign Missions, American Missions, Inner Missions, Education, Publication, Deaconess, Women's Missionary Society, Luther League, Lutheran Brotherhood, Laymen's Movement, Committee of Fifteen.

Following the presentation and discussion of the present educational plans of the different boards and agencies as now used in the congregations the following action was taken:

"Moved that a Committee of Five be appointed at this meeting to study the question of the Education of the Church along the lines of the Bible, Faith and Works, and that this committee prepare and submit to this group at a subsequent meeting plans for the co-ordination of the educational efforts of the boards and all other agencies of the Church."

The Committee of Five made a thorough survey and study of the entire situation and reported their findings to a second meeting of the representatives of boards and agencies held in the Muhlenberg Building, Philadelphia, Pa., March 11, 1930. The report of this Committee of Five was adopted as follows:

Your committee appointed to study the question of the education of the Church along the lines of Bible, Faith and Works, and to prepare and submit to this group at a subsequent meeting plans for the co-ordination of the educational efforts of the boards and all other agencies of the Church, begs leave to submit the following paper:

I. In making our study we recognize at least four educational factors and agencies entering into the educational program of the parish:

1. The Parish School as it is guided and directed by the Parish and Church School Board. This includes the Sunday school, the Weekday Church School and the Vacation Church School.

2. The auxiliaries recognized by the United Lutheran Church in America, namely, the Luther League, the Women's Missionary Society and the Men's Brotherhood.

3. The official papers and the other authorized publications of the United Lutheran Church in America.

4. The educational work of the boards and committees to which have been assigned certain days and seasons of the Church year for the presentation of their causes.

II. In our study we recognize certain values in each of the four, yet whose full value is not realized because of a lack of co-ordination of work and programs:

1. The Parish and Church School Board is best prepared to carry through a program of education because it has recognized educational standards and is a Board of the Church established for this particular purpose.

2. The auxiliaries have an educational value, not alone through information, but in the cultivation of certain church knowledge and church usages, and in their social opportunities.

3. We also recognize the invaluable educative influence of our official church papers and other authorized publications.
4. In the educational work of the boards and agencies of the Church, programs for special days and seasons as authorized by the United Lutheran Church in America have value and inspiration and, in these assigned tasks, much has been accomplished.

III. As a result of our study of the problem as it involves these factors, we recommend that the following resolution be adopted by this conference as its recommendation to the Parish and Church School Board.

"*Whereas,* the Parish and Church School Board has responsibility for the working out of a complete, correlated and progressive plan of parish education for all ages; and

"*Whereas* the formation of an integrated program for the parish involves features of promotion and organization on the part of the boards and agencies of the Church which apparently lie outside the sphere of the Parish and Church School Board; and

"*Whereas* it is also true that the solution of the problem requires continued time and study, we recommend:

1. That the Executive Board appoint a committee which shall study the problem of parish education in all its phases.
2. That this committee shall advise with all boards, committees, and agencies, concerning the correlation and co-ordination of all promotional and educational activities affecting the parish.
3. That this committee shall report its findings to the Executive Board and shall make such recommendations as seem advisable for such correlation and co-ordination.

The above report of the Committee of Five adopted by the representatives of boards and agencies at the meeting in Philadelphia, Pa., March 11, 1930, was considered by the Parish and Church School Board at its meeting on May 7, 1930, and the following action was taken:

"*Whereas* upon mature deliberation, it has been found that it is impossible to formulate a comprehensive plan of parish education because of the entrance of promotional features over which this Board has no jurisdiction, we recommend that the United Lutheran Church instruct its Executive Board to define the educational and promotional rights of the various boards and agencies of the Church, after which the Parish and Church School Board stands ready to undertake the work of formulating a comprehensive plan of parish education.

FRANK M. URICH, *President.*
D. BURT SMITH, *Acting Secretary.*

REPORT OF TREASURER OF THE PARISH AND CHURCH SCHOOL BOARD

CASH ACCOUNT

For the year ended June 30, 1929

Cash balance, July 1, 1928 .... $11,345.02
Receipts:
United Lutheran Church, on apportionment $12,240.00
Interest on bank balances 182.56
                                                           12,422.56
                                                          ─────────
                                                          $23,767.58

Disbursements:
```
Salaries of field secretaries .....................   $6,900.00
Expenses of field secretaries ...................      679.32
Expenses of members of board and committees..    1,222.98
Expenses of board meetings ...................       894.80
Literature and survey expense ................       387.35
Advertising ....................................        75.00
Honorarium, Lutheran Leadership Training Camp       250.00
Camera and projector .........................      278.10
Auditing .......................................        25.00
Premium on surety bond .....................          25.00
                                                 ————————   10,737.5:
```
Cash balance, June 30, 1929 .... $13,030.03

CASH ACCOUNT
For the year ended June 30, 1930

```
Cash balance, July 1, 1929......................................   $ 13,030.03
Receipts:
  United Lutheran Church, on apportionment...........$ 12,960.00
  Interest on bank balances ...........................      209.24
                                                     ————————   13,169.24
                                                              ————————
                                                              $26,199.27
```

DISBURSEMENTS

```
Salaries of field secretaries ........................................$   7,175.00
Expenses of field secretaries ...........................        943.73
Expenses of members of board and committees........        955.77
Expenses of board meetings ............................        719.01
Literature and survey expense .........................         88.79
Pro rata portion, Every Member Canvass Handbook        171.73
Lutheran Leadership Training Camp:
  Salary of director ...........................................$375.00
  Expenses ...................................................... 290.76
                                                          ————————
                                                               665.76
Auditing ...................................................................        25.00
Premium on surety bond ................................         25.00
                                                              ————————   10,769.79
```

Cash balance, June 30, 1930 .... $ 15,429.48

Respectfully submitted,
GEORGE M. JONES, *Treasurer.*

Philadelphia, August 1, 1930.

We have audited the accounts of the Parish and Church School Board of the United Lutheran Church in America for the years ended June 30, 1929, and June 30, 1930, and we certify that the foregoing Cash Statements of the Treasurer are in accordance with the books of account and, in our opinion, are correct.

LYBRAND, ROSS BROS., & MONTGOMERY,
Accountants and Auditors.

The report of the auditors was accepted.

In connection with this report the Secretary read Resolution No. 5 of the report of the Board of Education, which had been deferred until this time, also memorial 9 (5) from the Ministerium of Pennsylvania. On motion of the Rev. A. R. Wentz, the following substitute for the last paragraph of the report of the Parish and Church School Board and Resolution No. 5 of the report of the Board of Education was adopted.

Resolved, First, That the Parish and Church School Board be instructed
(1) to gather from the following boards and agencies all possible information pertaining to the educational program of the parish: Foreign Missions, American Missions, Inner Mission, Education, Publication, Deaconess Work, Women's Missionary Society, Luther League, Lutheran Brotherhoods, Laymen's Movement, Common Service Book Committee; and then
(2) to formulate a comprehensive plan of parish education including definition of the educational and promotional rights and duties of the various boards and agencies of the Church,
(3) to submit this plan to the Executive Board and
(4) after approval of the plan by the Executive Board, to put the plan into execution; it being understood that in the formulation of the plan the Board of Education, through a special committee, shall furnish all possible information concerning policies, programs and curricula of the higher educational institutions of The United Lutheran Church in America as they affect the educational program of the parish.

Resolved, Second, That the Board of Education be instructed to prepare and report at the next convention an inclusive educational plan for the Church which will include the educational plan for the parish as formulated by the Parish and Church School Board in accordance with Resolution 1.

The reply to Memorial No. 9, (5), from the Ministerium of Pennsylvania, was then adopted.

The Secretary submitted item IV, B, 8, of the report of the Executive Board and the recommendations were adopted.

The Rev. A. R. Wentz presented the report of the Executive Committee of the Lutheran World Convention.

REPORT OF THE PRESIDENT OF THE EXECUTIVE COMMITTEE OF THE LUTHERAN WORLD CONVENTION

On the basis of the commonly accepted confession of the faith of the Gospel as expressed in the historic symbols of the Evangelical Lutheran

Church,—a faith which has been fruitful in common works of brotherly love among us, we greet you in Christ's name and wish you, assembled in this Seventh Biennial Convention, God's guidance and richest blessing. With gratitude to Him, we recall the fact that the United Lutheran Church shared in the initiation of the Lutheran World Convention movement, was represented by official delegates at the First World Convention at Eisenach in 1923 and at the Second Lutheran World Convention at Copenhagen in 1929, and throughout the intervening years has helped in bearing its burdens and furthering its work. Inasmuch as more than one year has passed since the Second Lutheran World Convention at Copenhagen in 1929, it does not seem uncalled for that, in addition to the report of your official delegation, the Executive Committee for Continuation Work shall also submit to the United Lutheran Church, as to other participating Lutheran Church Bodies throughout the world, a brief account of its stewardship. Certainly, it is a pleasure to do so in accordance with the expressed wishes of the officers of the United Lutheran Church.

ORGANIZATION OF THE EXECUTIVE COMMITTEE

The Executive Committee for Continuation Work, which was appointed by the Second Lutheran World Convention to function until another ecumenical gathering of the representatives of the Lutheran Churches of the world can be held, met on July 4th in Copenhagen and July 6th to 8th of the past year in Orebro, Sweden, for organization. The undersigned was made president of the committee, Bishop Dr. Ludwig Ihmels and Dr. Per Pehrsson were elected vice-presidents, Baron Wilhelm v. Pechmann was chosen recording secretary, Dr. Alfred Th. Jörgensen was made treasurer, and Dr. L. W. Boe was elected assistant treasurer.

During the current year Baron Wilhelm v. Pechmann, on account of his advanced years and serious ill-health, has resigned from his position in the Executive Committee. The German delegations to the Copenhagen Convention have nominated as his successor the Rt. Rev. Bishop Dr. Marahrens, of the Evangelical Lutheran Church of Hanover, Germany. This nomination has been favorably received by the Executive Committee for Continuation Work, which has unanimously elected Bishop Marahrens as the successor of Baron v. Pechmann, the value of whose peculiar gifts during the formative period of the Lutheran World Convention movement is gratefully acknowledged.

LUTHERAN WORLD CONVENTION COMMITTEES

An elaborate Lutheran world organization would be contrary to the genius of the Evangelical Lutheran Church. The Lutheran World Conventions themselves are of the nature of free conferences. Without interfering in any way with the complete autonomy of any Evangelical Lutheran Church, the Lutheran World Convention movement and its committee or committees seek only to become the servants of all. But order, method, and simple machinery for service are necessary. The First Lutheran World Convention at Eisenach appointed a simple executive committee to carry forward its work during the interim between conventions. The Copenhagen Convention decided upon the continuance of this plan. In addition, action was taken inviting participating Lutheran Church Bodies to constitute severally Lutheran World Convention Committees of their own to co-operate with the general Executive Committee for Continuation Work. The action of the Second Lutheran World Convention on this subject is as follows:

"The Large Committee shall not be renewed in the form which it has hitherto had. In its stead there are to be organized within the churches and church territories larger and smaller special committees, which, in connection with the Executive Committee, are to be active in the cause sponsored by the World Convention within their respective churches. Each church or church territory shall regulate the extent, composition, order of business, method of operation, and name of its special committee, according to its own best judgment, as its own peculiar circumstances may indicate as being appropriate and conducive to the attainment of its objects. The chairman of each special committee shall keep the president of the Executive Committee informed concerning the organization of such special committee and of all important items pertaining to its work." (See item "7," page 207, English edition of *Second Lutheran World Convention*.)

The appointment according to their own wishes and wisdom of such special Lutheran World Convention Committees by or within the Evangelical Lutheran Churches of the world is proceeding encouragingly. For example, within the Church of Denmark, the following Lutheran World Convention Committee has been appointed: Bishop Dr. H. Ostenfeld, chairman; Bishop Chr. Ludwigs of Aalborg, Pastor C. Holt of Copenhagen, Propst Chr. Winther of Copenhagen, Mr. O. Lohse of Copenhagen, Dean Dr. H. Ussing of Copenhagen, Prof. J. Oskar Andersen, D.D., of Copenhagen, and Dr. Alfred Th. Jörgensen. Within the Church of Sweden the following Special National Lutheran World Convention Committee has been constituted: Archbishop Dr. Nathan Söderblom of Upsala, chairman; Bishop Dr. Stadener of Strangans, vice-chairman; Dompropst Dr. Lars Wollmer, secretary-treasurer; additional members including Bishop Block of Gothenburg, Bishop Dr. Rodhe of Lund, Bishop Dr. Reuterskiöld of Vaxjo, Propst Dr. Per Pehrsson of Gothenburg, Pastor Concricus of Eldsberger, Director Dr. Björkquist of Sigtuna, and Director v. Reis of Hindas.

Since the appointment of these special co-operating committees has been completed or is being completed in the countries of Europe, it is hoped that the participating Lutheran Church Bodies in America at their annual conventions during the current year will also be pleased, as they have already begun to do, to constitute similar committees in harmony with resolution "7" adopted by the Second Lutheran World Convention at Copenhagen.

THE WORLD-WIDE CELEBRATION OF THE QUADRICENTENNIAL OF THE AUGSBURG CONFESSION ENCOURAGED

In harmony with the specific action of the Second Lutheran World Convention, it became the duty of the Executive Committee to invite and encourage all Evangelical Lutheran Churches throughout the world to join heartily in the celebration of the Quadricentennial of the Augsburg Confession in the year 1930. Early in the current year, an official call to the observance of the jubilee of the *Confessio Augustana,* which ventured to motivate the celebration, was sent out to the heads of all Lutheran churches throughout the earth and to the editors of the church press. It is the conviction of the committee that the re-study and the re-assimilation of the biblical truth-content of the Augsburg Confession can only lead to the spiritual enrichment of the Church and its individual membership that the Word of God may dwell in them more richly and that they may be fully furnished unto every good work, especially for the making of a good confession and witness in this age of rationalism, religious indifferentism, and militant atheism. Moreover, it is believed that with God's blessing and through the gracious working of the Holy Spirit such a celebration, centered upon the fuller mastery of the faith of the Church and its assimilation unto the deepening of the spiritual life of all, is the true way to conscious inner unity among us and the inward spiritual consolidation of the forces of the Evangelical Lutheran Churches of the world. It is cheering to state that from the heads of the Lutheran churches in every quarter of the globe there have come encouraging reports of plans for such a spiritually helpful celebration of the four hundredth anniversary of the Augsburg Confession.

THE RELIEF AND ASSISTANCE OF WEAK, SUFFERING, AND ENDANGERED LUTHERAN CHURCHES

The Executive Committee is giving assiduous attention to the task of the relief, aid and encouragement of weak, suffering and endangered Evangelical Lutheran churches. The course of history in recent years and the consequent call of God's Providence have made the exercise of Christian brotherly love for the moral and material support of distressed fellow Lutherans a common responsibility resting upon the Lutheran Church as a whole. Hence the ministry of mercy and practical helpfulness for needy fellow believers has of necessity stood in the foreground of the work of the Executive Committee since the Copenhagen Convention. The program of work has been formulated briefly as follows:

I. The relief and assistance of the suffering and persecuted Evangelical Lutheran Church of Russia and the care of Russian refugee Lutherans migrating to other lands.

II. The relief, aid and strengthening of the Lutheran churches in the "second line of defense," namely, in the border countries of Esthonia, Latvia, Lithuania, Poland, Czecho-Slovakia, Austria, Hungary, Jugoslavia, and Roumania.

III. The aid of the local Lutheran Committee in Galicia in the task of giving the full Gospel as the Evangelical Lutheran Church confesses it to the Ukrainian people seeking it at the hands of the Church of the Reformation.

In view of the bitter pressure against and persecution of the Christian churches in Russia, including our own Evangelical Lutheran Church there, as an emergency matter the president of the Executive Committee sent an appeal to the heads of all Lutheran churches throughout the world to request pastors and congregations to make intercessory prayer for suffering fellow Christians in Russia. There has been a world-wide response to this suggestion. Unofficially and individually, the members of the Executive Committee have labored in their several countries to the end of the development through the co-operation of pastors and people of a lively and wholesome public opinion in favor of the guarantee of religious rights and religious freedom to all peoples. It is gratifying to report also that the prayers of God's people and their moral influence for the aid of oppressed Lutheran and other Christian churches have been followed by generous gifts for their material assistance. For example, gifts in the amount of approximately $31,190 for the relief and assistance of suffering churches have been contributed since February 1st from the Lutheran churches and relief organizations of fourteen countries of the world. Of this amount, $1,184.89 was contributed from the Church of Norway, $1,623.26 from the Church of Sweden, $11,000 from the Church of Denmark and $1,100 by the *Lutherischen Gotteskasten* of Germany. The concentration of the prayers and gifts of the Lutheran churches of the world through a common channel to meet a critical emergency like that in Russia is of the greatest significance and practical value. Of course the National Lutheran Council of America is one of the major agencies co-operating in the Lutheran relief programs of the Executive Committee, as is gratefully acknowledged. The continuous generous support of the National Lutheran Council is, humanly speaking, indispensable that this saving work of Christian mercy may go on. Lutheran world co-operation for the relief and aid of suffering churches has enabled the Executive Committee to finance the Lutheran Seminary in Leningrad, which the Church of Russia heroically continues under the greatest difficulties; to assist needy pastors and their families in many weak and suffering churches; to aid promising students for the ministry; to help the widow, the orphan and the inner mission institution; to have translated and distributed an edition of Luther's Small Catechism in the Ukrainian language, and to accomplish a multitude of other important services for the strengthening of the weak, the relief of the distressed, and the extension of the Evangelical Lutheran Church.

As a watchman on the walls of Zion, the Executive Committee, seeking accurate knowledge concerning the condition, progress, handicaps, problems and needs of the Lutheran churches throughout the world, is thus endeavoring to serve as the agency for the relief of the distressed, for the strengthening of the weak, for the freedom of the oppressed, and for the improvement of the position of the Lutheran Church as a whole on the earth. We are grateful to God for the growing and extending co-operation of Lutheran Church Bodies, large and small, in this unselfish and highly important common task. Special attention is earnestly called to the necessity of sustained, adequate and generous moral and material support of the suffering Lutheran Church of Russia. This noble enterprise of church relief and reconstruction in Russia is of far-reaching importance. The rescue, rebuilding and development of the Lutheran Church in Russia; the future of organized religion in that country; and the conquest of Russia for Christ are the issues involved. Moreover, the successful establishment in Russia of religious rights in theory and practice and therewith the opportunity of the free development of Christian churches will have no small significance in keeping open the doors for Christian missions in other countries of the Near and Far East. Looking to God, the Lutherans of the world will gladly do their part along with other Christian churches.

LOOKING TO INCREASED ACTIVITY UNDER DEFINITE INSTRUCTION OF THE SECOND LUTHERAN WORLD CONVENTION

The Executive Committee is giving thorough study to the problem of extending approved activities, including the perfecting of a generally useful international Lutheran news service, the visitation of Lutheran churches in the various countries of the world, co-operation in the care of migrating Lutherans, the discussion of conditions under which larger Lutheran participation in the International Missionary Council may be secured, and many other particularly assigned tasks too numerous to mention in detail. Through the generosity of the National Lutheran Council, provisions have been made by which the president of the Executive Committee is enabled to give all of his time to the work of the Lutheran World Convention, pending the proposal and acceptance of an adequate annual budget by the participating Lutheran Church Bodies throughout the earth. The Executive Committee is profoundly grateful to the co-operating Lutheran Church Bodies in America for this generous action through the National Lutheran Council. In consequence the Executive Committee will be enabled to prosecute its world-wide work more intensively and efficiently.

THE MEETING OF THE EXECUTIVE COMMITTEE FOR 1930

The Executive Committee for Continuation Work of the Lutheran World Convention has accepted the invitation of Bishop Johan Lunde to meet in Norway in September. This invitation includes participation in the convention of the clergy and representatives of all Scandinavian Lutheran Churches at Nidaros, September 2nd to 5th, although the main sessions of the annual meeting of the Executive Committee for the year are to be held at Oslo the following week. At this important meeting in Norway, the Executive Committee will take under advisement its program of work for the ensuing five years. At the Orebro meeting last year, activities approved or suggested by the Copenhagen Convention were assigned to individual members for study and report at the 1930 meeting. Hence the coming Norway meeting of your committee will be faced with important issues and responsibilities. As has been customary in past years, deputations of the committee will be appointed to visit Lutheran churches on invitation in adjacent countries, including Esthonia, Latvia, Lithuania, and possibly Finland.

A FINAL WORD

The Lutheran World Convention movement stands definitely for positive Christianity in harmony with the Word of God according to the witness of the historic confessions of the Evangelical Lutheran Church. Its influence is clearly and strongly for confessional Lutheranism and for genuine inner unity on that basis. Bishop Stadener of Sweden in a recent letter speaks of the Lutheran World Convention movement as "our joy and our hope." Your abiding interest and continued prayers are requested that God may guide the Executive Committee and the co-operating committees in all their work for the establishment of the faith of the Church, for the furtherance of conscious inner unity in the faith and for the increase of free co-operation among the Lutheran churches of the world in the approved field unto the welfare of the Church as a whole and the advancement of Christ's Kingdom.

Respectfully submitted,
JOHN A. MOREHEAD,
For the Executive Committee of the Lutheran World Convention.

The Rev. C. P. Swank presented the report of the Committee on President's Report. With the consent of the Convention the President withdrew from his report those phrases which were not a part of the substitute offered by the Rev. Henry H. Bagger for recommendation No. 5 of the Commission on Theological Education.

Dr. Swank then read the report of the Committee on President's Report as follows:

REPORT OF THE COMMITTEE ON PRESIDENT'S REPORT

The report of our President, we believe, is of special significance to this Convention. It not only reveals, as records testify, the diligence with which our President has discharged his duties, but it is laden with a burden of solicitude for a more nearly perfect ministry, in personal character and example, as well as in the educational processes of its training.

We should like to lay every possible emphasis upon the four-fold ideal of the Psalm 24, set forth by the President in a very forceful and practical manner, holding before the leaders of the Church the necessity of "clean hands," "pure hearts," a "soul without vanity " and a "tongue purged of all deceitfulness. " In this day of moral delinquency there can be no other hope for influential Christian leadership than this motto. How these ideals can best be placed impressively before our ministers was the cause of much consideration by your committee.

Our President has spoken earnestly concerning the educational training of our pastors and workers. The co-ordination and unification of these processes has given the Church much concern for several years and still leaves some things to be desired. Attention is called by the President to the obligation laid upon the United Lutheran Church by its constitution for efficiency in this vital spot of our church life. In a previous action of this convention the purpose and plan proposed by our President in his recommendation in this direction has virtually been accomplished. This action, your committee believes to be a plan most practicable in co-operation with present operating agencies and most hopeful of results.

We therefore recommend the following:

That every pastor of the United Lutheran Church read and give serious thought to the ideals set forth in the President's Report for a strong and efficient ministry.

Recommendation adopted.

The Rev. Wm. Freas presented the report of the Committee on Army and Navy Work as follows:

REPORT OF THE COMMITTEE ON ARMY AND NAVY WORK

Your committee appointed after the last convention carried over its organization from the previous biennium.

Rev. C. D. Trexler, D.D., served as chairman, Rev. Wm. Freas, D.D., as secretary, and with Mr. Chas. H. Dahmer formed the Executive Committee, and Rev G. M. Diffenderfer, D.D., as special Washington representative.

During the first year of the biennium but little activity for chaplains was possible. This was caused by preference of the chiefs of chaplains of the Army and Navy to deal directly with individuals rather than through the organizations of the Church. Men were sought out and appointed without the knowledge of the Church.

In the second year, however, the Chaplains' Corps in both Army and Navy had new chiefs. In the Army, Chaplain Yates, and in the Navy,

Chaplain Evans. With both of these men valuable contacts have been established. They are men sympathetic to the desires of our church. They will accept only properly qualified men. They are still desiring applications from Lutheran pastors for chaplaincy in both the regular and reserve service. Before a year is over there will be a possible opportunity for appointment of two Lutheran chaplains in the Army and one in the Navy.

We still receive a few requests for the Army and Navy Service Book, the supply of which is exhausted. Certain inquiries came concerning men in the service, one of them as far back as the Spanish War, and an effort was made to be of service.

I. REGULAR CHAPLAINS

During the biennium two Lutherans have been appointed as chaplains in the Army, both of them from the United Lutheran Church in America. They are Rev. J. E. Ensrud, D.D., and Rev. H. C. Moehlmann. During this same period three applicants have been rejected—one by this committee, two at Washington, one on account of being over age and the third because of failure to pass the physical examination. It is interesting to note that four young men in our seminaries have written concerning the possibility of entering the chaplaincy directly upon graduation. As both the services require some pastoral experience except in the cases of men of very unusual promise the desire of these young men has had to be discouraged.

A matter of some concern in the appointment of regular chaplains is that one of the chief's desires to have three or four men appear before him as candidates so that he may choose one from the number. As this practice is not in harmony with our polity as a church we have explained our position in this matter and urged that it be taken into consideration. Both chiefs are eager that the Lutheran quota should be filled.

Recent information indicates that since January 1st eight men have been refused appointment in the Army and Navy because of their failure to pass the physical examination. We have been asked as a committee to be cautious in recommending only men who may be able to meet the physical requirements.

We now have eight chaplains in the Army, five being from the United Lutheran Church in America. In the Navy we have two chaplains, one being from the United Lutheran Church in America.

II. RESERVE CHAPLAINS

During the biennium your committee has investigated and approved for appointment as chaplains in the Officers' Reserve Corps, sixteen men. Of this number fourteen are members of the United Lutheran Church in America. The total number of Lutheran pastors now members of the Officers' Reserve Corps as chaplains is 87. Of this number 53 are members of the United Lutheran Church in America. Many of these men are in the habit of serving actively for two weeks at some camp, naval vessel or port during the summer.

III. CAMPS AND POSTS

Your committee is urging that pastors of our Lutheran Church shall visit posts or camps in his vicinity for the purpose of a spiritual service to the men. There are many smaller posts where there is no regular chaplain. Some of them are located beyond the reach of our Church. Others, however, might well be served by them. Where a regular chaplain is on duty, if proper approach is made, the co-operation and service of local pastors will be welcomed. In posts without chaplains it is desirable first of all to seek out the commanding officer and secure his authority before attempting to do anything in such camps.

Pastor St. Clair is active as our only Lutheran civilian chaplain. He is doing a most splendid work at the Speedway Hospital in Chicago. He is supported by the churches of Chicago, several of the General Lutheran Bodies being represented.

Respectfully submitted,
WILLIAM FREAS, Secretary.

The Rev. Paul E. Scherer presented the report of the Committee on Conference with the Y. M. C. A.

REPORT ON THE COUNSELLING COMMISSION OF THE CHURCHES WITH THE Y. M. C. A.

Since the last convention of the United Lutheran Church two meetings of the Commission have been held, November 20, 1928, and November 7, 1929. Mr. Fred W. Ramsey, of Cleveland, has succeeded Dr. John R. Mott as General Secretary of the National Board, and Dr. W. I. Chamberlain has been elected Chairman of the Commission. Dr. D. G. Latshaw has withdrawn from active work as Secretary of the Department of Relations to Church and Interchurch Bodies of the National Council, but is made a permanent member of the Counselling Commission in view of his intimate acquaintance during five years with the work of the Commission.

In the 1928 meeting one of the most important matters discussed was the question of Leadership at Student Conferences. Mr. Elliott, of the Student Division, reported that in face of difficulties earnest efforts were being made to have the Church more adequately represented.

Mr. Irving, Secretary for the Evangelistic Emphasis of the National Council, called the attention of the Commission to the increasingly Christ-centered character of the Association program.

In 1929 an Ad Interim Committee of three (with two ex-officio members) was appointed by the Chairman to act between meetings of the Commission and to be available for conference.

The day was spent in the discussion of problems with regard to co-operation, especially in religious education and recreation. Frank reports were made, and every evidence given on the part of the Association of a genuine desire to be of service.

Your committee recommends the continuance of the relationship between the United Lutheran Church and the Counselling Commission.

Respectfully submitted,

PAUL E. SCHERER, *Chairman.*

Moved and carried, That the Committee be continued.

It was moved and carried to continue the session until the business of the Convention is completed.

The Rev. C. M. Jacobs announced that the Committee on Church and State had no report to offer.

The Secretary presented the report of the Committee on Transportation.

REPORT OF TRANSPORTATION COMMITEE

The Transportation Committee has been active throughout the biennium and through its activities, especially those of the Rev. J. M. Bramkamp, D.D., Western Secretary of the Committee, has secured a number of passes, both annual and trip, which have resulted in a great saving to the Church. The Chairman of the Committee, Mr. Harvey C. Miller, has rendered very valuable service in connection with the transportation of delegates to this Convention, and in gathering and certifying certificates for validation by the special agent appointed by the railroads for this purpose. The thanks of the Convention are due to Dr. Bramkamp and Mr. Miller.

M. G. G. SCHERER,
Secretary of the Committee.

A vote of thanks and appreciation of the services of Mr. Harvey C. Miller and the Rev. John M. Bramkamp was adopted.

The Rev. W. C. Davis submitted the report of the Committee on Leave of Absence.

REPORT OF COMMITTEE ON LEAVE
OF ABSENCE

Your Committee on Leave of Absence begs to report as follows:

1. Every synod of the United Lutheran Church has reported. This is the first time a 100 per cent return has been made since the present plan went into effect in 1924.

2. The following synods have had a 100 per cent attendance at the Convention of both clerical and lay delegates:

Alleghany   Mississippi
Florida   Nova Scotia
Manitoba   Rocky Mountain
                    Texas

3. The following synodical delegations asked for excuses:

(a) Full time:

California—one delegate   North Carolina—two delegates
Canada—one delegate   Ohio—two delegates
Michigan—one delegate   South Carolina—one delegate
New York—six delegates   Wartburg—three delegates

(b) Part time:

California—one delegate   New York—five delegates
Canada—one delegate   North Carolina—four delegates
East Penna.—four delegates   Northwest—one delegate
Georgia-Alabama—one delegate   Ohio—five delegates
German Nebraska—two delegates   Pacific—two delegates
Illinois—six delegates   Pittsburg—nine delegates
Indiana—two delegates   Slovak Zion—three delegates
Iowa—two delegates   South Carolina—three delegates
Kansas—one delegate   Susquehanna—one delegate
Maryland—three delegates   Virginia—two delegates
Ministerium of Penna.—   Wartburg—three delegates
     fourteen delegates   West Penna.—two delegates
Michigan—six delegates   West Virginia—three delegates
Nebraska—three delegates

4. Out of a possible 277 clerical delegates, 277 are reported registered. Out of a possible 272 lay delegates, 255 were registered as present. Total attendance was 532 out of a possible 549, which is 98 per cent plus.

5. Your committee would express its deep appreciation of the careful work done by the chairmen of synodical groups, whose careful reports balance with the registration of the Convention, and we recommend the continuance of the present system.

6. Your committee recommends that the action of the United Lutheran Church taken at the 1926 convention be put into operation, namely,

"We recommend that the Executive Board prepare a uniform report blank for the use of the chairmen of delegations, to be used in making their reports to the Committee on Leave of Absence."

Respectfully submitted,

W. C. DAVIS
Chairman of the Committee.

Recommendation adopted.

The Rev. A. R. Wentz presented the report of the Lutheran Historical Society which was received as follows:

MINUTES OF THE LUTHERAN HISTORICAL SOCIETY

HOTEL SCHROEDER
Milwaukee, Wisconsin
October 10, 1930

The Society was called to order by President Manhart.

The report of Professor A. R. Wentz, the Curator, was read and adopted, as follows:

The Library of the Society has continued to receive the Lutheran publications, books, periodicals and synodical minutes that have come from the press of this country. In addition a valuable collection of books, periodicals, pictures and pamphlets has been received from the library of the late Dr. F. G. Gotwald and that of his father, the late Dr. Luther A. Gotwald. Much work has been done during the biennium in card-indexing the thousands of pamphlets in the possession of the Society. The Library has received a constant stream of inquiries and visits from students of Lutheran history.

The report of the Treasurer, Mr. J. E. Musselman, together with the report of the auditors, was presented and adopted, showing a balance of $285.20 to meet the needs of the next biennium.

The following officers were elected:

President—Rev. F. P. Manhart, D.D., LL.D.
Vice-Presidents—Mr. H. M. M. Richards, Litt.D.; Rev. W. J. Finck, D.D.
Curator—Rev. Prof A. R. Wentz, Ph.D., D.D.
Secretary—Rev. Prof. H. C. Alleman, D.D.
Treasurer—Mr. J. Elmer Musselman.

Extra Members of the Executive Committee—Rev. Pres. G. Morris Smith and Rev. Prof. H. D. Hoover, Ph.D., D.D., S.T.D.

The minutes were read and approved.

The Society adjourned.

H. C. ALLEMAN, *Secretary.*

The Rev. G. H. Bechtold presented the report of the Lutheran Church Book and Literature Society which was received.

REPORT OF LUTHERAN CHURCH BOOK AND LITERATURE SOCIETY

The Society was reorganized on January 13, 1930, at which time the following officers were elected: Honorary President, the Rev. F. H. Knubel, D.D.; president, the Rev. P. Z. Strodach, D.D.; recording secretary, the Rev. W. H. C. Lauer; corresponding secretary, the Rev. Gustav H. Bechtold; treasurer, Mr. H. Torrey Walker.

With the resumption of work, distribution of Common Service Books and Parish and Church School Hymnals was begun. Books have thus far been sent as far north as Canada and as far west as the State of Washington. *The Lutheran* has been placed in libraries of seventy-six different communities.

Committees have been formed to expand the work of the Society through the Luther League, through the publication of new tracts and other literature that will stimulate the interest of non-Lutherans in our Church.

The Society solicits the interest and contributions of pastors and people in behalf of this work.

G. H. BECHTOLD, *Secretary.*

REPORT OF THE ARCHIVIST

The Archivist respectfully submits the following report:

Since the last Convention of the United Lutheran Church, the following items have been received and placed in the Archives:

Official Minutes of the 1926 Convention.
Official correspondence of the President, 1924-26.
Minute books (vols. 2-4) of the Board of Northwest Missions.
Ordination certificate of Otto C. Meyer.

LUTHER D. REED,
Archivist.

It was moved and carried that the matter of approving the Minutes of the final session of this Convention and also the printing of the Minutes be referred to the Executive Board.

The Convention was closed at 12:15 P. M. with the Order for the Closing of Synods.

M. G. G. SCHERER, *Secretary.*

LIST OF BOARDS AND ELECTIVE COMMITTEES

1. Executive Board.
2. Commission of Adjudication.
3. Board of Foreign Missions.
4. Board of American Missions.
5. Board of Northwestern Missions.
6. Immigrants Mission Board.
7. West Indies Mission Board.
8. Board of Education.
9. Inner Mission Board.
10. Board of Publication.
11. Board of Ministerial Pensions and Relief.
12. Parish and Church School Board.
13. Board of Deaconess Work.
14. National Lutheran Home for the Aged.
15. Committee on Church Papers.
16. Executive Committee of the Laymen's Movement.

LIST OF STANDING COMMITTEES, COMMISSIONS, ETC.

1. Statistical and Church Year Book Committee.
2. Committee on Common Service Book.
3. Committee on Church Music.
4. Committee on German Interests.
5. Committee on Lutheran Brotherhoods.
6. Committee on Women's Work.
7. Committee on Associations of Young People.
8. Committee on Army and Navy Work.
9. Committee on Moral and Social Welfare.
10. Committee on Evangelism.
11. Committee on Church Architecture.
12. Committee on Publicity.
13. Committee on Transportation.
14. Necrologist.
15. Archivist.
16. Such other Standing Committees as may be provided for
from time to time.

SPECIAL COMMITTEES

1.   Committee to Conduct the Opening and Closing Services of Each Session.
2.   Committee on Leave of Absence.
3.   Committee on Proceedings of District Synods.
4.   Committee of Reference and Counsel.
5.   Committee to Nominate Executive Committee of Laymen's Movement.
6.   Committee to Nominate Members of Boards.
7.   Committee to Nominate Members of Executive Board and all Elective Commissions or Committees.
8.   Committee of Tellers.

BOARDS AND ELECTIVE COMMITTEES
EXECUTIVE BOARD

President—Rev. F. H. Knubel, D.D., LL.D., S.T.D., 39 East Thirty-fifth Street, New York City.

Secretary—Rev. M. G. G. Scherer, D.D., 39 East Thirty-fifth Street, New York City.

Treasurer—E. Clarence Miller, LL.D., 1508 Walnut Street, Philadelphia, Pa.

Term Expires 1934

Rev. Marion J. Kline, D.D.; Rev. J. L. Morgan, D.D.; Rev. Rees Edgar Tulloss, D.D., Ph.D., LL.D.; Mr. John Greiner, Jr.; Mr. B. B. Miller; Mr. Wm. H. Stackel.

Term Expires 1932

Rev. A. C. R. Keiter; Rev. Charles D. Trexler. D.D.; Rev. A. R. Wentz, D.D., Ph.D.; Hon. Wm. E. Hirt; Hon. John F. Kramer; George E. Neff, Esq.

COMMISSION OF ADJUDICATION

President—Rev. A. G. Voigt, D.D., LL.D., Columbia, S. C.

Vice-President—Rev. Luther Kuhlman, D.D., 106 Carlisle St., Gettysburg, Pa.

Secretary—Rev. H. C. Roehner, D.D., 30 S. Mulberry St., Mansfield, Ohio.

Clerk—Hon. E. K. Strong, Columbia City, Ind.

Term Expires 1936

Rev. E. B. Burgess, D.D., LL.D.; Rev. H. C. Roehner, D.D.; Robbin B. Wolf, Esq.

Term Expires 1934

Rev. George Gebert, D.D.; Rev. A. G. Voigt, D.D., LL.D.; Hon. E. K. Strong.

Term Expires 1932

Rev. Luther Kuhlman, D.D.; Rev. W. F. Rangeler, D.D.; Hon. C. M. Efird, LL.D.

BOARD OF FOREIGN MISSIONS

President—Rev. S. W. Herman, D.D., 121 State St., Harrisburg, Pa.

Executive Secretary—Rev. Paul W. Koller, D.D., 18 E. Mt. Vernon Place, Baltimore, Md.

Recording Secretary—Rev. George Drach, D.D., 18 E. Mt. Vernon Place, Baltimore, Md.

Treasurer—Mr. Geo. R. Weitzel, 18 E. Mt. Vernon Place, Baltimore, Md.

General Secretaries in Charge of Departments of Work—Rev. George Drach, D.D., Literature, India and Japan; Rev. L. B. Wolf, D.D., Home Base, China and South America; Rev. M. Edwin Thomas, D.D., Special Gifts and Africa.

Term Expires 1936

Rev. Oscar A. Benson; Rev. E. E. Fischer, D.D.; Rev. G. Albert Getty, D.D.; Rev. J. L. Morgan, D.D.; Rev. Clarence M. Snyder; Rev. H. W. Snyder, D.D.; Mr. H. Torrey Walker.

Term Expires 1934

Rev. H. C. Brillhart, D.D.; Rev. G. A. Greiss, D.D.; Rev. E. R. Jaxheimer; Mr. A. Y. Leech, Jr.; Paul Van Reed Miller, Esq.; Mr. W. A. Rast.

Term Expires 1932

Rev Charles A. Dennig; Rev. S. W. Herman, D.D.; Rev. S. T. Nicholas, D.D.; Rev. J. L. Sieber, D.D.; Mr. Martin H. Buehler; Mr. Charles H. Dahmer; Mr. William H. Menges.

BOARD OF AMERICAN MISSIONS

President—Rev. J. B. Markward, D.D., 914 N. Fountain Avenue, Springfield, Ohio.

Vice-President—Rev. H. W. A. Hanson, D.D., LL.D., Gettysburg, Pa.

Secretary—Mr. H. F. Heuer, 52 E. Sedgwick St., Philadelphia, Pa.

Treasurer—Rev. Zenan M. Corbe, D.D., 39 East 35th Street, New York City.

Executive Secretary—Rev. F. F. Fry, D.D., 39 East 35th Street, New York City.

Divisional Secretary of English Missions—Rev. J. F. Seibert, D.D., 860 North Wabash Avenue, Chicago, Ill.

General Superintendents, Division of English Missions—Rev. G. H. Hillerman, D.D., 2505 Woolsey St., Berkeley, Calif.; Rev. A. D. R. Hancher, D.D., 139 E. Monroe St., Jacksonville, Fla.; Rev. I. Chantry Hoffman, D.D., 319 E. Walnut Lane, Philadelphia, Pa.

Divisional Secretary, Linguistic Interests—Rev. E. A. Tappert, D.D., 39 East 35th Street, New York City.

General Superintendent, Division of Linguistic Interests—Rev. Paul Ludwig, 860 N. Wabash Avenue, Chicago, Ill.

Departmental Secretary of Church Extension and Finance—Rev. Zenan M. Corbe, D.D., 39 East 35th Street, New York City.

Term Expires 1936

Rev. G. A. Benze, D.D.; Rev. H. W. A. Hanson, D.D., LL.D.; Rev. J. B. Markward, D.D.; Rev. Jacob Maurer, D.D.; Mr. A. Raymond Bard; Grant Hultberg, D.C.L.; Mr. H. L. Snyder.

Term Expires 1934

Rev. A. E. Bell, D.D.; Rev. C. A. Freed, D.D.; Rev. G. K. Rubrecht, D.D.; Rev. J. C. Seegers, D.D.; Mr. A. H. Durboraw; Mr. Wm. Eck; Mr. S. F. Telleen.

Term Expires 1932

Rev. F. O. Evers; Rev. J. M. Francis, D.D.; Rev. L. H. Lar-

imer, D.D., LL.D.; Rev. L. W. Steckel, D.D.; Mr. H. F. Heuer;
John A. Hoober, Esq.; Mr. Charles Lehmann.
Advisory Members—Mrs. A. B. Leamer; Mrs. H. C. Michael.

BOARD OF NORTHWESTERN MISSIONS
Term Expires 1936
Rev. G. A. Benze, D.D.; Rev. H. W. A. Hanson, D.D., LL.D.;
Rev. J. B. Markward, D.D.; Rev. Jacob Maurer, D.D.; Mr. A.
Raymond Bard; Grant Hultberg, D.C.L.; Mr. H. L. Snyder.

Term Expires 1934
Rev. A. E. Bell, D.D.; Rev. C. A. Freed, D.D.; Rev. G. K.
Rubrecht, D.D.; Rev. J. C. Seegers, D.D.; Mr. A. H. Durboraw;
Mr. Wm. Eck; Mr. S. F. Telleen.

Term Expires 1932
Rev. S. G. R. von Bosse; Rev. F. O. Evers; Rev. M. Koolen,
D.D.; Rev. G. H. Michelmann, D.D.; Mr. Henry S. Albers, Sr.;
Mr. Aug. Becker.

IMMIGRANTS MISSION BOARD
Term Expires 1936
Rev. H. W. A. Hanson, D.D., LL.D.; Rev. J. B. Markward,
D.D.; Mr. A. Raymond Bard; Grant Hultberg, D.C.L.

Term Expires 1934
Rev. A. E. Bell, D.D.; Rev. C. A. Freed, D.D.; Mr. Wm. Eck;
Mr. S. F. Telleen.
Term Expires 1932
Rev. S. N. Carpenter, D.D.; Rev. George H. Rhodes; Mr.
Frank L. Fox; Mr. Jacob Umlauf.

WEST INDIES MISSION BOARD
President—Rev. H. W. A. Hanson, D.D., LL.D.
Secretary—Mr. H. F. Heuer.

Term Expires 1936
Rev. G. A. Benze, D.D.; Rev. H. W. A. Hanson. D.D., LL.D.;

Rev. J. B. Markward, D.D.; Rev. Jacob Maurer, D.D.; Mr. A. Raymond Bard; Grant Hultberg, D.C.L.; Mr. H. L. Snyder.

Term Expires 1934

Rev. A. E. Bell, D.D.; Rev. C. A. Freed, D.D.; Rev. G. K. Rubrecht, D.D.; Rev. J. C. Seegers, D.D.; Mr. A. H. Durboraw; Mr. Wm. Eck; Mr. S. F. Telleen.

Term Expires 1932

Rev. J. A. Eckstrom, B.D.; Rev. F. O. Evers; Rev. H. T. Weiskotten, Ph. D.; Rev. J. A. Weyl; Mr. James Gear; Mr. H. F. Heuer; Mr. Charles Lehmann.

BOARD OF EDUCATION

President—Rev. Augustus Steimle, D.D., 174 W. 93rd Street, New York City.

Vice-President—Prof. Hugo C. M. Wendel, Ph.D., Long Island University, Brooklyn, N. Y.

Recording Secretary—Rev. N. J. Gould Wickey, Ph.D., 1415 K Street, N. W., Washington, D. C.

Treasurer—Mr. Thomas P. Hickman, 1415 K Street, N.W., Washington, D. C.

Executive Secretary—Rev. N. J. Gould Wickey, Ph.D., 1415 K Street, N.W., Washington, D. C.

Secretaries—Rev. Carolus P. Harry, D.D., 1415 K Street, N.W., Washington, D. C.; Miss Mary E. Markley, Litt.D., 1415 K Street, N.W., Washington D. C.; Miss Mildred E. Winston, 1415 K Street, N.W., Washington, D. C.

Term Expires 1936

Rev. H. J. Black, D.D.; Rev. Franklin K. Fretz, D.D., Ph.D.; Rev. H. R. Gold; Rev. W. H. Greever, D.D.; Henry W. Bikle, LL.D.; Mr. Frederick Henrich; Prof. R. S. Saby, Ph.D.

Term Expires 1934

Rev. Henry H. Bagger; Rev. E. C. Herman, D.D.; Rev. M. L. Stirewalt, D.D.; Rev. A. A. Zinck, D.D.; S.T.D.; Mrs. Adelaide Burge; W. J. Showalter, Sc.D.; Hon. Charles Steele.

Term Expires 1932

Rev. Charles R. Bowers, D.D.; Rev. G. M. Diffenderfer, D.D.; Rev. Paul H. Krauss; Prof. Hugo C. M. Wendel, Ph.D.; Mr. J. H. Dingle; Mr. C. J. Driever, Ralph D. Owen, Ph.D.

INNER MISSION BOARD

President—Carl M. Distler, Esq., 401 American Life Bldg., Baltimore, Md.

Vice-President—Rev. F. B. Clausen, Waterloo College, Waterloo, Ont., Canada.

Executive Secretary and Treasurer—Rev. Wm. Freas, D.D., 39 East 35th Street, New York City.

Secretary for Immigrant Work—Rev. E. A. Sievert, 218 Seventh Avenue, New York City.

Term Expires 1936

Rev. G. H. Bechtold; Rev. Herman Brezing, D.D.; Rev. P. D. Brown, D.D.; Carl M. Distler, Esq.; Mr. T. C. Rohrbaugh.

Term Expires 1934

Rev. F. B. Clausen; Rev. J. F. Fedders, D.D.; Rev. J. S. Schantz; Mr. A. H. Durboraw; Mr. Thos. P. Hickman.

Term Expires 1932

Rev. H. Brueckner, D.D.; Rev. S. E. Greenawalt, D.D.; Rev. J. J. Scherer, Jr.; D.D.; Mr. Robert F. Bowe; Harry C. Hoffman, M.D.

BOARD OF PUBLICATION

President—Mr. D. F. Yost, 1616 DeKalb St., Norristown, Pa.

Vice-President—Mr. E. G. Hoover, 25 North Third Street, Harrisburg, Pa.

Secretary—Rev. S. W. Herman, D.D., 121 State St., Harrisburg, Pa.

Treasurer—Mr. John M. Snyder, Elkins Park, Pa.

Business Manager—Mr. Grant Hultberg, D.C.L., 1228 Spruce Street, Philadelphia, Pa.

Term Expires 1936

Rev. Oscar F. Blackwelder, D.D.; Rev. Stewart W. Herman, D.D.; Rev. J. J. Scherer, Jr., D.D.; L. Russell Alden, Esq.; F. Wm. Cappelmann, Esq.; Mr. E. G. Hoover; Mr. Einar Schatvet.

Term Expires 1934

Rev. H. C. Alleman, D.D.; Rev. A. H. Holthusen, Ph.D.; Rev. G. W. Nicely, D.D.; Mr. Croll Keller; Mr. J. C. Lynch; Mr. Otto W. Osterlund; Mr. D. F. Yost.

Term Expires 1932

Rev. Henry Anstadt, D.D.; Rev. Stanley Billheimer, D.D.; Rev. John W. Horine, D.D.; Rev. C. M. Jacobs, D.D., LL.D., L.H.D.; Charles Baum, M.D.; Mr. John M. Snyder; Mr. M. P. Moller, Jr.

BOARD OF MINISTERIAL PENSIONS AND RELIEF

President—Mr. Paul F. Myers, Munsey Bldg., Washington, D. C.

Vice-President.—Hon. H. W. Harter, 1543 Market St., Canton, Ohio.

Executive Secretary—Mr. Harry Hodges, 1228 Spruce Street, Philadelphia, Pa.

Treasurer—Mr. Peter P. Hagan, Kensington Avenue & Butler Street, Philadelphia, Pa.

Term Expires 1936

Rev. J. H. Reble; Rev. Ross H. Stover, D.D.; Wm. A. Granville, Ph.D., LL.D.; Mr. H. J. Herbst; W. T. Stauffer, Esq.

Term Expires 1934

Rev. Otto Kleine; Mr. A. Raymond Bard; Mr. J. L. Fisher; Hon. Henry W. Harter; Mr. M. P. Moller, Sr.

Term Expires 1932

Mr. Peter P. Hagan; Mr. J. Elsie Miller; Mr. Paul F. Myers; Mr. William F. Schneider; Mr. A. F. Sittloh.

PARISH AND CHURCH SCHOOL BOARD

President—Rev. F. M. Urich, D.D., 2336 S. 18th St., Philadelphia, Pa.

Vice-President—Rev. F. R. Knubel, 1225 Park Avenue, Rochester, N. Y.

Secretary—Rev. D. Burt Smith, D.D., 1228 Spruce Street, Philadelphia, Pa.

Treasurer—George M. Jones, Esq., 52 N. Fourth Street, Reading, Pa.

Field Secretaries—Rev. D. Burt Smith, D.D., 1228 Spruce Street, Philadelphia, Pa.; Rev. C. H. B. Lewis, D.D., 748 E. Military Ave., Fremont, Nebr.; Rev. S. White Rhyne, Box 171, Charlotte, N. C.; Rev. Paul E. Keyser, 162 East Lakeview Avenue, Columbus, Ohio.

Term Expires 1936

Rev. Paul H. Heisey, Ph.D., D.D.; Rev. George H. Rhodes, D.D.; Rev. Wm. C. Schaeffer, Jr., D.D.; Mr. Clarence C. Dittmer.

Term Expires 1934

Rev. P. D. Brown, D.D.; Rev. A. J. Turkle, D.D.; Rev. F. M. Urich, D.D.; Grant Hutlberg, D.C.L.

Term Expires 1932

Rev. J. D. M. Brown, Litt.D.; Rev. M. Hadwin Fischer, Ph.D., Th.D.; Rev. F. R. Knubel; George M. Jones Esq.

BOARD OF DEACONESS WORK

President—Rev. William A Wade, D.D., 505 Harwood Avenue, Baltimore, Md.

Vice-President—Rev. U. S. G. Rupp, D.D., Frederick, Md.

Secretary—Rev. Foster U. Gift, D.D., 2500 W North Avenue, Baltimore, Md.

Treasurer—Mr. Pearre E. Crowl, Greenway Apartments, 34th and Charles Streets, Baltimore, Md.

Term Expires 1936

Rev. Allen L. Benner, D.D.; Rev. C. T. Benze, D.D.; Rev. L. A. Thomas, D.D.; Mr. E. S. Gerberich; Frederick J. Singley, Esq.

Term Expires 1934

Rev. Earl J. Bowman, S.T.M.; Rev. U. S. G. Rupp, D.D.; Rev. W. C. Schaeffer, Jr., D.D.; Prof. J. C. Kinard, LL.D.; Mr. Frederick H. Wefer.

Term Expires 1932

Rev. George N. Lauffer, D.D.; Rev. William A. Wade, D.D.; Mr. Pearre E. Crowl; Mr. I. Searles Runyon; Edgar W. Young, Esq.

Advisory Members—Rev. Foster U. Gift, D.D.; Rev. E. F. Bachman, D.D.; Rev. Charles E. Hay, D.D.; Sister Sophia Jepson; Sister Anna Ebert; Mrs. W. P. M. Braun; Mrs. A. M. Obenauf.

NATIONAL LUTHERAN HOME FOR THE AGED

President—Rev. John Weidley, D.D., 233 Second Street, S.E., Washington, D.C.

Vice-President—Rev. J. E. Harms, D.D., Hagerstown, Md.

Recording Secretary—Rev. Richard Schmidt, D.D., 308 Buchanan St., N.W., Washington, D. C.

Corresponding Secretary—W. H. Finckel, Esq., 918 F Street, N.W., Washington, D. C.

Treasurer—H. T. Domer, Litt.D., 727 Fifteenth Street, N.W., Washington, D. C.

Rev. Henry Anstadt, D.D.; Rev. Oscar F. Blackwelder, D.D.; Rev. J. L. Frantz; Rev. J. E. Harms, D.D.; Rev. J. T. Huddle, D.D.; Rev. Richard Schmidt, D.D.; Rev. H. E. Snyder; Rev. F. Wagner, D.D.; Rev. John Weidley, D.D.; L. Russell Alden, Esq.; W. M. Butler, M.D.; F. E. Cunningham, Esq.; Harry T. Domer, Litt.D.; W. H. Finckel, Esq.; Mr. John H. Jones; Mr. F. W. Kakel; Mr. H. L. Snyder.

COMMITTEE ON CHURCH PAPERS

Chairman—Rev. H. Offermann, D.D., 7206 Boyer Street, Mt. Airy, Philadelphia, Pa.

Secretary—Rev. E. P. Pfatteicher, D.D., Ph.D., 1228 Spruce Street, Philadelphia, Pa.

Term Expires 1936

Rev. John Aberly, D.D.; Rev. J. W. Horine, D.D.; Wm. J. Showalter, Sc.D.

Term Expires 1934

Rev. P. D. Brown, D.D.; Rev. J. A. Leas, D.D.; Rev. H. Offermann, D.D.

Term Expires 1932

Rev. M. R. Hamsher; Rev. E. P. Pfatteicher, D.D.. Ph.D.; Mr. I. Searles Runyon.

EXECUTIVE COMMITTEE OF THE LAYMEN'S MOVEMENT

Chairman—Mr. J. L. Clark, Ashland, Ohio.

Vice-Chairman—Mr. E. J. Young, Wadsworth, Ohio.

Executive Secretary—Mr. Arthur P. Black, 706 Our Home Life Bldg., Washington, D. C.

Treasurer—Mr. P. H. Glatfelter, Spring Grove, Pa.

Chairman of the Administrative Committee — Mr. Wm. H. Hager, Lancaster, Pa.

Mr. F. W. Albrecht; Mr. J. L. Clark; Mr. C. J. Driever; Mr. Peter P. Hagan; Hon. Henry W. Harter; Mr. E. G. Hoover; E. Clarence Miller, LL.D.; Mr. Harvey C. Miller; George E. Neff, Esq.; Hon. John L. Zimmerman, LL.D.

STANDING COMMITTEES

STATISTICAL AND CHURCH YEAR BOOK COMMITTEE

Rev. G. H. Schnur, D.D., (Convener), 709 East 11th Street, Erie, Pa.; Rev. Ira F. Frankenfield; Rev. G. L. Kieffer, D.D., Litt.D.; Rev. J. D. Krout; Rev. C. W. Leitzell, D.D.; Rev. C. J. Rockey, D.D.; Mr. Harry E. Pugh; also Secretary of The United Lutheran Church in America (ex-officio).

COMMITTEE ON COMMON SERVICE BOOK

Rev. L. D. Reed, D.D., (Convener), 7204 Boyer Street, Mt. Airy, Philadelphia, Pa.; Rev. R. D. Clare, D.D.; Rev. E. E. Fischer, D.D.; Rev. W. E. Fischer, D.D.; Rev. Carl R. Simon; Rev. H. D. Hoover, Ph.D., D.D., S.T.D.; Rev. H. E. Jacobs, D.D., LL.D., S.T.D.; Rev. J. C. Mattes, D.D.; Rev. J. F. Ohl, D.D., Mus.D.; Rev. G. C. Rees, D.D.; Rev. George R. Seltzer; Rev. R. M. Smith, Ph.D., D.D.; Rev. A. Steimle, D.D.; Rev. M. L. Stirewalt, D.D.; Rev. P. Z. Strodach, D.D.

COMMITTEE ON CHURCH MUSIC

Rev. G. C. Rees, D.D., (Convener), 211 South Main Street, North Wales, Pa.; Rev. C. T. Benze, D.D.; Rev. J. D. M. Brown, Litt.D.; Rev. E. F. Krauss, D.D.; Rev. H. K. Lantz; Rev. George R. Seltzer; Rev. E. A. Trabert; Prof. Frederick Lewis Bach, Mus.D.; Mr. William Benbow; Mr. Ralph P. Lewars; Harold K. Marks, Mus.D.; Mr. Rob Roy Peery; Prof. Carl P. Pfatteicher, Th.D.; Mr. Henry F. Seibert; Harry A. Sykes, Mus.D.

COMMITTEE ON GERMAN INTERESTS

Rev. E. C. J. Kraeling, D.D., (Convener), 132 Henry Street, Brooklyn, N. Y.; Rev. G. A. Benze, D.D.; Rev. F. H Bosch, D.D.; Rev. S. G. R. von Bosse; Rev. F. O. Evers; Rev. R. H. Ischinger; Rev. O. Kleine; Rev. J. L. Neve, D.D., D.Th.; Rev. F. E. Oberlander, D.D.; Rev. T. O. Posselt, D.D.; Rev. J. Reble; Rev. C. R. Tappert, D.D.; Rev. J. A. Weyl, D.D.

Corresponding Members — The Presidents of the German Nebraska, Manitoba, Texas and Wartburg Synods.

COMMITTEE ON LUTHERAN BROTHERHOODS

Rev. David A. Davy, D.D., (Convener), 5402 Magnolia Avenue, Chicago, Ill.; Rev. J. S. Blank; Rev. Mark O. Heller; Rev. W. C. Schaeffer, Jr., D.D.; Mr. William B. Ahlgren; Mr. P. R. Boubel; Mr. J. Milton Deck; Mr. Paul T. Fretz; Mr. E. B. Graeber; Mr. George H. Hollenberg; Dr. T. J. Seiler; Mr. W. B. Shealy; Mr. Albert F. Sittloh; Mr. Joseph Tate; Mr. Karl Weichers; Hon. John L. Zimmerman, LL.D.

COMMITTEE ON WOMEN'S WORK

Rev. Frank M. Urich, D.D., (Convener), 2336 South 18th Street, Philadelphia, Pa.; Rev. W. G. Boomhower, D.D.; Rev. F. A. Kahler, D.D., LL.D.; Rev. S. J. McDowell, D.D.; Rev. J. E. Rudisill; Rev. D. Bruce Young, D.D.

COMMITTEE ON ASSOCIATIONS OF YOUNG PEOPLE

Rev. H. C. Roehner, D.D., (Convener), 30 S. Mulberry Street, Mansfield, Ohio; Rev. Oscar F. Blackwelder, D.D.; Rev. G. Franklin Gehr, D.D.; Rev. L. M. Kuhns, D.D., Litt.D.; Rev. L. H. Lesher; Rev. H. L. Saul; Rev. John Schmieder; Rev. Chester Simonton; Mr. Austin Howard; Mr. Alvin Schaediger.

COMMITTEE ON ARMY AND NAVY WORK

Rev. Charles D. Trexler, D.D., (Convener), 28 East 73rd Street, New York City; Rev. J. F. Fedders, D.D.; Rev. Wm. Freas, D.D.; Rev. R. H. Gearhart; Rev. Henry Manken, Jr.; Rev. H. S. Miller; Rev. Emil W. Weber; Mr. C. H. Dahmer; Mr. W. A. G. Lape.

COMMITTEE ON MORAL AND SOCIAL WELFARE

Rev. W. H. Greever, D.D., (Convener), Drawer 300, Columbia, S. C.; Rev. O. E. Brandorff; Rev. E. C. Dinwiddie, D.D.; Prof. E. E. Flack, S.T.D.; Rev. J. H. Harms, D.D.; Rev. P. H. Heisey, Ph.D., D.D.; Rev. L. S. Keyser, D.D.; Rev. W. A. Sadtler, Ph.D., D.D.; Rev. H. W. Tope, D.D.; Rev. N. Willison, Litt.D.; Mr. W. H. Hager.

COMMITTEE ON EVANGELISM

Rev. J. C. Seegers, D.D., (Convener), 7322 Boyer Street, Mt. Airy, Philadelphia, Pa.; Rev. Russell F. Auman; Rev. S. D. Daugherty, D.D.; Rev. W. C. Davis, D.D.; Rev. Franklin C. Fry; Rev. G. Arthur Fry, D.D.; Rev. A. Pohlman, D.D., M.D.; Rev. C. F. Stickles; Rev. F. Wolford, D.D.; Mr. F. Stussy, Jr.

COMMITTEE ON CHURCH ARCHITECTURE

Rev. L. D. Reed, D.D., (Convener), 7204 Boyer Street, Mt. Airy, Philadelphia, Pa.; Rev. Wm. H. Cooper; Rev. J. L. Deaton,

Jr.; Rev. H. S. Kidd; Rev. E. F. Krauss, D.D.; Rev. G. H. Schnur, D.D.; Rev. E. A. Trabert; Mr. J. Horace Frank; Mr. Charles Z. Klauder; Prof. Warren P. Laird, ScD.; Mr. Luther M. Leisenring; Mr. Charles F. Obenhack; Mr. Albert F. Schenck; Mr. Charles A. Scheuringer.

COMMITTEE ON PUBLICITY

Rev. Howard R. Gold (Convener), 15 Vaughan Avenue, Winyah Woods, New Rochelle, N. Y.; Rev. M. Luther Canup, D.D.; Rev. C. K. Fegley; Rev. G. F. Genszler; Rev. Arthur Herbert; Rev. A. F. Klepfer; Rev. Geo. C. Koehler; Rev. A. R. Naus; Rev. L. W. Rupp; Mr. Edward E. Croll; Mr. Jesse R. Hildebrand; Mr. Oscar H. Lindow; Wm. J. Showalter, Sc.D.

COMMITTEE ON TRANSPORTATION

Mr. Harvey C. Miller (Convener), 319 Commercial Trust Bldg., Philadelphia, Pa.; Rev. J. M. Bramkamp, D.D., 860 N. Wabash Avenue, Chicago, Ill., and the Secretary of The United Lutheran Church in America (ex-officio).

NECROLOGIST

Rev. James F. Lambert, D.D., 415 Howertown Avenue, Catasauqua, Pa.

ARCHIVIST

Rev. L. D. Reed, D.D., 7204 Boyer Street, Mt. Airy, Philadelphia, Pa.

STATISTICAL SECRETARY

Rev. G. L. Kieffer, D.D., Litt.D., 39 East 35th Street, New York City.

COMMISSIONERS TO THE NATIONAL LUTHERAN COUNCIL

Rev. C. M. Jacobs, D.D., LL.D., L.H.D., (Convener), 7335 Germantown Avenue, Mt. Airy, Philadelphia, Pa.; Rev. E. B. Burgess, D.D., LL.D.; Rev. C. A. Freed, D.D.; Rev. J. A. W. Haas, D.D., LL.D.; Rev. P. W. Koller, D.D.; Rev. E. P. Pfatteicher, Ph.D., D.D.; Rev. M. G. G. Scherer, D.D.; Rev. L. W. Steckel, D.D.; Hon. E. F. Eilert, C.S.D.; G. F. Greiner, Esq.

REPRESENTATIVE ON THE ADVISORY COMMITTEE OF THE AMERICAN BIBLE SOCIETY

Rev. H. C. Alleman, D.D., Gettysburg, Pa.

CONSULTATIVE REPRESENTATIVES TO COMMISSIONS OF THE FEDERAL COUNCIL OF CHURCHES

Administrative Committee—Rev. G. U. Wenner, D.D., LL.D., L.H.D., 355 East 19th Street, New York City; Rev. A. Steimle, D.D.

Washington Committee—Rev. Wm. Freas, D.D., 39 East 35th Street, New York City; Rev. Henry Manken, Jr.; Rev. Emil W. Weber.

Commission on International Justice and Good Will—Rev. E. P. Pfatteicher, Ph.D., D.D., 1228 Spruce Street, Philadelphia, Pa.; Rev. E. H. Delk, D.D.; Rev. L. B. Wolf, D.D.

Committee on Mercy and Relief—Rev. F. H. Knubel, D.D., LL.D., S.T.D., 39 East 35th Street, New York City; Rev. Amos J. Traver.

COMMITTEE ON CONFERENCE WITH Y. M. C. A.

Rev. Paul E. Scherer, D.D., (Chairman), 3 West 65th Street, New York City; Rev. R. E. Tulloss, Ph.D., D.D., LL.D.; Mr. W. H. Hager; Robbin B. Wolf, Esq.

COMMITTEE TO PREPARE A STATEMENT CONCERNING RELATIONS OF CHURCH AND STATE

Rev. C. M. Jacobs, D.D., LL.D., L.H.D., 7335 Germantown Avenue, Mt. Airy, Philadelphia, Pa.; Rev. J. A. W. Haas, D.D., LL.D.; Rev. F. K. Fretz, Ph.D., D.D.; Rev. A. R. Wentz, Ph.D., D.D.

COMMISSION ON WORLD CONFERENCE ON FAITH AND ORDER

Rev. M. G. G. Scherer, D.D., 39 East 35th Street, New York City; Rev. John Aberly, D.D.; Rev. Holmes Dysinger, D.D., LL.D.; Rev. W. H. Greever, D.D.; Rev. A. Steimle, D.D.

COMMISSION ON LUTHERAN CHURCH UNITY

Rev. Paul E. Scherer, D.D., 3 West 65th Street, New York City; Rev. C. M. Jacobs, D.D., LL.D., L.H.D.; Rev. R. E. Tulloss, Ph.D., D.D., LL.D.; Hon. E. F. Eilert, C.S.D.; W. A. Granville, Ph.D., LL.D.; Mr. J. K. Jensen.

COMMISSION ON INVESTMENTS

(To be appointed by the Executive Board).

COMMITTEE ON THE OFFICE OF THE MINISTRY

Rev. H. Anstadt, D.D., (Convener), 170 South Second Street, Chambersburg, Pa.; Rev. H. Offermann, D.D.; Rev. A. H. Smith, D.D.; Rev. A. Steimle, D.D.; Rev. M. L. Stirewalt, D.D.

COMMITTEE ON WOMEN AS CONGREGATIONAL REPRESENTATIVES

Rev. Stanley Billheimer, D.D., (Convener), 26 College Street, Palmyra, Pa.; Rev. J. C. Mattes, D.D.; Rev. Ray T. Stamm, Ph.D.; Hon. Claude T. Reno; Miss Flora Prince.

COMMITTEE ON PLAN OF APPORTIONMENT

(To be appointed later).

APPENDIX

CORPORATE TITLES

The United Lutheran Church in America, 39 East 35th Street, New York City.

The Board of Foreign Missions of the United Lutheran Church in America, 18 East Mt. Vernon Place, Baltimore, Md.

The Board of American Missions of the United Lutheran Church in America, 39 East 35th St., New York City.

The Board of Education of the United Lutheran Church in America, 1415 K Street, N. W., Washington, D. C.

The Inner Mission Board of the United Lutheran Church in America, 39 East 35th Street, New York City.

The Board of Publication of the United Lutheran Church in America, 1228 Spruce Street, Philadelphia, Pa.

Board of Ministerial Pensions and Relief of the United Lutheran Church in America, 1228 Spruce St., Philadelphia, Pa.

The Parish and Church School Board of the United Lutheran Church in America, 1228 Spruce Street, Philadelphia, Pa.

The Board of Deaconess Work of the United Lutheran Church in America, 2500 W. North Avenue, Baltimore, Md.

Evangelical Lutheran Seminary of Canada, Waterloo, Ontario, Canada.

The Theological Seminary of the Evangelical Lutheran Church at Chicago, Ill., 11th Avenue & Harrison Street, Maywood, Ill.

The Theological Seminary of the General Synod of the Evangelical Lutheran Church in the United States and of the United Lutheran Church in America, Gettysburg, Pa.

The Hartwick Seminary, 259 Washington Ave., Brooklyn, N. Y.

Martin Luther Seminary of the German Evangelical Lutheran Synod of Nebraska, Lincoln, Nebr.

Northwestern Lutheran Theological Seminary, 1018 Nineteenth Ave., N. E., Minneapolis, Minn.

Pacific Theological Seminary of the Evangelical Lutheran Church, 4300 E. 45th St., Seattle, Wash.

The Lutheran Theological Seminary at Philadelphia, 7301 Germantown Avenue, Mt. Airy, Philadelphia, Pa.

The Lutheran College and Seminary, Saskatoon, Sask., Canada.

Trustees of the Lutheran Theological Southern Seminary, at Columbia, S. C.

The Western Theological Seminary of the United Lutheran Church in America, Fremont, Nebr.

Carthage College, Carthage, Ill.

North Carolina College (called Collegiate Institute), Mt. Pleasant, N. C.

Gettysburg College, Gettysburg, Pa.

Irving Female College, Mechanicsburg, Pa.

Lenoir-Rhyne College, Hickory, N. C.

Marion Female College (known as Marion Junior College), Marion, Va.

Midland College of the United Lutheran Church in America, Fremont Nebr.

Muhlenberg College, Located at Allentown, Lehigh County, Pennsylvania.

Newberry College, Newberry, S. C.

The Trustees of Roanoke College, at Salem, Va.

Susquehanna University, Selinsgrove, Pa.

Trustees of Thiel College of the Evangelical Lutheran Church, Greenville, Pa.

Wagner Memorial Lutheran College, Staten Island, N. Y.

The Board of Directors of Wittenberg College, Springfield, Ohio.

Hartwick College, Oneonta, N. Y.

Hartwick Academy, Hartwick Seminary, N. Y.

———————◆———————

Lutheran Orphans' Home in Berks County, Pennsylvania.

Tressler Orphans' Home of the Evangelical Lutheran Church of the General Synod in the United States of America, Loysville, Pa.

The Zelienople Orphans' Home Board of Directors of the Pittsburgh Synod of the Evangelical Lutheran Church, Zelienople, Pa.

The Oesterlen Orphans' Home of the United Lutheran Church of North America located at Springfield, Ohio.

The Lutheran Orphan Home of the South, located at Salem, Va.

The Nachusa Lutheran Orphanage, Nachusa, Ill.

Wartburg Orphans' Farm School of the Evangelical Lutheran Church, in the State of New York, Mount Vernon, N. Y.

Evangelical Lutheran St. John's Orphan Home at Buffalo and Sulphur Springs, N. Y., "Station D," Buffalo, N. Y.

Old People's Home of the Pittsburgh Synod of the Evangelical Lutheran Church, at Zelienople, Pa.

Evangelical Lutheran Charities Society of Charleston, S. C., (for The Jacob Washington Franke Lutheran Hospital and Home), Charleston, S. C.

The Association of the Lutheran Church Home for the Aged and Infirm of Buffalo, N. Y.

The Lutheran Church Home for the Aged and Infirm of Central New York, Inc., Clinton, N. Y. (Office at Utica, N. Y.)

The National Lutheran Home for the Aged, Washington, D. C.

The Feghtly Lutheran Home, Tippecanoe City, Ohio.

Lowman Home for Aged and Helpless, White Rock, S. C.

Lutheran Home for the Aged, of Erie, Pennsylvania.

Lutheran Inner Mission Society of the State of Connecticut, Inc. Owner of "Lutheran Home for the Aged, Southbury, Conn."

Tabitha Home, Lincoln, Nebr.

Emaus Orphan House, Middletown, Pa.

Orphans' Home and Asylum for the Aged and Infirm of the Evangelical Lutheran Church, Philadelphia, 6950 Germantown Avenue, Philadelphia, Pa.

The Good Shepherd Home, Allentown, Pa.

The Auxiliary Board of the Passavant Memorial Homes for the Care of Epileptics, Rochester, Pa.

INDEX